An Atypical ASP.NET Core 6 Design Patterns Guide

Second Edition

A SOLID adventure into architectural principles and design patterns using .NET 6 and C# 10

Carl-Hugo Marcotte

BIRMINGHAM—MUMBAI

An Atypical ASP.NET Core 6 Design Patterns Guide
Second Edition

Senior Publishing Product Manager: Suman Sen
Acquisition Editor – Peer Reviews: Gaurav Gavas
Project Editor: Amisha Vathare
Content Development Editor: Edward Doxey
Copy Editor: Safis Editing
Technical Editor: Tejas Mhasvekar
Proofreader: Safis Editing
Indexer: Hemangini Bari
Presentation Designer: Ganesh Bhadwalkar

First published: December 2020
Second edition: March 2022

Production reference: 2280622

Published by Packt Publishing Ltd.
Livery Place
35 Livery Street
Birmingham
B3 2PB, UK.

ISBN 978-1-80324-984-1

www.packt.com

Foreword

After 10 years of abiding partnership with Carl-Hugo, I still remember the production support project that ushered this partnership in—the application's accuracy and reliability were the overriding factors, providing the final product's competitive edge. This project brought to light Carl-Hugo's talent and his solid grasp of the .NET programming platform, which spurred me on to entrust him with more sensitive and crucial projects, laying the groundwork for our extended partnership.

We started tackling projects that had been on hold for a long time, requiring deep analysis, and more importantly, acute imagination to put them across using .NET programs. Once again, Carl-Hugo's knowledge and skills stood out, leading to robust and flexible .NET application designs.

Carl-Hugo has consolidated his expertise by spending several years teaching programming. His book *An Atypical ASP.NET Core 6 Design Patterns Guide, Second Edition* unites that experience with his long-term expertise in the field. I highly recommend reading the book and putting it into practice as I've already had the opportunity to attend some of his training sessions and bear witness to this manual's consistency and practical features.

Abdelhamid Zebdi

IT Director at Nortek Air Solutions (2007-2017), IT OPS Management at House of Commons of Canada (2017-present).

Contributors

About the author

Carl-Hugo Marcotte has been developing, designing, and architecting web applications professionally since 2005, wrote his first line of code at about eight years old, and holds a bachelor's degree in computer science.

After working at a firm for a few years, he became an independent consultant, and developed projects of different sizes for SMEs and educational institutions. He is now a Senior Solutions Architect at Export Development Canada and is passionate about software architecture, C#, ASP.NET Core, and the Cloud.

He loves to share his knowledge, which led him to teach programming, write a blog, and create, maintain, and contribute to multiple open-source projects.

I want to thank everyone who supported me during my journey into the world of authoring, especially my other half and partner in life, Cathie, who is always there no matter the idea I pursue.

About the reviewer

Damir Arh has many years of experience with software development and maintenance; from complex enterprise software projects to modern consumer-oriented mobile applications. Although he has worked with a wide spectrum of different languages, his favorite language remains C#. In his drive towards better development processes, he is a proponent of test-driven development, continuous integration, and continuous deployment. He shares his knowledge by speaking at local user groups and conferences, blogging, and writing articles. He has received the prestigious Microsoft MVP award for developer technologies 10 times in a row. In his spare time, he's always on the move: hiking, geocaching, running, and rock climbing.

Join our book's Discord space

Join the book's Discord workspace for *Ask me Anything* session with the authors:

https://packt.link/ASPdotNET6DesignPatterns

Table of Contents

Chapter 3: Architectural Principles   41

Section 2: Designing for ASP.NET Core

Chapter 4: The MVC Pattern Using Razor   93

Chapter 8: Options and Logging Patterns 195

Section 3: Designing at Component Scale

Chapter 9: Structural Patterns   239

Section 4: Designing at Application Scale

Chapter 12: Understanding Layering   323

Chapter 13: Getting Started with Object Mappers   357

Appendices

Preface

Design patterns are a set of solutions to many of the common problems occurring in software development. They are essential for any experienced developer and professionals crafting software solutions of any scale.

We start by exploring basic design patterns, automated testing, the SOLID architectural principles, dependency injection, and other ASP.NET Core mechanisms. Then we explore component-scale patterns oriented toward small chunks of software. Next, we move on to application-scale patterns and techniques, where we explore higher-level patterns and how to structure the application as a whole. The book covers many fundamental Gang of Four (GoF) patterns, such as strategy, singleton, decorator, façade, and composite. The chapters are organized based on scale and topics, allowing you to start small with a strong base and build slowly on top of it, the same way you would build a program. Many use cases in the book combine more than one design pattern to display alternate usage. It also shows that design patterns are tools to be used, not complex concepts to be feared. Finally, we tackle the client side to connect the dots and make ASP.NET Core a viable full stack alternative.

This book is a journey to learn the reasoning behind the craft. By the end of the book, you will be able to mix and match design patterns and will have learned how to think about architecture. You will learn techniques to help you create the building blocks that you need to solve your unique day-to-day design problems.

Who this book is for

The book is intended for intermediate software and web developers with an understanding of .NET who want to write flexible, maintainable, and robust code for building scalable web applications. The book assumes knowledge of C# programming and an understanding of web concepts such as HTTP.

What this book covers

Section 1, Principles and Methodologies

This section contains the book's foundations: an overview of unit testing and xUnit, the **SOLID** principles, and some theory and examples on how to design software.

Chapter 1, *Introduction*, contains the prerequisites and an explanation of how the book works as well as a few important topics that will be useful to a software developer.

Chapter 2, Automated Testing, introduces you to the basics of unit testing and the xUnit testing framework as well as to some good practices and methodologies to help write unit tests.

Chapter 3, Architectural Principles, lays the architectural groundwork with crucial principles used throughout the book and extremely important to any engineer trying to write SOLID code.

Section 2, Designing for ASP.NET Core

This section introduces ASP.NET Core-specific subjects, including Model-View-Controller (MVC), View Models, Data Transfer Objects (DTO), and other classic design patterns. We also deep dive into dependency injection and explore the evolved usage of certain patterns in ASP.NET Core as pillars of modern software engineering.

Chapter 4, The MVC Pattern Using Razor, introduces you to the MVC and the View Model design patterns to render views using Razor and ASP.NET Core MVC.

Chapter 5, The MVC Pattern for Web APIs, takes you further on the ASP.NET Core MVC journey, focusing on web APIs. We explore the DTO pattern and API contracts.

Chapter 6, Understanding the Strategy, Abstract Factory, and Singleton Design Patterns, introduces you to the traditional implementation of three GoF design patterns: Strategy, Abstract Factory, and Singleton.

Chapter 7, Deep Dive into Dependency Injection, takes the ASP.NET Core dependency injection container for a ride, introducing you to one of the most important aspects of modern software development. This chapter connects ASP.NET Core and the SOLID principles. Once the basics of dependency injection are laid out, we review the previous three GoF design patterns and revisit them using dependency injection, opening the way to build testable, flexible, and reliable software.

Chapter 8, Options and Logging Patterns, takes ASP.NET Core-related subjects and digs into them. We cover different options patterns and the abstraction provided to us. We also explore how to leverage logging in .NET 6.

Section 3, Designing at Component Scale

This section focuses on component design, where we study how an individual piece of software can be crafted to achieve a particular goal. We explore a few more GoF patterns that should help you design SOLID data structures and components as well as simplify the complexity of our code by encapsulating our logic in smaller units.

Chapter 9, Structural Patterns, introduces four new GoF structural design patterns and a few variants, such as transparent façades and opaque façades. It also introduces you to Scrutor, an open source project that adds support for the dependency injection of decorators.

Chapter 10, Behavioral Patterns, introduces two GoF behavioral design patterns and concludes by mixing them together as a final improvement on the code sample's design.

Chapter 11, Understanding the Operation Result Design Pattern, covers multiple variants of the Operation Result design pattern, structuring a result object to carry more than a simple result.

Section 4, Designing at Application Scale

This section takes a step toward application design and introduces layering, vertical slices, and microservices. We overview each technique making sure you know how to get started. We also cover different component-level patterns that help put those architectural styles together.

Chapter 12, Understanding Layering, introduces you to layering and clean architecture, covering the primary objectives behind the presentation, domain, data (persistence) layers, and their clean architecture counterparts, which is the apogee of layering. It also highlights the evolution of application design in the last few decades, helping you understand where it started (the beginning of the chapter) and where it is now (the end of the chapter).

Chapter 13, Getting Started with Object Mappers, covers object mapping (that is, copying an object into another), also known as the Translator pattern, the Mapper pattern, and Entity Translator. The chapter introduces AutoMapper at the end, an open source library, to help us cover the most common scenarios automatically.

Chapter 14, Mediator and CQRS Design Patterns, introduces the Command Query Responsibility Segregation (CQRS) and the Mediator patterns. After covering those two patterns, we explore an open source tool called MediatR, which is foundational to many subsequent subjects.

Chapter 15, Getting Started with Vertical Slice Architecture, introduces Vertical Slice Architecture. It uses a number of the previous patterns and tools that we have explored to piece together a different way to see the design of an application. It also introduces FluentValidation, which gets added to MediatR and AutoMapper.

Chapter 16, Introduction to Microservices Architecture, introduces microservices, what they are, what they are not, and talks about a few related patterns. It introduces many concepts, such as message queues, events, Publish-Subscribe, and Gateway patterns. We also revisit CQRS at cloud scale.

Section 5, Designing the Client Side

This section introduces multiple UI patterns that we can use when developing ASP.NET Core 6 applications, such as Blazor, Razor Pages, and various types of components. It overviews what ASP. NET Core 6 offers in terms of UIs, leading to additional learning paths if you are interested.

Chapter 17, ASP.NET Core User Interfaces, explores most of the UI elements available to us in ASP.NET Core 6, such as Razor Pages, Partial Views, Tag Helpers, View Components, Display Templates, and Editor Templates.

Chapter 18, A Brief Look into Blazor, touches upon Blazor Server quickly, then explores Blazor WebAssembly (Wasm) to complete our journey and transform C#/.NET into a full-stack alternative to other JavaScript technologies. We explore Razor Components and the Model-View-Update design pattern. We end the chapter with a medley of possibilities you can start digging into.

Appendices

The appendices contain additional information about supporting subjects related to the technology used and explored in the book.

Appendix A explores numerous C# features spanning a wide range of versions, including .NET 6 and C# 10. If you don't understand a piece of code in the book, that feature is most likely covered in _Appendix A_. Even if you understood all the code, you should find some good tips there.

Appendix B covers additional microservices-related topics like an overview of containers with a cheat sheet-like list of useful Docker commands, an overview of orchestration, and some notions related to scaling applications.

To get the most out of this book

You must know C# and how to program. Boolean logic, loops, and other basic programming constructs should be mastered, including object-oriented programming basics. Some knowledge of ASP.NET will be beneficial. Knowing how to read UML class and sequence diagrams is an asset, but not required.

The code samples and resources are available on GitHub (`https://adpg.link/net6`). The `README.md` file at the root of the repository is filled with information to help you find the code and resources you are looking for.

Most links are shortened in the form of `https://adpg.link/****` so readers of a physical copy can easily type URLs quickly.

In the book, I use a mix of Visual Studio 2022 (which has a free version) and Visual Studio Code (free). I recommend that you use one or both of those. The IDE is unrelated to most of the content. You could use Notepad if you are impetuous enough (I don't recommend that). Unless you install Visual Studio, which comes with the .NET SDK, you may need to install the .NET 6 SDK. The SDK comes with the dotnet CLI as well as the building tools for running and testing your programs. I develop on Windows, but you should be able to use another OS. OS-related topics are very limited, even inexistent. The code compiles on both Windows and Linux.

Download the example code files

The code bundle for the book is hosted on GitHub at `https://github.com/PacktPublishing/An-Atypical-ASP.NET-Core-6-Design-Patterns-Guide`. We also have other code bundles from our rich catalog of books and videos available at `https://github.com/PacktPublishing/`. Check them out!

Download the color images

We also provide a PDF file that has color images of the screenshots/diagrams used in this book. You can download it here: `https://static.packt-cdn.com/downloads/9781803249841_ColorImages.pdf`.

Conventions used

There are a number of text conventions used throughout this book.

`CodeInText`: Indicates code words in text, database table names, folder names, filenames, file extensions, pathnames, dummy URLs, user input, and Twitter handles. For example, "Mount the downloaded `WebStorm-10*.dmg` disk image file as another disk in your system."

A block of code is set as follows:

```
public class FactTest
{
    [Fact]
    public void Should_be_equal()
    {
        var expectedValue = 2;
        var actualValue = 2;
        Assert.Equal(expectedValue, actualValue);
    }
}
```

When we wish to draw your attention to a particular part of a code block, the relevant lines or items are set in bold:

```
public class AsyncFactTest
{
    [Fact]
    public async Task Should_be_equal()
    {
        var expectedValue = 2;
        var actualValue = 2;
        await Task.Yield();
        Assert.Equal(expectedValue, actualValue);
    }
}
```

Any command-line input or output is written as follows:

```
Passed!  - Failed:      0, Passed:     23, Skipped:      0, Total:     23,
Duration: 22 ms - MyApp.Tests.dll (net6.0)
```

Bold: Indicates a new term, an important word, or words that you see on the screen, for example, in menus or dialog boxes, also appear in the text like this. For example: "Select **System info** from the **Administration** panel."

 Warnings or important notes appear like this.

 Tips and tricks appear like this.

Get in touch

Feedback from our readers is always welcome.

General feedback: Email `feedback@packtpub.com`, and mention the book's title in the subject of your message. If you have questions about any aspect of this book, please email us at `questions@packtpub.com`.

Errata: Although we have taken every care to ensure the accuracy of our content, mistakes do happen. If you have found a mistake in this book we would be grateful if you would report this to us. Please visit, `http://www.packtpub.com/submit-errata`, selecting your book, clicking on the Errata Submission Form link, and entering the details.

Piracy: If you come across any illegal copies of our works in any form on the Internet, we would be grateful if you would provide us with the location address or website name. Please contact us at `copyright@packtpub.com` with a link to the material.

If you are interested in becoming an author: If there is a topic that you have expertise in and you are interested in either writing or contributing to a book, please visit `http://authors.packtpub.com`.

For more information about Packt, please visit `packtpub.com`.

Share your thoughts

Once you've read *An Atypical ASP.NET Core 6 Design Patterns Guide, Second Edition*, we'd love to hear your thoughts! Scan the QR code below to go straight to the Amazon review page for this book and share your feedback.

https://packt.link/r/1803249846

Your review is important to us and the tech community and will help us make sure we're delivering excellent quality content.

Section 1: Principles and Methodologies

This section focuses on architectural principles and development methodologies that we use throughout the book. These introductory chapters are essential for progressing toward making great architectural decisions.

We first look at how to approach the book itself, explore prerequisites, and see a few helpful topics. Then, we cover automated testing and xUnit, to finally jump into the architectural principles, where we begin our study of the fundamentals of modern software engineering.

This section comprises the following chapters:

- *Chapter 1, Introduction*
- *Chapter 2, Automated Testing*
- *Chapter 3, Architectural Principles*

1

Introduction

The goal of this book is not to create yet another design pattern book; instead, the chapters are organized according to scale and topic, allowing you to start small with a strong foundation and build slowly upon it, in just the same way that you would build a program.

Instead of this being a guide that covers a few ways of applying a design pattern, we will explore the thought processes behind the systems we are designing from a software engineer's point of view.

This is not a magic recipe book, and from experience, there is no magic recipe when designing software; there is only your logic, knowledge, experience, and analytical skills. Let's define "experience" as *your past successes and failures*. And don't worry, you will fail during your career, but don't get discouraged by it. The faster you fail, the faster you can recover and learn, leading to successful products. Many techniques covered in this book should help you achieve that goal. Everyone has failed and made mistakes; you aren't the first, and you certainly won't be the last. To paraphrase a well-known saying of Roosevelt's, the people that never fail are the ones who never do anything.

The high-level plan looks like this:

- We will explore basic patterns, unit testing, architectural principles, and some crucial ASP.NET Core mechanisms.
- Then, we will move up to the component scale, exploring patterns oriented toward small chunks of software and individual units.
- After that, we will move to application-scale patterns and techniques, where we explore higher-level patterns and how to structure an application as a whole.
- Afterward, we will tackle the client side to connect the dots and make ASP.NET a viable full stack alternative.

Many subjects covered throughout the book could have a book of their own. Once you are done with this book, you should have plenty of ideas about where to continue your journey into software architecture.

Here are a few pointers that I believe are worth stating:

- The chapters are organized to start with small-scale patterns and then progress to higher-level ones, making the learning curve easier.
- Instead of giving you a recipe, the book focuses on the thinking behind things and shows the evolution of some techniques to help you understand why the evolution happened.
- Many use cases combine more than one design pattern to illustrate alternate usage, so that you can understand the patterns and use them efficiently. This also shows that design patterns are not beasts to tame but tools to use, manipulate, and bend to your will.
- As in real life, no textbook solution can solve all our problems, and real problems are always more complicated than what's explained in textbooks. In this book, my goal is to show you how to mix and match patterns to think "architecture," instead of giving you step-by-step instructions to reproduce.

This chapter introduces the different concepts that we will be exploring throughout the book, including refreshers on a few notions. We will also cover .NET and its tooling, as well as the technical requirements, such as where the source code is located.

The following topics will be covered in this chapter:

- What is a design pattern?
- Anti-patterns and code smells
- Understanding the web – request/response
- Getting started with .NET

What is a design pattern?

Since you just purchased a book about design patterns, I guess that you have some idea of what design patterns are, but let's just make sure that we are on the same page.

Abstract definition: A design pattern is a proven technique that can be used to solve a specific problem.

In this book, we will apply different patterns to solve different problems and leverage some open source tools to go further, faster! Abstract definitions make people sound intelligent and all, but there is no better way to learn than by experimenting with something, and design patterns are no different.

If that definition does not make sense to you yet, don't worry. You should have enough information by the end of the book to correlate the multiple practical examples and explanations with that definition, making it clear enough.

I like to compare programming to playing with LEGO® because what you have to do is generally the same: put small pieces together to create something bigger. It could be a castle, a spaceship, or something else that you want to build. With that analogy in mind, a design pattern is a plan to assemble a solution that fits one or more scenarios; a tower or a reactor, for example. Therefore, if you lack imagination or skills in the case of LEGO®, possibly because you are too young, your castle might not look as good as someone else's who has more experience. Design patterns give you the tools you need, helping you put beautiful and reliable pieces together to improve your masterpiece.

However, instead of snapping LEGO® blocks together, you nest code blocks and interweave objects in a virtual environment!

Before going into more detail, well-thought-out applications of design patterns should improve your application designs. That is true whether you are designing a small component or a whole system. However, be careful: throwing patterns into the mix just to use them can lead to the opposite result. Aim to write readable code that solves the issue at hand, not at over-engineering systems with as many patterns as you can.

As we have briefly mentioned, there are design patterns that are applicable to multiple software engineering levels, and in this book, we will start small and grow to cloud scale! We will follow a smooth learning curve, starting with simpler patterns and code samples that bend good practices to focus on the patterns, and finally ending with more advanced full stack topics, integrating multiple patterns and good practices.

Of course, some subjects are overviews more than deep dives, like automated testing, because no one can fit it all in a single book. Nonetheless, I've done my best to give you as much information about as many architecture-related subjects as I can, and I hope you'll find this book a helpful and enjoyable read.

Let's start with the opposite of design patterns because it is essential to identify wrong ways of doing things if you want to avoid making those mistakes or correct them when you see them. Knowing the right way to overcome specific problems using design patterns is crucial.

Anti-patterns and code smells

Anti-patterns and code smells are architectural bad practices or tips about possible bad design. Learning about best practices is as important as learning about bad ones, which is where we start. There are multiple anti-patterns and code smells throughout the book to help you get started.

Anti-patterns

An **anti-pattern** is the opposite of a design pattern: it is a proven flawed technique that will most likely cause you some trouble and cost you time and money (and probably give you a headache or two along the way).

An anti-pattern is a pattern that seems to be a good idea and that seems to be the solution you were looking for, but that in the end will most likely cause more harm than good. Some anti-patterns started as legitimate design patterns and were labeled anti-patterns later. Sometimes, it is a matter of opinion, and sometimes the classification can be influenced by the programming language.

Let's look at an example next. We will explore some other anti-patterns throughout the book.

Anti-pattern – God Class

A **God class** is a class that handles way too many things. It is usually a central class that many other classes inherit from or use; it is the class that knows and manages everything in the system; it is *the* class. On the other hand, it is also the class that nobody wants to update, and the class that breaks the application every time somebody touches it: **it is an evil class!**

The best way to fix this is to separate responsibilities and distribute them to multiple classes instead of only one. We will see how to split responsibilities throughout the book, which helps create more robust software.

If you have a personal project with a *God class* at its core, start by reading the book, and then try to apply the principles and patterns that you learn to divide that class into multiple smaller classes that interact together. Try to organize those new classes into cohesive units, modules, or assemblies.

We will be getting into architectural principles very soon, which will open the way to concepts such as responsibility segregation.

Code smells

A **code smell** is an indicator of a possible problem. It points to areas of your design that could benefit from a redesign. By "code smell," we mean "code that stinks" or "code that does not smell right."

It is important to note that a code smell only indicates the possibility of a problem; it does not mean that there is a problem. They usually are good indicators though, so it is worth taking the time to analyze a "smelly" part of your software.

An excellent example of this is when many comments are being used to explain the logic of a method. That often means that the code could be split into smaller methods with proper names, leading to more readable code and allowing you to get rid of those pesky comments.

Another note about comments is that they don't evolve, so what often happens is that the code described by the comments changes but the comment remains the same. That leaves a false or obsolete description of a block of code that can lead a developer astray.

The same is also true with method names. Sometimes, the method's name and its body tell a different story, leading to the same issues. Nevertheless, it is rare that this will happen since programmers tend to read and write code better than spoken language comments. Nonetheless, keep both in mind when reading, writing, or reviewing code.

Code smell – Control Freak

An excellent example of a code smell is when you use the new keyword. This is an indication of a hardcoded dependency where the creator controls the new object and its lifetime. This is also known as the **Control Freak anti-pattern**, but I prefer to box it as a code smell instead of an anti-pattern since the new keyword is not intrinsically wrong.

At this point, you may be wondering how it is possible not to use the new keyword in object-oriented programming, but rest assured, we will cover that and expand on the control freak code smell in *Chapter 7, Deep Dive into Dependency Injection*.

Code smell – Long Methods

The **long methods** code smell is when a method starts to extend to more than 10 to 15 lines of code. That is a good indicator that you should think about that method differently. Having comments that separate multiple code blocks is a good indicator of a method that may be too long.

Here are a few examples of what might be the case:

- The method contains complex logic intertwined in multiple conditional statements.
- The method contains a big `switch` block.
- The method does too many things.
- The method contains duplications of code.

To fix this, you could do the following:

- Extract one or more private methods.
- Extract some code to new classes.
- Reuse the code from external classes.
- If you have a lot of conditional statements or a huge `switch` block, you could leverage a design pattern such as the Chain of Responsibility, or CQRS, which you will learn about in *Chapter 10, Behavioral Patterns*, and *Chapter 14, Mediator and CQRS Design Patterns*.

Usually, each problem has one or more solutions; you need to spot the problem and then find, choose, and implement one of the solutions. Let's be clear here: a method containing 16 lines does not necessarily need refactoring; it could be OK. Remember that a code smell indicates that there *might* be a problem, not that there necessarily *is* one—apply common sense.

Understanding the web — request/response

Before going any further, it is imperative to understand the basic concept of the web. The idea behind HTTP 1.X is that a client sends an HTTP request to a server, and then the server responds to that client. That can sound trivial if you have web development experience. However, it is one of the most important web programming concepts, irrespective of whether you are building web APIs, websites, or complex cloud applications.

Let's reduce an HTTP request lifetime to the following:

1. The communication starts.
2. The client sends a request to the server.
3. The server receives the request.
4. The server most likely does something (executes some code/logic).
5. The server responds to the client.
6. The communication ends.

After that cycle, the server is no longer aware of the client. Moreover, if the client sends another request, the server is unaware that it responded to a request earlier for that same client because **HTTP is stateless**.

There are mechanisms for creating a sense of persistence between requests for the server to be "aware" of its clients. The most well known of these is probably cookies.

If we dig a little deeper, an HTTP request is composed of a header and an optional body. The most commonly used HTTP methods are `GET` and `POST`. Made popular by web APIs, we could also add `PUT`, `DELETE`, and `PATCH` to that list.

Although not every HTTP method accepts a body, can respond with a body, or should be idempotent, here is a quick reference table:

Method	Request has body	Response has body	Idempotent
GET	No*	Yes	Yes
POST	Yes	Yes	No
PUT	Yes	No	Yes
PATCH	Yes	Yes	No
DELETE	May	May	Yes

 * Sending a body with a GET request is not forbidden by the HTTP specifications, but the semantics of such a request is not defined either. It is best to avoid sending GET requests with a body.

An **idempotent** request is a request that always yields the same result, whether it is sent once or multiple times. For example, sending the same POST request multiple times should create multiple similar entities, while sending the same DELETE request multiple times should delete a single entity. The status code of an idempotent request may vary, but the server state should remain the same. We will explore some of those concepts in more depth in *Chapter 5, The MVC Pattern for Web APIs*.

Here is an example of a GET request (without a body since that's not allowed for GET requests):

```
GET http://www.forevolve.com/ HTTP/1.1
Host: www.forevolve.com
Connection: keep-alive
Upgrade-Insecure-Requests: 1
User-Agent: Mozilla/5.0 (Windows NT 10.0; Win64; x64)
AppleWebKit/537.36 (KHTML, like Gecko) Chrome/70.0.3538.110 Safari/537.36
Accept: text/html,application/xhtml+xml,application/xml;q=0.9,image/webp,image/
apng,*/*;q=0.8
Accept-Encoding: gzip, deflate
Accept-Language: en-US,en;q=0.9,fr-CA;q=0.8,fr;q=0.7
Cookie: ...
```

The HTTP header is composed of a list of key/value pairs representing metadata that a client wants to send to the server. In this case, I queried my blog using the GET method and Google Chrome attached some additional information to the request. I replaced the Cookie header's value with ... because cookies can be quite large and are irrelevant to this sample. Nonetheless, cookies are passed back and forth like any other HTTP header.

Important note about cookies

The client sends cookies, and the server returns them for every request-response cycle. This could kill your bandwidth or slow down your application if you pass too much information back and forth (cookies or otherwise). One good example would be a serialized identity cookie that is very large.

Another example, one that is unrelated to cookies but that created such a back and forth, was the good old Web Forms `ViewState`. This was a hidden field sent with every request. That field could become very large when left unchecked.

Nowadays, with high-speed internet, it is easy to forget about those issues, but they can significantly impact the user experience of a client using a slow network.

When the server decides to respond to the request, it returns a header and an optional body, following the same principles as the request. The first line indicates the status of the request: whether it was successful. In our case, the status code was `200`, which indicates success. Each server can add more or less information to their response, as can you in your code.

Here is the response to the previous request:

```
HTTP/1.1 200 OK
Server: GitHub.com
Content-Type: text/html; charset=utf-8
Last-Modified: Wed, 03 Oct 2018 21:35:40 GMT
ETag: W/"5bb5362c-f677"
Access-Control-Allow-Origin: *
Expires: Fri, 07 Dec 2018 02:11:07 GMT
Cache-Control: max-age=600
Content-Encoding: gzip
X-GitHub-Request-Id: 32CE:1953:F1022C:1350142:5C09D460
Content-Length: 10055
Accept-Ranges: bytes
Date: Fri, 07 Dec 2018 02:42:05 GMT
Via: 1.1 varnish
Age: 35
Connection: keep-alive
X-Served-By: cache-ord1737-ORD
X-Cache: HIT
X-Cache-Hits: 2
X-Timer: S1544150525.288285,VS0,VE0
Vary: Accept-Encoding
X-Fastly-Request-ID: 98a36fb1b5642c8041b88ceace73f25caaf07746

<Response body truncated for brevity>
```

Now that the browser has received the server's response, in the case of HTML pages, it starts rendering it. Then, for each resource, it sends another HTTP call to its URI and loads it. A resource is an external asset, such as an image, a JavaScript file, a CSS file, or a font.

After the response, the server is no longer aware of the client; the communication has ended. It is essential to understand that to create a pseudo-state between each request, we need to use an external mechanism. That mechanism could be the *session-state* leveraging cookies, simply using cookies, or some other ASP.NET Core mechanisms; or we could create a stateless application. I recommend going stateless whenever you can.

> **Note**
>
> If you are interested in learning more about session and state management, I left a link in the *Further reading* section at the end of the chapter.

As you can imagine, the backbone of the internet is its networking stack. The **Hypertext Transfer Protocol (HTTP)** is the highest layer of that stack (layer 7). HTTP is an application layer built on the **Transmission Control Protocol (TCP)**. TCP (layer 4) is the transport layer, which defines how data is moved over the network (for instance, the transmission of data, the amount of transmitted data, and error checking). TCP uses the **Internet Protocol (IP)** layer to reach the computer it tries to talk to. IP (layer 3) represents the network layer, which handles packet IP addressing.

A packet is a chunk of data that is transmitted over the wire. We could send a large file directly from a source to a destination machine, but that is not practical, so the network stack breaks down large items into smaller packets. For example, the source machine breaks a file into multiple packets, sends them to the target machine, and then the target reassembles them back into the source file. This process allows numerous senders to use the same wire instead of waiting for the first transmission to be done. If a packet gets lost in transit, the source machine can also send only that packet back to the target machine.

Rest assured, you don't need to understand every detail behind networking to program web applications, but it is always good to know that HTTP uses TCP/IP and chunks big payloads into smaller packets. Moreover, HTTP/1 allows a limited number of parallel requests that a browser can open. This knowledge can help you optimize your apps. For example, a high number of assets to load, their size, and the order in which they are sent to the browser can increase the page load time, the perceived page load time, or paint time.

To conclude this subject and not dig too deep into networking, HTTP/1 is older but foundational. HTTP/2 is more efficient and supports streaming multiple assets using the same TCP connection. It also allows the server to send assets to the client before it requests the resources, called a server push.

If you find HTTP interesting, HTTP/2 is an excellent place to start digging deeper, as well as the newest experimental HTTP/3 specifications.

Getting started with .NET

A bit of history: .NET Framework 1.0 was first released in 2002. .NET is a managed framework that compiles your code into an **Intermediate Language** (IL) named **Microsoft Intermediate Language** (**MSIL**). That IL code is then compiled into native code and executed by the **Common Language Runtime** (**CLR**). The CLR is now known simply as the **.NET runtime**. After releasing several versions of .NET Framework, Microsoft never delivered on the promise of an interoperable stack. Moreover, many flaws were built into the core of .NET Framework, tying it to Windows.

Mono, an open source project, was developed by the community to enable .NET code to run on non-Windows OSes. Mono was used and supported by Xamarin, acquired by Microsoft in 2016. Mono enabled .NET code to run on other OSes like Android and iOS. Later, Microsoft started to develop an official cross-platform .NET SDK and runtime they named .NET Core.

The .NET team did a magnificent job building ASP.NET Core from the ground up, cutting out compatibility with the older .NET Framework versions. That brought its share of problems at first, but .NET Standard alleviated the interoperability issues between the old .NET and the new .NET.

After years of improvements and two major versions in parallel (Core and Framework), Microsoft reunified most .NET technologies into .NET 5 (now .NET 6) and the promise of a shared **Base Class Library** (**BCL**). With .NET 5, .NET Core simply became .NET while ASP.NET Core remained ASP.NET Core. There is no .NET Core 4, to avoid any potential confusion with .NET Framework 4.X.

New major versions of .NET should release every year now. Even-number releases are **Long-Term Support** (**LTS**) releases with free support for 3 years, and odd-number releases (Current) have free support for only 18 months.

The good thing behind this book is that the architectural principles and design patterns covered should remain relevant in the future and are not tightly coupled with the versions of .NET you are using. Minor changes to the code samples should be enough to migrate your knowledge and code to new versions.

Now, let's cover some key information about the .NET ecosystem.

.NET SDK versus runtime

You can install different binaries grouped under SDKs and runtimes. The SDK allows you to build and run .NET programs, while the runtime only allows you to run .NET programs.

As a developer, you want to install the SDK on your deployment environment. On the server, you want to install the runtime. The runtime is lighter, while the SDK contains more tools, including the runtime.

.NET 5+ versus .NET Standard

When building .NET projects, there are multiple types of projects, but basically, we can separate them into two categories:

*   Applications
*   Libraries

Applications target a version of .NET, such as `net5.0` and `net6.0`. Examples of that would be an ASP.NET application or a console application.

Libraries are bundles of code compiled together, often distributed as a NuGet package. .NET Standard class library projects allow code to be shared between .NET Core, .NET 5+, and .NET Framework projects. .NET Standard came into play to bridge the compatibility gap between .NET Core and .NET Framework, which eased the transition. Things were not easy when .NET Core 1.0 first came out.

With .NET 5 unifying all the platforms and becoming the future of the unified .NET ecosystem, .NET Standard is no longer needed. Moreover, app and library authors should target the base **Target Framework Moniker (TFM)**, as in `net5.0` and `net6.0`. You should target `netstandard2.0` or `netstandard2.1` only when needed, for example, to share code with .NET Framework, and avoid targeting .NET Standard 1.X. Microsoft also introduced OS-specific TFMs with .NET 5 and 6 that allow code to use OS-specific APIs like `net6.0-android` and `net6.0-tvos`. You can also target multiple TFMs when needed.

Note

I'm sure that we are going to see .NET Standard libraries stick around for a while. All projects are not just going to migrate from .NET Framework to .NET 5 magically, and people are likely to want to continue sharing code between the two.

The next versions of .NET should be built over .NET (Core) 5, while .NET Framework 4.X is going to stay where it is today, receiving only security patches and minor updates. For example, .NET 6 is built over .NET 5.

Visual Studio Code versus Visual Studio versus the command-line interface

How can one of these projects be created? .NET Core comes with the `dotnet` **command-line interface (CLI)**, which exposes multiple commands, including `new`. Running the `dotnet new` command in a terminal generates a new project.

To create an empty class library, we can run the following commands:

```
md MyProject
cd MyProject
dotnet new classlib
```

That would generate an empty class library in the newly created `MyProject` directory. The `-h` option can come in handy when discovering available commands and their options. You can use `dotnet -h` to find the available SDK commands, or `dotnet new -h` to find out about options and available templates.

The CLI enables us to automate our workflows in **continuous integration (CI)** pipelines, while developing locally, or through any other process.

The CLI also makes it easier to write documentation that anyone can follow; it is way easier and faster to write a few commands in a terminal than install programs like Visual Studio and emulators.

Visual Studio Code is my favorite text editor. I don't use it much for .NET coding, but I still do to reorganize projects, when it's CLI time, or for any other task that is easier to complete using a text editor, such as writing documentation using Markdown, writing JavaScript or TypeScript, or managing JSON, YAML, or XML files. To create a project or solution, or to add a NuGet package using Visual Studio Code, open a terminal and use the CLI.

As for **Visual Studio**, my favorite IDE, it uses the CLI under the hood to create the same projects, making it consistent between tools. Visual Studio adds a user interface over the CLI, which is a good example of leveraging it.

You can also create and install additional dotnet new project templates in the CLI or even create global tools. Those topics are beyond the scope of this book.

An overview of project templates

Here is an example of the templates that are installed (dotnet new --list):

```
Windows PowerShell         X    +    v

These templates matched your input:

Template Name                                     Short Name       Language       Tags
----------------------------------------------    -------------    -----------    -----------------------------
ASP.NET Core Empty                                web              [C#],F#        Web/Empty
ASP.NET Core gRPC Service                         grpc             [C#]           Web/gRPC
ASP.NET Core Web API                              webapi           [C#],F#        Web/WebAPI
ASP.NET Core Web App                              razor,webapp     [C#]           Web/MVC/Razor Pages
ASP.NET Core Web App (Model-View-Controller)      mvc              [C#],F#        Web/MVC
ASP.NET Core with Angular                         angular          [C#]           Web/MVC/SPA
ASP.NET Core with React.js                        react            [C#]           Web/MVC/SPA
ASP.NET Core with React.js and Redux              reactredux       [C#]           Web/MVC/SPA
Blazor Server App                                 blazorserver     [C#]           Web/Blazor
Blazor WebAssembly App                            blazorwasm       [C#]           Web/Blazor/WebAssembly/PWA
Class Library                                     classlib         [C#],F#,VB     Common/Library
Console App                                       console          [C#],F#,VB     Common/Console
dotnet gitignore file                             gitignore                       Config
Dotnet local tool manifest file                   tool-manifest                   Config
```

Figure 1.1: Project templates

A study of all the templates is beyond the scope of this book, but I'd like to visit the few that are worth mentioning, some of which we will use later:

- dotnet new console creates a console application
- dotnet new classlib creates a class library
- dotnet new xunit creates an xUnit test project
- dotnet new web creates an empty web project
- dotnet new mvc scaffolds an MVC application
- dotnet new webapi scaffolds a web API application

Running and building your program

If you are using Visual Studio, you can always hit the play button, or *F5*, and run your app. If you are using the CLI, you can use one of the following commands (and more). Each of them also offers different options to control their behavior. Add the -h flag with any command to get help on that command, such as `dotnet build -h`:

Command	Description
`dotnet restore`	Restore the dependencies (a.k.a. NuGet packages) based on the `.csproj` or `.sln` file present in the current dictionary.
`dotnet build`	Build the application based on the `.csproj` or `.sln` file present in the current dictionary. It implicitly runs the `restore` command first.
`dotnet run`	Run the current application based on the `.csproj` file present in the current dictionary. It implicitly runs the `build` and `restore` commands first.
`dotnet watch run`	Watch for file changes. When a file has changed, the CLI updates the code from that file using the hot-reload feature. When that is impossible, it rebuilds the application and then reruns it (equivalent to executing the `run` command again). If it is a web application, the page should refresh automatically.
`dotnet test`	Run the tests based on the `.csproj` or `.sln` file present in the current directory. It implicitly runs the `build` and `restore` commands first. We cover testing in the next chapter.
`dotnet watch test`	Watch for file changes. When a file has changed, the CLI reruns the tests (equivalent to executing the `test` command again).
`dotnet publish`	Publish the current application, based on the `.csproj` or `.sln` file present in the current directory, to a directory or remote location, such as a hosting provider. It implicitly runs the `build` and `restore` commands first.
`dotnet pack`	Create a NuGet package based on the `.csproj` or `.sln` file present in the current directory. It implicitly runs the `build` and `restore` commands first. You don't need a `.nuspec` file.
`dotnet clean`	Clean the build(s) output of a project or solution based on the `.csproj` or `.sln` file present in the current directory.

Technical requirements

Throughout the book, we will explore and write code. I recommend that you install Visual Studio, Visual Studio Code, or both to help with that. Other alternatives are Visual Studio for Mac, Riders, or any other text editor of your choice. I use Visual Studio and Visual Studio Code.

Unless you install Visual Studio, which comes with the .NET SDK, you may need to install it. The SDK comes with the CLI that we explored earlier, as well as the build tools for running and testing your programs. Have a look at the README.md file in the GitHub repository for more information and links to those resources.

The source code of all chapters is available for download on GitHub at the following address: `https://adpg.link/net6`.

Summary

In this chapter, we took a look at design patterns, anti-patterns, and code smells. We also explored a few of them. We then moved on to a recap of the request/response cycle of a typical web application.

We continued by exploring .NET essentials, such as SDK versus runtime and app targets versus .NET Standard. This has set us up to explore the different possibilities we have when building our .NET applications. We then dug a little more into the .NET CLI, where I laid down a list of essential commands, including `dotnet build` and `dotnet watch run`. We also covered how to create new projects.

In the next two chapters, we explore automated testing and architectural principles. These are foundational chapters for anyone wishing to build robust, flexible, and maintainable applications.

Questions

Let's take a look at a few practice questions:

1. Can we add a body to a `GET` request?
2. Why are long methods a code smell?
3. Is it true that .NET Standard should be your default target when creating libraries?
4. What is a code smell?

Further reading

Here are some links to consolidate what has been learned in the chapter:

- Overview of how .NET is versioned: `https://adpg.link/n52L`
- .NET CLI overview: `https://adpg.link/Lzx3`
- Custom templates for dotnet new: `https://adpg.link/74i2`
- Session and state management in ASP.NET Core: `https://adpg.link/Xzgf`

Join our book's Discord space

Join the book's Discord workspace for *Ask me Anything* session with the authors:

https://packt.link/ASPdotNET6DesignPatterns

2

Automated Testing

This chapter focuses on automated testing and how helpful it can be for crafting better software. It also covers a few different types of tests and the foundation of **test-driven development** (**TDD**). We also outline how testable ASP.NET Core is and how much easier it is to test ASP.NET Core applications than old ASP.NET MVC applications. This chapter is an overview of automated testing, its principles, xUnit, and more. While other books cover this topic more in-depth, this chapter covers the foundational aspect of automated testing, built upon throughout the book.

In this chapter, we cover the following topics:

- An overview of automated testing
- Testing .NET applications
- Important testing principles

An overview of automated testing

Testing is an integral part of the development process, and automated testing becomes crucial in the long run. You can always run your ASP.NET Core website, open a browser, and click everywhere to test your features. That's a legitimate approach, but it is harder to test individual rules or more complex algorithms that way. Another downside is the lack of automation; when you first start with a small app containing a few pages, a few endpoints, or a few features, it may be fast to perform those tests manually. However, as your app grows, it becomes more tedious, takes longer, and the likelihood of making a mistake increases. Don't get me wrong here; you will always need real users to test out your applications, but you may want those tests to focus on the UX, the content, or on some experimental features that you are building instead of bug reports that automated tests could have caught early on.

There are multiple types of tests, and developers are very creative at finding new ways to test things. Here is a list of three broad categories that represent how we can divide automated testing from a code correctness standpoint:

- Unit tests
- Integration tests
- **End-to-end** (**E2E**) tests

The test pyramid is a good way of explaining a few concepts around automated testing. You want different granularity of tests, and you want a different number of tests depending on their complexity. The following test pyramid shows the three types of tests stated above. However, you can add all the other types of tests in there if you want to. Moreover, that's just an abstract guideline to give you an idea. The most important aspect is the **return on investment (ROI)**. If you can write one integration test that covers a large surface and is fast enough, this might be worth doing instead of multiple unit tests.

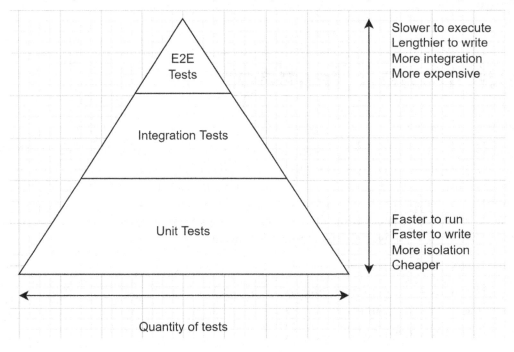

Figure 2.1: The test pyramid

Unit testing

Unit tests focus on individual units, like testing the outcome of a method. Unit tests should be fast and should not rely on any infrastructure such as a database. Those are the kinds of tests you want the most because they run fast, and each one tests a precise code path. They should also help you design your application better because you use your code in the tests, so you become its first consumer, leading to you finding some design flaws and making your code better. If you don't like using your code in your tests, that is a good indicator that nobody else will. Unit tests should focus on testing algorithms (the ins and outs) and domain logic, not the code itself; how you wrote the code should have no impact on the intent of the test. For example, you are testing that a Purchase method executes the logic required to purchase one or more items, not that you created the variable X or Y or Z inside that method. Don't discourage yourself if you find it challenging; writing a good test suite is not as easy as it sounds.

Integration testing

Integration tests focus on the interaction between components, such as what happens when a component queries the database or what happens when two components interact with each other.

Integration tests often require some infrastructure to interact with, which makes them slower to run. By following the classic testing model, you want integration tests, but you want fewer of them than unit tests. An integration test can be very close to an E2E test but without using a production-like environment.

> **Note**
>
> We break the test pyramid rule later, so always be critical of rules and principles; sometimes, it can be better to break or bend them. For example, having one good integration test can be better than N unit tests; don't discard that fact when writing your tests.

End-to-end testing

End-to-end tests focus on application-wide behaviors, such as what happens when a user clicks on a specific button, navigates to a particular page, posts a form, or sends a PUT request to some web API endpoint. E2E tests focus on testing the whole application from the user's perspective, not just part of it, as unit and integration tests do. E2E tests are usually run on actual infrastructure to test your application and your deployment.

Other types of tests

There are other types of automated tests. For example, we could do load testing, performance testing, regression testing, contract testing, penetration testing, functional testing, smoke testing, and more. You can automate tests for almost anything you want to validate, but some tests are more challenging to automate or more fragile than others, such as UI tests. That said, if you can automate a test in a reasonable timeframe, do it! In the long run, it should pay off.

One more thing; don't blindly rely on metrics such as code coverage. Those metrics make for cute badges in your GitHub project's `readme.md` file but can lead you off track, resulting in you writing useless tests. Don't get me wrong, code coverage is a great metric when used correctly, but remember that one good test can be better than a lousy test suite covering 100% of your codebase.

Writing good tests is not easy and comes with practice.

> **Note**
>
> One piece of advice: keep your test suite healthy by adding missing test cases and removing obsolete or useless tests. Think about use case coverage, not about how many lines of code are covered by your tests.

Before moving forward to testing styles, let's inspect a hypothetical system and explore a more efficient way to test it.

Picking the right test style

Next is a dependency map of a hypothetical system. We use that diagram to pick the most meaningful type of test possible for each piece of the program. In real life, that diagram will most likely be in your head, but in this case, I drew it out. Let's inspect that diagram before I explain its content:

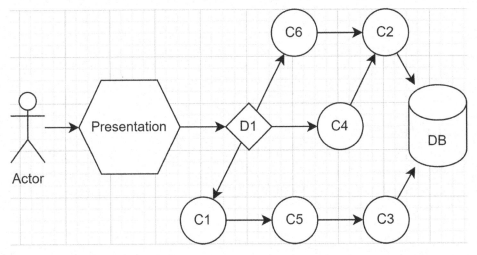

Figure 2.2: Dependency map of a hypothetical system

In the diagram, the **Actor** can be anything from a user to another system. **Presentation** is the piece of the system that the **Actor** is interacting with that forwards the request to the system itself (this could be a user interface). **D1** is a component that has to decide what to do next based on the user input. **C1** to **C6** are other components of the system (could be classes, for example). **DB** is a database.

D1 must choose between three code paths: interact with the components C1, C4, or C6. This type of logic is usually a good subject for unit tests, ensuring the algorithm yields the correct result based on the input parameter. Why pick a unit test? We can test multiple scenarios very quickly, try extreme cases, out-of-bound data cases, and more. We usually mock the dependencies away in this type of test and assert that the subject under test made the expected call on the desired component.

Then, if we look at the other code paths, we could write one or more integration tests for component C1, testing the whole chain in one go (C1, C5, and C3) instead of writing multiple mock-heavy unit tests for each component. If there is any logic that we need to test in components C1, C5, or C3, we can always add a few unit tests; that's what they are for.

Finally, C4 and C6 are both using C2. Depending on the code (that we don't have here), we could write integration tests for C4 and C6, testing C2 simultaneously. Another way would be to unit test C4 and C6, and then write integration tests between C2 and the DB. If C2 has no logic, the latter could be the best and the fastest, while the former will most likely yield results that give you more confidence in your test suite in a continuous delivery model.

When it is an option, I recommend evaluating the possibility of writing fewer meaningful integration tests that assert the correctness of a use case over a suite of mock-heavy unit tests.

That may seem to go "against" the test pyramid, but does it? If you spend less time (thus lower costs) testing more use cases (adding more value), that sounds like a win to me. Moreover, we must not forget that mocking dependencies tends to make you waste time fighting the framework or other libraries instead of testing something meaningful.

Now that we have explored the fundamentals of automated testing, it is time to explore testing approaches and TDD, which is a way to apply those testing concepts.

Testing approaches

There are various approaches to testing, such as **behavior-driven development (BDD)**, **acceptance test-driven development (ATDD)**, and **test-driven development (TDD)**. The DevOps culture brings a mindset to the table that focuses on embracing automated testing in line with its **continuous integration (CI)** and **continuous deployment (CD)** ideals. CD is really where a robust and healthy suite of tests shine, giving you a high degree of confidence in your code, high enough to deploy the program when all tests pass.

TDD is a method of developing software that states that you should write one or more tests before writing the actual code. In a nutshell, you invert your development flow by following the **Red-Green-Refactor** technique, which goes like this:

1. You write a failing test (red).
2. You write just enough code to make your test pass (green).
3. You refactor that code to improve the design by ensuring that all of the tests are still passing.

 Note

We explore the meaning of **refactoring** in the next section.

ATDD is similar to TDD but focuses on acceptance (or functional) tests instead of software units and involves multiple parties like customers, developers, and testers.

BDD is another complementary technique originating from TDD and ATDD. BDD focuses on formulating test cases around application behaviors using spoken language and also involves multiple parties like customers, developers, and testers. Moreover, practitioners of BDD often leverage the *given–when–then* grammar to formalize their test cases. Because of that, BDD output is in a human-readable format allowing stakeholders to consult such artifacts.

The given–when–then template defines the way to describe the behavior of a user story or acceptance test, like this:

*   *Given* one or more preconditions (context)
*   *When* something happens (behavior)
*   *Then* one or more observable changes are expected (measurable side effects)

For the sake of simplicity, we stick to unit testing, integration testing, and a tad of TDD in the book. ATDD and BDD are great areas to dig deeper into and can help design better apps; defining precise user-centric specifications can help build only what is needed, prioritize better, and improve communication between parties. Nonetheless, let's go back to the main track and define refactoring.

Refactoring

Refactoring is about (continually) improving the code without changing its behavior.

Having an automated test suite should help you achieve that goal and should help you discover when you break something. No matter whether you do TDD or not, I do recommend refactoring as often as possible; this helps clean your codebase, and it should also help you get rid of some technical debt at the same time.

Okay, but what is **technical debt**?

Technical debt

Technical debt represents the corners you cut short while developing a feature or a system. That happens no matter how hard you try because life is life, and there are delays, deadlines, budgets, and people, including developers.

The most important point is to understand that you cannot avoid technical debt altogether, so it's better to embrace that fact and learn to live with it instead of fighting it. From that point forward, you can only try to limit the amount of technical debt that you, or someone else, generates.

One way to limit the piling up of technical debt is to refactor the code often. So, factor the refactoring time into your time estimates. Another way is to improve collaboration between all the parties involved. Everyone must work toward the same goal if you want your projects to succeed.

You will at some point cut the usage of best practices short due to external forces like people or time constraints. The key is to come back at it as soon as possible to repay that technical debt, and automated tests are there to help you refactor that code and get rid of that debt elegantly. Depending on the size of your workplace, there will be more or fewer people between you and that decision.

Tip

I realize that some of these things might be out of your control, so you may have to live with more technical debt than you had hoped for. However, even when things are out of your control, nothing stops you from becoming a pioneer and working toward changing the enterprise's culture for the better. Don't be afraid to become a leader, an agent of change.

Nevertheless, don't let the technical debt pile up too high, or you may not be able to pay it back, and at some point, that's where a project begins to break and fail. Don't be mistaken; a project in production can be a failure. Delivering a product does not guarantee success, and I'm talking about the quality of the code here, not the amount of generated revenue (I'll leave that to other people to evaluate).

Next, we look at testing ASP.NET Core applications.

Testing .NET applications

The ASP.NET Core team made our life easier by designing ASP.NET Core for testability; most testing is way easier than before the ASP.NET Core era. Back when .NET Core was in pre-release, I discovered that the .NET team was using **xUnit** to test their code and that it was the only testing framework available. xUnit has become my favorite testing framework, and I use it throughout the book.

We are not going into full TDD mode, as it would deviate our focus from the matter at hand, but I did my best to tag automated testing along for the ride! Why are we talking about tests in an architectural book? Because testability is usually the sign of a good design, which allows some concepts to be proven by using tests instead of words.

Moreover, in many code samples, the test cases are the consumers, making the program lighter without building an entire user interface over it. That allows us to focus on the patterns we are exploring instead of getting our focus scattered over some boilerplate code.

Let's start by creating a test project.

Creating an xUnit test project

To create a new xUnit test project, you can run the `dotnet new xunit` command, and the CLI does the job for you by creating a project containing a `UnitTest1` class. That command does the same as creating a new xUnit project from Visual Studio.

For unit testing projects, name the project the same as the project you want to test and append `.Tests` to it. For example, `MyProject` would have an associated `MyProject.Tests` project associated with it. We explore more details in the *Organizing your tests* section below.

The template already defines all the required NuGet packages, so you can start testing right away; after adding a reference to your project under test, of course.

Next, we explore some xUnit features.

Getting started with xUnit

In xUnit, the `[Fact]` attribute is the way to create unique test cases, while the `[Theory]` attribute is the way to make data-driven test cases. Let's start with facts.

Facts

Any method with no parameter can become a test method by decorating it with a `[Fact]` attribute, like this:

```
public class FactTest
{
    [Fact]
    public void Should_be_equal()
    {
        var expectedValue = 2;
```

```
        var actualValue = 2;
        Assert.Equal(expectedValue, actualValue);
    }
}
```

You can also decorate asynchronous methods with the fact attribute when the code under test needs it:

```
public class AsyncFactTest
{
    [Fact]
    public async Task Should_be_equal()
    {
        var expectedValue = 2;
        var actualValue = 2;
        await Task.Yield();
        Assert.Equal(expectedValue, actualValue);
    }
}
```

In the preceding code, the highlighted line conceptually represents an asynchronous operation and does nothing more than allow the use of the `async`/`await` keywords.

Note

The test classes are nested in the `xUnitFeaturesTest` class, part of the `MyApp` namespace, and under the `MyApp.Tests` project.

From the Visual Studio Test Explorer, that test case looks like this:

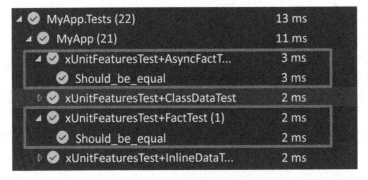

Figure 2.3: Test results in Visual Studio

Running the `dotnet test` CLI command should yield a result similar to the following:

```
Passed!  - Failed:     0, Passed:    23, Skipped:     0, Total:    23,
Duration: 22 ms - MyApp.Tests.dll (net6.0)
```

As we can read from the preceding output, all tests are passing, none have failed, and none were skipped. It is as simple as that to create test cases using xUnit.

Have you noticed the `Assert` keyword? If you are not familiar with it, we explore assertions next.

Assertions

We just learned about facts and will head toward theories next. Meanwhile, let's visit a few ways to assert correctness. We use barebone xUnit functionality in this section, but you can bring in the assertion library of your choice if you have one.

In xUnit, the assertion throws an exception when it fails. You do not have to handle those; that's the mechanism to propagate the failure result up to the test runner.

We won't explore all possibilities here, but let's start with a few common use cases. The code is broken down to make the explanations clearer:

```
public class AssertionTest
{
    [Fact]
    public void Exploring_xUnit_assertions()
    {
        object obj1 = new MyClass { Name = "Object 1" };
        object obj2 = new MyClass { Name = "Object 1" };
        object obj3 = obj1;
        object? obj4 = default(MyClass);
```

In the preceding code, we declare a few objects that are used by the assertions next. All variables are of the `object` type to leverage the `IsType` method later. The `MyClass` class is defined after the assertions:

```
        Assert.Equal(expected: 2, actual: 2);
        Assert.NotEqual(expected: 2, actual: 1);
```

The preceding two assertions are explicit and compare whether the actual value is equal, or not equal, to the expected value. `Assert.Equal` is probably the most commonly used assertion method.

Tip

As a rule of thumb, it is better to assert a result (`Equal`) than assert that the value is different (`NotEqual`). Except in a few rare cases, asserting equality will yield more accurate results and close the door to missing defects.

```
        Assert.Same(obj1, obj3);
        Assert.NotSame(obj2, obj3);
        Assert.Equal(obj1, obj2);
```

The first two assertions are very similar to the equality ones, but assert that the objects are the same instance, or not (have the same reference or not). The third one asserts that the two objects are equals and leverages record classes to make it that easy; obj1 and obj2 are not the same but are equal (see *Appendix A* for more information on record classes):

```
Assert.Null(obj4);
Assert.NotNull(obj3);
```

These two are also very explicit, asserting that the value is null or not:

```
var instanceOfMyClass = Assert.IsType<MyClass>(obj1);
Assert.Equal(expected: "Object 1", actual: instanceOfMyClass.Name);
```

The first preceding line asserts that obj1 is of the MyClass type and then returns the argument (obj1) converted to the asserted type (MyClass). If the type is incorrect, the IsType method will throw an exception:

```
var exception = Assert.Throws<SomeCustomException>(
    testCode: () => OperationThatThrows("Toto")
);
Assert.Equal(expected: "Toto", actual: exception.Name);

static void OperationThatThrows(string name)
{
    throw new SomeCustomException { Name = name };
}
```

The highlighted line of the preceding code asserts that the testCode argument throws an exception of the SomeCustomException type. The testCode argument is executing the OperationThatThrows inline function, which does just that. What is often very important is to test the fact that the exception properties, like the message, are well-formatted. Whether you want to assert the error message or another property of the exception, it is a well-used pattern that the Throws method allows us to do easily, as the second line does by asserting that the value of the exception.Name property is equal to the one passed as an argument of the inline function ("Toto"). The same behavior as IsType happens here; if the exception is of the wrong type or no exception is thrown at all, the Throws method will throw an exception:

```
}
private record class MyClass
{
    public string? Name { get; set; }
}
```

```
        private class SomeCustomException : Exception
        {
            public string? Name { get; set; }
        }
    }
}
```

The remaining two classes are utilities used in the tests with nothing special to them; their purpose was to help us play with xUnit assertions.

We covered a few assertion methods, but many others are part of xUnit, like the Collection, Contains, False, and True methods. We use many assertions throughout the book, so if these are still unclear, you will have a chance to learn more about them.

Next, let's look at data-driven test cases using theories.

Theories

For more complex test cases, we can use theories. A theory is defined in two parts:

- A [Theory] attribute.
- At least one of the three following data attributes: [InlineData], [MemberData], or [ClassData].

Interestingly, you are not limited to only one type of data attribute; you can use as many as you need to suit your needs and feed a theory with the appropriate data.

When writing a theory, your primary constraint is to ensure that the number of values matches the number of parameters defined in the test method. For example, a theory with one parameter must be fed with one value. Let's look at some examples.

The [InlineData] attribute is the most suitable for constant values or smaller sets of values. Inline data is the most straightforward way of the three because of the proximity of the test values and the test method.

Here is an example of a theory using inline data:

```
public class InlineDataTest
{
    [Theory]
    [InlineData(1, 1)]
    [InlineData(2, 2)]
    [InlineData(5, 5)]
    public void Should_be_equal(int value1, int value2)
    {
        Assert.Equal(value1, value2);
    }
}
```

That test method yields three test cases in the Test Explorer, where each can pass or fail individually:

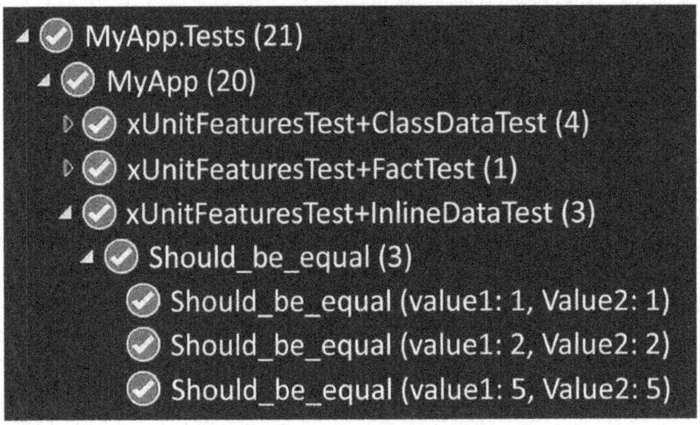

Figure 2.4: Test results

Then, the [MemberData] and [ClassData] attributes can be used to simplify the test method's declaration. When it is impossible to instantiate the data in the attribute, reuse the data in multiple test methods, or encapsulate the data away from the test class.

Here is an example of [MemberData] usage:

```
public class MemberDataTest
{
    public static IEnumerable<object[]> Data => new[]
    {
        new object[] { 1, 2, false },
        new object[] { 2, 2, true },
        new object[] { 3, 3, true },
    };

    public static TheoryData<int, int, bool> TypedData =>new TheoryData<int,
int, bool>
    {
        { 3, 2, false },
        { 2, 3, false },
        { 5, 5, true },
    };

    [Theory]
    [MemberData(nameof(Data))]
    [MemberData(nameof(TypedData))]
    [MemberData(nameof(ExternalData.GetData), 10, MemberType =
typeof(ExternalData))]
```

```
    [MemberData(nameof(ExternalData.TypedData), MemberType =
typeof(ExternalData))]
    public void Should_be_equal(int value1, int value2, bool shouldBeEqual)
    {
        if (shouldBeEqual)
        {
            Assert.Equal(value1, value2);
        }
        else
        {
            Assert.NotEqual(value1, value2);
        }
    }


    public class ExternalData
    {
        public static IEnumerable<object[]> GetData(int start) => new[]
        {
            new object[] { start, start, true },
            new object[] { start, start + 1, false },
            new object[] { start + 1, start + 1, true },
        };
        public static TheoryData<int, int, bool> TypedData => new
TheoryData<int, int, bool>
        {
            { 20, 30, false },
            { 40, 50, false },
            { 50, 50, true },
        };
    }
}
```

The preceding test case should yield 12 results. If we break it down, the code starts by loading three sets of data from the IEnumerable<object[]> Data property by decorating the test method with the [MemberData(nameof(Data))] attribute. This is how to load data from a member of the class the test method is declared in.

Then, the second property is very similar to the Data property, but replaces IEnumerable<object[]> with a TheoryData<…> class, making it more readable and type-safe. This is my preferred way of defining member data and what I recommend you to do. Like the first one, we feed those three sets of data to the test method by decorating it with the [MemberData(nameof(TypedData))] attribute. Once again, it is part of the test class.

The third data feeds three more sets of data to the test method. However, that data originates from the GetData method of the ExternalData class, sending 10 as an argument during the execution (the start parameter). To do that, we must specify the MemberType instance where the method is located so xUnit knows where to look. In this case, we pass the argument 10 as the second parameter of the MemberData constructor. However, in other cases, you can pass zero or more arguments there.

Finally, we are doing the same for the ExternalData.TypedData property, which is represented by the [MemberData(nameof(ExternalData.TypedData), MemberType = typeof(ExternalData))] attribute. Once again, the only difference is that the property is defined using TheoryData instead of IEnumerable<object[]>, which makes its intent clearer.

When running the tests, the data provided by the [MemberData] attributes is combined, which yields the following result in the Test Explorer:

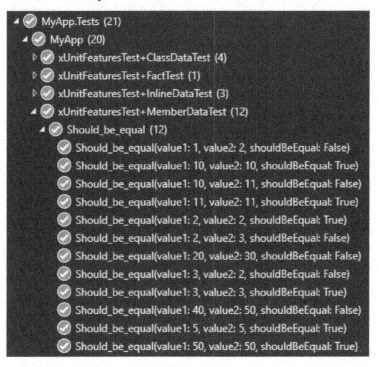

Figure 2.5: Test results

These are only a few examples of what we can do with the [MemberData] attribute. The goal is to cover just enough cases to get you started.

Last but not least, the [ClassData] attribute gets its data from a class implementing IEnumerable<object[]> or inheriting from TheoryData<…>. The concept is the same as the other two. Here is an example:

```
public class ClassDataTest
{
```

```csharp
[Theory]
[ClassData(typeof(TheoryDataClass))]
[ClassData(typeof(TheoryTypedDataClass))]
public void Should_be_equal(int value1, int value2, bool shouldBeEqual)
{
    if (shouldBeEqual)
    {
        Assert.Equal(value1, value2);
    }
    else
    {
        Assert.NotEqual(value1, value2);
    }
}
public class TheoryDataClass : IEnumerable<object[]>
{
    public IEnumerator<object[]> GetEnumerator()
    {
        yield return new object[] { 1, 2, false };
        yield return new object[] { 2, 2, true };
        yield return new object[] { 3, 3, true };
    }
    IEnumerator IEnumerable.GetEnumerator() => GetEnumerator();
}
public class TheoryTypedDataClass : TheoryData<int, int, bool>
{
    public TheoryTypedDataClass()
    {
        Add(102, 104, false);
    }
}
}
```

These are very similar to [MemberData], but instead of pointing to a member, we point to a type.

In TheoryDataClass, implementing the IEnumerable<object[]> interface makes it easy to yield return the results. On the other hand, in the TheoryTypedDataClass class, by inheriting TheoryData, we can leverage a list-like Add method. Once again, I find inheriting from TheoryData more explicit, but either way works with xUnit. You have many options, so choose the best one for your use case.

Here is the result in the Test Explorer, which is very similar to the other attributes:

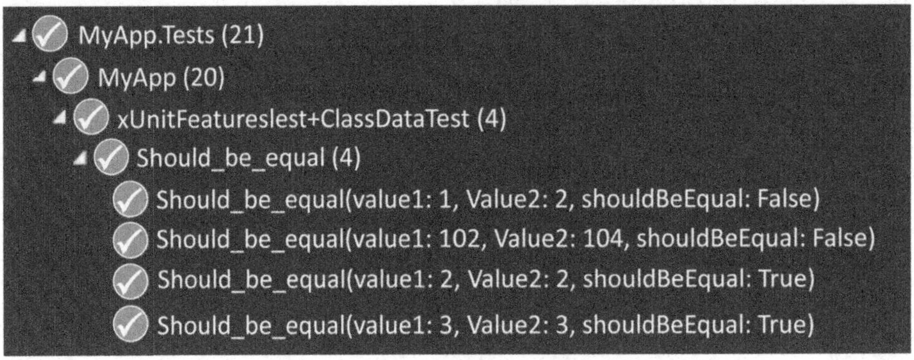

Figure 2.6: Test Explorer

That's it for the theories—next, a few last words before organizing our tests.

Closing words

Now that facts, theories, and assertions are out of the way, xUnit offers other mechanics to allow developers to inject dependencies into their test classes. These are named fixtures. Fixtures allow dependencies to be reused by all of the test methods of a test class by implementing the IClassFixture<T> interface. Fixtures are very helpful for costly dependencies, like creating an in-memory database. With fixtures, you can create the dependency once and use it multiple times. The ValuesControllerTest class in the MyApp.IntegrationTests project shows that in action.

It is important to note that xUnit creates an instance of the test class for every test run, so your dependencies are recreated every time if you are not using the fixtures.

You can also share the dependency provided by the fixture between multiple test classes by using ICollectionFixture<T>, [Collection], and [CollectionDefinition] instead. We won't get into the details here, but at least you know it's possible and know what types to look for when you need something similar.

Finally, if you have worked with other testing frameworks, you might have encountered **setup** and **teardown** methods. In xUnit, there are no particular attributes or mechanisms for handling setup and teardown code. Instead, xUnit uses existing OOP concepts:

* To set up your tests, use the class constructor.
* To tear down (clean up) your tests, implement IDisposable or IAsyncDisposable and dispose of your resources there.

That's it, xUnit is very simple and powerful, which is the main reason why I adopted it as my main testing framework several years ago and why I chose it for this book.

Next, we learn to write readable test methods.

Arrange, Act, Assert

One well-known method for writing readable tests is **Arrange, Act, Assert (AAA or 3A)**. This technique allows you to clearly define your setup (arrange), the operation under test (act), and your assertions (assert). One efficient way to use this technique is to start by writing the 3A as comments in your test case and then write the test code in between. Here is an example:

```
[Fact]
public void Should_be_equals()
{
    // Arrange
    var a = 1;
    var b = 2;
    var expectedResult = 3;

    // Act
    var result = a + b;

    // Assert
    Assert.Equal(expectedResult, result);
}
```

Of course, that test case cannot fail, but the three blocks are easily identifiable with the 3A comments.

In general, **you want the Act block of your unit tests to be a single line,** making the test focus clear. If you need more than one line, the chances are that something is wrong in the test or the design.

One last tip before learning to organize tests into projects, directories, and files: when the tests are very small (only a few lines), getting rid of the comments might help readability. Furthermore, when you don't need the Arrange block, please don't leave the comment there; delete it.

Organizing your tests

There are many ways of organizing test projects inside a solution, and I tend to create a unit test project for each project in the solution and one or more integration test projects. It depends on the type of project.

Since unit tests are directly related to single units of code, it makes sense to organize them into a one-on-one relationship. Since integration tests could also span multiple projects, it is hard to put a hard rule in place. One integration test project could be fine, while one integration test project per project under test could be better in another context. Trust your judgment and change the solution structure if your first choice causes you trouble later.

Note

Some people may recommend creating a single unit test project per solution instead of one per project, and I think that for most solutions, it is a matter of preference. If you have a preferred way to organize yours, by all means, use that approach instead! That said, I find that one unit test project per assembly is more portable and easier to navigate.

Folder-wise, at the solution level, creating the application and its related libraries in an src directory helps isolate the actual solution code from the test projects created under a test directory, like this:

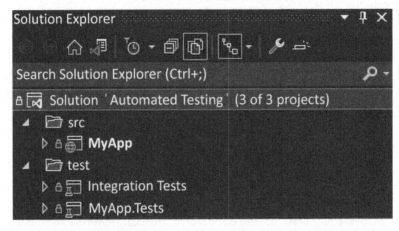

Figure 2.7: The Automated Testing Solution Explorer, displaying how the projects are organized

That's a well-known and effective way of organizing a solution in the .NET world.

However, sometimes, it is not possible to do that. One such use case would be microservices written under a single solution. In that case, you might want the tests to live closer to your microservices, and not split them between a root src and test folders.

Let's now dig deeper into organizing unit tests.

Unit tests

I find it convenient to create unit tests in the same namespace as the subject under test when creating unit tests. That helps get tests and code aligned without adding any additional using statements. To make it easier when creating files, you can change the default namespace used by Visual Studio when creating a new class in your test project by adding <RootNamespace>[Project under test namespace]</RootNamespace> to a PropertyGroup of the test project file (*.csproj), like this:

```
<PropertyGroup>
  ...
  <RootNamespace>MyApp</RootNamespace>
</PropertyGroup>
```

By convention, I name test classes [`class under test`]`Test.cs` and create them in the same directory as in the original project, depicted by the following solution with the `ValuesController` class:

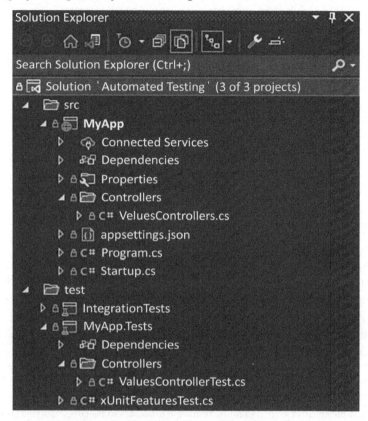

Figure 2.8: The Automated Testing Solution Explorer, displaying how tests are organized

Finding tests is easy when you follow that simple rule. For the test code itself, I follow a multi-level structure similar to the following:

- One test class is named the same as the class under test

  - One nested test class per method to test from the class under test

    - One test method per test case of the method under test

I find this helps to organize tests efficiently by test case while keeping a clear hierarchy. Let's look at a small test class:

```
namespace MyApp.IntegrationTests.Controllers
{
    public class ValuesControllerTest
    {
        public class Get : ValuesControllerTest
        {
```

```
        [Fact]
        public void Should_return_the_expected_strings()
        {
            // Arrange
            var sut = new ValuesController();
            // Act
            var result = sut.Get();
            // Assert
            Assert.Collection(result.Value,
                x => Assert.Equal("value1", x),
                x => Assert.Equal("value2", x)
            );
        }
    }
}
```

This convention allows you to set up tests step by step. For example, by inheriting the outer class (the `ValuesControllerTest` class here), you can create top-level private mocks or classes shared by all nested classes. Then, for each method to test, you can modify the setup or create other private test elements in the nested classes (the `Get` class here). Finally, you can do more configuration per test case inside the test method (the `Should_return_the_expected_strings` method here).

One word of advice: don't go too hard on reusability inside your test classes as it can make tests harder to read from an external eye, such as a reviewer or another developer that needs to play there. Unit tests should remain clear, small, and easy to read: a unit of code testing another unit of code.

Now that we have explored organizing unit tests, let's have a look at integration tests.

Integration tests

Integration tests are harder to organize because they depend on multiple units and can cross project boundaries and interact with various dependencies.

As mentioned before, you can create one integration test project for most simple solutions or many for more complex scenarios. When writing many integration tests without crossing project boundaries, I'd look at creating one integration test project per project to test by following a similar convention as with unit tests: `[Project under test].IntegrationTests`.

Inside those projects, it depends on how you want to attack the problem and the structure of the solution itself. Start by identifying the features under test. Name the test classes in a way that mimics your requirements, organize those into sub-folders (maybe a sub-unit of the requirements), and code test cases as methods. You can also leverage nested classes, as we did with unit tests.

Next, we implement an integration test by leveraging ASP.NET Core features.

ASP.NET Core integration testing

Microsoft built ASP.NET Core from the ground up. They fixed and improved so many things that I cannot enumerate them all here, including testability. Let's start by talking about the structure of a .NET program. There are two ways to structure your program:

- The classic ASP.NET Core `Program` and the `Startup` classes. You might find this model in existing projects (created prior to .NET 6).
- The minimal hosting model introduced in .NET 6 encourages you to write the start up code in the `Program.cs` file by leveraging top-level statements. You will most likely find this model in new projects (created after the release of .NET 6).

No matter how you choose to write your program, that's the place to define how the application boots and its composition. Moreover, we can leverage the same testing tools more or less seamlessly.

The scope of our integration test is to call the endpoint of a controller over HTTP and assert the response. Luckily, in .NET Core 2.1, the .NET team added the `WebApplicationFactory<TEntry>` class to make the integration testing of web applications easier. With that class, we can boot up an ASP.NET Core application in-memory and query it using the supplied `HttpClient`—all of that in just a few lines of code. The test classes also provide extension points to configure the server, such as replacing implementations with mocks, stubs, or any other test-specific elements that we may require.

Classic web application

In a classic ASP.NET Core application, the `TEntry` generic parameter is usually the `Startup` or `Program` class of your project under test but could be anything. I created a few test cases in the `Automated Testing` solution under the `MyApp.IntegrationTests` project to show you this functionality.

Here is the broken-down code:

```
namespace MyApp.IntegrationTests.Controllers
{
    public class ValuesControllerTest :
    IClassFixture<WebApplicationFactory<Startup>>
    {
        private readonly HttpClient _httpClient;

        public ValuesControllerTest(WebApplicationFactory<Startup>
                                    webApplicationFactory)
        {
            _httpClient = webApplicationFactory.CreateClient();
        }
```

In the preceding class declaration, we are injecting a `WebApplicationFactory<Startup>` object into the constructor. That is possible because the class is implementing the `IClassFixture<T>` interface. We could also use the factory to configure the test server, but since it was not needed here, we only keep a reference on the `HttpClient`, preconfigured to connect to the in-memory test server:

```csharp
public class Get : ValuesControllerTest {
    public Get(WebApplicationFactory<Startup> webApplicationFactory) :
base(webApplicationFactory) { }
    [Fact]
    public async Task Should_respond_a_status_200_OK()
    {
        // Act
        var result = await _httpClient.GetAsync("/api/values");
        // Assert
        Assert.Equal(HttpStatusCode.OK, result.StatusCode);
    }
```

In the preceding test case, we use `HttpClient` to query the `http://localhost/api/values` URI, accessible through the in-memory server. Then, we assert that the status code of the HTTP response was a success (`200 OK`):

```csharp
    [Fact]
    public async Task Should_respond_the_expected_strings()
    {
        // Act
        var result = await _httpClient
            .GetFromJsonAsync<string[]>("/api/values");
        // Assert
        Assert.Collection(result,
            x => Assert.Equal("value1", x),
            x => Assert.Equal("value2", x)
        );
    }
}}}
```

This last test sends an HTTP request to the in-memory server, like the previous one, but deserializes the body's content as a `string[]` to ensure the values are the same as expected instead of validating the status code. If you've worked with an `HttpClient` before, this should be very familiar to you.

When running those tests, an in-memory web server starts. Then, HTTP requests are sent to that server, testing the complete application. In this case, the tests are simple, but you can create more complex test cases in more complex programs.

You can run .NET tests within Visual Studio or use the CLI by running the dotnet test command. In VS Code, you can use the CLI or find an extension to help with test runs.

Next, we explore how to do the same for minimal APIs.

Minimal hosting

If you are using minimal hosting, you must use a workaround. We explore a few workarounds here and leverage minimal APIs, allowing you to pick the one you prefer. These work with regular MVC projects as well.

The **first workaround** is to use any other class in the assembly as the `TEntryPoint` of `WebApplicationFactory<TEntryPoint>` instead of the `Program` or `Startup` class. This makes what `WebApplicationFactory` does a little less explicit, but that's all.

The **second workaround** is to add a line at the bottom of the `Program.cs` file (or anywhere else in the project for that matter) to make the `internal` autogenerated program class `public` so that the compiler does not complain about inconsistent accessibility.

Here is the complete `Program.cs` file with that added line (highlighted):

```
var builder = WebApplication.CreateBuilder(args);
var app = builder.Build();
app.MapGet("/", () => "Hello World!");
app.Run();
public partial class Program { }
```

Then, the test cases are very similar to the ones of the classic web application that we just explored:

```
namespace MyMinimalApiApp.IntegrationTests
{
    public class ProgramTest : IClassFixture<WebApplicationFactory<Program>>
    {
        private readonly HttpClient _httpClient;
        public ProgramTest(WebApplicationFactory<Program>
webApplicationFactory)
        {
            _httpClient = webApplicationFactory.CreateClient();
        }

        public class Get : ProgramTest
        {
            public Get(WebApplicationFactory<Program> webApplicationFactory) :
base(webApplicationFactory) { }

            [Fact]
            public async Task Should_respond_a_status_200_OK()
            {
                var result = await _httpClient.GetAsync("/");
```

```
                    Assert.Equal(HttpStatusCode.OK, result.StatusCode);
            }
            [Fact]
            public async Task Should_respond_hello_world()
            {
                var result = await _httpClient
                    .GetStringAsync("/");
                Assert.Equal("Hello World!", result );
            }
        }
    }
}
```

The only change is the expected result as the endpoint returns a text/plain string instead of a collection of strings serialized as JSON. If the two endpoints were producing the same thing, those parts of the tests would have also been the same.

The **third workaround** is to instantiate WebApplicationFactory manually. However, instead of using the Program class, which should not exist or be inaccessible, we can use the AutoGeneratedProgram class or any other class from that assembly. I prefer the Program or AutoGeneratedProgram class to make the intent clearer, but I ran into some issues when using AutoGeneratedProgram with .NET 6 builds.

Experiment

I found that executing the two tests under ProgramTestWithoutFixture always takes a few more milliseconds than using the IClassFixture. The same happened for the tests in the ProgramTestWithoutFixtureNoReuse class, which always takes a few more milliseconds than the other two classes. This experiment led me to think it could get way worse with more than two tests, so I recommend sticking to class fixtures.

The code is very similar to the previous workaround, but WebApplicationFactory is instantiated manually instead:

```
public class ProgramTestWithoutFixture : IAsyncDisposable
{
    private readonly WebApplicationFactory<SomeOtherClass> _webApplicationFactory;
    private readonly HttpClient _httpClient;

    public ProgramTestWithoutFixture()
    {
        _webApplicationFactory = new WebApplicationFactory<SomeOtherClass>();
```

```
            _httpClient = _webApplicationFactory.CreateClient();
    }
    //...
}
```

I omitted the test cases in the preceding code block because they are the same as the previous workarounds. The full source code is available on GitHub: https://adpg.link/vzkr.

And that's it. We have covered multiple ways to work around integration testing minimal APIs simplistically and elegantly. Next, we explore a few testing principles before moving to architectural principles in the next chapter.

Important testing principles

One essential thing to remember when writing tests is to test use cases, not the code itself; we are testing features' correctness, not code correctness. Of course, if the expected outcome of a feature is correct, that also means the codebase is correct. However, it is not always true for the other way around; correct code may yield an incorrect outcome. Also, remember that code costs money to write while features deliver value.

To help with that, the test requirements usually revolve around the **inputs and outputs**. When specific values go into your subject under test, you expect particular values to come out. Whether you are testing a simple Add method where the ins are two or more numbers and the out is the sum of those numbers, or a more complex feature where the ins come from a form and the out is the record getting persisted in a database, most of the time, we are testing the ins and outs.

That's the first principle you must know about. The interaction between two components or two systems should always be tied to a **data contract**, whether using a classic request/response model over a REST API where the data contract is the API signature, or using an event-driven architecture approach and the data contract is the event signature or, even simpler, ComponentA returns an object that is injected into ComponentB; the correctness of those interactions gravitates around the ins and outs. Test those as units or test the integration between those units, and you should be on the right way to writing strong test suites.

The second concept I want you to learn is a trick to divide those units: everything in a program is a query or a command. No matter how you organize your code, from a simple single-file application to a microservices architecture-base Netflix clone, all operations, single or compounded, are queries or commands. Thinking about a system this way should help you test the ins and outs.

But what's a query? A query means getting some ins, like the unique identifier of a database record, and getting some outs, like the record itself. It could also be some part of the code asking how many times it should retry an HTTP GET request when it fails. These are the easiest to test: you push some ins and receive some outs to assert.

And what's a command? We could see a command as a unit of code that mutates the state of an entity. A command could be to hide a panel in a GUI or update a record in a database. It does not matter what the command does as much as the fact that it changes something somewhere.

Now that we have laid this out, it should become easier to write tests if you divide your code into small units, like commands and queries. But what if a unit must perform multiple operations, such as read from a database, and then send multiple commands? Well, if you create multiple smaller units, and then another unit that interacts with those other building blocks, you should be able to test each piece in isolation and integrate them together.

In a nutshell, when writing automated tests, we assert the output of the unit undergoing testing. That unit optionally had some input parameters and is a query or a command.

We explore numerous techniques throughout the book to help you achieve that level of separation, starting with architectural principles in the next chapter.

Summary

This chapter covered automated testing such as unit and integration tests. We also briefly covered end-to-end tests, but it would be tough to cover that in a few pages since this is tied to an application and its implementation. Nonetheless, all is not lost since the notions covered to write integration tests can also be used for end-to-end testing.

We looked at xUnit, the testing framework used throughout the book, and a way of organizing tests. We explored ways to pick the correct type of test and some guidelines about choosing the right quantity of each kind of test. Then we saw how ASP.NET Core makes it easier than ever before to test our web applications by allowing us to mount and run our ASP.NET Core application in memory. Finally, we explored some high-level concepts that should guide you in writing testable, flexible, and reliable programs.

Now that we have talked about testing, we are ready to explore a few architectural principles to help us increase programs' testability. Those are a crucial part of modern software engineering and go hand in hand with automated testing.

Questions

Let's take a look at a few practice questions:

1. Is it true that in TDD, you write tests before the code to be tested?
2. What is the role of unit tests?
3. How big can a unit test be?
4. What type of test is usually used when the subject under test has to access a database?
5. Is doing TDD required?

Further reading

Here are some links to build upon what we have learned in the chapter:

- xUnit: `https://xunit.net/`
- If you use Visual Studio, I have a few handy snippets to help improve productivity. They are available on GitHub: `https://adpg.link/5TbY`

3

Architectural Principles

This chapter focuses on fundamental architectural principles. The reason behind this is simple: those principles are the foundation of modern software engineering. Moreover, we apply these principles throughout the book to make sure that we write better code and make better design decisions by the end.

In this chapter, we cover the following topics:

- The **SOLID** principles and their importance
- The separation of concerns principle
- The **DRY** principle
- The **KISS** principle

The SOLID principles

SOLID is an acronym representing five principles that extend the basic OOP concepts of **Abstraction**, **Encapsulation**, **Inheritance**, and **Polymorphism**. They add more details about what to do and how to do it, guiding developers toward more robust and flexible designs.

It is also important to note that they are principles, not rules to follow at all costs. Weigh the cost in the context of what you are building. If you are building a small tool, it may be OK to cut it short more than when designing a business-critical application. For the latter case, you may want to consider being stricter. However, following them is usually a good idea, irrespective of the size of your application, which is the main reason to cover them here, in the beginning, before digging into design patterns.

The SOLID acronym represents the following:

- Single responsibility principle
- Open/Closed principle
- Liskov substitution principle
- Interface segregation principle
- Dependency inversion principle

By following these principles, your systems should become easier to test and maintain.

Single responsibility principle (SRP)

Essentially, the SRP means that a single class should hold one, and only one, responsibility, leading me to the following quote:

> *"There should never be more than one reason for a class to change."*
>
> — *Robert C. Martin, originator of the single responsibility principle*

OK, but why? Before giving you the answer, think about one or more times a specification was added, updated, or removed from one project you worked on. Then, think about how easier it would have been if every class in your system had only a single responsibility: one reason to change.

I don't know if you visualized that clearly or not, but I can think of a few projects off the top of my head that would have benefited from this principle. Software maintainability problems can be due to both tech and non-tech people. I think that nothing is black or white and that most situations are gray; sometimes, it is of a darker or lighter gray, but gray nonetheless. That lack of absoluteness is also true when designing software: do your best, learn from your mistakes, and be humble.

Let's review why that principle exists:

- Applications are born to change.
- To make our classes more reusable and create more flexible systems.
- To help maintain applications. Since you know the only thing a class does before updating it, you can quickly foresee the impact on the system, unlike with classes that hold many responsibilities, where updating one can break one or more other parts.
- To make our classes more readable. Fewer responsibilities lead to less code, and less code is simpler to visualize in a few seconds, leading to a quicker understanding of that piece of software.

Let's try this out in action.

Project — BookStore

I have written some horrible code that violates a few principles, including the SRP. Let's start by analyzing the code to partially fix it so that it no longer violates the SRP.

The following is an example of poorly written code:

```
public class Book
{
    public int Id { get; set; }
    public string? Title { get; set; }
    private static int _lastId = 0;
    public static List<Book> Books { get; }
    public static int NextId => ++_lastId;
    static Book()
    {
        Books = new List<Book>
```

```
        {
            new Book
            {
                Id = NextId,
                Title = "Some cool computer book"
            }
        };
    }
    public Book(int? id = null)
    {
        Id = id ?? default;
    }
    public void Save()
    {
        // Create the book if it does not exist,
        // otherwise, find its index and replace it
        // by the current object.
        if (Books.Any(x => x.Id == Id))
        {
            var index = Books.FindIndex(x => x.Id == Id);
            Books[index] = this;
        }
        else
        {
            Books.Add(this);
        }
    }
    public void Load()
    {
        // Validate that an Id is set
        if (Id == default(int))
        {
            throw new Exception("You must set the Id to the Book Id you want to
load.");
        }
        // Get the book
        var book = Books.FirstOrDefault(x => x.Id == Id);
        // Make sure it exist
        if (book == null)
        {
            throw new Exception("This book does not exist");
```

```
            }
            // Copy the book properties to the current object
            Id = book.Id; // this should already be set
            Title = book.Title;
        }
        public void Display()
        {
            Console.WriteLine($"Book: {Title} ({Id})");
        }
    }
}
```

That class contains all the responsibilities of that super small console application. There is also the Program class, which includes a quick and dirty user interface, the consumer of the Book class.

The program offers the following options:

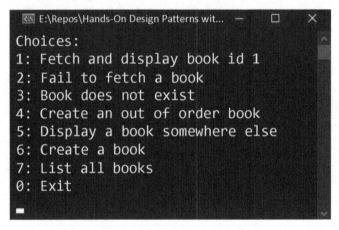

Figure 3.1: The program's user interface

The Program class structure is as follows:

```
public class Program
{
    public static void Main(string[] args)
    {
        // Omitted code
    }
    // The methods we explore next go here
}
```

I omitted the Main method code because it is just a big switch statement with Console.WriteLine calls. It dispatches the user input to the other methods (explained later) when a user makes a choice. See https://adpg.link/jpxa for more information on the Main method. Next, the method called when a user chooses 1:

```
private static void FetchAndDisplayBook()
{
    var book = new Book(id: 1);
    book.Load();
    book.Display();
}
```

The `FetchAndDisplayBook()` method loads the book instance with an `id` equal to 1 and then displays it in the console. Next, the method called when a user chooses 2:

```
private static void FailToFetchBook()
{
    var book = new Book();
    book.Load(); // Exception: You must set the Id to the Book Id you want to
Load.
    book.Display();
}
```

The `FailToFetchBook()` method loads a book instance without specifying an `id`, which results in an exception thrown when loading the data; refer to the `book.Load()` method (preceding code block, first highlight). Next, the method called when a user chooses 3:

```
private static void BookDoesNotExist()
{
    var book = new Book(id: 999);
    book.Load();
    book.Display();
}
```

The `BookDoesNotExist()` method loads a book instance that does not exist, leading to an exception being thrown when loading the data; refer to the `book.Load()` method (preceding code block, second highlight). Next, the method called when a user chooses 4:

```
private static void CreateOutOfOrderBook()
{
    var book = new Book
    {
        Id = 4, // this value is not enforced by anything and will be
overridden at some point.
        Title = "Some out of order book"
    };
    book.Save();
    book.Display();
}
```

The `CreateOutOfOrderBook()` method creates a book instance specifying an `id` manually. That ID could be overridden by the auto-incremental mechanism of the `Book` class. Here is a sequence that shows how to achieve such an override:

1. Start the program; there is one book: `ID:` 1.
2. Choose option 4; there are two books: `ID:` 1 and 4.
3. Choose option 6 and enter any title; there are three books: `ID:` 1, 4, and 2.
4. Choose option 6 and enter any title; there are four books: `ID:` 1, 4, 2, and 3.
5. Choose option 6 and enter any title; there are still four books, but the second one's title (`ID:` 4) was updated instead of creating a fifth book.

These kinds of behaviors are good indicators of a problem in the design of a program. Next, the method called when a user chooses 5:

```
private static void DisplayTheBookSomewhereElse()
{
    Console.WriteLine("Oops! Can't do that, the Display method only write to
the \"Console\".");
}
```

The `DisplayTheBookSomewhereElse()` method points to another problem with that design. We cannot display the books anywhere else other than in the console because the `Book` class owns the display mechanism; refer to the `book.Display()` method. Next, the method called when a user chooses 6:

```
private static void CreateBook()
{
    Console.Clear();
    Console.WriteLine("Please enter the book title: ");
    var title = Console.ReadLine();
    var book = new Book {
        Id = Book.NextId,
        Title = title
    };
    book.Save();
}
```

The `CreateBook()` method lets us create new books. It uses the `Book.NextId` static property, which increments the `Id`. That breaks encapsulation and leaks the creation logic to the consumer, which is another problem associated with the design that we will fix later. Next, the method called when a user chooses 7:

```
private static void ListAllBooks()
{
    foreach (var book in Book.Books)
    {
```

```
        book.Display();
    }
}
```

The ListAllBooks() method displays all of the books that we have created in the program.

Before going further, I'd like you to think about what is wrong in the Book class and how many responsibilities there are that violate the SRP. Once done, please continue reading.

OK, let's start by isolating the features:

- The class is a data structure that represents a book (Id, Title).
- It saves and loads data, including keeping a list of all existing books (Books, Save(), Load()).
- It "manages" auto-incremented IDs by exposing the NextId property that hacks the feature into the program.
- It plays the presenter role, outputting a book in the console with its Display() method.

From those four points, what roles could we extract?

- It is a book.
- It performs data access (manages the data).
- It presents the book to the user by outputting itself in the console.

These three elements are responsibilities, which is an excellent starting point for splitting the Book class. Let's look at those three classes:

- We can keep the Book class and make it a simple data structure that represents a book.
- We can create a BookStore class whose role is to access the data.
- We can create a BookPresenter class that outputs (presents) a book on the console.

Here are those three classes:

```
public class Book
{
    public int Id { get; set; }
    public string? Title { get; set; }
}
public class BookStore
{
    private static int _lastId = 0;
    private static List<Book> _books;
    public static int NextId => ++_lastId;
    static BookStore()
    {
        _books = new List<Book>
        {
```

```
                new Book
                {
                    Id = NextId,
                    Title = "Some cool computer book"
                }
            };
    }
    public IEnumerable<Book> Books => _books;
    public void Save(Book book)
    {
        // Create the book when it does not exist,
        // otherwise, find its index and replace it
        // by the specified book.
        if (_books.Any(x => x.Id == book.Id))
        {
            var index = _books.FindIndex(x => x.Id == book.Id);
            _books[index] = book;
        }
        else
        {
            _books.Add(book);
        }
    }
    public Book? Load(int bookId)
    {
        return _books.FirstOrDefault(x => x.Id == bookId);
    }
}
public class BookPresenter
{
    public void Display(Book book)
    {
        Console.WriteLine($"Book: {book.Title} ({book.Id})");
    }
}
```

That does not fix every problem yet, but at least it is a good start. By extracting the responsibilities, we have achieved the following:

- The FailToFetchBook() use case has been fixed (see the Load() method).
- Fetching a book is now more elegant and more intuitive.
- We also opened a possibility about the DisplayTheBookSomewhereElse() use case (to be revisited later).

From an SRP standpoint, we still have a problem or two:

- The auto-incremented ID is still exposed publicly, and BookStore is not managing it, meaning the responsibility leaks to consumers.
- The Save() method handles adding and updating books, which seems like two responsibilities, not one.

For the following updates, we focus on those two problems that share a synergy, making them easier to fix independently than together (dividing responsibility between the methods).

What we are about to do is the following:

1. Hide the BookStore.NextId property to fix encapsulation (not the SRP, but it is essential nonetheless).
2. Split the BookStore.Save() method into two methods: Add() and Replace().
3. Update our user interface: Program.cs.

After hiding the NextId property, we need to move that feature inside the BookStore class. The most logical place would be the Save() method (not yet split in two) since we want a new unique identifier for each new book. Here are the changes:

```
public class BookStore
{
    ...
    private static int NextId => ++_lastId;
    ...
    public void Save(Book book)
    {
        ...
        else
        {
            book.Id = NextId;
            _books.Add(book);
        }
    }
}
```

The auto-incremented identifier is still a half-baked feature. To help improve it more, let's split the Save() method into two. By looking at the resulting code, we can imagine that handling both use cases was easier to write. It is also easier to read and clearer to use for any developer who may come into contact with that code in the future. See for yourself:

```
public void Add(Book book)
{
    if (book.Id != default)
    {
```

```
            throw new Exception("A new book cannot be created with an id.");
    }
    book.Id = NextId;
    _books.Add(book);
}
public void Replace(Book book)
{
    if (!_books.Any(x => x.Id == book.Id))
    {
        throw new Exception($"Book {book.Id} does not exist!");
    }
    var index = _books.FindIndex(x => x.Id == book.Id);
    _books[index] = book;
}
```

Now we are beginning to get somewhere. We have successfully split the responsibilities into three classes and split the Save() method, such that both handle only a single operation.

The Program members now look like this:

```
private static readonly BookStore _bookStore = new BookStore();
private static readonly BookPresenter _bookPresenter = new BookPresenter();
//...
private static void FetchAndDisplayBook()
{
    var book = _bookStore.Load(1);
    _bookPresenter.Display(book!);
    // In the preceding line, the null forgiving operator ('!')
    // tells the analyzer that the 'book' variable is not null
    // because we know it isn't. In a more dynamic scenario, we
    // should validate if the book variable is not null.
}
private static void FailToFetchBook()
{
    // This cannot happen anymore,
    // this has been fixed automatically.
}
private static void BookDoesNotExist()
{
    var book = _bookStore.Load(999);
    if (book == null)
    {
        // Book does not exist
```

```
        }
    }
    private static void CreateOutOfOrderBook()
    {
        var book = new Book
        {
            Id = 4,
            Title = "Some out of order book"
        };
        _bookStore.Add(book); // Exception: A new book cannot be created with an
id.
        _bookPresenter.Display(book);
    }
    private static void DisplayTheBookSomewhereElse()
    {
        Console.WriteLine("This is now possible, but we need a new Presenter; not
100% there yet!");
    }
    private static void CreateBook()
    {
        Console.Clear();
        Console.WriteLine("Please enter the book title: ");
        var title = Console.ReadLine();
        var book = new Book { Title = title };
        _bookStore.Create(book);
    }
    private static void ListAllBooks()
    {
        foreach (var book in _bookStore.Books)
        {
            _bookPresenter.Display(book);
        }
    }
}
```

Apart from automatically fixing the FailToFetchBook method, I found the code easier to read. For example, the first following line (Fixed Program) is explaining the intent better than the next two (Initial Program):

```
// Fixed Program
// Intent: loads a book from a bookstore
var book = _bookStore.Load(999);
```

```
// Initial Program
// Intent: loads a book; unclear
var book = new Book(id: 999);
book.Load();
```

Aside from readability, the `Program` class of the `Fixed Program` project no longer manages the book's ID when creating a book. It is now only managing the user interface and interaction with the bookstore API.

To conclude, one thing to be careful about when thinking about the SRP is not to over-separate classes. The more classes in a system, the more complex to assemble the system can become, and the harder it can be to debug or to follow the execution paths. On the other hand, many well-separated responsibilities should lead to a better, more testable system.

How to describe "one reason" or "a single responsibility" is unfortunately impossible to define, and I don't have a hard guideline to give you here. As a rule of thumb, aim at packing a cohesive set of functionalities in a single class that revolves around its responsibility. Any excess logic should be stripped out and missing pieces added in.

A good indicator of the SRP violation is when you don't know how to name an element, like a class. That is often a good pointer that the element should not reside there, should be extracted, or split into multiple smaller pieces.

Another good indicator is when a method becomes too big, maybe containing many `if` statements or loops. In that case, you should split that method into multiple smaller methods, classes, or any other construct that suits your requirements. That should make the code easier to read and make the initial method's body cleaner. It often also helps you get rid of useless comments and improve testability. Remember that naming methods and other elements clearly is very important.

Next, we explore how to change behaviors without modifying code, but before that, let's have a look at interfaces.

What is an interface?

Interfaces are one of the most useful tools in the C# box for creating flexible and maintainable software alike. I'll try to give you a clear definition of an interface, but don't worry; it is tough to understand and grasp the power of interfaces from an explanation:

- The role of an interface is to define a cohesive contract (public methods, properties, and events). In its theoretical form, there is no code in an interface; it is only a contract. In practice, since C# 8, we can create default implementation in interfaces, which could be helpful to limit breaking changes in a library (such as adding a method to an interface without breaking any class implementing that interface).
- An interface should be small (ISP), and its members should align toward a common goal (cohesion) and share a single responsibility (SRP).
- In C#, a class can implement multiple interfaces, exposing multiples of those public contracts, or, more accurately, be any and all of them. By leveraging polymorphism, a class can be used as any of the interfaces it implements as well as its supertype (if any).

Let's be honest. That definition is still a bit abstract, but rest assured, we use interfaces intensively throughout the book, so by the end, interfaces should not hold many secrets for you.

On another more fundamental note

A class does not inherit from an interface; it implements an interface. However, an interface can inherit from another interface.

Open/Closed principle (OCP)

Let's start this section with a quote from Bertrand Meyer, the person who first wrote the term open/closed principle in 1988:

> *"Software entities (classes, modules, functions, and so on) should be open for extension but closed for modification."*

OK, but what does that mean? It means that you should be able to change the class behaviors from the outside without altering the code itself.

The best way to pull that off is to assemble the application using multiple well-designed units of code, sewed together using dependency injection.

To illustrate that, let's play with a ninja, a sword, and a shuriken, but be careful; that's dangerous ground! There are two versions of the project in GitHub, one that does not leverage the OCP (NinjaBeforeOCP) and another that does (NinjaOCP). In the chapter, we explore both versions in order.

Project — IAttacker

The example is a small hypothetical game where an implementation of an IAttacker interface can attack any implementation of the IAttackable interface, as shown below:

```
public interface IAttacker : IAttackable
{
    AttackResult Attack(IAttackable target);
}
public interface IAttackable
{
    string Name { get; }
    Vector2 Position { get; set; }
}
```

Of course, for a ninja to attack another ninja, they must have access to weapons. Here is the Weapon base class:

```
public abstract class Weapon
{
    public abstract float MinRanged { get; }
```

```
    public abstract float MaxRanged { get; }

    public virtual string Name => GetType().Name;
    public virtual bool CanHit(float distance)
        => distance >= MinRanged && distance <= MaxRanged;
}
```

The preceding code shows that derived types are responsible for setting the MinRanged and MaxRanged properties, while the Weapon class is responsible for computing if it can hit at a certain distance or not.

As for the implementations, in the first part of the example, we use two weapons: Sword and Shuriken. In the next iteration, we add the Pistol. Here is the code that covers all of those weapons:

```
public class Sword : Weapon
{
    public override float MinRanged { get; } = 0;
    public override float MaxRanged { get; } = Vector2.Distance(Vector2.Zero,
Vector2.One);
}
public class Shuriken : Weapon
{
    public override float MinRanged { get; } = Vector2.Distance(Vector2.Zero,
Vector2.One);
    public override float MaxRanged { get; } = 20;
}
public class Pistol : Weapon
{
    public override float MinRanged { get; } = Vector2.Distance(Vector2.Zero,
Vector2.One);
    public override float MaxRanged { get; } = 50;
}
```

Those three classes are very thin and barely contain any code. The only logic is that the melee weapon can hit from a range of 0 to Vector2.Distance(Vector2.Zero, Vector2.One), while the range weapons can hit from a range of Vector2.Distance(Vector2.Zero, Vector2.One) to 20 for the shuriken or 50 for the pistol.

Distances

When I coded this, I saw each unit as one meter, so a sword can reach around the attacker's position while the ranged weapons can hit targets at longer distances. Those distances are arbitrary and are not supposed to be realistic.

Finally, the last pieces of code shared by both versions of the project are the `AttackResult` class, which we use to display the results, and the `AttackableExtensions` class, which helps with distance computation and movement:

```
public class AttackResult
{
    public string Weapon { get; }
    public string Attacker { get; }
    public string Target { get; }
    public bool Succeeded { get; }
    public float Distance { get; }

    public AttackResult(Weapon weapon, IAttacker attacker, IAttackable target)
    {
        Weapon = $"{weapon.Name} (Min: {weapon.MinRanged}, Max: {weapon.MaxRanged})";
        Attacker = $"{attacker.Name} (Position: {attacker.Position})";
        Target = $"{target.Name} (Position: {target.Position})";
        Distance = attacker.DistanceFrom(target);
        Succeeded = weapon.CanHit(Distance);
    }
}
public static class AttackableExtensions
{
    public static float DistanceFrom(this IAttackable attacker, IAttackable target)
    {
        return Vector2.Distance(attacker.Position, target.Position);
    }
    public static IAttackable MoveTo(this IAttackable target, float x, float y)
    {
        target.Position = new Vector2(x, y);
        return target;
    }
}
```

In the preceding code, the `AttackResult` class is responsible for keeping a hold on the result of an attack.

Note

In our case, we only need to display strings. However, in a more advanced program, we might need more than this. In that case, be careful about parameters that are passed by references like what we are injecting in the `AttackResult` constructor, as they can continue to change after object creation. For example, if we create the result of an attack and then move the target before displaying the result, the target's position change could wield an inconsistent result.

As we can see in the following consumer code, we display the results right away, not keeping hold of those values. Nevertheless, since we computed strings and are not referencing any external object, we don't have the problem described in the previous note; we flattened our "point in time:"

```csharp
public static async Task ExecuteSequenceAsync<T>(T theBluePhantom, T
theUnseenMirage, Func<string, Task> writeAsync)
    where T : IAttackable, IAttacker
{
    // The Blue Phantom attacks The Unseen Mirage with a first attack
    var result = theBluePhantom.Attack(theUnseenMirage);
    await PrintAttackResultAsync(result);

    // The Unseen Mirage moves away from The Blue Phantom
    theUnseenMirage.MoveTo(5, 5);
    await PrintMovementAsync(theUnseenMirage);

    // The Blue Phantom attacks The Unseen Mirage with a second attack
    var result2 = theBluePhantom.Attack(theUnseenMirage);
    await PrintAttackResultAsync(result2);

    // The Unseen Mirage moves further away from The Blue Phantom
    theUnseenMirage.MoveTo(20, 20);
    await PrintMovementAsync(theUnseenMirage);

    // The Blue Phantom attacks The Unseen Mirage with a third attack
    var result3 = theBluePhantom.Attack(theUnseenMirage);
    await PrintAttackResultAsync(result3);

    // The Unseen Mirage strikes back at The Blue Phantom from a distance
    var result4 = theUnseenMirage.Attack(theBluePhantom);
    await PrintAttackResultAsync(result4);

    // Output
```

```
    async Task PrintAttackResultAsync(AttackResult attackResult)
    {
        if (attackResult.Succeeded)
        {
            await writeAsync($"{attackResult.Attacker} hits {attackResult.
Target} using {attackResult.Weapon} at distance {attackResult.
Distance}!{Environment.NewLine}");
        }
        else
        {
            await writeAsync($"{attackResult.Attacker} misses {attackResult.
Target} using {attackResult.Weapon} at distance {attackResult.Distance}...
{Environment.NewLine}");
        }
    }

    async Task PrintMovementAsync(IAttackable ninja)
    {
        await writeAsync($"{ninja.Name} moved to {ninja.Position}.{Environment.
NewLine}");
    }
}
```

The preceding code shows the sequence of events that both the pre- and post-OCP code samples use. In a nutshell, that code makes the ninjas attack each other. It's like a video game, but without the controls, graphics, and interactive elements that make a game a game.

OK, now that all that code is out of the way, let's look at the initial implementation of the Ninja class before improving it to follow the OCP:

```
namespace NinjaBeforeOCP;
public class Ninja : IAttackable, IAttacker
{
    private readonly Weapon _sword = new Sword();
    private readonly Weapon _shuriken = new Shuriken();

    public string Name { get; }
    public Vector2 Position { get; set; }

    public Ninja(string name, Vector2? position = null)
    {
        Name = name;
        Position = position ?? Vector2.Zero;
```

```
    }

    public AttackResult Attack(IAttackable target)
    {
        var distance = this.DistanceFrom(target);
        if (_sword.CanHit(distance))
        {
            return new AttackResult(_sword, this, target);
        }
        else
        {
            return new AttackResult(_shuriken, this, target);
        }
    }
}
```

In the preceding code, the highlighted lines show the two weapons the ninja can use. The shuriken is a ranged weapon, while the sword is a melee weapon.

Next, let's look at the program code that consumes the `Ninja` class before we execute it:

```
var builder = WebApplication.CreateBuilder(args);
var app = builder.Build();
app.MapGet("/", async (HttpContext context) =>
{
    // Create actors
    var target = new Ninja("The Unseen Mirage");
    var ninja = new Ninja("The Blue Phantom");

    // Execute the sequence of actions
    await Logic.ExecuteSequenceAsync(ninja, target, writeAsync: s => context.
Response.WriteAsync(s));
});
app.Run();
```

When we execute that version of the program and navigate to `https://localhost:3001/`, we get the following results:

```
The Blue Phantom (Position: <0, 0>) hits The Unseen Mirage (Position: <0, 0>)
using Sword (Min: 0, Max: 1.4142135) at distance 0!
The Unseen Mirage moved to <5, 5>.
The Blue Phantom (Position: <0, 0>) hits The Unseen Mirage (Position: <5, 5>)
using Shuriken (Min: 1.4142135, Max: 20) at distance 7.071068!
The Unseen Mirage moved to <20, 20>.
```

```
The Blue Phantom (Position: <0, 0>) misses The Unseen Mirage (Position: <20,
20>) using Shuriken (Min: 1.4142135, Max: 20) at distance 28.284271...
The Unseen Mirage (Position: <20, 20>) misses The Blue Phantom (Position: <0,
0>) using Shuriken (Min: 1.4142135, Max: 20) at distance 28.284271...
```

The above result makes sense; it is what we built. However, I have the following questions for you (try to answer the first one before reading the second one):

• Are there any issues with that code, and if so, what could they be?

• How can a ninja use a pistol instead of a shuriken?

To answer those questions, based on the Ninja class we covered, we must modify the class or create a new one that defines a different set of weapons. This is a problem as in most games, you can loot new items. If we think about it, with this design, we would need to create one ninja class per item set, which is not a viable option for any game bigger than this.

To fix this, we apply the OCP and open the Ninja class to create ninjas with different weapon sets. We want to **compose** the Ninja instances instead of relying on a hardcoded set of weapons.

Composition over inheritance

Composition improves code reuse since multiple classes can use those other smaller classes. We are using this principle throughout the book, including in this example. The idea is to have an object use other objects to achieve the correct behaviors instead of inheriting a base class. For example, the first Ninja implementation is composed of a set of hardcoded weapons, and after applying the OCP, the second Ninja class (that we explore next) is composed dynamically using dependency injection. None of them inherit a base class; they implement two interfaces instead and leverage other classes, such as the Weapon class, to handle part of its behavior.

The best way of implementing this is the **Strategy pattern**, which we explore in more detail in *Chapter 6, Understanding the Strategy, Abstract Factory, and Singleton Design Patterns*, and *Chapter 7, Deep Dive into Dependency Injection*. For now, let's forget about those fancy names, and let's look at the updated version of the Ninja class after applying the OCP:

```
public class Ninja : IAttackable, IAttacker
{
    private readonly Weapon _meleeWeapon;
    private readonly Weapon _rangedWeapon;

    public string Name { get; }
    public Vector2 Position { get; set; }

    public Ninja(string name, Weapon meleeWeapon, Weapon rangedWeapon, Vector2?
position = null)
```

```
    {
        Name = name;
        Position = position ?? Vector2.Zero;
        _meleeWeapon = meleeWeapon;
        _rangedWeapon = rangedWeapon;
    }

    public AttackResult Attack(IAttackable target)
    {
        var distance = this.DistanceFrom(target);
        if (_meleeWeapon.CanHit(distance))
        {
            return new AttackResult(_meleeWeapon, this, target);
        }
        else
        {
            return new AttackResult(_rangedWeapon, this, target);
        }
    }
}
```

I tried to keep the code as close to the first code sample as possible to make it easier to focus on the differences. The highlighted lines of the preceding code point to the following differences:

- The _shuriken field was renamed _rangedWeapon, and _sword was renamed _meleeWeapon.
- The weapons are set through constructor parameters during the instantiation of the Ninja class instead of hardcoded.

That's it. The rest of the class remained the same. The first change makes the code more readable, helping to understand what each field holds. Now that we can set the weapons, it is not necessarily a sword and a shuriken anymore; it can be what we set them to be during the object construction.

The second change is the key here. It is one way of applying the OCP, showing the concept. It allows consumers to change the behavior of the Ninja class without modifying the code itself. To prove that, let's visit and execute the following endpoint and then inspect the result:

```
app.MapGet("/old", async (HttpContext context) =>
{
    // Create actors
    var target = new Ninja("The Unseen Mirage", new Sword(), new Shuriken());
    var ninja = new Ninja("The Blue Phantom", new Sword(), new Shuriken());

    // Execute the sequence of actions
```

```
    await Logic.ExecuteSequenceAsync(ninja, target, writeAsync: s => context.
Response.WriteAsync(s));
});
```

By running the program and navigating to the https://localhost:3002/old URL, we obtain the same result as before because both ninjas are identical, holding a sword and a shuriken.

Now, let's try that pistol by giving it to *The Unseen Mirage*. I highlighted the only change in the following endpoint code:

```
app.MapGet("/", async (HttpContext context) =>
{
    // Create actors
    var target = new Ninja("The Unseen Mirage", new Sword(), new Pistol());
    var ninja = new Ninja("The Blue Phantom", new Sword(), new Shuriken());

    // Execute the sequence of actions
    await Logic.ExecuteSequenceAsync(ninja, target, writeAsync: s => context.
Response.WriteAsync(s));
});
```

By navigating to the https://localhost:3002/ URL, we can notice a subtle but important difference:

```
The Blue Phantom (Position: <0, 0>) hits The Unseen Mirage (Position: <0, 0>)
using Sword (Min: 0, Max: 1.4142135) at distance 0!
The Unseen Mirage moved to <5, 5>.
The Blue Phantom (Position: <0, 0>) hits The Unseen Mirage (Position: <5, 5>)
using Shuriken (Min: 1.4142135, Max: 20) at distance 7.071068!
The Unseen Mirage moved to <20, 20>.
The Blue Phantom (Position: <0, 0>) misses The Unseen Mirage (Position: <20,
20>) using Shuriken (Min: 1.4142135, Max: 20) at distance 28.284271...
The Unseen Mirage (Position: <20, 20>) hits The Blue Phantom (Position: <0, 0>)
using Pistol (Min: 1.4142135, Max: 50) at distance 28.284271!
```

Have you spotted the difference? The Unseen Mirage hits The Blue Phantom at a distance of 28.284271 instead of missing. Due to the OCP, we can now change the program's behavior by creating and using new weapons without altering the Ninja class code.

In a more complex application, combining **composition** and **dependency injection** could allow changing the behaviors of the whole program from a single place, called the composition root, without changing our existing code; "open for extension, but closed for modification." To add new weapons, we can create new classes and do not need to modify existing ones, which we are doing in a later example.

Those new terms could be overwhelming at first, but we cover them in more detail in subsequent chapters and use those techniques extensively throughout the book. The crucial part is the OCP concepts, not the fancy names.

A bit of history

The first appearance of the OCP, in 1988, was referring to inheritance, and OOP has evolved a lot since then. You should, most of the time, opt for composition over inheritance. Inheritance is still a useful concept, but you should be careful when using it; it is a concept that is easy to misuse, creating direct coupling between classes and deep hierarchy. We explore that more throughout the book.

Next, we explore the principle we could perceive as the most complex of the five.

Liskov substitution principle (LSP)

The LSP emanated from Barbara Liskov at the end of the '80s and was revisited during the '90s by both Liskov and Jeannette Wing to create the principle that we know and use today. It is also similar to *Design by contract*, by Bertrand Meyer.

The LSP focuses on preserving subtype behaviors, which leads to system stability. Before going any further, let's start with the formal definition introduced by Wing and Liskov:

> *Let $\emptyset(x)$ be a property provable about objects x of type T. Then, $\emptyset(y)$ should be true for objects y of type S, where S is a subtype of T.*

This means that you should be able to swap an object of type T with an object of type S, where S is the subtype of T, without breaking your program's correctness.

Without putting in some effort, you can't violate the following rules in C#, but they are still worth mentioning:

- The contravariance of method arguments in the subtype.
- The covariance of return types in the subtype.

Before moving on with the LSP, let's look at covariance and contravariance. We won't go too deep into this, so we don't move too far away from the LSP, but in a nutshell, covariance and contravariance represent specific polymorphism scenarios. They allow reference types to be converted into other types implicitly. They apply to generic type arguments, delegates, and array types. Chances are, you will never need to remember this.

Let's start with the class hierarchy we are using in the covariance and contravariance examples:

```
public class Weapon { }
public class Sword : Weapon { }
public class TwoHandedSword : Sword { }
```

Covariance means you can **return (output) the instance of a subtype as its supertype**. Here is an example:

```
[Fact]
public void Covariance_tests()
```

```
{
    Assert.IsType<Sword>(Covariance());
    Assert.Throws<InvalidCastException>(() => BreakCovariance());
}


// We can return a Sword into a Weapon
private Weapon Covariance()
    => new Sword();


// We cannot return a Sword into a TwoHandedSword
private TwoHandedSword BreakCovariance()
    => (TwoHandedSword)new Sword();
```

As shown in the preceding example, one way to break covariance is to return a supertype as a subtype.

On the other hand, **contravariance** means you can **input the instance of a subtype as its supertype.** It is basically the same thing but for inputs, like this:

```
[Fact]
public void Contravariance_tests()
{
    // We can pass a Sword as a Weapon
    Contravariance(new Sword());

    // We cannot pass a Weapon as a Sword
    BreakContravariance(new Weapon()); // Compilation error
}
private void Contravariance(Weapon weapon) { }
private void BreakContravariance(Sword weapon) { }
```

The same polymorphic rule applies, as we can see from the preceding code. We can use a subtype as a supertype.

Note

I left a link in the *Further reading* section that explains covariance and contravariance if you want to know more since we just covered the basics here.

Then, we must follow a few more rules to prove subtype correctness. Subtype correctness means a subtype will not break the program more than its supertype if one is swapped by the other.

Any precondition implemented in a supertype should yield the same outcome in its subtypes, but subtypes can be less strict about it, never more. For example, if a supertype validates that an argument cannot be null, the subtype could remove that validation but not add stricter validation rules.

Any postcondition implemented in a supertype should yield the same outcome in its subtypes, but subtypes can be more strict about it, never less. For example, if the supertype never returns null, the subtype should not return null either or risk breaking the consumers of the object that are not testing for null. On the other hand, if the supertype does not guarantee the returned value cannot be null, then a subtype could decide never to return null, making both instances interchangeable.

Subtypes must preserve the invariance of the supertype. In other words, the behaviors of the supertype must not change. For example, a subtype must pass all the tests written for the supertype, so there is no variance between them (they don't vary/they react the same).

Finally, we must add the "history constraint" to that list of rules, which states that what would happen in the supertype must still happen in the subtype. While subtypes can add new properties (state) and methods (behaviors), they must not modify the supertype state in any new way.

OK, at this point, you are right to feel that this is rather complex. Rest assured that this is the less important of those principles, yet the more complex, and we are moving as far as we can from inheritance, so this should not apply often.

That said, I'd summarize all that previous complexity by the following:

In your subtypes, add new behaviors; don't change existing ones.

By doing that, you should be able to swap an instance of a class for one of its subclasses without breaking anything.

It is important to note that changing existing behaviors also means throwing new exceptions in subtypes. A supertype can throw subtyped exceptions because the error handling of existing consumers will catch the subtyped exceptions.

As a side note, before even bothering with the LSP, start by applying the "is-a" rule from inheritance; if a subtype is not a supertype, don't use inheritance or rethink your inheritance chain.

To make a LEGO® analogy: LSP is like swapping a 4x2 blue block with a 4x2 green block: neither the structural integrity of the structure nor the role of the block changed, just its color.

Tip

An excellent way of enforcing those behavioral constraints is automated testing. You could write a test suite and run it against all subclasses of a specific supertype to enforce the preservation of behaviors.

Let's jump into some code to visualize that in practice.

Project — HallOfFame

Now, let's see what this looks like in code. We explore a hall of fame feature of a fictive game that we are working on.

Feature description: the game should accumulate the number of enemies killed during the game session. At the end of a game session where you killed at least 100 enemies, your ninja should reach the hall of fame. The hall of fame should be ordered from the best score to the worst.

We created the following automated tests to enforce those rules, with sut (subject under test) being of the HallOfFame type. Here is the empty implementation of the HallOfFame class:

```
public class HallOfFame
{
    public virtual void Add(Ninja ninja)
        => throw new NotImplementedException();
    public virtual IEnumerable<Ninja> Members
        => throw new NotImplementedException();
}
```

Note

In the following test code, I'm not following the convention about writing tests that I explained in the previous chapter because I need inheritance to reuse my test suite for the three versions of the code. That was impossible to do using nested classes due to how C# works. As the saying goes, that is the exception that proves the rule.

The Add() method should add ninjas that killed more than 100 enemies:

```
public static TheoryData<Ninja> NinjaWithAtLeast100Kills => new
TheoryData<Ninja>
{
    new Ninja { Kills = 100 },
    new Ninja { Kills = 101 },
    new Ninja { Kills = 200 },
};
// The following theory is executed three times.
// Once with 100 kills, then 101, then 200 as
// defined in the preceding property.
[Theory]
[MemberData(nameof(NinjaWithAtLeast100Kills))]
public void Add_should_add_the_specified_ninja(Ninja expectedNinja)
{
    // Act
    sut.Add(expectedNinja);

    // Assert
    Assert.Collection(sut.Members,
```

```
            ninja => Assert.Same(expectedNinja, ninja)
    );
}
```

The `Add()` method should not add a ninja more than once:

```
[Fact]
public void Add_should_not_add_existing_ninja()
{
    // Arrange
    var expectedNinja = new Ninja { Kills = 200 };

    // Act
    sut.Add(expectedNinja);
    sut.Add(expectedNinja);

    // Assert
    Assert.Collection(sut.Members,
        ninja => Assert.Same(expectedNinja, ninja)
    );
}
```

The `Add()` method should validate that a ninja has at least 100 kills before adding it to the `Members` collection of the `HallOfFame` instance under test:

```
[Fact]
public void Add_should_not_add_ninja_with_less_than_100_kills()
{
    // Arrange
    var ninja = new Ninja { Kills = 99 };

    // Act
    sut.Add(ninja);

    // Assert
    Assert.Empty(sut.Members);
}
```

The `Members` property of the `HallOfFame` class should return the ninja ordered by their number of kills, from the most to the least:

```
[Fact]
public void Members_should_return_ninja_ordered_by_kills_desc()
{
```

```
    // Arrange
    sut.Add(new Ninja { Kills = 100 });
    sut.Add(new Ninja { Kills = 150 });
    sut.Add(new Ninja { Kills = 200 });

    // Act
    var result = sut.Members;

    // Assert
    Assert.Collection(result,
        ninja => Assert.Equal(200, ninja.Kills),
        ninja => Assert.Equal(150, ninja.Kills),
        ninja => Assert.Equal(100, ninja.Kills)
    );
}
```

The test cases we explored prove the correctness of the hall of fame feature we are about to develop. We created the tests first, as prescribed by **test-driven development (TDD)**, and now, it is time to look at the implementation of the HallOfFame class:

```
public class HallOfFame
{
    protected HashSet<Ninja> InternalMembers { get; } = new();
    public virtual void Add(Ninja ninja)
    {
        if (InternalMembers.Contains(ninja))
        {
            return;
        }
        if (ninja.Kills >= 100)
        {
            InternalMembers.Add(ninja);
        }
    }
    public virtual IEnumerable<Ninja> Members
        => new ReadOnlyCollection<Ninja>(
            InternalMembers
                .OrderByDescending(x => x.Kills)
                .ToArray()
        );
}
```

Now that we have completed our feature and pushed our changes, we demo the hall of fame to our stakeholders. The feature works as expected, and we are now ready to break the LSP before fixing the issues.

Update 1: Adding a hall of heroes

After the demo, an idea arises: why not add a *hall of heroes* for players who do not qualify for the hall of fame? After deliberation, we decided that we should implement that feature.

Feature description: the game should accumulate the number of enemies killed during the game session (already done) and add all ninjas to the hall of heroes, no matter the score. The results should be ordered by the best score first, in descending order, and each ninja should only be present once.

The first idea that arises to implement this feature quickly is to reuse the hall of fame code. In *step one*, we decide to create a HallOfHeroes class that inherits the HallOfFame class and rewrite the Add() method to support the new specifications.

Note

Do you think the hall of heroes *is a* hall of fame? Have we broken the first rule of inheritance? Nevertheless, we continue with this debatable choice with a focus on learning the LSP.

After thinking about it, do you think that change would break the LSP?

Before giving you the answer, let's look at that HallOfHeroes class:

```
namespace LSP.Examples.Update1;
public class HallOfHeroes : HallOfFame
{
    public override void Add(Ninja ninja)
    {
        if (InternalMembers.Contains(ninja))
        {
            return;
        }
        InternalMembers.Add(ninja);
    }
}
```

Since the LSP states that *subclasses can be less strict about preconditions*, removing the number of kill preconditions should be acceptable.

Now, if we run the tests built for HallOfFame using HallOfHeroes instead, the only test that fails is related to our precondition, so the subclass changed no behavior, and all use cases are still valid.

To test our features more efficiently, we can encapsulate all shared tests into a base class but keep Add_should_not_add_ninja_with_less_than_100_kills only for the HallOfFame tests.

With that in place to validate our code, we can begin to explore the role of the LSP as we can use an instance of HallOfHeroes everywhere our program expects a HallOfFame instance without breaking it.

Next, we explore the test classes that we use to test the HallOfFame and HallOfHeroes classes. Let's start with the complete BaseLSPTest class that we broke down previously:

```
namespace LSP.Examples;
public abstract class BaseLSPTest
{
    protected abstract HallOfFame sut { get; }
    public static TheoryData<Ninja> NinjaWithAtLeast100Kills => new()
    {
        new Ninja { Kills = 100 },
        new Ninja { Kills = 101 },
        new Ninja { Kills = 200 },
    };

    [Fact]
    public virtual void Add_should_not_add_existing_ninja()
    {
        // Arrange
        var expectedNinja = new Ninja { Kills = 200 };

        // Act
        sut.Add(expectedNinja);
        sut.Add(expectedNinja);

        // Assert
        Assert.Collection(sut.Members,
            ninja => Assert.Same(expectedNinja, ninja)
        );
    }

    [Theory]
    [MemberData(nameof(NinjaWithAtLeast100Kills))]
    public void Add_should_add_the_specified_ninja(Ninja expectedNinja)
    {
        // Act
        sut.Add(expectedNinja);
```

```
        // Assert
        Assert.Collection(sut.Members,
            ninja => Assert.Same(expectedNinja, ninja)
        );
    }


    [Fact]
    public void Members_should_return_ninja_ordered_by_kills_desc()
    {
        // Arrange
        sut.Add(new Ninja { Kills = 100 });
        sut.Add(new Ninja { Kills = 150 });
        sut.Add(new Ninja { Kills = 200 });

        // Act
        var result = sut.Members;

        // Assert
        Assert.Collection(result,
            ninja => Assert.Equal(200, ninja.Kills),
            ninja => Assert.Equal(150, ninja.Kills),
            ninja => Assert.Equal(100, ninja.Kills)
        );
    }
}
```

Now, let's look at the new `HallOfFameTest` class, which is way simpler and looks like the following:

```
namespace LSP.Examples;
public class HallOfFameTest : BaseLSPTest
{
    protected override HallOfFame sut { get; } = new HallOfFame();

    [Fact]
    public void Add_should_not_add_ninja_with_less_than_100_kills()
    {
        // Arrange
        var ninja = new Ninja { Kills = 99 };

        // Act
        sut.Add(ninja);
```

```
        // Assert
        Assert.Empty(sut.Members);
    }
}
```

The preceding test class tests the HallOfFame class and inherits from BaseLSPTest. It adds one test case that only applies to itself: a ninja must have at least 100 kills to be added to the hall of fame.

Finally, the HallOfHeroesTest class is almost empty:

```
namespace LSP.Examples.Update1;
public class HallOfHeroesTest : BaseLSPTest
{
    protected override HallOfFame sut { get; }
        = new HallOfHeroes();
}
```

In the preceding code, there is nothing more to add; the tests from the inherited BaseLSPTest class are covering the whole feature. The highlighted line represents the subject under test, which is the HallOfHeroes class this time instead of the HallOfFame class.

That new feature is implemented, but we are not done yet. Everything is still working as intended, no issues with the LSP, we have not broken the principle yet, but that's what we are doing next.

Update 2: Breaking the LSP

Later on, the game uses those classes. However, another developer, Joe, decides to use HallOfHeroes in a new feature, but he needs to know when duplicated ninjas are added, so he decides to replace the return; statement with throw new DuplicateNinjaException() instead. He is proud of this feature and shows that to the team.

Do you think Joe's update is breaking the LSP?

The class looks like this after the changes:

```
namespace LSP.Examples.Update2;
public class HallOfHeroes : HallOfFame
{
    public override void Add(Ninja ninja)
    {
        if (InternalMembers.Contains(ninja))
        {
            throw new DuplicateNinjaException();
        }
        InternalMembers.Add(ninja);
    }
}
```

```
public class DuplicateNinjaException : Exception
{
    public DuplicateNinjaException()
        : base("Cannot add the same ninja twice!") { }
}
```

Yes, it is violating the LSP. Moreover, if our engineer had run the tests, it would have been clear that one test was failing!

What do you think is violating the LSP?

The existing code was not expecting a `DuplicateNinjaException` to be thrown anywhere by a `HallOfFame` instance, which could have created runtime crashes, possibly breaking the game. Throwing new exceptions in subclasses is forbidden as per the LSP.

Update 3: Back on track with the LSP

To fix his mistake and conform to the LSP, our engineer decides to add an `AddingDuplicateNinja` event to the `HallOfHeroes` class and then subscribes to that event instead of catching the `DuplicateNinjaException`.

Would that fix the previous LSP violation?

The updated code looks like this:

```
namespace LSP.Examples.Update3;
public class HallOfHeroes : HallOfFame
{
    public event EventHandler<AddingDuplicateNinjaEventArgs>
    AddingDuplicateNinja;

    public override void Add(Ninja ninja)
    {
        if (InternalMembers.Contains(ninja))
        {
            OnAddingDuplicateNinja(new AddingDuplicateNinjaEventArgs(ninja));
            return;
        }
        InternalMembers.Add(ninja);
    }

    protected virtual void OnAddingDuplicateNinja(AddingDuplicateNinjaEventArgs e)
    {
        AddingDuplicateNinja?.Invoke(this, e);
    }
```

```
}
public class AddingDuplicateNinjaEventArgs : EventArgs
{
    public Ninja DuplicatedNinja { get; }

    public AddingDuplicateNinjaEventArgs(Ninja ninja)
    {
        DuplicatedNinja = ninja ?? throw new
ArgumentNullException(nameof(ninja));
    }
}
```

Yes, that fix allowed the existing code to run smoothly while adding the new feature that Joe (our fictive dev) required. Publishing an event instead of throwing an Exception was just one way to fix our fictional problem. In a real-life scenario, you should choose the solution that fits your problem best. In our case, it was a straightforward and low-effort fix, which was perfect.

The important part of the example is that introducing a new exception type can seem harmless, but can actually cause much harm. The same goes for other LSP violations.

Conclusion

Once again, this is only a principle, not a law. A good tip would be to see the violation of the LSP as a *code smell*. From there, perform some analysis to see whether you have a design problem and the impact. Use your analytical skills on a case-by-case basis and conclude whether or not it would be acceptable to break the LSP in that specific case.

We could also name this principle the *backward-compatibility principle* because everything that worked in a way before should still work at least the same after the substitution, which is why this principle is important.

The more we advance, the more we move away from inheritance and the less we need this principle. Don't get me wrong here; if you use inheritance, do your best to apply the LSP, and you will most likely be rewarded by doing so.

Interface segregation principle (ISP)

Let's start with another famous quote by Robert C. Martin:

> *"Many client-specific interfaces are better than one general-purpose interface."*

What does that mean? It means the following:

*   You should create interfaces.
*   You should value small interfaces more.
*   You should not try to create a multipurpose interface as "an interface to rule them all".

An interface could refer to a class interface here (all exposed elements of a class), but I prefer to focus on C# interfaces instead, as we use them a lot throughout the book. If you know C++, you could see an interface as a header file.

Project — Ninja versus Pirate

Let's have a second look at the code shared by the two versions of the OCP ninja example, where we can find multiple granular interfaces. The IAttacker interface defines an Attack method to target an IAttackable instance. The IAttacker interface is also an IAttackable interface as attackers should be attackable; if you can attack, you can be attacked. The IAttackable interface exposes a name and a position but could also include other properties, such as hit points and defense.

By dividing functionalities into multiple interfaces, we can more easily reuse or extend them. Let's extend the code sample by creating a Pirate class, its new pirate arsenal, and new default behavior. Let's start by looking at the new pirate weapons:

```
public class Kick : Weapon
{
    public override float MinRanged { get; } = 0;
    public override float MaxRanged { get; } = 0;
}


public class Cutlass : Sword { }
public class BoardingAxe : Weapon
{
    public override float MinRanged { get; } = 0;
    public override float MaxRanged { get; } = 5;
}


public class Blunderbuss : Weapon
{
    public override float MinRanged { get; } = 3;
    public override float MaxRanged { get; } = 100;
}
```

The weapons are very simple and don't require further explanation. The class that interests us most is the Pirate class itself:

```
public class Pirate : IAttackable, Iattacker
{
    private readonly List<Weapon> _weapons;
    public Pirate(string name, params Weapon[] weapons)
    {
        _weapons = new(weapons);
        Name = name;
```

```
    }

    public string Name { get; }
    public Vector2 Position { get; set; }

    public AttackResult Attack(Iattackable target)
    {
        var distance = this.DistanceFrom(target);
        foreach (var weapon in _weapons)
        {
            if(weapon.CanHit(distance))
            {
                return new AttackResult(weapon, this, target);
            }
        }
        return new(new NoWeapon(), this, target);
    }

    private class NoWeapon : Weapon
    {
        public override float MinRanged => 0;
        public override float MaxRanged => 0;
        public override string Name { get; } = "Nothing";
        public override bool CanHit(float distance) => false;
    }
}
```

The preceding code shows a similar implementation to the `Ninja` class, but owning more than two weapons. Moreover, the highlighted line points to the new default behavior of the pirate, in case no weapon can hit the target. That was an easy way to implement that use case using only a few lines of code.

So far, there is nothing new here but a few different implementation details. Let's get another entity into the world now; a barrel:

```
public class Barrel : IAttackable
{
    public string Name => nameof(Barrel);
    public Vector2 Position { get; set; }
}
```

The `Barrel` class is a little different from the `Pirate` and `Ninja` classes because it only implements the `IAttackable` interface; a barrel cannot attack and just stands there.

We can see that the ISP comes into play in the program, where a pirate starts to attack a ninja and a barrel:

```
app.MapGet("/", async (HttpContext context) =>
{
    // Create actors
    var theUnseenMirage = new Ninja("The Unseen Mirage", new Sword(), new
Pistol());
    var blackbeard = new Pirate("Blackbeard", new Kick(), new Cutlass(), new
BoardingAxe(), new Blunderbuss());
    var barrel = new Barrel().MoveTo(20, 45);

    // Execute a sequence of actions
    await PrintAttackResultAsync(blackbeard.Attack(theUnseenMirage));
    await PrintMovementAsync(theUnseenMirage.MoveTo(1, 1));
    await PrintAttackResultAsync(theUnseenMirage.Attack(blackbeard));
    await PrintAttackResultAsync(blackbeard.Attack(theUnseenMirage));
    await PrintMovementAsync(theUnseenMirage.MoveTo(3, 3));
    await PrintAttackResultAsync(theUnseenMirage.Attack(blackbeard));
    await PrintAttackResultAsync(blackbeard.Attack(theUnseenMirage));
    await PrintMovementAsync(theUnseenMirage.MoveTo(5, 5));
    await PrintAttackResultAsync(theUnseenMirage.Attack(blackbeard));
    await PrintAttackResultAsync(blackbeard.Attack(theUnseenMirage));
    await PrintMovementAsync(theUnseenMirage.MoveTo(40, 40));
    await PrintAttackResultAsync(theUnseenMirage.Attack(blackbeard));
    await PrintAttackResultAsync(blackbeard.Attack(theUnseenMirage));
    await PrintMovementAsync(theUnseenMirage.MoveTo(80, 80));
    await PrintAttackResultAsync(theUnseenMirage.Attack(blackbeard));
    await PrintAttackResultAsync(blackbeard.Attack(theUnseenMirage));
    await PrintAttackResultAsync(blackbeard.Attack(barrel));

    // Utilities
    async Task PrintAttackResultAsync(AttackResult attackResult){...}
    async Task PrintMovementAsync(IAttackable attackable){...}
});
```

In the preceding code, all the highlighted lines leverage the IAttackable interface. Without it, an instance of the Pirate class could not attack an instance of a Ninja class and vice versa.

The ISP is telling us to create a smaller cohesive set of functionalities that can be reused and extended, and that's what gave us the power to add a pirate so easily.

Looking back at the line that instantiates the barrel variable, we see the MoveTo extension method leveraging the ISP. The MoveTo extension method works on any instance of an IAttackable interface, another use of the separation into multiple interfaces, as dictated by the ISP.

We could do many things by leveraging those two interfaces that would have been impossible or had made less sense if we had a single INinja interface, for example. We could create more types of enemies, decor elements, and add new features by introducing new interfaces.

Nevertheless, I hope this visual explanation of the ISP helps you visualize the concept. Next, we explore another sample that extends our bookstore project.

Project – Bookstore update

Context: We are building a web application with different roles; some users are administrators, and some consume the app. The administrators can read and write all of the data in the system while the normal users can only read. UI-wise, there are two distinct parts: the public UI and an admin panel.

Since users are not allowed to write data, we don't want to expose those methods there just in case certain developers decide to use them at some point in time. We don't want unused code to linger around in places where that code should not be used. On the other hand, we don't want to create two classes either, one that reads and one that writes; we prefer keeping only one data access class, which should be easier to maintain.

To do that, let's start by remodeling the earlier BookStore class by extracting an interface. To improve readability, let's rename the Load() method to Find(), and then let's add a Remove() method, which was missing before. The new interface looks like this:

```
public interface IBookStore
{
    IEnumerable<Book> Books { get; }
    Book? Find(int bookId);
    void Create(Book book);
    void Replace(Book book);
    void Remove(Book book);
}
```

Then, to ensure that consumers cannot alter our IBookStore instances from the outside (encapsulation), let's also update the Books property of our BookStore class to return a ReadOnlyCollection<Book> type instead of the _books field directly. This only affects the implementation, but allows me to introduce the concept (see note).

Note

The `System.Collections.ObjectModel` namespace contains a few read-only classes:

a) `ReadOnlyCollection<T>`

b) `ReadOnlyDictionary<TKey,TValue>`

c) `ReadOnlyObservableCollection<T>`

Those are very useful for exposing data to the clients without allowing them to modify it. In our example, the `IEnumerable<Book>` instance is of the `ReadOnlyCollection<Book>` type. We could have kept returning our internal `List<Book>` instances but some clever developer could have figured this out, cast `IEnumerable<Book>` to a `List<Book>`, and added some books to it, thereby breaking encapsulation!

Now, let's look at that updated `BookStore` class:

```
public class BookStore : IBookStore
{
    private static int _lastId = 0;
    private static List<Book> _books;
    private static int NextId => ++_lastId;
    static BookStore()
    {
        _books = new List<Book>
        {
            new Book
            {
                Id = NextId,
                Title = "Some cool computer book"
            }
        };
    }
    public IEnumerable<Book> Books => new ReadOnlyCollection<Book>(_books);
    public Book? Find(int bookId)
    {
        return _books.FirstOrDefault(x => x.Id == bookId);
    }
    public void Create(Book book)
    {
        if (book.Id != default(int))
        {
            throw new Exception("A new book cannot be created with an id.");
```

```
            }
            book.Id = NextId;
            _books.Add(book);
        }
        public void Replace(Book book)
        {
            if (!_books.Any(x => x.Id == book.Id))
            {
                throw new Exception($"Book {book.Id} does not exist!");
            }
            var index = _books.FindIndex(x => x.Id == book.Id);
            _books[index] = book;
        }
        public void Remove(Book book)
        {
            if (!_books.Any(x => x.Id == book.Id))
            {
                throw new Exception($"Book {book.Id} does not exist!");
            }
            var index = _books.FindIndex(x => x.Id == book.Id);
            _books.RemoveAt(index);
        }
    }
```

When looking at that code, if we expose the interface in the public UI, we also expose the write methods we want to avoid.

To solve our design problem, we can use the ISP and start by splitting the IBookStore interface into two: IBookReader and IBookWriter:

```
public interface IBookReader
{
    IEnumerable<Book> Books { get; }
    Book? Find(int bookId);
}
public interface IBookWriter
{
    void Create(Book book);
    void Replace(Book book);
    void Remove(Book book);
}
```

By following the ISP, we could split `IBookWriter` into three interfaces: `IBookCreator`, `IBookReplacer`, and `IBookRemover`. A word of warning: We must be careful because doing ultra-granular interface segregation like that could create quite a mess in your system, but it could also be super beneficial, depending on the context and your goals.

> **Tip**
>
> Be careful not to overuse this principle blindly. Think about cohesion and what you are trying to build, and not about how granular an interface can blindly become. The finer-grained your interfaces, the more flexible your system could be, but remember that flexibility has a cost, and that cost can become very high, very quickly.

Now, we need to update our `BookStore` class. First, we have to implement our two new interfaces:

```
public class BookStore : IBookReader, IBookWriter
{
    // ...
}
```

That was easy! With that new `BookStore` class, we can use `IBookReader` and `IBookWriter` independently like this:

```
IBookReader reader = new BookStore();
IBookWriter writer = new BookStore();
// ...
var book3 = reader.Find(3);
// ...
writer.Create(new Book { Title = "Some nice new title!" });
// ...
```

If we focus on the `reader` and `writer` variables, we can see that we can now use only the `IBookReader` interface on the public side, hiding the `BookStore` implementation behind the interface. On the administrator side, we could use both interfaces to manage books.

Conclusion

To summarize the idea behind the ISP, if you have multiple smaller interfaces, it is easier to reuse them and expose only the features you need instead of exposing APIs that are not needed. This is the goal: **only depend on interfaces that you consume**. Furthermore, it is easier to compose bigger pieces using multiple specialized interfaces by implementing them as needed than remove methods from a big interface if we don't need them in one of its implementations.

If you don't see all of the benefits yet, don't worry. All the pieces should come together as we move on to the next principle, dependency injection, and the rest of the book.

Dependency inversion principle (DIP)

And yet another quote, from Robert C. Martin (including the implied context from Wikipedia):

> *One should "depend upon abstractions, [not] concretions."*

In the previous section, I introduced you to interfaces with the SRP and the ISP. Interfaces are one of the pivotal elements of our SOLID arsenal! Moreover, using interfaces is the best way to approach the DIP. Of course, abstract classes are also abstractions, but you should depend on interfaces whenever possible instead.

Why not use abstract classes, you might think? An abstract class is an abstraction but is not 100% abstract, and if it is, you should replace it with an interface. Abstract classes are used to encapsulate default behaviors that you can then inherit in sub-classes. They are helpful, but interfaces are more flexible, more powerful, and better suited to design contracts. Nonetheless, don't just discard abstract classes. To extrapolate on this, I'd say: never discard anything blindly.

Moreover, using interfaces can save you countless hours of struggling and complex workaround when programming unit tests. That is even more true if you are building a framework or library that other people use. In that case, please be kind and provide your consumers with interfaces to mock if they need to.

All of that talk about interfaces is nice, but how can the flow of dependencies be inverted? Let's begin by comparing a direct dependency and an inverted dependency.

Direct dependency

If we have a Ninja class using a Sword instance, the dependency graph should look like this because the Ninja class directly depends on the Sword class:

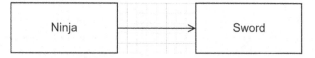

Figure 3.2: Direct dependency schema

Inverted dependency

As you can see in the following diagram, the Ninja class now depends only on the new IWeapon interface. We achieved this by inverting the dependency flow. Doing this gives us the flexibility to change the type of weapon without any impact on the system's stability and without altering the Ninja class, especially if we also followed the OCP. Indirectly, Ninja still uses a Weapon class instance, thereby breaking the direct dependency.

Here is the updated schema:

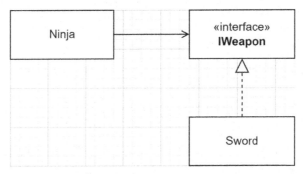

Figure 3.3: Indirect dependency schema

Inverting subsystems using DIP

To go a little further, you can also isolate and decouple a complete subsystem this way by creating two or more assemblies:

1. An abstraction assembly containing only interfaces.
2. One or more other assemblies that contain the implementation of the contracts from that first assembly.

There are multiple examples of this in .NET, such as the `Microsoft.Extensions.DependencyInjection.Abstractions` and `Microsoft.Extensions.DependencyInjection` assemblies. We are also exploring this concept in *Chapter 12, Understanding Layering*.

Before jumping into more code, let's take a look at another schema representing this idea. This time, it is related to abstracting data access from the database itself (we also talk more about this later):

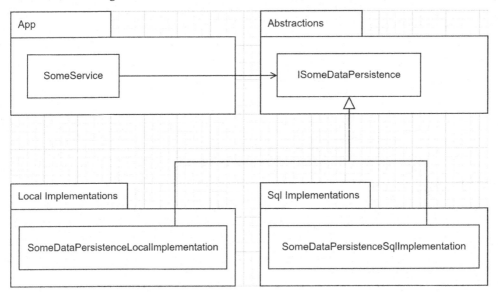

Figure 3.4: Diagram representing how to break tight coupling by inverting dependencies

In the diagram, the App package directly depends on the Abstractions package, while two implementations are available: Local and Sql. From there, we should be able to swap one implementation for the other without breaking the App. The reason is that we depend on the abstractions and coded the app using those abstractions. No matter what implementations are used, the program should run just fine unless something is wrong with the implementation itself.

Another example that I recently designed in a microservices-based application is a Publish-Subscribe (Pub-Sub) communication library. There are some abstractions that the microservices use, and there are one or more implementations that are swappable, so one microservice could use a provider, while another microservice could use another provider without depending on it directly. We discuss the Pub-Sub pattern and microservices architecture in *Chapter 16, Introduction to Microservices Architecture*. Until then, think of a microservice as a small application.

Packages

The packages described here could be namespaces as well as assemblies. By dividing responsibilities around assemblies, it creates the possibility to load only the implementations that need to be loaded. For example, one app could load the "local" assembly, and another app could load the "SQL" assembly, while a third app could load both.

Project – Dependency inversion

Context: We just learned about the DIP and want to apply it to our bookstore app. Since we do not have any real user interface yet, we believe it makes sense to create multiple reusable assemblies that our ASP.NET Core app can use later, allowing us to swap one GUI with another. Meanwhile, we are going to test our code using a little console application.

There are three projects:

- GUI: the console app
- Core: the application logic
- Data: the data access

Layering

This concept is called layering. We visit layering in more depth later. For now, you can think of it as splitting responsibilities into different assemblies.

Using a classical dependency hierarchy, we would end up with the following dependency graph:

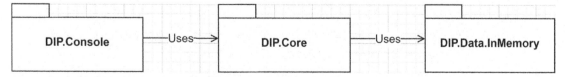

Figure 3.5: Diagram representing assemblies that directly depend on the next assembly

This is not very flexible as all assemblies are directly linked to the next in line, creating a strong, unbreakable bond between them. Let's now revisit this using the DIP.

> **Note**
>
> To keep it simple and to focus on only one portion of the code, I only abstracted the data portion of the program. We explore dependency inversion in more depth further on in the book, along with dependency injection.
>
> For now, we focus on the DIP.Data and DIP.Data.InMemory projects of the current code sample.

In the solution, there are four projects; three libraries and one console. Their goals are as follows:

- DIP.Console is the entry point, the program. Its role is to compose and run the application. It uses DIP.Core and defines what implementation should be used to cover the DIP.Data interfaces, in this case, DIP.Data.InMemory.
- DIP.Core is the program core, the shared logic. Its only dependency is on DIP.Data, abstracting away the implementation.
- DIP.Data contains persistence interfaces: IBookReader and IBookWriter. It also contains the data model (the Book class).
- DIP.Data.InMemory is a concrete implementation of DIP.Data.

To visualize the assemblies' relationships, let's take a look at the following diagram:

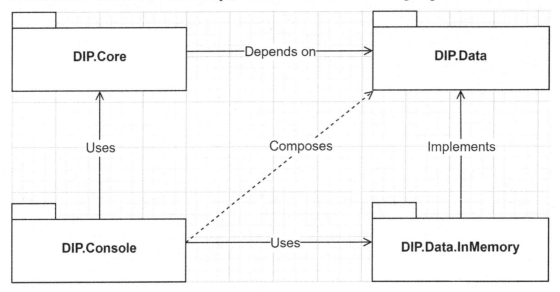

Figure 3.6: Diagram representing assemblies that invert the dependency flow, breaking coupling between DIP.Core and DIP.Data.InMemory

The preceding diagram shows that the Core assembly depends on the Data assembly but gets the Data. InMemory assembly to work with at runtime because the Console composed the application this way.

This would allow the Console to compose the program differently while not changing the Core library. For example, the Console program could use another implementation, say, Data.SqlServer (not in the diagram) instead of Data.InMemory. This example represents dependency inversion; Core does not depend directly on the implementation (Data.InMemory), but on the abstractions (Data) instead. Next, we look at some code to understand the concept.

If we start by looking at the PublicService class of the Core project, we can see that it only depends on the Data project's IBookReader interface:

```
namespace DIP.Core;
public class PublicService
{
    private readonly IBookReader _bookReader;
    public PublicService(IBookReader bookReader)
    {
        _bookReader = bookReader;
    }
    public Task<IEnumerable<Book>> FindAllAsync()
    {
        return Task.FromResult(_bookReader.Books);
    }
    public Task<Book?> FindAsync(int bookId)
    {
        var book = _bookReader.Find(bookId);
        return Task.FromResult(book);
    }
}
```

The PublicService class defines a few methods that use the IBookReader abstraction to query books. PublicService plays the consumer role and doesn't know about any concrete class. Even if we wanted to, the implementation is not accessible from this project. We succeeded; we inverted the dependency. Yes, as easy as that.

Note

Having a public field such as _bookReader breaks encapsulation, so don't do that in your projects. I just wanted to keep the focus of the example on the DIP. We see how to take advantage of the DIP using good practices later, including leveraging dependency injection.

Without any concrete implementation, an interface does nothing, so the other part of the DIP is to configure the consumer by defining the implementations that back those abstractions. To help us out, let's create a private class named Composer inside Program to centralize that step.

That is, once again, not something you usually want to do in a real project, but until we cover dependency injection, we have to rely on a more manual approach, so let's take a look at that light version, focusing on PublicService:

```
private static class Composer
{
    private readonly static BookStore BookStore = new();
    // ...
    public static PublicService CreatePublicService()
    {
        return new PublicService(
            bookReader: BookStore
        );
    }
}
```

The CreatePublicService() method is responsible for building the PublicService instance. In it, we assign an instance of the concrete class, BookStore, to the public IBookReader _bookReader; field, leaving PublicService unaware of its _bookReader implementation.

This little sample shows how to invert dependency, making sure of the following:

- The code always depends on abstraction (interfaces).
- The projects also depend on abstractions (depending on DIP.Data instead of DIP.Data.InMemory).

Conclusion

The conclusion of this principle is strongly tied to what is coming next. Nevertheless, the idea is to depend on abstractions (interfaces or abstract classes). Try to stick to interfaces as much as possible. They are pure contracts, which makes them more flexible than abstract classes. Abstract classes are still useful, and we explore ways to leverage them in the book.

Depending upon concretions creates tight coupling between classes, which leads to a system that can be harder to maintain. The cohesion between your dependencies plays an essential role in whether the coupling will help or hurt you in the long run. More on that later. Once again, don't discard concrete types everywhere blindly.

What's next?

The words *dependency injection* came out a few times, and you may be curious about it, so let's take a peek at what that is. Dependency injection, or **Inversion of Control (IoC)**, is a mechanism (a concept) that is a first-class citizen of ASP.NET Core. It allows you to map abstractions to implementations, and when you need a new type, the whole object tree gets created automatically for you by following your configuration. Once you get used to it, you cannot go back; but beware of the challenges as you may need to "unlearn" a part of what you know to embrace this new technique.

Enough talking. Let's get through those last sections before getting too excited about dependency injection. We start that journey in *Chapter 7, Deep Dive into Dependency Injection*.

Other important principles

I found a few other principles to talk about briefly before going further:

- Separation of concerns
- **Don't repeat yourself (DRY)**
- **Keep it simple, stupid (KISS)**

Of course, after reading the SOLID principles, you may find these more basic, but they are still complementary to what we just learned.

> **Note**
>
> There are many other principles, some that you may already know, some that you will most likely learn about later, but at some point, I have to choose the subjects or face writing an encyclopedia-sized book.

Separation of concerns

The idea is to separate your software into logical blocks, where each block is a concern; this can go from factoring a program into modules to applying the SRP to some subsystems. That can be applied to any programming paradigm. How to encapsulate a specific concern depends on the paradigm and the concern's level. The higher the level, the broader the solution; the lower the level, the more granular it becomes.

For example, the following applies:

- By using **aspect-oriented programming (AOP)**, we could see security or logging as cross-cutting concerns, encapsulating the code in an aspect.
- By using **object-oriented programming (OOP)**, we could also see security or logging as a cross-cutting concern, encapsulating shared logic in an ASP.NET Core filter.
- By using OOP again, we could see the rendering of a web page and the handling of an HTTP request as two concerns, leading to the MVC pattern; the view "renders" the page, while the controller handles the HTTP request.
- By using any paradigm, we could see adding extension points as a concern, leading to a plugin-based design.
- Using any paradigm again, we could see a component responsible for copying an object into another as a concern. In contrast, another component's responsibility could be to orchestrate those copies efficiently by following some rules, such as limiting the amount of copy that can happen in parallel, queuing the overflowing operations, and more.

As you may have noticed with those examples, a concern can be a significant matter or a tiny detail; nonetheless, it is imperative to consider concerns when dividing your software into pieces to create cohesive units. A good separation of concerns should help you create modular designs and help you face design dilemmas more effectively.

Don't repeat yourself (DRY)

OK, this principle's name is self-explanatory, and, as we already saw with the SRP and the OCP, we can, and should, extend and encapsulate logic into smaller units, aiming at reusability and lower maintenance costs.

The DRY principle explains it more or less the other way around by stating the following:

When you have duplicated logic in your system, encapsulate it and reuse that new encapsulation in multiple places instead.

The goal is to avoid making multiple changes when a specification changes. Why? To avoid forgetting to make one or to avoid creating inconsistencies and bugs in the program.

It is imperative to regroup duplicated logic by concern, not only by the similarities of code itself. Let's look at those two methods from the Program class of a previous sample:

```
private static async Task PublicAppAsync()
{
    var publicService = Composer.CreatePublicService();
    var books = await publicService.FindAllAsync();
    foreach (var book in books)
    {
        presenter.Display(book);
    }
}
private static async Task AdminAppAsync()
{
    var adminService = Composer.CreateAdminService();
    var books = await adminService.FindAllAsync();
    foreach (var book in books)
    {
        presenter.Display(book);
    }
}
```

The code is very similar, but extracting a single method out of those would be a mistake. Why? Because the public program and the admin program can have different reasons to change (adding filters in the admin panel, but not in the public section, for example).

However, we could create a display method in the presenter class that handles a collection of books, replacing the `foreach` loop with a `presenter.Display(books)` call. We could then move those two methods out of `Program` without much impact. In the future, that would allow us to support multiple implementations, one for the admins and one for the public users for added flexibility.

> **Tip**
>
> I have told you this already, but here I go again. When you don't know how to name a class or a method, you may have isolated an invalid or an incomplete concern. This is a good indicator that you should go back to the drawing board. That said, naming is hard, so sometimes that's just it.

Keep it simple, stupid (KISS)

This is probably one of the most straightforward principles, yet one of the most important. Like in the real world, the more moving pieces, the more chances something breaks. This principle states to keep your systems simple and that the best solutions are often the simplest.

Of course, adding interfaces, abstraction layers, and complex object hierarchy adds complexity, but what are the added benefits of that complexity? If we take interfaces as an example, they add flexibility and testability but break the code into more pieces and make the program flow harder to follow.

So if you can write the same program with less complexity, I'd say do it. That's also why anticipating future needs is often a bad thing and could make you introduce complexity for features that may never come.

That said, I think I talked enough about this one, and I'll leave you to it.

Summary

In this chapter, we covered many architectural principles. We began by exploring the five SOLID principles and their importance in modern software engineering to jump to the DRY, KISS, and separation of concerns principles, which add some more guidance to the mix. By following those principles, you should be able to build better, more maintainable software.

As we also covered, principles are only principles, not laws. You must always be careful not to abuse them, so they remain helpful instead of harmful. The context is always important; internal tools and critical business apps require different levels of tinkering. Try not to over-engineer everything and try to keep it simple, stupid.

With all of those principles in our toolbox, we are now ready to jump into design patterns and get our design level one step further! In the next few chapters, we explore how to implement some of the most frequently used Gang of Four (GoF) patterns and how those are applied at another level with dependency injection. Dependency injection is going to help follow the SOLID principles in our day-to-day designs, but before that, in the next two chapters, we explore ASP.NET Core MVC.

Questions

Let's take a look at a few practice questions:

1. How many principles are represented by the SOLID acronym?

2. Is it true that when following the SOLID principles, the idea is to create bigger components that can each manage more elements of a program by creating God-sized classes?

3. By following the DRY principle, you want to remove all code duplication from everywhere, irrespective of the source, and encapsulate that code into a reusable component. Is this affirmation correct?

4. Is it true that the ISP tells us that creating multiple smaller interfaces is better than creating one large one?

5. What principle tells us that creating multiple smaller classes that handle a single responsibility is better than one class handling multiple responsibilities?

Further reading

- Covariance and contravariance (C#): `https://adpg.link/BxBG`

Join our book's Discord space

Join the book's Discord workspace for *Ask me Anything* session with the authors:

`https://packt.link/ASPdotNET6DesignPatterns`

Section 2: Designing for ASP.NET Core

This section introduces ASP.NET Core Model View Controller (MVC) and its web API counterpart. We explore Razor Pages, MVC, and HTTP-based RESTful services. Then we explore a number of more advanced techniques used to push the MVC pattern further, such as view models and data transfer objects.

Afterward, we dig into some classic design patterns to warm us up. Finally, we take those patterns to the next level using dependency injection, which is at the core of modern ASP.NET Core applications. Those subjects lay out the fundamental knowledge that we build upon until the end of the book and, most likely, for the rest of your career as an ASP.NET Core developer.

Finally, we dig into some ASP.NET Core-specific patterns, such as the options pattern and the .NET logging abstractions.

This section comprises the following chapters:

- *Chapter 4, The MVC Pattern using Razor*
- *Chapter 5, The MVC Pattern for Web APIs*
- *Chapter 6, Understanding the Strategy, Abstract Factory, and Singleton Design Patterns*
- *Chapter 7, Deep Dive into Dependency Injection*
- *Chapter 8, Options and Logging Patterns*

The MVC Pattern Using Razor

This chapter explains the **Model View Controller (MVC)** and **View Model** design patterns and contains an overview of the ASP.NET Core MVC framework pieces in case you are not familiar with them. MVC segregates the responsibilities of rendering a user interface into three parts: the model, the view, and a controller.

The MVC pattern is probably one of the most extensively adapted architectural patterns for displaying web user interfaces. Why? Because it matches the concept behind HTTP/1 and the classic web almost to perfection. MVC might serve you well for a typical server-rendered web application using the request-response pattern. A **single-page application (SPA) framework** could be best for more user-intensive user interfaces. For page-oriented applications, **Razor Pages** is a strong contestant.

From the old ASP.NET MVC to ASP.NET Core, the MVC framework is cleaner, leaner, faster, and more flexible than ever before. Moreover, dependency injection is now built into the heart of ASP.NET, which helps leverage its power. We cover dependency injection in *Chapter 7, Deep Dive into Dependency Injection*.

The ASP.NET Core pipeline uses a series of middleware to handle cross-cutting concerns, such as authentication and routing. MVC is an opt-in feature now, like pretty much everything else. You can opt in to MVC, Razor Pages, or web APIs and configure them with only a few statements.

In this chapter, we cover the following topics:

- The Model View Controller design pattern
- The View Model design pattern

The Model View Controller design pattern

When using ASP.NET Core MVC, there are two broad usages of the MVC framework:

- The first use is to display a web user interface, using a classic client-server application model where the page is composed on the server. The result is then sent back to the client. To build this type of application, you can use Razor, which allows developers to mix C# and HTML to build rich user interfaces elegantly. From my perspective, Razor is the technology that made me embrace MVC in the first place when ASP.NET MVC 3 came out in 2011.

- The second use of MVC is to build web APIs. The presentation (or the view) becomes a data contract in a web API instead of a user interface. The contract is defined by the expected input and output, as with any API. The most significant difference is that a web API acts as a remote API. Essentially, inputs and outputs are serialized data structures, usually JSON or XML, mixed with HTTP verbs such as GET and POST. More on that in *Chapter 5, The MVC Pattern for Web APIs*.

Goal

In a classic server-rendered web user interface, the objective of the MVC pattern is to separate the rendering of a page into three distinct components that interact with each other. Doing this helps have smaller pieces that are easier to maintain instead of one bigger piece.

Design

MVC divides the application into three distinct parts, where each has a single responsibility:

- **Model:** The model is a data structure representing the domain that we are modeling.
- **View:** The view's responsibility is to present a model to a user, in our case, as a web user interface, so mainly HTML, CSS, and JavaScript.
- **Controller:** The controller is the key component of MVC. It plays a coordinating role between the request from a user and its response. The controller's code should remain minimal and should not include complex logic or manipulation. The controller's primary responsibility is to handle requests and dispatch responses. The controller is an HTTP bridge.

> **Note**
>
> Throughout the book, we explore multiple alternatives to move the complex logic out of the controllers, especially in *Section 4: Designing at Application Scale*. In a nutshell, you can leverage many patterns that we cover in this book to achieve that, including the **Command Query Separation** (**CQS**), Mediator, and Layering patterns.

If we put all of that back together, the controller is the entry point of every request, the view composes the response (the user interface that shapes the user's experience), and both share the model. The model is fetched or manipulated by the controller and sent to the view for rendering. The user then sees the requested resource in their browser.

The following diagram illustrates the MVC concept:

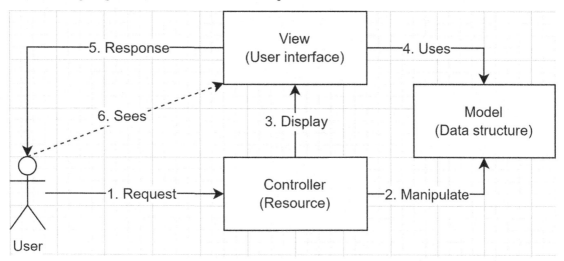

Figure 4.1: MVC workflow

We can interpret *Figure 4.1* as the following:

1. The user requests an HTTP resource (routed to an action of a controller).
2. The controller reads or updates the model to be used by the view.
3. The controller then dispatches the model to the view for rendering.
4. The view uses the model to render the HTML page.
5. That rendered page is sent to the user over HTTP.
6. The user's browser displays the page like any other web page; it is only HTML after all.

Next, we look into ASP.NET Core MVC itself, how the directories are organized by default, what controllers are, and how routing works.

Anatomy of ASP.NET Core MVC

We use the default template to explore MVC anatomy. To generate a new MVC project, you can execute the dotnet new mvc command or use Visual Studio. In this section, we explore the pieces the template generates to understand how they fit together.

The first piece is the entry point; the Program class. Since .NET 6, there is no more Startup class by default in many templates, and the Program class is autogenerated. Using top-level statements and the minimal hosting model leads to a simplified Program.cs file (see *Appendix A* for more information).

Here is an example:

```
var builder = WebApplication.CreateBuilder(args);
// Add services to the container.
builder.Services.AddControllersWithViews();

var app = builder.Build();
if (!app.Environment.IsDevelopment())
{
    app.UseExceptionHandler("/Home/Error");
    app.UseHsts();
}
app.UseHttpsRedirection();
app.UseStaticFiles();
app.UseRouting();
app.UseAuthorization();
app.MapControllerRoute(
    name: "default",
    pattern: "{controller=Home}/{action=Index}/{id?}");
app.Run();
```

In the preceding code, the `Program.cs` file, we have the same control over the building blocks but they are centralized in a single file. The highlighted lines are the MVC pieces' registration. As it explicitly states, the `AddControllersWithViews` method adds support for controllers and views while the other lines add middlewares that enable routing, static files (like CSS, images, and JavaScript), and the default route.

> **Note**
>
> In the previous model containing two files, the `builder` variable was instantiated in the `Program` class while the `builder.Services` property and the `app` variable were managed in the `Startup` class. If you are more fond of the `Startup` class, you can still create one.

Next, let's look at how the files are organized.

Directory structure

The default ASP.NET Core MVC directory structure is very explicit. There is a `Controllers` directory, a `Models` directory, and a `Views` directory. By convention, we create controllers in the `Controllers` directory, models in the `Models` directory, and views in the `Views` directory.

However, the `Views` directory is a little different. To keep your project organized, each controller has its own subdirectory under `Views`. For example, the views for `HomeController` are found in the `Views/Home` directory.

The Views/Shared directory is a particular case. The views in that subdirectory are accessible by all other views and controllers alike. In that directory, we usually create global views, such as layouts, menus, and other similar elements.

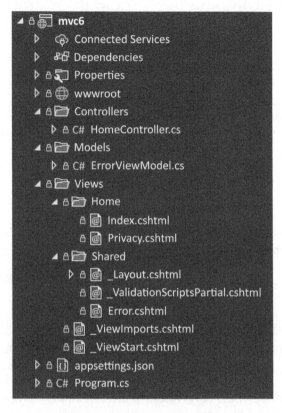

Figure 4.2: MVC directory structure

You can create your controller classes anywhere; they don't need to be in any specific folder. You can leverage sub directory structures or areas to help keep a clean project structure and organize your controllers. The same goes for the model classes.

Controller

The easiest way to create a controller is to create a class inheriting from Microsoft.AspNetCore.Mvc. Controller. By convention, the class's name is suffixed by Controller. That base class adds all the utility methods you should need to return the appropriate view, like the View() method.

Once you have a controller class, you need to add actions. Actions are public methods that represent the operations that a user can perform.

More precisely, the following define a controller:

- A controller exposes one or more actions.
- An action can take zero or more input parameters.
- An action can return zero or one output value.

- The action is what handles the actual request.
- We can group cohesive actions under the same controller, thus creating a unit.

For example, the following represents the `HomeController` class containing a single `Index` action:

```
public class HomeController : Controller
{
    public IActionResult Index() => View();
}
```

That `Index` method (action) returns its default view by leveraging the `View` method offered by the `Controller` class. In this case, MVC will serve the `Home/Index.cshtml` view to the user, which usually represents the home page.

Let's look at the model next.

Model

An MVC model is a class that contains properties or methods, like any other class. Let's inspect the `ErrorViewModel` class, which represents a model created by the default template:

```
namespace MVC6.Models;
public class ErrorViewModel
{
    public string? RequestId { get; set; }
    public bool ShowRequestId => !string.IsNullOrEmpty(RequestId);
}
```

The preceding code shows that the `ErrorViewModel` class contains two properties, the `ShowRequestId` property computed automatically and the `RequestId` property.

If you wonder where the parentheses of the namespace declaration went, that's new syntactic sugar from C# 10 where we can make a file-scoped namespace declaration like this. See *Appendix A* for more information about C# features.

To send a model to the view, we pass it as an argument of the `View` method. Here is the `Error` action of the `HomeController` class from the MVC template:

```
public IActionResult Error()
{
    return View(new ErrorViewModel { RequestId = Activity.Current?.Id ??
HttpContext.TraceIdentifier });
}
```

In the preceding code, we leverage the same `View` method as the `Index` action but pass an `ErrorViewModel` instance as an argument. The code sets the `RequestId` property to either `Activity.Current?.Id` (an optional distributed trace activity) or `HttpContext.TraceIdentifier` (the request ID generated by Kestrel).

As simple as that, the Error action sends the ErrorViewModel model to the Shared/Error.cshtml view to display an error page to the user. Of course, the real challenge is designing those models according to your domain.

Next, let's look at the structure of a view.

View

Razor is a C#-based templating language that allows creating HTML-like pages and views (there is also a VB.NET version). Razor is a very convenient way of writing complex web UI logic productively. Razor views are stored in .cshtml files. The Razor view engine compiles that markup to C# classes that ASP.NET Core MVC leverages to render the HTML to the users.

Note

Setting the EmitCompilerGeneratedFiles property to true in the csproj file tells the compiler to write the generated cshtml.g.cs files to disk. Doing this is a good way to inspect how .NET magically generates those views. The default directory is under obj/[configuration]/[version]/generated/.

Let's look at the Error action's view as an example:

```
@model ErrorViewModel
@{
    ViewData["Title"] = "Error";
}
@if (Model?.ShowRequestId ?? false)
{
    <p>
        <strong>Request ID:</strong>
        <code>@Model?.RequestId</code>
    </p>
}
```

I omitted most of the HTML in the preceding code to keep the noise to a minimum. Nevertheless, the first line of the view defines the type of model it expects using the @model directive. In this case, the view expects the model to be an instance of the ErrorViewModel class.

Then, highlighted in the code, the Model property can be used to access the properties of the model using the Razor syntax.

Now that we have explored the core mechanics, let's look at routing.

Default routing

ASP.NET Core has a routing mechanism that allows developers to define one or more routes to know which controller should handle a specific HTTP request. A route is a URL template that maps HTTP requests to C# code.

The MVC template defines the following `default` pattern:

```
app.MapControllerRoute(
    name: "default",
    pattern: "{controller=Home}/{action=Index}/{id?}");
```

The first fragment is about controllers, where the following apply:

- `{controller}` maps the request to a `{controller}Controller` class. For example, Home would map to the `HomeController` class.
- `{controller=Home}` means that the `HomeController` class is the default controller, which is used if no `{controller}` is supplied.

The second fragment is about actions:

- `{action}` maps the request to a controller method (the action).
- Like its controller counterpart, `{action=Index}` means that the `Index` method is the default action. For example, if we had a `ProductsController` class in our application, making a `GET` request to `https://localhost/Products` would make MVC invoke the `ProductsController.Index()` method.

 Note

In a **Create, Read, Update, Delete (CRUD)** controller, `Index` is where you usually define your list.

The last fragment is about an optional `id` parameter:

- `{id}` means that any value following the action name maps to the `id` parameter of that action method.
- The `?` in `{id?}` means the parameter is optional.

Let's look at some examples to wrap up our study of the default routing template:

- Calling `/Some/Action` would map to `SomeController.Action()`.
- Calling `/Some` would map to `SomeController.Index()`.
- Calling `/` would map to `HomeController.Index()`.
- Calling `/Some/Action/123` would map to `SomeController.Action(123)`.

Conclusion

We could talk about MVC for the remainder of the book, but we would be missing the point. This chapter and the next aim to cover the possibilities to help you understand the MVC pattern and ASP.NET Core, but nothing too in depth regarding the framework itself.

We covered the different building blocks and mechanisms of MVC, which should be enough to continue. We use ASP.NET Core throughout the book, covering many aspects in different contexts.

Using the MVC pattern helps us follow the SOLID principles in the following ways:

- **S**: The MVC pattern divides the rendering of a page into three different roles.
- **O**: N/A
- **L**: N/A
- **I**: The MVC pattern helps divide one responsibility into three smaller ones (SRP), up to a certain extent creating three smaller interfaces. However, controllers can become bloated with capabilities and contain many actions. For example, a simple CRUD controller has a total of eight actions to begin with: one action for the list and the details page, and two actions for the create, edit, and delete pages. From there if you add more capabilities, the controller will just become fatter and fatter. One way to help is to create reusable components. We explore ways to create and reuse smaller pieces of UI in *Chapter 17, ASP.NET Core User Interfaces*, but that may not fix this potential problem entirely. Razor Pages might be a good alternative to investigate as well. The other two pieces (the views and models) should have a smaller API surface (interface) with the MVC pattern.
- **D**: N/A

Next, we improve the M part of the MVC pattern.

The View Model design pattern

The **View Model** pattern is used when building ASP.NET Core MVC applications but can be applied to other technologies. Typically, you access data from a data source and then render a view based on that data. That is where the view model comes into play. Instead of sending the raw data directly to the view, you copy the required data to another class that carries only the required information to render that view, nothing more.

Using this technique, you can even compose a complex view model, adding filtering, sorting, and more without altering your data or domain models. Those features are presentation-centric and, as such, the view model's responsibility is to meet the view's requirements in terms of the presentation of information, which is in line with the **Single Responsibility Principle** (**SRP**) explored in *Chapter 3, Architectural Principles*.

Goal

The goal of the View Model pattern is to **create a model specific to a view**, decoupling the other parts of the software from the view. As a rule of thumb, you want each view to be strongly typed with its own view model class to make sure that views are not coupled with each other, thereby causing possible maintenance issues in the long run.

View models allow developers to gather data in a particular format and send it to the view in another format that's better suited for rendering that specific view. That improves the application's testability, which in turn should increase the overall code quality and stability.

In other words, the view model is the data contract that a controller's action uses to communicate information to a view.

Design

Here is a revised MVC workflow that supports view models:

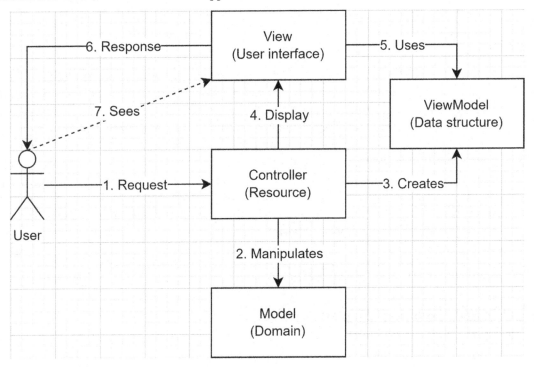

Figure 4.3: MVC workflow with view models

We can interpret *Figure 4.3* as follows:

1. The user requests an HTTP resource (routed to the action of a controller).
2. The controller reads or updates the model.
3. The controller creates the view model.
4. The controller dispatches the view model to the view for rendering.
5. The view uses the view model to render the HTML page.
6. That rendered page is sent to the user over HTTP.
7. The browser displays the page like any other web page.

In the previous diagram, have you noticed that the model is now decoupled from the view? That's what the View Model pattern brings to the table: a clear line between the user interfaces and the domain.

Project – View models (a list of students)

Context: We must build a list of students. Each list item must display a student's name and the number of classes that student is registered in.

The UI/UX experts came up with the following list that includes badges to improve the customer experience (I know, what a sophisticated design, right?):

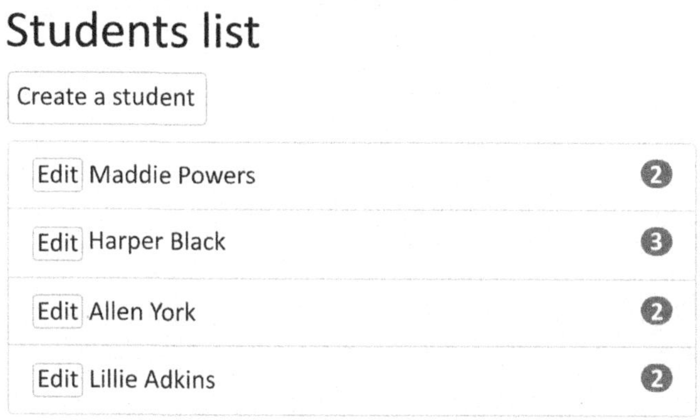

Students list

Create a student

Edit Maddie Powers	2
Edit Harper Black	3
Edit Allen York	2
Edit Lillie Adkins	2

Figure 4.4: Students list with their number of classes

To keep things simple and create our prototype, we load in-memory data through the `StudentService` class.

It is important to remember that the view model must only contain the required information to display the view. The view model classes, located in `StudentListViewModels.cs`, look like the following:

```
namespace ViewModels;

public record class StudentListViewModel(
    IEnumerable<StudentListItemViewModel> Students
);
public record class StudentListItemViewModel(
    int Id,
    string Name,
    int ClassCount
);
```

This is one of the scenarios where keeping more than one class in the same file makes sense, hence the plural filename. That said, if you can't stand having multiple classes in a single file, feel free to split them up in your project. You can refer to *Appendix A* for more information about `record class`.

> **Note**
>
> In a larger application, we could create subdirectories or use namespaces to keep our view model classes' names unique and organized, for example, /Models/Students/ListViewModels.cs.
>
> Another alternative is to create view models in a /ViewModels/ directory instead of the default /Models/ one. We could also create the view model classes as nested classes under their controller.
>
> For example, a StudentsController class could have a nested ListViewModel class, callable like this: StudentsController.ListViewModel.
>
> These are all valid options. Once again, do as you prefer and what suits your project best.

The StudentController class is the key element and has an Index action that handles GET requests. Each request fetches the students, creates the view model, and then dispatches it to the view. Here is the controller code:

```
namespace ViewModels.Controllers;
public class StudentsController : Controller
{
    private readonly StudentService _studentService = new();
    public async Task<IActionResult> IndexAsync()
    {
        // Get data from the data store
        var students = await _studentService.ReadAllAsync();

        // Create the ViewModel, based on the data
        var viewModel = new StudentListViewModel(
            Students: students.Select(student => new StudentListItemViewModel(
                Id: student.Id,
                Name: student.Name,
                ClassCount: student.Classes.Count()
            ))
        );

        // Return the View
        return View(viewModel);
    }
}
```

The view renders the students as a Bootstrap 3 list-group, using a badge to display the ClassCount property, as defined by our initial specifications.

```
@model StudentListViewModel
@{
    ViewData["Title"] = "Students";}
<h2>Students list</h2>
<ul class="list-group">
    @foreach (var item in Model!.Students)
    {
        <li class="list-group-item">
            <span class="badge">@Html.DisplayFor(modelItem => item.
ClassCount)</span>
            @Html.DisplayFor(modelItem => item.Name)
        </li>
    }
</ul>
```

With the preceding few lines of code and the View Model pattern, we decoupled the Student model from the view with the StudentListViewModel class, serving as a transitory model. Moreover, we limit the amount of information passed to the view by replacing the Student.Classes property with the StudentListItemViewModel.ClassCount property, which only contains the required information to render the view (the number of classes a student is in).

> **Bootstrap 3**
>
> It is important to note that new .NET projects reference a more recent version of Bootstrap, which can translate into minor differences. We used Bootstrap only to make the UI look better; it was not part of the subject we are studying, hence keeping the older version.

Conclusion

If you are still uncertain about this pattern, we use view models and other similar concepts throughout the book. That said, when you choose one pattern over another, it is essential to review the requirements of that specific project or feature as it dictates whether your choice is rational.

For example, if the following apply to your project:

- It is a simple data-driven user interface, tightly coupled with a database.
- It has no or minimal logic.
- It is not going to evolve (this one rarely happens and is very hard to predict).

In that case, view models may only add development time to your project, while you could have Visual Studio almost scaffold it all for you instead. Nothing stops you from using a view model or two when you need it, such as creating a dashboard or some more complex views.

> **Tip**
>
> For scaffolding-heavy projects, you can customize the templates Visual Studio uses to make it even faster.

For non-trivial projects, I recommend defaulting to view models. We explore multiple ways of organizing and building applications later in *Section 4: Designing at Application Scale* of the book.

Using the View Model pattern helps us follow the SOLID principles in the following ways:

- S: A view model adds clear boundaries between the domain model and the view, leading to two distinct responsibilities to help keep things isolated.
- O: N/A
- L: N/A
- I: A view model allows us to limit the amount of information sent to the view, keeping that information to a minimum. The View Model pattern introduces two possibly smaller interfaces: one for the view and one for the domain.
- D: N/A

Summary

In this chapter, we explored ASP.NET Core MVC, which allows us to create rich web user interfaces with Razor and C#.

We saw how to decouple the model from the presentation using view models. View models are classes specially crafted around a view. For example, rather than passing a data or domain model to a view and letting the view do calculations, the controller does the calculation instead and passes the results to the view. This way, the view only has one responsibility: displaying the user interface, the page.

In the next chapter, we explore the web API counterpart to the MVC and View Model patterns. We then look at our first **Gang of Four** (**GoF**) design patterns and deep dive into ASP.NET Core dependency injection. All of that pushes us further down the path of designing better applications.

Questions

Let's take a look at a few practice questions:

1. What is the role of the **controller** in the MVC pattern?
2. What Razor directive indicates the type of **model** that a view accepts?
3. With how many views should a **view model** be associated?
4. Can a **view model** add flexibility to a system?
5. Can a **view model** add robustness to a system?

Further reading

- Routing in ASP.NET Core: https://adpg.link/YHVJ

5

The MVC Pattern for Web APIs

In the previous chapter, we explored displaying web user interfaces with the Model View Controller (MVC) pattern using Razor. This chapter covers the web API version of the ASP.NET Core MVC framework, which is a crucial part of most modern technology stacks. A web API allows us to send data to the user, usually another machine, instead of a user interface, as we did in the previous chapter. Moreover, we use the technologies and patterns learned in this chapter throughout the book. Avoiding user interfaces makes code easier to follow.

Web APIs are used in projects of all types and sizes, from microservices to mobile apps, passing by single-page applications (SPA).

In this chapter, we cover the following topics:

- An overview of REST
- The Model View Controller design pattern
- Anatomy of ASP.NET Core web APIs
- The Data Transfer Object design pattern
- API contracts

An overview of REST

REST, or **Representational State Transfer**, is a way to create internet-based services, known as web services or web APIs, that commonly use HTTP as their transport protocol. It allows the well-known HTTP specifications to be reused instead of recreating new ways of exchanging data. For example, returning an HTTP status code 200 OK indicates success, while 400 Bad Request indicates failure.

In a nutshell, we can state the following:

- Each HTTP endpoint is a resource.
- Each resource can be secured independently.
- Calling the same resource twice should result in the same operation executed twice. For example, executing two POST /entities should result in two new entities, while fetching GET /entities/some-id should return the same entity twice.

- The service should be stateless, meaning that it does not persist information about its clients between requests.
- The response from a RESTful service (GET) should be cacheable.

There are multiple other elements that we could talk about here, but those are the fundamental ones that should allow a neophyte to get a good initial idea of what a RESTful service is.

Web APIs are probably the most commonly used way to create interoperable web services for other machines to interact with our system. We could write entire books devoted to web APIs and REST, but the goal is to know just enough to get started. Nevertheless, here is some broadly applicable guidance about RESTful APIs to kickstart you.

HTTP methods

The HTTP methods, known as *verbs*, should define what operation an endpoint performs. It helps to make the intent clear. Here is a list of the most frequently used methods, what they are for, and their expected success status code:

Method	Typical role	Success status code
GET	Read data: a list or a single entity.	200 OK
POST	Create a new entity.	201 CREATED
PUT	Replace an entity.	200 OK or 204 No Content
DELETE	Delete an entity.	200 OK or 204 No Content
PATCH	Partially update an entity.	200 OK

With these, we can start describing our API endpoints. But what are those status codes? That's what we briefly explore next.

Status code

HTTP status codes are the way to transmit what happened during an operation back to the consumer. The following table explains some common ones:

Status code	Role
200 OK	Tells the client the request has succeeded. It usually includes data related to an operation or an entity in the body of the response.
201 CREATED	Tells the client the request has succeeded and the system created a resource. It should also include a Location HTTP header pointing to the newly created resource and including the new entity in the response body.
202 ACCEPTED	Tells the client the request has been accepted for processing but is not processed yet. In an event-driven system (see *Chapter 16, Introduction to Microservices Architecture*), this could mean that an event has been published, the current resource has completed its job (published the event), but to know more, the client needs to contact another resource, wait for a notification, just wait, or can't know.

204 NO CONTENT	Tells the client the request has succeeded with no content in the response body.
302 FOUND	Tells the client to follow the specified `Location` header, which represents the redirection target.
400 BAD REQUEST	Tells the client about a validation error, generally related to badly formatted input data, missing data, or something similar.
401 UNAUTHORIZED	Tells the client that it must authenticate to access the resource.
403 FORBIDDEN	Tells the client that it does not have the required rights to access the resource (authorization).
404 NOT FOUND	Tells the client that the resource does not exist or was not found.
409 CONFLICT	Tells the client that a conflict has occurred. A typical scenario would be that the entity has changed between its last `GET` and its current operation (likely a `PUT` request).
500 INTERNAL SERVER ERROR	Tells the client that an unhandled error occurred on the server side and prevented it from fulfilling the request.

Those status codes are not entirely arbitrary, and there is a logic behind classifying them. The status codes touching similar subjects are grouped under the same "hundredth," for example:

- The 1XX status code (omitted from the preceding table) represents informational continuation results, usually handled automatically by the server, such as **100 Continue** and **101 Switching Protocols**.
- 2XX are successful results.
- 3XX are related to redirections.
- 4XX are request errors (from the client side), usually introduced by the user, such as an empty required field.
- 5XX are server-side errors that the client cannot do anything about.

Next, keeping status codes in mind, we overview how to pass more metadata between the client and the server.

HTTP headers

Web services, like RESTful and web APIs, leverage HTTP headers to transmit clients' information and describe their options and capabilities. Some headers are part of the request, while some are part of the response.

One well-known header is the `Location` header that we use for different purposes. For example:

- After creating an entity (`201 Created`), the `Location` header should point to the `GET` endpoint where the client can access that new entity.

- After starting an asynchronous operation (202 `Accepted`), the `Location` header could point to the status endpoint where you can poll for the state of the operation (has it completed, failed, or is it still ongoing).

- When redirecting a client, the `Location` header contains the destination URL. The following status codes are the most common for redirections: 301 `Moved` `Permanently`, 302 `Found`, 303 `See` `Other`, 307 `Temporary` `Redirect`, and 308 `Permanent` `Redirect`.

The `Retry-After` header can also come in handy when mixed with 202 `Accepted`, 301 `Moved` `Permanently`, 429 `Too` `Many` `Requests`, or 503 `Service` `Unavailable`. The `ETag` header identifies the version of the entity and can be used in conjunction with `If-Match` to avoid *mid-air collisions*. The `ETag` and `If-Match` headers form a sort of *optimistic concurrency* method that prevents *request two* from overwriting changes made by *request one* when changes are happening simultaneously or not in the expected order; a.k.a. a way to manage conflicts. We can also add the following to the mix as an example of HTTP headers that describe a REST endpoint: `Allow`, `Authorization`, and `Cache-Control`. The list is very long, and it would help no one to enumerate all HTTP headers here. Nonetheless, I hope this gives you a clear-enough idea to get started.

Next, we look at versioning because nothing stays the same forever, business needs change, entities are modified, and APIs must evolve.

Versioning

Versioning is a crucial aspect of a REST API. Unless you are your only consumer, you'll need a way for the API clients to query specific API versions when the contract changes. Whether the version of the API is long-lived or transitory (during the decommissioning cycle of an old endpoint, for example), both ends of the pipe must know what to expect; what API contract to respect.

Next, we explore a few ways to think about our versioning strategy.

Default versioning strategy

The first thing to think about when versioning is the default strategy. What happens when no version is specified? Will the endpoint return an error, return the first version, or return the latest version?

If the API returns an error, chances are you put that versioning strategy in place from day one, so clients are already aware that a version is required. In this case, there is no real drawback. On the other hand, putting this default strategy in place after the fact will most likely break all clients that are not up to date, which might not be the best idea (a good deployment strategy could help mitigate problems).

The next way is always to return the first version. This method is an excellent way to preserve backward compatibility. You can add more endpoint versions without breaking your consumers.

The opposite way is always to return the latest version. For consumers, this means specifying a version to consume or be up to date or break, and this might not be the best user experience to provide to your consumers. Nonetheless, many have opted for this default strategy.

You could also pick any version as the default for the API (like version 3.2, for example) or even choose a different version per endpoint. No matter what you choose, always think it through by weighing the pros and cons.

Next, we explore ways to define those versions.

Versioning strategy

Of course, there are multiple ways to think this through. You can leverage URL patterns to define and include the API version, like `https://localhost/v2/some-entities`. This is easier to query from a browser, making it simple to know the version at a glance, but the endpoint is not pointing to a unique resource anymore (a key principle of REST) as each resource has one endpoint for each version. Nonetheless, this way of versioning an API is used extensively and is one of the most popular, if not *the* most popular, ways of doing REST versioning, even if it violates one of its core principles.

The other way is to use HTTP headers. You can use a custom header like `api-version` or `Accept-version`, for example, or the `Accept` standard header. This allows resources to have unique endpoints while enabling multiple versions of each entity (multiple versions of each API contract describing the same entity).

For example, a client could specify an HTTP header while calling the endpoint like this (custom header):

```
GET https://localhost/some-entities
Accept-version: v2
```

Or like the following, by leveraging the `Accept` header for *content negotiation*:

```
GET https://localhost/some-entities
Accept: application/vnd.yourapp.v2+json
```

Whether you are using one way or another, headers or URLs, you'll most likely need to version your APIs at some point. It does not matter much the way you choose. Some people are strong advocates of one way or the other, but in the end, the decision should be taken on a case-by-case basis; what best covers your needs and capacities: simplicity, formality, or a mix of both.

Wrapping up

With a method (verb), the client (and the endpoint) can express the intent to create, update, read, or delete an entity. With a status code, the endpoint can tell the client the state of the operation. By adding more headers, both clients and endpoints can add more metadata to the request or response. Finally, by adding versioning, the endpoint can evolve without breaking existing clients while giving options to consumers about the version they want to consume.

With what we just covered, you should have more than what's needed to follow along with the examples in this book. However, if you are interested in RESTful services, I recommend learning more on that subject after completing this book.

The Model View Controller design pattern

Now that we have explored the basics of ASP.NET Core MVC in *Chapter 4, The MVC Pattern Using Razor*, and REST, it is time to jump into ASP.NET Core web APIs and return data instead of a user interface.

In the past few years, the number of web APIs just exploded to a gazillion; everybody builds APIs nowadays, not because people are blindly following a trend but based on good reasons. Here are a few examples of what makes web APIs so appealing:

- It is an efficient way of sharing data between systems.
- It allows interoperability between technologies by dialoguing in universal languages, such as JSON or XML.
- It allows your backend to be centralized and shared with multiple frontends such as mobile, desktop, and web applications.
- It allows you to gate (secure, protect, or hide) downstream systems, with APIs acting as gateways.
- It allows the encapsulation of units of logic in reusable, independent, and possibly even tiny systems.

Those reasons make it easier to reuse backend systems and share them with multiple user interfaces or other backends. For example, think of any mobile app you know; it probably has an iOS, Android, and web app to maintain. In that case, sharing part of the backend can be an excellent way to save time and money.

Goal

In a web API, the objective of the MVC pattern is to separate displaying (serializing) an entity into three distinct components that interact with each other. Doing this helps have smaller pieces that are easier to maintain and test than big bloated ones that are very hard to test in isolation.

Design

MVC divides the application into three distinct parts, where each has a single responsibility:

- **Model:** The model is a data structure representing the domain that we are modeling.
- **View:** The view's responsibility is to present a model to a user; in this case, the view is a serialized model.
- **Controller:** The controller is the key component of MVC. It plays the coordinator role between a request from a user to its response. The code of a controller should remain minimal and should not include complex logic or manipulation. The controller's primary responsibility is to handle a request and dispatch a response. The controller is an HTTP bridge.

Here is an updated diagram that represents the MVC flow of a web API:

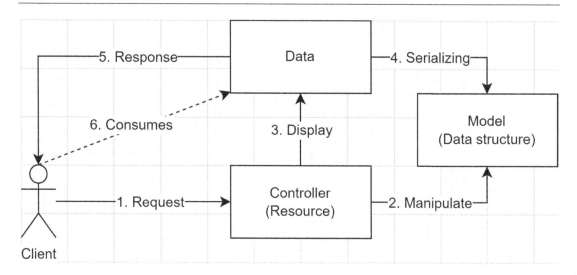

Figure 5.1: Workflow of a web API

There are only a couple of differences between rendering a user interface and building a web API:

- Instead of sending HTML to the browser, the API outputs a serialized data structure.
- The client wants to consume the data instead of having a browser display it.

Based on this diagram, we are sending our model directly to the client. In most scenarios, we don't want to do that, and instead, we want to send only the portion of the data we need in the format we want. We will be covering this next with the DTO pattern, but first, let's dig into ASP.NET Core web APIs.

Anatomy of ASP.NET Core web APIs

We use the default template to explore web APIs' anatomy. To generate a new web API project, you can execute the dotnet new webapi command or use Visual Studio. This section explores the pieces the template generates to understand how they fit together, leading to a good starting point.

The entry point

The first piece is the entry point: the Program class. Since .NET 6, there is no more Startup class by default in many templates, and the Program class is autogenerated. Using top-level statements and the minimal hosting model leads to a simplified Program.cs file (see *Appendix A* for more information).

Here is an example:

```
var builder = WebApplication.CreateBuilder(args);

// Add services to the container.
builder.Services.AddControllers();
builder.Services.AddEndpointsApiExplorer();
builder.Services.AddSwaggerGen();

var app = builder.Build();
// Configure the HTTP request pipeline.
if (app.Environment.IsDevelopment())
{
    app.UseSwagger();
    app.UseSwaggerUI();
}
app.UseHttpsRedirection();
app.UseAuthorization();
app.MapControllers();
app.Run();
```

In the preceding code, the `Program.cs` file is very similar to what the MVC template generated. We also have the same control over the building blocks as before .NET 6, but everything is centralized in a single file. The highlighted lines are the web API pieces' registration.

The default template also registers **Swagger** to generate **OpenAPI** specs automatically and a UI to visualize them. More on that in the *API contracts* section at the end of the chapter.

Directory structure

The default directory structure is a lightweight version of what the MVC template generates. It contains a single `Controllers` folder. However, you could create a `Models` folder to store your models or use any other structure you prefer. The only piece tied to a directory structure was the views, which are not part of web APIs. We explore many ways of designing applications in *Section 4, Designing at Application Scale*.

That's it for the directory structure. Next, we look at the central part of this pattern—the controllers.

Controller

The easiest way to create a controller is to create a class inheriting from `ControllerBase`. However, while `ControllerBase` adds many beneficial methods, the only requirement is to decorate the controller class with the `[ApiController]` attribute. As with MVC, by convention, the controller's class name is suffixed by `Controller`.

Note

ControllerBase, ApiControllerAttribute, and attribute routing classes come from the Microsoft.AspNetCore.Mvc namespace.

The endpoints are exposed by creating action methods like MVC. The difference is that instead of returning a view, an action returns data. We look at that next.

Returning values

The objective of building a web API is to return data to its consumers and execute remote operations securely. Most of the plumbing is done for us by the ASP.NET Core code, including serialization. Most of the ASP.NET Core pipeline is customizable, which is out of the scope of this chapter.

That said, before returning values, let's look at a few helpers provided by the ControllerBase class. These are very valuable, even if not necessary:

- The StatusCode method allows specifying the status code that you want to return. You can use constants defined in the StatusCodes class to help or pass an int directly. You can also optionally pass a second argument that will be serialized as the body of the response.
- The Ok method allows returning a status code 200 OK with an optional body.
- The Created, CreatedAtAction, and other similar methods allow returning a status code 201 Created, including different options to craft the Location URL representing the newly created resource and optionally serialize that new entity as part of the response body.
- The NoContent method allows returning a status code 204 No Content and an empty body.
- The NotFound method allows returning a status code 404 Not Found with an optional body.
- The BadRequest method allows returning a status code 400 Bad Request with an optional body representing the problems.
- The Redirect, RedirectPermanent, and other similar methods allow returning a redirection status code like 302 Found and 301 Moved Permanently while exposing different options to craft the Location URL representing the redirection the client should follow.
- The Accepted, AcceptedAtAction, and other similar methods allow the status code 202 Accepted to be returned, along with an optional body and different options to craft the Location URL representing the status endpoint.
- The Conflict method allows the status code 409 Conflict to be returned with an optional body representing the error.

There are other methods as part of the ControllerBase class that are self-discoverable using IntelliSense (code completion). Those helper methods create the return value for you, which you could manually do yourself. You could even create your own classes that extend IActionResult. Customization aside, you should go a long way with the helper methods that the ControllerBase class exposes. Now that we explored these, let's look at ways to return data to the client:

- You can return the model directly.
- You can return an `ActionResult<TValue>` class.
- You can return an `ActionResult` class.
- You can return an `IActionResult` interface.

Starting with the last two, the `IActionResult` interface and the `ActionResult` class are more abstract. They are constraining you to use the helper methods exposed by `ControllerBase` or construct the resulting instances yourself to return values. Moreover, they are not auto-discoverable by OpenAPI tools like Swagger.

Here is an example (without routing) based on the `WeatherForecastController` generated, where the actions return a collection of `WeatherForecast` objects, leveraging the `Ok` method (highlighted code):

```
public class WeatherForecastController : ControllerBase
{
    public IActionResult InterfaceAction()
        => Ok(GetWeatherForecasts());


    public ActionResult ClassAction()
        => Ok(GetWeatherForecasts());


    private static WeatherForecast[] GetWeatherForecasts()
        => Enumerable.Range(1, 5)
            .Select(index => new WeatherForecast
            {
                Date = DateTime.Now.AddDays(index),
                TemperatureC = Random.Shared.Next(-20, 55),
                Summary = _summaries[Random.Shared.Next(_summaries.Length)]
            })
            .ToArray();
}
```

The problem with the preceding code is API discoverability. However, we could decorate our actions with the `ProducesResponseType` attribute to circumvent that, like this:

```
[ProducesResponseType(typeof(WeatherForecast[]), StatusCodes.Status200OK)]
public IActionResult InterfaceAction() { ... }
```

In the preceding code, we specify the return type as the first argument and the status code as the second, using the `StatusCodes` class constants. We can add multiples of those to define alternate states, such as `404` and `400`. We can also define conventions that apply more broad rules, which we won't cover here (refer to the *Further reading* section at the end of the chapter).

All other actions use the `GetWeatherForecasts` method. The critical part of that method is that it returns a collection of `WeatherForecast` objects.

Next, let's explore returning the model directly (without the routing):

```
public IEnumerable<WeatherForecast> Get()
    => GetWeatherForecasts();
```

As we can see from the preceding code, the Get action method is nothing more than any other method. However, the response is a 200 OK status code and a WeatherForecast JSON array body that looks like this:

```
[
  {
    "date": "2021-11-13T10:39:48.857043-05:00",
    "temperatureC": -4,
    "temperatureF": 25,
    "summary": "Cool"
  },
  ...
]
```

Thanks to **class conversion operators** (see *Appendix A* for more info), we can do the same with ActionResult<T> as well, like this:

```
public ActionResult<IEnumerable<WeatherForecast>> GenericClassActionDirect()
    => GetWeatherForecasts();
```

Moreover, with ActionResult<T>, we can return other results. Here is an example using the Ok method (highlighted):

```
public ActionResult<IEnumerable<WeatherForecast>> GenericClassActionOk()
    => Ok(GetWeatherForcasts());
```

To prove that point, here is a similar method that returns a 404 Not Found response:

```
public ActionResult<IEnumerable<WeatherForecast>> GenericClassActionNotFound()
    => NotFound();
```

To conclude returning values, we have multiple ways of doing it, with ActionResult<T> being the most flexible in terms of feature support. On the other hand, IActionResult is the most abstract one.

Next, we look at routing requests to those action methods.

Attribute routing

Attribute routing maps an HTTP request to a controller action. Those attributes decorate the controllers and the actions to create the complete routes. To cover attribute routing, let's use the following controller without any implementation code to focus only on attributes:

```
[ApiController]
[Route("[controller]")]
```

```
public class ValuesController : ControllerBase
{
    [HttpGet]
    public ActionResult<IEnumerable<string>> Get() => default!;
    [HttpGet("{id}")]
    public ActionResult<string> Get(int id) => default!;
    [HttpPost]
    public void Post([FromBody] string value) { }
    [HttpPut("{id}")]
    public void Put(int id, [FromBody] string value) { }
    [HttpDelete("{id}")]
    public void Delete(int id) { }
}
```

The Route attributes and Http[Method] attributes define what a user should query to reach a specific resource. The Route attribute allows us to define a routing pattern, like MVC, that applies to all HTTP methods under the decorated controller. The Http[Method] attributes define the HTTP method used to reach that action method. They also offer the possibility to set an optional route pattern to handle more complex routes, including passing parameters. Those attributes are very helpful in crafting concise and clear URLs while keeping the routing system close to the controller. All routes must be unique.

Based on the code, [Route("[controller]")] means that the actions of this controller are reachable through /values (the Controller suffix is ignored, as with MVC). Then, the other attributes tell ASP.NET to map specific requests to specific methods. For example, [HttpGet] tells ASP.NET that GET /values should map to the Get() method. The [HttpGet("{id}")] attribute tells the routing engine that GET /values/1 requests should be routed to the Get(int id) method instead. Both are mapping the GET method, but the id parameter helps differentiate them. The other attributes are doing the same but aim at a different HTTP method.

The FromBody attribute tells the model binder to use the HTTP request body for that value. Other attributes tell the model binder where to look to fetch the decorated value. Here is the list:

- FromBody, to look at the body and choose a formatter based on Content-Type.
- FromForm, to look at the form collection; the fields of an HTML form.
- FromHeader, to look at the HTTP headers.
- FromQuery, to look at the query string.
- FromRoute, to look at the MVC route data.
- FromServices, to inject a service from the dependency injection container.

If we look back at ValuesController, it defines the following endpoints:

URL	Action/Method
GET /values	Get()
GET /values/1	Get(int id)

POST /values	void Post([FromBody] string value)
PUT /values/1	void Put(int id, [FromBody] string value)
DELETE /values/1	void Delete(int id)

When designing a web API, the URL leading to your endpoints should be clear and concise, making it easier for consumers to discover and learn the API. You want to group your resources by concern, hierarchically, to create a cohesive URI space that is easy to use and understand. Clients must be able to understand the logic behind the endpoints easily. Think about your endpoints as a consumer of the web API. I would even extend that suggestion to any API; always think about the consumer of your code to create the best possible API.

Conclusion

As for MVC, we could talk about web APIs for the remainder of the book, but we would be missing the point. Hopefully, the subset of features we covered here was enough to fill the gap you might have had. Otherwise, we are not done with web APIs, so more knowledge pieces will likely fall in place.

In this MVC section oriented toward web APIs, we explored the pattern itself, the default template, how to create controllers and action methods, as well as how to route requests to those actions.

Using the MVC pattern helps us follow the SOLID principles in the following ways:

- **S**: The MVC pattern divides the rendering of a data structure into three different roles. Based on what we explored so far, the framework handles the "View" (serialization) part, leaving us only two pieces to manage: the Model and the Controller.
- **O**: N/A
- **L**: N/A
- **I**: As with MVC, controllers can become bloated with capabilities. However, unlike MVC, web API controllers don't have those views to render, making them leaner by keeping their interface more cohesive. We could also leverage Minimal APIs to skip the need for controllers altogether.
- **D**: N/A

Next, we explore the **Data Transfer Object** pattern to isolate the API's model from the domain. We dig deeper into models, data, and domains in *Chapter 12, Understanding Layering*.

The Data Transfer Object design pattern

The **Data Transfer Object** (DTO) pattern is the equivalent of the View Model pattern, but for web APIs. Instead of targeting a view, we are targeting the consumers of a web API endpoint.

Goal

The goal is to *control the inputs and outputs of an endpoint* by decoupling the API contract from the application's inner workings. DTOs empower us to define our APIs without thinking about the underlying data structures, leaving us the choice to craft our web services the way we want. More precisely, we can craft them the way we want the consumers to interact with them. So, no matter the underlying system, we can use DTOs to design endpoints that are easier to consume, maintain, and evolve.

Other possible objectives are to save bandwidth by limiting the amount of information that the API transmits, flatten the data structure, or add API-only features.

Design

Let's start by analyzing a schema, which you may find similar to the one we saw when visiting view models:

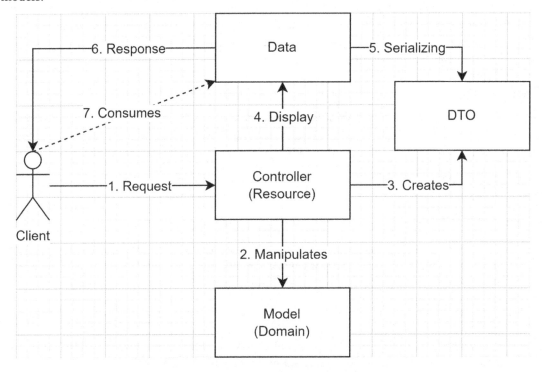

Figure 5.2: MVC workflow with a DTO

The same few differences between view models and DTOs can be applied here, following the same idea: decoupling the domain from the view (data). These design patterns are the same, but one targets a view and the other the input and output of a web service.

Project — DTO

Context: In a new application, our UX experts figured that displaying statistics about our customers' contracts on a new dashboard would be a fantastic idea, and that would save lots of time for the managers. In addition to that, when a user clicks on a customer, our UX experts decided it would be best to display the customer's full details when the manager needs to dig deeper into that customer's data.

The system is composed of multiple user interfaces querying a single web API. To keep it simple, we focus on the backend part of the system.

Next are the expected output from our two endpoints, starting with the first endpoint that should return a list of customers comprising the following information:

```json
[
    {
        "id": 0,
        "name": "...",
        "totalNumberOfContracts": 0,
        "numberOfOpenContracts": 0
    }
]
```

The second endpoint should return the details of the specified customer with its complete list of contracts. We need to provide the information in the following format:

```json
{
    "id": 0,
    "name": "...",
    "contracts":
    [
        {
            "id": 0,
            "name": "...",
            "description": "...",
            "workTotal": 0,
            "workDone": 0,
            "workState": "New|InProgress|Completed",
            "primaryContactFirstname": "...",
            "primaryContactLastname": "...",
            "primaryContactEmail": "..."
        }
    ]
}
```

Our data structure looks like this:

```
namespace DTOs.Models;
public record class Customer(
    int Id,
    string Name,
    List<Contract> Contracts
);

public record class Contract(
    int Id,
```

```
    string Name,
    string Description,
    ContractWork Work,
    ContactInformation PrimaryContact
);

public record class ContractWork(int Total, int Done)
{
    public WorkState State =>
        Done == 0 ? WorkState.New :
        Done == Total ? WorkState.Completed :
        WorkState.InProgress;
}

public record class ContactInformation(
    string Firstname,
    string Lastname,
    string Email
);

public enum WorkState
{
    New,
    InProgress,
    Completed
}
```

A problem arose when analyzing the feature: our domain model and the model we needed to provide to the UIs differ.

If we use our data structure directly, the user interfaces would have to make multiple HTTP requests to build the dashboard. That would push the logic to the UIs and most likely even duplicate it. That could become tedious to maintain, especially if we add other user interfaces.

Solution: Create two specialized resources in our web API that run the computation and return only the required data.

Note

To keep it simple and abstract away the data access logic from the controller, we moved that code to the `CustomerRepository` class, which provides static data to the controller, omitted here.

For the first endpoint, let's create a new record class named `CustomerSummaryDto` that holds our two statistics and our customer info:

```
public record class CustomerSummaryDto(
    [property: JsonPropertyName("id")]
    int Id,
    [property: JsonPropertyName("name")]
    string Name,
    [property: JsonPropertyName("totalNumberOfContracts")]
    int TotalNumberOfContracts,
    [property: JsonPropertyName("numberOfOpenContracts")]
    int NumberOfOpenContracts
);
```

Note

The properties decorated with `JsonPropertyName` attributes define the serialized property name explicitly. That is one of the advantages of the DTO pattern. Since the DTOs are unrelated to our other objects, we can manipulate them without any impact on the data source, lowering the chance of unforeseen consequences, such as updating a DTO and breaking the database. For example, adding `JsonPropertyName` attributes to a property of the `CustomerSummaryDto` class has no impact on the `Customer` class.

In our case, the default serializer handles the naming convention automatically, so the `JsonPropertyName` attributes are not adding any value other than academic (if you did not know, now you know they exist). Nonetheless, it is good to know the options for scenarios where the name must be changed manually (or other scenarios). This independence is one of the key advantages.

The action that returns the data, representing our first endpoint, goes as follows:

```
namespace DTOs.Controllers;

[Route("[controller]")]
[ApiController]
public class CustomersController : ControllerBase
{
    private readonly CustomerRepository _customerRepository = new();
    // GET customers
    [HttpGet]
    public ActionResult<IEnumerable<CustomerSummaryDto>> Get()
    {
        var customers = _customerRepository.ReadAll();
        var dto = customers.Select(customer => new CustomerSummaryDto(
```

```
            Id: customer.Id,
            Name: customer.Name,
            TotalNumberOfContracts: customer.Contracts.Count,
            NumberOfOpenContracts: customer.Contracts.Count(x => x.Work.State
!= WorkState.Completed)
        )).ToArray();
        return dto;
    }
    // Omitted the second endpoint
}
```

What is happening is this:

1. We read the data from the `CustomerRepository` instance (could be from a database).
2. We transform it into an array of DTO objects (copying the data into new objects).
3. We return that DTO to the client.

If we run the application and navigate to GET `/customers`, we should see the following output:

```
[
    {
        "id": 1,
        "name": "Jonny Boy Inc.",
        "totalNumberOfContracts": 2,
        "numberOfOpenContracts": 1
    },
    {
        "id": 2,
        "name": "Some mega-corporation",
        "totalNumberOfContracts": 1,
        "numberOfOpenContracts": 1
    }
]
```

Now that the first endpoint is working, let's attack the second one. Based on our requirements, we need to create two classes for this one:

```
namespace DTOs.Models;

public record class CustomerDetailsDto(
    [property: JsonPropertyName("id")]
    int Id,
    [property: JsonPropertyName("name")]
    string Name,
```

```
        [property: JsonPropertyName("contracts")]
        IEnumerable<ContractDetailsDto> Contracts
);
public record class ContractDetailsDto(
        [property: JsonPropertyName("id")]
        int Id,
        [property: JsonPropertyName("name")]
        string Name,
        [property: JsonPropertyName("description")]
        string Description,
        [property: JsonPropertyName("workTotal")]
        int WorkTotal,
        [property: JsonPropertyName("workDone")]
        int WorkDone,
        [property: JsonPropertyName("workState")]
        [property: JsonConverter(typeof(JsonStringEnumConverter))]
        WorkState WorkState,
        [property: JsonPropertyName("primaryContactFirstname")]
        string PrimaryContactFirstname,
        [property: JsonPropertyName("primaryContactLastname")]
        string PrimaryContactLastname,
        [property: JsonPropertyName("primaryContactEmail")]
        string PrimaryContactEmail
);
```

This time, we used the `[JsonConverter(typeof(JsonStringEnumConverter))]` attribute on the `ContractDetailsDto.WorkState` property to tell the serializer that the `WorkState` enumeration should be serialized as a `string` instead of a numeric index.

Note

In the past, ASP.NET Core used JSON.NET as the underlying JSON serializer. Since .NET Core 3.0, they added the `System.Text.Json` namespace, which contains a brand new serializer. The new serializer is faster, but has fewer features. If you need JSON.NET features, or for compatibility reasons, you can use it by referencing the `Microsoft.AspNetCore.Mvc.NewtonsoftJson` NuGet package. Then, add a call to the `AddNewtonsoftJson()` extension method on your `IMvcBuilder` object, like `services.AddControllers().AddNewtonsoftJson();`.

Now that we have a data structure to represent our DTO, let's look at the controller's code:

```
// GET customers/1
[HttpGet("{id}")]
```

```
public ActionResult<CustomerDetailsDto> Get(int id)
{
    var customer = _customerRepository.ReadOne(id);
    if (customer == default)
    {
        return NotFound();
    }
    var dto = new CustomerDetailsDto(
        Id: customer.Id,
        Name: customer.Name,
        Contracts: customer.Contracts.Select(contract => new
ContractDetailsDto(
            Id: contract.Id,
            Name: contract.Name,
            Description: contract.Description,

            // Flattening PrimaryContact
            PrimaryContactEmail: contract.PrimaryContact.Email,
            PrimaryContactFirstname: contract.PrimaryContact.Firstname,
            PrimaryContactLastname: contract.PrimaryContact.Lastname,

            // Flattening Work
            WorkDone: contract.Work.Done,
            WorkState: contract.Work.State,
            WorkTotal: contract.Work.Total
        ))
    );
    return Ok(dto);
}
```

That action flattens the details of a `Customer` into a `CustomerDetailsDto` and returns 404 `Not Found` if the `Customer` does not exist. For example, we moved the `PrimaryContact` object from the contracts to the `ContractDetailsDto` object, flattening the data structure. The same happened with the `Work` object.

If we run the application and navigate to `GET /customers/2`, we should have the following output:

```
{
    "id": 2,
    "name": "Some mega-corporation",
    "contracts": [
        {
            "id": 3,
            "name": "Huge contract",
```

```
            "description": "This is a huge contract of Some mega-corporation.",
            "workTotal": 15000,
            "workDone": 0,
            "workState": "New",
            "primaryContactFirstname": "Kory",
            "primaryContactLastname": "O'Neill",
            "primaryContactEmail": "kory.oneill@megacorp.com"
        }
    ]
}
```

And voilà! Our little application is working as expected and without much effort. We took some data, converted it into a different format, computed some statistics, flattened some objects, and serialized that as JSON so consumers could start using those two endpoints. All of that was made without any alteration to our initial model but by creating DTOs instead.

Note

I would recommend moving as much logic as possible out of the controller in a more significant project because we don't want to break the single responsibility principle. However, flattening the model into a DTO could arguably be considered the responsibility of the controller. We could also use AutoMapper, a third-party library, to do that. More on that in *Chapter 13, Getting Started with Object Mappers*.

Think of a controller as a bridge between HTTP and your application logic, or if you prefer, a very thin layer allowing users to access your software over HTTP.

Minimal APIs

If you are interested in minimal APIs, I also implemented the DTO example without using MVC. The code is available in the GitHub repo: `https://adpg.link/mRMf`.

Now that we have explored DTOs, let's dig deeper and discuss API contracts, which define our web APIs.

Conclusion

A data transfer object allows us to design an API endpoint with a specific data contract (input and output) instead of exposing the domain model. This separation between the presentation and the domain is a crucial element that leads to having multiple independent components instead of a bigger, more fragile one.

We mostly focused on outputting DTOs, but we can also use DTOs to control the inputs. We leverage that in *Section 4, Designing at Application Scale*.

Using the MVC pattern helps us follow the SOLID principles in the following ways:

- **S:** A DTO adds clear boundaries between the domain model and the API contract, dividing one model into two distinct responsibilities to help keep things isolated.
- **O:** N/A
- **L:** N/A
- **I:** A DTO is a smaller, specifically crafted model that serves a clear purpose. With a DTO, we now have two models, one for the domain and one for the view (API), leading to two specialized interfaces instead of a generic one.
- **D:** N/A

Note

Most objects were record classes in the example, but you could also use normal classes to achieve the same result. That should rarely be the case with DTOs, but maybe you have other constraints, such as inheriting a non-record class or using an older version of .NET/C#. Just in case, I included a normal class for each DTO, including the `Json*Attributes` in the same file (commented out), available in GitHub.

I'm sure you have at least a small understanding of what an API contract is by now. Nonetheless, we explore that subject in more detail next to make that understanding clearer.

API contracts

An API contract is the definition of a web API. Like any standard API, a consumer should know how to call an endpoint and what to expect from it in return. Each endpoint should have a signature, like a method, and should enforce that signature.

Using DTOs as input and output makes them part of that contract, adding even more value to them, locking in place the contract instead of using a more volatile model shared across multiple parts (layers) of the system. From this point forward, a DTO is more than a simple "object used to transfer data." It becomes an integral part of the contract, and the only reason for a DTO to change is directly linked to that contract (and vice versa).

Now that we have an idea of what an API contract is, let's see how to define those contracts to improve teamwork, system collaboration, and discoverability for consumers of APIs.

To define API contracts, we could do the following:

- Open any text editor, such as MS Word or Notepad, and start writing out a document describing our web APIs; this is probably the most tedious and least flexible way of doing it.
- Use Markdown for written specs and save those files within your project repo for easy discoverability. Very similar to MS Word, but easier to have other devs consume those specs.
- Use an existing standard, such as the OpenAPI specification (formerly Swagger). This is more complex to learn but yields better machine-to-machine consumption options.

- Use any other tools that fit our requirements.

> **Tip**
>
> Postman is a fantastic tool for building web APIs documentation, test suites, and experimenting with your APIs. It supports OpenAPI specifications, allows you to create mock servers, supports environments, and more.

Some people go even further when defining API contracts, but once again, it depends on each project, your team, or the company you are working for. For now, let's stay minimalist and define an API contract as the API surface: its URL, method, input, and output.

Let's analyze the preceding DTO sample. From a developer perspective, a contract is a model associated with a URI and an HTTP method. For example, if we dissect `CustomersController`, we end up with the two following endpoints:

- Read all customers
- Read one customer

"Read all customers" uses the `GET` method and listens to the `/customers` URL. It has no input parameter, and it returns a collection of `CustomerSummaryDto`.

"Read one customer" also uses the `GET` method but listens to the `/customers/{id}` URI. The discriminator between the two `GET` actions is the `id` parameter. When successful, the action returns an instance of `CustomerDetailsDto`.

These are the contracts defining our API in a textual format. That is not the most technical way of sharing this information, but it hopefully helped you understand the idea. Nonetheless, when you cannot explain an idea using spoken language, it may indicate that your understanding is incomplete.

One way to be more formal about the API contracts is by leveraging the OpenAPI format. To do that, we have two choices:

- Design the contract first, and then build the APIs.
- Build the APIs and extract the contract for others to consume it.

To design the contract first, you'll need to familiarize yourself with the OpenAPI specification. I left a link in the *Further reading* section below.

On the other hand, to automatically extract the OpenAPI specifications, you have nothing specific to do, but ensure your endpoints are discoverable by the .NET `ApiExplorer`. The default template registered Swagger for us, highlighted in the following code:

```
var builder = WebApplication.CreateBuilder(args);
builder.Services.AddControllers();
builder.Services.AddEndpointsApiExplorer();
builder.Services.AddSwaggerGen();

var app = builder.Build();
```

```
if (app.Environment.IsDevelopment())
{
    app.UseSwagger();
    app.UseSwaggerUI();
    app.UseDeveloperExceptionPage();
}
else
{
    app.UseHsts();
}
app.UseHttpsRedirection();
app.MapControllers();
app.Run();
```

With those few lines, when navigating to the /swagger/v1/swagger.json URL of the running web API project, you can consult the API contracts defined with the OpenAPI standard. I won't paste 187 lines of JSON here, so I'll leave you to access it. Meanwhile, here is a high-level overview of the file:

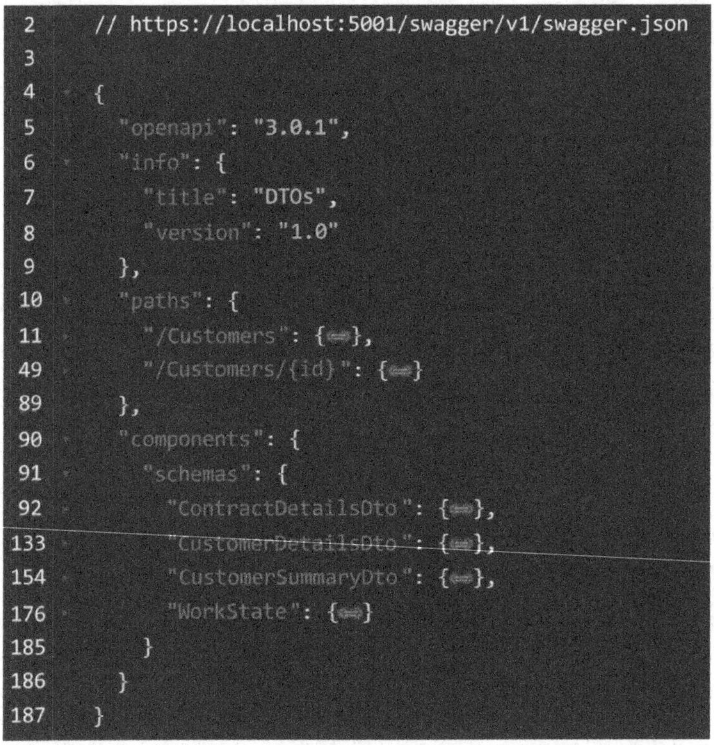

```
2      // https://localhost:5001/swagger/v1/swagger.json
3
4      {
5        "openapi": "3.0.1",
6        "info": {
7          "title": "DTOs",
8          "version": "1.0"
9        },
10       "paths": {
11         "/Customers": {…},
49         "/Customers/{id}": {…}
89       },
90       "components": {
91         "schemas": {
92           "ContractDetailsDto": {…},
133          "CustomerDetailsDto": {…},
154          "CustomerSummaryDto": {…},
176          "WorkState": {…}
185        }
186      }
187    }
```

Figure 5.3: High-level view of the autogenerated OpenAPI document

Now that we know this, one of those four lines (app.UseSwaggerUI();) is registering a user interface to consult the preceding JSON from a nice-looking UI that also allows the endpoints to be tested.

When navigating to the `/swagger/index.html` URL of the running web API project, you should have access to the following page:

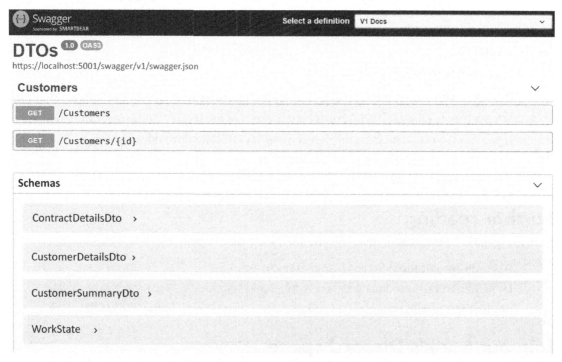

Figure 5.4: Swagger UI generated using OpenAPI

Now that we have peeked at the pieces from the default template, including the autogeneration of an OpenAPI document and UI, it is time to move to the summary.

Summary

This chapter explored how easy it is to leverage web APIs and create web services that expose REST endpoints to share data over HTTP. We also saw how to decouple the model from the "presentation" using DTOs.

DTOs are the equivalent of view models, but for web services. They are classes specially crafted around a specific resource: an HTTP endpoint. Instead of returning raw data to the client, a DTO can encapsulate the result of computations, limit the number of exposed properties, aggregate results, and flatten data structures to carefully craft the API contract representing the input and output of its endpoint.

Then we dug a little further along that path by defining that DTOs are part of the API contract defining our web API, so its consumers know how to communicate with it. We also peeked at OpenAPI to help share the contracts in a more standard way.

Now that we explored principles and methodologies as well as a few ASP.NET Core bases like MVC, it is time to continue our learning and tackle some more design patterns and features.

In the following two chapters, we explore our first **Gang of Four** (**GoF**) design patterns and take a deep dive into ASP.NET Core **dependency injection** (**DI**). All of this will help us to continue on the path we started: **to design better software**.

Questions

Let's look at a few practice questions:

1. In a REST API, what is the most common status code sent after creating an entity?
2. What attribute tells ASP.NET Core to bind the data of the request body to a parameter?
3. If you want to read data from the server, what HTTP method would you use?
4. Can DTOs add flexibility and robustness to a system?
5. Are DTOs part of an API contract?

Further reading

Here are some links to build on what we have learned in the chapter:

- OpenAPI specification: `https://adpg.link/M4Uz`
- Using web API conventions: `https://adpg.link/ioKV`
- Getting started with Swashbuckle and ASP.NET Core: `https://adpg.link/ETja`

Join our book's Discord space

Join the book's Discord workspace for *Ask me Anything* session with the authors:

`https://packt.link/ASPdotNET6DesignPatterns`

6

Understanding the Strategy, Abstract Factory, and Singleton Design Patterns

This chapter explores object creation using a few classic, simple, and yet powerful design patterns from the **Gang of Four** (**GoF**). These patterns allow developers to encapsulate behaviors, centralize object creation, add flexibility to their design, or control object lifetime. Moreover, they will most likely be used in all software you build directly or indirectly in the future.

GoF

Erich Gamma, Richard Helm, Ralph Johnson, and John Vlissides are the authors of *Design Patterns: Elements of Reusable Object-Oriented Software* (1994), and are also known as the **GoF**. In that book, they introduce 23 design patterns, some of which we look at in this book.

Why are they that important? Because they are the building blocks of robust object composition and they help to create flexibility and reliability. Moreover, in *Chapter 7, Deep Dive into Dependency Injection*, we leverage dependency injection to make those patterns even more powerful!

But first things first. The following topics will be covered in this chapter:

- The Strategy design pattern
- The Abstract Factory design pattern
- The Singleton design pattern

The Strategy design pattern

The Strategy pattern is a behavioral design pattern that allows us to change object behaviors at runtime. We can also use this pattern to compose complex object trees and rely on it to follow the **Open/Closed Principle** (**OCP**) without much effort.

As a follow-up on that last point, the Strategy pattern plays a significant role in the *composition over inheritance* way of thinking. In this chapter, we focus on the behavioral part of the Strategy pattern. In the next chapter, we cover how to use the Strategy pattern to compose systems dynamically.

Goal

The Strategy pattern's goal is to extract an algorithm (strategy) from the host class needing it (the context). That allows the consumer to decide on the strategy (algorithm) to use at runtime.

For example, we could design a system that fetches data from two different types of databases. Then we could apply the same logic over that data and use the same user interface to display it. To achieve this, using the Strategy pattern, we could create two strategies, one named FetchDataFromSql and the other FetchDataFromCosmosDb. Then we could plug the strategy that we need at runtime in the context class. That way, when the consumer calls the context, the context does not need to know where the data comes from, how it is fetched, or what strategy is in use; it only gets what it needs to work, delegating the fetching responsibility to an abstracted strategy.

Design

Before any further explanation, let's take a look at the following class diagram:

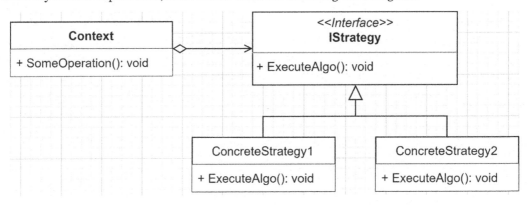

Figure 6.1: Strategy pattern class diagram

The building blocks of the Strategy pattern go as follows:

- Context is a class that delegates one or more operations to an IStrategy implementation.
- IStrategy is an interface defining the strategies.
- ConcreteStrategy1 and ConcreteStrategy2 represent one or more different concrete implementations of the IStrategy interface.

In the following diagram, we explore what happens at runtime. The actor represents any code consuming the Context object.

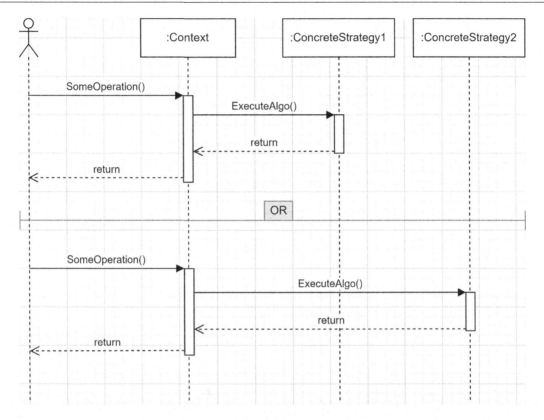

Figure 6.2: Strategy pattern sequence diagram

When the consumer calls the `Context.SomeOperation()` method, it does not know which implementation is executed, which is an essential part of this pattern. `Context` should not be aware of the strategy being used either. It should execute it through the interface without any knowledge of the implementation past that point. That is the strength of the Strategy pattern: it abstracts the implementation away from both the `Context` and the consumer. Because of that, we can change the strategy during either the object creation or at runtime without the object knowing, changing its behavior on the fly.

 Note

We could even generalize that last sentence and extend it to the use of any interface. Using an interface removes the ties between the consumer and the implementation by relying on the abstraction instead.

Project — Strategy

Context: We want to sort a collection using different strategies. Initially, we want to support sorting the elements of a list in ascending or descending order.

To achieve this, we need to implement the following building blocks:

- The Context is the `SortableCollection` class.
- The Strategy is the `ISortStrategy` interface.
- The concrete strategies are:

     a.   `SortAscendingStrategy`

     b.   `SortDescendingStrategy`

The consumer is a small program that allows the user to choose a strategy, sort the collection, and display the items. Let's start with the `ISortStrategy` interface:

```
public interface ISortStrategy
{
    IOrderedEnumerable<string> Sort(IEnumerable<string> input);
}
```

That interface contains only one method that expects a collection of strings as input, and that returns an ordered collection of strings. Now let's inspect the two implementations:

```
public class SortAscendingStrategy : ISortStrategy
{
    public IOrderedEnumerable<string> Sort(IEnumerable<string> input)
        => input.OrderBy(x => x);
}
public class SortDescendingStrategy : ISortStrategy
{
    public IOrderedEnumerable<string> Sort(IEnumerable<string> input)
        => input.OrderByDescending(x => x);
}
```

Both implementations are super simple as well, using **Language Integrated Query** (**LINQ**) to sort the input and return the result directly. Both implementations use **expression-bodied methods**, which we talked about in *Chapter 4, The MVC Pattern Using Razor*.

Tip

When using expression-bodied methods, please ensure that you do not make the method harder to read for your colleagues by creating very complex one-liners. Writing multiple lines often makes the code clearer except in the case of tiny methods like in the preceding example.

The next building block to inspect is the `SortableCollection` class. It is not a collection in itself (it does not implement `IEnumerable` or other collection interfaces), but it is composed of multiple string items (the `Items` property) and can sort them using an `ISortStrategy`, like this:

```
public sealed class SortableCollection
{
    public ISortStrategy? SortStrategy { get; set; }
    public IEnumerable<string> Items { get; private set; }

    public SortableCollection(IEnumerable<string> items)
    {
        Items = items;
    }

    public void Sort()
    {
        if (SortStrategy == null)
        {
            throw new NullReferenceException("Sort strategy not found.");
        }
        Items = SortStrategy.Sort(Items);
    }
}
```

This class is the most complex one so far, so let's take a more in-depth look:

- The SortStrategy property holds a reference to an ISortStrategy implementation (that can be null).
- The Items property holds a reference to the collection of strings contained in the SortableCollection class.
- We set the initial IEnumerable<string> when creating an instance of SortableCollection, through its constructor.
- The Sort method uses the current SortStrategy property to sort the Items. When there is no strategy set, it throws a NullReferenceException.

With that code, we can see the Strategy pattern in action. The SortStrategy property represents the current algorithm, respecting an ISortStrategy contract, which is updatable at runtime. The SortableCollection.Sort() method delegates the work to that ISortStrategy implementation (the concrete strategy). Therefore, changing the value of the SortStrategy property leads to a change of behavior of the Sort() method, making this pattern very powerful yet simple.

Let's experiment with this by looking at MyConsumerApp, a console application that uses the previous code:

```
public class Program
{
    private static readonly SortableCollection _data = new
SortableCollection(new[] { "Lorem", "ipsum", "dolor", "sit", "amet." });
```

The _data instance represents the **context**, our sortable collection of items. Next, an empty `Main` method:

```
public static void Main(string[] args) { /*...*/ }
```

To keep it focused on the pattern, I took away the console logic from the book, which is irrelevant for now, but the code is available in the GitHub repository.

```
private static string SetSortAsc()
{
    _data.SortStrategy = new SortAscendingStrategy();
    return "The sort strategy is now Ascending";
}
```

The preceding method sets the **strategy** to a new instance of `SortAscendingStrategy`.

```
private static string SetSortDesc()
{
    _data.SortStrategy = new SortDescendingStrategy();
    return "The sort strategy is now Descending";
}
```

The preceding method sets the **strategy** to a new instance of `SortDescendingStrategy`.

```
private static string SortData()
{
    try
    {
        _data.Sort();
        return "Data sorted";
    }
    catch (NullReferenceException ex)
    {
        return ex.Message;
    }
}
```

The SortData method calls the Sort() method, which delegates the call to an optional ISortStrategy implementation.

```
private static string PrintCollection()
{
    var sb = new StringBuilder();
    foreach (var item in _data.Items)
    {
        sb.AppendLine(item);
    }
    return sb.ToString();
}
}
```

This last method displays the collection in the console to visually validate the correctness of the code.

When we run the program, the following menu appears:

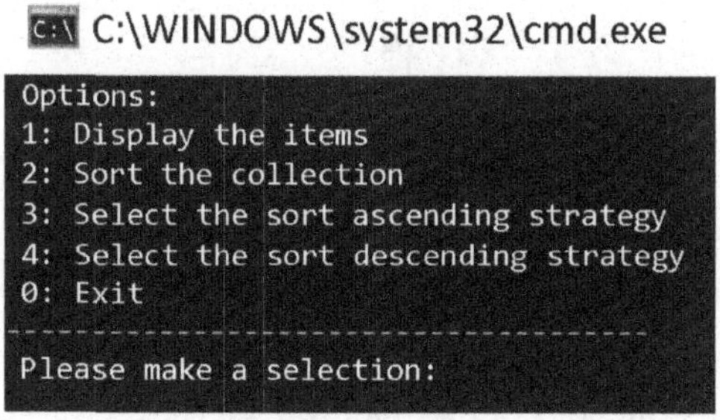

Figure 6.3: Output showing the Options menu

When a user selects an option, the program calls the appropriate method, as described earlier.

When executing the program, if you display the items (1), they appear in their initial order. If you assign a strategy (3 or 4), sort the collection (2), then display the list again, the order will have changed and will now be different, based on the selected algorithm.

Let's analyze the sequence of events when you select the following options:

1. Select the sort ascending strategy (**3**).
2. Sort the collection (**2**).

Next is a sequence diagram that represents this:

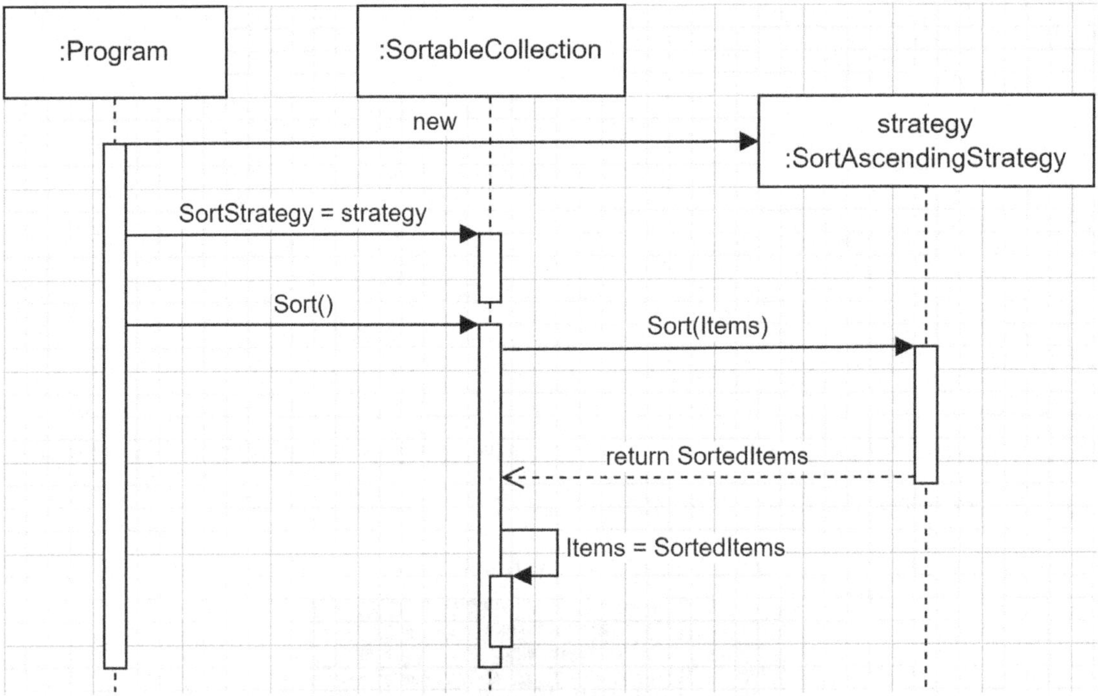

Figure 6.4 : Sequence diagram sorting the items using the "sort ascending" strategy (options 3 then 2)

The preceding diagram shows the Program creating a strategy and assigning it to SortableCollection. Then, when the Program calls the Sort() method, the SortableCollection instance delegates the sorting computation to the underlying algorithm implemented by the SortAscendingStrategy class, a.k.a. the **strategy**.

From the pattern standpoint, the SortableCollection class, a.k.a. the **context**, is responsible for keeping a hold on the current **strategy** and for using it.

Conclusion

The Strategy design pattern is very effective at delegating responsibilities to other objects, allowing you to delegate the responsibility of an algorithm to other objects while keeping its usage trivial. It also allows having a rich interface (context) with behaviors that can change during the program's execution.

The strategy does not have to be exposed directly; it can also be private to the class, hiding its presence to the outside world (the consumers); we talk more about this in the next chapter. Meanwhile, the Strategy pattern is excellent at helping us follow the **SOLID** principles:

- **S:** It helps to extract responsibilities to external classes and use them, interchangeably, later.
- **O:** It allows extending classes without updating its code by changing the current strategy at runtime.

- **L:** It does not rely on inheritance. Moreover, it plays a large role in the *composition over inheritance principle*, helping us avoid inheritance altogether and, at the same time, the LSP.

- **I:** By creating smaller strategies based on lean and focused interfaces, the Strategy pattern is an excellent enabler for respecting the ISP.

- **D:** The creation of dependencies is moved from the class using the strategy (the context) to the class's consumer. That makes the context depend on abstraction instead of implementation, inverting the flow of control.

C# Features

If you looked at the implementation of the Main method (omitted here), you might have noticed that I used a few newer C# features like **default literal expressions, switch expressions,** and **discards.** Those are covered in *Appendix A*.

Next, let's explore the Abstract Factory pattern.

The Abstract Factory design pattern

The Abstract Factory design pattern is a creational design pattern from the GoF. We use creational patterns to create other objects, and factories are a very popular way of doing that.

The Strategy pattern is the backbone of dependency injection, enabling the composition of complex object trees, while factories are used to create some of those complex objects that can't be assembled automatically by a dependency injection library. More on that in the next chapter.

Goal

The Abstract Factory pattern is used to abstract the creation of a family of objects. It usually implies the creation of multiple object types within that family. A family is a group of related or dependent objects (classes).

Let's think about creating automotive vehicles. There are multiple types of vehicles, and for each type, there are multiple models. We can use the Abstract Factory pattern to make our life easier for this type of scenario.

Note

There is also the *Factory Method* pattern, which focuses on creating a single type of object instead of a family. We only cover Abstract Factory here, but we use other types of factories later in the book.

Design

With Abstract Factory, the consumer asks for an abstract object and gets one. The factory is an abstraction, and the resulting objects are also abstractions, decoupling the object creation from the consumers.

That allows adding or removing families of objects produced together without impacting the consumers (all actors communicate through abstractions).

In our case, the family (the object set the factory can produce) is composed of a car and a bike, and each factory (family) must produce both of those objects.

If we think about vehicles, we could have the ability to create low- and high-grade models of each vehicle type. Here is a diagram representing how to achieve that using the Abstract Factory pattern:

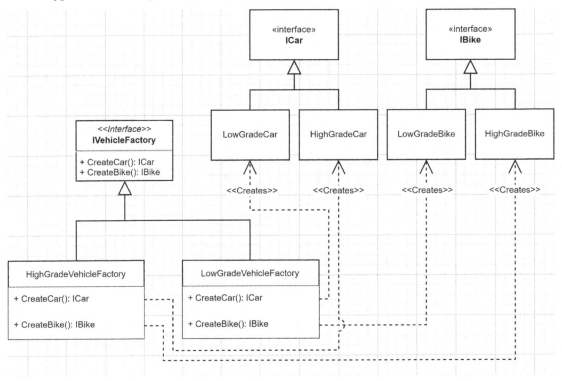

Figure 6.5: Abstract Factory class diagram

In the diagram, we have the following:

- `IVehicleFactory` is an Abstract Factory defining two methods: one that creates cars of type `ICar` and another that creates bikes of type `IBike`.

- `HighGradeVehicleFactory` is an implementation of the Abstract Factory that handles high-grade vehicle model creation. This concrete factory returns instances of type `HighGradeCar` or `HighGradeBike`.

- `LowGradeVehicleFactory` is an implementation of our Abstract Factory that handles low-grade vehicle model creation. This concrete factory returns instances of type `LowGradeCar` or `LowGradeBike`.

- `LowGradeCar` and `HighGradeCar` are two implementations of `ICar`.

- `LowGradeBike` and `HighGradeBike` are two implementations of `IBike`.

Based on that diagram, a consumer uses the IVehicleFactory interface and should not be aware of the concrete factory used underneath, abstracting away the vehicle creation process.

Project — AbstractVehicleFactory

Context: We need to support the creation of multiple models of vehicles. We also need to be able to add new models as they become available without impacting the system. To begin with, we only support high-grade and low-grade models and the program only supports the creation of cars and bikes.

For the sake of our demo, the vehicles are just empty classes and interfaces:

```
public interface ICar { }
public interface IBike { }
public class LowGradeCar : ICar { }
public class LowGradeBike : IBike { }
public class HighGradeCar : ICar { }
public class HighGradeBike : IBike { }
```

Let's now look at the part that we want to study—the factories:

```
public interface IVehicleFactory
{
    ICar CreateCar();
    IBike CreateBike();
}
public class LowGradeVehicleFactory : IVehicleFactory
{
    public IBike CreateBike() => new LowGradeBike();
    public ICar CreateCar() => new LowGradeCar();
}
public class HighGradeVehicleFactory : IVehicleFactory
{
    public IBike CreateBike() => new HighGradeBike();
    public ICar CreateCar() => new HighGradeCar();
}
```

The factories are simple implementations that describe the pattern well:

- LowGradeVehicleFactory creates low-grade models.
- HighGradeVehicleFactory creates high-grade models.

The consumer is an xUnit test project. Unit tests are often your first consumers, especially if you are doing **test-driven development (TDD)**.

The `AbstractFactoryBaseTestData` class encapsulates some of our test data classes' utilities and is not relevant to our pattern study. Nevertheless, it can be useful to have all of the code on hand, and it is a very small class; so let's start there:

```
public abstract class AbstractFactoryBaseTestData : IEnumerable<object[]>
{
    private readonly TheoryData<IVehicleFactory, Type> _data = new
TheoryData<IVehicleFactory, Type>();
    protected void AddTestData<TConcreteFactory, TExpectedVehicle>()
        where TConcreteFactory : IVehicleFactory, new()
    {
        _data.Add(new TConcreteFactory(), typeof(TExpectedVehicle));
    }
    public IEnumerator<object[]> GetEnumerator() => _data.GetEnumerator();
    IEnumerator IEnumerable.GetEnumerator() => GetEnumerator();
}
```

That class is an `IEnumerable<object[]>` with a private collection of `TheoryData<T1, T2>`, and an `AddTestData<TConcreteFactory, TExpectedVehicle>()` method that is used by other classes, to feed our theories.

The data inheriting from the `AbstractFactoryBaseTestData` class that we are going to feed to our theories looks like this:

```
public class AbstractFactoryTestCars : AbstractFactoryBaseTestData
{
    public AbstractFactoryTestCars()
    {
        AddTestData<LowGradeVehicleFactory, LowGradeCar>();
        AddTestData<HighGradeVehicleFactory, HighGradeCar>();
    }
}
public class AbstractFactoryTestBikes : AbstractFactoryBaseTestData
{
    public AbstractFactoryTestBikes()
    {
        AddTestData<LowGradeVehicleFactory, LowGradeBike>();
        AddTestData<HighGradeVehicleFactory, HighGradeBike>();
    }
}
```

With the implementation details abstracted, the preceding code is straightforward. If we take a closer look at the `AbstractFactoryTestCars` class, it creates two sets of test data:

- A `LowGradeVehicleFactory` that should create a `LowGradeCar` instance.

- A HighGradeVehicleFactory that should create a HighGradeCar instance.

The same goes for the AbstractFactoryTestBikes data:

- A LowGradeVehicleFactory that should create a LowGradeBike instance.
- A HighGradeVehicleFactory that should create a HighGradeBike instance.

Now, let's look at the test class and theories using that test data:

```
public class AbstractFactoryTest
{
    [Theory]
    [ClassData(typeof(AbstractFactoryTestCars))]
    public void Should_create_a_Car_of_the_specified_type(IVehicleFactory
vehicleFactory, Type expectedCarType)
    {
        // Act
        ICar result = vehicleFactory.CreateCar();
        // Assert
        Assert.IsType(expectedCarType, result);
    }
    [Theory]
    [ClassData(typeof(AbstractFactoryTestBikes))]
    public void Should_create_a_Bike_of_the_specified_type(IVehicleFactory
vehicleFactory, Type expectedBikeType)
    {
        // Act
        IBike result = vehicleFactory.CreateBike();
        // Assert
        Assert.IsType(expectedBikeType, result);
    }
}
```

In the preceding code, we have two theories that each use the data contained in the class, defined by the [ClassData(...)] attribute (see the highlighted code). That data is used by the test runner to populate the value of the test method's parameters. So the test runner executes a test once per set of data. In this case, each method runs twice.

The execution of each test method goes as follows:

- We use the Abstract Factory IVehicleFactory vehicleFactory to create an ICar or an IBike instance.
- We test that instance against the expected concrete type to ensure it is the right type; that type is specified by Type expectedCarType or Type expectedBikeType, depending on the test method.

Note

I used `ICar` and `IBike` to type the variables instead of `var`, to make the type of the `result` variable clearer. In another context, I would have used `var` instead.

We now have four tests; two bike tests (`Vehicles.AbstractFactoryTest.Should_create_a_Bike_of_the_specified_type`) executed with the following arguments:

```
(vehicleFactory: HighGradeVehicleFactory { }, expectedBikeType:
typeof(Vehicles.Models.HighGradeBike))
(vehicleFactory: LowGradeVehicleFactory { }, expectedBikeType: typeof(Vehicles.
Models.LowGradeBike))
```

And two car tests (`Vehicles.AbstractFactoryTest.Should_create_a_Car_of_the_specified_type`) executed with the following arguments:

```
(vehicleFactory: HighGradeVehicleFactory { }, expectedCarType: typeof(Vehicles.
Models.HighGradeCar))
(vehicleFactory: LowGradeVehicleFactory { }, expectedCarType: typeof(Vehicles.
Models.LowGradeCar))
```

If we review the tests' execution, both test methods are unaware of types. They use the Abstract Factory (`IVehicleFactory`) and test the `result` against the expected type without any knowledge of what they were testing, but the abstraction (or contract). That shows how loosely coupled the consumers (tests) and factories are.

In a real program, we would use the `ICar` or the `IBike` instances to execute some logic, compute statistics, or do anything relevant to that program. Maybe that could be a racing game or a rich person's garage management system, who knows!

The important part of this project is the abstraction of the object creation process. The consumer code was not aware of the implementations.

Note

The code of the second part of the project is part of another solution, named `MiddleEndVehicleFactory`, so you can compare the first version with its evolution.

To prove our design's flexibility, based on the Abstract Factory pattern, let's add a new concrete factory named `MiddleEndVehicleFactory`. That factory should return a `MiddleEndCar` or a `MiddleEndBike` instance. Once again, the car and bike are just empty classes (of course, in your programs they will do something):

```
public class MiddleGradeCar : ICar { }
public class MiddleGradeBike : IBike { }
```

The new `MiddleEndVehicleFactory` looks pretty much the same as the other two:

```
public class MiddleEndVehicleFactory : IVehicleFactory
{
    public IBike CreateBike() => new MiddleGradeBike();
    public ICar CreateCar() => new MiddleGradeCar();
}
```

As for the test class, we don't need to update the test methods (the consumers); we only need to update the setup to add new test data (see the highlighted lines):

```
public class AbstractFactoryTestCars : AbstractFactoryBaseTestData
{
    public AbstractFactoryTestCars()
    {
        AddTestData<LowGradeVehicleFactory, LowGradeCar>();
        AddTestData<HighGradeVehicleFactory, HighGradeCar>();
        AddTestData<MiddleEndVehicleFactory, MiddleGradeCar>();
    }
}
public class AbstractFactoryTestBikes : AbstractFactoryBaseTestData
{
    public AbstractFactoryTestBikes()
    {
        AddTestData<LowGradeVehicleFactory, LowGradeBike>();
        AddTestData<HighGradeVehicleFactory, HighGradeBike>();
        AddTestData<MiddleEndVehicleFactory, MiddleGradeBike>();
    }
}
```

If we run the tests, we now have six passing tests (two theories with three test cases each). So, without updating the consumer (the `AbstractFactoryTest` class), we were able to add a new family of vehicles, the middle-end cars and bikes; kudos to the Abstract Factory pattern for that wonderfulness!

Conclusion

Abstract Factory is an excellent pattern to abstract away the creation of object families, isolating each family and its concrete implementation, leaving the consumers unaware of (decoupled from) the family being created at runtime.

We talk more about factories in the next chapter; meanwhile, let's see how the Abstract Factory pattern can help us follow the **SOLID** principles:

- **S**: Each concrete factory has the sole responsibility of creating a family of objects. You could combine Abstract Factory with other creational patterns such as the **Prototype** and **Builder** patterns for more complex creational needs.

- **O:** The consumer is open to extension but closed for modification; as we did in the "expansion" sample, we can add new families without modifying the code that uses it.
- **L:** We are aiming at composition, so there's no need for any inheritance, implicitly discarding the need for the LSP. If you use abstract classes in your design, you need to make sure you don't break the LSP when creating new abstract factories.
- **I:** By extracting an abstraction that creates other objects, it makes that interface very focused on one task, which is in line with the ISP, creating flexibility at a minimal cost.
- **D:** By depending only on interfaces, the consumer is not aware of the concrete types that it is using.

Next, we explore the last design pattern of the chapter.

The Singleton design pattern

The Singleton design pattern allows creating and reusing a single instance of a class. We could use a static class to achieve almost the same goal, but not everything is doable using static classes. For example, implementing an interface or passing the instance as an argument cannot be done with a static class; you cannot pass static classes around, you can only use them directly.

We are exploring the Singleton pattern in this chapter because it relates to dependency injection. Knowing about the patterns in this order should help you with the next chapter.

In my opinion, the Singleton pattern in C# is an anti-pattern. Unless I cannot rely on dependency injection, I don't see how this pattern can serve a purpose. That said, it is a classic, so let's start by studying it, then move to a better alternative in the next chapter.

Here are a few reasons why we are covering this pattern:

- It translates into a singleton scope in the next chapter.
- Without knowing about it, you cannot locate it, nor try to remove it, nor avoid its usage.
- It is a simple pattern to explore, which is excellent for a first chapter about design patterns.
- It leads to other patterns, such as the **Ambient Context** pattern.

Goal

The Singleton pattern limits the number of instances of a class to one. Then, the idea is to reuse the same instance subsequently. A singleton encapsulates both the object logic itself and its creational logic. For example, the Singleton pattern could lower the cost of instantiating an object with a large memory footprint since it's instantiated only once.

Can you think of a SOLID principle that gets broken right there?

The Singleton pattern promotes that one object must have two responsibilities, breaking the **Single Responsibility Principle (SRP)**. A singleton is the object and its own factory.

Design

This design pattern is straightforward and is limited to a single class. Let's start with a class diagram:

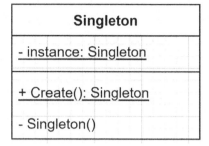

Figure 6.6: Singleton pattern class diagram

The Singleton class is composed of the following:

- A private static field that holds its unique instance.
- A public static Create() method that creates or returns the unique instance.
- A private constructor, so external code cannot instantiate it without passing by the Create method.

> **Note**
>
> You can name the Create() method anything or even get rid of it, as we see in the next example. We could name it GetInstance(), or it could be a static property named Instance or bear any other relevant name.

Now, in code, it can be translated to the following:

```
public class MySingleton
{
    private static MySingleton? _instance;
    private MySingleton() { }
    public static MySingleton Create()
    {
        if(_instance == default(MySingleton))
        {
            _instance = new MySingleton();
        }
        return _instance;
    }
}
```

We can see in the following unit test that `MySingleton.Create()` always returns the same instance:

```
public class MySingletonTest
{
    [Fact]
    public void Create_should_always_return_the_same_instance()
    {
        var first = MySingleton.Create();
        var second = MySingleton.Create();
        Assert.Same(first, second);
    }
}
```

And voilà! We have a working Singleton pattern, which is extremely simple—probably the most simple design pattern that I can think of.

Here is what is happening under the hood:

1. The first time that a consumer calls `MySingleton.Create()`, it creates the first instance of `MySingleton`. Since the only constructor is `private`, it can only be created from the inside. You cannot instantiate `MySingleton` (using `new MySingleton()`) from the outside of the class because there is no public constructor.
2. That first instance is then persisted to the `_instance` field for future use.
3. When a consumer calls `MySingleton.Create()` a second time, it returns the `_instance` field, reusing the previous (and only) instance of the class.

If you want your singleton to be thread-safe, you may want to `lock` the instance creation, like this:

```
public class MySingletonWithLock
{
    private readonly static object _myLock = new();
    private static MySingletonWithLock? _instance;
    private MySingletonWithLock() { }
    public static MySingletonWithLock Create()
    {
        lock (_myLock)
        {
            if (_instance == default)
            {
                _instance = new MySingletonWithLock();
            }
        }
        return _instance;
    }
}
```

In the preceding code, we make sure two threads are not attempting to access the Create method simultaneously, to ensure that they are not getting different instances. We could use **double-checked locking** to optimize that pattern, but instead, we explore another, shorter way of achieving thread safety.

An alternate (better) way

Previously, we used the "long way" of implementing the Singleton pattern and had to implement a thread-safe mechanism. Now that classic is behind us. We can shorten that to get rid of the Create() method, like this:

```
public class MySimpleSingleton
{
    public static MySimpleSingleton Instance { get; } = new
MySimpleSingleton();
    private MySimpleSingleton() { }
}
```

This way, you can use the singleton instance directly through its Instance property, like this:

```
MySimpleSingleton.Instance.SomeOperation();
```

We can prove the correctness of that claim by executing the following test method:

```
[Fact]
public void Create_should_always_return_the_same_instance()
{
    var first = MySimpleSingleton.Instance;
    var second = MySimpleSingleton.Instance;
    Assert.Same(first, second);
}
```

By doing this, our singleton becomes thread-safe as the property initializer creates the singleton instance instead of nesting it inside an if statement. It is usually best to delegate responsibilities to the language or the framework whenever possible.

Beware of the arrow operator

It may be tempting to use the arrow operator => to initialize the Instance property like this: public static MySimpleSingleton Instance => new MySimpleSingleton();, but doing so would return a new instance every time. This would defeat the purpose of what we want to achieve. On the other hand, the property initializer is run only once.

The arrow operator makes the Instance property an expression-bodied member, which is the equivalent of creating the following getter: get { return new MySimpleSingleton(); }. Consult *Appendix A* for more information about expression-bodies statements.

The use of a static constructor would also be a valid, thread-safe alternative, once again delegating the job to the language.

Code smell – Ambient Context

That last implementation of the **Singleton** pattern led us to the **Ambient Context** pattern. We could even call the Ambient Context an anti-pattern, but let's just state that it is a consequential code smell.

I don't like ambient contexts for multiple reasons. First, I do my best to stay away from anything global. Globals can be very convenient at first because they are easy to use. They are always there and accessible whenever needed: easy. However, they can have many drawbacks in terms of flexibility and testability.

When using an ambient context, the following occurs:

- The system will most likely become **less flexible**. A global object is harder to replace and cannot easily be swapped for another object. Also, the implementation cannot be different based on its consumer.
- Global objects are hard to mock, which can lead to a system that is **hard to test**.
- The system can become **brittle**; for example, if some part of your system messes up your global object, that may have unexpected consequences on other parts of your system, and you may have a hard time finding out the root cause of those errors.
- Another thing that does not help is the lack of isolation since consumers are usually directly coupled with the ambient context. Not being able to isolate components from those global objects can be a hassle, as stated in the previous points.

Fun fact

Many years ago, before the JavaScript frameworks era, I ended up fixing a bug in a system where some function was overriding the value of undefined due to a subtle error. This is an excellent example of how global variables could impact your whole system and make it more brittle. The same is true for the Ambient Context and Singleton patterns in C#; globals can be dangerous and annoying.

Rest assured that, nowadays, browsers won't let developers update the value of undefined, but back then, it was possible.

Now that we've talked about globals, an ambient context is a global instance, usually available through a static property. The Ambient Context pattern is not purely evil, but it is a code smell that smells bad. There are a few examples in .NET Framework, such as System.Threading.Thread.CurrentPrincipal and System.Threading.Thread.CurrentThread, that are scoped to a thread instead of being purely global like most static members. An ambient context does not have to be a singleton, but that is what they are most of the time. Creating a non-global (scoped) ambient context is harder, requires more work, and is out of the scope of this book.

Is the Ambient Context pattern good or bad? I'd go with both! It is useful primarily because of its convenience and ease of use while it is usually global. Most of the time, it could and should be designed differently to reduce the drawbacks that globals bring.

There are many ways of implementing an ambient context; it can be more complicated than a simple singleton, and it can aim at another, more dynamic scope than a single global instance. However, to keep it brief and straightforward, we are focusing only on the singleton version of the ambient context, like this:

```
public class MyAmbientContext
{
    public static MyAmbientContext Current { get; } = new MyAmbientContext();
    private MyAmbientContext() { }
    public void WriteSomething(string something)
    {
        Console.WriteLine($"This is your something: {something}");
    }
}
```

That code is an exact copy of the MySimpleSingleton class, with a few subtle changes:

- Instance is named Current.
- The WriteSomething method is new but has nothing to do with the Ambient Context pattern itself; it is just to make the class do something.

If we take a look at the test method that follows, we can see that we use the ambient context by calling MyAmbientContext.Current, just like we did with the last singleton implementation:

```
[Fact]
public void Should_echo_the_inputted_text_to_the_console()
{
    // Arrange (make the console write to a StringBuilder
    // instead of the actual console)
    var expectedText = "This is your something: Hello World!" + Environment.
NewLine;
    var sb = new StringBuilder();
    using (var writer = new StringWriter(sb))
    {
        Console.SetOut(writer);
        // Act
        MyAmbientContext.Current.WriteSomething("Hello World!");
    }
    // Assert
    var actualText = sb.ToString();
    Assert.Equal(expectedText, actualText);
}
```

The property could include a public setter (`public static MyAmbientContext Current { get; set; }`), and it could support more complex mechanics. As always, it is up to you and your specifications to build the right classes exposing the right behaviors.

To conclude this interlude: try to avoid ambient contexts and use instantiable classes instead. We see how to replace a singleton with a single instance of a class using dependency injection in the next chapter. That gives us a more flexible alternative to the Singleton pattern.

Conclusion

The Singleton pattern allows the creation of a single instance of a class for the whole lifetime of the program. It leverages a `private static` field and a `private` constructor to achieve its goal, exposing the instantiation through a `public static` method or property. We can use a field initializer, the `Create` method itself, a static constructor, or any other valid C# options to encapsulate the initialization logic.

Now let's see how the Singleton pattern can help us (not) follow the SOLID principles:

- S: The singleton violates this principle because it has two clear responsibilities:
  a. It has the responsibility for which it has been created (not illustrated here), like any other class.
  b. It has the responsibility of creating and managing itself (lifetime management).

- O: The Singleton pattern also violates this principle. It enforces a single static instance, locked in place by itself, which limits extensibility. The class must be modified to be updated, impossible to extend without changing the code.

- L: There is no inheritance directly involved, which is the only good point.

- I: There is no interface involved, which is a violation of this principle.

- D: The singleton class has a rock-solid hold on itself. It also suggests using its static property (or method) directly without using an abstraction, breaking the DIP with a sledgehammer.

As you can see, the Singleton pattern does violate all the SOLID principles but the LSP and should be used with caution. Having only a single instance of a class and always using that same instance is a legitimate concept. However, we see how to properly do this in the next chapter, leading me to the following advice: do not use the Singleton pattern, and if you see it used somewhere, try refactoring it out. Another good idea is to avoid the use of `static` members as much as possible as they create global elements that can make your system less flexible and more brittle. There are occasions where `static` members are worth using, but try keeping their number as low as possible. Ask yourself if that `static` member or class could be replaced with something else before coding one.

Some may argue that the Singleton design pattern is a legitimate way of doing things. However, in ASP.NET Core I cannot agree with them: we have a powerful mechanism to do it differently, called dependency injection. When using other technologies, maybe, but not with .NET.

Summary

In this chapter, we explored our first GoF design patterns. These patterns expose some of the essential basics of software engineering, not necessarily the patterns themselves, but the concepts behind them:

- The Strategy pattern is a behavioral pattern that we use to compose most of our future classes. It allows swapping behavior at runtime by composing an object with small pieces and coding against interfaces, following the SOLID principles.

- The Abstract Factory pattern brings the idea of abstracting away object creation, leading to a better separation of concerns. More specifically, it aims to abstract the creation of object families and follow the SOLID principles.

- Even if we defined it as an anti-pattern, the Singleton pattern brings the application-level objects to the table. It allows creating a single instance of an object that lives for the whole lifetime of a program. The pattern violates most SOLID principles.

We also peeked at the Ambient Context code smell, which is used to create an omnipresent entity accessible from everywhere. It is often implemented as a singleton and is a global object usually defined using the `static` modifier.

In the next chapter, we finally jump into dependency injection to see how it helps us compose complex yet maintainable systems. We also revisit the Strategy, the Factory, and the Singleton patterns to see how to use them in a dependency-injection-oriented context and how powerful they really are.

Questions

Let's take a look at a few practice questions:

1. Why is the Strategy pattern a behavioral pattern?
2. How could we define the goal of the creational patterns?
3. If I write the code `public MyType MyProp => new MyType();`, and I call the property twice (`var v1 = MyProp; var v2 = MyProp;`), are `v1` and `v2` the same instance or two different instances?
4. Is it true that the Abstract Factory pattern allows us to add new families of elements without modifying the existing consuming code?
5. Why is the Singleton pattern an anti-pattern?

7

Deep Dive into Dependency Injection

In this chapter, we explore the ASP.NET Core **Dependency Injection** (**DI**) system and how to leverage it efficiently, along with its limits and its capabilities. We also cover how to compose objects using DI, the meaning of inversion of control, and how to use the built-in DI container. We cover the concepts behind DI, too, and we also revisit our first three GoF design patterns using DI. This chapter is crucial to your journey into modern application design.

The following topics will be covered in this chapter:

- What is dependency injection?
- Revisiting the Strategy pattern
- Revisiting the Singleton pattern
- Understanding the Service Locator pattern
- Revisiting the Factory pattern

What is dependency injection?

DI is a way to apply the **Inversion of Control** (**IoC**) principle. We could regard IoC as a broader version of the dependency inversion principle (the D in SOLID).

The idea behind DI is to move the creation of dependencies from the objects themselves to the program's entry point (the composition root). That way, we can delegate the management of dependencies to an IoC container (also known as a DI container), which does the heavy lifting.

For example, object A should not know about object B that it is using. Instead, A should use an interface, I, implemented by B, and B should be resolved and injected at runtime.

Let's decompose this:

- Object A should depend on interface I instead of concretion B.
- Instance B, injected into A, should be resolved at runtime by the IoC container.
- A should not be aware of the existence of B.
- A should not control the lifetime of B.

To go all out LEGO®, we could see IoC as drawing a plan to build a castle: you draw it, make or buy the blocks, and then you press the start button and the blocks assemble themselves as per your plan. By following that logic, you could create a new 4x4 block with a unicorn painted on its side, update your plan, and then press the restart button to rebuild the castle with that new block inserted into it, replacing an old one without affecting the structural integrity of the castle. By respecting the 4x4 block contract, everything should be updatable without impacting the rest of the castle.

By following that idea, if we needed to manage every single LEGO® block one by one, it would become incredibly complex very quickly! Therefore, managing all dependencies by hand in a project would be super tedious and error-prone, even in the smallest program. To help us solve this issue, IoC containers come into play.

> **Note**
>
> A DI container or IoC container is the same thing—they're just different words that people use. I use both interchangeably in real life, but I'll do my best to stick with IoC container in this book.
>
> I chose the term *IoC container* because it seems more accurate than "DI container." IoC is the concept (the principle), while DI is a way of inverting the flow of control (applying IoC). For example, you apply the IoC principle (inverting the flow) by injecting dependencies at runtime (doing DI) using a container.

The role of an IoC container is to manage objects for you. You configure them and then, when you ask for some abstraction, the associated implementation is resolved by the container. Moreover, the container manages the lifetime of dependencies, leaving your classes to do only one thing, the job you designed them for, without thinking about their dependencies, their implementation, or their lifetime!

The bottom line is that an IoC container is a DI framework that does the autowiring for you. We could regard DI as follows:

1. The *consumer* of a dependency states its needs about one or more dependencies.
2. The IoC container injects that dependency (implementation) upon creating the *consumer*, fulfilling its needs at runtime.

Next, we explore different DI areas: where to configure the container, available options, and a common object-oriented technique that is now a code smell.

The composition root

One of the first concepts behind DI is the composition root. The composition root is where you tell the container about your dependencies: where you compose your dependency trees. The composition root should be as close to the starting point of the program as possible.

From ASP.NET Core 6 onward, the composition root is in the Program.cs file, while previously it was in either Program.cs or Startup.cs, or both.

> **Note**
>
> As a LEGO® analogy, the composition root could be the paper sheet on which you draw your plan.

The starting point of an ASP.NET Core application is the Program class, which is now autogenerated by default. We must first create a WebApplicationBuilder (highlighted), and then we can use its Services property to register our dependencies, like this:

```
var builder = WebApplication.CreateBuilder(args);
builder.Services.AddSingleton<Dependency1>();
builder.Services.AddSingleton<Dependency2>();
builder.Services.AddSingleton<Dependency3>();
builder.Services.AddDemoFeature();
```

Once that is done, we must create WebApplication itself (highlighted) to configure the ASP.NET Core middleware pipeline. You can write any code before the Run method call that starts the application, but this place is usually reserved for configuring the pipeline:

```
var app = builder.Build();
app.MapGet("/", () => "Hello World!");
// You can write any code here
app.Run();
```

It is imperative to remember that your program's composition should be done in the composition root. That removes the need for all of those pesky new keywords spread around your code base and all the responsibilities that come with them. It centralizes the application's composition into that location (that is, creating the plan to assemble the LEGO® blocks).

Registering your features elegantly

As we just saw, you should register dependencies in the composition root, but you can still organize your registration code. For example, you could split your application's composition into multiple methods or classes, and then call them from your composition root. You could also use an auto-discovery mechanism to automate the registration of some services; we use packages that do that in subsequent chapters.

Note

The critical part remains centralizing the program composition.

As an example, most features of ASP.NET Core and other popular libraries provide one or more `Add[Feature name]()` extension methods to manage the registration of their dependencies, allowing you to register a "bundle of dependencies" with one method call. That's very useful for organizing program composition into smaller, more cohesive units, such as by feature.

Side Note

A feature is the correct size as long as it stays cohesive. If your feature becomes too big, does too many things, or starts to share dependencies with other features, it may be the time for a redesign before losing control over it. That's usually a good indicator of undesired coupling.

Using extension methods makes it reasonably easy to build such a bundle of dependencies to register a feature. As a rule of thumb, you should do the following:

1. Create a static class named `[subject]Extensions`.
2. As per the Microsoft recommendation, create that class in the `Microsoft.Extensions.DependencyInjection` namespace (the same as `IServiceCollection`).
3. From there, create your `IServiceCollection` extension methods. Unless you need to return something else like a builder interface (see below), make sure to return the extended `IServiceCollection`; this allows method calls to be chained.

Note

Builder interfaces are used to configure more complex features, like ASP.NET Core MVC. For example, the `AddControllers` extension method returns an `IMvcBuilder` interface that contains a `PartManager` property. Moreover, there are extension methods that target the `IMvcBuilder` interface, allowing further configuration of the feature by requiring its registration first; that is, you can't configure `IMvcBuilder` before calling `AddControllers`. You can also design your features to leverage that pattern when needed.

For example, if my feature were named `Demo Feature`, I'd write the following extension method:

```
using CompositionRoot.DemoFeature;
namespace Microsoft.Extensions.DependencyInjection
{
    public static class DemoFeatureExtensions
    {
        public static IServiceCollection AddDemoFeature(this IServiceCollection
services)
        {
            return services
                .AddSingleton<MyFeature>()
                .AddSingleton<IMyFeatureDependency, MyFeatureDependency>()
            ;
        }
    }
}
```

Then, to use it, we could enter the following in the composition root:

```
public void ConfigureServices(IServiceCollection services)
{
    services.AddDemoFeature();
}
```

If you are not familiar with extension methods, they come in handy for extending existing classes, like what we just did. For example, you could build a sophisticated library and a set of easy-to-use extension methods that allow consumers to learn and use your library easily while keeping advanced options and customization opportunities to a maximum; think ASP.NET Core MVC or `System.Linq`.

Object lifetime

I've talked about this a few times already: no more `new`; that time is over! From now on, the IoC container should do most of the jobs related to instantiating and managing objects for us.

However, before trying this out, we need to cover one last thing: object lifetime. When you create instances manually, using the `new` keyword, you create a hold on that object; you know when you create them and when you destroy them. That leaves no chance to control these objects from the outside, enhance them, intercept them, or swap them for another implementation. This is known as the **Control Freak** anti-pattern or code smell, explained in the *Code smell – Control Freak* section.

When using DI, you need to forget about controlling objects and start to think about using dependencies — more explicitly, using their interfaces. In ASP.NET Core, there are three possible lifetimes to choose from:

Lifetime	Description	Code sample
Transient	The container creates a new object every time you ask for one.	```services.AddTransient<ISomeService, SomeService>();```
Scoped	The container creates an object per HTTP request and passes that object around to all other objects that want to use it.	```services.AddScoped<ISomeService, SomeService>();```
Singleton	The container creates a single instance of that dependency and always passes that unique object around.	```services.AddSingleton<ISomeService, SomeService>();```

From now on, we manage most of our objects using one of those three scopes. Here are some questions to help you choose:

- Do I need a single instance of my dependency? Yes? Use the **singleton** lifetime.
- Do I need a single instance of my dependency shared over an HTTP request? Yes? Use the **scoped** lifetime.
- Do I need a new instance of my dependency every time? Yes? Use the **transient** lifetime.

If you need a more complex lifetime, you may need to swap the built-in container to a third-party one (see the *Using external IoC container* section) or create your dependency tree manually in the composition root.

> **Note**
>
>
>
> A more general approach to object lifetime is to design the components to be *singletons*. When we can't, then go for *scoped*. When *scoped* is also impossible, go for *transient*. This way, we maximize instance reuse, lower the overhead of creating objects, lower the memory cost of keeping those objects in memory, and lower the amount of garbage collection needed to remove unused instances.
>
> For example, we can pick *singleton* blindly for stateless objects.
>
> For stateful objects, where multiple consumers use the same instance of an object having a lifetime of *singleton* or *scoped*, we must ensure that the object is thread-safe since multiple consumers could try to access it simultaneously.
>
> For stateful objects, an important reason is around the data contained in that object (its state). Say we load data that relates to the current user. In this case, we must make sure that data does not get leaked to other users. To do so, we can define the lifetime of that object to *scoped* when we want to allow reusing that state between multiple consumers. If that's not the case, we can choose a *transient* lifetime to ensure every consumer gets their own instance. When that state object is reused often during a single request, a *scoped* lifetime should improve the performance.
>
> Another point around long-lived objects is that they are inspected only once in a while by the garbage collector, while short-lived ones are often scanned and disposed of.

There are multiple variants of the three preceding examples, but the lifetimes remain. We use the built-in container throughout the book with many of its registration methods, so you should grow familiar with it by the end. The system offers good discoverability, so you could explore the possibilities by using IntelliSense or by reading the documentation.

Code smell – Control Freak

We've already stated that using the new keyword is a code smell or even an anti-pattern. However, do not ban the new keyword just yet. Instead, every time you use it, ask yourself whether the object you instantiated using the new keyword is a dependency that could be managed by the container and injected instead.

To help out with that, I borrowed two terms from Mark Seemann's book *Dependency Injection in .NET*; the name *Control Freak* also comes from that book. He describes the following two categories of dependencies:

- Stable dependencies
- Volatile dependencies

Stable dependencies are dependencies that should not break your application when a new version of it is released. They should use deterministic algorithms (input X should always produce output Y; a.k.a. respecting the **Liskov Substitution Principle (LSP)**, and you should not expect to change them with something else in the future. I'd say that most data structures could fall into this category: **Data Transfer Objects (DTOs)**, List<T>, and so on. You can still instantiate objects using the new keyword when they fall into this category; it is acceptable since they are not likely to break anything or to change. But be careful because foreseeing whether a dependency is likely to change or not is very hard, even impossible, as we can't know for sure what the future has to offer. For example, elements that are part of .NET could be considered stable dependencies.

Volatile dependencies are dependencies that can change, behaviors that could be swapped, or elements you may want to extend, basically, most of the classes you create for your programs such as data access and business logic classes. These are the dependencies that you should no longer instantiate using the new keyword. The primary way to break the tight coupling between implementations is to rely on interfaces instead.

To conclude this interlude: don't be a control freak anymore, those days are behind you!

Tip

When in doubt, inject the dependency instead of using the new keyword.

Next, we briefly explore an ASP.NET Core extension point before revisiting three design patterns, but this time, by exploiting DI.

Using external IoC containers

ASP.NET Core provides an extensible built-in IoC container out of the box. It is not the most powerful IoC container because it lacks some advanced features, but it can do the job for most applications.

Rest assured, if it does not, you can change it for another. If you are used to another IoC container and want to stick to it or require some missing advanced features, you might want to do that.

As of today, Microsoft recommends using the built-in container first. If you don't know ahead of time all the DI features that you will need, I'd go with the following strategy:

1. Use the built-in container.

2. When something cannot be done with it, look at your design and see if you can redesign your feature to work with the built-in container. This could help simplify your design and, at the same time, help maintain your software in the long run.

3. If it is impossible to achieve your goal, then swap it for another IoC container.

Assuming the container supports it, it is super simple to swap. The third-party container must implement the `IServiceProviderFactory<TContainerBuilder>` interface. Then, in the `Program.cs` file, we must register that factory using the `UseServiceProviderFactory<TContainerBuilder>` method, like this:

```
var builder = WebApplication.CreateBuilder(args);
builder.Host.UseServiceProviderFactory<ContainerBuilder>(new
ContainerBuilderFactory());
```

In this case, the `ContainerBuilder` and `ContainerBuilderFactory` classes are just wrappers around ASP.NET Core, but your third-party container of choice should provide you with those types. I suggest you visit their documentation to know more.

Once that factory is registered, we can configure the container using the `ConfigureContainer<TContainerBuilder>` method as usual, like this:

```
builder.Host.ConfigureContainer<ContainerBuilder>((context, builder) =>
{
    builder.Services.AddSingleton<Dependency1>();
    builder.Services.AddSingleton<Dependency2>();
    builder.Services.AddSingleton<Dependency3>();
});
```

That's the only difference; the rest of the `Program.cs` file is as usual.

As I sense that you don't feel like implementing your own IoC container just yet (or even ever), don't worry; multiple third-party integrations already exist. Here is a non-exhaustive list:

- Autofac
- DryIoc
- Grace
- LightInject
- Lamar
- Stashbox
- Unity

Some libraries extend the default container and add functionalities to it, which is an option that we explore in *Chapter 9, Structural Patterns*.

Next, we revisit the Strategy pattern, which will become the primary tool to compose our applications and add flexibility to our systems.

Revisiting the Strategy pattern

In this section, we leverage the Strategy pattern to compose complex object trees and use DI to dynamically create those instances without using the new keyword, moving away from being control freaks and toward writing DI-ready code.

The Strategy pattern is a behavioral design pattern that we can use to compose object trees at runtime, allowing extra flexibility and control over objects' behavior. Composing our objects using the Strategy pattern should make our classes easier to test and maintain and put us on a SOLID path.

From now on, we want to compose objects and lower the amount of inheritance to a minimum. We call that principle **composition over inheritance**. The goal is to inject dependencies (composition) into the current class instead of depending on base class features (inheritance). Moreover, that allows behaviors to be extracted in external classes (SRP/ISP) and then reused in one or more other classes (composition) through their interface (DIP).

The following list covers the most popular ways of injecting dependencies into objects:

- Constructor injection
- Property injection
- Method injection

We can also ask the container directly to resolve a dependency, which is known as the Service Locator (anti-)pattern. We explore the Service Locator pattern later in this chapter.

Let's look at some theory and then jump into the code to see DI in action.

Constructor injection

Constructor injection consists of injecting dependencies into the constructor as parameters. This is the most popular and preferred technique by far. Constructor injection is useful for injecting required dependencies; you can add null checks to ensure that, also known as the guard clause (see the *Adding a guard clause* section).

Property injection

The built-in IoC container does not support **property injection** out of the box. The concept is to inject **optional dependencies** into properties. Most of the time, you want to avoid doing this because property injection leads to optional dependencies, leading to nullable properties, more null checks, and often avoidable code complexity. So when we think about it, it is good that ASP.NET Core left this one out of the built-in container.

You can usually remove the property injection requirements by reworking your design, leading to a better design. If you cannot avoid using property injection, you must use a third-party container or find a way to build the dependency yourself (maybe leveraging a factory).

Nevertheless, from a high-level view, the container would do something like this:

1. Create a new instance of the class and inject all required dependencies into the constructor.

2. Find extension points by scanning properties (this could be attributes, contextual bindings, or something else).

3. For each extension point, inject (set) a dependency, leaving unconfigured properties untouched, hence its definition of an optional dependency.

There are a couple of exceptions to the previous statement regarding the lack of support:

*   Razor components (Blazor) support property injection through the use of the [Inject] attribute.

*   Razor contains the @inject directive, which generates a property to hold a dependency (ASP.NET Core manages to inject it).

We can't call that property injection per se because they are not optional but required, and the @inject directive is more about generating code than doing DI. They are more about an internal workaround than "real" property injection. That said, that is as close as .NET can get to property injection.

Tip

I recommend aiming for constructor injection instead. Not having property injection should not cause you any problems.

Method injection

ASP.NET Core supports method injection only at a few locations, such as in a controller's actions (methods), the Startup class (if you are using the pre-.NET 6 hosting model), and the middlewares' Invoke or InvokeAsync methods. You are not able to liberally use method injection in your classes without some work on your part.

Method injection is also used to inject **optional dependencies** into classes. We can also validate those at runtime using null checks or any other required logic.

Tip

I recommend aiming for constructor injection whenever you can. Only rely on method injection when it is the only way or if it adds something. For example, in a controller, injecting a transient service in the only action that needs it instead of the constructor could save a lot of useless object instantiation and, by doing so, increase performance (less instantiation and less garbage collection).

Project – Strategy

In the Strategy project, we use the Strategy pattern and constructor injection to add (compose) a
IHomeService dependency to the HomeController class.

The goal is to inject a dependency of the IHomeService type into the HomeController class. Then, send
a view model to the view to render the page.

The service goes like this:

```
namespace Strategy.Services
{
    public interface IHomeService
    {
        IEnumerable<string> GetHomePageData();
    }

    public class HomeService : IHomeService
    {
        public IEnumerable<string> GetHomePageData()
        {
            yield return "Lorem";
            yield return "ipsum";
            yield return "dolor";
            yield return "sit";
            yield return "amet";
        }
    }
}
```

The IHomeService interface is the dependency that we want the HomeController class to have. The
HomeService class is the implementation that we want to inject when instantiating HomeController,
thereby inverting the flow of dependency.

To do that, we inject IHomeService into the controller using constructor injection, leading to the
following steps:

1. Create a private IHomeService field in the HomeController class.
2. Create a HomeController constructor with a parameter of the IHomeService type.
3. Assign the argument to the field.

In code, it looks like this:

```
using Strategy.Services;
namespace Strategy.Controllers;
public class HomeController : Controller
```

```
{
    private readonly IHomeService _homeService;
    public HomeController(IHomeService homeService)
    {
        _homeService = homeService;
    }
    // Omitted action methods
}
```

The use of `private readonly` fields is beneficial for two reasons:

- They are `private`, so you do not expose your dependencies outside of the class (encapsulation).
- They are `readonly`, so you can only set the value during the initialization; usually only once. In the case of constructor injection, this ensures that the injected dependency, referenced by the `private` field, cannot be changed by other parts of the class.

If we run the application now, we get the following error:

```
InvalidOperationException: Unable to resolve service for type
'Strategy.Services.IHomeService' while attempting to activate
'Strategy.Controllers.HomeController'.
```

This error tells us that we forgot about something essential: to tell the container about the dependency.

To do that, we need to map the injection of `IHomeService` to an instance of `HomeService`. Due to our class's nature, we are safe to use the singleton lifetime (one single instance). Using the extension methods provided, in the composition root, we only need to add the following line:

```
builder.Services.AddSingleton<IHomeService, HomeService>();
```

Now, if we rerun the app, the home page should load. That tells ASP.NET to inject a `HomeService` instance when a class depends on the `IHomeService` interface.

We have just completed our first implementation of constructor injection using ASP.NET Core—it's as easy as that.

To recap constructor injection, we need to do the following:

1. Create a dependency and its interface.
2. Inject that dependency into another class through its constructor.
3. Create a binding that tells the container how to handle the dependency.

Note

We can also inject classes directly, but until you feel that you've mastered the SOLID principles, I'd recommend sticking with injecting interfaces.

Next, we practice the use of view models.

Adding the View Model

Now that we've injected the service that contains the data to display in the `HomeController` class, we need to display it. To achieve that, we decided to use the View Model pattern. The view model's goal is to create a view-centric model and then use it to render that view.

Here is what we need to do:

1. Create a View Model class (`HomePageViewModel`).
2. Update the `Home/Index` view to use the view model and display the information that it contains.
3. Create and send an instance of `HomePageViewModel` to the view from the controller.

The `HomePageViewModel` class is exposing the `SomeData` property publicly and expects that data to be injected when instantiated. The code looks like this:

```
namespace Strategy.Models;
public class HomePageViewModel
{
    public IEnumerable<string> SomeData { get; }
    public HomePageViewModel(IEnumerable<string> someData)
    {
        SomeData = someData ?? throw new
ArgumentNullException(nameof(someData));
    }
}
```

That's another example of constructor injection.

Then, after a few updates (highlighted), the `Views/Home/Index.cshtml` view looks like this:

```
@model HomePageViewModel
@{
    ViewData["Title"] = "Home Page";
}
<div class="text-center">
    <h1 class="display-4">Welcome</h1>
    @if(Model != null)
    {
        <p>Here are your data:</p>
        <ul class="list-group">
        @foreach (var item in Model.SomeData)
        {
            <li class="list-group-item">@item</li>
        }
        </ul>
    }
</div>
```

Now we need to pass an instance of `HomePageViewModel` to the view. We are doing that in the `Index` action, like this:

```
public IActionResult Index()
{
    var data = _homeService.GetHomePageData();
    var viewModel = new HomePageViewModel(data);
    return View(viewModel);
}
```

In that code, we used the `_homeService` field to retrieve the data through the `IHomeService` interface. It is important to note that at this point, the controller is not aware of the implementation; it depends only on the contract (the interface). Then we create the `HomePageViewModel` class using that data. Finally, we dispatch the instance of `HomePageViewModel` to the view for rendering.

> **Note**
>
> As you may have noticed, I used the new keyword here. In this case, I find that instantiating a view model inside the controller's action is acceptable. However, we could have used method injection or any other technique to help with object creation, such as a factory.

Next, we leverage a guard clause to make `homeService` mandatory.

Adding a guard clause

We've already stated that constructor injection is reliable and is used to inject the required dependencies. However, one thing bothers me from the last code sample: nothing guarantees us that `_homeService` is not `null`.

We could check for nulls in the `Index` method, like this:

```
public IActionResult Index()
{
    var data = _homeService?.GetHomePageData();
    var viewModel = new HomePageViewModel(data);
    return View(viewModel);
}
```

But as the controller grows, we may write null checks for that dependency many times in multiple locations. Then we should do the same null check in the view. Otherwise, we would loop a `null` value, which could cause a runtime error.

To avoid that duplication of logic and the number of possible errors that could come with it at the same time, we can add a **guard clause**.

A guard clause does as its name implies: it guards against invalid values. Most of the time, it guards against null. When you pass a `null` dependency into an object, the guard clause testing that parameter should throw an `ArgumentNullException`.

By using a `throw` expression, from C# 7 (See *Appendix A* for more information), we can simply write this:

```csharp
public HomeController(IHomeService homeService)
{
    _homeService = homeService ?? throw new
ArgumentNullException(nameof(homeService));
}
```

This throws an `ArgumentNullException` when `homeService` is `null`; otherwise, it assigns the `homeService` parameter value to the `_homeService` field. Of course, with the introduction of the nullable reference types (see *Appendix A*), the possibility of receiving a `null` argument is less likely, but it is still possible that it happens at runtime.

Important Note

A built-in container will automatically throw an exception if it can't fulfill all dependencies during the instantiation of a class (such as `HomeController`). That said, it does not mean that all third-party containers act the same. Moreover, that does not protect you from passing `null` to a manually instantiated instance (even if we should use DI, it does not mean it won't happen). As a matter of preference, I like to add them no matter what, but they are not required.

We can apply a guard clause to the `HomePageViewModel` class as well, but it would be redundant to go over that same process a second time.

We now have everything that we need to render the home page. More importantly, we achieved that without directly coupling the `HomeController` class with `HomeService`. Instead, we depend only on the `IHomeService` interface—a contract. By centralizing composition into the composition root, we could change the resulting home page by swapping the `IHomeService` implementation in the `Program.cs` file without impacting the controller or the view.

Conclusion

In this section, we saw that the strategy pattern went from a simple behavioral GoF pattern to the cornerstone of DI. We explored different ways of injecting dependencies with a strong focus on constructor injection.

Constructor injection is the most commonly used approach as it injects required dependencies, which are the ones we most often need. Method injection allows injecting algorithms, shared states, or contexts in a method that could not otherwise access that information. We can use property injection to inject optional dependencies, which should happen as rarely as possible.

You can see optional dependencies as code smells because if the class has an optional role to play, it also has a primary role leading to two responsibilities. Moreover, it could be better to move that optional role to another class if it's optional or redesign that part of the system.

To practice what you just learned, I invite you to create a class that implements IHomeService and changes the mapping in the Program.cs file from HomeService to your new class and see how easy it is to change the home page's list. To go even further, you could connect your implementation to a database, Azure Table, Redis, a JSON file, or any other data source that you can think of.

Next, we revisit a design pattern that is now an anti-pattern while exploring the singleton lifetime replacing it.

Revisiting the Singleton pattern

The Singleton pattern is obsolete, goes against the SOLID principles, and we replace it with a lifetime, as we've already seen. This section explores that lifetime and recreates the good old application state, which turns out to be nothing more than a singleton scoped dictionary.

We explore two examples here: one about the application state, in case you were wondering where that feature disappeared to. Then, the Wishlist project also uses the singleton lifetime to provide an application-level feature. There are also a few unit tests to play with the testability and to allow safe refactoring.

Project – Application state

You might remember the application state if you programmed ASP.NET using .NET Framework or the "good" old classic ASP with VBScript. If you don't, the application state was a key/value dictionary that allowed you to store data globally in your application, shared between all sessions and requests. That is one of the things that ASP always had and other languages, such as PHP, did not (or does not easily allow).

For example, I remember designing a generic reusable typed shopping cart system with classic ASP/ VBScript. VBScript was not a strongly typed language and had limited object-oriented capabilities. The shopping cart fields and types were defined at the application level (once per application), and then each user had their own "instance" containing the products in their "private shopping cart" (created once per session).

In ASP.NET Core, there is no more Application dictionary. To achieve the same goal, you could use a static class or static members, which is not the best approach; remember that global objects (static) make your application harder to test and less flexible. We could also use the Singleton pattern or create an ambient context, which would allow us to create an application-level instance of an object. We could even mix that with a factory to create end user shopping carts, but we won't; these are not the best solution either. Another way could be to use one of the ASP.NET Core caching mechanisms, memory cache, or distributed cache, but this is a stretch.

We could also save everything in a database to persist the shopping cart between visits, but that is not related to the application state and requires a user account, so we will not do that either.

We could save the shopping cart on the client-side using cookies, local storage, or any other modern mechanism to save data on the user's computer. However, we'd get even further from the application state than using a database.

For most cases requiring an application state-like feature, the best approach would be to create a standard class and an interface and then register the binding with a singleton lifetime in the container. Finally, you inject it into the component that needs it, using constructor injection. Doing so allows the mocking of dependencies and changing the implementations without touching the code but the composition root.

> **Tip**
>
> Sometimes, the best solution is not the technically complex one or design pattern-oriented; the best solution is often the simplest. Less code means less maintenance and fewer tests, resulting in a simpler application.

Let's implement a small program that simulates the application state. The API is a single interface with two implementations. The program also exposes part of the API over HTTP, allowing users to get or set a value associated with the specified key. We use the singleton lifetime to make sure the data is shared between all requests.

The interface looks like the following:

```
public interface IApplicationState
{
    TItem? Get<TItem>(string key);
    bool Has<TItem>(string key);
    void Set<TItem>(string key, TItem value) where TItem : notnull;
}
```

We can get the value associated with a key, associate a value with a key (set), and validate whether a key exists.

The Program.cs file contains the code responsible for handling HTTP requests. It is not using MVC, but minimal APIs. The two implementations can be swapped by commenting or uncommenting the first line of the Program.cs file, which is #define USE_MEMORY_CACHE. That changes the dependency registration, as highlighted in the following code:

```
var builder = WebApplication.CreateBuilder(args);
#if USE_MEMORY_CACHE
        builder.Services.AddMemoryCache();
        builder.Services.AddSingleton<IApplicationState,
ApplicationMemoryCache>();
#else
        builder.Services.AddSingleton<IApplicationState,
```

```
ApplicationDictionary>();
#endif
var app = builder.Build();
app.MapGet("/", (IApplicationState myAppState, string key) =>
{
    var value = myAppState.Get<string>(key);
    return $"{key} = {value ?? "null"}";
});
app.MapPost("/", (IApplicationState myAppState, SetAppState dto) =>
{
    myAppState.Set(dto.Key, dto.Value);
    return $"{dto.Key} = {dto.Value}";
});
app.Run();


public record class SetAppState(string Key, string Value);
```

The first implementation uses the memory cache system, and I thought it would be educational to show that to you. Caching data in memory is something you might need to do sooner rather than later. Second, we are hiding the cache system behind our implementation, which is also educational. Finally, we needed two implementations, and using the cache system was a pretty straightforward implementation.

Here is the ApplicationMemoryCache class:

```
public class ApplicationMemoryCache : IApplicationState
{
    private readonly IMemoryCache _memoryCache;

    public ApplicationMemoryCache(IMemoryCache memoryCache)
    {
        _memoryCache = memoryCache ?? throw new
ArgumentNullException(nameof(memoryCache));
    }

    public TItem Get<TItem>(string key)
    {
        return _memoryCache.Get<TItem>(key);
    }

    public bool Has<TItem>(string key)
    {
        return _memoryCache.TryGetValue<TItem>(key, out _);
```

```
    }

    public void Set<TItem>(string key, TItem value)
    {
        _memoryCache.Set(key, value);
    }
}
```

> **Note**
>
> The `ApplicationMemoryCache` class is a thin layer over `IMemoryCache`, hiding the implementation details. That type of class is called a façade. We talk more about the Façade design pattern in *Chapter 9, Structural Patterns*.

The second implementation uses `ConcurrentDictionary<string, object>` to store the application state data and ensure thread safety as multiple users could simultaneously use the application state. The `ApplicationDictionary` class is almost as simple as `ApplicationMemoryCache`:

```
public class ApplicationDictionary : IApplicationState
{
    private readonly ConcurrentDictionary<string, object> _memoryCache = new();

    public TItem? Get<TItem>(string key)
    {
        if (!Has<TItem>(key))
        {
            return default;
        }
        return (TItem)_memoryCache[key];
    }

    public bool Has<TItem>(string key)
    {
        return _memoryCache.ContainsKey(key) && _memoryCache[key] is TItem;
    }

    public void Set<TItem>(string key, TItem value)
        where TItem : notnull
```

```
    {
        _memoryCache[key] = value;
    }
}
```

We can now use any of the two implementations without impacting the rest of the program. That demonstrates the strength of DI when it comes to dependency management. Moreover, we control the lifetime of the dependencies from the composition root.

If we were to use the IApplicationState interface in another class, say SomeConsumer, its usage could look similar to the following:

```
namespace ApplicationState;
public class SomeConsumer
{
    private readonly IApplicationState _myApplicationWideService;

    public SomeConsumer(IapplicationState myApplicationWideService)
    {
        _myApplicationWideService = myApplicationWideService ?? throw new
ArgumentNullException(nameof(myApplicationWideService));
    }

    public void Execute()
    {
        if (_myApplicationWideService.Has<string>("some-key"))
        {
            var someValue = _myApplicationWideService.Get<string>("some-key");
            // Do something with someValue
        }
        // Do something else like:
        _myApplicationWideService.Set("some-key", "some-value");
        // More logic here
    }
}
```

In that code, SomeConsumer depends only on the IApplicationState interface, not on IMemoryCache or Dictionary<string, object>. Using DI allows us to hide the implementation by inverting the control of dependencies. It also breaks direct coupling between concrete implementations, programming against interfaces like the DIP prescribes.

Here is a diagram illustrating our application state system, making it visually easier to notice how it breaks coupling:

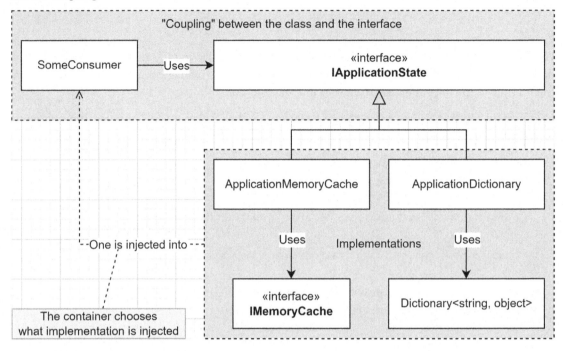

Figure 7.1: DI-oriented diagram representing the application state system

From this sample, let's remember that the singleton lifetime allows us to reuse objects between requests and share them application-wide. Moreover, hiding implementation details behind interfaces can improve the flexibility of our design.

Project – Wishlist

Let's get into another sample to illustrate the use of the singleton lifetime and DI. Seeing DI in action should help with understanding it, and then leveraging it to create SOLID software.

Context: The application is a site-wide wishlist where users can add items. Items should expire every 30 seconds. When a user adds an existing item, the system should increment the count and reset the item's expiration time. That way, popular items stay on the list longer, making it to the top. The system should sort the items by count (highest first) when displayed.

> **Note**
>
> 30 seconds is very fast, but I'm sure that you don't want to wait for days before an item expires when running the app.

The program is a tiny web API that exposes two endpoints:

- Add an item to the wishlist (POST).

- Read the wishlist (GET).

The wishlist interface looks like this:

```
public interface IWishList
{
    Task<WishListItem> AddOrRefreshAsync(string itemName);
    Task<IEnumerable<WishListItem>> AllAsync();
}
public record class WishListItem(string Name, int Count, DateTimeOffset
Expiration);
```

The two operations are there, and by making them async (returning a Task<T>), we could implement another version that relies on a remote system, such as a database, instead of an in-memory store. Then, the WishListItem record class is part of the IWishList contract; it is the model. To keep it simple, the wishlist only stores the names of items.

Note

Trying to foresee the future is not usually a good idea, but designing APIs to be awaitable is generally a safe bet. Other than this, I'd recommend you stick to your specifications and use cases. When you try to solve problems that do not exist yet, you usually end up coding a lot of useless stuff, leading to additional unnecessary maintenance and testing time.

In the composition root, we must set the IWishList implementation instance to a singleton scope, so all users share the same instance. Meanwhile, let's look at the minimal APIs that handle the HTTP requests, highlighted below. To make it easier for you, here is the whole Program.cs file:

```
var builder = WebApplication.CreateBuilder(args);
builder.Services
    .ConfigureOptions<InMemoryWishListOptions>()
    .AddTransient<IValidateOptions<InMemoryWishListOptions>,
InMemoryWishListOptions>()
    .AddSingleton(serviceProvider => serviceProvider.
GetRequiredService<IOptions<InMemoryWishListOptions>>().Value)

    // The singleton registration
    .AddSingleton<IWishList, InMemoryWishList>()
;
```

Note

If you are wondering where IConfigureOptions, IValidateOptions, and IOptions come from, we are covering the ASP.NET Core Options pattern in the next chapter.

```
var app = builder.Build();
app.MapGet("/", async (IWishList wishList) => await wishList.AllAsync());
app.MapPost("/", async (IWishList wishList, CreateItem? newItem) =>
{
    if (newItem?.Name == null)
    {
        return Results.BadRequest();
    }
    var item = await wishList.AddOrRefreshAsync(newItem.Name);
    return Results.Created("/", item);
});
app.Run();
public record class CreateItem(string? Name);
```

The GET endpoint delegates the logic to the injected IWishList implementation and returns the result, while the POST endpoint also validates the CreateItem DTO.

Note

As of .NET 6, we can't use **DataAnnotations** to validate minimal APIs. At the end of the chapter, I left a few links that explain the differences between minimal APIs and Controllers/MVC. Moreover, we explore **FluentValidation** in *Chapter 15, Getting Started with Vertical Slice Architecture*, that we can leverage for more complex validation. In this case, it was fairly simple to validate the input manually using a single if statement.

To help us implement the InMemoryWishList class, we started by writing some tests to back our specifications up. Since static members are hard to configure in tests (remember globals?), we borrowed a concept from the ASP.NET Core memory cache and created an ISystemClock interface that abstracts away the static call to DateTimeOffset.UtcNow. This way, we can program the value of UtcNow in our tests to create expired items. Here's the clock interface and implementation:

```
namespace Wishlist.Internal;
public interface ISystemClock
{
    DateTimeOffset UtcNow { get; }
}
public class SystemClock : ISystemClock
{
    public DateTimeOffset UtcNow => DateTimeOffset.UtcNow;
}
```

The unit tests file would be many pages long, so here is the outline:

```
namespace Wishlist;
public class InMemoryWishListTest
{
    // Constructor and private fields omitted
    public class AddOrRefreshAsync : InMemoryWishListTest
    {
        [Fact]
        public async Task Should_create_new_item();
        [Fact]
        public async Task Should_increment_Count_of_an_existing_item();
        [Fact]
        public async Task Should_set_the_new_Expiration_date_of_an_existing_
item();
        [Fact]
        public async Task Should_set_the_Count_of_expired_items_to_1();
        [Fact]
        public async Task Should_remove_expired_items();
    }
    public class AllAsync : InMemoryWishListTest
    {
        [Fact]
        public async Task Should_return_items_ordered_by_Count_Descending();
        [Fact]
        public async Task Should_not_return_expired_items();
    }
    // Private helper methods omitted
}
```

Let's analyze that code (see the source code on GitHub: https://adpg.link/ywy8). We mocked the ISystemClock interface in the tests and programmed it to obtain the desired results based on each test case. We also programmed some helper methods to make the tests easier to read. Those helpers use tuples to return multiple values (See *Appendix A* for more information). Here is an example of such a method setting the clock to the past:

```
// Mock definition:
private readonly Mock<ISystemClock> _systemClockMock = new();
// Lots of omitted code here
private (DateTimeOffset UtcNow, DateTimeOffset ExpectedExpiryTime)
SetUtcNowToExpired()
```

```
{
    var delay = -(_options.ExpirationInSeconds * 2);
    var utcNow = DateTimeOffset.UtcNow.AddSeconds(delay);
    _systemClockMock.Setup(x => x.UtcNow).Returns(utcNow);
    var expectedExpiryTime = utcNow.AddSeconds(_options.ExpirationInSeconds);
    return (utcNow, expectedExpiryTime);
}
```

Now that we have those failing tests, here is the implementation of the `InMemoryWishList` class:

```
namespace Wishlist;
public class InMemoryWishList : IWishList
{
    private readonly InMemoryWishListOptions _options;
    private readonly ConcurrentDictionary<string, InternalItem> _items = new();
    public InMemoryWishList(InMemoryWishListOptions options)
    {
        _options = options ?? throw new ArgumentNullException(nameof(options));
    }
    public Task<WishListItem> AddOrRefreshAsync(string itemName)
    {
        var expirationTime = _options.SystemClock.UtcNow.AddSeconds(_options.
ExpirationInSeconds);
        _items
            .Where(x => x.Value.Expiration < _options.SystemClock.UtcNow)
            .Select(x => x.Key)
            .ToList()
            .ForEach(key => _items.Remove(key, out _))
        ;
        var item = _items.AddOrUpdate(
            itemName,
            new InternalItem(Count: 1,Expiration: expirationTime),
            (string key, InternalItem item) => item with { Count = item.Count +
1, Expiration = expirationTime }

        );
        var wishlistItem = new WishListItem(
            Name: itemName,
            Count: item.Count,
            Expiration: item.Expiration
        );
        return Task.FromResult(wishlistItem);
```

```
    }
    public Task<IEnumerable<WishListItem>> AllAsync()
    {
        var items = _items
            .Where(x => x.Value.Expiration >= _options.SystemClock.UtcNow)
            .Select(x => new WishListItem(
                Name: x.Key,
                Count: x.Value.Count,
                Expiration: x.Value.Expiration
            ))
            .OrderByDescending(x => x.Count)
            .AsEnumerable()
        ;
        return Task.FromResult(items);
    }
    private record class InternalItem(int Count, DateTimeOffset Expiration);
}
```

The `InMemoryWishList` class uses `ConcurrentDictionary<string, InternalItem>` internally to store the items and make the wishlist thread-safe. It also uses a `with` expression to manipulate and copy the `InternalItem` record class.

The `AllAsync` method filters out expired items, while the `AddOrRefreshAsync` method removes expired items. This might not be the most advanced logic ever, but that does the trick.

Exercise

You might have noticed the code is not the most elegant of all code, and I left it this way on purpose. While using the test suite, I invite you to refactor the methods of the `InMemoryWishList` class into more readable code.

I took a few minutes to refactor it myself and saved it as `InMemoryWishListRefactored`. You can also uncomment the first line of `InMemoryWishListTest.cs` to test that class instead of the main one. My refactoring is a way to make the code cleaner, to give you ideas. It is not the only way, nor the best way, to write that class (the "best way" being subjective).

Back to DI, the line that makes the wishlist shared between users is in the composition root that we explored earlier. As a reference, here it is:

```
builder.Services.AddSingleton<IWishList, InMemoryWishList>();
```

Yes, only that line makes all the difference between creating multiple instances and a single shared instance. By setting the lifetime to Singleton, you can open multiple browsers and share the wishlist.

To POST to the API, I recommend using the Postman collection (`https://adpg.link/postman6`) that comes with the book. The collection already contains multiple requests that you can execute in batches or individually. You can also use the Swagger UI that I added to the project. I left the code out of the chapter as it was not useful, but that's the default URL that should open when starting the project. If you prefer working in a terminal, you can use `curl` or `Invoke-WebRequest`, depending on your OS.

That's it! All that code to demo what a single line can do, and we have a working program, as tiny as it is.

Conclusion

This section explored how to replace the classic Singleton pattern with a class registered with a singleton lifetime. We looked at the old application state, learned that was no more, and implemented two versions of it. We no longer need that, but it was a good way of learning about singletons.

We then implemented a wishlist system as a second example and concluded that the whole thing was working due to, and managed by, a single line of the composition root: the call to the `AddSingleton` method. Changing that line could drastically change the behavior of the system, even making it unusable.

From now on, you can see the Singleton pattern as an anti-pattern in .NET, and unless you find strong reasons to implement it, you should stick to normal classes and DI instead. Doing this moves the creation responsibility from the singleton class to the composition root, which is the composition root's responsibility, leaving the class only one responsibility: perfectly in line with the Single Responsibility Principle.

Next, we explore the Service Locator anti-pattern/code smell.

Understanding the Service Locator pattern

Service Locator is an anti-pattern that reverts the IoC principle to its Control Freak roots. The only difference is using the IoC container to build the dependency tree instead of the new keyword.

There is some use of this pattern in ASP.NET, and some may argue that there are some reasons for one to use the Service Locator pattern, but it should happen very rarely or never. For that reason, in this book, let's call Service Locator a **code smell** instead of an **anti-pattern**.

The DI container uses the Service Locator pattern internally to find dependencies, which is the correct way of using it. In your applications, you want to avoid injecting an `IServiceProvider` to get the dependencies you need from it, which revert to the classic flow of control.

My strong recommendation is *don't use Service Locator* unless you know what you are doing and have no other option. A good use of Service Locator could be to migrate a legacy system that is too big to rewrite. So you could build the new code using DI and update the legacy code using the Service Locator pattern, allowing both systems to live together or migrate one into the other, depending on your goal.

Project — ServiceLocator

The best way to avoid something is to know about it, so let's see how to implement the Service Locator pattern using `IServiceProvider` to find a dependency.

The service we want to use is an implementation of `IMyService`. Let's start with the interface:

```
namespace ServiceLocator;
public interface IMyService : IDisposable
{
    void Execute();
}
```

The interface implements the `IDisposable` interface and contains a single `Execute` method. Here is the implementation, which does nothing more than throw an exception if the instance has been disposed of:

```
namespace ServiceLocator;
public class MyServiceImplementation : IMyService
{
    private bool _isDisposed = false;
    public void Dispose() => _isDisposed = true;

    public void Execute()
    {
        if (_isDisposed)
        {
            throw new NullReferenceException("Some dependencies have been
disposed.");
        }
    }
}
```

Then, let's add a controller that implements the Service Locator pattern:

```
namespace ServiceLocator;
public class MyController : ControllerBase
{
    private readonly IServiceProvider _serviceProvider;
    public MyController(IServiceProvider serviceProvider)
    {
        _serviceProvider = serviceProvider ?? throw new
ArgumentNullException(nameof(serviceProvider));
    }
    [Route("/service-locator")]
    public IActionResult Get()
    {
        using var myService = _serviceProvider.
GetRequiredService<IMyService>();
```

```
            myService.Execute();
            return Ok("Success!");
    }
}
```

In that code sample, instead of injecting `IMyService` into the constructor, we are injecting `IServiceProvider`. Then, we use it (highlighted line) to locate the `IMyService` instance. Doing so shifts the responsibility for creating the object from the container to the consumer (`MyController`, in this case). `MyController` should not be aware of `IServiceProvider` and should let the container do its job without interference.

What could go wrong? If we run the application and navigate to /service-locator, everything works as expected. However, if we reload the page, we get an error thrown by the `Execute()` method because we called `Dispose()` during the previous request. `MyController` should not control its injected dependencies, which is the point that I am trying to emphasize here: leave the container to control the lifetime of dependencies rather than trying to be a control freak. Using the Service Locator pattern opens pathways toward those wrong behaviors, which will most likely cause more harm than good in the long run.

Moreover, even though the ASP.NET Core container does not natively support this, we lose the ability to inject dependencies contextually when using the Service Locator pattern because the consumer controls its dependencies. What do I mean by contextually? One could inject instance A into a class but instance B into another class.

Before exploring ways to fix this, here is the `Program.cs` code that powers this program:

```
var builder = WebApplication.CreateBuilder(args);
builder.Services
    .AddSingleton<IMyService, MyServiceImplementation>()
    .AddControllers()
;
var app = builder.Build();
app.MapControllers();
app.Run();
```

There is nothing fancy in the preceding code apart from enabling controller support and registering our service. To fix the controller, we need to either remove the `using` statement or move away from Service Locator and inject our dependencies instead. I picked moving away from the Service Locator pattern, and we will tackle the following:

- Method injection
- Constructor injection
- Minimal API

Implementing method injection

Let's start by using *method injection* to demonstrate its use:

```
public class MethodInjectionController : ControllerBase
{
    [Route("/method-injection")]
    public IActionResult GetUsingMethodInjection([FromServices]IMyService
myService)
    {
        ArgumentNullException.ThrowIfNull(myService, nameof(myService));
        myService.Execute();
        return Ok("Success!");
    }
}
```

Let's analyze the code:

- The `FromServicesAttribute` class tells the model binder about method injection. We can inject zero or more services into any action by decorating its parameters with [`FromServices`].
- We added a guard clause to protect us from `null`. We leverage the `ThrowIfNull` method instead of manually checking for `null` then throwing an exception (see *Appendix A*).
- Finally, we kept the original code except for the `using` statement.

 Note

Method injection like this would be of good use for a controller with multiple actions, but that uses `IMyService` in only one of them.

Implementing constructor injection

Let's continue by implementing the same solution using constructor injection. Our new controller looks like this:

```
namespace ServiceLocator;
public class ConstructorInjectionController : ControllerBase
{
    private readonly IMyService _myService;
    public ConstructorInjectionController(IMyService myService)
    {
        _myService = myService ?? throw new
ArgumentNullException(nameof(myService));
    }
    [Route("/constructor-injection")]
```

```
    public IActionResult GetUsingConstructorInjection()
    {
        _myService.Execute();
        return Ok("Success!");
    }
}
```

When using constructor injection, we ensure that `IMyService` is not `null` upon class instantiation. Since it is a class member, it is even less tempting to call its `Dispose()` method in an action, leaving that responsibility to the container (as it should be).

Both techniques are an acceptable replacement for the Service Locator anti-pattern. Let's analyze the code before moving to the next possibility:

*   We implemented the strategy pattern with constructor injection.
*   We added a guard clause to ensure that no `null` value could get in at runtime.
*   We simplified the action to what it should do: to a bare minimum.

Implementing a minimal API

Minimal APIs allow us to implement method injection the same way we did previously but without creating a controller. This approach is very beneficial for code samples, educational material, and APIs representing a very thin controller layer. Here is the code to add to the `Program.cs` file:

```
app.MapGet("/minimal-api", (IMyService myService) =>
{
    myService.Execute();
    return "Success!";
});
```

That code does the same as the method injection sample without the guard clause that I omitted because no external consumer is likely to inject nulls into it: the endpoint is a delegate that is passed directly to the `MapGet` method. In other cases, where your delegates can be called by external code, you could add a guard clause there as well.

Conclusion

Most of the time, by following the Service Locator anti-pattern, we only hide the fact that we are taking control of objects instead of decoupling our components. The last example demonstrated a problem when disposing of an object, which could happen using constructor injection. However, when thinking about it, it is more tempting to dispose of an object that we create than one that is injected.

Moreover, the service locator takes control away from the container and moves it into the consumer, against the **Open-Closed Principle**. You should be able to update the consumer by updating the composition root's bindings. In this case, we could change the binding, and it would work. In a more advanced case, when requiring contextual injection, we would have difficulty binding two implementations to the same interface, one for each context; it could even be impossible.

The IoC container is responsible for weaving the program's thread, connecting its pieces together where each independent piece should be as clueless as possible about the others.

This anti-pattern also complicates testing. When unit testing your class, you need to mock a container that returns a mocked service instead of mocking only the service.

One place where I can see its usage justified is in the composition root, where bindings are defined, and sometimes, especially when using the built-in container, we can't avoid it. Another place would be a library that adds functionalities to the container. Other than that, try to stay away!

 Beware

Moving the service locator elsewhere does not make it disappear; it only moves it around, like any dependency.

Next, we revisit our third and final pattern of this chapter.

Revisiting the Factory pattern

In the Strategy pattern example, we implemented a solution that instantiated HomePageViewModel using the new keyword. While doing that is acceptable, we could use method injection instead, mixed with the use of a factory. The Factory patterns are handy tools when the time comes to construct objects. Let's look at a few rewrites of the Strategy project using factories to explore some possibilities.

Project – Factory

Let's start by mixing a factory with method injection and injecting the view model directly into our method instead of injecting IHomeService. To achieve this, we rewrite the Index method of the HomeController class to this:

```
public class HomeController : Controller
{
    public IActionResult Index([FromServices]HomePageViewModel viewModel)
    {
        return View(viewModel);
    }
    // Omitted Privacy() and Error()
}
```

The FromServicesAttribute class tells the ASP.NET Core pipeline to inject an instance of HomePageViewModel directly into the method. Unfortunately, the IoC container is not yet aware of how to create such an instance. Now, we use a factory instead of a static binding to explain to the container what to do. Here is the Project.cs file (factory highlighted):

```
using Factory.Models;
using Factory.Services;
```

```
var builder = WebApplication.CreateBuilder(args);
builder.Services
    .AddSingleton<IHomeService, HomeService>()
    .AddTransient(serviceProvider =>
    {
        var homeService = serviceProvider.GetRequiredService<IHomeService>();
        var data = homeService.GetHomePageData();
        return new HomePageViewModel(data);
    })
    .AddSingleton<IHomeViewModelFactory, HomeViewModelFactory>()
    .AddControllersWithViews()
;
var app = builder.Build();
app.MapDefaultControllerRoute();
app.Run();
```

In the preceding code, we used another overload of the AddTransient() extension method and passed Func<IServiceProvider, TService> implementationFactory as an argument. The highlighted code represents our factory, and that factory is implemented as a service locator using the IServiceProvider instance to create the IHomeService dependency that we use to instantiate HomePageViewModel.

We are using the new keyword here, but is this wrong? The composition root is where elements should be created (or configured), so instantiating objects there is okay, as it is to use the Service Locator pattern. However, you should aim to avoid it whenever possible. It is harder to avoid when using the default container versus a full-featured third-party one, but we can avoid it in many cases.

We could also create a factory class to keep our composition root clean as we do with the HomeViewModelFactory soon. While that is true, we would only move the code around, adding more complexity to our program. That is the reason why creating view models inside your controller's actions is acceptable to reduce unnecessary complexity.

Moreover, creating view models inside actions should not negatively impact the program's maintainability in most cases since a view model is bound to a single view, controlled by a single action, leading to a one-on-one relationship. Furthermore, it is way cheaper to implement, and it is also easier to understand than roaming around the code to find what binding does what. However, the biggest downside of instantiating view models manually in the action method is testability. It is easier to inject the data we want from a test case than dealing with hardcoded object creation. Nonetheless, the extra complexity that we are implementing here is rarely worth it for a view model but is a good way to demonstrate the use of factories.

We could create a class to handle the factory logic for more complex scenarios or to clean the composition root. We could also create a class and an interface to directly use the factory inside our other classes. This approach comes in handy for creating your dependencies only when you need them; this is also known as lazy loading. Lazy loading means to create the object only when needed, deferring the overhead of doing so to the time of use or during its first use.

Note

There is an existing `Lazy<T>` class to help with lazy loading, but that is not the point of this code sample. The idea is the same, though: we create the object only when first needed.

Unless you need to reuse that creation logic in multiple places, creating a factory class may not be worth it. Nevertheless, this is a convenient pattern worth remembering. Here is how to implement a factory that returns an instance of `PrivacyViewModel`:

```
namespace Factory.Services;
public interface IHomeViewModelFactory
{
    PrivacyViewModel CreatePrivacyViewModel();
}
public class HomeViewModelFactory : IHomeViewModelFactory
{
    public PrivacyViewModel CreatePrivacyViewModel() => new()
    {
    Title = "Privacy Policy (from IHomeViewModelFactory)",
    Content = new HtmlString("<p>Use this page to detail your site's privacy
policy.</p>")
    };
}
```

The preceding code encapsulates the creation of `PrivacyViewModel` instances into `HomeViewModelFactory`. The code is very basic; it creates an instance of the `PrivacyViewModel` class and fills its properties with hardcoded values.

Now, to use that new factory, we update the controller, use constructor injection to inject `IHomeViewModelFactory` into `HomeController`, and then use it from the `Privacy()` action method, like this:

```
private readonly IHomeViewModelFactory _homeViewModelFactory;
public HomeController(IHomeViewModelFactory homeViewModelFactory)
{
    _homeViewModelFactory = homeViewModelFactory ?? throw new
ArgumentNullException(nameof(homeViewModelFactory));
}
// Omitted action methods
public IActionResult Privacy()
{
    var viewModel = _homeViewModelFactory.CreatePrivacyViewModel();
    return View(viewModel);
}
```

The preceding code is clear, simple, and easy to test.

By using this technique, we are not limited to one method. We can write multiple methods that each encapsulate their own creational logic in the same factory. We could also pass additional objects to the `Create[object to create]()` method (highlighted), like this:

```
public HomePageViewModel CreateHomePageViewModel(IEnumerable<string> someData)
    => new(someData);
```

The possibilities are almost endless when you think about it, so now that you've seen a few in action, you may find other uses for a factory when you need to inject some classes with complex instantiation logic into other objects.

One advantage of using factories like this is to inject dependencies into them and use them for that complex instantiation logic. For example, you could inject a class that connects to a database and leverage that data to build the object. Without a factory, the controller (in our case) would have that added responsibility.

Conclusion

The use of a factory can be considered for multiple scenarios. Our example covered the fact that we could create a factory in the composition root to instantiate dependencies (a `Func<IServiceProvider, TService>`). We leveraged method injection to get that view model instance, and we saw that sometimes, the `new` keyword should be used directly instead of trying to implement more complex code that would, in the end, only move the problem around, leading to false decoupling with added complexity.

As a rule of thumb, creating view models in controller actions is acceptable, and classes containing logic are the ones we want to inject to break tight coupling with. Just keep in mind that *moving code around your codebase does not make that code, logic, dependencies, or coupling disappear*.

Moreover, we explored the creation of a factory class backed by an interface. Those are very helpful for more complex instantiation, removing inlined factories from the composition root, or depending on other services, like access to a database.

We use factories often, and now that you know more about them, I'm sure you'll start to see them in the .NET APIs if you have not already.

Summary

This chapter covered the basics of **Dependency Injection** and how to leverage it to follow the **Dependency Inversion Principle** helped by the **Inversion of Control** principle. We then revisited the **Strategy** design pattern, and saw how to use it to create a flexible, DI-ready system. We also revisited the **Singleton** pattern, seeing that we can inject the same instance, system-wide, by using the singleton lifetime when configuring dependencies in the container. We finally saw how to leverage factories to handle complex object creation logic.

We also talked about moving code around, the illusion of improvement, and the cost of engineering. We saw that the new keyword could help reduce complexity when the construction logic is simple enough and that it could save time and money. On the other hand, we also explored a few techniques to handle object creation complexity to create maintainable and testable programs, such as factories, and get away from the **Control Freak** code smell. We also visited the guard clause, which guards our injected dependencies against null. This way, we can demand some required services using constructor injection and use them from the class methods without testing for null every time.

We explored how the **Service Locator** (anti-)pattern can be harmful and how it can be leveraged from the composition root to create complex objects dynamically. We also discussed why to keep its usage frequency as close to never as possible. Understanding these patterns and code smells is very important when it comes to keeping your systems maintainable as your programs grow in size. For programs that require complex DI logic, conditional injection, multiple scopes, auto-implemented factories, and other advanced features, we saw that it is possible to use third-party containers instead of the built-in one.

In subsequent sections, we will explore tools that add functionality to the default container, reducing the need to swap it for another. If you are building multiple smaller projects (microservices) instead of a big one (a monolith), that may save you from requiring those extra features, but nothing is free, and everything has a cost; more on this in *Chapter 16, Introduction to Microservices Architecture*.

In the next chapter, we are going to explore options and logging patterns. These ASP.NET Core patterns aim to make our lives easier when managing such common problems.

Questions

Let's take a look at a few practice questions:

1. What are the three DI lifetimes that we can assign to objects in ASP.NET Core?
2. What is the composition root for?
3. Is it true that we should avoid the new keyword when instantiating volatile dependencies?
4. What is the pattern that we revisited in this chapter that helps compose objects to eliminate inheritance?
5. Is the Service Locator pattern a design pattern, a code smell, or an anti-pattern?

Further reading

Here are some links to build upon what we have learned in the chapter:

*   Start up environment-specific composition root: https://adpg.link/GdjP
*   If you need more options, such as contextual injection, you can check out an open source library that I built. It adds support for new scenarios: https://adpg.link/S3aT
*   Minimal APIs overview: https://adpg.link/q5pc
*   Tutorial: Creating a minimal web API with ASP.NET Core: https://adpg.link/w32e

Join our book's Discord space

Join the book's Discord workspace for *Ask me Anything* session with the authors:

https://packt.link/ASPdotNET6DesignPatterns

8

Options and Logging Patterns

This chapter covers .NET-specific patterns that close the *Designing for ASP.NET Core* section of the book. The Options pattern and logging features are two more building blocks of most applications that come built in and that are extensible. We explore these abstractions while keeping it to a level where we use them, not master every aspect of them. Once you've read this chapter, you should know how to leverage the .NET options and settings infrastructure, as well as how to write application logs. We also briefly explore how to customize those systems.

The following topics will be covered in this chapter:

- The Options pattern
- Becoming familiar with .NET logging abstractions

Let's get started!

The Options pattern

With ASP.NET Core, we can use predefined mechanisms to enhance the usage of application settings. These allow us to divide our configuration into multiple smaller objects, configure them during multiple stages of the startup flow, validate them, and even watch for runtime changes with minimal effort.

The Options pattern's goal is to use settings at runtime, allowing changes to the application to happen without changing the code. The settings could be as simple as a `string`, a `bool`, a database connection string, or a complex object that holds an entire subsystem's configuration.

This section explores different tools offered by ASP.NET Core to manage, inject, and load configurations and options into our programs. We will tackle different scenarios, from common ones to more advanced ones.

Getting started

The Options pattern in ASP.NET Core allows us to seamlessly load settings from multiple sources. We can customize these sources when creating `IHostBuilder`, or even use the default ones set by calling `WebApplication.CreateBuilder(args)`.

The default sources, in order, are as follows:

- `appsettings.json`
- `appsettings.{Environment}.json`
- User secrets; these are only loaded when the environment is `Development`
- Environment variables
- Command-line arguments

The order is also very important as the last to be loaded overrides any previous values. For example, you can set a value in `appsettings.json` and override it in `appsettings.Staging.json` by redefining the value in that file, user secrets, an environment variable or by passing it as a command-line argument when you run your application.

There are four main ways to use settings: `IOptionsMonitor<TOptions>`, `IOptionsFactory<TOptions>`, `IOptionsSnapshot<TOptions>`, and `IOptions<TOptions>`. In all these cases, we can inject that dependency into a class to use the available settings. `TOptions` is the type that represents the settings that we want to access.

The framework often returns an empty instance of your options class if you don't configure it. We will learn how to configure options properly in the next subsection, but keep in mind that using property initializers inside your options class can also be a great way to ensure certain defaults are used. Don't use initializers for default values that change based on the environment (dev, staging, or production) or for secrets such as connection strings and passwords. You can also use constants to centralize those defaults somewhere in your codebase (making them easier to maintain). Nevertheless, proper configuration and validation are always preferred, but both combined can add a safety net.

Based on the `MyListOption` class, because the default value of an `int` is 0, the default number of items to display per page would be 0, leading to an empty list. However, we can configure this using a property initializer, as shown in the example below:

```
public class MyListOption
{
    public int ItemsPerPage { get; set; } = 20;
}
```

The default number of items to display per page is now 20.

> **Note**
>
> In the source code for this chapter, I've included a few tests in the `CommonScenarios.Tests` project that assert the lifetime of the different options interfaces. I haven't included this code here for brevity, but it describes the behavior of the different options via unit tests. See `https://adpg.link/T8Ro` for more information.

Next, we explore the different interfaces provided by .NET.

IOptionsMonitor<TOptions>

This interface is the most versatile of them all. It allows us to receive notifications about reloading the configuration. It also supports caching and can have multiple configurations, each associated with a name (named configuration). The injected IOptionsMonitor<TOptions> instance is always the same (**singleton lifetime**). It also supports default settings (without a name) through its Value property.

> **Note**
>
> You receive an empty TOptions instance (new TOptions()) if you only configured named options or configured no instance at all.

IOptionsFactory<TOptions>

This interface is a factory, as we saw in *Chapter 6, Understanding the Strategy, Abstract Factory, and Singleton Design Patterns*, and *Chapter 7, Deep Dive into Dependency Injection*. We use factories to create instances; this one is no different. Unless it's absolutely necessary, I'd suggest sticking with IOptionsMonitor<TOptions> or IOptionsSnapshot<TOptions> instead.

One use of this factory could be to create multiple instances of settings while injecting only one dependency, but that sounds more like a design flaw than a solution to me. Nevertheless, this could be useful in some rare situations. Why a flaw? You revert to controlling your dependencies instead of doing IoC.

How it works is simple: a new factory is created every time you ask for one (transient lifetime), and each factory creates a new options instance every time you call its Create(name) method (**transient lifetime**).

> **Note**
>
> You receive an empty TOptions instance (new TOptions()) if you only configured the named options or configured no instance at all when calling factory.Create(Options.DefaultName).

Options.DefaultName is the name that's given to non-named options; this is usually handled for you by the framework.

IOptionsSnapshot<TOptions>

This interface is useful when you need a snapshot of the settings, and is created once per request (**scoped lifetime**). We can use it to get named options as well, such as IOptionsMonitor<TOptions>. We can access the default options with the CurrentValue property.

> **Note**
>
> You receive an empty TOptions instance (new TOptions()) if you only configured the named options or configured no instance at all.

IOptions<TOptions>

This interface is the first that was added to ASP.NET Core. It does not support advanced scenarios such as what snapshots and monitors do. Whenever you request an IOptions<TOptions> instance, you get the same instance (**singleton lifetime**).

> **Note**
>
> IOptions<TOptions> does not support named options, so you can only access the default options.

Next, we explore how to leverage those interfaces.

Project – CommonScenarios

This first example covers multiple basic use cases, such as injecting options, using named options, and storing options values in settings.

Let's start by learning how to leverage IOptions<TOptions>, which is the first and simplest interface that comes out of .NET Core. We also define the groundwork of multiple subsequent scenarios. Like most things we program from now on, the examples leverage dependency injection.

Let's go over the process step by step:

1. Create an interface for the service classes, named IMyNameService.
2. Create options classes.
3. Code some unit tests against that interface. We reuse these tests for each implementation.
4. Code the first implementation.
5. Run our tests against that implementation.

Our interface is very simple and looks like this:

```
public interface IMyNameService
{
    string? GetName(bool someCondition);
}
```

It contains a single GetName method that takes someCondition as a parameter and returns a string, from which we can expect its content to be a name.

Next, we create two options classes: one for this scenario and one for the others. The class that we will use in the other scenarios is as follows:

```
public class MyOptions
{
    public string? Name { get; set; }
}
```

The class that we will use in this scenario is as follows:

```
public class MyDoubleNameOptions
{
    public string? FirstName { get; set; }
    public string? SecondName { get; set; }
}
```

Note

I have shown both classes here to save space later, so that I don't have to copy the same tests again while only making a small change. Moreover, they are small and straightforward classes.

Now, as practitioners of **test-driven design** (**TDD**), let's see the unit tests that act as our initial code consumers. Our simple specifications are that when `someCondition` is `true`, `GetName` returns the value of `Option1Name`, but when `someCondition` is `false`, `GetName` returns the value of `Option2Name`.

Note

`Option1Name` and `Option2Name` are two constants containing irrelevant values (but different ones so that we can compare their output).

Let's begin with our unit test:

```
public abstract class MyNameServiceTest<TMyNameService>
    where TMyNameService : class, IMyNameService
{
    protected readonly IMyNameService _sut;

    public const string Option1Name = "Options 1";
    public const string Option2Name = "Options 2";

    public MyNameServiceTest()
    {
        var services = new ServiceCollection();
        services.AddTransient<IMyNameService, TMyNameService>();
        services.Configure<MyOptions>("Options1", myOptions =>
        {
            myOptions.Name = Option1Name;
        });
        services.Configure<MyOptions>("Options2", myOptions =>
        {
```

```
        myOptions.Name = Option2Name;
    });
    services.Configure<MyDoubleNameOptions>(options =>
    {
        options.FirstName = Option1Name;
        options.SecondName = Option2Name;
    });
    _sut = services.BuildServiceProvider()
        .GetRequiredService<IMyNameService>();
}
```

Let's analyze the first part of our test class:

- Our test class is abstract and generic, making it the base class of all `IMyNameService` tests.
- We created our subject under test by using the generic `TMyNameService` type as our implementation.
- We configured two named `MyOptions` and one `MyDoubleNameOptions`. These are injected into the service's implementations; more on that later. In this case, we have configured the options' properties manually. In programs, we usually move those values to configuration files or other providers, such as `appsettings.json`; more on that later.

Note

The name of each option is passed as an argument to the `services.Configure<MyOptions>("name", ...)` method.

Then, we need to create the two test cases we discussed earlier:

```
    [Fact]
    public void GetName_should_return_Name_from_options1_when_someCondition_is_
true()
    {
        var result = _sut.GetName(true);
        Assert.Equal(Option1Name, result);
    }
    [Fact]
    public void GetName_should_return_Name_from_options2_when_someCondition_is_
false()
    {
        var result = _sut.GetName(false);
        Assert.Equal(Option2Name, result);
    }
}
```

Now, let's create our implementation, named `MyNameServiceUsingDoubleNameOptions`. It uses the `IOptions<MyDoubleNameOptions>` interface, which make it the simplest implementation we can use:

```
public class MyNameServiceUsingDoubleNameOptions : IMyNameService
{
    private readonly MyDoubleNameOptions _options;

    public MyNameServiceUsingDoubleNameOptions(IOptions<MyDoubleNameOptions> options)
    {
        _options = options.Value;
    }

    public string? GetName(bool someCondition)
    {
        return someCondition ? _options.FirstName : _options.SecondName;
    }
}
```

This is a fairly simple implementation; we inject `IOptions<MyDoubleNameOptions>` into the constructor and use the tertiary operator to return the first or second name from the options. Now that we have our reusable tests and the `MyNameServiceUsingDoubleNameOptions` class, we can add the concrete test class, which runs the actual tests against our implementation:

```
public class MyNameServiceUsingDoubleNameOptionsTest :
MyNameServiceTest<MyNameServiceUsingDoubleNameOptions> { }
```

Yes, that's it; all the plumbing has been done in the base test. When running the tests, everything should be green! By injecting options this way, we control their values from the composition root, allowing us to configure them as we wish without impacting the consumers' code of such options. Let's continue to explore more options, starting by naming options objects.

Named options

Using the Options pattern, we can register multiple instances of the same type and access them by name.

Note

Doing this breaks the inversion of control, dependency inversion, and open/closed principles by giving back the dependencies' creation control to the consuming class instead of moving that responsibility out of it, up to the composition root.

Since the .NET teams deemed it appropriate to implement named options, we are going to cover it here. Instead of hardcoding a magic string inside constructors, we could use this pattern to build a dynamic application without compromising any principles by dynamically accessing the name of the options to create.

This could use a database or some other settings, for example. The feature is not wrong in itself, but problems could arise based on its usage.

For this example, we are going to create three different implementations: one using IOptionsFactory<MyOptions>, one using IOptionsMonitor<MyOptions>, and one using IOptionsSnapshot<MyOptions>. All three use the test suite we created in the previous sample. Let's take a look at the code:

```
public class MyNameServiceUsingNamedOptionsFactory : IMyNameService
{
    private readonly MyOptions _options1;
    private readonly MyOptions _options2;

    public MyNameServiceUsingNamedOptionsFactory(IOptionsFactory<MyOptions>
myOptions)
    {
        _options1 = myOptions.Create("Options1");
        _options2 = myOptions.Create("Options2");
    }

    public string? GetName(bool someCondition)
    {
        return someCondition ? _options1.Name : _options2.Name;
    }
}

public class MyNameServiceUsingNamedOptionsMonitor : IMyNameService
{
    private readonly MyOptions _options1;
    private readonly MyOptions _options2;

    public MyNameServiceUsingNamedOptionsMonitor(IOptionsMonitor<MyOptions>
myOptions)
    {
        _options1 = myOptions.Get("Options1");
        _options2 = myOptions.Get("Options2");
    }

    public string? GetName(bool someCondition)
    {
```

```
            return someCondition ? _options1.Name : _options2.Name;
    }
}


public class MyNameServiceUsingNamedOptionsSnapshot : IMyNameService
{
    private readonly MyOptions _options1;
    private readonly MyOptions _options2;

    public MyNameServiceUsingNamedOptionsSnapshot(IOptionsSnapshot<MyOptions>
myOptions)
    {
        _options1 = myOptions.Get("Options1");
        _options2 = myOptions.Get("Options2");
    }
    public string? GetName(bool someCondition)
    {
        return someCondition ? _options1.Name : _options2.Name;
    }
}
```

These three classes are very similar, except for their constructors; each is expecting a different dependency.

Note

My note about magic strings may make more sense now; each class requests a specific set of options using a hardcoded name; that is, a *magic string*. Doing so limits our ability to change the injected options in any single class from the composition root. To make a change, we need to open the class, change the magic strings, save the class, and then recompile. Moreover, strings are not automatically refactored using the tooling, leading to inconsistencies and runtime errors. We can also make typos when writing those magic strings, leading to unexpected runtime errors or behaviors. So, all in all, magic strings are harder to maintain and should be avoided as much as possible.

Next, we need to create the following three simple classes:

```
public class MyNameServiceUsingNamedOptionsFactoryTest :
MyNameServiceTest<MyNameServiceUsingNamedOptionsFactory> {}


public class MyNameServiceUsingNamedOptionsMonitorTest :
MyNameServiceTest<MyNameServiceUsingNamedOptionsMonitor> {}
```

```
public class MyNameServiceUsingNamedOptionsSnapshotTest :
MyNameServiceTest<MyNameServiceUsingNamedOptionsSnapshot> {}
```

Running these tests proves that our three new classes respect our use cases. With that, we have created multiple classes that use named options.

With these, we explored the named options semantic behind each interface. If you can't avoid using named options, remember to pick the interface that has the correct lifetime for your use case. Moreover, centralizing the names in constants should help you limit magic string issues. Unless you build a more complex system, chances are that you are breaking many SOLID principles just by using named options.

Of course, building options manually like that is good for tests but in programs, you most likely have one or more sources from where those options come from, which is what we explore next.

Using settings

Now that we've explored how to create options manually, let's explore how to make that happen in an ASP.NET Core application using appsettings.json instead.

The appsettings.json file allows you to define any setting, structured as you want, in the JSON syntax. It is a great improvement from the key/value settings that we had in the web.config file before ASP.NET Core. You can now define complex object hierarchies, which allow for better organization. You also don't need to program complex plumbing code, like you had to do to create custom web.config sections.

Here are our JSON settings (default settings are omitted):

```
{
  "options1": {
    "name": "Options 1"
  },
  "options2": {
    "name": "Options 2"
  },
  "myDoubleNameOptions": {
    "firstName": "Options 1",
    "secondName": "Options 2"
  }
}
```

The data structures here are the same as our previously defined classes; that is, MyOptions and MyDoubleNameOptions. That's because we are about to load (deserialize) those settings into our classes using the utilities provided by .NET.

Here is the first half of the Program.cs file, where we register our program dependencies:

```
var builder = WebApplication.CreateBuilder(args);
builder.Services
```

```
    .Configure<MyOptions>(
        "Options1",
        builder.Configuration.GetSection("options1"))
    .Configure<MyOptions>(
        "Options2",
        builder.Configuration.GetSection("options2"))
    .Configure<MyDoubleNameOptions>(
        builder.Configuration.GetSection("myDoubleNameOptions"))
    .AddTransient<MyNameServiceUsingDoubleNameOptions>()
    .AddTransient<MyNameServiceUsingNamedOptionsFactory>()
    .AddTransient<MyNameServiceUsingNamedOptionsMonitor>()
    .AddTransient<MyNameServiceUsingNamedOptionsSnapshot>()
;
```

We are using two different extension methods here instead of configuring the options manually, as we did previously. The `builder.Configuration` property is an instance of `ConfigurationManager` that implements the `IConfiguration` interface, which allows us to access the application settings. Calling `builder.Configuration.GetSection("key")` gives us another `IConfiguration` object—more precisely, an `IConfigurationSection` object—where the keys match our settings. After that, we registered our four services with a transient lifetime.

Note

If you need to access a subsection, you can use the : sign. For example, with a configuration that looks like { "object1": { "object2": {} } }, you could use `GetSection("object1:object2")` to get the nested configuration object directly.

Once this is done, we can inject any of those dependencies anywhere we want to. For this example, I've decided to leverage minimal APIs, leading to the following extremely simple endpoints (the other half of the `Program.cs` file):

```
var app = builder.Build();
app.MapGet("/options/{someCondition}", (bool someCondition,
MyNameServiceUsingDoubleNameOptions service)
    => new { name = service.GetName(someCondition) });

app.MapGet("/factory/{someCondition}", (bool someCondition,
MyNameServiceUsingNamedOptionsFactory service)
    => new { name = service.GetName(someCondition) });

app.MapGet("/monitor/{someCondition}", (bool someCondition,
MyNameServiceUsingNamedOptionsMonitor service)
    => new { name = service.GetName(someCondition) });
```

```
app.MapGet("/snapshot/{someCondition}", (bool someCondition,
MyNameServiceUsingNamedOptionsSnapshot service)
    => new { name = service.GetName(someCondition) });
app.Run();
```

Each endpoint takes a bool (from the route) and a service (from the IoC container) as parameters. Each endpoint dispatches that bool to the injected service and returns an anonymous object that has a name property. That object gets serialized as JSON with a 200 OK status code, thanks to minimal APIs.

Note

I also added an endpoint that responds with a list of links when a user calls GET /. I omitted the code as it is not relevant to the example, but it is convenient when running it. If you have a plugin in your browser that formats the JSON string for you, the links should be clickable. I use *JSON Viewer*, an open source project, in both Chrome and Edge on Chromium for this.

That's it! We've loaded options from JSON to our objects using a few lines of code. Feel free to run the code, add breakpoints, and explore how the app behaves.

We connected the dots with those few additional lines by registering the dependencies with the IoC container. We loaded the values from the appsettings.json file using the .NET configuration API and can now consume those options using dependency injection.

These are very simple scenarios that allowed us to explore the basics of the .NET options. Moving options to external sources, like in the appsettings.json file, opens the possibility to configure our program without the need to recompile it. For example, we can have development settings, development secrets (credentials for example), staging settings, production settings, and so on. Layering settings the .NET way allows controlling the settings at different levels, including not committing credentials to your Git repository or limiting access to production credentials.

Loading options from settings like we did here is a very likely scenario that happens in most programs. Of course, there are even more options, leading us next to looking at different ways to configure options objects.

Project – OptionsConfiguration

Now that we have covered some simple scenarios, let's attack some more advanced possibilities, such as creating types that will help configure, initialize, and validate our options, starting with configuration.

We can create types that implement IConfigureOptions<TOptions>, then register these implementations as services to dynamically configure our options.

Note

We can implement IConfigureNamedOptions<TOptions> for named options as well.

First, we must lay out the groundwork for our little program:

1. The first building block is the options class that we want to configure:

```
namespace OptionsConfiguration;
public class ConfigureMeOptions
{
    public string? Title { get; set; }
    public IEnumerable<string> Lines { get; set; } = Enumerable.
Empty<string>();
}
```

2. Now, let's define our application settings in the appsettings.json file (default settings omitted):

```
{
  "configureMe": {
    "title": "Configure Me!",
    "lines": [
      "This comes from appsettings!"
    ]
  }
}
```

3. Next, let's make an endpoint that accesses the settings, serializes the result to a JSON string, and then writes it to the response stream:

```
app.MapGet("/configure-me", (IOptionsMonitor<ConfigureMeOptions> options)
=> options);
```

This endpoint displays the latest options, even if we change the content of appsettings.json without changing the code or restarting the server.

4. Before we can run the program, we need to tell ASP.NET about those settings:

```
builder.Services.Configure<ConfigureMeOptions>(builder.Configuration.
GetSection("configureMe"));
```

5. Now, when running the program and navigating to /configure-me, we should see the following:

```
{
  "CurrentValue": {
    "Title": "Configure Me!",
    "Lines": [
      "This comes from appsettings!"
    ]
  }
}
```

CurrentValue is the property name and can be accessed from IOptionsMonitor<TOptions>. Besides that, the rest of the JSON code looks very similar to the value we configured in the appsettings.json file.

Now that we've created the option class, configured the IoT container, added an endpoint, and set values in the settings.json file, we are ready to implement our first object to configure the ConfigureMeOptions instances.

Implementing a configurator object

Now, let's configure our options in another class, enforcing the single responsibility principle. We have an option object and another object that configures such options.

Let's start by creating the Configure1ConfigureMeOptions class that adds a line to the ConfigureMeOptions instance dynamically. To achieve this, we must create a class that implements the IConfigureOptions<TOptions> interface, like this:

```
public class Configure1ConfigureMeOptions :
IConfigureOptions<ConfigureMeOptions>
{
    public void Configure(ConfigureMeOptions options)
    {
        options.Lines = options.Lines.Append("Added line 1!");
    }
}
```

We must then register it with the service collection:

```
builder.Services.AddSingleton<IConfigureOptions<ConfigureMeOptions>,
Configure1ConfigureMeOptions>();
```

From there, navigating to /configure-me should output the following:

```
{
  "currentValue": {
    "title": "Configure Me!",
    "lines": [
      "This comes from appsettings!",
      "Added line 1!"
    ]
  }
}
```

And voilà—we have a neat result that took almost no effort. This can lead to so many possibilities! Implementing IConfigureOptions<TOptions> is the best way to configure the default values of an options class. Next, we explore how a system reacts when having multiple of those configurators.

Using multiple configurator objects

As fun as the previous example was, we now explore how we can register many ICongigureOptions<TOptions> for the same TOptions instance as easily as registering a new service binding.

For our purposes, let's create another class that adds another line to the array. This allows us to follow what is happening in the background (running a sort of trace):

```
public class Configure2ConfigureMeOptions :
IConfigureOptions<ConfigureMeOptions>
{
    public void Configure(ConfigureMeOptions options)
    {
        options.Lines = options.Lines.Append("Added line 2!");
    }
}
```

Now, we can register it:

```
builder.Services.AddSingleton<IConfigureOptions<ConfigureMeOptions>,
Configure2ConfigureMeOptions>();
```

The new output should be as follows:

```
{
  "currentValue": {
  "title": "Configure Me!",
  "lines": [
    "This comes from appsettings!",
    "Added line 1!",
    "Added line 2!"
    ]
  }
}
```

It is important to note that the dependencies that have been registered with IServiceCollection are ordered, so by swapping the registration of Configure1ConfigureMeOptions and Configure2ConfigureMeOptions, we would end up with the following output instead:

```
{
  "currentValue": {
    "title": "Configure Me!",
    "lines": [
      "This comes from appsettings!",
      "Added line 2!",
      "Added line 1!"
```

```
    ]
  }
}
```

Great, right? Now that we know we can create and use multiple configurator objects, we could have many of those configurator objects that each configure part of a bigger options object or change options objects we don't control by creating a new configurator object. Next, we explore a few more possibilities before looking at validating those options.

Exploring other configuration possibilities

There are other ways to configure options; for instance:

- We can call the `Configure` extension methods multiple times.

- `ConfigureAll` allows us to run configuration on all the options of any given `TOptions`. This is primarily used to configure named options, but unnamed options are just named options associated with the default name, so in our example, this works as well.

- `PostConfigure` and `PostConfigureAll` are the equivalents of `Configure` and `ConfigureAll`, respectively, but they run at the end of the initialization process.

To demonstrate that, let's add the following lines to the composition root:

```
builder.Services.Configure<ConfigureMeOptions>(options
    => options.Lines = options.Lines.Append("Another Configure call"));
builder.Services.PostConfigure<ConfigureMeOptions>(options
    => options.Lines = options.Lines.Append("What about PostConfigure?"));
builder.Services.PostConfigureAll<ConfigureMeOptions>(options
    => options.Lines = options.Lines.Append("Did you forgot about
PostConfigureAll?"));
builder.Services.ConfigureAll<ConfigureMeOptions>(options
    => options.Lines = options.Lines.Append("Or ConfigureAll?"));
```

When executing the program, we now end up with the following output:

```
{
  "currentValue": {
    "title": "Configure Me!",
    "lines": [
      "This comes from appsettings!",
      "Added line 1!",
      "Added line 2!",
      "Another Configure call",
      "Or ConfigureAll?",
      "What about PostConfigure?",
      "Did you forgot about PostConfigureAll?"
```

```
        ]
    }
}
```

The registration order matters here because, under the hood, the framework is creating instances that implement IConfigureOptions<ConfigureMeOptions> and registers them with the service collection.

The post-configuration extension points are a bit of a rule-breaker as they run after the configure methods, but the order between them also matters. If options configuration is still unclear, please play around with this example. I find experimentation to be one of the best ways to learn and improve.

Now that we know the options interface types, their lifetimes, and many ways to configure their values, it is time to validate them and enforce a certain level of integrity in our programs.

Project – OptionsValidation

Another feature that comes out of the box is options validation, which allows us to run validation code when a TOptions object is created. This code is guaranteed to run the first time an option is created and does not account for subsequent options modifications. If the lifetime is transient, the validation runs every time you get an options object. If its lifetime is scoped, it runs once per scope (once per HTTP request in the case of ASP.NET Core). If its lifetime is singleton, it runs once per application.

To validate options, we can create validation types that implement the IValidateOptions<TOptions> interface or use data annotations such as [Required]. Implementing the interface works very similarly to the options configuration.

Eager validation

Eager validation has been added to .NET 6 and allows catching incorrectly configured options at startup time, in a fail-fast mindset.

The Microsoft.Extensions.Hosting assembly adds the ValidateOnStart extension method to the OptionsBuilder<TOptions> type.

There are different ways of using this, including the following, which binds a configuration section to an option class:

```
services.AddOptions<Options>()
    .Configure(o => /* Omitted configuration code */)
    .ValidateOnStart()
;
```

The highlighted line is all we need to apply our validation rules during startup. I recommend using this as your new default, so you know at startup time that options are misconfigured instead of later at runtime, limiting unexpected issues.

Now that we know that, let's look at how to configure options validation.

Data annotations

Let's start by using `System.ComponentModel.DataAnnotations` types to decorate our options with validation attributes. To demonstrate this, let's look at two small tests:

```
using Microsoft.Extensions.DependencyInjection;
using Microsoft.Extensions.Options;
using System.ComponentModel.DataAnnotations;
using Xunit;

namespace OptionsValidation;

public class ValidateOptionsWithDataAnnotations
{
    [Fact]
    public void Should_pass_validation()
    {
        var services = new ServiceCollection();
        services.AddOptions<Options>()
            .Configure(o => o.MyImportantProperty = "Some important value")
            .ValidateDataAnnotations();
        var serviceProvider = services.BuildServiceProvider();
        var options = serviceProvider.
GetRequiredService<IOptionsMonitor<Options>>();
        Assert.Equal("Some important value", options.CurrentValue.
MyImportantProperty);
    }


    [Fact]
    public void Should_fail_validation()
    {
        var services = new ServiceCollection();
        services.AddOptions<Options>()
            .ValidateDataAnnotations();
        var serviceProvider = services.BuildServiceProvider();
        var options = serviceProvider.
GetRequiredService<IOptionsMonitor<Options>>();
        var error = Assert.Throws<OptionsValidationException>(() => options.
CurrentValue);
        Assert.Collection(error.Failures,
            f => Assert.Equal("DataAnnotation validation failed for 'Options'
members: 'MyImportantProperty' with the error: 'The MyImportantProperty field
is required.'.", f)
```

```
        );
    }

    private class Options
    {
        [Required]
        public string? MyImportantProperty { get; set; }
    }
}
```

From these tests, we can see that setting MyImportantProperty allows us to use our options object, while not setting it throws an OptionsValidationException, alerting us of the error.

To tell .NET to validate data annotations on options, we must call the ValidateDataAnnotations extension method, which is available from the Microsoft.Extensions.Options.DataAnnotations assembly, like this:

```
services
    .AddOptions<Options>()
    .ValidateDataAnnotations()
;
```

That's it—.NET does the job for us from there and validates our instance of the Options class using the data annotation, like you can do when using EF Core or MVC model binding. In our case, .NET validates that the value of the MyImportantProperty property is not null or empty ([Required] attribute).

From there, if we were running that code in an actual web app, we could add eager validation by calling the ValidateOnStart method like this:

```
services.AddOptions<Options>()
    .ValidateDataAnnotations()
    .ValidateOnStart() // eager validation
;
```

Now that we know how to validate our options objects using data annotations, let's see how to leverage validation classes instead. Data annotations are good, but adding metadata to types is not always the most flexible way of doing things, and requires reflection, which is sometimes less instinctive than object-oriented programming. Reflection is also slower, but that is not as much of a concern nowadays as it was years ago; nevertheless, keep an eye out when writing code that uses reflection, and don't worry about what the framework offers you.

Validation types

To implement validation types for options (options validators), we can create a class that implements one or more IValidateOptions<TOptions> interfaces. One type can validate multiple options, and multiple types can validate the same options, so the possible combinations should be covering all possible use cases.

Using a custom class is no harder than using data annotations. However, it allows us to remove the validation concerns away from the options class itself and code more complex validation logic. You should pick the way that makes the most sense for your project.

Here is how to do this via code:

```csharp
using Microsoft.Extensions.DependencyInjection;
using Microsoft.Extensions.Options;
using Xunit;

namespace OptionsValidation;

public class ValidateOptionsWithTypes
{
    [Fact]
    public void Should_pass_validation()
    {
        var services = new ServiceCollection();
        services.AddSingleton<IValidateOptions<Options>, OptionsValidator>();
        services.AddOptions<Options>()
            .Configure(o => o.MyImportantProperty = "Some important value")
            .ValidateOnStart()
        ;
        var serviceProvider = services.BuildServiceProvider();
        var options = serviceProvider.
GetRequiredService<IOptionsMonitor<Options>>();
        Assert.Equal("Some important value", options.CurrentValue.
MyImportantProperty);
    }

    [Fact]
    public void Should_fail_validation()
    {
        var services = new ServiceCollection();
        services.AddSingleton<IValidateOptions<Options>, OptionsValidator>();
        services.AddOptions<Options>().ValidateOnStart();
        var serviceProvider = services.BuildServiceProvider();
        var options = serviceProvider.
GetRequiredService<IOptionsMonitor<Options>>();
        var error = Assert.Throws<OptionsValidationException>(() => options.
CurrentValue);
        Assert.Collection(error.Failures,
            f => Assert.Equal("'MyImportantProperty' is required.", f)
```

```
        );
    }

    private class Options
    {
        public string? MyImportantProperty { get; set; }
    }

    private class OptionsValidator : IValidateOptions<Options>
    {
        public ValidateOptionsResult Validate(string name, Options options)
        {
            if (string.IsNullOrEmpty(options.MyImportantProperty))
            {
                return ValidateOptionsResult.Fail("'MyImportantProperty' is
required.");
            }
            return ValidateOptionsResult.Success;
        }
    }
}
```

As you can see, this is the same options class we used in the previous example, without the data annotation, and both test cases are very similar as well. The difference is that instead of using the [Required] attribute, we created the OptionsValidator class, which contains the validation logic.

OptionsValidator implements IValidateOptions<Options>, which only contains the ValidateOptionsResult Validate(string name, Options options) method. This method allows named and default options to be validated. The name argument represents the options' names. In our case, we implemented the required logic for all options. The ValidateOptionsResult class exposes a few members to help us out, such as the Success and Skip fields, as well as two Fail() methods.

ValidateOptionsResult.Success indicates success. ValidateOptionsResult.Skip indicates that the validator did not validate the options, most likely because it only validates certain named options but not the given one. For failure, we can fail with either a single message or a collection of messages by calling ValidateOptionsResult.Fail(message) or ValidateOptionsResult.Fail(messages).

The next step is to make the validator available in the IoC container. In our case, we could do this using a simple services.AddSingleton<IValidateOptions<Options>, OptionsValidator>() call, but we could also scan one or more assemblies to register all our validators "automagically."

Then, as with the data annotations, the validation is executed against that instance when we first use the options. Using types to validate options is handy when you don't want to use data annotations, can't use data annotations, or need to implement certain logic that is easier with a class than with attributes.

Next, we glance at how to leverage options with FluentValidation.

Project — OptionsValidationFluentValidation

In this project, we validate options classes using FluentValidation. FluentValidation is a popular open source library that provides a validation framework different from data annotations. We explore FluentValidation more in *Chapter 15, Getting Started with Vertical Slice Architecture*, but that should not hinder you from following along with this example.

There are existing packages built by different people around using FluentValidation to validate options, but I want to show you how to leverage a few patterns that we've learned so far to implement it ourselves with only a few lines of code. In this micro-project, we leverage:

- Dependency injection
- The Strategy design pattern
- The Options pattern
- Options validation: validation types
- Options validation: eager validation

Let's start with the options class itself:

```
public class MyOptions
{
    public string? Name { get; set; }
}
```

The options class is very thin, containing only a nullable `Name` property. Next, let's look at the FluentValidation validator, which validates that the `Name` property is not empty:

```
public class MyOptionsValidator : AbstractValidator<MyOptions>
{
    public MyOptionsValidator()
    {
        RuleFor(x => x.Name).NotEmpty();
    }
}
```

If you have never used FluentValidation before, the `AbstractValidator<T>` class implements the `IValidator<T>` interface and adds utility methods like `RuleFor`.

To make ASP.NET Core validate `MyOptions` instances using FluentValidation, we can implement an `IValidateOptions<TOptions>` interface as we did in the previous example, inject our validator, and then leverage it to ensure the validity of `MyOptions` objects.

Here is a generic implementation of such a class that could be reused for any type of options:

```
public class FluentValidateOptions<TOptions> : IValidateOptions<TOptions>
    where TOptions : class
```

```
{
    private readonly IValidator<TOptions> _validator;
    public FluentValidateOptions(IValidator<TOptions> validator)
    {
        _validator = validator;
    }

    public ValidateOptionsResult Validate(string name, TOptions options)
    {
        var validationResult = _validator.Validate(options);
        if (validationResult.IsValid)
        {
            return ValidateOptionsResult.Success;
        }
        var errorMessages = validationResult.Errors.Select(x =>
x.ErrorMessage);
        return ValidateOptionsResult.Fail(errorMessages);
    }
}
```

In the preceding code, the `FluentValidateOptions<TOptions>` class adapts the `IValidateOptions<TOptions>` interface to the `IValidator<TOptions>` interface by leveraging FluentValidation in the `Validate` method. In a nutshell, we use the output of one system and make it an input of another system.

 This type of adaptation is known as the Adapter design pattern. We explore the Adapter pattern in the next chapter.

Now that we have all the building blocks, let's have a look at the composition root:

```
using FluentValidation;
using Microsoft.Extensions.Options;

var builder = WebApplication.CreateBuilder(args);
builder.Services
    .AddSingleton<IValidator<MyOptions>, MyOptionsValidator>()
    .AddSingleton<IValidateOptions<MyOptions>,
FluentValidateOptions<MyOptions>>()
;
builder.Services
    .AddOptions<MyOptions>()
```

```
    // Uncomment the following line to make the application start
    //.Bind(builder.Configuration.GetSection("MyOptions"))
    .ValidateOnStart()
;
var app = builder.Build();
app.MapGet("/", () => "Hello World!");
app.Run();
```

The highlighted code is the key to this system. It registers the FluentValidation `MyOptionsValidator` that contains the validation rules. Then it registers the generic `FluentValidateOptions<MyOptions>` instance as an `IValidateOptions<MyOptions>` interface that .NET will use to validate the `MyOptions` options. The `FluentValidateOptions` class uses the `MyOptionsValidator` to internally validate the options.

When running the program, unless you uncomment the `Bind` line, the console yields the following error:

```
Unhandled exception. Microsoft.Extensions.Options.OptionsValidationException:
'Name' must not be empty.
```

This is a good use case that can leverage validation types instead of data annotations. Moreover, it took around 50 lines of code to write a generic wrapper around FluentValidation and use it to validate our options class.

Now that we've explored many ways to configure and validate options objects, it is time to look at a way to inject options classes directly either by choice or to work around a library capability issue.

Workaround – Injecting options directly

The only negative point about the .NET Options pattern is that we need to tie our code to the framework's interfaces, meaning that we need to inject an interface like `IOptionsMonitor<Options>` instead of the `Options` class itself. By letting the consumers choose the interface, we let them control the lifetime of the options.

> **Note**
>
> As we explored in the *Getting started* section of this chapter, the `IOptions`, `IOptionsFactory`, `IOptionsMonitor`, and `IOptionsSnapshot` interfaces define the options object's lifetime.

In most cases, I prefer to inject `Options` directly, controlling its lifetime from the composition root, instead of letting the class itself control its dependencies. I'm a little *anti-control-freak*, I know.

It just so happens that we can circumvent this easily with a little trick. Here, we need to do two things:

1. Set up the `Options` pattern, as shown previously in this chapter.
2. Create a dependency binding that tells the container how to inject the options class that we want directly.

The following code from the OptionsValidation project does the same thing as our previous examples and uses scopes to demonstrate scoping:

```
using Microsoft.Extensions.DependencyInjection;
using Microsoft.Extensions.Options;
using Xunit;

namespace OptionsValidation
{
    public class ByPassingInterfaces
    {
        [Fact]
        public void Should_support_any_scope()
        {
            var services = new ServiceCollection();
            services.AddOptions<Options>()
                .Configure(o => o.MyImportantProperty = "Some important
value");
```

Here, we are registering the Options class and then configuring the default value of MyImportantProperty like we did in previous examples:

```
            services.AddScoped(sp =>
    sp.GetRequiredService<IOptionsSnapshot<Options>>().Value);
```

In the preceding code block, we registered the Options class using a factory method. That way, we can inject the Options class directly (with a scoped lifetime). We control the creation and the lifetime from that delegate (highlighted code).

And voilà, we can now inject Options directly into our system without the need to tie our classes with any .NET-specific options interface. Next, we test that out:

```
            var serviceProvider = services.BuildServiceProvider();
            using var scope1 = serviceProvider.CreateScope();
            var options1 = scope1.ServiceProvider. GetService<Options>();
            var options2 = scope1.ServiceProvider. GetService<Options>();
            Assert.Same(options1, options2);
```

The preceding code asserts that the two instances acquired from the same scope are the same:

```
            using var scope2 = serviceProvider.CreateScope();
            var options3 = scope2.ServiceProvider. GetService<Options>();
            Assert.NotSame(options2, options3);
        }
```

The preceding code asserts that the options from two different scopes are not the same:

```
private class Options
{
    public string? MyImportantProperty { get; set; }
}
    }
}
```

Finally, we had our `Options` class, which allowed us to write those tests.

This can also be a good workaround for an existing system that could benefit from the Options pattern without us having to update its code, assuming the system is dependency injection-ready. We can also use this trick to compile an assembly that does not depend on `Microsoft.Extensions.Options`. By using this trick, we can set the lifetime of the options from the composition root (here we used scoped), which is a more classic dependency injection-enabled flow.

Conclusion

The Options pattern is a great way to inject strongly typed options classes to configure our applications. We first explored the following options interfaces:

- `IOptionsMonitor<TOptions>` or `IOptions<TOptions>` for singleton
- `IOptionsSnapshot<TOptions>` for scoped
- `IOptionsFactory<TOptions>` for transient

We also covered multiple ways to configure and validate our options classes. We can load settings from a file or configure them using custom classes that implement the `IConfigureOptions<TOptions>` interface. We can then validate options using data annotations or custom classes that implement the `IValidateOptions<TOptions>` interface.

All in all, these .NET options provide us with very flexible ways to inject options into our systems, and I strongly recommend that you start using them today, if you are not already. This can help improve the testability of your systems, and it also makes it easier to manage the changes of your applications since we can configure options from the composition root.

Finally, we explored a trick to bypass injecting the framework's interfaces and injected the options classes directly instead, leading to controlling the lifetime and the instantiation of options classes from the composition root instead of from the consumer class.

The Options pattern helps us stay in line with the **SOLID** principles, as follows:

- **S:** The Options pattern divides managing settings into multiple pieces where each has a single responsibility. Loading unmanaged settings into strongly typed classes is one responsibility, validating options using classes is another, and configuring options from multiple independent sources is one more. On the other hand, I find data annotations validation to mix two responsibilities in the options class, bending this principle. If you like data annotations, I don't want to stop you from using them.

Data annotations can improve development speed but make the validation rules harder to test. For example, it is easier to test a `Validate` method that returns a `ValidateOptionsResult` object than attributes.

- **O**: The different `IOptions[*]<Toptions>` interfaces break this principle by forcing the consumer to decide what lifetime the options should have and what capabilities. To change the lifetime of a dependency, we must update the consuming class when using the default interfaces. On the other hand, we explored an easy and flexible workaround that allows us to bypass this issue for many scenarios and inject the options directly, inverting the dependency flow again, leading to open/closed consumers.

- **L**: N/A

- **I**: The `IValidateOptions<TOptions>` and `IconfigureOptions<TOptions>` interfaces are two good examples of segregating a system into smaller interfaces where each has a single purpose.

- **D**: The Options framework is built around interfaces, allowing us to depend on abstractions. The `IOptions[*]<Toptions>` interfaces are the exceptions to this. Even if they are interfaces, they tie us to implementation details like the options lifetime. In this case, I think it is more beneficial to inject the options object directly (a data contract) instead of those interfaces.

Next, we explore .NET logging, which is another very important aspect of building applications; good traceability can make all the difference when observing or debugging applications.

Becoming familiar with .NET logging abstractions

Another improvement of .NET Core over .NET Framework is its logging abstractions. Instead of relying on third-party libraries, the new, uniform system offers clean interfaces that are backed by a flexible and robust mechanism that helps implement logging into your application. It also supports third-party libraries that are streamlined through that abstraction. Before we look at the implementation in more detail, let's talk about logging.

About logging

Logging is the practice of writing messages into a log and cataloging information for later use. That information can be used to debug errors, trace operations, analyze usage, or any other reason that creative people can come up with. Logging is a cross-cutting concern, meaning it applies to every piece of your application. We talk about layers in *Chapter 12, Understanding Layering*, but until then, let's just say that a cross-cutting concern affects all layers and cannot be centralized in just one.

A log is made up of log entries. We can view each log entry as an event that happened during the program's execution. Those events are then written to the log. This log can be a file, a remote system, simply `stdout`, or a combination of multiple destinations.

When creating a log entry, we must also think about the level of that log entry. In a way, this level represents the type of message or the level of importance that we want to log. It can also be used to filter those logs. `Trace`, `Error`, and `Debug` are examples of log entry levels. Those levels are defined in the `Microsoft.Extensions.Logging.LogLevel` enum.

Another important aspect of a log entry is how it is structured. You can log a single string. Everyone on your team could log single strings in their own way. But what happens when someone searches for information? Chaos ensues! There's the stress of not finding what that person is looking for and the displeasure of the log's structure, as experienced by that same person. One way to fix this is by using structured logging. It is simple yet complex; you need to create a structure that every log entry follows. That structure could be more or less complex. It could be serialized into JSON. The important part is that the log entries are structured. We won't get into this subject here, but if you have to decide on a logging strategy, I recommend digging into structured logging first. If you are part of a team, then chances are someone else already did. If that's not the case, you can always bring it up. Continuous improvement is a key aspect of life.

We could write a whole book on logging, best logging practices, structured logging, and distributed logging, but this chapter aims to teach you how to use .NET logging abstractions.

Writing logs

First, the logging system is provider-based, meaning that you must register one or more `ILoggerProvider` instances if you want your log entries to go somewhere. By default, when calling `Host.CreateDefaultBuilder(args)` or `WebApplication.CreateBuilder(args)`, it registers the Console, Debug, EventSource, and EventLog (Windows only) providers, but this list can be modified. You can add and remove providers if you need to. The required dependencies for using logging in the application are also registered as part of this process.

> **Note**
>
> The default configurations are part of the `ConfigureDefaults` extension method in the `HostingHostBuilderExtensions` class (see GitHub: `https://adpg.link/A5nF`).

Before we look at the code, let's learn how to create log entries, which is the objective behind logging. To create an entry, we can use one of the following interfaces: `ILogger`, `ILogger<T>`, or `ILoggerFactory`. Let's take a look at them in more detail:

- `ILogger` is the base abstraction.
- `ILogger<T>` uses `T` to automatically create the logging *category*.
- `ILoggerFactory` allows us to create an `ILogger` with a custom category name.

The following is the more commonly used pattern, which consists of injecting an `ILogger<T>` interface and storing it in an `ILogger` field before using it, like this:

```
public class Service : IService
{
    private readonly ILogger _logger;
    public Service(ILogger<Service> logger)
    {
        _logger = logger ?? throw new ArgumentNullException(nameof(logger));
```

```
    }
    public void Execute()
    {
        _logger.LogInformation("Service.Execute()");
    }
}
```

In the preceding code, we have the private `ILogger` `_logger` field in the `Service` class. We inject an `ILogger<Service>` logger that we store in that field and then use that member in the `Execute` method to write an information-level message to the log.

The `IService` interface is very simple and only exposes a single `Execute` method for testing purposes:

```
public interface IService
{
    void Execute();
}
```

I loaded a small library that I created to test this out, which provides additional logging providers for testing purposes. With that, we are creating a generic host (`IHost`) since we don't need a `WebApplication` in our tests, then we configure it:

```
namespace Logging;
public class BaseAbstractions
{
    [Fact]
    public void Should_log_the_Service_Execute_line()
    {
        // Arrange
        var lines = new List<string>();
        var host = Host.CreateDefaultBuilder()
            .ConfigureLogging(loggingBuilder =>
            {
                loggingBuilder.ClearProviders();
                loggingBuilder.AddAssertableLogger(lines);
            })
            .ConfigureServices(services =>
            {
                services.AddSingleton<IService, Service>();
            })
            .Build();
        var service = host.Services.GetRequiredService<IService>();

        // Act
```

```
        service.Execute();

        // Assert
        Assert.Collection(lines,
            line => Assert.Equal("Service.Execute()", line)
        );
    }
    // Omitted IService, Service, and WebApplication test
}
```

In the `Arrange` phase of the test, we create some variables, configure `IHost`, and get an instance of `IService` that we want to use to test the logging capabilities that we programmed in it.

The highlighted code removes all providers using the `ClearProviders` method and uses the `AddAssertableLogger` extension method from the library that we loaded to add a new provider. We could have just added a new provider if we wanted to, but I wanted to show you how to remove existing providers so that we can start from a clean slate. That's something you might need someday.

Note

The library that I loaded is available on NuGet and is named `ForEvolve.Testing.Logging`, but this is irrelevant to understanding logging abstractions.

In the `Act` phase, we call the `Execute` method of our service. This method logs a line to the `ILogger` implementation that is injected upon instantiation. Then, we assert that the line was written in the `lines` list (that's what `AssertableLogger` does; that is, it writes to a `List<string>`). From an ASP.NET Core application, all that logging will go to the console by default. Logging is a great way to know what is happening in the background when running the application.

The `Service` class is a simple consumer of an `ILogger<Service>` and uses that `ILogger`. You can do the same for any class that you want to add logging support to. Change `Service` by the name of that class to have a logger configured for your class. That generic argument becomes the category name the logger uses when writing log entries.

Since ASP.NET Core uses a `WebApplication` instead of a generic `IHost`, here is the same test code using that construct (usually written in `Program.cs`):

```
[Fact]
public void Should_log_the_Service_Execute_line_using_WebApplication()
{
    // Arrange
    var lines = new List<string>();
    var builder = WebApplication.CreateBuilder();
    builder.Logging.ClearProviders()
        .AddAssertableLogger(lines);
```

```
    builder.Services.AddSingleton<IService, Service>();
    var app = builder.Build();
    var service = app.Services.GetRequiredService<IService>();

    // Act
    service.Execute();

    // Assert
    Assert.Collection(lines,
        line => Assert.Equal("Service.Execute()", line)
    );
}
```

I highlighted the changes in the preceding code. In a nutshell, the extension methods used on the generic host have been replaced by WebApplicationBuilder properties like Logging and Services. Finally, the Create method creates a WebApplication instead of an IHost, exactly like in the Program.cs file.

To wrap this up, these test cases allowed us to implement the most commonly used logging pattern in ASP.NET Core and add a custom provider to make sure that we logged the correct information. Logging is very important and adds visibility to production systems. Without logs, you don't know what is happening in your system, unless you are the only one using it, which is very unlikely. You can also log what is happening in your infrastructure and run security scans in real time on those log streams to quickly identify security breaches or system failures. These subjects are out of the scope of this book, but having strong logging capabilities at the application level can only help your overall logging strategy.

Before moving on to the next subject, let's explore an example that leverages the ILoggerFactory interface, sets a custom category name, and uses an ILogger instance to log a message. This should be very similar to the previous example. Here's the whole code:

```
namespace Logging;
public class LoggerFactoryExploration
{
    private readonly ITestOutputHelper _output;
    public LoggerFactoryExploration(ITestOutputHelper output)
    {
        _output = output ?? throw new ArgumentNullException(nameof(output));
    }

    [Fact]
    public void Create_a_ILoggerFactory()
    {
        // Arrange
```

```
        var lines = new List<string>();
        var host = Host.CreateDefaultBuilder()
            .ConfigureLogging(loggingBuilder => loggingBuilder
                .AddAssertableLogger(lines)
                .AddxUnitTestOutput(_output))
            .ConfigureServices(services => services.AddSingleton<Service>())
            .Build()
        ;
        var service = host.Services.GetRequiredService<Service>();

        // Act
        service.Execute();

        // Assert
        Assert.Collection(lines,
            line => Assert.Equal("LogInformation like any ILogger<T>.", line)
        );
    }

    public class Service
    {
        private readonly ILogger _logger;
        public Service(ILoggerFactory loggerFactory)
        {
            ArgumentNullException.ThrowIfNull(loggerFactory);
            _logger = loggerFactory.CreateLogger("Some custom category name");
        }

        public void Execute()
        {
            _logger.LogInformation("LogInformation like any ILogger<T>.");
        }
    }
}
```

The preceding code should look very familiar. Let's focus on the highlighted lines, which relate to the current pattern:

1. We inject the `ILoggerFactory` interface into the `Service` class constructor (instead of an `ILogger<Service>`).
2. We create an `ILogger` instance with the `"Some custom category name"` category name.
3. That logger is assigned to the `_logger` field.
4. We then use that `ILogger` like any other logger.

As a rule of thumb, I suggest you stick with ILogger<T> as much as possible, but if you ever need a more dynamic way for setting the category name for your logs, you can leverage the ILoggerFactory instead. By default, when using ILogger<T>, the category name is the T parameter. The ILoggerFactory interface is more of an internal piece than something made for us to consume; nonetheless, it exists and could satisfy some use cases.

> **Note**
>
> In the preceding example, the ITestOutputHelper interface is part of the Xunit. Abstractions assembly and allows us to write lines as *standard output* to the test log. That output is available in the Visual Studio Test Explorer.

Now that we have covered how to write log entries, and since all log entries are not created equal, let's look at **log levels** next.

Log levels

In the previous examples, we used the LogInformation method to log information messages, but there are other levels as well, shown in the following table:

Level	Method	Description	Production
Trace	LogTrace	This is used to capture detailed information about the program, instrument execution speed, and debugging. You can also log sensitive information when using traces.	Disabled.
Debug	LogDebug	This is used to log debugging and development information.	Disabled unless troubleshooting.
Information	LogInformation	This is used to track the flow of the application. Normal events that occur in the system are often information-level events, such as the system started, the system stopped, and a user has signed in.	Enabled.
Warning	LogWarning	This is used to log abnormal behavior in the application flow that does not cause the program to stop, but that may need to be investigated; for example, handled exceptions, failed network calls, and accessing resources that do not exist.	Enabled.
Error	LogError	This is used to log errors in the application flow that do not cause the application to stop. Errors must usually be investigated. Examples include the failure of the current operation and an exception that cannot be handled.	Enabled.

Critical	LogCritical	This is used to log errors that require immediate attention and represent a catastrophic state. The program is most likely about to stop, and the integrity of the application might be compromised; for example, a hard drive is full, the server is out of memory, or the database is in a deadlocked state.	Enabled with some alerts that could be configured to trigger automatically.

Those log levels tell the logger what severity a log entry is. Then, we can configure the system to log only entries of at least a certain level, so we don't fill out production logs with traces, for example. As described in the preceding table, each log level serves one or more purposes. Nonetheless, your project, team, or enterprise might have different guidelines in place.

In a project that I led, we benchmarked multiple ways to log simple and complex messages using ASP.NET Core because we wanted to build clear and optimized guidelines around that. We could not reach a fair conclusion when the messages were logged due to too much time variance between benchmark runs. However, we observed a constant trend when messages were not logged (*trace* logs with the minimum logging level configured to *debug* for example).

Based on that conclusion, I recommend logging the Trace and Debug messages using the following construct instead of interpolation, string.Format, or other means. That may sound strange to optimize for *not logging something*, but if you think about it, those log entries will be skipped in production, so optimizing them will save your production app a few milliseconds of computing time here and there.

Let's look at the fastest way to *not write log entries*:

```
_logger.LogTrace("Some: {variable}", variable);
// Or
_logger.LogTrace("Some: {0}", variable);
```

When the log level is disabled, such as in production, you only pay the price of a method call because no processing is done on your log entries. On the other hand, if we use interpolation, the processing is done, so that one argument is passed to the Log[Level] method, leading to a higher cost in processing power for each log entry.

For lines that we know the program will log, like warnings, the way to go does not matter much since the processing has to be done no matter how. Therefore, using interpolation in the code or letting the logger do it later should yield a similar result. Of course, all other non-logging-specific optimization applies, which is out of the scope of this book.

Note

One last note. I suggest you don't try to over-optimize your code before there is a need for that. The action of investing a lot of effort in optimizing something that does not need optimizing is known as **premature optimization**. The idea is to optimize just enough, bottlenecks, or when needed instead.

Now that we know the log levels that .NET offers us, let's overview the available logging providers.

Logging providers

To give you an idea of the possible built-in logging providers, here is a list from the official documentation (see the *Further reading* section at the end of this chapter):

- Console
- Debug
- EventSource
- EventLog (Windows only)
- ApplicationInsights

The following is a list of third-party logging providers, also from the official documentation:

- elmah.io
- Gelf
- JSNLog
- KissLog.net
- Log4Net
- Loggr
- NLog
- Sentry
- Serilog
- Stackdriver

Now, if you need any of those or if your favorite logging library is part of the preceding list, you know that you can use it. If it is not, maybe it supports ASP.NET Core but was not part of the documentation when I consulted it.

Next, let's learn how to configure the logging system.

Configuring logging

As with most of ASP.NET Core, we can configure logging. The default `IHostBuilder`, created when calling `Host.CreateDefaultBuilder(args)`, and the `WebApplicationBuilder`, created when calling `WebApplication.CreateBuilder`, do a lot for us.

As we saw earlier, those methods register many configuration providers and load the `Logging` section of the configuration. That section is present, by default, in the `appsettings.json` file. Like all configurations, it is cumulative, so we can redefine part of it in another file or another provider.

I don't want to spend too many pages on this, but it is good to know that you can customize the minimum level of what you are logging. You can also use transformation files (such as `appsettings.Development.json`) to customize those levels per environment.

For example, you can define your defaults in `appsettings.json`, then update a few for development purposes in `appsettings.Development.json`, change production settings in `appsettings.Production.json`, then change the staging settings in `appsettings.Staging.json`, and add some testing settings in `appsettings.Testing.json`. Moreover, you can use environment variables or even secrets managers like Azure Key Vault for more sensitive settings.

Before we move on, let's take a peek at the default settings:

```json
{
  "Logging": {
    "LogLevel": {
      "Default": "Information",
      "Microsoft": "Warning"
    }
  }
}
```

We can define default levels (using `Logging:LogLevel:Default`) and a custom level for each category (such as `Logging:LogLevel:Microsoft`) representing base namespaces. For example, from that configuration file, the minimum level is `Information`, while every item that is part of the `Microsoft` or `Microsoft.*` namespaces have a minimum level of `Warning`. That allows removing noise when running the application. We can also leverage these configurations to debug certain parts of the application by lowering the log level to `Debug` or `Trace` for only a subset of items (items from one or more namespaces, for example).

We can also filter what we want to log on a provider basis, using configuration or code. In the configuration file, we can change the default level of the console provider to `Trace`, like this:

```json
{
  "Logging": {
    "LogLevel": {
      "Default": "Information",
      "Microsoft": "Warning"
    },
    "Console": {
      "LogLevel": {
        "Default": "Trace"
      }
    }
  }
}
```

We kept the same default values but added the `Logging:Console` section (see highlighted code) with a default `LogLevel` set to `Trace`. We could have defined more settings here, but that's outside the scope of this book.

Instead, we can use one of the AddFilter extension methods, as shown in the following experimental test code, or in conjunction with configurations.

Here is the service class that logs data:

```
public interface IService
{
    void Execute();
}
public class Service : IService
{
    private readonly ILogger _logger;
    public Service(ILogger<Service> logger)
    {
        _logger = logger ?? throw new ArgumentNullException(nameof(logger));
    }
    public void Execute()
    {
        _logger.LogInformation("[info] Service.Execute()");
        _logger.LogWarning("[warning] Service.Execute()");
    }
}
```

The preceding class is like other classes we used during the chapter but logs messages using two different levels: Information and Warning. Here is a test case in which we leverage the AddFilter method:

```
[Fact]
public void Should_filter_logs_by_provider()
{
    // Arrange
    var lines = new List<string>();
    var host = Host.CreateDefaultBuilder()
        .ConfigureLogging(loggingBuilder =>
        {
            loggingBuilder.ClearProviders();
            loggingBuilder.AddConsole();
            loggingBuilder.AddAssertableLogger(lines);
            loggingBuilder.AddxUnitTestOutput(_output);
            loggingBuilder
                .AddFilter<XunitTestOutputLoggerProvider>(
                    level => level >= LogLevel.Warning
                );
        })
```

```
        .ConfigureServices(services =>
        {
            services.AddSingleton<IService, Service>();
        })
        .Build();
    var service = host.Services.GetRequiredService<IService>();

    // Act
    service.Execute();

    // Assert
    Assert.Collection(lines,
        line => Assert.Equal("[info] Service.Execute()", line),
        line => Assert.Equal("[warning] Service.Execute()", line)
    );
}
```

We created a generic host in the preceding test code and added three providers: the console and two test providers — one that logs to a list and another that logs to the xUnit output. Then, we told the system to filter out everything that is not at least a Warning from XunitTestOutputLoggerProvider (see highlighted code); other providers are unaffected by that code.

Note

In the code, the _output variable is an ITestOutputHelper, like we used previously in this chapter.

We now know of two options to set the minimum logging levels:

*   Code
*   Configuration

You can tweak the way you configure your logging policies as needed. Code can be more testable, while configurations can be updated at runtime without the need for deployment. Moreover, with the cascading model, which allows us to override configuration, we can cover most use cases using configurations. The biggest downside of configuration is that writing strings in a JSON file is more error-prone than writing code (assuming you are not reverting to using strings there either).

That said, I usually stick with configurations to set those values as they do not change often. If you prefer code, I'm not aware of any drawbacks, and it's just a matter of preference.

Next, let's look at a brief example of structured logging.

Structured logging

As stated at the beginning, structured logging can become very important and open opportunities. Querying a data structure is always more versatile than querying a single line of text. That is even more true if there is no clear guideline around logging, whether a line of text or a JSON-formatted data structure.

To keep it simple, we leverage a built-in formatter (highlighted line below) that serializes our log entries into JSON. Here is the `Program.cs` file:

```
var builder = WebApplication.CreateBuilder(args);
builder.Logging.AddJsonConsole();

var app = builder.Build();
app.MapGet("/", (ILoggerFactory loggerFactory) =>
{
    const string category = "root";
    var logger = loggerFactory.CreateLogger(category);
    logger.LogInformation("You hit the {category} URL!", category);
    return "Hello World!";
});
app.Run();
```

That transforms the console to logging JSON. For example, every time we hit the / URL, the console displays the following JSON (but minified):

```
{
  "EventId": 0,
  "LogLevel": "Information",
  "Category": "root",
  "Message": "You hit the root URL!",
  "State": {
    "Message": "You hit the root URL!",
    "category": "root",
    "{OriginalFormat}": "You hit the {category} URL!"
  }
}
```

Without that formatter, the usual output would have been:

```
info: root[0]
      You hit the root URL!
```

Based on that comparison, it is easy to see that even if the JSON payload does not add much additional information, it is easier to programmatically query.

The biggest benefit of structured logging is improved searchability. You can run more precise queries at scale with a predefined data structure.

Of course, if you are setting up a production system, you would probably want more information attached to such log items like the correlation ID of the request, optionally some information about the current user, the server's name on which the code is running, and possibly more details depending on the application.

To take full advantage of structured logging, you may need more than the out-of-the-box features. Some third-party libraries like Serilog offer those additional capabilities. However, defining the way to send plain text to the logger could also be a start.

Each project should dictate the needs and depth of each of its features, including logging. Moreover, structured logging is a broader subject that merits studying on its own. Nonetheless, I wanted to touch on this subject a bit, and hopefully, you learned enough about logging to get started.

Conclusion

Logging is essential, and ASP.NET Core gives us various ways to log independently of third-party libraries while allowing us to use our favorite logging framework. We can customize the way the logs are written and categorized. We can use zero or more logging providers. We can also create custom logging providers. Finally, we can use configurations or code to filter logs and much more.

What you must remember the most is the following pattern:

1. Inject an `ILogger<T>`, where `T` is the type of the class into which the logger is injected. `T` becomes the category.
2. Save a reference of that logger into a `private readonly ILogger` field.
3. Use that logger in your methods to log messages using the appropriate log level.

With the .NET logging abstractions we covered in this chapter, you should have enough to get started. Let's recap what we explored in the chapter before learning about some structural design patterns.

Summary

.NET Core added many features, such as configuration and logging, that are now part of .NET. The new APIs are better and provide more value than the old .NET Framework ones. Most of the boilerplate code is gone, and almost everything is on an opt-in basis.

Options allows us to load and compose configurations from multiple sources while using those easily in our systems through simple C# objects. It removes the hassle of the previous configuration from `web.config` and makes it easy to use. No more complex boilerplate code is needed to create custom `web.config` sections; just add a JSON object to `appsettings.json`, tell the system what section to load, what the type should be, and voilà — you have your strongly typed options! The same simplicity applies to consuming settings: inject the desired interface or the class itself and use it. With that, you are up and running; no more static `ConfigurationManager` or other structures that are hard to test.

Logging is also a great addition; it allows us to standardize the logging mechanism, making our systems easier to maintain in the long run. For example, if you want to use a new third-party library or even a custom-made one, you can load the provider into your `Program`, and the entire system will adapt and start using it without any further changes. That's what well-designed abstractions are supposed to bring to a system.

This chapter closes the second section of this book that had ASP.NET Core at its center. In the next three chapters, we explore design patterns to design flexible and robust components.

Questions

Let's take a look at a few practice questions:

1. What is the lifetime of `IOptionsMonitor<TOptions>`?
2. What is the lifetime of `IOptionsSnapshot<TOptions>`?
3. What is the lifetime of `IOptionsFactory<TOptions>`?
4. Can we write log entries to the console and a file at the same time?
5. Is it true that we should log the trace- and debug-level log entries in a production environment?

Further reading

Here are some links to build upon what we learned in the chapter:

- [Official docs] *Logging in .NET Core and ASP.NET Core*: https://adpg.link/MUVG
- [Official docs] *Options pattern in ASP.NET Core*: https://adpg.link/RTGc

Section 3: Designing at Component Scale

This section focuses on component design, where we study how an individual piece of software can be crafted to achieve a specific goal. We do that by exploring a few structural Gang of Four patterns to help design SOLID data structures and components. They also help simplify the complexity of our code by encapsulating our logic in smaller units.

We continue with two behavioral patterns that help manage shared logic or simplify the efforts needed to manage complex logic. We end the section by exploring how to transmit structured information between components regarding operations' errors and successes.

This section comprises the following chapters:

- *Chapter 9, Structural Patterns*
- *Chapter 10, Behavioral Patterns*
- *Chapter 11, Understanding the Operation Result Design Pattern*

Structural Patterns

This chapter explores four design patterns from the well-known **Gang of Four (GoF)**. We use structural patterns to create complex, flexible, and fine-grained classes.

Structural patterns help us build and organize complex object hierarchies in a maintainable fashion. They allow us to add behaviors to existing classes dynamically, whether we designed the initial system this way or as an afterthought that emerges out of necessity later in the program's lifecycle.

The following topics will be covered in this chapter:

- Implementing the Decorator design pattern
- Implementing the Composite design pattern
- Implementing the Adapter design pattern
- Implementing the Façade design pattern

The first two patterns help us extend a class dynamically and efficiently manage a complex object structure. The last two help us adapt an interface to another or shield a complex system with a simple interface. Let's begin!

Implementing the Decorator design pattern

The Decorator pattern allows us to extend objects at runtime while separating responsibilities. It is a simple but powerful pattern. In this section, we explore how to implement this pattern in the traditional way and how to leverage an open source tool named **Scrutor** to help us create powerful dependency injection-ready decorators using .NET.

Goal

The decorator's goal is to extend an existing object, at runtime, without changing its code. Moreover, the decorated object should not be aware that it is being decorated, leaving it as a great candidate for long-lived or complex systems that need to evolve. This pattern fits systems of all sizes.

I often use this pattern to add flexibility and create adaptability to a program for next to no cost. In addition, small classes are easier to test, so the Decorator pattern adds ease of testability into the mix, making it worth mastering.

The Decorator pattern makes it easier to encapsulate responsibilities into multiple classes, instead of packing multiple responsibilities inside a single class. Having multiple classes that each holds a single responsibility makes the system easier to manage.

Design

A **decorator** class must both implement and use the interface that's being implemented by the **decorated** class. Let's see this step by step, starting with a non-decorated class design:

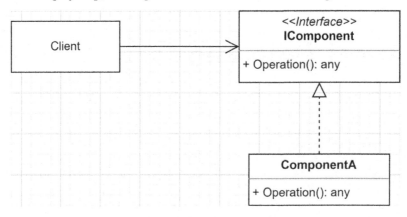

Figure 9.1: A class diagram representing the ComponentA class implementing the IComponent interface

In the preceding diagram, we have the following components:

- A client that calls the Operation() method of IComponent.
- ComponentA, which implements the IComponent interface.

This translates into the following sequence diagram:

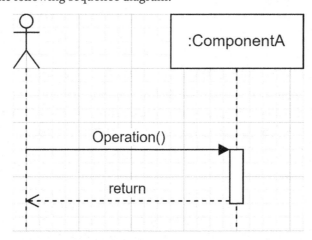

Figure 9.2: A sequence diagram showing a consumer calling the Operation method of the ComponentA class

Now, say that we want to add some new behavior to ComponentA, but only in some cases. In other cases, we want to keep the initial behavior. To do so, we could choose the Decorator pattern and implement it as follows:

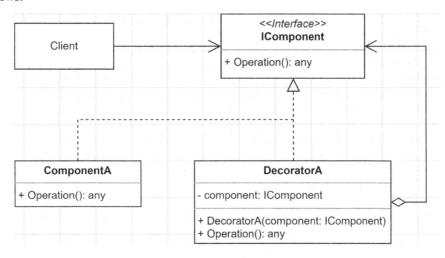

Figure 9.3: Decorator class diagram

Instead of modifying the ComponentA class, we created DecoratorA, which implements IComponent as well. This way, Client can use an instance of DecoratorA instead of ComponentA and have access to the new behavior, without impacting the other consumers of ComponentA. Then, to avoid rewriting the whole component, an implementation of IComponent is injected when creating a new DecoratorA instance (constructor injection). This new instance is stored in the component field and used by the Operation() method (implicit use of the **Strategy** pattern).

We can translate the updated sequence like so:

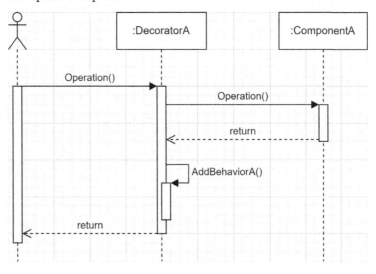

Figure 9.4: Decorator sequence diagram

In the preceding diagram, instead of calling ComponentA directly, Client calls DecoratorA, which in turn calls ComponentA. Finally, DecoratorA does some postprocessing by calling its private method; that is, AddBehaviorA().

> **Note**
>
> Nothing from the Decorator pattern limits us from doing preprocessing, postprocessing, wrapping the decorated class's call (the Operation method in this example) with some logic (like an if statement or a try-catch), or all of that combined.

To show you how powerful the Decorator pattern is before we jump into the code, know this: we can chain decorators! Since our decorator depends on the interface (not the implementation), we could inject another decorator, say DecoratorB, inside DecoratorA (or vice versa). We could then create an infinite chain of rules that decorate one another, leading to a very powerful yet simple design.

Let's take a look at the following class diagram, which represents our chaining example:

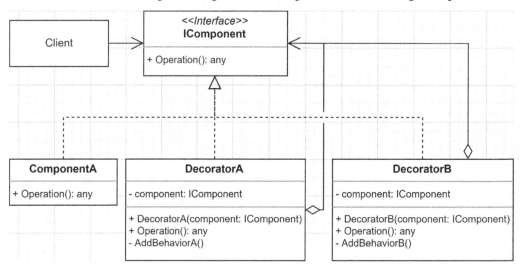

Figure 9.5: Decorator class diagram, including two decorators

Here, we created the DecoratorB class, which looks very similar to DecoratorA but has a private AddBehaviorB() method instead of AddBehaviorA().

> **Note**
>
> The way we implement the decorator's changes in behavior or state is irrelevant to the pattern, which is why I excluded the AddBehaviorA() method from the initial class diagram: to show you only the pattern. However, I added it to this one (*Figure 9.5*) to make the idea behind having a second decorator clearer.

Let's take a look at the sequence diagram for this:

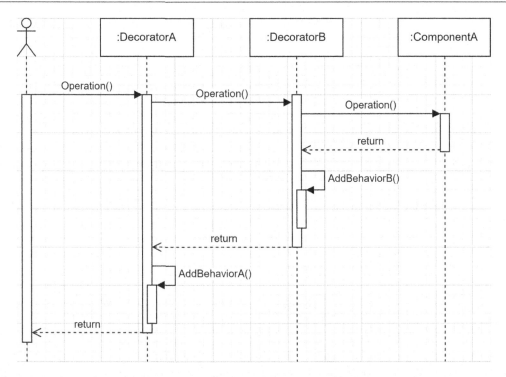

Figure 9.6: Sequence diagram of two nested decorators

With this, we are beginning to see the power of decorators. In the preceding diagram, we can assess that the behaviors of ComponentA have been changed twice without Client knowing about it. All those classes are unaware of the next IComponent in the chain. They don't even know that they are being decorated. They only play their role in the plan—that's all.

It is also important to note that the decorator's power resides in its dependency on the interface, not on an implementation, making it reusable. Based on that fact, we could swap DecoratorA and DecoratorB to invert the order the new behaviors are applied without touching the code itself. We could also apply the same decorator (say DecoratorC) to multiple IComponent implementations, like decorating both DecoratorA and DecoratorB.

Project – Adding behaviors

To help visualize the Decorator pattern, let's implement the previous example, which adds some arbitrary behaviors. Each Operation() method returns a string that is then outputted to the response stream. It is not fancy, but it shows how this works.

First, let's look at the IComponent interface and the ComponentA class:

```
public interface IComponent
{
    string Operation();
}
public class ComponentA : IComponent
```

```
{
    public string Operation()
    {
        return "Hello from ComponentA";
    }
}
```

The `IComponent` interface only states that an implementation should have an `Operation()` method that returns a `string`. The `Operation()` method implementation of the `ComponentA` class returns a literal string.

Now that we described the first pieces, let's look at the consumer, which is a minimal API endpoint:

```
var builder = WebApplication.CreateBuilder(args);
builder.Services.AddSingleton<IComponent, ComponentA>();

var app = builder.Build();
app.MapGet("/", (IComponent component) => component.Operation());
app.Run();
```

In the `Program.cs` file above, we register `ComponentA` as the implementation of `IComponent`, with a singleton lifetime. We then inject an `IComponent` implementation when an HTTP request hits the / endpoint. The delegate then calls the `Operation()` method (see highlight).

At this point, running the application (from any URL) will result in the following output:

```
Hello from ComponentA
```

This happened because the system injected an implementation of the `IComponent` interface of type `ComponentA` into the / delegate, so the client outputs the result of `ComponentA`.

Next, we add the first decorator.

DecoratorA

Here, we want to modify the response without touching `ComponentA`. To do so, let's create a decorator named `DecoratorA` that wraps the `Operation()` result into a `<DecoratorA>` tag:

```
public class DecoratorA : IComponent
{
    private readonly IComponent _component;
    public DecoratorA(IComponent component)
    {
        _component = component ?? throw new
ArgumentNullException(nameof(component));
    }
    public string Operation()
    {
```

```
            var result = _component.Operation();
            return $"<DecoratorA>{result}</DecoratorA>";
    }
}
```

DecoratorA depends on an implementation of IComponent. It uses that IComponent in the Operation() method and wraps its result in an HTML-like (XML) tag.

Now that we have a decorator, we need to tell the IoC container to send an instance of DecoratorA instead of ComponentA when injecting an IComponent interface.

DecoratorA should decorate ComponentA; or, more precisely, ComponentA should be injected into DecoratorA.

To achieve this, we could register it as follows:

```
builder.Services.AddSingleton<IComponent>(serviceProvider => new DecoratorA(new
ComponentA()));
```

Here, we are telling ASP.NET Core to inject an instance of DecoratorA that decorates an instance of ComponentA when injecting an IComponent interface. When we run the application, we should see the following result in the browser:

```
<DecoratorA>Hello from ComponentA</DecoratorA>
```

Note

You may have noticed a few new keywords there, but even though it is not very elegant, we can manually create new instances in the composition root without jeopardizing our application's health. We learn how to get rid of some of them later with the introduction of Scrutor.

Next, we create a second decorator.

DecoratorB

Now that we have a decorator, it is time to create a second decorator to demonstrate the power of chaining decorators.

Context: At some point, we need to wrap that content once again, but we don't want to modify any existing classes. To achieve this, we concluded that creating a second decorator would be perfect, so we created the following DecoratorB class:

```
public class DecoratorB : IComponent
{
    private readonly IComponent _component;
    public DecoratorB(IComponent component)
    {
```

```
            _component = component ?? throw new
    ArgumentNullException(nameof(component));
        }
        public string Operation()
        {
            var result = _component.Operation();
            return $"<DecoratorB>{result}</DecoratorB>";
        }
    }
}
```

It is very similar to DecoratorA, but the HTML-like tag is DecoratorB instead. The important and similar part here is that we always depend on the IComponent abstraction, never on any concrete class. This is what gives us the flexibility of decorating any IComponent, and this is what enables us to chain decorators.

To complete this example, we need to update our composition root like this:

```
builder.Services.AddSingleton<IComponent>(serviceProvider => new DecoratorB(new
DecoratorA(new ComponentA())));
```

Now, we can decorate DecoratorA with DecoratorB, which, in turn, decorates ComponentA. Upon running the application, you should see the following output:

```
<DecoratorB><DecoratorA>Hello from ComponentA</DecoratorA></DecoratorB>
```

And voilà! These decorators allowed us to modify the behavior of ComponentA without having an impact on the code. However, our composition root is beginning to get messy as we are instantiating multiple dependencies inside each other. This could make our application harder to maintain. Moreover, the code is becoming harder to read. Furthermore, the code would be even harder to read if the decorators were depending on other classes as well.

As we mentioned previously, you can use decorators to change the behavior or state of an object; be creative. For example, you could create a class that queries remote resources, say over HTTP, and then decorate that class with a small component that manages a memory cache of the results, limiting the round trip to the remote server. You could then create another decorator that monitors the time needed to query those resources and then log that somewhere. This could be a nice exercise to code if you are looking to practice.

Next, we get rid of the new keywords.

Project – Decorator using Scrutor

The objective of this update is to simplify the composition of the system we just created. To achieve this, we use **Scrutor**, an open source library that allows us to do just that, among other things.

The first thing we need to do is install the NuGet package using Visual Studio or the CLI. When using the CLI, run the following command:

```
dotnet add package Scrutor
```

Once Scrutor has been installed, you can use the `Decorate<TService, TDecorator>()` extension method on `IServiceCollection` to add decorators.

By using Scrutor, we can update the following messy line:

```
builder.Services.AddSingleton<IComponent>(serviceProvider => new DecoratorB(new
DecoratorA(new ComponentA())))
```

And convert it into these three more elegant lines:

```
builder.Services
    .AddSingleton<IComponent, ComponentA>()
    .Decorate<IComponent, DecoratorA>()
    .Decorate<IComponent, DecoratorB>()
;
```

OK; what happened here?

We registered `ComponentA` as the implementation of `IComponent`, with a singleton lifetime, just like the first time.

Then, by using Scrutor, we told the IoC container to override that first binding and to decorate the already registered `IComponent` (`ComponentA`) with an instance of `DecoratorA` instead. Then, we overrode the second binding by telling the IoC container to return an instance of `DecoratorB` that decorates the last known binding of `IComponent` instead (`DecoratorA`).

The result is the same as what we did previously, but is now written in a more elegant and flexible manner. The IoC container injects the equivalent of the following `instance` with a singleton lifetime:

```
var instance = new DecoratorB(new DecoratorA(new ComponentA()));
```

Note

Why am I saying that it is more elegant and flexible? This is a simple example, but if we start adding other dependencies to those classes, it could quickly end up as a complex code block that could turn into a maintenance nightmare, become very hard to read, and have manually managed lifetimes. Of course, if the system is simple, you can always instantiate the decorators manually without loading an external library. Using methods to encapsulate the initialization of some part of the system is also an option.

Whenever possible, keep your code simple. Using Scrutor is one way to achieve this. Code simplicity helps in the long run as it is easier to read and follow, even for someone else reading it. Always consider the fact that someone else may maintain your code.

To validate that both programs behave the same, with or without Scrutor, the following integration test runs for both projects and ensures their correctness. See `StartupTest.cs` (https://adpg.link/Tbeh):

```
[Fact]
public async Task Should_return_a_double_decorated_string()
{
    // Arrange
    var client = _webApplicationFactory.CreateClient();
    // Act
    var response = await client.GetAsync("/");
    // Assert
    response.EnsureSuccessStatusCode();
    var body = await response.Content.ReadAsStringAsync();
    Assert.Equal(
        "Operation: <DecoratorB><DecoratorA>Hello from ComponentA</
DecoratorA></DecoratorB>",
        body
    );
}
```

The preceding test sends an HTTP request to one of the applications running in memory and compares the server response to the expected value. Since both projects should have the same output, that test is reused in both `DecoratorPlainStartupTest` and `DecoratorScrutorStartupTest`.

Scrutor

You can also do assembly scanning using Scrutor (`https://adpg.link/xvfS`), which allows you to perform automatic dependency registration. This is outside the scope of this chapter, but it is worth looking into. Scrutor allows you to use the built-in IoC container for more complex scenarios, postponing the need to replace it with a third-party one.

Conclusion

The Decorator pattern is one of the simplest but most powerful design patterns out there. It augments existing classes without modifying them. Moreover, if you don't need to decorate all instances of X by Y, you can encapsulate small blocks of logic, then create complex and granular object trees to fit different needs; this can even be modified at runtime.

The Decorator pattern helps us stay in line with the **SOLID** principles, as follows:

- **S**: The Decorator pattern suggests creating small classes to add behaviors to other classes, which segregates responsibilities.
- **O**: Decorators add behaviors to other classes without modifying them, which is literally the definition of the OCP.
- **L**: N/A

- **I**: By following the ISP, it should be easy to create decorators for your specific needs. If your interfaces are too complex, packing in too many responsibilities, using decorators could be harder. Having a hard time creating a decorator is a good indicator that something is wrong with the design. A well-segregated interface should be easy to decorate.
- **D**: Depending on abstractions is the key to the Decorator's power.

Next, we explore the Composite pattern, which helps us manage complex objects' structures in a different way than how the decorator does.

Implementing the Composite design pattern

The Composite design pattern is another structural GoF pattern that helps us manage complex object structures.

Goal

The goal behind the Composite pattern is to create a hierarchical data structure where you don't need to differentiate groups of elements from a single element, making the hierarchy easy to use for its consumers.

You could think of the Composite pattern as a way of building a graph or a tree with self-managing nodes.

Design

The design is straightforward; we have *components* and *composites*. Both implement a common interface that defines the shared operations. The *components* are the single nodes, while the *composites* are collections of *components*. Let's take a look at a diagram:

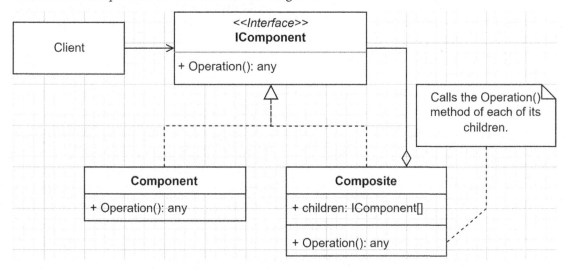

Figure 9.7: Composite class diagram

In the preceding diagram, `Client` depends on an `IComponent` interface. By doing so, it is unaware of the implementation it is using; it could be a `Component` or a `Composite`. Then, we have two implementations:

- `Component` represents a single element; a leaf.
- `Composite` represents a collection of `IComponent`. The `Composite` object uses its children to manage the hierarchy's complexity by delegating part of the process to them.

Those three pieces, when put together, create the Composite design pattern. Considering that it is possible to add `Composite` and `Component` as children of other `Composite` objects, it is possible to create complex, non-linear, and self-managed data structures with next to no effort.

Note

You are not limited to one implementation of `Component` and one implementation of `Composite`; you can create as many implementations of `IComponent` as you need to, based on your use case. Then, you can mix and match them so your data structure fits your needs. We explore how to display complex composites in *Chapter 17, ASP.NET Core User Interfaces*.

Project – BookStore

Let's revisit the bookstore that we built in *Chapter 3, Architectural Principles*.

Context: The store is going so well that our little program is not enough anymore. Our fictional company now owns multiple stores, so they need to divide those stores into sections, and they need to manage book sets and single books. After a few minutes of gathering information, we realize that they can have sets of sets, subsections, and possibly sub-stores, so we need a flexible design.

Let's use the Composite pattern to solve this problem. The user interface that we are aiming to build looks like this:

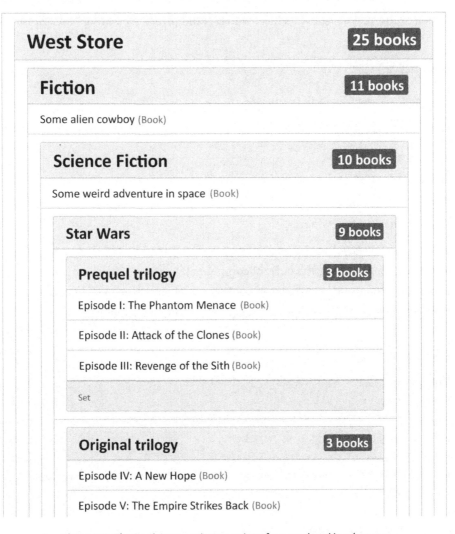

Figure 9.8: The Bookstore project user interface rendered in a browser

First, let's look at the IComponent interface, which is the primary building block of the Composite pattern:

```
public interface IComponent
{
    void Add(IComponent bookComponent);
    void Remove(IComponent bookComponent);
    string Display();
    int Count();
    string Type { get; }
}
```

This interface defines the following:

- The Add() and Remove() sub-components.
- Display(), for displaying the current component.
- Count(), for counting the number of books available from the current component.
- Knowing the Type of the component (displayed in the card's footer).

From there, we need components. First, let's focus on the BookComposite class, which abstracts away most of the composite logic:

```
public abstract class BookComposite : IComponent
{
    protected readonly List<IComponent> children = new();
    public BookComposite(string name)
    {
        Name = name ?? throw new ArgumentNullException(nameof(name));
    }

    public string Name { get; }
    public virtual string Type => GetType().Name;

    // Not part of the IComponent interface.
    // Sets a different heading tag per sub-class,
    // see the AppendHeader method.
    protected abstract string HeadingTagName { get; }

    public virtual void Add(IComponent bookComponent)
    {
        children.Add(bookComponent);
    }

    public virtual int Count()
```

```csharp
    {
        return children.Sum(child => child.Count());
    }

    public virtual string Display()
    {
        var sb = new StringBuilder();
        sb.Append("<section class=\"card\">");
        AppendHeader(sb);
        AppendBody(sb);
        AppendFooter(sb);
        sb.Append("</section>");
        return sb.ToString();
    }
    private void AppendHeader(StringBuilder sb)
    {
        sb.Append($"<{HeadingTagName} class=\"card-header\">");
        sb.Append(Name);
        sb.Append($"<span class=\"badge badge-secondary float-right\">{Count()}
books</span>");
        sb.Append($"</{HeadingTagName}>");
    }
    private void AppendBody(StringBuilder sb)
    {
        sb.Append($"<ul class=\"list-group list-group-flush\">");
        children.ForEach(child =>
        {
            sb.Append($"<li class=\"list-group-item\">");
            sb.Append(child.Display());
            sb.Append("</li>");
        });
        sb.Append("</ul>");
    }
    private void AppendFooter(StringBuilder sb)
    {
        sb.Append("<div class=\"card-footer text-muted\">");
        sb.Append($"<small class=\"text-muted text-right\">{Type}</small>");
        sb.Append("</div>");
    }

    public virtual void Remove(IComponent bookComponent)
```

```
    {
        children.Remove(bookComponent);
    }
}
```

> **Note**
>
> In this case, to focus on the Composite pattern, `IComponent`'s implementations handle how its data is presented. However, most of the time, I would not recommend doing so. Why? Because we are giving too many responsibilities to those classes since we are tightly coupling them with the HTML language. It makes the components harder to reuse. Think Single-Responsibility Principle (SRP). We revisit these concepts in subsequent chapters and fix this problem.

The `BookComposite` class implements the following shared features:

*   Children management (highlighted in the code).
*   Setting the `Name` property of the composite object.
*   Automatically finding the `Type` name of its derived class.
*   Counting the number of children (and, implicitly, the children's children).
*   Displaying the composite and its children.

> **Note**
>
> Using the LINQ `Sum()` extension method in the `children.Sum(child => child.Count());` expression allowed us to replace a more complex `for` loop and an accumulator variable.

Now, let's take a look at a more complex composite example. By creating multiple classes, we can pinpoint what responsibilities we have. In a real scenario, we may need to handle more than a name and a count. Moreover, it shows how flexible the Composite pattern is.

Here is the full hierarchy that represents our bookstore:

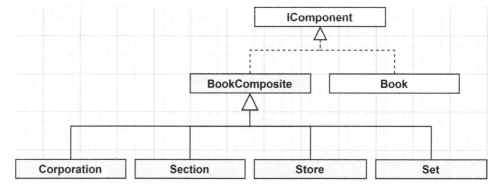

Figure 9.9: Inheritance hierarchy of the BookStore project

Under `BookComposite`, we have the following:

- `Corporation`, which represents the corporation that owns multiple stores. However, it is not limited to owning stores; a corporation could own other corporations and stores, or any other `IComponent` for that matter.
- `Section`, which is a section of a bookstore, or a category of books.
- `Store`, which represents a bookstore.
- `Set`, which is a book set, such as a trilogy.

All of these can be composed of any `IComponent`, making this an ultra-flexible data structure. Before we move on, let's look at the code for these `BookComposite` subclasses:

```csharp
public class Corporation : BookComposite
{
    public Corporation(string name) : base(name) { }
    protected override string HeadingTagName => "h1";
}
public class Store : BookComposite
{
    public Store(string name) : base(name) { }
    protected override string HeadingTagName => "h2";
}
public class Section : BookComposite
{
    public Section(string name) : base(name) { }
    protected override string HeadingTagName => "h3";
}
public class Set : BookComposite
{
    public Set(string name, params IComponent[] books)
        : base(name)
    {
        foreach (var book in books)
        {
            Add(book);
        }
    }
    protected override string HeadingTagName => "h4";
}
```

As you can see, the code is straightforward; the subclasses inherit from `BookComposite`, which does most of the work, leaving them to specify only the value of the `HeadingTagName` property. `Set` is different and allows us to inject other `IComponent` objects into its constructor. This is going to be convenient later when we assemble the tree (Hint: A book set contains multiple books).

The last part of our Composite pattern's implementation is the Book class:

```
public class Book : IComponent
{
    public Book(string title)
    {
        Title = title ?? throw new ArgumentNullException(nameof(title));
    }
    public string Title { get; set; }
    public string Type => "Book";
    public int Count() => 1;
    public string Display() => $"{Title} <small class=\"text-muted\">({Type})</
small>";
    public void Add(IComponent bookComponent) => throw new
NotSupportedException();
    public void Remove(IComponent bookComponent) => throw new
NotSupportedException();
}
```

The Book class is a little different as it is not a collection of other objects, but a single node. Let's look at the differences:

- It has a Title property, instead of Name. How to name a component is not defined in the IComponent interface, so we can do what we want; in this case, a book has a title, not a name.
- It returns "Book" as the value of its Type property.
- It tells the callers that both the Add() and Remove() operations are not supported by throwing an exception.
- Its Count() method always returns 1 because an instance of the Book class represents a single book and, by extension, only represent themselves: one book; this is the leaf.
- The Display() method is also way simpler because it only needs to handle itself; there are no children.

Before we jump into the program, let's look at the last part that was added to help encapsulate the data structure's creation. This is not part of the Composite pattern, but now that we know what a factory is, we can use one to encapsulate the creation logic of our data structure. The factory interface looks like the following:

```
public interface ICorporationFactory
{
    Corporation Create();
}
```

The default concrete implementation of ICorporationFactory is DefaultCorporationFactory, and it creates the following structure (visual representation; see https://adpg.link/2Vqw for the full-size image):

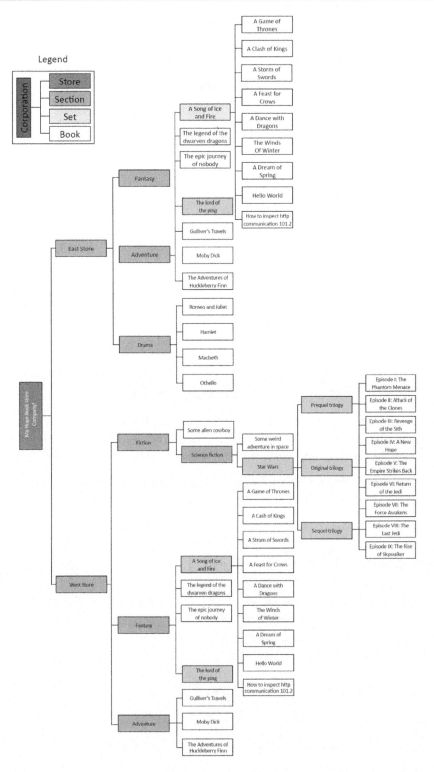

Figure 9.10: A representation of the data that the DefaultCorporationFactory class creates

If we take a close look, we can see that the structure is non-linear. There are sections, subsections, sets, and subsets. We could even add books directly to the store if we want. This whole structure is defined using our composite model in `DefaultCorporationFactory`.

To keep it simple, let's focus on the West Store's Fiction section:

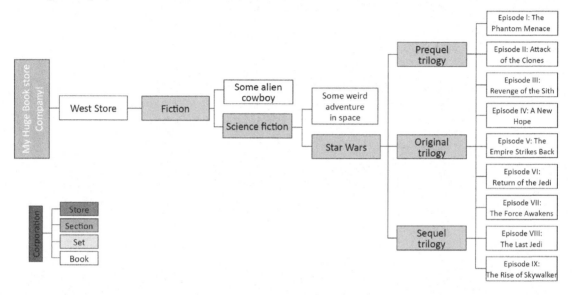

Figure 9.11: The Fiction section of the West Store data

In the West Store, we have a section that contains a fabricated book and a subsection named Science fiction. In Science fiction, there is another fabricated book and a set of books named Star Wars. Three subsets represent the three trilogies under the Star Wars set, which reveal the flexibility of the design.

Let's take a look at the code that builds that section in isolation. Feel free to consult the full source code for the complete example (`https://adpg.link/DD8e`). Here is the code:

```
public class DefaultCorporationFactory : ICorporationFactory
{
    public Corporation Create()
    {
        var corporation = new Corporation("My Huge Book Store Company!");
        corporation.Add(CreateEastStore());
        corporation.Add(CreateWestStore());
        return corporation;
    }
    private IComponent CreateWestStore()
    {
        var store = new Store("West Store");
        store.Add(CreateFictionSection());
        store.Add(CreateFantasySection());
```

```
            store.Add(CreateAdventureSection());
            return store;
        }
    private IComponent CreateFictionSection()
    {
            var section = new Section("Fiction");
            section.Add(new Book("Some alien cowboy"));
            section.Add(CreateScienceFictionSection());
            return section;
        }
    private IComponent CreateScienceFictionSection()
    {
            var section = new Section("Science Fiction");
            section.Add(new Book("Some weird adventure in space"));
            section.Add(new Set(
                "Star Wars",
                new Set(
                    "Prequel trilogy",
                    new Book("Episode I: The Phantom Menace"),
                    new Book("Episode II: Attack of the Clones"),
                    new Book("Episode III: Revenge of the Sith")
                ),
                new Set(
                    "Original trilogy",
                    new Book("Episode IV: A New Hope"),
                    new Book("Episode V: The Empire Strikes Back"),
                    new Book("Episode VI: Return of the Jedi")
                ),
                new Set(
                    "Sequel trilogy",
                    new Book("Episode VII: The Force Awakens"),
                    new Book("Episode VIII: The Last Jedi"),
                    new Book("Episode IX: The Rise of Skywalker")
                )
            ));
            return section;
        }
    // ...
}
```

I find the preceding code very exhaustive, making the creation of this part of the data structure clear. Now that we've read part of the code of the factory, let's head back to the Composite pattern and learn how to display it. In short, we only need to call the `Display()` method of the root node of our composite model (highlighted), like this:

```
using Composite.Services;

var builder = WebApplication.CreateBuilder(args);
builder.Services.AddSingleton<ICorporationFactory,
DefaultCorporationFactory>();

var app = builder.Build();
app.MapGet("/", async (HttpContext context, ICorporationFactory
corporationFactory) =>
{
    var compositeDataStructure = corporationFactory.Create();
    var output = compositeDataStructure.Display();
    context.Response.Headers.Add("Content-Type", "text/html; charset=utf-8");
    await context.Response.WriteAsync("[HTML removed for brevity]");
    await context.Response.WriteAsync(output);
    await context.Response.WriteAsync("[HTML removed for brevity]");
});
app.Run();
```

Let's take a look at what's happening in the preceding code:

- We are telling the IoC container to bind the `DefaultCorporationFactory` class to the `ICorporationFactory` interface.
- In the minimal API delegate, we inject an implementation of `ICorporationFactory`, build the data structure, and display it. This is the part that represents the consumer of our Composite pattern implementation.

Now, let's analyze the content of the `MapGet` delegate in more detail:

1. We use the injected `ICorporationFactory` `corporationFactory` parameter to create the data structure.
2. We call the `Display()` method to generate the output; the highlighted line. This is where the composite magic happens.
3. Finally, we write that output to the response stream by calling `await context.Response.WriteAsync(output);`. We wrap the content of the `output` variable with omitted HTML that adds the default tags like `<html>`, `<head>`, and `<body>`, registers Bootstrap, and so on.

The Composite pattern allowed us to render a complex data structure in a small method call. Since each component handles itself in an autonomous fashion, the burden of handling this complexity is taken away from the consumer.

In another scenario, we could have used the data instead of blindly displaying it; we could have also implemented a way of browsing that data or any other use cases that may come to mind. In this code example, I added a bit of complexity on purpose so that we could experiment with the Composite pattern in a more complex scenario while keeping extraneous details away from the code as much as possible.

I encourage you to play around with the existing data structure so that you understand the pattern. You could also try adding a `Movie` class to manage movies; a bookstore must diversify its activities. You could also differentiate movies from books so that customers are not confused. The bookstores could have physical and digital books as well.

If, after all of that, you are still looking for more, try building a new application from scratch and using the Composite pattern to create, manage, and display a multi-level menu.

Conclusion

The Composite pattern is very effective at building, managing, and maintaining complex non-linear data structures. Its power is primarily in its self-management capabilities. Each node, component, or composite is responsible for its own logic, leaving little to no work for the composite's consumers.

Using the Composite pattern helps us follow the **SOLID** principles in the following ways:

- **S**: It helps divide multiple elements of a complex data structure into small classes, in order to split responsibilities.
- **O**: By allowing us to "mix and match" different implementations of `IComponent`, the Composite pattern allows us to extend the data structure without impacting the other existing classes. For example, you could create a new class that implements `IComponent` and start using it right away, with no need to modify any other component classes.
- **L**: N/A
- **I**: The Composite pattern may violate the ISP when single items implement operations that only impact the collections.
- **D**: All of the Composite pattern actors depend solely on `IComponent`.

Next, we move to a different type of structural pattern that adapts one interface to another.

Implementing the Adapter design pattern

The Adapter pattern is another structural GoF pattern that helps adapt the API of one class to the API of another interface.

Goal

The adapter's goal is to plug in a component that does not respect the expected contract and adapt it so that it does. The adapter comes in handy when you cannot change the adaptee's code or if you do not want to change it.

Design

Think of the adapter as a power outlet's universal adapter; you can connect a North American device to a European outlet by connecting it to the adapter and then connecting it to the power outlet. The Adapter design pattern does exactly that, but for APIs.

Let's start by looking at the following diagram:

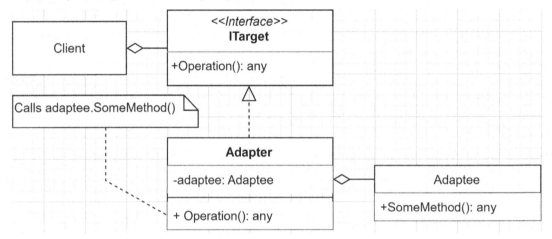

Figure 9.12: Adapter class diagram

In the preceding diagram, we have the following actors:

- ITarget, which is the interface that holds the contract that we want (or have) to use.
- Adaptee, which is the concrete component that we want to use that does not conform to ITarget.
- Adapter, which adapts the Adaptee class to the ITarget interface.

There is a second way of implementing the Adapter pattern that implies inheritance. If you can go for composition, go for it, but if you need access to protected methods or other internal states of Adaptee, you can go for inheritance instead, like this:

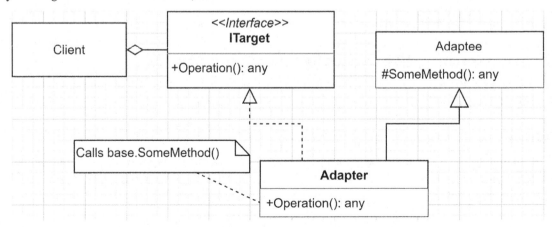

Figure 9.13: Adapter class diagram inheriting the Adaptee

The actors are the same, but instead of composing `Adapter` with `Adaptee`, `Adapter` inherits from `Adaptee`. This makes `Adapter` become both an `Adaptee` and an `ITarget`.

Project — Greeter

Context: We've programmed a highly sophisticated greeting system that we want to reuse in a new program. However, its interface does not match the new design, and we cannot modify it because other systems use that greeting system.

To fix this problem, we decided to apply the Adapter pattern. Here is the code of the external greeter (`ExternalGreeter`), and the new interface (`IGreeter`) used in the new system. This code must not directly modify the `ExternalGreeter` class to prevent any breaking changes from occurring in other systems:

```
public interface IGreeter
{
    string Greeting();
}
public class ExternalGreeter
{
    public string GreetByName(string name)
    {
        return $"Adaptee says: hi {name}!";
    }
}
```

Next is how the external greeter is adapted to meet the latest requirements:

```
public class ExternalGreeterAdapter : IGreeter
{
    private readonly ExternalGreeter _adaptee;
    public ExternalGreeterAdapter(ExternalGreeter adaptee)
    {
        _adaptee = adaptee ?? throw new ArgumentNullException(nameof(adaptee));
    }
    public string Greeting()
    {
        return _adaptee.GreetByName("ExternalGreeterAdapter");
    }
}
```

In the preceding code, the actors are as follows:

- `IGreeter`, which represents `ITarget`. This is the interface that we want to use.

- ExternalGreeter, which represents Adaptee. This is the external component that already contains all the logic that's been programmed and tested. This could be located in an external assembly, maybe even installed from NuGet.

- ExternalGreeterAdapter, which represents Adapter. This is where the adapter's job is done: ExternalGreeterAdapter.Greeting() calls ExternalGreeter.GreetByName("ExternalGreeterAdapter"), which implements the greeting logic.

Now, we can call the IGreeter.Greeting() method and get the result of the ExternalGreeter.GreetByName("ExternalGreeterAdapter") call. With this in place, we can reuse the existing logic. We can test any IGreeter consumers by mocking the IGreeter interface, without caring about the ExternalGreeterAdapter class.

I have to admit that the "complex logic" in this case is pretty simple, but we are here for the Adapter pattern, not for imaginary business logic. Now, let's take a look at the consumer:

```
var builder = WebApplication.CreateBuilder(args);
builder.Services.AddSingleton<ExternalGreeter>();
builder.Services.AddSingleton<IGreeter, ExternalGreeterAdapter>();

var app = builder.Build();
app.MapGet("/", (IGreeter greeter) => greeter.Greeting());
app.Run();
```

In the preceding code, we composed our application by specifying that the same instance of ExternalGreeterAdapter should be provided every time we ask for an IGreeter interface (singleton). We also told the container to provide a single instance of ExternalGreeter whenever it's requested (in this case, it's injected into ExternalGreeterAdapter).

Then, the consumer (**Client** in the preceding class diagrams) is the app.MapGet("/", ...) delegate (see the highlighted code of the preceding code block). IGreeter is injected as a parameter of the delegate when an HTTP call is made to /. Then, the delegate calls the Greeting method on that injected instance. Finally, it outputs the greeting to the response stream automatically.

The following diagram represents what's happening in this system:

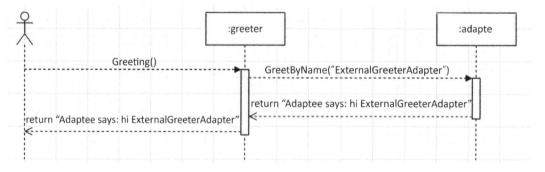

Figure 9.14: Greeter system sequence diagram

And voilà! We've adapted the ExternalGreeterAdapter class to the IGreeter interface with little effort.

Conclusion

The Adapter pattern is another simple pattern that offers flexibility. With it, we can use older or non-conforming components without rewriting them. Of course, depending on the ITarget and Adaptee interfaces, you may need to put more or less effort into writing the code of the Adapter class.

Now, let's learn how the Adapter pattern can help us follow the **SOLID** principles:

- **S:** The Adapter pattern has only one responsibility: make an interface work with another interface.
- **O:** The Adapter pattern allows us to modify the Adaptee's interface without the need to modify its code.
- **L:** Inheritance is not much of a concern when it comes to the Adapter pattern, so once again, this principle does not apply. If Adapter inherits from Adaptee, the goal is to change its interface, not its behavior, which should conform to the LSP.
- **I:** Since we could see the Adapter class as a means to an end where ITarget is the end, the Adapter pattern is directly depending on the design of ITarget and has no direct impact on it (good or bad). Your only concern for this principle is to design ITarget well enough so that it follows the ISP, which is not part of the pattern, but the reason to use the pattern.
- **D:** The Adapter pattern introduces only an implementation of the ITarget interface. Even if the adapter depends on a concrete class, its goal is to break the direct dependency on that external component by adapting it to the ITarget interface.

Next, we explore the last structural pattern of the chapter that teaches foundational concepts.

Implementing the Façade design pattern

The Façade pattern is another structural GoF pattern, similar to the Adapter pattern. It creates a wall (a façade) between one or more subsystems. The big difference between the adapter and the façade is that instead of adapting an interface to another, the façade simplifies the use of a subsystem, typically by using multiple classes of that subsystem.

Note

The same idea can be applied to shielding one or more programs, but in this case, the façade is called a gateway—more on that in *Chapter 16, Introduction to Microservices Architecture*.

The Façade pattern is an extremely useful pattern that can be adapted to multiple situations.

Goal

The goal of the Façade pattern is to simplify the use of one or more subsystems by providing an interface that is easier to use than the subsystems themselves, shielding the consumers from that complexity.

Design

We could create multiple diagrams representing a multitude of subsystems, but let's keep things simple here. Remember that you can replace the single subsystem shown in the following diagram with as many subsystems as you need to adapt:

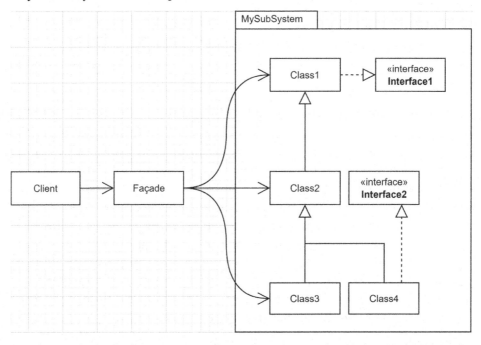

Figure 9.15: A class diagram representing a Façade object that hides a complex subsystem

As we can see, **Façade** plays the intermediary between **Client** and the subsystem, simplifying its usage. Let's see this in action as a sequence diagram:

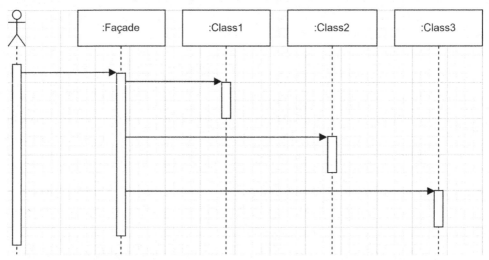

Figure 9.16: A sequence diagram representing a Façade object that interacts with a complex subsystem

In the preceding diagram, **Client** calls **Façade** once, while **Façade** places multiple calls against different classes.

There are multiple ways of implementing a façade:

- **Opaque façades:** In this form, the `Façade` class is inside the subsystem. All other classes of the subsystem have an `internal` visibility modifier. This way, only the classes inside the subsystem can interact with the other internal classes, forcing the consumers to use the `Façade` class.
- **Transparent façades:** In this form, the classes can have a `public` modifier, allowing the consumers to use them directly or to use the `Façade` class. This way, we can create the `Façade` class inside or outside the subsystem.
- Static façades: In this form, the `Façade` class is `static`. We can implement a static façade as opaque or transparent. Use this approach only as a last resort because global (`static`) elements tend to limit flexibility and testability.

Project – The façades

In this example, we will play with three C# projects:

- An ASP.NET Core application leveraging minimal APIs to expose four HTTP endpoints. Two endpoints aim at `OpaqueFacadeSubSystem`, while the other two endpoints aim at `TransparentFacadeSubSystem`. This is our consumer.
- The `OpaqueFacadeSubSystem` class library implements an **opaque façade**.
- The `TransparentFacadeSubSystem` class library implements a **transparent façade**.

Let's start with the class libraries.

Note

To follow the SOLID principles, adding some interfaces representing the elements of the subsystem seemed appropriate. In subsequent chapters, we explore how to organize our abstractions to be more reusable, but for now, both abstractions and implementations are in the same assembly.

Opaque façade

In this assembly, only the façade is public; all the other classes are internal, which means they are hidden from the external world. In most cases, this is not ideal; hiding everything makes the subsystem less flexible and harder to extend.

However, in some scenarios, you may want to control access to your internal APIs. This may be because they are not mature enough and you don't want any third party to depend on them, or for any other reasons you may deem appropriate for your specific use case.

Let's start by taking a look at the following subsystem code:

```csharp
// An added interface for flexibility
public interface IOpaqueFacade
{
    string ExecuteOperationA();
    string ExecuteOperationB();
}
// A hidden component
internal class ComponentA
{
    public string OperationA() => "Component A, Operation A";
    public string OperationB() => "Component A, Operation B";
}
// A hidden component
internal class ComponentB
{
    public string OperationC() => "Component B, Operation C";
    public string OperationD() => "Component B, Operation D";
}
// A hidden component
internal class ComponentC
{
    public string OperationE() => "Component C, Operation E";
    public string OperationF() => "Component C, Operation F";
}
// The opaque façade using the other hidden components
public class OpaqueFacade : IOpaqueFacade
{
    private readonly ComponentA _componentA;
    private readonly ComponentB _componentB;
    private readonly ComponentC _componentC;
    // Using constructor injection
    internal OpaqueFacade(ComponentA componentA, ComponentB componentB,
ComponentC componentC)
    {
        _componentA = componentA ?? throw new
ArgumentNullException(nameof(componentA));
        _componentB = componentB ?? throw new
ArgumentNullException(nameof(componentB));
        _componentC = componentC ?? throw new
ArgumentNullException(nameof(componentC));
```

```
    }
    public string ExecuteOperationA()
    {
        return new StringBuilder()
            .AppendLine(_componentA.OperationA())
            .AppendLine(_componentA.OperationB())
            .AppendLine(_componentB.OperationD())
            .AppendLine(_componentC.OperationE())
            .ToString();
    }
    public string ExecuteOperationB()
    {
        return new StringBuilder()
            .AppendLine(_componentB.OperationC())
            .AppendLine(_componentB.OperationD())
            .AppendLine(_componentC.OperationF())
            .ToString();
    }
}
```

As you can see, the `OpaqueFacade` class is coupled with `ComponentA`, `ComponentB`, and `ComponentC` directly. There was no point in extracting any `internal` interfaces since the subsystem is not extensible anyway. We could have done this to offer some kind of internal flexibility, but in this case, there was no advantage in doing so.

Besides this coupling, `ComponentA`, `ComponentB`, and `ComponentC` define two methods each, which returns a string describing their source. With that code in place, we can observe what is happening and how the final result was composed.

`OpaqueFacade` also exposes two methods, but each composes a different message by using the underlying subsystem's components. This is a classic use of a façade; the façade queries other objects in a more or less complicated way and then does something with the results, taking away the caller's burden of knowing the subsystem.

Moreover, to register the `OpaqueFacadeSubSystem` façade against the IoC container, we needed some "magic" to overcome the `internal` visibility modifiers. To solve this problem, I added the following extension method that registers the dependencies, as we explored in *Chapter 7, Deep Dive into Dependency Injection*. The extension method is accessible by the consumer application:

```
public static class StartupExtensions
{
    public static IServiceCollection AddOpaqueFacadeSubSystem(this
    IServiceCollection services)
    {
        services.AddSingleton<IOpaqueFacade>(serviceProvider
```

```
            => new OpaqueFacade(new ComponentA(), new ComponentB(), new
    ComponentC()));
            return services;
        }
    }
```

Next, to the transparent façade implementation.

Transparent façade

The transparent façade is the most flexible type of façade, extremely suitable for a system that leverages dependency injection. The implementation is very similar to the opaque façade, but the `public` visibility modifier changes how consumers can access the class library elements. For this system, it was worth adding interfaces to allow the consumers of the subsystem to extend it when needed.

First, let's take a look at the abstractions:

```
namespace TransparentFacadeSubSystem.Abstractions
{
    public interface ITransparentFacade
    {
        string ExecuteOperationA();
        string ExecuteOperationB();
    }
    public interface IComponentA
    {
        string OperationA();
        string OperationB();
    }
    public interface IComponentB
    {
        string OperationC();
        string OperationD();
    }
    public interface IComponentC
    {
        string OperationE();
        string OperationF();
    }

}
```

The API of this subsystem is the same as the opaque façade. The only difference is how we can use the subsystem and extend it (from a consumer standpoint). The implementations are mostly the same as well, but the classes implement the interfaces and are `public`; the highlighted elements represent the changes that have been made:

```csharp
namespace TransparentFacadeSubSystem
{
    public class ComponentA : IComponentA
    {
        public string OperationA() => "Component A, Operation A";
        public string OperationB() => "Component A, Operation B";
}
    public class ComponentB : IComponentB
    {
        public string OperationC() => "Component B, Operation C";
        public string OperationD() => "Component B, Operation D";
    }
    public class ComponentC : IComponentC
    {
        public string OperationE() => "Component C, Operation E";
        public string OperationF() => "Component C, Operation F";
    }
    public class TransparentFacade : ITransparentFacade
    {
        private readonly IComponentA _componentA;
        private readonly IComponentB _componentB;
        private readonly IComponentC _componentC;
    public TransparentFacade(IComponentA componentA, IComponentB
componentB, IComponentC componentC)
    {
        _componentA = componentA ?? throw new
ArgumentNullException(nameof(componentA));
        _componentB = componentB ?? throw new
ArgumentNullException(nameof(componentB));
        _componentC = componentC ?? throw new
ArgumentNullException(nameof(componentC));
    }
        public string ExecuteOperationA()
        {
            return new StringBuilder()
                .AppendLine(_componentA.OperationA())
                .AppendLine(_componentA.OperationB())
                .AppendLine(_componentB.OperationD())
                .AppendLine(_componentC.OperationE())
                .ToString();
        }
```

```
        public string ExecuteOperationB()
        {
            return new StringBuilder()
                .AppendLine(_componentB.OperationC())
                .AppendLine(_componentB.OperationD())
                .AppendLine(_componentC.OperationF())
                .ToString();
        }
    }
}
```

Before going further, note that the following extension method was also created to simplify the use of the subsystem. However, everything that's defined there can be overridden (which is not the case for the opaque façade):

```
public static class StartupExtensions
{
    public static IServiceCollection AddTransparentFacadeSubSystem(this
    IServiceCollection services)
    {
        services.AddSingleton<ITransparentFacade, TransparentFacade>();
        services.AddSingleton<IComponentA, ComponentA>();
        services.AddSingleton<IComponentB, ComponentB>();
        services.AddSingleton<IComponentC, ComponentC>();
        return services;
    }
}
```

As you can see, all the new elements are gone and have been replaced by simple dependency registration (singleton lifetimes, in this case). These little differences give you the tools to reimplement any part of the subsystem if you want to; see the following subsection for an example.

Note

In the transparent façade code, we can register bindings because classes and interfaces are `public`. In the opaque façade, we had to define the constructor of the `OpaqueFacade` class as `internal` because the type of its parameters (`ComponentA`, `ComponentB`, and `ComponentC`) are internal. Changing the visibility modifier of the constructor from `internal` to `public` yields a *CS0051 Inconsistent accessibility* error.

Besides those differences, the transparent façade plays the same role as the opaque façade, outputting the same result.

The program

Now, let's analyze the consumer that is a micro-ASP.NET Core application that forwards HTTP requests to the façades.

The first step is to register the dependencies (in the composition root), like this:

```
var builder = WebApplication.CreateBuilder(args);
builder.Services
    .AddOpaqueFacadeSubSystem()
    .AddTransparentFacadeSubSystem()
;
```

> **Note**
>
> With these extension methods, the application root is so clean that it is hard to know that we registered two subsystems against the IoC container. This is a good way of keeping your code organized and clean, especially when you're building class libraries.

Now that everything has been registered, the second thing we need to do is route those HTTP requests to the façades. Let's take a look at the code first:

```
var app = builder.Build();
app.MapGet("/opaque/a", (IOpaqueFacade opaqueFacade) => opaqueFacade.
ExecuteOperationA());
app.MapGet("/opaque/b", (IOpaqueFacade opaqueFacade) => opaqueFacade.
ExecuteOperationB());
app.MapGet("/transparent/a", (ITransparentFacade transparentFacade) =>
transparentFacade.ExecuteOperationA());
app.MapGet("/transparent/b", (ITransparentFacade transparentFacade) =>
transparentFacade.ExecuteOperationB());
app.Run();
```

In the preceding block (see highlighted code), we define four routes. Each route dispatches the request to one of the façade's methods. A façade is injected in each delegate, and thanks to the minimal API feature, this code is indeed minimal and very clean.

If you run the program and navigate to `https://localhost:9004/transparent/a`, the page should display the following:

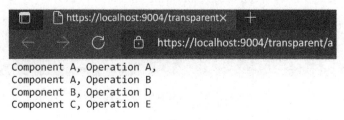

Figure 9.17: The result of executing the ExecuteOperationA method of the ITransparentFacade instance

What happened is located inside the delegates. It uses the injected `ITransparentFacade` service and calls its `ExecuteOperationA()` method, and then outputs the `result` variable to the response stream.

Now, let's define how `ITransparentFacade` is composed:

- `ITransparentFacade` is an instance of `TransparentFacade`.
- We inject `IComponentA`, `IComponentB`, and `IComponentC` in the `TransparentFacade` class.
- These dependencies are instances of `ComponentA`, `ComponentB`, and `ComponentC`, respectively.

Visually, the following flow happens:

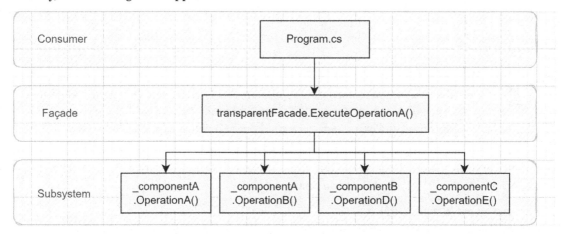

Figure 9.18: A representation of the call hierarchy that occurs when the consumer executes the ExecuteOperationA method

In the preceding diagram, we can see the shielding that's done by the façade and how it has made the consumer's life easier. Here, there's one call instead of four.

Note

One of the hardest parts of using dependency injection is its abstractness. If you are not sure how all those parts are assembled, add a breakpoint into Visual Studio (let's say, on the `var result = transparentFacade.ExecuteOperationA()` line) and run the application in debug mode. From there, **Step Into** each method call. That should help you figure out what is happening. Using the debugger to find the concrete types and their states can help find details about a system or diagnose bugs.

To use **Step Into**, you can use the following button or hit **F11**:

Figure 9.19: The Visual Studio Step Into (F11) button

Next, we update the result without changing the component's code.

Flexibility in action

Now, let's see the added flexibility of the transparent façade in action.

Context: We want to change the behavior of the `TransparentFacade` class. At the moment, the result of the `transparent/b` endpoint looks like this:

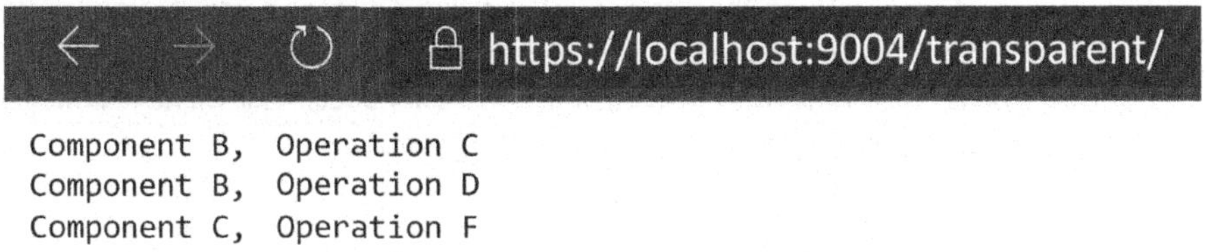

```
← → ○    🔒 https://localhost:9004/transparent/
```

```
Component B, Operation C
Component B, Operation D
Component C, Operation F
```

Figure 9.20: The result of executing the ExecuteOperationB method of the ITransparentFacade instance

To demonstrate that we can extend and change the hidden sub-system (transparent façade), we want to change the output to the following:

```
← → ○    🔒 https://localhost:9004/transparent/
```

```
Flexibility
Design Pattern
Component C, Operation F
```

Figure 9.21: The expected result once the change has been made

We also want to achieve this result without modifying `ComponentB`. To do this, we execute the following steps:

1. Create the following class:

   ```
   public class UpdatedComponentB : IComponentB
   {
       public string OperationC() => "Flexibility";
       public string OperationD() => "Design Pattern";
   }
   ```

2. Tell the IoC container about it, like this:

   ```
   services
       .AddRouting()
       .AddOpaqueFacadeSubSystem()
       .AddTransparentFacadeSubSystem()
       .AddSingleton<IComponentB, UpdatedComponentB>()
   ;
   ```

3. From there, if you run the program, you should see the desired result!

> **Note**
>
> Adding a dependency for a second time makes that dependency resolved by the container, thus overriding the first one. However, both registrations remain present in the services collection; for example, calling `GetServices<IComponentB>()` on `IServiceProvider` would return two dependencies. Do not confuse the `GetServices()` and `GetService()` methods (plural versus singular); one returns a collection while the other returns a single instance. That single instance is always the last that has been registered.

That's it! We updated the system without modifying it. This is what dependency injection can do for you when you're designing a program around it.

Alternative façade patterns

One alternative would be to create a *hybrid between a transparent façade and an opaque façade* by exposing the abstractions using the `public` visibility modifier (all of the interfaces) while keeping the implementations hidden under an `internal` visibility modifier. This hybrid design offers the right balance between **control and flexibility**.

Another alternative would be to create *a façade outside of the subsystem*. In the previous examples, we created the façades inside the class libraries, but this is not mandatory; the façade is just a class that creates an accessible wall between your system and one or more subsystems. It should be located wherever you see fit. Creating external façades like this would be especially useful when you do not control the source code of the subsystem(s), such as if you only have access to the binaries. This could also be used to create project-specific façades over the same subsystem, giving you extra flexibility without cluttering your subsystems with multiple façades, shifting the maintenance cost from the subsystems to the client applications that use them.

This one is more of a note than an alternative: you do not need to create an assembly per subsystem. I did it because it helped me explain different concepts to you in the examples, but you could create multiple subsystems in the same assembly. You could even create a single assembly that includes all your subsystems, façades, and the client code (all in a single project).

Conclusion

The Façade pattern is handy for simplifying consumers' lives as it allows you to hide subsystems' implementation details behind a wall. There are multiple flavors to it; the two most prominent ones are:

- The **transparent façade**, which increases flexibility by exposing at least part of the subsystem(s)
- The **opaque façade**, which controls access by hiding most of the subsystem(s)

Now, let's see how the **transparent façade** pattern can help us follow the **SOLID** principles:

- **S**: A well-designed **transparent façade** serves this exact purpose by providing a cohesive set of functionalities to its clients by hiding overly complex subsystems or internal implementation details

- **O**: A well-designed **transparent façade** and its underlying subsystem's components can be extended without direct modification, as we saw in the *Flexibility in action* section

- **L**: N/A

- **I**: By exposing a façade that uses different smaller objects implementing small interfaces, we could say that the segregation is done at both the façade and the component levels

- **D**: The Façade pattern does not specify anything about interfaces, so it is up to the developers to enforce this principle by using other patterns, principles, and best practices

Finally, let's see how the **opaque façade** pattern can help us follow the **SOLID** principles:

- **S**: A well-designed **opaque façade** serves this exact purpose by providing a cohesive set of functionalities to its clients by hiding overly complex subsystems or internal implementation details.

- **O**: By hiding the subsystem, the **opaque façade** limits our ability to extend it. However, we could implement a **hybrid façade** to help with that.

- **L**: N/A

- **I**: The **opaque façade** does not help nor diminish our ability to apply the ISP.

- **D**: The Façade pattern does not specify anything about interfaces, so it is up to the developers to enforce this principle by using other patterns, principles, and best practices.

Summary

In this chapter, we covered multiple fundamental GoF structural design patterns. They help us extend our systems from the outside, without modifying the actual classes, leading to a higher degree of cohesion by composing our object graph dynamically.

We started with the Decorator pattern, which extends other objects, at runtime, by using them internally. Decorators can also be chained, allowing even greater flexibility (decorating other decorators). We also used an open source tool named Scrutor that simplifies the decorator pattern usage by extending the built-in ASP.NET Core dependency injection system.

Then, we covered the Composite pattern, which allows us to create complex and flexible data structures. To make the life of its consumer easier, the composite delegates the navigation responsibility to each component.

After that, we covered the Adapter pattern, which allows us to adapt an object to another interface. This pattern is very helpful when we need to adapt the components of external systems that we have no control over.

Finally, we dug into the Façade pattern, which is similar to the Adapter pattern, but at the subsystem level. It allows us to create a wall in front of one or more subsystems, simplifying its usage. It could also be used to hide a subsystem from its consumers.

In the next chapter, we explore two GoF behavioral design patterns: the Template method and the Chain of Responsibility design pattern.

Questions

Here are a few revision questions:

1. Can we decorate a decorator with another decorator?
2. Name one of the advantages of the Composite pattern.
3. Can we use the Adapter pattern to migrate an old API to a new system in order to adapt its APIs before rewriting it?
4. Why should we use a façade?
5. What is the difference between the Adapter and the Façade patterns?

Further reading

*   To learn more about Scrutor, please visit `https://adpg.link/xvfS`

Join our book's Discord space

Join the book's Discord workspace for *Ask me Anything* session with the authors:

`https://packt.link/ASPdotNET6DesignPatterns`

10

Behavioral Patterns

In this chapter, we explore two new design patterns from the well-known **Gang of Four** (GoF). They are behavioral patterns, which means that they help simplify the management of system behaviors.

Often, you need to encapsulate some core algorithm while allowing other pieces of code to extend that implementation. That is where the **Template Method** pattern comes into play.

Other times, you have a complex process with multiple algorithms that all apply to one or more situations and you need to organize it in a testable and extensible fashion. This is where the **Chain of Responsibility** pattern can help. For example, the ASP.NET Core middleware pipeline is a Chain of Responsibility where all the middleware inspects the request and acts on it.

The following topics are covered in this chapter:

- Implementing the Template Method pattern
- Implementing the Chain of Responsibility pattern
- How to mix them

Implementing the Template Method pattern

The **Template Method** is a GoF behavioral pattern that uses inheritance to share code between the base class and its subclasses. It is a very powerful, yet simple, design pattern.

Goal

The goal of the Template Method pattern is to encapsulate the outline of an algorithm in a base class while leaving some parts of that algorithm open for modification by the subclasses, which adds flexibility at a low cost.

Design

As mentioned earlier, the design is simple but extensible. First, we need to define a base class that contains the `TemplateMethod()` method and then defines one or more sub-operations that need to be implemented by its subclasses (`abstract`), or that can be overridden (`virtual`).

Using UML, it looks like this:

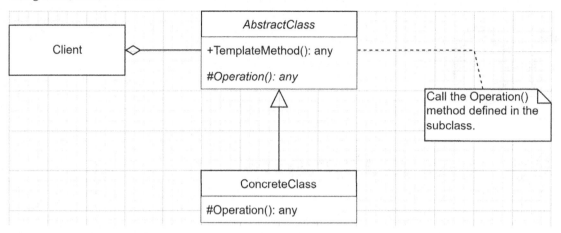

Figure 10.1: Class diagram representing the Template Method pattern

How does this work?

- `AbstractClass` implements the shared code: the algorithm.
- `ConcreteClass` implements its specific part of the algorithm.
- `Client` calls `TemplateMethod()`, which calls the subclass implementation of one or more specific algorithm elements.

Note

We could also extract an interface from `AbstractClass` to allow even more flexibility, but that's beyond the scope of the Template Method pattern.

Let's now get into some code to see the Template Method pattern in action.

Project – Building a search machine

Let's start with a simple, classic example to demonstrate how the Template Method pattern works.

Context: We want to use a different search algorithm depending on the collection to be searched. When the collection is sorted, we want to use a binary search, but when it is not, we want to use a linear search.

Let's start with the consumer, `Program.cs`:

```
var builder = WebApplication.CreateBuilder(args);
builder.Services
    .AddSingleton<SearchMachine>(x => new LinearSearchMachine(1, 10, 5, 2, 123,
333, 4))
    .AddSingleton<SearchMachine>(x => new BinarySearchMachine(1, 2, 3, 4, 5, 6,
7, 8, 9, 10))
;
```

```
var app = builder.Build();
app.MapGet("/", (IEnumerable<SearchMachine> searchMachines) =>
{
    var sb = new StringBuilder();
    var elementsToFind = new int[] { 1, 10, 11 };
    foreach (var searchMachine in searchMachines)
    {
        var heading = $"Current search machine is {searchMachine.GetType().
Name}";
        sb.AppendLine("".PadRight(heading.Length, '='));
        sb.AppendLine(heading);
        foreach (var value in elementsToFind)
        {
            var index = searchMachine.IndexOf(value);
            var wasFound = index.HasValue;
            if (wasFound)
            {
                sb.AppendLine($"The element '{value}' was found at index
{index!.Value}.");
            }
            else
            {
                sb.AppendLine($"The element '{value}' was not found.");
            }
        }
    }
    return sb.ToString();
});
app.Run();
```

In the consumer code, we configure `LinearSearchMachine` and `BinarySearchMachine` as two `SearchMachine` implementations. Each instance is initialized using a different sequence of numbers.

We then inject all registered `SearchMachine` services into the / delegate (highlighted in the code block). That handler iterates all `SearchMachine` instances and tries to find all elements of the `elementsToFind` array, before outputting the `text/plain` results.

Next, let's explore the `SearchMachine` class:

```
namespace TemplateMethod;
public abstract class SearchMachine
{
    protected int[] Values { get; }
    protected SearchMachine(params int[] values)
```

```
    {
        Values = values ?? throw new ArgumentNullException(nameof(values));
    }
    public int? IndexOf(int value)
    {
        if (Values.Length == 0) { return null; }
        var result = Find(value);
        return result;
    }
    protected abstract int? Find(int value);
}
```

The `SearchMachine` class represents `AbstractClass`. It exposes the `IndexOf()` template method, which uses the required hook represented by the abstract `Find()` method (see highlighted code). The hook is required because each subclass must implement that method, thereby making that method a required extension point (or hook).

Next, we explore our first implementation of `ConcreteClass`, the `LinearSearchMachine` class:

```
namespace TemplateMethod;
public class LinearSearchMachine : SearchMachine
{
    public LinearSearchMachine(params int[] values)
        : base(values) { }

    protected override int? Find(int value)
    {
        var index = 0;
        foreach (var item in Values)
        {
            if (item == value) { return index; }
            index++;
        }
        return null;
    }
}
```

The `LinearSearchMachine` class is a `ConcreteClass` representing the linear search implementation used by `SearchMachine`. It's part of the algorithm implemented by the `Find` method.

Finally, we move on to the `BinarySearchMachine` class:

```
namespace TemplateMethod;
public class BinarySearchMachine : SearchMachine
{
```

```
    public BinarySearchMachine(params int[] values)
        : base(values.OrderBy(v => v).ToArray()) { }

    protected override int? Find(int value)
    {
        var index = Array.BinarySearch(Values, value);
        return index == -1 ? null : index;
    }
}
```

The BinarySearchMachine class is a ConcreteClass representing the binary search implementation of SearchMachine. As you may have noticed, we skipped the binary search algorithm's implementation by delegating it to the built-in Array.BinarySearch method. Thanks to the .NET team!

Important

For a binary search algorithm to work, the collection must be sorted, hence the sorting that is done in the constructor when passing the values to the base class (OrderBy). That may not be the most performant way of ensuring the array is sorted (precondition/guard), but it is a very fast and readable way to write it. Moreover, in our case, performance should not be an issue. Furthermore, to optimize such an algorithm, you need to test a large set of data and leverage parallelism (multithreading).

Now that we have defined the actors and explored the code, let's see what is happening in client:

1. client uses the registered SearchMachine instances and searches for a set of values (1, 10, and 11).

2. Once that is done, client displays to the user whether the numbers were found or not.

In this case, the template method and the Find method return null when a value is not found.

By running the program, we get the following output:

```
================================================
Current search machine is LinearSearchMachine
The element '1' was found at index 0.
The element '10' was found at index 1.
The element '11' was not found.
================================================
Current search machine is BinarySearchMachine
The element '1' was found at index 0.
The element '10' was found at index 9.
The element '11' was not found.
```

The preceding output shows the two algorithms at play. Both `SearchMachine` implementations did not contain the value 11. They both contained the values 1 and 10 placed at a different position of their respective arrays. Here is a reminder of the values:

```
new LinearSearchMachine(1, 10, 5, 2, 123, 333, 4)
new BinarySearchMachine(1, 2, 3, 4, 5, 6, 7, 8, 9, 10)
```

The consumer was iterating the `SearchMachine` registered with the IoC container. The base class implements the `IndexOf` but delegates the search (`Find`) algorithm to the subclasses. The preceding output shows that each `SearchMachine` was able to execute the expected task by implementing only the `Find` piece of the algorithm.

And voilà! We have covered the Template Method pattern, as easy as that. Of course, our algorithm was very simple, but the concept remains.

We could add `virtual` methods in the base class to create optional hooks. Those methods would become optional extension points that subclasses can implement or not. That would allow a more complex and more versatile scenario to be supported. We will not cover this here because it is not part of the pattern itself, even if very similar. There are many examples in the .NET **base class library** (BCL), like most methods of the `ComponentBase` class (in the `Microsoft.AspNetCore.Components` namespace). For example, when we override the `OnInitialized` method in a Blazor component, we leverage such an optional extension hook. The base method does nothing and is there only for extensibility purposes, allowing us to run code as part of the component's lifecycle. You can consult the `ComponentBase` class code in the official .NET repo on GitHub: `https://adpg.link/1WYq`.

Conclusion

The Template Method is a powerful and easy-to-implement design pattern that allows subclasses to reuse the algorithm's skeleton while implementing (`abstract`) or overriding (`virtual`) some of its subparts. Allowing implementation-specific classes to extend the core algorithm can reduce the duplication of logic and improve maintainability while not cutting out any flexibility in the process. There are many examples in the .NET BCL, and we leverage this pattern at the end of the chapter, based on a real-world scenario.

Now, let's see how the Template Method pattern can help us follow the **SOLID** principles:

- **S**: The Template Method pushes algorithm-specific portions of the code to subclasses while keeping the core algorithm in the base class. By doing that, it helps follow the **single responsibility principle** (SRP) by distributing responsibilities.

- **O**: By opening extension hooks, it opens the template for extensions (allowing subclasses to extend it) and closes it from modifications (no need to modify the base class since the subclasses can extend it).

- **L**: Since the subclasses are the implementations, there are no base behaviors to enforce in subclasses, so following the **Liskov substitution principle** (LSP) should not be a problem when implementing the Template Method pattern. That said, this principle is tricky, so it could be possible to create a subclass (or a subclass of a subclass) that breaks the LSP, thereby altering the program logic.

- **I:** As long as the base class implements the smallest cohesive surface possible, using the Template Method pattern should not negatively impact the program.
- **D:** The Template Method pattern is based on an abstraction, so as long as consumers depend on that abstraction, it should help to get in line with the **dependency inversion principle (DIP)**.

Next, we move to the Chain of Responsibility design pattern before mixing the Template Method and the Chain of Responsibility pattern to improve our code.

Implementing the Chain of Responsibility pattern

The **Chain of Responsibility** is a GoF behavioral pattern that chains classes to handle complex scenarios efficiently, with limited effort. Once again, the goal is to take a complex problem and break it into multiple smaller units.

Goal

The goal of the Chain of Responsibility pattern is to chain multiple handlers that each solve a limited number of problems. If a handler cannot solve the specific problem, it passes the resolution to the chain's next handler. There could be a default handler executing some logic at the end of the chain, such as throwing a custom exception (for example, `OperationNotHandledException`) or a handler that makes sure of the opposite (in other words, that nothing happens, especially no exception).

Design

The most basic Chain of Responsibility starts by defining an interface that handles a request (`IHandler`). Then we add classes that handle one or more scenarios (`Handler1` and `Handler2`):

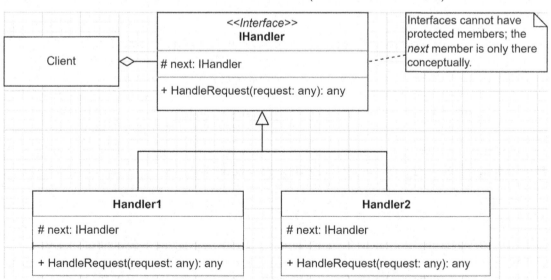

Figure 10.2: Class diagram representing the Chain of Responsibility pattern

Tip

When creating the chain of responsibility, you can order the handlers so that the most requested handlers are closer to the beginning of the chain and the least requested handlers are closer to the end. This helps limit the number of "chain links" that are visited for each request before reaching the right handler.

A big difference between the Chain of Responsibility pattern and many other patterns is that no central dispatcher knows the handlers; all handlers are independent. The consumer receives a handler and tells it to handle the request, no more complexity than this. Each handler is also simple, handling the request or not, and then passing it, or not, to the next handler in the chain. This allows us to divide complex logic into multiple pieces that handle a single responsibility, improving testability, reusability, and extensibility in the process. Since there is no orchestrator, each chain element is independent, leading to a cohesive and loosely coupled design.

Enough theory. Let's look at some code.

Project – Message interpreter

Context: We need to create the receiving end of a messaging application where each message is unique, making it impossible to create a single algorithm to handle them all.

After analyzing the problem, we decided to build a chain of responsibility where each handler can manage a single message. The pattern seems more than perfect!

Background

This project is based on something that I built years ago. Physical (IoT) devices were sending bytes (messages) due to limited bandwidth. Then, in a web application, we had to associate those bytes with real values. Each message had a fixed header size, but a variable body size. The headers were handled in a base handler (template method), and each individual handler in the chain was managing a different message type. For the current example, we keep it simpler than parsing bytes, but the concept is the same.

For our demo application, the messages are as simple as this:

```
namespace ChainOfResponsibility;
public record class Message(string Name, string? Payload);
```

The `Name` property is used as a discriminator to differentiate messages, and each handler's responsibility is to do something with the `Payload` property. We won't do anything with the payload as it is irrelevant to the pattern, but conceptually, that's what should happen.

The handlers are also very simple:

```
namespace ChainOfResponsibility;
public interface IMessageHandler
{
    void Handle(Message message);
}
```

The only thing a handler can do is handle a message. Our initial application can handle the following messages:

- The `AlarmTriggeredHandler` class handles `AlarmTriggered` messages.
- The `AlarmPausedHandler` class handles `AlarmPaused` messages.
- The `AlarmStoppedHandler` class handles `AlarmStopped` messages.

The three handlers are very similar and share quite a bit of logic, but we fix that later. In the meantime, we have the following:

```
public class AlarmTriggeredHandler : IMessageHandler
{
    private readonly IMessageHandler? _next;
    public AlarmTriggeredHandler(IMessageHandler? next = null)
    {
        _next = next;
    }
    public void Handle(Message message)
    {
        if (message.Name == "AlarmTriggered")
        {
            // Do something clever with the Payload
        }
        else if (_next != null)
        {
            _next.Handle(message);
        }
    }
}
public class AlarmPausedHandler : IMessageHandler
{
    private readonly IMessageHandler? _next;
    public AlarmPausedHandler(IMessageHandler? next = null)
    {
```

```
            _next = next;
        }
        public void Handle(Message message)
        {
            if (message.Name == "AlarmPaused")
            {
                // Do something clever with the Payload
            }
            else if (_next != null)
            {
                _next.Handle(message);
            }
        }
    }
    public class AlarmStoppedHandler : IMessageHandler
    {
        private readonly IMessageHandler? _next;
        public AlarmStoppedHandler(IMessageHandler? next = null)
        {
            _next = next;
        }
        public void Handle(Message message)
        {
            if (message.Name == "AlarmStopped")
            {
                // Do something clever with the Payload
            }
            else if (_next != null)
            {
                _next.Handle(message);
            }
        }
    }
```

Each handler does two things:

- It allows an optional "next handler" to be injected into its constructor (highlighted in the code). The handler classes use that _next member in the Handle method.
- It handles only the request that it knows about, delegating the others to the next handler in the chain (the Handle method).

In this case, if the next handler is null, nothing happens. In a real scenario, you may want to know that a handler is missing or that the message was invalid. Let's add a fourth handler that notifies us of invalid requests:

```
public class DefaultHandler : IMessageHandler
{
    public void Handle(Message message)
    {
        throw new NotSupportedException($"Messages named '{message.Name}' are
not supported.");
    }
}
```

That new default handler throws an exception that notifies the consumer of the Chain of Responsibility about the error.

Note

We can create custom exceptions to make it easier to differentiate between system errors and application errors. But sometimes, throwing a system exception is good enough. For example, here are a few exceptions that are often thrown as is: `NotSupportedException`, `NotImplementedException`, and `ArgumentNullException`.

Let's use `Program.cs` as the consumer of the Chain of Responsibility (the client) and use HTTP requests as the way to interface with our program and build the message.

Tip

Usually, the `GET` method is used to read data, while other methods, such as `POST`, `PUT`, and `PATCH`, are used to create, replace, or update data. For testing purposes, it is easier to send arbitrary data to our Chain of Responsibility by using `GET` (I recommend that you don't do that in your apps), so we are cheating on this one.

Here is our program, using minimal APIs and top-level statements:

```
var builder = WebApplication.CreateBuilder(args);
// Create the chain of responsibility,
// ordered by the most called (or the ones to execute earlier)
// to the less called handler (or the ones that take more time to execute),
// followed by the DefaultHandler.
builder.Services.AddSingleton<IMessageHandler>(new AlarmTriggeredHandler(new
AlarmPausedHandler(new AlarmStoppedHandler(new DefaultHandler()))));
```

In the preceding code, we manually create the Chain of Responsibility and register it as a singleton of IMessageHandler. In that registration code, each handler is injected in the previous constructor manually (created with the new keyword).

The next code represents a list of relative URLs that are displayed when calling /, for convenience purposes:

```
var app = builder.Build();

// "Menu" endpoint
app.MapGet("/", () => new[] {
    "/handle/AlarmTriggered",
    "/handle/AlarmPaused",
    "/handle/AlarmStopped",
    "/handle/SomeUnhandledMessageName",
});
```

The following code is the consumer of the chain:

```
// Consumer (client) endpoint
app.MapGet("/handle/{name}", (string name, string? payload, IMessageHandler
messageHandler) =>
{
    var message = new Message(name, payload);
    try
    {
        // Send the message into the chain of responsibility
        messageHandler.Handle(message);
        return $"Message '{message.Name}' handled successfully.";
    }
    catch (NotSupportedException ex)
    {
        return ex.Message;
    }
});
app.Run();
```

The consumer is reachable through the /handle/{name} URL. The delegate expects the name, an optional payload, and an IMessageHandler implementation to be injected. For every request, it does the following:

1. Creates a Message based on the name and payload parameters.
2. Passes that message to the first handler of the chain of responsibility (injected into the /handle/ {name} delegate): messageHandler.Handle(message);.

3.   Writes an error message when a `NotSupportedException` has been thrown, or a success
     message otherwise.

When running the application, we should expect the following "menu" when calling
`https://localhost:10001/`:

```
4    [
5        "/handle/AlarmTriggered",
6        "/handle/AlarmPaused",
7        "/handle/AlarmStopped",
8        "/handle/SomeUnhandledMessageName"
9    ]
```

Figure 10.3: The root endpoint JSON response that represents a menu

By specifying a valid `name` such as `AlarmTriggered`, we should obtain the following result:

```
URL: https://localhost:10001/AlarmTriggered
Message 'AlarmTriggered' handled successfully.
```

By specifying an invalid `name` such as `SomeUnhandledMessageName`, we should obtain the following
result:

```
URL: https://localhost:10001/SomeUnhandledMessageName
Messages named 'SomeUnhandledMessageName' are not supported.
```

And voilà. We have built a simple Chain of Responsibility that handles messages. Next, let's use both the
Template Method and Chain of Responsibility patterns to encapsulate our handlers' duplicated logic.

Project – Improved message interpreter

Now that we know both the **Chain of Responsibility** and the **Template Method** patterns, it is time to
DRY out our handlers by extracting the shared logic into an abstract base class using the Template
Method pattern and providing extension points to the subclasses.

DRY

We covered the **Don't Repeat Yourself (DRY)** principle in *Chapter 3, Architectural Principles*.

OK, so what has been duplicated?

*   The next handler injection code has been duplicated, and, as an important part of the pattern,
    could be encapsulated into the base class.
*   The logic testing whether the current handler can handle the message has been duplicated.

The new base class looks like this:

```
namespace ImprovedChainOfResponsibility;
public abstract class MessageHandlerBase : IMessageHandler
{
    private readonly IMessageHandler? _next;
    public MessageHandlerBase(IMessageHandler? next = null)
    {
        _next = next;
    }
    public void Handle(Message message)
    {
        if (CanHandle(message))
        {
            Process(message);
        }
        else if (HasNext())
        {
            _next.Handle(message);
        }
    }
    [MemberNotNullWhen(true, nameof(_next))]
    private bool HasNext()
    {
        return _next != null;
    }
    protected virtual bool CanHandle(Message message)
    {
        return message.Name == HandledMessageName;
    }
    protected abstract string HandledMessageName { get; }
    protected abstract void Process(Message message);
}
```

Based on those few changes, what is the template method, and what are the extension points (hooks)?

The MessageHandlerBase class adds the Handle template method. That template method's algorithm is easier to read than it was before. Then, MessageHandlerBase exposes the following extension points:

- CanHandleMessage(Message message) tests whether HandledMessageName is equal to message.Name. This could be overridden if a handler required more complex comparison logic.
- HandledMessageName must be implemented by all subclasses, driving the default logic of CanHandleMessage.

- `Process(Message message)` must be implemented by all subclasses, allowing them to run logic against the message.

Let's now take a look at the three simplified alarm handlers:

```
public class AlarmTriggeredHandler : MessageHandlerBase
{
    protected override string HandledMessageName => "AlarmTriggered";
    public AlarmTriggeredHandler(IMessageHandler? next = null)
        : base(next) { }
    protected override void Process(Message message)
    {
        // Do something clever with the Payload
    }
}
public class AlarmPausedHandler : MessageHandlerBase
{
    protected override string HandledMessageName => "AlarmPaused";
    public AlarmPausedHandler(IMessageHandler? next = null)
        : base(next) { }
    protected override void Process(Message message)
    {
        // Do something clever with the Payload
    }
}
public class AlarmStoppedHandler : MessageHandlerBase
{
    protected override string HandledMessageName => "AlarmStopped";
    public AlarmStoppedHandler(IMessageHandler? next = null)
        : base(next) { }
    protected override void Process(Message message)
    {
        // Do something clever with the Payload
    }
}
```

As we can see from the updated alarm handlers, they are now limited to a single responsibility: processing the messages they can handle. In contrast, `MessageHandlerBase` now handles the chain of responsibility's plumbing. We left the `DefaultHandler` class unchanged since it is the end of the chain and does not support having a next handler.

By mixing those two patterns, we created a complex messaging system that divides responsibilities into handlers. There is one handler per message, and the chain logic is pushed into a base class.

The beauty of such a system is that we don't have to think about all the messages at once; we can focus on just one message at a time. When dealing with a new type of message, we can concentrate on that precise message, implement its handler, and forget about the N other types. The consumers can also be super dumb, sending the request into the pipe without knowing about the Chain of Responsibility, and like magic, the right handler shall prevail!

Project — A final, finer-grained design

In the last example, we were using `HandledMessageName` and `CanHandleMessage` to decide whether a handler could handle a request. There is one problem with that code: if a subclass decides to override `CanHandleMessage`, and then decides that it no longer requires `HandledMessageName`, we would end up having a lingering, unused property in our system.

Note

There are worse situations, but we are talking component design here, so why not push that system a little further toward a better design?

One way to fix this is to create a finer-grained class hierarchy, as follows:

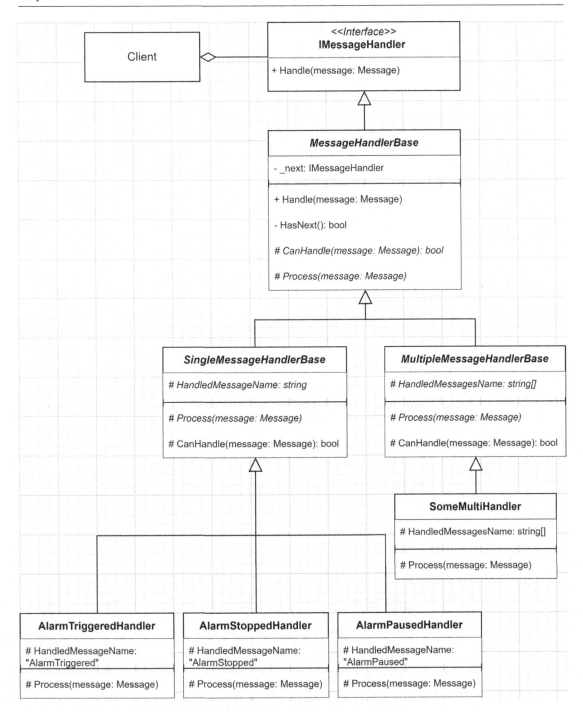

Figure 10.4: Class diagram representing the design of the finer-grained project that implements the
Chain of Responsibility and Template Method patterns

That looks more complicated than it is, really. Before digging into what it actually does, let's take a look at the refactored code:

```csharp
namespace FinalChainOfResponsibility;
public interface IMessageHandler
{
    void Handle(Message message);
}

public abstract class MessageHandlerBase : IMessageHandler
{
    private readonly IMessageHandler? _next;
    public MessageHandlerBase(IMessageHandler? next = null)
    {
        _next = next;
    }

    public void Handle(Message message)
    {
        if (CanHandle(message))
        {
            Process(message);
        }
        else if (HasNext())
        {
            _next.Handle(message);
        }
    }

    [MemberNotNullWhen(true, nameof(_next))]
    private bool HasNext()
    {
        return _next != null;
    }

    protected abstract bool CanHandle(Message message);
    protected abstract void Process(Message message);
}

public abstract class SingleMessageHandlerBase : MessageHandlerBase
{
    public SingleMessageHandlerBase(IMessageHandler? next = null)
```

```
        : base(next) { }

    protected override bool CanHandle(Message message)
    {
        return message.Name == HandledMessageName;
    }
    protected abstract string HandledMessageName { get; }
}


public abstract class MultipleMessageHandlerBase : MessageHandlerBase
{
    public MultipleMessageHandlerBase(IMessageHandler? next = null)
        : base(next) { }

    protected override bool CanHandle(Message message)
    {
        return HandledMessagesName.Contains(message.Name);
    }
    protected abstract string[] HandledMessagesName { get; }
}
```

The omitted `AlarmPausedHandler`, `AlarmStoppedHandler`, and `AlarmTriggeredHandler` classes now inherit from `SingleMessageHandlerBase` instead of `MessageHandlerBase`, but nothing else has changed. `DefaultHandler` has not changed either. For demonstration purposes, I added the `SomeMultiHandler` class to simulate a message handler that can handle "Foo", "Bar", and "Baz" messages. That looks like the following:

```
namespace FinalChainOfResponsibility
{
    public class SomeMultiHandler : MultipleMessageHandlerBase
    {
        public SomeMultiHandler(IMessageHandler? next = null)
            : base(next) { }
        protected override string[] HandledMessagesName
            => new[] { "Foo", "Bar", "Baz" };
        protected override void Process(Message message)
        {
            // Do something clever with the Payload
        }
    }
}
```

Now that we have seen the code and the UML representation of the class hierarchy, let's analyze the actors of the new structure:

- `MessageHandlerBase` manages the Chain of Responsibility by handling the next handler logic and by exposing two hooks (the Template Method pattern) for subclasses to extend:

    a. `bool CanHandle(Message message)`

    b. `void Process(Message message)`

- `SingleMessageHandlerBase` inherits from `MessageHandlerBase` and implements (override) the `bool CanHandle(Message message)` method. It implements the logic related to it and adds the `abstract string HandledMessageName { get; }` property that subclasses must define (override) for the `CanHandle` method to work (a required extension point).

- The subclasses of `SingleMessageHandlerBase` implement the `HandledMessageName` property, which returns the message name that they can handle and implements the handling logic by overriding the `void Process(Message message)` method.

- `MultipleMessageHandlerBase` does the same as `SingleMessageHandlerBase`, but it uses a string array instead of a single string, supporting multiple handler names.

This may sound complicated, but what we did was to allow extensibility without the need to keep any unnecessary code in the process, leaving each class with a single responsibility:

- `MessageHandlerBase` handles _next.
- `SingleMessageHandlerBase` handles the `CanHandle` method of handlers, supporting just a single message.
- `MultipleMessageHandlerBase` handles the `CanHandle` method of handlers supporting multiple messages.
- Other classes must implement their version of `void Process(Message message)` to handle one or more messages.

And voilà! This is another example demonstrating the strength of the Template Method and Chain of Responsibility patterns put together. That last example also emphasizes the importance of the SRP by allowing greater flexibility while keeping the code reliable and maintainable.

Another strength of that design is the interface at the top. Anything that does not fit the class hierarchy can be implemented directly from the interface instead of trying to adapt logic from inappropriate structures—tricking code into doing your bidding often leads to half-baked solutions that become hard to maintain. The `DefaultHandler` class is a good example of that.

Conclusion

The Chain of Responsibility pattern is another great GoF pattern. It divides a large problem into smaller, cohesive units, each doing one job: handling its specific request(s). Mixed with the Template Method pattern, it can become even simpler to handle the chain, moving each part closer toward single responsibilities.

Now, let's see how the Chain of Responsibility pattern can help us follow the **SOLID** principles:

- **S:** The Chain of Responsibility pattern aims toward this exact principle, making it a perfect SRP advocate: single units of logic per class!
- **O:** The Chain of Responsibility pattern allows the addition, removal, and reordering of handlers without touching the code, but by altering the composition of the chain (in the composition root).
- **L:** N/A
- **I:** By creating a small interface with multiple handlers (implementations), the Chain of Responsibility pattern should help with the ISP. The handler interface is not limited to a single method; it can expose multiple methods as long as they aim toward the same responsibility. Cohesion is key.
- **D:** By using the handler interface, no element of the chain, nor the consumers, depends on a specific handler; they only depend on the interface, which helps with the DIP.

Summary

In this chapter, we covered two GoF behavioral patterns. These patterns can help us create a flexible, yet easy-to-maintain system. As the name suggests, behavioral patterns aim at encapsulating application behaviors into cohesive software pieces.

First, we looked at the Template Method pattern, which allows us to encapsulate an algorithm's core inside a base class. It then allows its subclasses to fill in the gaps and extend that algorithm at predefined locations. These locations can be required (`abstract`) or optional (`virtual`).

Then, we explored the Chain of Responsibility pattern, which opens the possibility of chaining multiple small handlers into a chain of processing, inputting the message to be processed at the beginning of the chain, and waiting for one or more handlers to execute the actual logic related to that message against it. That is an important nuance: you don't have to stop the chain's execution at the first handler. In some cases, the Chain of Responsibility could become more like a pipeline than a clear association of one message to one handler.

Lastly, using the Template Method pattern to encapsulate the Chain of Responsibility's chaining logic led us to a simpler implementation without any sacrifices.

In the next chapter, we are going to dig into the Operation Result design pattern to discover efficient ways of managing return values.

Questions

Let's take a look at a few practice questions:

1. Is it true that we can only add one `abstract` method when implementing the Template Method design pattern?
2. Can we use the Strategy pattern in conjunction with the Template Method pattern?
3. Is it true that there is a limit of 32 handlers in a Chain of Responsibility?
4. In a Chain of Responsibility, can multiple handlers process the same message?
5. In what way can the Template Method help implement the Chain of Responsibility pattern?

11

Understanding the Operation Result Design Pattern

This chapter explores the **Operation Result** pattern, starting simple and progressing to more complex cases. An operation result aims at communicating the success or the failure of an operation to its caller. It also allows that operation to return both a value and one or more messages to the caller.

Imagine any system in which you want to display user-friendly error messages, achieve some small speed gain, or even handle failure easily and explicitly. The **Operation Result** design pattern can help you achieve these goals. One way to use it is to handle the result of a remote operation, such as after querying a remote web service.

This pattern builds upon foundational object-oriented programming concepts. Having a whole chapter about it allows us to iterate and design different possibilities incrementally. Of course, the final design should always be based on your needs, so learning multiple options should help you make the right choices.

The following topics are covered in this chapter:

- The Operation Result design pattern basics
- The Operation Result design pattern returning a value
- The Operation Result design pattern returning error messages
- The Operation Result design pattern returning messages with severity levels
- Using sub-classes and static factory methods for better isolation of successes and failures

The Operation Result pattern

The Operation Result design pattern can be very simple to more complex. In this section, we explore multiple ways to use that pattern. We start with its simplest form and build on that until we can return messages, values, and add severity levels as the result of an operation.

Goal

The role of the **Operation Result** pattern is to give an operation (a method) the possibility to return a complex result (an object), which allows the consumer to:

- [Mandatory] Access the success indicator of the operation (that is, whether the operation succeeded or not).
- [Optional] Access the result of the operation if there is one (the return value of the method).
- [Optional] Access the cause of the failure if the operation was not successful (error messages).
- [Optional] Access other information that documents the operation's result. This could be as simple as a list of messages or as complex as multiple properties.

This can go even further, such as returning the severity of a failure or adding any other relevant information for the specific use case. The success indicator could be binary (`true` or `false`), or there could be more than two states, such as success, partial success, and failure. Your imagination (and your needs) is your limit!

> **Tip**
>
> Focus on your needs first, then use your imagination to reach the best possible solution. Software engineering is not only about applying techniques that others told you to. It's an art! The difference is that you are crafting software instead of painting or woodworking. And that most people won't see any of that art (code).

Design

It is easy to rely on throwing exceptions when an operation fails. However, the Operation Result pattern is an alternative way of communicating success or failure between components when you don't want to use exceptions. One such reason could be that the messages are not errors or that treating an erroneous result is part of the main flow, not part of a side `catch` flow.

To be used effectively, a method must return an object containing one or more elements presented in the *Goal* section. As a rule of thumb, a method returning an operation result should not throw an exception. This way, consumers don't have to handle anything other than the operation result itself. For special cases, you could allow exceptions to be thrown, but at that point, it would be a judgment call based on clear specifications or facing a real problem.

Instead of walking you through all of the possible UML diagrams, let's jump into the code and explore multiple smaller examples after taking a look at the basic sequence diagram that describes the simplest form of this pattern, applicable to all examples:

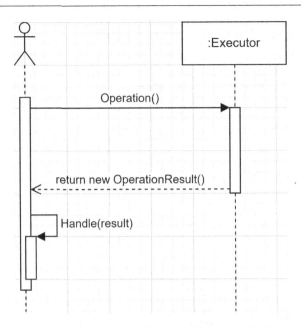

Figure 11.1: Sequence diagram of the Operation Result design pattern

As we can see from the diagram, an operation returns a result (an object), and then the caller can handle that result. What can be included in that result object is covered in the following examples.

Project – Implementing different Operation Result patterns

In this project, a consumer routes the HTTP requests to the right handler. We are visiting each of those handlers one by one, which will help us implement simple to more complex operation results. This should show you many ways to implement the Operation Result pattern to help you understand it, make it your own, and implement it as required in your projects.

The consumer

The consumer of all examples is the Program.cs file. The / URL lists all the consumers. The following code, from Program.cs, routes the HTTP requests toward a handler:

```
app.MapGet("/simplest-form", ...);
app.MapGet("/single-error", ...);
app.MapGet("/single-error-with-value", ...);
app.MapGet("/multiple-errors-with-value", ...);
app.MapGet("/multiple-errors-with-value-and-severity", ...);
app.MapGet("/static-factory-methods", ...);
```

Next, we cover each use case one by one.

The simplest form of the Operation Result pattern

The following diagram represents the simplest form of the Operation Result pattern:

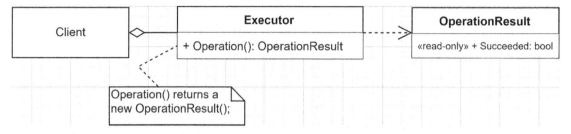

Figure 11.2: Class diagram of the Operation Result design pattern

We can translate that class diagram into the following blocks of code:

```
app.MapGet("/simplest-form", (OperationResult.SimplestForm.Executor executor)
=>
{
    var result = executor.Operation();
    if (result.Succeeded)
    {
        // Handle the success
        return "Operation succeeded";
    }
    else
    {
        // Handle the failure
        return "Operation failed";
    }
});
```

The preceding code handles the /simplest-form HTTP requests. The highlighted code in the preceding
code snippet is the consumer of the following operation:

```
namespace OperationResult.SimplestForm;
public class Executor
{
    public OperationResult Operation()
    {
        // Randomize the success indicator
        // This should be real logic
        var randomNumber = new Random().Next(100);
        var success = randomNumber % 2 == 0;
```

```
        // Return the operation result
        return new OperationResult(success);
    }
}

public record class OperationResult(bool Succeeded);
```

The `Executor` class contains the operation to execute represented by the `Operation` method. That method returns an instance of the `OperationResult` class. The implementation is based on a random number. Sometimes it succeeds, and sometimes it fails. You would usually code some application logic in that method instead. Moreover, the method should hold a proper name that represents the operation itself in an actual program.

The `OperationResult` record class represents the result of the operation. In this case, it is a simple read-only Boolean value stored in the `Succeeded` property. I chose a record class because there is no reason for the result to change. To know more about record classes, have a look at *Appendix A*.

In this form, the difference between the `Operation` method returning a `bool` and an instance of `OperationResult` is small, but it exists nonetheless. By returning an `OperationResult` object, you can extend the return value over time, adding properties and methods to it, which you cannot do with a `bool` without updating all consumers.

Next, we add an error message to the result.

A single error message

Now that we know whether the operation succeeded or not, we want to know what went wrong. To do that, we add an `ErrorMessage` property to the `OperationResult` record class.

With that in place, we no longer need to set whether the operation succeeded or not; we can compute that using the `ErrorMessage` property instead. The logic behind this improvement goes as follows:

*   When there is no error message, the operation succeeded.
*   When there is an error message, the operation failed.

The `OperationResult` record class implementing this logic looks like the following:

```
namespace OperationResult.SingleError
public record class OperationResult
{
    public bool Succeeded => string.IsNullOrWhiteSpace(ErrorMessage);
    public string? ErrorMessage { get; init; }
}
```

In the preceding code, we have the following:

*   The `Succeeded` property, which checks for an `ErrorMessage`.
*   The `ErrorMessage` property, which contains an `ErrorMessage`, settable when instantiating the object.

The executor of that operation looks similar but uses the new constructor, setting an error message instead of directly setting the success indicator:

```
namespace OperationResult.SingleError
public class Executor
{
    public OperationResult Operation()
    {
        // Randomize the success indicator
        // This should be real logic
        var randomNumber = new Random().Next(100);
        var success = randomNumber % 2 == 0;

        // Return the operation result
        return success
            ? new()
            : new() { ErrorMessage = $"Something went wrong with the number
'{randomNumber}'." };
    }
}
```

The consuming code does the same as in the previous sample but writes the error message in the response output instead of a generic failure string:

```
app.MapGet("/single-error", (OperationResult.SingleError.Executor executor) =>
{
    var result = executor.Operation();
    if (result.Succeeded)
    {
        // Handle the success
        return "Operation succeeded";
    }
    else
    {
        // Handle the failure
        return result.ErrorMessage;
    }
});
```

When looking at that example, we can begin to comprehend the Operation Result pattern's usefulness. It gets us further away from the simple success indicator that looked like an overcomplicated Boolean. Furthermore, this is not the end of our exploration because many more forms can be designed and used in more complex scenarios.

Next, we add the possibility of setting a value when the operation succeeds.

Adding a return value

Now that we have a reason for failure, we may want the operation to return a value. To achieve this, let's build over the previous example and add a `Value` property to the `OperationResult` class:

```
namespace OperationResult.SingleErrorWithValue;
public record class OperationResult
{
    public bool Succeeded => string.IsNullOrWhiteSpace(ErrorMessage);
    public string? ErrorMessage { get; init; }
    public int? Value { get; init; }
}
```

By adding a second init-only property, we can set the `Value` property when the operation succeeds and fails.

> **Note**
>
> In a real-world scenario, that `Value` property could be `null` in the case of an error, hence the nullable `int` property.

The operation is also very similar, but we are setting the `Value` property as well as using the object initializer in both cases (highlighted lines):

```
namespace OperationResult.SingleErrorWithValue;
public class Executor
{
    public OperationResult Operation()
    {
        // Randomize the success indicator
        // This should be real logic
        var randomNumber = new Random().Next(100);
        var success = randomNumber % 2 == 0;

        // Return the operation result
        return success
            ? new() { Value = randomNumber }
            : new()
            {
                ErrorMessage = $"Something went wrong with the number '{randomNumber}'.",
                Value = randomNumber,
```

```
                };
        }
}
```

With that in place, the consumer can use the Value. In our case, the program displays it when the operation succeeds:

```
app.MapGet("/single-error-with-value", (OperationResult.SingleErrorWithValue.
Executor executor) =>
{
    var result = executor.Operation();
    if (result.Succeeded)
    {
        // Handle the success
        return $"Operation succeeded with a value of '{result.Value}'.";
    }
    else
    {
        // Handle the failure
        return "Operation failed";
    }
});
```

As we can see from this sample, we can display a custom error message when the operation fails or use the Value property when it succeeds (or even when it fails in this case). We could also leverage the ErrorMessage property as we did in the preceding single-error sample. With this, the power of the Operation Result pattern continues to emerge.

Rest assured, we are not done yet, so let's jump into the next evolution.

Multiple error messages

Now we are at the point where we can transfer a Value and an ErrorMessage to the operation consumers, but what about transferring multiple errors, such as validation errors? To achieve this, we can convert our ErrorMessage property from a string to an IEnumerable<string> or another type of collection that fits your needs better. Here I chose ImmutableList<string> so we know that external actors can't mutate the results:

```
namespace OperationResult.MultipleErrorsWithValue;
public record class OperationResult
{
    public OperationResult()
    {
        Errors = ImmutableList<string>.Empty;
    }
```

```
    public OperationResult(params string[] errors)
    {
        Errors = errors.ToImmutableList();
    }


    public bool Succeeded => !HasErrors();
    public int? Value { get; init; }


    public ImmutableList<string> Errors { get; init; }
    public bool HasErrors()
    {
        return Errors?.Count > 0;
    }
}
```

Let's look at the new pieces in the preceding code before continuing:

- The errors are now stored in `ImmutableList<string>`.
- The `Succeeded` property was updated to account for a collection instead of a single message and follows the same logic.
- The `HasErrors` method was added for convenience.
- A default constructor (success) and one that takes error messages as parameters (failure) have been added to populate the `Errors` property.

Now that the operation result is updated, the operation itself can stay the same. The consumer stays almost the same (see the highlight in the code below), but we need to tell ASP.NET how to serialize the result:

```
app.MapGet("/multiple-errors-with-value", (OperationResult.
MultipleErrorsWithValue.Executor executor) =>
{
    var result = executor.Operation();
    if (result.Succeeded)
    {
        // Handle the success
        return $"Operation succeeded with a value of '{result.Value}'.";
    }
    else
    {
        // Handle the failure
        return result.Errors as object;
    }
});
```

By converting `result.Errors` to an object (see the highlighted code), ASP.NET understands that the return value of our delegate is an object. Without that, the return type could not be inferred, and the code would not compile. That makes sense since the function is returning a `string` in one path and an `ImmutableList<string>` in another.

During the executing, ASP.NET serializes the `ImmutableList<string> Errors` property to JSON before outputting it to the client to help visualize the collection.

> **Tip**
>
> Returning a `plain/text` string when the operation succeeds and an `application/json` array when it fails is usually not a good idea. I suggest not doing something like this in a real application. Either return JSON or plain text. Try not to mix content types in a single endpoint. In most cases, mixing content types will only create avoidable complexity and confusion. We could say that reading the `content-type` header and the status code would be enough to know what has been returned by the server, and that's the purpose of those headers in the HTTP specifications. But, even if that is true, it is way easier for your fellow developers to always be able to expect the same content type when consuming your APIs.
>
> When designing system contracts, consistency and uniformity are usually better than incoherency, ambiguity, and variance.

Our Operation Result pattern implementation is getting better and better but still lacks a few features. One of those features is the possibility to propagate messages that are not errors, such as information messages and warnings, which we implement next.

Adding message severity

Now that our operation result structure is materializing, let's update our last iteration to support message severity.

First, we need a severity indicator. An enum is a good candidate for this kind of work, but it could also be something else. In our case, we leverage an enum that we name `OperationResultSeverity`.

Then we need a message class to encapsulate both the message and the severity level; let's name that class `OperationResultMessage`. The new code looks like this:

```
namespace OperationResult.WithSeverity;
public record class OperationResultMessage
{
    public OperationResultMessage(string message, OperationResultSeverity
severity)
    {
        Message = message ?? throw new ArgumentNullException(nameof(message));
        Severity = severity;
    }

    public string Message { get; }
```

```
    [JsonConverter(typeof(JsonStringEnumConverter))]
    public OperationResultSeverity Severity { get; }
}

public enum OperationResultSeverity
{
    Information = 0,
    Warning = 1,
    Error = 2
}
```

As you can see, we have a simple data structure to replace our string messages.

Then we need to update the OperationResult class to use that new OperationResultMessage class instead. We then need to ensure that the operation result indicates a success only when there is no OperationResultSeverity.Error, allowing it to transmit the OperationResultSeverity.Information and OperationResultSeverity.Warnings messages (we could implement different logic here):

```
namespace OperationResult.WithSeverity;
public record class OperationResult
{
    public OperationResult()
    {
        Messages = ImmutableList<OperationResultMessage>.Empty;
    }
    public OperationResult(params OperationResultMessage[] messages)
    {
        Messages = messages.ToImmutableList();
    }

    public bool Succeeded => !HasErrors();
    public int? Value { get; init; }

    public ImmutableList<OperationResultMessage> Messages { get; init; }
    public bool HasErrors()
    {
        return FindErrors().Any();
    }

    private IEnumerable<OperationResultMessage> FindErrors()
        => Messages.Where(x => x.Severity == OperationResultSeverity.Error);
}
```

The highlighted lines represent the updated logic that sets the success state of the operation. The operation is considered a success only when no error is present in the `Messages` list. The `FindErrors` method returns messages that have an `Error` severity while the `HasErrors` method bases its decision on that method's output.

With that in place, the `Executor` class is also revamped. Let's have a look at those changes:

```
namespace OperationResult.WithSeverity;
public class Executor
{
    public OperationResult Operation()
    {
        // Randomize the success indicator
        // This should be real logic
        var randomNumber = new Random().Next(100);
        var success = randomNumber % 2 == 0;

        // Some information message
        var information = new OperationResultMessage(
            "This should be very informative!",
            OperationResultSeverity.Information
        );

        // Return the operation result
        if (success)
        {
            var warning = new OperationResultMessage(
                "Something went wrong, but we will try again later
automatically until it works!",
                OperationResultSeverity.Warning
            );
            return new OperationResult(information, warning) { Value =
randomNumber };
        }
        else
        {
            var error = new OperationResultMessage(
                $"Something went wrong with the number '{randomNumber}'.",
                OperationResultSeverity.Error
            );
            return new OperationResult(information, error) { Value =
randomNumber };
        }
```

```
        }
    }
```

As you may have noticed, we removed the tertiary operator and made use of all severity levels.

Tip

You should always aim to write code that is easy to read. It is OK to use language features, but nesting statements over statements on a single line has its limits and can quickly become a mess.

In that last code block, both successes and failures return two messages:

- When it is successful, the severity of those messages is information and a warning.
- When it is unsuccessful, the severity of those messages is information and an error.

From the consumer standpoint, nothing has changed from the previous example but once again could be handled differently in a real application that needs to know about those messages:

```
app.MapGet("/multiple-errors-with-value-and-severity", (OperationResult.
WithSeverity.Executor executor) =>
{
    var result = executor.Operation();
    if (result.Succeeded)
    {
        // Handle the success
    }
    else
    {
        // Handle the failure
    }
    return result;
});
```

As you can see, it is still as easy to use, but now with more flexibility added to it. We could do something with the different types of messages, such as displaying them to the user, retrying the operation, and more.

For now, if you run the application and call that endpoint, successful calls should return a JSON string that looks like the following:

```
{
    "succeeded": true,
    "value": 56,
    "messages": [
        {
```

```
        "message": "This should be very informative!",
        "severity": "Information"
    },
    {
        "message": "Something went wrong, but we will try again later
automatically until it works!",
        "severity": "Warning"
    }
    ]
}
```

Failures should return a JSON string that looks like this:

```
{
    "succeeded": false,
    "value": 19,
    "messages": [
        {
            "message": "This should be very informative!",
            "severity": "Information"
        },
        {
            "message": "Something went wrong with the number '19'.",
            "severity": "Error"
        }
    ]
}
```

One more idea to improve this design would be to add a `Status` property that returns a complex success result based on each message's severity level. To do that, we could create another enum:

```
public enum OperationStatus { Success, Failure, PartialSuccess }
```

Then we could access that value through a new property named `Status`, on the `OperationResult` class. With this, a consumer could handle partial successes without digging into the messages themselves. I will leave you to play with this one on your own; for example, the `Status` property could replace the `Succeeded` property, or the `Succeeded` property could leverage the `Status` property similarly to what we did with the errors. The most important part is to define what would be a success, a partial success, and a failure. Think of a database transaction, for example; one failure could lead to the rollback of the transaction, while in another case, one failure could be acceptable.

Now that we've expanded our simple example into this, what happens if we want the `Value` to be optional? To do that, we could create multiple operation result classes that each hold more or less information (properties); let's try that next.

Sub-classes and factories

In this iteration, we keep all the properties, but we instantiate the `OperationResult` objects using static factories. Moreover, we hide certain properties away in the sub-classes, so each type of result only contains the data it needs to be correct. The `OperationResult` class itself only exposes the `Succeeded` property in this scenario.

A **static factory method** is nothing more than a static method responsible for creating objects. It can be handy because it is easy to use as you are about to see. As always, I cannot stress this enough: be careful when designing something `static`, or it could haunt you later; `static` members are not extensible and can make their consumers harder to test.

The `OperationResultMessage` class and the `OperationResultSeverity` enum remain unchanged. In the following code block, the severity is not considered when computing the operation's success or failure state. Instead, we create an abstract `OperationResult` class with two sub-classes:

- `SuccessfulOperationResult`, which represents successful operations.
- `FailedOperationResult`, which represents failed operations.

Then the next step is to force the use of the specifically designed classes by creating two static factory methods:

- `public static OperationResult Success()`, which returns a `SuccessfulOperationResult`.
- `public static OperationResult Failure(params OperationResultMessage[] errors)`, which returns a `FailedOperationResult`.

Doing this moves the responsibility of deciding whether the operation is a success or not from the `OperationResult` class itself to the `Operation` method that creates the result explicitly.

The following code block shows the new `OperationResult` implementation (the static factories are highlighted):

```
namespace OperationResult.StaticFactoryMethod;
public abstract record class OperationResult
{
    private OperationResult() { }

    public abstract bool Succeeded { get; }

    public static OperationResult Success(int? value = null)
    {
        return new SuccessfulOperationResult { Value = value };
    }

    public static OperationResult Failure(params OperationResultMessage[]
errors)
    {
```

```
            return new FailedOperationResult(errors);
    }

    private record class SuccessfulOperationResult : OperationResult
    {
        public override bool Succeeded { get; } = true;
        public virtual int? Value { get; init; }
    }

    private record class FailedOperationResult : OperationResult
    {
        public FailedOperationResult(params OperationResultMessage[] errors)
        {
            Messages = errors.ToImmutableList();
        }

        public override bool Succeeded { get; } = false;
        public ImmutableList<OperationResultMessage> Messages { get; }
    }
}
```

After analyzing the code, there are a few closely related particularities:

- The OperationResult class has a private constructor.
- Both the SuccessfulOperationResult and FailedOperationResult classes are nested inside OperationResult.
- They both inherit from the OperationResult class.
- Both classes are private.

Nested classes are the only way to inherit from the OperationResult class because, like other members of the class, nested classes have access to their private members, including the constructor. Otherwise, it is impossible to inherit from OperationResult. Moreover, as private classes, they can only be accessed internally from the OperationResult class for the same reason and become inaccessible from the outside.

Since the beginning of the book, I have repeated **flexibility** many times; but you don't always want flexibility. Sometimes you want control over what you expose and what you allow consumers to do, whether to protect internal mechanisms (encapsulation) or for maintainability reasons. For example, allowing consumers to change the internal state of an object can lead to unexpected behaviors. Another example, when managing a library, the larger the public API, the more chances of introducing a breaking change. Nonetheless, over-hiding elements can be a detrimental experience for the consumers; if you need something somewhere, the chances are that someone else will too (eventually).

In this case, we could have used a protected constructor instead or implemented a fancier way of instancing success and failure instances. However, I decided to use this opportunity to show you how to lock an implementation in place without needing the `sealed` modifier, making it impossible to extend by inheritance from the outside. We could have built mechanisms in our classes to allow controlled extensibility, but for this one, let's keep it locked in tight!

From there, the only missing pieces are the operation itself and the consumer of the operation. Let's look at the operation first:

```csharp
namespace OperationResult.StaticFactoryMethod;
public class Executor
{
    public OperationResult Operation()
    {
        // Randomize the success indicator
        // This should be real logic
        var randomNumber = new Random().Next(100);
        var success = randomNumber % 2 == 0;

        // Return the operation result
        if (success)
        {
            return OperationResult.Success(randomNumber);
        }
        else
        {
            var error = new OperationResultMessage(
                $"Something went wrong with the number '{randomNumber}'.",
                OperationResultSeverity.Error
            );
            return OperationResult.Failure(error);
        }
    }
}
```

The two highlighted lines in the preceding code block show the elegance of this new improvement. I find this code very easy to read, which was the objective. We now have two methods that clearly define our intentions when using them: `Success` or `Failure`.

The consumer uses the same code that we saw before in other examples, so I'll omit it here. However, the output is different for a successful or a failed operation. Here is a successful output:

```
{
    "succeeded": true,
```

```
    "value": 80
}
```

Here is a failed output:

```
{
    "succeeded": false,
    "messages": [
        {
            "message": "Something went wrong with the number '37'.",
            "severity": "Error"
        }
    ]
}
```

As we can see from the two preceding JSON outputs, the properties of each object are different (that was not a serialization trick). The only shared property of the two is Succeeded. Beware that this type of class hierarchy is harder to consume since the interface (the OperationResult class) has a minimal API surface (good in theory), and each sub-class adds different properties (hidden to the consumers); it would be hard to use the Value property of a successful operation. When doing this, the additional properties of each object should be optional information. For example, we could send the result to another system over HTTP, return the result object directly (like we do now), or publish an event (see *Chapter 16, Introduction to Microservices Architecture*, where we tackle event-driven architecture). It is helpful to know how to manipulate classes using polymorphism techniques like what we explored here for the day you need them.

Next, let's peek at some advantages and disadvantages of the Operation Result pattern.

Advantages and disadvantages

Here are a few advantages and disadvantages that come with the Operation Result design pattern.

Advantages

It is more explicit than throwing an Exception since the operation result type is specified explicitly as the method's return type. That makes it more evident than knowing what type of exceptions the operation and its dependencies can throw.

Another advantage is the execution speed; returning an object is faster than throwing an exception. Not that much faster, but faster nonetheless.

Using operation results allows managing different message types like warnings and information, compared to exceptions.

Disadvantages

Using operation results is more complex than throwing exceptions because we must *manually propagate it up the call stack* (i.e. the result object is returned by the callee and handled by the caller).

This is especially true if the operation result must go up multiple levels, which could be an indicator not to use the pattern.

It is easy to expose members that are not used in all scenarios, creating a bigger API surface than needed, where some parts are used only in some cases. But, between this and spending countless hours designing the perfect system, sometimes exposing an `int? Value { get; }` property can be a viable option. From there, you have lots of options to reduce that surface to a minimum. Use your imagination and your design skills to overcome those challenges!

Summary

In this chapter, we visited multiple forms of the Operation Result pattern, from an augmented Boolean to a complex data structure containing messages, values, and success indicators. We also explored static factories and private constructors to control external access. Furthermore, after all of that exploring, we can conclude that there are almost endless possibilities around the Operation Result pattern. Each specific use case should dictate how to make it happen. From here, I am confident that you have enough information about the pattern to explore the many more possibilities by yourself, and I highly encourage you to.

The Operation Result pattern is perfect for crafting strongly typed return values that self-manage multiple states (error and success) or support complex states (like partial success). It is also ideal for transporting messages that are not necessarily errors, like information messages. Even in its simplest form, we can leverage the Operation Result pattern as a base for extensibility since we can add members to the result class over time, which would be impossible for a primitive type (or any type that we don't control).

Note

The `HttpResponseMessage` class returned by the methods of the `HttpClient` class is an excellent example of a concrete implementation of the Operation Result pattern. It contains a single message exposed through the `ReasonPhrase` property. It exposes a complex success state through the `StatusCode` property and a simple success indicator through its `IsSuccessStatusCode` property. It also contains more information about the request and response through other properties.

At this point, we would usually explore how the **Operation Result** pattern can help us follow the SOLID principles. However, it depends too much on the implementation, so here are a few key points instead:

- The `OperationResult` class encapsulates the result, extracting that responsibility from the other system's components (SRP).
- We violated the ISP with the `Value` property in multiple examples. This was minor and could have been done differently, which could lead to a more complex design.

- We could compare an **operation result** to a **view model** or a **DTO** but returned by an operation (method). From there, we could add an abstraction or stick with returning a concrete class, which we could see as a violation of the DIP. Sometimes using concrete types makes the system simpler and easier to maintain.

- When the advantages surpass the minor and limited impacts of those two violations, I don't mind letting them slide (principles are ideals not applicable in every scenario; not laws).

This chapter concludes the *Designing at Component Scale* section and leads to the *Designing at Application Scale* section, in which we explore higher-level design patterns.

Questions

Let's take a look at a few practice questions:

1. Is returning an operation result when doing an asynchronous call, such as an HTTP request, a good idea?

2. What is the name of the pattern that we implemented using static methods?

3. Is it faster to return an operation result than throw an exception?

Further reading

Here are some links to build on what we learned in this chapter:

- An article on my blog about exceptions (title: *A beginner guide to exceptions | The basics*): `https://adpg.link/PpEm`

- An article on my blog about Operation Result (title: *Operation result | Design Pattern*): `https://adpg.link/4o2q`

Join our book's Discord space

Join the book's Discord workspace for *Ask me Anything* session with the authors:

`https://packt.link/ASPdotNET6DesignPatterns`

Section 4: Designing at Application Scale

In this section, we enter the realm of application design. Instead of focusing on a smaller part of an application, we look at how we want to design the application itself. We start by looking into layering, which exposes the bases of application design, where we focus on the three most common layers used in layered applications before moving toward the evolution of layering. We explore two ways of modeling the domain model. We then explore a way to encapsulate and lower the burden of layering and model copy before moving on to newer architectural styles, such as vertical slice and microservices.

Each of these chapters could make a book by themselves, so we explore them at a higher level, helping you make more informed decisions when the time to choose an architectural style arrives. This section is a starting point to further reading while still filled with helpful content, patterns, tips, and technologies to use straight away in your everyday projects.

The goal is to cover as many application-level patterns as possible. The reason is that knowing a little about many techniques helps choose the right method for the job at hand instead of picking the same one every time. Getting better at something is easier when you know where to start but impossible if you don't know what options are available.

This section comprises the following chapters:

- *Chapter 12, Understanding Layering*
- *Chapter 13, Getting Started with Object Mappers*
- *Chapter 14, Mediator and CQRS Design Patterns*
- *Chapter 15, Getting Started with Vertical Slice Architecture*
- *Chapter 16, Introduction to Microservices Architecture*

12

Understanding Layering

In this chapter, we explore the inherent concepts behind layering. Layering is a popular way of organizing computer systems by encapsulating major concerns into layers. Those concerns are related to a computer vocation such as data access instead of a business concern such as inventory. It is essential to understand the concepts behind layering as other concepts were born from layers, and they are very common.

We start this chapter by exploring the initial ideas behind layering. Then, we explore alternatives that can help us solve different problems. We use both **anemic and rich models** and expose both pros and cons in action. Finally, we quickly explore **Clean Architecture**, which is what I call an evolution of layering.

This chapter lays out the evolution of layering, starting with basic, restrictive, even flawed techniques, then gradually moves toward more modern patterns. This journey should help you understand the concepts and practices behind layering, giving you a stronger understanding than just learning one way of doing things.

The following topics are covered in this chapter:

- Introducing layering
- Responsibilities of the common layers
- Abstract layers
- Shared model
- Clean Architecture

Let's get started!

Introducing layering

Now that we've explored a few design patterns and played with ASP.NET Core a little, it is time to jump into layering. In most computer systems, there are layers. Why? Because it is an efficient way to partition and organize units of logic together. We could conceptually represent layers as horizontal chunks of software, each encapsulating a concern.

Classic layering model

Let's start by examining a classic three-layer application design:

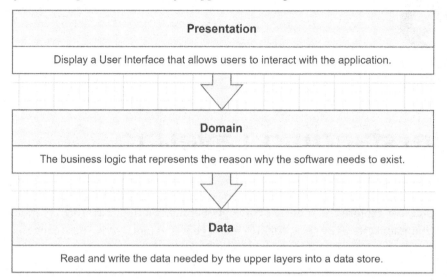

Figure 12.1: A classic three-layer application design

The **presentation layer** represents any user interface that a user can interact with to reach the **domain**. In our case, it could be an ASP.NET Core web application. However, anything from WPF to WinForms to Android could be a valid non-web presentation layer alternative.

The **domain layer** represents the core logic driven by the business rules; this is the solution to the application's problem. The domain layer is also called the **business logic layer** (**BLL**).

The **data layer** represents the bridge between the data and the application. The data could be stored in a SQL Server database, hosted elsewhere, a NoSQL database hosted in the cloud, a mix of all of those, or anything else that fits the business needs. The data layer is also called the **data access layer** (**DAL**) and the **persistence layer**.

Let's jump to an example. Given that a user has been authenticated and authorized, here is what happens when they want to create a book in a bookstore application built using those three layers:

1. The user requests the page by sending a `GET` request to the server.
2. The server handles that `GET` request (**presentation layer**) and then returns the page to the user.
3. The user fills out the form and sends a `POST` request back to the server.
4. The server handles the `POST` request (**presentation layer**) and then sends it to the **domain layer** for processing.
5. The **domain layer** executes the logic required to create a book, then tells the **data layer** to persist that data.
6. After unrolling to the presentation layer, the server returns the appropriate response to the user, most likely a page containing a list of books and a message telling them that the operation was successful.

Following a classic layering architecture, a layer can only talk to the next layer in the stack—**presentation** talks to **domain**, which talks to **data**, and so on. The important part is that **each layer must be independent and isolated to limit tight coupling.**

In this classic layering model, each layer should own its **model**. For example, **view models** should not be sent to the **domain**; only **domain objects** should be used there. The opposite is also true: since the **domain** returns its own objects to the **presentation layer**, the **presentation layer** should not leak them to the **views**, but organize the required information into **view models** instead.

Here is a visual example:

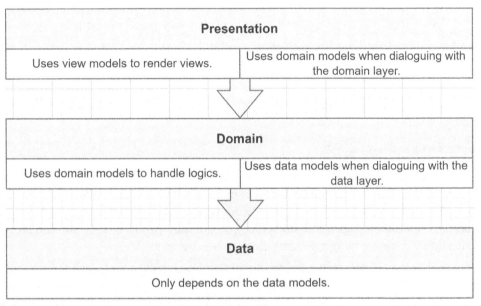

Figure 12.2: Diagram representing how the layers interact with one another

I'd like to point out that even if three is probably the most popular number of layers, we can create as many as we need; we are not limited to three layers.

Let's examine the advantages and disadvantages of classic layering, starting with the advantages:

- Knowing the purpose of a layer makes it easy to understand. For example, it is easy to guess that the data layer components read or write some data somewhere.
- It creates a cohesive unit built around a single concern. For example, our **data layer** should not render any user interface; it should stick to accessing data.
- It allows us to decouple the layer from the rest of the system (the other layers). You can isolate and work with a layer without any knowledge of the others. For example, suppose you are tasked with optimizing a query in a data access layer. In that case, you don't need to know about the user interface that eventually displays that data to a user. You only need to focus on that element, optimize it, test it in isolation, and then ship the layer or redeploy the application.

- Like any other isolated unit, it should be possible to reuse a layer. For example, we could reuse our **data access layer** in another application that needs to query the same database for a different purpose (a different **domain layer**).

> **TIP**
>
> Some layers are theoretically easier to reuse than others, and reusability could add more or less value, depending on the software you are building. I have never seen a layer being integrally reused in practice, and I've rarely heard or read about such a situation—each time rather ends in a not-so-reusable-after-all situation.
>
> Based on my experience, I would strongly suggest not over-aiming at reusability when it is not a precise specification that adds value to your application. By limiting your overengineering endeavors, you and your employers could save a lot of time and money. We must not forget that our job is to deliver value.
>
> As a rule of thumb, do what needs to be done, not more, but do it well.

OK, now, let's look at the drawbacks:

- By splitting your software horizontally into layers, each feature crosses all of the layers. This often leads to cascading changes between layers. For example, if we decide to add a field to our bookstore database, we would need to update the database, the code that accesses it (**data layer**), the business logic (**domain layer**), and the user interface (**presentation layer**). With volatile specs or low-budget projects, this can become painful!
- It could be more challenging for newcomers to implement a full-stack feature because it crosses all layers.
- Since a layer directly depends on the layer under it, dependency injection is impossible without introducing an **abstraction layer** or referencing lower layers from the **presentation layer**. For example, if the **domain layer** depends on the **data layer**, changing the data layer would require rewriting all of that coupling from the **domain** to the **data**.
- Since each layer owns its entities, the more layers you add, the more copies there are of the entities, leading to minor performance loss. For example, the **presentation layer** takes a **view model** and copies it to a **domain object**. Then, the **domain layer** copies it to a **data object**. Finally, the **data layer** translates it into SQL to persist it into a **database** (SQL Server, for example). The opposite is also true when reading from the database.

We explore ways to combat some of those drawbacks later.

I strongly recommend that you don't do what we just explored. It is an old, more basic way of doing layering. We are looking at multiple improvements to this layering system during this chapter, so keep reading before jumping to a conclusion. I decided to explore layering from the beginning in case you have to work with that kind of application. Furthermore, studying its chronological evolution, fixing some flaws, and adding options should help you understand the concepts instead of just knowing a single way of doing things. Understanding the patterns is the key to software architecture, not just learning how to apply them.

Splitting the layers

Now that we've discussed layers and saw them as big horizontal slices of responsibilities, we can organize our applications more granularly by splitting those big slices vertically, creating multiple smaller layers. This can help us organize applications by features or by bounding context, and it could also allow us to compose various user interfaces using the same building blocks, which would be easier than reusing colossal-size layers.

Here is a conceptual representation of this idea:

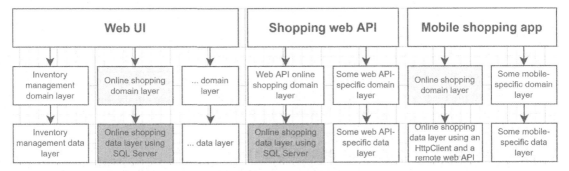

Figure 12.3: Organizing multiple applications using smaller partially shared layers

We can split an application into multiple features (vertically) and divide each into layers (horizontally). Based on the previous diagram, we named those features as follows:

- Inventory management
- Online shopping
- Others

So, we can bring in the online shopping domain and data layers to our Shopping web API without bringing everything else with it. Moreover, we can bring the online shopping domain layer to the mobile app and swap its data layer for another that talks to the web API.

We could also use our web API as a plain and simple data access application with different logic attached to it while keeping the shopping data layer underneath.

We could end up with the following recomposed applications (this is just one possible outcome):

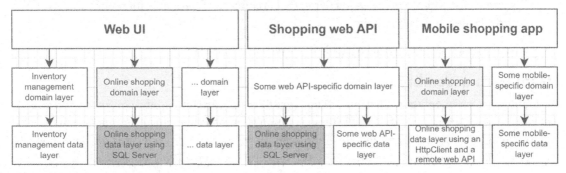

Figure 12.4: Organizing multiple applications using smaller partially shared layers

These are just examples of what we can conceptually do with layers. However, the most important thing to remember is not how the diagrams are laid out but the specifications of the applications you are building. Only those specs and good analyses can help you create the best possible design for that exact problem. Here, I used a hypothetical shopping example, but it could have been anything.

By splitting huge horizontal slices vertically, each piece becomes easier to reuse and share. This improvement can yield interesting results, especially if you have multiple frontend apps or plan to migrate away from a monolith in the future.

Note

A **monolithic application** (or monolith) is a program deployed as a single integrated piece (one-tier; we explore tiers next), and that is not modular (no reuse and low interoperability). A monolith can leverage layers or not. People often compare monolithic applications to microservices applications because they are antipodes. We explore microservices in *Chapter 16, Introduction to Microservices Architecture*.

Layers versus tiers versus assemblies

So far in this chapter, we have been talking about layers without talking about making them into code. Before we jump into that subject, I'd like to talk about **tiers**. You may have seen the term **3-tier architecture** somewhere before or heard people talking about **tiers** and **layers**, and possibly even interchanging them in the same context as synonyms. However, they are not the same. Let's take a look:

- **Tiers** are **physical**; each **tier** can be deployed on its own machine. For example, you could have a database server, a server hosting your web API that contains the business logic (the **domain**), and another server that serves an Angular application (**presentation**); these are three tiers (three distinct machines), and each **tier** can scale independently.

- **Layers** are **logical**; each **layer** is only the logical organization of code, with concerns organized and divided in a layered fashion. For example, you may create one or more projects in Visual Studio and organize your code into three layers. For example, a Razor Pages application depends on a business logic layer that depends on a data access layer. When you deploy that application, all these layers, including the database, are deployed together on the same server. This would be one tier and three layers. Of course, nowadays, chances are you have a cloud database somewhere, which adds a second tier to that architecture: the application tier (which still has three layers) and database tier.

Now that we've talked about **tiers**, let's look at a **layer** versus an **assembly**.

What is an assembly?

Assemblies are commonly compiled into `.dll` or `.exe` files; you can compile and consume them directly. For most cases, each project of a Visual Studio solution gets compiled into an assembly. You can also deploy them as NuGet packages and consume them from `nuget.org` or a custom NuGet repository of your choosing. But there is no one-to-one relationship between a layer and an assembly or a tier and an assembly; assemblies are only a consumable unit of compiled code: a library or a program.

Moreover, you do not need to split your layers into different assemblies; you can have your three layers residing in the same assembly. It can be easier to create undesirable coupling this way, with all of the code being in the same project, but it is a viable option with some rigor, rules, and conventions. Moving each layer to an assembly does not necessarily make the application better; the code inside each of those layers (or assemblies) can become mixed up and coupled with other parts of the system.

Don't get me wrong here: you can create an assembly per layer; I even encourage you to do so in most cases, but doing so does not mean the layers are not tightly coupled. A layer is simply a logical unit of organization, so each contributor's responsibility is to make sure the layer's code stays healthy.

Responsibilities of the common layers

In this section, we explore each of the most commonly used layers in more depth. We do not dig too deep into each one, but that overview should help you understand the essential ideas behind layering.

Presentation

The **presentation layer** is probably the easiest layer to understand because it is the only one we can see: the user interface. However, the presentation layer can also be the data contracts in case of a REST, OData, GraphQL, or other types of web service. The presentation layer is what the user uses to access your program. As another example, a CLI program can be a presentation layer. You write commands in a terminal, and the CLI dispatches those commands to its **domain layer**, which executes the required business logic.

The key of a maintainable presentation layer is to keep it as focused on displaying the user interface as possible with as little business logic as possible.

Now, let's take a look at the **domain layer** to see where these calls are going.

Domain

The **domain layer** is where the software's value resides; it is also where most of the complexity lies. The **domain layer** is the home of your business logic rules.

Unfortunately, it is easier to sell a **user interface** than a **domain layer**, since users connect to the domain through the presentation. However, it is important to remember that the domain is responsible for solving the problems and automating the solutions; the **presentation layer** only links users' actions to the **domain**.

There are two primary points of view about how to build the domain layer:

- Using a rich model.
- Using an anemic model.

No matter which one you choose, the domain layer is usually built around a domain model. You can leverage **Domain-Driven Design (DDD)** to build that model and the program around it. DDD goes hand in hand with rich models, and a well-crafted model should simplify the maintenance of the program. Doing DDD is not mandatory, and you can achieve the required level of correctness without it.

Another dilemma is whether to **persist the domain model directly into the database or use an intermediate data model**. We talk about that in more detail in the *Data* section.

Next, we look at the two primary ways to think about the domain model, starting with the rich domain model, before exploring the service layer.

Rich domain model

A rich domain model is more object-oriented, in the "purest" sense of the term, and encapsulates the domain logic as part of the model inside methods. For example, the following class represents the rich version of a minimal `Product` class that contains only a few properties:

```
public class Product
{
    public Product(string name, int quantityInStock, int? id = null)
    {
        Name = name ?? throw new ArgumentNullException(nameof(name));
        QuantityInStock = quantityInStock;
        Id = id;
    }

    public int? Id { get; init; }
    public string Name { get; init; }
    public int QuantityInStock { get; private set; }

    public void AddStock(int amount)
    {
        if (amount == 0) { return; }
        if (amount < 0) { throw new NegativeValueException(amount); }
        QuantityInStock += amount;
    }

    public void RemoveStock(int amount)
    {
        if (amount == 0) { return; }
        if (amount < 0) { throw new NegativeValueException(amount); }
        if (amount > QuantityInStock) { throw new
NotEnoughStockException(QuantityInStock, amount); }
        QuantityInStock -= amount;
    }
}
```

The `AddStock` and `RemoveStock` methods represent the domain logic of adding and removing stock for the product inventory. Of course, we only increment and decrement a property's value in this case, but the concept would be the same in a more complex model.

We could add a **service layer** in front of such a **rich model**, taking the input, mutating the domain object, and updating the database. We explore the service layer after the models.

The biggest advantage of this approach is that most of the logic is built into the model, making this very domain-centric with operations programmed on model entities as methods. Moreover, it reaches the basic ideas behind object-oriented design, where behaviors should be part of the objects, making them a virtual representation of their real-life counterparts.

The biggest drawback is the accumulation of responsibilities by a single class. Even if object-oriented design tells us to put logic into the objects, this does not mean that it is always a good idea. If flexibility is important for your system, hardcoding logic into the domain model may hinder your ability to evolve business rules without changing the code itself (it can still be done). If the domain must be robust and fixed, then a rich model might be a good choice for your project.

A relative drawback of this approach is that injecting dependencies into the domain model is harder to do than into other objects, such as services, possibly reducing flexibility once again or increasing the complexity of creating the models.

If you are building a stateful application where the domain model can live in memory longer than the time of an HTTP request, a rich domain model could be of use to you. Other patterns, such as **Model-View-View-Model** (**MVVM**) and **Model-View-Update** (**MVU**), also help you with that. We tackle MVU in *Chapter 18, A Brief Look into Blazor*.

If you believe that your application would benefit from keeping the data and the logic together, then a rich domain model is most likely a good idea for your project. If you are practicing DDD, I probably don't have to tell you that a rich model is the way to go. Without the notions of DDD it might be harder to achieve a maintainable and flexible rich model.

A rich model could be a good option if your program is built around a complex domain model and persists those classes directly to your database using an **object-relational mapper** (**ORM**). Using Cosmos DB, Firebase, MongoDB, or any other document database could make it very easy to store complex models as a single document instead of a collection of tables (this applies to anemic models too).

As you may have noticed, there is a lot of "ifs" in this section because I don't think there is an absolute answer to whether a rich model is better or not, and it is more a question of whether it is better for your specific case than better overall. You also need to take your personal preferences and skills into account.

Experience is most likely your best ally here, so I'd recommend coding, coding, and coding more applications to acquire that experience. Leverage your colleagues' experiences as well.

Anemic domain model

An anemic domain model usually does not contain methods but only getters and setters. Such models must not contain business logic rules. The `Product` class we had previously would look like this:

```
public class Product
{
    public int? Id { get; set; }
    public string Name { get; set; } = "";
```

```
    public int QuantityInStock { get; set; }
}
```

As you can see, there is no method in the class anymore, only the three properties with public setters. The logic should now be part of the service layer.

A **service layer** in front of such an **anemic model** would take the input, mutate the domain object, and update the database. The difference is that the service owns the logic, while in the case of the rich model, the model owns the logic.

With the anemic model, separating the operations from the data can help us add flexibility to a system. However, it can be harder to enforce the model's state at any given time since external actors (services) are modifying the model instead of the model managing itself.

Encapsulating logic into smaller units makes it easier to manage each of them, and it is easier to inject those dependencies into the service classes than injecting them into the entities themselves. Having more smaller units of code can make a system more dreadful for a newcomer as it can be more complex to understand since it has more moving parts. On the other hand, if the system is built around well-defined abstractions, it can be easier to test each unit in isolation.

However, the tests can be quite different. In the case of our rich model, we can test the rules and the persistence separately. We call this **persistence ignorance**, which allows us to test business rules in isolation. Then we could create integration tests to cover the persistence aspect of the service layer and more unit and integration tests on the data and domain levels. With an anemic model, we test both the business rules and the persistence simultaneously with integration tests at the service layer level or test only the business rules in unit tests that mock the persistence part away. Since the model is just a data bag without logic, there is nothing to test there.

All in all, if the same rigorous domain analysis process is followed, the business rules of an anemic model backed by a service layer should be as complex as a rich domain model. The biggest difference should be in which classes the methods are located.

For stateless systems, such as RESTful APIs, an anemic model is a good option. Since you have to recreate the model's state for every request, an anemic model can offer you a way to recreate a smaller portion of the model with smaller classes optimized for each use case independently. Stateless systems require a more procedural type of thinking than a purely object-oriented approach, leaving the anemic models as excellent candidates for that.

> **Note**
>
> I personally love anemic models behind a service layer, but some people would not agree with me. I recommend choosing what you think is best for the system you are building instead of doing something based on what someone else said about another system.
>
> Another good tip is to let the refactoring flow *top-down* to the right location. For example, if you feel that a method is bound to an entity, nothing stops you from moving that piece of logic into that entity instead of a service class. If a service is more appropriate, then move the logic to a service class. This approach is instrumental to the Vertical Slice architecture, which we cover in *Chapter 15, Getting Started with Vertical Slice Architecture*.

Next, let's go back to the **domain layer** and explore a pattern that emerged over the years to shield the **domain model** using a **service layer**, splitting the **domain layer** into two distinct pieces.

Service layer

The **service layer** shields the domain model and encapsulates domain logic. The service layer is usually designed to be highly reusable, orchestrating the complex interactions with the model or external resources such as databases. Multiple components can then use the service layer while having limited knowledge of the model:

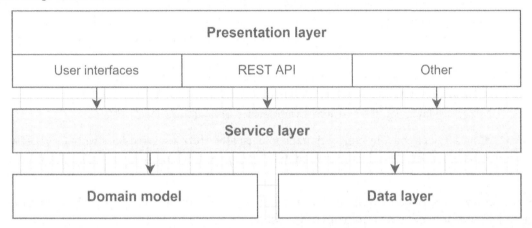

Figure 12.5: Service layer relationships with other layers

As shown in the preceding diagram, the presentation layer talks to the service layer, which manages the domain model and implements the business logic.

The **service layer** contains services, which are classes that interact with other **domain objects**, such as the **domain model** and the **data layer**.

We can divide services into two categories, **domain services** and **application services**:

- **Domain services** are those services we are talking about here. They contain domain logic and allow consumers from the presentation layer to read or write data. They access and mutate the domain model.
- **Application services** are services that are not related to the domain, such as [I]EmailService, a class/interface that sends emails. These could live in the domain layer or not, depending on their use. Since they are not tied to the domain (no domain logic), it can be wise to extract them into a library to share them between the domain and other layers or with other applications (why rewrite an email service for every project, right?).

As with other layers, your service layer could expose its own model, shielding its consumers from domain model (internal) changes. In other words, the service layer should only expose its contracts and interfaces (keyword: shield). **A service layer is a form of façade.**

There are many ways to interpret this layer, and I'll try to illustrate as many as possible in a condensed manner (from simpler to more complex ones). Let's get started:

- The classes and interfaces of the service layer could be part of the domain layer's assembly, created in a *Services* directory, for example. This is less reusable, but it paves the way to sharing services in the future without managing multiple projects at first. It needs rigor to not to depend on what you should not.

- The service layer could be an assembly containing interfaces and implementation. This is a great compromise between reusability and maintenance time. Chances are you will never need two implementations (see the next point) because the services are tied to the logic, which makes the domain. You could even hide the implementation, as we did with the **opaque façade** in *Chapter 9, Structural Patterns*.

- The service layer could be divided into two assemblies -- one containing abstractions (referenced by consumers) and one containing implementations.

- The service layer could be an actual web service tier (such as a web API).

When writing services code, by convention, people usually suffix a service class with `Service`, such as `ProductService` and `InventoryService`; the same goes for interfaces (`IProductService` and `IInventoryService`).

No matter which technique you choose, keep in mind that the service layer contains the domain logic and shields the domain model from direct access.

To conclude, the service layer is an amazing addition that shields and encapsulates the logic for manipulating an anemic domain model. It can defeat the purpose of a rich domain model if it's just a pass-through but can be very useful to handle complex, non-atomic business rules that affect multiple domain objects.

The primary decider of whether or not to add a service layer is tied to the complexity of your project's domain. The more complex, the more it makes sense, the more trivial, the less sense. Here are a few tips:

- Add a service layer when using an anemic model.
- Add a service layer for very complex domains.
- Do not add a service layer for low-complexity domains or *façade over database* applications.

Now, let's look at the data layer.

Data

The **data layer** is where the persistence code goes. In most programs, we need some kind of persistence to store our application data, which is often a database. Several patterns come to mind when discussing the data layer, including the **Unit of Work** and **Repository patterns**, which are very common. We cover these two patterns very briefly at the end of this subsection.

We can persist our **domain model** as is or create a **data model** that is more suited to be stored. For example, a many-to-many relationship is not a thing in the object-oriented world, while it is from a relational database standpoint.

You can view a **data model** like a **view model** or a DTO, but for data. The **data model** is the way the data is stored in your data store; that is, how you modeled your data or what you have to live with.

In a classic layering project, you have no choice but to have a data model. However, you may find better solutions as we continue to explore additional options.

> **Note**
>
> An **ORM** is a piece of software that translates objects into a database language such as SQL. It allows mutating data, querying data, loading that data into objects, and more.

Modern data layers usually leverage an **ORM** such as **Entity Framework Core** (**EF Core**), which does a big part of our job, making our lives easier. In the case of **EF Core**, it allows us to choose between multiple providers, from SQL Server to Cosmos DB, passing by the in-memory provider. The great thing about EF Core is that it already implements the **Unit of Work** and the **Repository** patterns for us, among other things. In the book, we use the in-memory provider to cut down setup time and run integration tests.

> **Note**
>
> If you've used EF6 before and dread Entity Framework, know that EF Core is lighter, faster, and easier to test. Feel free to give it a second shot. EF Core's performance is very high now too. However, if you want complete control over your SQL code, look for Dapper (not to be confused with **Dapr**).

I don't want to go into too much detail about these patterns, but they are important enough to deserve an overview. I've written a multi-part article series about the Repository pattern (see the *Further reading* section). As I mentioned before, EF Core already implements these patterns, so we don't have to deal with them. Moreover, using such patterns is not always desirable, can be hard to implement right, and can lead to bloated data access layers, but can also be very useful.

In the meantime, let's at least study their goals to know what they are for, and if the situation arises where you need to write such components, you know where to look.

Repository pattern

The goal of the Repository pattern is to allow consumers to query the database in an object-oriented way. Usually, this implies caching objects and filtering data dynamically. EF Core represents this concept with a `DbSet<T>` and provides dynamic filtering using LINQ and the `IQueryable<T>` interface.

People also use the term **repository** to represent the **Table Data Gateway pattern**, which is another pattern that models a class that gives us access to a single table in a database and provides access to operations such as creating, updating, deleting, and fetching entities from that database table. Both patterns are from the *Patterns of Enterprise Application Architecture*.

Homegrown custom implementations usually follow the Table Data Gateway pattern more than the Repository one. They are based on an interface that looks like the following code and contains methods to create, update, delete, and read entities. They can have a base entity or not, in this case, `IEntity<TId>`. The `Id` property can also be generic or not:

```
public interface IRepository<T, TId>
    where T : class, IEntity<TId>
{

    Task<IEnumerable<T>> AllAsync(CancellationToken cancellationToken);
    Task<T?> GetByIdAsync(TId id, CancellationToken cancellationToken);
    Task<T> CreateAsync(T entity, CancellationToken cancellationToken);
    Task UpdateAsync(T entity, CancellationToken cancellationToken);
    Task DeleteAsync(TId id, CancellationToken cancellationToken);
}
public interface IEntity<TId>
{
    TId Id { get; }
}
```

One thing that often happens with those table data gateways is that people add a save method to the interface. As long as you update a single entity, it should be fine, but that makes transactions that cross multiple repositories harder to manage or dependent on the underlying implementation (breaking abstraction). To commit or revert such transactions, we can leverage the Unit of Work pattern, moving the save method from the table data gateway there.

For example, when using EF Core, we can use `DbSet<Product>` (the `db.Products` property) to add new products to the database, like this:

```
db.Products.Add(new Data.Product
{
    Id = 1,
    Name = "Banana",
    QuantityInStock = 50
});
```

For the querying part, the easiest way to find a single product is to use it like this:

```
var product = _db.Products.Find(productId);
```

However, we could use LINQ instead:

```
_db.Products.Single(x => x.Id == productId);
```

These are some of the querying capabilities that a **repository** should provide. EF Core seamlessly translates LINQ into the configured provider expectations like SQL, adding extended filtering capabilities.

Of course, with EF Core, we can query collections of items, fetching all products and projecting them as domain objects like this (in case the model is not shared between both projects):

```
_db.Products.Select(p => new Domain.Product
{
    Id = p.Id,
    Name = p.Name,
    QuantityInStock = p.QuantityInStock
});
```

We can also filter further using LINQ here; for example, by querying all the products that are out of stock:

```
var outOfStockProducts = _db.Products
    .Where(p => p.QuantityInStock == 0);
```

We could also allow a margin for error, like so:

```
var mostLikelyOutOfStockProducts = _db.Products
    .Where(p => p.QuantityInStock < 3);
```

With that, we have briefly explored how to use the EF Core implementation of the Repository pattern, DbSet<T>. These few examples might seem trivial, but it would require considerable effort to implement custom repositories on par with EF Core's features.

EF Core's unit of work, DbContext, contains the save methods to persist the modifications done to all its DbSet<T> properties (the repositories). Homebrewed implementations often feature such methods on the repository itself, making cross-repository transactions harder to handle and leading to bloated repositories containing tons of operation-specific methods to handle such cases.

That's enough for the **Repository pattern**. Now, let's jump into an overview of the **Unit of Work pattern** before going back to layering.

Unit of Work pattern

A **unit of work** keeps track of the object representation of a transaction. In other words, it manages a registry of what objects should be created, updated, and deleted. It allows us to combine multiple changes in a single transaction (one database call), which offers multiple advantages over calling the database every time we make a change.

Assuming we are using a relational database, here are two advantages:

*   First, it can speed up data access; calling a database is slow, so limiting the number of calls and connections can improve performance.
*   Second, running a transaction instead of individual operations allows us to roll back all operations if one fails or commit the transaction as a whole if everything succeeds.

EF Core implements this pattern with the DbContext class and its underlying types, such as the DatabaseFacade and ChangeTracker classes.

We don't need transactions in our small applications, but the concept remains the same. Here is an example of what happens using EF Core:

```
var product = _db.Products.Find(productId);
product.QuantityInStock += amount;
_db.SaveChanges();
```

The preceding code does the following:

1. Queries the database for a single entity.
2. Changes the value of the QuantityInStock property.
3. Persists the changes back into the database.

In reality, what happened is closer to the following:

1. We ask EF Core for a single entity through the ProductContext (a unit of work), which exposes the DbSet<Product> property (the product repository). Under the hood, EF Core does the following:

    a. Queries the database.
    b. Caches the entity.
    c. Tracks changes for that entity.
    d. Returns it to us.

2. We changed the value of the QuantityInStock property; EF Core detects the change and marks the object as dirty.
3. We tell the unit of work to persist the changes that it tracked, saving the dirty product back to the database.

In a more complex scenario, we could have written the following code:

```
_db.Products.Add(newProduct);
_db.Products.Remove(productToDelete);
product.Name = "New product name";
_db.SaveChanges();
```

Here, the SaveChanges() method triggers saving the three operations instead of sending them one by one. You can control database transactions using the Database property of DbContext (see the *Further reading* section for more information).

Now that we've explored the **unit of work**, we could implement one by ourselves. Would that add value to our application? Probably not. If you want to build a custom **unit of work** or a wrapper over EF Core, there are plenty of existing resources to guide you. Unless you want to experiment or need a custom **unit of work** and **repository** (which is possible), I recommend staying away from doing that. Remember: **do only what needs to be done for your program to be correct.**

Tip

Don't get me wrong when I say *do only what needs to be done*; wild engineering endeavors and experimentations are a great way to explore, and I encourage you to do so. However, I recommend doing so in parallel so that you can innovate, learn, and possibly even migrate that knowledge to your application later instead of wasting time and breaking things. If you are using Git, a good way of doing this would be to create an experimental branch. You can then delete it when your experimentation does not work, or merge the branch if it yields positive results.

Now that we explored a high-level view of the Repository and Unit of Work patterns, and what those common layers are for, we can continue our journey of using layers in a robust, flexible, and efficient way.

Abstract layers

This section looks at abstract layers with an abstract data layer implementation. This type of abstraction can be very useful and is another step closer to **Clean Architecture**. Moreover, you can abstract pretty much anything this way, which is nothing more than applying the **Dependency Inversion Principle** (**DIP**).

Let's start with the problem: the **domain layer** is where the logic lies, and the UI links the user and the **domain**, exposing the features built into that **domain**. On the other hand, the **data layer** should be an implementation detail that the **domain** blindly uses. The **data layer** contains the code that knows where the data is stored, which should be irrelevant to the **domain**, but the **domain** directly depends on it.

The solution to **break the tight coupling** between the **domain** and the **data** persistence implementations is to create an additional abstract layer, as shown in the following diagram:

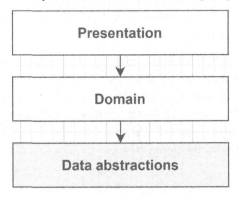

Figure 12.6: Replacing the data (persistence) layer with a data abstraction layer

New rule: **only interfaces and data model classes go into the data abstractions layer**. This new layer now defines our data access API and does nothing but expose a set of interfaces—the contract.

Then, **we can create one or more data implementations** based on that abstract layer contract, like using EF Core. The link between the abstractions and implementations is done with dependency injection bindings defined in the **composition root**, which explains the indirect link between the presentation and the data implementation.

The new dependency tree looks like this:

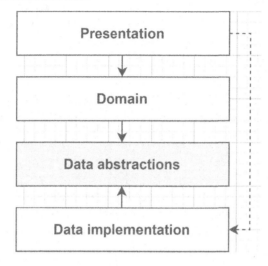

Figure 12.7: The relationships between layers

As just mentioned, the **presentation layer** references a **data implementation layer** for the sole reason of creating the DI bindings. We need those bindings to inject the correct implementation when creating **domain** classes. Besides that, **the presentation layer must not use the data layer's abstractions nor its implementation.**

I created a sample project that showcases this, but to save you from reading pages of code, it is not included in the book but is available on GitHub (`https://adpg.link/rZdN`). The most important piece is the dependency flow between the layers, not the code itself.

In that project, the program injects an instance of the `EF.ProductRepository` class when a consumer asks for an object that implements the `IProductRepository` interface. In that case, the consuming class is `ProductService` and only depends on the `IProductRepository` interface. The `ProductService` class is not aware of the implementation itself: it leverages only the interface. The same goes for the program that loads a `ProductService` class but knows only about the `IProductService` interface. Here is a visual representation of that dependency tree:

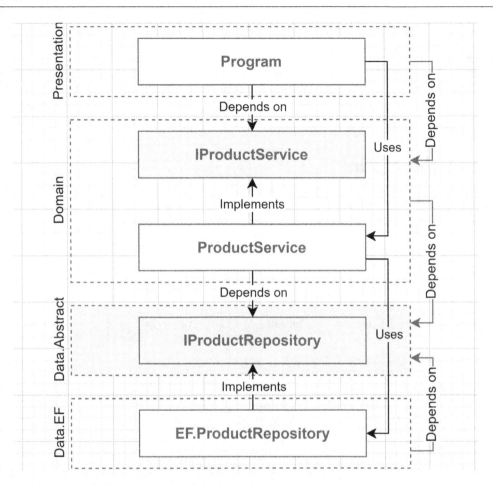

Figure 12.8: The dependency flow between layers, classes, and interfaces

In the preceding diagram, look at how dependencies converge on the Data.Abstract layer. The dependency tree ends up on that abstract data layer.

With this applied piece of architectural theory, we are inverting the flow of dependencies on the data layer by following the **DIP**. We also cut out the direct dependency on EF Core, allowing us to implement a new data layer and swap it without impacting the rest of the application or update the implementation without affecting the domain. As I mentioned previously, swapping layers should not happen very often, if ever. Nonetheless, this is an important part of the evolution of layering, and more importantly, we can apply this technique to any layer or project, not just the data layer, so it is imperative to understand how to invert the dependency flow.

Note

To test the APIs, you can use the Postman collection that comes with the book; visit
`https://adpg.link/postman6` or GitHub (`https://adpg.link/net6`) for more info.

Next, let's explore how to share and persist a rich domain model.

Sharing the model

Now we have explored strict layering, but we still have multiple models. An alternative to copying
models from one layer to another is to share a model between multiple layers, generally as an assembly.
Visually, it looks like this:

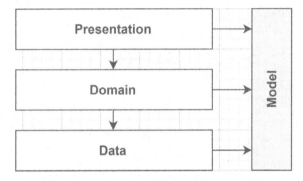

Figure 12.9: Sharing a model between all three layers

There are pros and cons to everything, so no matter how much time this can save you at first, it will
come back to haunt you and become a pain point later as the project advances and becomes more
complex.

Suppose you feel that sharing a model is worth it for your application. In that case, I recommend
using **view models** or **DTOs** at the presentation level to control and keep the input and output of
your application loosely coupled from your model. This way of shielding your lower layers can be
represented as follows:

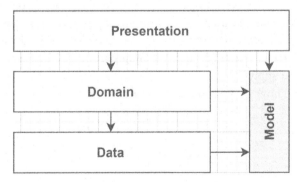

Figure 12.10: Sharing a model between the domain and data layers

By doing that, you may save some time initially by sharing your model between your domain and data layers. The good thing is that by hiding that shared model under the presentation layer, you should dodge many problems in the long run, making this a good compromise between quality and development time. Moreover, since your presentation layer shields your application from the outside world, you can rework or rewrite your other layers without impacting your consumers.

> **Note**
>
> This is pretty much how Clean Architecture does it but represented differently. Using that, the model is at the center of the application, and is manipulated and persisted. While the layers have different names, the concept remains very similar. More on that later.

View models and **DTOs** are key elements to successful programs and developers' sanity; they should save you many headaches for long-running projects. We revisit and explore the concepts of controlling the input and output later in *Chapter 14, Mediator and CQRS Design Patterns*, where inputs become **commands** and **queries**.

Meanwhile, let's merge that concept with an abstraction layer. In the previous project, the **data abstraction layer** owned the **data model**, and the **domain layer** owned the **domain model**.

In this architectural alternative, we are sharing the model between the two layers. The presentation layer can indirectly use that shared model to dialog with the domain layer without exposing it externally. The objective is to directly persist the **domain model** and skip the copy from the **domain** to the **data layer** while having that data abstraction layer that breaks the tight coupling between the domain logic and the persistence.

Here is a visual representation of that:

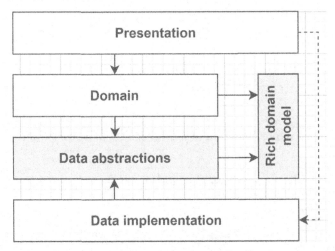

Figure 12.11: Diagram representing a shared rich model

It is well suited for **rich models,** but we can do this for **anemic models** too. With a **rich domain model,** you delegate the job of reconstructing the model to the ORM and immediately start calling its methods.

The ORM also recreates the anemic model, but those classes just contain data, so you need to call other pieces of the software that contain the logic to manipulates those objects.

In the code sample, the **data abstraction layer** now contains only the data access abstractions, such as the repositories, and it references the new Model project that is now the persisted model.

Conceptually, it cleans up a few things:

- The data abstraction layer's only responsibility is to contain data access abstractions.
- The domain layer's only responsibility is to implement the domain services and domain logic that is not part of that rich model.
- In the case of an anemic model, the domain layer's responsibility would be to encapsulate all the domain logic.
- The Model project contains the entities.

Once again, I skip publishing most of the code here as it is irrelevant to the overall concept. If you think reading the code would help you, you can consult and explore the sample on GitHub (https://adpg.link/VTgt). Using an IDE to browse the code should help you understand the flow, and as with the abstract layer, the dependencies between the projects, classes, and interfaces are the key to this.

Nevertheless, here is the StockService class that uses that shared model so you can peek at some code that directly relates to the explanations:

```
namespace Domain.Services;

public class StockService : IStockService
{
    private readonly IProductRepository _repository;
    public StockService(IProductRepository repository)
    {
        _repository = repository ?? throw new
ArgumentNullException(nameof(repository));
    }
```

Above, we are injecting an implementation of the IProductRepository interface that we use in the next two methods.

```
    public async Task<int> AddStockAsync(int productId, int amount,
    CancellationToken cancellationToken)
    {
        var product = await _repository.FindByIdAsync(productId,
    cancellationToken);
        if (product == null)
        {
            throw new ProductNotFoundException(productId);
```

```
        }
        product.AddStock(amount);
        await _repository.UpdateAsync(product, cancellationToken);

        return product.QuantityInStock;
    }
```

The fun starts in the preceding code, which does the following:

- The repository recreates the product (model) that contains the logic.
- It validates that the product exists.
- It uses that model and calls the AddStock method (encapsulated domain logic).
- It tells the repository to update the product.
- It returns the updated product's QuantityInStock to the consumer of the service.

```
    public async Task<int> RemoveStockAsync(int productId, int amount,
CancellationToken cancellationToken)
    {
        var product = await _repository.FindByIdAsync(productId,
cancellationToken);
        if (product == null)
        {
            throw new ProductNotFoundException(productId);
        }
        product.RemoveStock(amount);
        await _repository.UpdateAsync(product, cancellationToken);

        return product.QuantityInStock;
    }
}
```

The same logic as the AddStock method was applied to RemoveStock, but it called the Product.RemoveStock method instead. From the StockService class, we can see the service gating the access to the domain model (the product), fetching and updating the model through the abstract data layer, manipulating the model by calling its methods, and returning domain data (an int in this case, but could be an object).

Note

This type of design can be either very helpful or undesirable. Too many projects depending on and exposing a shared model can lead to leaking part of that model to consumers, for example exposing properties that shouldn't be, exposing the whole domain model as output, or the very worst, exposing it as an input and opening exploitable holes and unexpected bugs. Be careful not to expose your shared model to the presentation layer consumers.

Pushing logic into the model is not always possible or desirable, which is why we are exploring multiple types of domain models and ways to share them. Making a good design is often about options and making the right decision about what option to use for each scenario. There are also tradeoffs to make between flexibility and robustness.

The rest of the code is very similar to the abstract layer project, but the classes were moved around slightly. Feel free to explore the source code (`https://adpg.link/VTgt`) and compare it with the other projects. The best way to learn is to practice, so play with the samples, add features, update the current features, remove stuff, or even build your own project. Understanding these concepts should help you apply them to different scenarios, sometimes creating unexpected but efficient constructs.

Now, let's look at the final evolution of layering: Clean Architecture.

Clean Architecture

Now that we've covered many layering approaches, it is time to combine them into **Clean Architecture**, also known as Hexagonal Architecture, Onion Architecture, Ports and Adapters, and more. Clean Architecture is an evolution of the layers, yet very similar to what we just built. Instead of presentation, domain, and data (or persistence), Clean Architecture suggests **UI**, **Core**, and **Infrastructure**.

As we saw previously, we can design a layer so that it contains abstractions or implementations. Then, when implementations depend only on abstractions, that inverts the flow of dependency. Clean Architecture emphasizes such layers but with its own set of guidance about organizing them.

We also explored the theoretical concept of breaking layers into smaller ones (or multiple projects), thus creating "fractured layers" that are easier to port and reuse. Clean Architecture leverages that concept at the infrastructure layer level.

There are probably as many points of view and variants of this as there are names for it, so I'll try to be as general as possible while keeping the essence. By doing this, if you are interested in this type of architecture, you'll be able to pick a resource and dig deeper into it, following the style that you prefer.

Let's take a look at a diagram that resembles what we can find online:

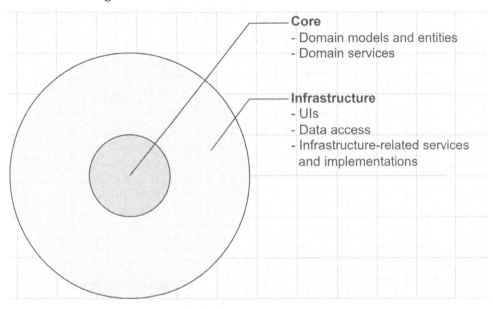

Figure 12.12: A diagram representing the most basic Clean Architecture layout

From a layering diagram-like standpoint, the preceding diagram could look like this:

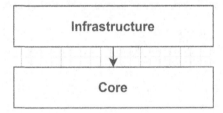

Figure 12.13: A two-layer view of the previous Clean Architecture diagram

From here, depending on what method you choose, you can split those layers into multiple other sublayers. One thing that we often see is to divide the **Core** layer into **Entities** and **Use cases**, like this:

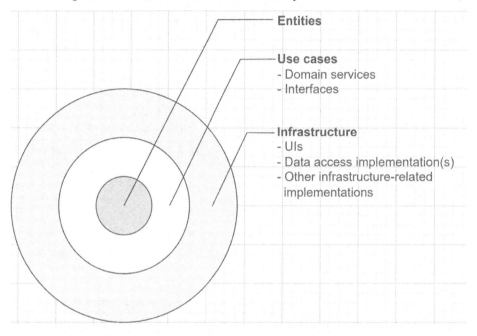

Figure 12.14: Widespread Clean Architecture layout diagram

Since people in the tech industry are creative, there are many names for many things, but the concepts remain the same. From a layering diagram-like standpoint, that diagram could look like this:

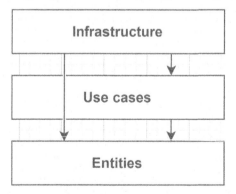

Figure 12.15: A layer-like view of the previous Clean Architecture diagram

The infrastructure layer is conceptual and can represent multiple projects, such as an infrastructure assembly containing EF Core implementations and a website project representing the web UI. We could also add more projects to the infrastructure layer.

The dependency rule of Clean Architecture states that dependencies can only point inward, from the outer layers to the inner layers. This means that abstractions lie inside, and concretions lie outside. Based on the preceding layer-like diagram, inside translates to downward. That means a layer can use any direct or transitive dependencies, which means that infrastructure can depend on use cases and entities.

Clean Architecture follows all the principles that we've been discussing since the beginning of this book, such as decoupling our implementations using abstractions, dependency inversion, and separation of concerns. These implementations are glued over abstractions using dependency injection (this is not mandatory, but it should help).

I've always found those circle diagrams a bit confusing, so here is my take on an updated, more linear diagram:

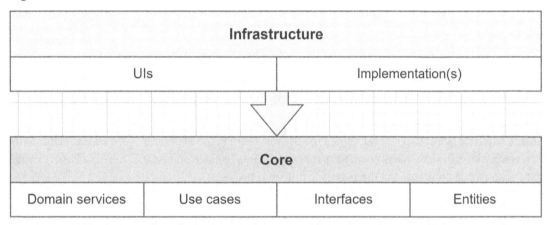

Figure 12.16: A two-layer view of Clean Architecture's common elements

Now, let's revisit our layered application using Clean Architecture, starting with the **core layer**. The core project contains the domain model, the use cases (services), and the interfaces needed to fulfill those use cases.

No external resource should be accessed here: no database calls, no disk access, and no HTTP requests. This layer contains the interfaces that expose such interaction, but the implementations must live in the **infrastructure layer**.

The presentation layer was renamed Web and lives in the outer layer with the EF Core implementation. The Web project depends only on the Core project. Once again, since the composition root is in this project, it must load the EF Core implementation project to configure the IoC container.

Here is a diagram representing the relation between the shared model and the new Clean Architecture project structure:

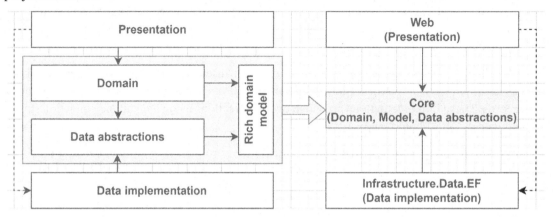

Figure 12.17: From shared project to the Clean Architecture project structure

In the preceding diagram, note that I took the center of the solution and merged the layers into a single Core project. I also renamed the project, so linking them to Clean Architecture is easier, but you can name your projects however you want.

Most of the code is not that relevant since the biggest point is the dependency flow and relationships between projects (link to this project: `https://adpg.link/QRrR`). Nonetheless, here is a list of changes that I made aside from moving the pieces to different projects:

- I removed the `ProductService` class and `IProductService` interface and used the `IProductRepository` interface directly from the `StockService` class (Core project) and the `/products` endpoint (Web project: `Program.cs`)
- I removed the `IStockService` interface and now both the add and remove stocks endpoints (Web project: `Program.cs`) depend directly on the `StockService` class

Why use the `IProductRepository` interface directly, you might wonder? Since the Web project (**infrastructure layer**) depends on the **core layer**, we can leverage the inward dependency flow. It is acceptable to use a repository directly as long as the feature has no business logic. Programming empty shells and pass-through services only adds useless complexity. However, as soon as business logic is involved, create a service or any other domain entity you deem necessary for that scenario. Don't pack business logic into your controllers or minimal API delegates.

I removed the `IStockService` interface since the `StockService` class contains concrete business rules that can be consumed as is from the infrastructure layer. I know we have emphasized using interfaces since the beginning of the book, but I also often said that principles are not laws. All in all, there is nothing to abstract away: if the business rules change, the old ones won't be needed anymore. On the other hand, you could keep the interface if you'd prefer to.

To wrap this up, Clean Architecture is a proven pattern for building applications that is fundamentally an evolution of layering. Many variants can help you manage use cases, entities, and infrastructure; however, we will not cover those here.

If you think this is a great fit for you, your team, your project, or your organization, feel free to dig deeper and adopt this pattern. In subsequent chapters, we explore some patterns, such as CQRS, Publish-Subscribe, and events, that can be used with Clean Architecture to add more flexibility and robustness. These become particularly useful as your system grows in size or complexity.

Implementing layering in real life

Now that we have covered all of this, it is important to note that on the one hand there is theory, and on the other there is life hitting you in the face. If you are working in a big enterprise, chances are your employer can pour hundreds of thousands or even millions of dollars into a feature to run experiments, spend months designing every little piece, and make sure everything is perfect. Even then, is achieving perfection even possible? Probably not.

For companies that don't have that type of capital, you must build entire products for a few thousand dollars sometimes because they are not trying to resell them but just need that tool built. That is where your architectural skills come in handy. How do you design the least-worst product in a maintainable fashion while meeting stakeholders expectations? The most important part of the answer is to set expectations correctly. Moreover, never forget that someone needs to maintain and make changes to the software over time.

Tip

If you are in a position where you must evaluate the feasibility of products and features in this context, setting expectations lower can be a good way to plan for the unplannable. It is easier to overdeliver than justify why you underdelivered.

Let's dig deeper into this and look at a few tricks to help you out. Even if you are working for a larger enterprise, you should get something out of it.

To be or not to be a purist?

In your day-to-day work, you may not always need the rigidity of a **domain layer** creating a wall in front of your data. Maybe you just don't have the time or the money, or it's just not worth doing.

Taking the data and presenting it can often work well enough, especially for simple data-driven applications that are only a user interface over a database, as is the case for many internal tools.

The answer to the *"To be or not to be a purist?"* question is: it depends!

Here are a few examples of things that the answer depends on, to help you out:

- The project; for example:
  - **Domain-heavy or logic-intensive projects** will benefit from a domain layer, helping you centralize parts for an augmented level of reusability and maintainability.
  - **Data management projects** tend to have less or no logic in them. We can often build them without adding a domain layer as the **domain** is often only a tunnel from the **presentation** to the **data**; a pass-through layer. We can often simplify those systems by dividing them into two layers: **data** and **presentation**.

- Your team; for example, a highly skilled team may tend to use advanced concepts and patterns more efficiently, and the learning curve for newcomers should be easier due to the number of seasoned engineers that can support them on the team. This does not mean that less skilled teams should aim lower; on the contrary, it may just be harder or take longer to start. Analyze each project individually and find the best patterns to drive them accordingly.

- Your boss; if the company you work for puts pressure on you and your team to deliver complex applications in record time and nobody tells your boss that it is impossible, you may need to cut corners a lot and enjoy many maintenance headaches with crashing systems, painful deployments, and more. That being said, if it is inevitable, for these types of projects, I'd go with a very simple design that does not aim at reusability—aim at low-to-average testability and code stuff that just works. I also suggest you continue reading and explore using the techniques from *Chapter 15, Getting Started with Vertical Slice Architecture*, to improve the design while keeping the design overhead low.

- Your budget; once again, this often depends on the people selling the application and the features. I often saw promises that were impossible to keep but were delivered anyway with a lot of effort, extra hours, and corner-cutting. The thing to keep in mind when going down that path is that at some point, there is no return from the amount of accumulated **technical debt**, and it will just get worse (this applies to all budgets).

- The audience; the people who use the software can make a big difference to how you build it: ask them. For example, if you are building a tool for your fellow developers, you can probably cut many corners that you would not for other, less technically skilled users. On the other hand, if you're aiming your application at multiple clients (web, mobile, and so on), isolating your application's components and focusing on reusability could be a winning design.

- The expected quality; you should not tackle the problem in the same way for building a prototype and a SaaS application. It is acceptable, even encouraged, for a prototype to have no tests and not follow best practices, but I'd recommend the opposite for a production-quality application.

- Any other things that life throws at you; yes, life is unpredictable, and no one can cover every possible scenario in a book, so just keep the following in mind when building your next piece of software:

    - Do not over-engineer your applications.
    - Only implement features that you need, not more, as per the **you aren't gonna need it (YAGNI)** principle.

I hope that you find this guidance good enough and that it will be helpful at some point in your career.

Building a façade over a database

Data-driven programs are a type of software that I often see in smaller enterprises. Those companies need to support their day-to-day operations with computers, not the other way around. Every company needs internal tools, and many needed them yesterday.

The reason is simple; every company is unique. Because it's unique, due to its business model, leadership, or employees, it also needs unique tools to help with its day-to-day operations. Often, those small tools are simple user interfaces over a database, controlling access to that data. In these cases, you don't need over-engineered solutions, as long as everyone is informed that the tool will not evolve beyond what it is: a small tool.

In real life, this one is tough to explain to non-programmers because they tend to see complex use cases as easy to implement and simple use cases as hard to implement. It's normal; they just don't know, and we all don't know something. In these scenarios, a big part of our job is also to educate people. Advising decision-makers about the differences in quality between a small tool and a large business application should help. By educating and working with stakeholders, they become aware of the situation and make decisions with you, leading to higher project quality that meets everyone's expectations. This can also reduce the *"it's not my fault"* syndrome from both sides.

I've found that immersing customers and decision-makers in the decision process and having them follow the development cycle helps them understand the reality behind the programs and helps both sides stay happy and grow more satisfied. Stakeholders not getting what they want is no better than you being super stressed over unreachable deadlines.

That said, our educational role does not end with decision-makers. Teaching new tools and techniques to your peers is also a major way to improve your team, peers, and yourself. Explaining concepts is not always as easy as it sounds.

Nevertheless, data-driven programs may be hard to avoid, especially if you are working for SMEs, so try to get the best out of it. Another tip is to remember that someday, someone will have to do maintenance on those small tools. Think of that person as being you, and think about how you'd like to have some guidelines or documentation to help you out. I'm not saying to over-document projects either, as documentation often gets out of sync with the code and becomes more of a problem than a solution. However, a simple `README.md` file at the root of the project explaining how to build and run the program and some general guidelines could be beneficial. Always think about documentation as if you were the one reading it. Most people don't like to spend hours reading documentation to understand something simple, so keep it simple.

When building a *façade over a database*, you want to keep it simple. Also, you should make it clear that it should not evolve past that role. One way to build this would be to use EF Core as your data layer and scaffold an MVC application as your presentation layer, shielding your database. If you need access control, you can use the built-in ASP.NET Core authentication and authorization mechanism. You can then choose role-based or policy-based access control, or any other way that makes sense for your tool and allows you to control access to the data the way you need to.

Keeping it simple should help you build more tools in less time, making everyone happy. Most likely, improving your non-tech colleagues' productivity, which should lead to more profit for the company, could lead to prosperity, which should mean more work for you; it should be a win-win situation.

From a layering standpoint, using my previous example, you will end up having two layers sharing the data model:

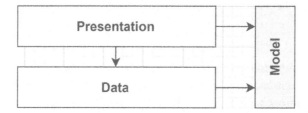

Figure 12.18: A façade-like presentation layer over a database application's design

Nothing stops you from creating a **view model** here and there for more complex views, but the key is to keep the logic's complexity to a minimum. Otherwise, you may discover the hard way that sometimes, rewriting a program from scratch takes less time than trying to fix it. Moreover, nothing stops you from using any other presentation tools and components available to you.

Using this data-driven architecture as a temporary application while the main application is in development is also a good solution. It takes a fraction of the time to build, and the users have access to it immediately. You can even get feedback from it, which allows you to fix any mistakes before they are implemented in the real (future) application, working like a living prototype.

> **Tip**
>
> A good database design in these sorts of applications can go a long way.

Not all projects are that simple, but still, many are; the key is to make the program good enough while making sure you cut the right corners. The presentation layer in these types of applications could leverage a low-code solution such as Power Apps, for example.

Summary

Layering is one of the most used architectural techniques when it comes to designing applications. An application is often split into multiple different layers, each managing a single responsibility. The three most popular layers are **presentation**, **domain**, and **data**. You are not limited to three layers, and you can split each one into smaller layers (or smaller pieces inside the same conceptual layer). This allows you to create composable, manageable, and maintainable applications.

Moreover, you can create abstraction layers to invert the flow of dependency and separate interfaces from implementations, as we saw in the *Abstract layers* section. You can persist the domain entities directly or create an independent model for the data layer. You can also use an anemic model (no logic or method) or a rich model (packed with entity-related logic). You can share that model between multiple layers or have each layer possess its own.

Out of layering was born Clean Architecture, which guides how you can organize your application into concentric layers, often dividing the application into use cases.

Let's see how this approach can help us move toward the **SOLID** principles at app scale:

- **S:** Layering leads us toward splitting responsibilities horizontally, with each layer oriented around a single macro-concern. The main goal of layering is responsibility segregation.
- **O:** Abstract layers enable consumers to act differently (change behaviors) based on the provided implementation (concrete layer).
- **L:** N/A
- **I:** Splitting layers based on features (or cohesive groups of features) is a way of segregating a system into smaller blocks (interfaces).
- **D:** Abstraction layers lead directly to the dependency flow's inversion, while classic layering leads to the opposite direction.

In the next chapter, we learn how to centralize the logic of copying objects (models) using object mappers and an open source tool to help us skip the implementation, also known as productive laziness.

Questions

Let's take a look at a few practice questions:

1. Is it true that, when creating a layered application, we must have presentation, domain, and data layers?
2. Is a rich domain model better than an anemic domain model?
3. Does EF Core implement the Repository and Unit of Work patterns?
4. Do we need to use an ORM in the data layer?
5. Can a layer in Clean Architecture access any inward layers?

Further reading

Here are a few links to help you build on what we learned in this chapter:

- **ExceptionMapper** is an ASP.NET Core middleware that reacts to `Exception`. You can map certain exception types to HTTP status codes and more. It is one of the open source projects that I created in 2020: `https://adpg.link/i8jb`.
- **Dapper** is a simple yet powerful ORM for .NET, made by the people of Stack Overflow. If you like writing SQL, but don't like mapping data to objects, this ORM might be for you: `https://adpg.link/pTYs`.
- An article that I wrote in 2017, talking about the Repository pattern; that is, *Design Patterns: ASP.NET Core Web API, services, and repositories | Part 5: Repositories, the ClanRepository, and integration testing*: `https://adpg.link/D53Z`.
- *Entity Framework Core – Using Transactions*: `https://adpg.link/gxwD`.

13

Getting Started with Object Mappers

In this chapter, we explore object mapping. As we saw in the previous chapter, working with layers often leads to copying models from one layer to another. Object mappers solve that problem. We first look at manually implementing an object mapper. Then, we improve our design by regrouping the mappers under a mapper service. Finally, we replace that with an open source tool that helps us generate business value instead of writing mapping code.

The following topics are covered in this chapter:

- Overview of object mapping and object mappers
- Implementing a simple object mapper
- Exploring the too-many-dependencies code smell
- Exploring the Aggregate Services pattern
- Implementing a Mapping Façade by leveraging the Façade pattern
- Using the Service Locator pattern to create a flexible Mapping Service in front of our mappers
- Using AutoMapper to map an object to another, replacing our homebrewed code

Object mapper

What is object mapping? In a nutshell, it is the action of copying the value of an object's properties into the properties of another object. But sometimes, properties' names do not match; an object hierarchy may need to be flattened and transformed. As we saw in the previous chapter, each layer can own its own model, which can be a good thing, but that comes at the price of copying objects from one layer to another. We can also share models between layers, but even then we need some sort of mapping at some point. Even if it's just to map your models to **Data Transfer Objects (DTOs)** or view models, it is almost inevitable unless you are building a tiny application, but even then, you may want or need DTOs and view models.

> **Note**
>
> Remember that DTOs define your API's contract. Having independent contract classes should help you maintain a system, making you choose when to modify them. If you skip that part, each time you change your model it automatically updates your endpoint's contract, possibly breaking some clients. Moreover, if you input your model directly, a malicious user could try to bind the values of properties that they should not, leading to potential security issues (known as **over-posting** or **over-posting attacks**). Having good data exchange contracts is one of the keys to designing robust systems.

In the previous projects, the mapping logic was done in the code, sometimes duplicating the mapping logic and adding additional responsibilities to the class doing the mapping. In this chapter, we are extracting the mapping logic into object mappers to fix that issue.

Goal

The object mapper's goal is to copy the value of an object's properties into the properties of another object. It encapsulates the mapping logic away from where the mapping takes place. The mapper is also responsible for transforming the values from the original format to the destination format when both objects do not follow the same structure. We might want to flatten the object hierarchy, for example.

Design

We can design object mappers in many ways. Here is the most basic object mapper design:

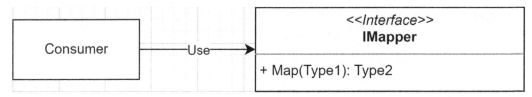

Figure 13.1: Basic design of the object mapper

In the diagram, the **Consumer** uses the IMapper interface to map an object of Type1 to an object of Type2. That's not very reusable, but it illustrates the concept. By using the power of **generics**, we can upgrade that simple design to this more reusable version:

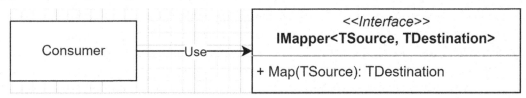

Figure 13.2: Generic object mapper design

With this design, we can map any TSource to any TDestination by implementing the IMapper<TSource, TDestination> interface once per mapping rule. One class could also implement multiple mapping rules. For example, we could implement the mapping of Type1 to Type2 and Type2 to Type1 in the same class (a bidirectional mapper).

We could also use the following design and create an IMapper interface with a single method that handles all of the application's mapping:

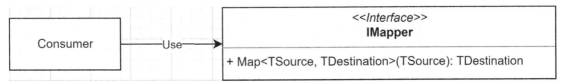

Figure 13.3: Object mapping using a single IMapper as the entry point

The biggest advantage of that last design is the ease of use. We always inject a single IMapper instead of one IMapper<TSource, TDestination> per type of mapping, which should reduce the number of dependencies and the complexity of consuming such a mapper.

You can implement object mapping in any way that your imagination allows, but the critical part to remember is that the mapper is responsible for mapping an object to another. A mapper should not do crazy stuff such as loading data from a database and whatnot. It should copy the values of one object into another: that's it. Think about the **Single Responsibility Principle** (SRP) here: the class must have a single reason to change, and since it's an object mapper, that reason should be object mapping.

Let's jump into some code to explore the designs in more depth with each project.

Project — Mapper

This project is an updated version of the Clean Architecture code from the previous chapter. The project aims to demonstrate the design's versatility of encapsulating entity mapping logic into mapper classes, moving that logic away from the consumers. Of course, the project is again focused on the use case at hand, making learning the topics easier.

First, we need an interface that resides in the Core project so the other projects can implement the mapping that they need. Let's adopt the second design that we saw:

```
namespace Core.Mappers;
public interface IMapper<TSource, TDestination>
{
    TDestination Map(TSource entity);
}
```

With that interface, we can start by creating the data mappers. But first, let's start by creating record classes instead of anonymous types to name the DTOs returned by the endpoints. Here are all the DTOs (from the `Program.cs` file):

```
// Input stock DTOs
public record class AddStocksCommand(int Amount);
public record class RemoveStocksCommand(int Amount);
// Output stock DTO
public record class StockLevel(int QuantityInStock);

// Output "read all products" DTO
public record class ProductDetails(int Id, string Name, int QuantityInStock);

// Output Exceptions DTO
public record class ProductNotFound(int ProductId, string Message);
public record class NotEnoughStock(int AmountToRemove, int QuantityInStock,
string Message);
```

Three of the four output DTOs need mapping:

- `Product` to `ProductDetails`
- `ProductNotFoundException` to `ProductNotFound`
- `NotEnoughStockException` to `NotEnoughStock`

Note

Why not map the `StockLevel` DTO? In our case, the `StockService` returns an `int` when we add or remove stocks, so converting a primitive value like an `int` into a `StockLevel` object does not require an object mapper. Moreover, creating such an object mapper adds no value and would just make the code more complex. If the service had returned an object, creating a mapper that maps an object to `StockLevel` would have made more sense.

Let's start with the product mapper (from the `Program.cs` file):

```
public class ProductMapper : IMapper<Product, ProductDetails>
{
    public ProductDetails Map(Product entity)
        => new(entity.Id ?? default, entity.Name, entity.QuantityInStock);
}
```

The preceding code is very straightforward; the `ProductMapper` class implements the `IMapper<Product, ProductDetails>` interface. The `Map` method returns a `ProductDetails` instance and makes sure the `Id` property's value is not `null` (highlighted), which should not happen. That workaround makes the static analyzer happy.

All in all, the Map method takes a `Product` as input and outputs a `ProductDetails` instance containing the same values.

Then let's continue with the exception mappers (from the `Program.cs` file):

```
public class ExceptionsMapper : IMapper<ProductNotFoundException,
ProductNotFound>, IMapper<NotEnoughStockException, NotEnoughStock>
{
    public ProductNotFound Map(ProductNotFoundException exception)
        => new(exception.ProductId, exception.Message);
    public NotEnoughStock Map(NotEnoughStockException exception)
        => new(exception.AmountToRemove, exception.QuantityInStock, exception.
Message);
}
```

Compared to the `ProductMapper` class, the `ExceptionsMapper` class implements the two remaining use cases, depicted by implementing the `IMapper<ProductNotFoundException, ProductNotFound>` and `IMapper<NotEnoughStockException, NotEnoughStock>` interfaces. The two Map methods handle mapping an exception to its DTO, leading to one class being responsible for mapping exceptions to the DTO.

Let's look at the products endpoint (original value from the `clean-architecture` project of *Chapter 12, Understanding Layering*):

```
app.MapGet("/products", async (
    IProductRepository productRepository,
    CancellationToken cancellationToken) =>
{
    var products = await productRepository.AllAsync(cancellationToken);
    return products.Select(p => new
    {
        p.Id,
        p.Name,
        p.QuantityInStock
    });
});
```

Before analyzing the code, let's look at the updated version (from the `Program.cs` file):

```
app.MapGet("/products", async (
    IProductRepository productRepository,
    IMapper<Product, ProductDetails> mapper,
    CancellationToken cancellationToken) =>
{
    var products = await productRepository.AllAsync(cancellationToken);
    return products.Select(p => mapper.Map(p));
}).Produces(200, typeof(ProductDetails[]));
```

In the preceding code, the request delegate uses the mapper to replace the copy logic (the highlighted lines of the original code). That simplifies the handler, moving the mapping responsibility into mapper objects instead (highlighted in the preceding code)—one more step toward the SRP (the "S" in SOLID).

Let's skip the add stocks endpoint since it is very similar to the remove stocks endpoint but simpler, and let's focus on the remove stocks endpoint (original value from the `clean-architecture` project of *Chapter 12, Understanding Layering*):

```
app.MapPost("/products/{productId:int}/remove-stocks", async (
    int productId,
    RemoveStocksCommand command,
    StockService stockService,
    CancellationToken cancellationToken) =>
{
    try
    {
        var quantityInStock = await stockService.RemoveStockAsync(productId,
command.Amount, cancellationToken);
        var stockLevel = new StockLevel(quantityInStock);
        return Results.Ok(stockLevel);
    }
    catch (NotEnoughStockException ex)
    {
        return Results.Conflict(new
        {
            ex.Message,
            ex.AmountToRemove,
            ex.QuantityInStock
        });
    }
    catch (ProductNotFoundException ex)
    {
        return Results.NotFound(new
        {
            ex.Message,
            productId,
        });
    }
});
```

Once again, before analyzing the code, let's look at the updated version (from the `Program.cs` file):

```
app.MapPost("/products/{productId:int}/remove-stocks", async (
    int productId,
    RemoveStocksCommand command,
    StockService stockService,
    IMapper<ProductNotFoundException, ProductNotFound> notFoundMapper,
    IMapper<NotEnoughStockException, NotEnoughStock> notEnoughStockMapper,
    CancellationToken cancellationToken) =>
{
    try
    {
        var quantityInStock = await stockService.RemoveStockAsync(productId,
command.Amount, cancellationToken);
        var stockLevel = new StockLevel(quantityInStock);
        return Results.Ok(stockLevel);
    }
    catch (NotEnoughStockException ex)
    {
        return Results.Conflict(notEnoughStockMapper.Map(ex));
    }
    catch (ProductNotFoundException ex)
    {
        return Results.NotFound(notFoundMapper.Map(ex));
    }
}).Produces(200, typeof(StockLevel))
  .Produces(404, typeof(ProductNotFound))
  .Produces(409, typeof(NotEnoughStock));
```

The same thing happened for this request delegate, but we injected two mappers instead of just one. The mapping logic was moved from inline using an anonymous type to the mapper objects. Nevertheless, a code smell is starting to emerge here; can you smell it? We investigate this after we are done with this project; meanwhile, keep thinking about the number of injected dependencies.

Note

Have you noticed the `Produces` method calls, chained after `MapGet` and `MapPost`? These allow us to add metadata to our endpoints, telling the `ApiExplorer` what return value comes with each status code. We can leverage this feature now that we have concrete DTOs, not just anonymous types. Those values add more details to the OpenAPI definition file generated by Swagger and displayed by Swagger UI when running the project. It has nothing to do with object mapping, yet is good to know.

Now that the delegates are depending on interfaces with object mappers encapsulating the mapping responsibility, we have to configure the composition root and bind the mapper implementations to the `IMapper<TSource, TDestination>` interface. The service bindings look like this:

```
.AddSingleton<IMapper<Product, ProductDetails>, ProductMapper>()
.AddSingleton<IMapper<ProductNotFoundException, ProductNotFound>,
ExceptionsMapper>()
.AddSingleton<IMapper<NotEnoughStockException, NotEnoughStock>,
ExceptionsMapper>()
```

Since `ExceptionsMapper` implements two interfaces, we bind both to that class. That is one of the beauties of abstractions; the remove stocks delegate asks for two mappers but receives an instance of `ExceptionsMapper` twice, without even knowing it.

We could also register the classes, so the same instance is injected twice, like this:

```
.AddSingleton<ExceptionsMapper>()
.AddSingleton<IMapper<ProductNotFoundException, ProductNotFound>,
ExceptionsMapper>(sp => sp.GetRequiredService<ExceptionsMapper>())
.AddSingleton<IMapper<NotEnoughStockException, NotEnoughStock>,
ExceptionsMapper>( sp => sp.GetRequiredService<ExceptionsMapper>())
```

In this case, we will stick with two instances of the same class.

> **Note**
>
> Yes, I did that double registration of the same class on purpose. That proves that we can compose an application as we want it without impacting the **consumers**. That is done by depending on abstractions instead of implementations, as per the **Dependency Inversion Principle (DIP**—the "D" in SOLID). Moreover, the division into small interfaces, as per the **Interface Segregation Principle (ISP**—the "I" in SOLID), makes that kind of scenario possible. Finally, all those pieces are put back together using the power of **Dependency Injection (DI)**.

Now that we've explored how to extract and use mappers, let's look at that code smell that emerged as we were using them.

Code smell – Too many dependencies

Using that kind of mapping could become tedious in the long run, and we would rapidly see scenarios such as injecting three or more mappers into a single request delegate or controller (yes, the same applies to MVC and web API controllers). The consumer would likely have other dependencies already, leading to four or more dependencies.

That should raise the following flag:

- Does the class do too much and have too many responsibilities?

In this case, the fine-grained IMapper interface pollutes our request delegates with tons of dependencies on mappers, which is not ideal and makes our code harder to read. The preferred solution would be to move the exception handling responsibility away from the delegates or controllers themselves, leveraging a middleware or an exception filter, for example. Anyhow, we explore more object mapping concepts to help us with this problem.

As a rule of thumb, you want to **limit the number of dependencies to three or less**. Over that number, ask yourself if there is a problem with that class; does it have too many responsibilities? Having more than three dependencies is not inherently bad; it is just an indicator that you should reconsider some part of the design. If nothing is wrong, keep it at 4 or 5 or 10; it does not matter.

If you don't like to have that many dependencies, you could extract service aggregates that encapsulate two or more of those dependencies and inject that aggregate instead. Beware that moving your dependencies around does not fix anything; it just moves the problem elsewhere if there was a problem in the first place. Using aggregates could increase the readability of the code, though.

Instead of blindly moving dependencies around, analyze the problem to see if you could create classes with actual logic that could do something useful to reduce the number of dependencies.

Next, let's have a quick look at aggregating services.

Pattern – Aggregate Services

Even if the Aggregate Services pattern is not a magic problem-solving pattern, it is a viable alternative to injecting tons of dependencies into another class. Its goal is to aggregate many dependencies in a class to reduce the number of injected services in other classes, grouping dependencies together. The way to manage aggregates would be to group them by concern or responsibility. Putting a bunch of services in another service just for the sake of it is rarely the way to go; aim for cohesion.

Note

Creating one or more aggregation services that expose other services can be a way to implement service discovery in a project. This may bring some issues to the table so don't put everything into an aggregate firsthand either; like always, analyze if the problem is not elsewhere first. Loading a service that exposes other services can be handy.

Here is an example of a hypothetical mapping aggregate to reduce the number of dependencies of an imaginary **Create-Read-Update-Delete (CRUD)** controller that allows the creation, updating, deletion, and reading of one, many, or all products. Here's the aggregate service code and a usage example:

```
public interface IProductMappers
{
    IMapper<Product, ProductDetails> EntityToDto { get; }
    IMapper<InsertProduct, Product> InsertDtoToEntity { get; }
    IMapper<UpdateProduct, Product> UpdateDtoToEntity { get; }
}
```

```csharp
public class ProductMappers : IProductMappers
{
    public ProductMappers(IMapper<Product, ProductDetails> entityToDto,
IMapper<InsertProduct, Product> insertDtoToEntity, IMapper<UpdateProduct,
Product> updateDtoToEntity)
    {
        EntityToDto = entityToDto ?? throw new
ArgumentNullException(nameof(entityToDto));
        InsertDtoToEntity = insertDtoToEntity ?? throw new
ArgumentNullException(nameof(insertDtoToEntity));
        UpdateDtoToEntity = updateDtoToEntity ?? throw new
ArgumentNullException(nameof(updateDtoToEntity));
    }
    public IMapper<Product, ProductDetails> EntityToDto { get; }
    public IMapper<InsertProduct, Product> InsertDtoToEntity { get; }
    public IMapper<UpdateProduct, Product> UpdateDtoToEntity { get; }
}
public class ProductsController : ControllerBase
{
    private readonly IProductMappers _mapper;
    // Constructor injection, other methods, routing attributes, ...
    public ProductDetails GetProductById(int id)
    {
        Product product = ...; // Fetch a product by id
        ProductDetails dto = _mapper.EntityToDto.Map(product);
        return dto;
    }
}
```

The IProductMappers aggregate could make sense from that example as it regroups all mappers used in the ProductsController class. It has the single responsibility of mapping ProductsController-related domain objects to DTOs and vice versa. You can create aggregates with anything, not just mappers. That's a fairly common pattern in DI-heavy applications, which can also point to some design flaws.

Note

As long as an aggregate service is not likely to change and implements no logic, we could omit the interface and directly inject the concrete type. Since we are focusing heavily on the SOLID principles here, I decided to include the interface (which is not a bad thing in itself). One advantage of not having an interface is that using the concrete type could reduce the complexity of mocking the aggregate in unit tests. And as long as you don't try to put logic in there, I see no drawback.

Now that we've explored the Aggregate Services pattern, let's explore how to make a mapping façade instead.

Pattern — Mapping Façade

We studied façades already; here we explore one other way of organizing our many mappers by leveraging that design pattern. Instead of what we just did, we could create a mapping façade instead of an aggregate. The code consuming the façade is more elegant because it uses the Map methods directly instead of passing by properties. The responsibility of the façade is the same as the aggregate, but it implements the interfaces instead of exposing properties.

Here is an example:

```
public interface IProductMapperService : IMapper<Product, ProductDetails>,
IMapper<InsertProduct, Product>, IMapper<UpdateProduct, Product>
{
}
public class ProductMapperService : IProductMapperService
{
    private readonly IMapper<Product, ProductDetails> _entityToDto;
    private readonly IMapper<InsertProduct, Product> _insertDtoToEntity;
    private readonly IMapper<UpdateProduct, Product> _updateDtoToEntity;
    // Omitted constructor injection code
    public ProductDetails Map(Product entity)
    {
        return _entityToDto.Map(entity);
    }
    public Product Map(InsertProduct dto)
    {
        return _insertDtoToEntity.Map(dto);
    }
    public Product Map(UpdateProduct dto)
    {
        return _updateDtoToEntity.Map(dto);
    }
}
```

In the preceding code, the ProductMapperService class implements IMapper interfaces through the IProductMapperService interface and delegates the mapping logic to each injected mapper: a façade wrapping multiple individual mappers. Next, we look at the ProductsController that consumes the façade:

```
public class ProductsController : ControllerBase
{
    private readonly IProductMapperService _mapper;
```

```
    // Omitted constructor injection, other methods, routing attributes, ...
    public ProductDetails GetProductById(int id)
    {
        Product product = ...; // Fetch a product by id
        ProductDetails dto = _mapper.Map(product);
        return dto;
    }
}
```

From the consumer standpoint (the `ProductsController` class), I find it cleaner to write `_mapper.Map(…)` instead of `_mapper.SomeMapper.Map(…)`. The consumer does not want to know what mapper is doing what mapping; it only wants to map what needs mapping. If we compare the Mapping Façade with the Aggregate Services of the previous example, the façade takes the responsibility of choosing the mapper and moves it away from the consumer. This design distributes the responsibilities between the classes better.

This was a good occasion to revisit the Façade design pattern, but now that we've covered a few mapping options and explored the *too-many-dependencies* code smell, it is time to continue our journey into object mapping, with a "mapping façade on steroids."

Project – Mapping service

The goal is to simplify the implementation of the Mapper façade with a universal interface. To achieve that, we are implementing the diagram shown in *Figure 13.3*. Here's a reminder:

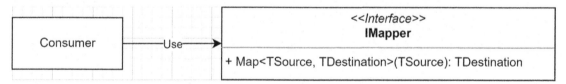

Figure 13.4: Object mapping using a single IMapper interface

Instead of naming the interface `IMapper`, `IMappingService` is more suitable because it is not mapping anything; it is a dispatcher servicing the mapping request to the right mapper. Let's take a look:

```
namespace Core.Mappers;
public interface IMappingService
{
    TDestination Map<TSource, TDestination>(TSource entity);
}
```

That interface is self-explanatory; it maps any TSource to any TDestination.

On the implementation side, we are leveraging the **Service Locator** pattern, so I called the class ServiceLocatorMappingService:

```
namespace Core.Mappers;
public class ServiceLocatorMappingService : IMappingService
{
    private readonly IServiceProvider _serviceProvider;
    public ServiceLocatorMappingService(IServiceProvider serviceProvider)
    {
        _serviceProvider = serviceProvider ?? throw new
ArgumentNullException(nameof(serviceProvider));
    }

    public TDestination Map<TSource, TDestination>(TSource entity)
    {
        var mapper = _serviceProvider.GetService<IMapper<TSource,
TDestination>>();
        if (mapper == null)
        {
            throw new MapperNotFoundException(typeof(TSource),
typeof(TDestination));
        }
        return mapper.Map(entity);
    }
}
```

The logic is simple:

- Find the appropriate IMapper<TSource, TDestination> service, then map the entity with it
- If you don't find any, throw a MapperNotFoundException

The key to that design is to register the mappers with the IoC container instead of with the service itself. Then we use the mappers without knowing every single one of them, like in the previous example. The ServiceLocatorMappingService class doesn't know any mappers; it just dynamically asks for one whenever needed.

> **Tip**
>
> I do not like the **Service Locator** pattern much in the application's code. The Service Locator is a code smell, and sometimes even worse, an anti-pattern. However, sometimes it can come in handy, as in this case. We are not trying to cheat DI here; on the contrary, we are leveraging its power. Moreover, that service location needs to be done somewhere. Usually, I prefer to let the framework do it for me, but in this case, we explicitly did it, which was fine.
>
> The use of a service locator is wrong when acquiring dependencies in a way that removes the possibility of controlling the program's composition from the composition root, which breaks the IoC principle.
>
> In this case, we load mappers dynamically from the IoC container, limiting the container's ability to control what to inject, but it is acceptable enough for this type of implementation since it has little to no negative impact on the maintainability, flexibility, and reliability of the program. Moreover, the mappers are registered and controlled by the container.

Now, we can inject that service everywhere we need mapping and then use it directly. We already registered the mappers, so we just need to bind the `IMappingService` to its `ServiceLocatorMappingService` implementation and update the consumers.

If we look at the new implementation of the remove stocks endpoint, we can see the number of dependencies was reduced to one:

```
app.MapPost("/products/{productId:int}/remove-stocks", async (
    int productId,
    RemoveStocksCommand command,
    StockService stockService,
    IMappingService mapper,
    CancellationToken cancellationToken) => {
    try
    {
        var quantityInStock = await stockService.RemoveStockAsync(productId,
command.Amount, cancellationToken);
        var stockLevel = new StockLevel(quantityInStock);
        return Results.Ok(stockLevel);
    }
    catch (NotEnoughStockException ex)
    {
        return Results.Conflict(mapper.Map<NotEnoughStockException,
NotEnoughStock>(ex));
    }
    catch (ProductNotFoundException ex)
    {
```

```
        return Results.NotFound(mapper.Map<ProductNotFoundException,
ProductNotFound>(ex));
    }
}).Produces(200, typeof(StockLevel))
  .Produces(404, typeof(ProductNotFound))
  .Produces(409, typeof(NotEnoughStock));
```

That code is very similar to the previous sample, but we replaced the mappers with the new service (the highlighted lines). The last piece is the DI binding:

```
.AddSingleton<IMappingService, ServiceLocatorMappingService>();
```

And that's it; we now have a universal mapping service that delegates the mapping to any mapper that we register with the IoC container.

> **Note**
>
> I used the singleton lifetime because `ServiceLocatorMappingService` has no state; it can be reused every time without impacting the mapping logic. Having no state is an easy reason to promote the service to a singleton lifetime but such a service could also define an application-wide shared state. In this case, the service could cache the mappers to facilitate reuse or improve the service location speed.
>
> The mappers from the other code samples of this chapter were also registered with a singleton lifetime for the same reason.

The nicest part is that this is not the end of our object mapping exploration. We have one tool to explore, AutoMapper, which does all the object mapping work for us. That said, we explored and revisited quite a few patterns and a code smell in that journey to mapping objects. Even if you are not likely to implement object mappers manually often, it was good to cover all of those topics, which should help you craft better software.

Project — AutoMapper

We just covered different ways to implement object mapping, but here we leverage an open source tool named AutoMapper that does it for us instead of us implementing our own.

Why bother learning all of that if there is a tool that already does it? There are a few reasons to do so:

- It is important to understand the concepts; you don't always need a full-fledged tool like AutoMapper.
- It gives us the chance to cover multiple patterns that we applied to the mappers that can also be applied elsewhere to any components with different responsibilities. So, all in all, you should have learned multiple new techniques during this object mapping progression.
- Lastly, we dug deeper into applying the SOLID principles to write better programs.

The AutoMapper project is also a copy of the Clean Architecture sample. The biggest difference between this project and the others is that we don't need to define any interface because AutoMapper exposes an IMapper interface with all the methods we need and more.

To install AutoMapper, you can install the AutoMapper NuGet package using the CLI (dotnet add package AutoMapper), Visual Studio's NuGet package manager, or by updating your .csproj manually.

The best way to define our mappers is by using AutoMapper's profile mechanism. A profile is a simple class that inherits from AutoMapper.Profile and contains maps from one object to another. We can use profiles to create groups, but in our case, with only three maps, I decided to create a single WebProfile class.

Finally, instead of manually registering our profiles, we can scan one or more assemblies to load all of the profiles into AutoMapper by using the AutoMapper.Extensions.Microsoft.DependencyInjection package.

Note

When installing the AutoMapper.Extensions.Microsoft.DependencyInjection package you don't have to load the AutoMapper package.

There is more to AutoMapper than this, but it has enough resources online, including the official documentation, to help you dig deeper into the tool. The goal of this project is to do basic object mapping.

In the *Web* project, we need to map Product to ProductDetails, NotEnoughStockException to NotEnoughStock, and ProductNotFoundException to ProductNotFound. To do that, we create the following WebProfile class (from the Program.cs file):

```
using AutoMapper;
public class WebProfile : Profile
{
    public WebProfile()
    {
        CreateMap<Product, ProductDetails>();
        CreateMap<NotEnoughStockException, NotEnoughStock>();
        CreateMap<ProductNotFoundException, ProductNotFound>();
    }
}
```

A profile in AutoMapper is nothing more than a class where you create maps in the constructor. The Profile class adds the required methods for you to do that, such as the CreateMap method. What does that do?

Invoking the method `CreateMap<Product, ProductDetails>()` tells AutoMapper to register a mapper that maps `Product` to `ProductDetails`. The other two `CreateMap` calls are doing the same for the other two maps. That's all we need for now because AutoMapper maps properties using conventions, and both our model and DTO classes have the same sets of properties with the same names.

> **Note**
>
> In the preceding examples, the mappers were defined in the `Core` layer. In this example, we are taking a dependency on a library, so it is even more important to think about the dependency flow. We are mapping objects only in the `Web` layer, so there is no need to put the dependency on AutoMapper in the `Core` layer. Remember that all layers depend directly or indirectly on `Core`, so having a dependency on AutoMapper from that layer means all layers would also depend on it. Therefore, in this example, we created the `WebProfile` class in the `Web` layer instead, limiting the dependency on AutoMapper to only that layer. Having only the `Web` layer depend on AutoMapper allows all outer layers (if we were to add more) to control how they are doing object mapping, giving more independence to each layer. It is also a best practice to limit object mapping as much as possible. I've added a link to *AutoMapper Usage Guidelines* in the *Further reading* section at the end of the chapter.

Now that we have one profile, we need to register it with the IoC container but rest assured that we don't have to do this by hand. We can scan for profiles from the composition root by using one of the `AddAutoMapper` extension methods to scan one or more assemblies:

```
builder.Services.AddAutoMapper(typeof(WebProfile).Assembly);
```

That method accepts a `params Assembly[] assemblies` argument, which means that we can pass multiple `Assembly` instances to it.

> **Note**
>
> That `AddAutoMapper` extension method comes from the `AutoMapper.Extensions.Microsoft.DependencyInjection` package.

Since we have only one profile in one assembly, we leverage that class to access the assembly by passing the `typeof(WebProfile).Assembly` argument to the `AddAutoMapper` method. From there, AutoMapper scans for profiles in that assembly and finds the `WebProfile` class. If there were more than one, it would register all it finds.

The beauty of scanning for types like this is that once you register AutoMapper with the IoC container, you can add profiles in any registered assemblies, and they get loaded automatically; there's no need to do anything else afterward but to write useful code. Scanning assemblies also encourages composition by convention, making it easier to maintain in the long run. The downside of assembly scanning is that it can be hard to debug when something is not registered.

Now that we've created the profiles and registered them with the IoC container, it is time to use AutoMapper. Let's look at the three endpoints we created initially (the `Produces` method calls are omitted to save space):

```
app.MapGet("/products", async (
    IProductRepository productRepository,
    IMapper mapper,
    CancellationToken cancellationToken) =>
{
    var products = await productRepository.AllAsync(cancellationToken);
    return products.Select(p => mapper.Map<Product, ProductDetails>(p));
});

app.MapPost("/products/{productId:int}/add-stocks", async (
    int productId,
    AddStocksCommand command,
    StockService stockService,
    IMapper mapper,
    CancellationToken cancellationToken) =>
{
    try
    {
        var quantityInStock = await stockService.AddStockAsync(productId,
command.Amount, cancellationToken);
        var stockLevel = new StockLevel(quantityInStock);
        return Results.Ok(stockLevel);
    }
    catch (ProductNotFoundException ex)
    {
        return Results.NotFound(mapper.Map<ProductNotFound>(ex));
    }
});

app.MapPost("/products/{productId:int}/remove-stocks", async (
    int productId,
    RemoveStocksCommand command,
    StockService stockService,
    IMapper mapper,
    CancellationToken cancellationToken) =>
{
    try
    {
        var quantityInStock = await stockService.RemoveStockAsync(productId,
command.Amount, cancellationToken);
```

```
            var stockLevel = new StockLevel(quantityInStock);
            return Results.Ok(stockLevel);
        }
        catch (NotEnoughStockException ex)
        {
            return Results.Conflict(mapper.Map<NotEnoughStock>(ex));
        }
        catch (ProductNotFoundException ex)
        {
            return Results.NotFound(mapper.Map<ProductNotFound>(ex));
        }
    });
```

The preceding code shows how similar it is to use AutoMapper to the other options. We inject an IMapper, then use it to map the entities. Instead of explicitly specifying both TSource and TDestination like in the previous example, when using AutoMapper we specify only TDestination, which reduces the complexity of the code from mapper.Map<ProductNotFoundException, ProductNotFound>(ex) to mapper.Map<ProductNotFound>(ex).

> **Note**
>
> If you are using AutoMapper on an IQueryable collection, you should use the ProjectTo<TDestination>(source) method to limit the number of queried fields when you don't need all of them in the destination class. In our case, that changes nothing because we need the whole entity. Here is an example that fetches all products from EF Core (_db.Products) and projects them to ProductDto instances:
>
> ```
> public IEnumerable<ProductDto> GetAllProducts()
> {
>     return _mapper.ProjectTo<ProductDto>(_db.Products);
> }
> ```
>
> Performance-wise, this is the recommended way to use AutoMapper with EF Core.

The last detail I'd like to add is that we can assert whether our mapper configurations are valid when the application starts. That will not point to missing mappers, but it validates that the registered ones are configured correctly. The recommended way of doing this is in a unit test. To make this happen, I made the autogenerated Program class public by adding the following line at the end:

```
public partial class Program { }
```

Then I created a test project named Web.Tests that contains the following code:

```
namespace Web;
public class StartupTest
{
```

```
[Fact]
public async Task AutoMapper_configuration_is_valid()
{
    // Arrange
    await using var application = new AutoMapperAppWebApplication();
    var mapper = application.Services.GetRequiredService<IMapper>();
    mapper.ConfigurationProvider.AssertConfigurationIsValid();
}
}
internal class AutoMapperAppWebApplication : WebApplicationFactory<Program>{}
```

In the preceding code, we validate that all the AutoMapper maps are valid. To make the test fail, you can uncomment the following line of the `WebProfile` class:

```
CreateMap<NotEnoughStockException, Product>();
```

The `AutoMapperAppWebApplication` class is there to centralize the initialization of the test cases when there is more than one.

In the test project, I created a second test case that ensures the `products` endpoint is reachable. For both tests to work together we must change the database name to avoid seeding conflicts so each test runs on its own database. This has to do with how we seed the database in the `Program.cs` file, which is not something we usually do except for development or proofs of concept. Nonetheless, testing against multiple databases is something that can come in handy to isolate tests.

Here's that second test case and updated `AutoMapperAppWebApplication` class to give you an idea:

```
public class StartupTest
{
    [Fact]
    public async Task The_products_endpoint_should_be_reachable()
    {
        await using var application = new AutoMapperAppWebApplication();
        using var client = application.CreateClient();
        using var response = await client.GetAsync("/products");
        response.EnsureSuccessStatusCode();
    }
    // Avoided AutoMapper_configuration_is_valid method
}
internal class AutoMapperAppWebApplication : WebApplicationFactory<Program>
{
    private readonly string _databaseName;
    public AutoMapperAppWebApplication([CallerMemberName]string? databaseName =
default)
```

```
    {
        _databaseName = databaseName ?? nameof(AutoMapperAppWebApplication);
    }
    protected override IHost CreateHost(IHostBuilder builder)
    {
        builder.ConfigureServices(services =>
        {
            services.AddScoped(sp =>
            {
                return new DbContextOptionsBuilder<ProductContext>()
                    .UseInMemoryDatabase(_databaseName)
                    .UseApplicationServiceProvider(sp)
                    .Options;
            });
        });
        return base.CreateHost(builder);
    }
}
```

Note

The `CallerMemberNameAttribute` used in the preceding code is part of the `System.Runtime.CompilerServices` namespace and allows its decorated member to access the name of the method that called it. In this case, the `databaseName` parameter receives the test method name.

And this closes the AutoMapper project. At this point, you should begin to be familiar with object mapping. I'd recommend you evaluate whether AutoMapper is the right tool for the job whenever a project needs object mapping. You can always load another tool or implement your own mapping logic if AutoMapper does not suit your needs. If too much mapping is done at too many levels, maybe another application architecture pattern would be better, or some rethinking is in order.

Final note

AutoMapper is convention-based and does a lot on its own without any configuration from us, the developers. It is also configuration-based, caching the conversions to improve performance. We can also create **type converters, value resolvers, value converters,** and more. AutoMapper keeps us away from writing that boring mapping code, and I have yet to find a better tool when object mapping is concerned.

Conclusion

Let's see how object mapping can help us follow the **SOLID** principles:

- **S:** It helps extract the mapping responsibility away from the other classes, encapsulating mapping logic into mapper objects or AutoMapper profiles.
- **O:** By injecting mappers, we can change the mapping logic without changing the code of their consumers.
- **L:** N/A
- **I:** We saw different ways of dividing mappers into smaller interfaces. AutoMapper is no different; it exposes the `IMapper` interface and uses other interfaces and implementations under the hood to add flexibility to how the mapping is done.
- **D:** All the code depends only on interfaces, moving the implementation's binding to the composition root. Moreover, the mapping service was literally looking up its mappers from the service provider through the Service Locator pattern.

That's it for object mapping; let's summarize what we learned before moving to the Mediator and CQRS design patterns.

Summary

Object mapping is an unavoidable reality in many cases. However, as we saw in this chapter, there are several ways of implementing object mapping, taking that responsibility away from the other components of our applications.

At the same time, we took the opportunity to explore the Aggregate Services pattern, which gives us a way to centralize multiple dependencies into one, lowering the number of dependencies needed in other classes. That pattern can help with the too-many-dependencies code smell, which, as a rule of thumb, states that we should investigate objects with more than three dependencies for design flaws. Like with any dependency, moving many dependencies into an aggregate may just be that: moving dependencies around. When doing so, make sure there is another reason or a certain cohesion within that aggregate or you risk adding unwanted complexity to your program.

We also explored how to leverage the Façade pattern to implement a mapping façade, which led to a more readable and elegant mapper, before implementing a mapper service that did the same thing, a bit less elegantly, but was way more flexible.

The last way we explored is AutoMapper, an open source tool that does object mapping for us, offering us many options to configure the mapping of our objects. As we explored, just using the default convention allowed us to eliminate all of our mapping code.

Hopefully, as we are putting more and more pieces together, you are starting to see what I had in mind at the beginning of this book when stating this was an architectural journey.

Now that we are done with object mapping, we explore the Mediator and CQRS patterns in the next chapter. Then we combine our knowledge to learn about a new style of application-level architecture named **Vertical Slice Architecture**.

Questions

Let's take a look at a few practice questions:

1. Is it true that injecting an Aggregation Service instead of multiple services makes our system better?
2. Is it true that using mappers helps us extract responsibilities from consumers to mapper classes?
3. Is it true that you should always use AutoMapper?
4. When using AutoMapper, should you encapsulate your mapping code into profiles?
5. How many dependencies should start to raise a flag telling you that you are injecting too many dependencies into a single class?

Further reading

Here are some links to build upon what we learned in the chapter:

- If you want more information on object mapping, I wrote an article about that in 2017, titled *Design Patterns: ASP.NET Core Web API, Services, and Repositories | Part 9: the NinjaMappingService and the Façade Pattern*: `https://adpg.link/hxYf`
- AutoMapper official website: `https://adpg.link/5AUZ`
- *AutoMapper Usage Guidelines* is an excellent do/don't list to help you do the right thing with AutoMapper, written by the library's author: `https://adpg.link/tTKg`

Join our book's Discord space

Join the book's Discord workspace for *Ask me Anything* session with the authors:

`https://packt.link/ASPdotNET6DesignPatterns`

14

Mediator and CQRS Design Patterns

This chapter covers the building blocks of the next chapter, which is about **Vertical Slice Architecture**. We begin with a quick overview of Vertical Slice Architecture to give you an idea of the end goal. Then, we explore the **Mediator** design pattern, which plays the role of the middleman between the components of our application. That leads us to the **Command Query Responsibility Segregation (CQRS)** pattern, which describes how to divide our logic into commands and queries. Finally, to piece all of that together, we explore MediatR, an open source implementation of the Mediator design pattern.

The following topics are covered in this chapter:

- A high-level overview of Vertical Slice Architecture
- Implementing the Mediator pattern
- Implementing the CQRS pattern
- Using MediatR as a mediator

Let's begin with the end goal.

A high-level overview of Vertical Slice Architecture

Before starting, let's look at the end goal of this chapter and the next. This way, it should be easier to follow the progress toward that goal throughout the chapter.

As we covered in *Chapter 12*, *Understanding Layering*, a layer groups classes together based on shared responsibilities. So, classes containing data access code are part of the data access layer (or infrastructure). In diagrams, layers are usually represented using horizontal slices, like this:

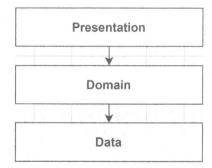

Figure 14.1: Diagram representing layers as horizontal slices

The "vertical slice" in "Vertical Slice Architecture" comes from that; a vertical slice represents the part of each layer that creates a specific feature. So, instead of dividing the application into layers, we divide it by feature. A feature manages its data access code, its domain logic, and possibly even its presentation code. We are decoupling the features from one another by doing this but keeping each feature's components close together. When we add, update, or remove a feature using layering, we change one or more layers. Unfortunately, "one or more layers" too often translates to "all layers."

On the other hand, with vertical slices, keeping features in isolation allows us to design them independently instead. From a layering perspective, it's like flipping your way of thinking about software to a 90° angle:

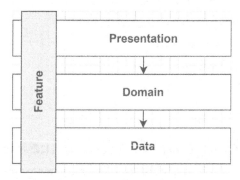

Figure 14.2: Diagram representing a vertical slice crossing all layers

Vertical Slice Architecture does not dictate the use of **CQRS**, the **Mediator** pattern, or **MediatR**, but these tools and patterns flow very well together, as we see in the next chapter. Nonetheless, these are just tools and patterns that you can use or change in your implementation using different techniques; it does not matter and does not change the concept.

The goal is to encapsulate features together, use CQRS to divide the application into requests (commands and queries), and use MediatR as the mediator of that CQRS pipeline, decoupling the pieces from one another.

You now know the plan—we will explore Vertical Slice Architecture later; meanwhile, let's start with the Mediator design pattern.

Implementing the Mediator pattern

The **Mediator** pattern is another GoF design pattern that controls how objects interact with one another (making it a behavioral pattern).

Goal

The mediator's role is to manage the communication between objects (colleagues). Those colleagues should not communicate together directly but use the mediator instead. The mediator helps break tight coupling between these colleagues.

A mediator is a middleman who relays messages between colleagues.

Design

Let's start with some UML diagrams. From a very high level, the Mediator pattern is composed of a mediator and colleagues:

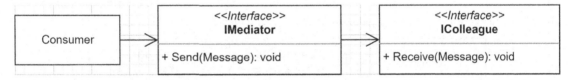

Figure 14.3: Class diagram representing the Mediator pattern

When an object in the system wants to send a message to one or more colleagues, it uses the mediator. Here is an example of how it works:

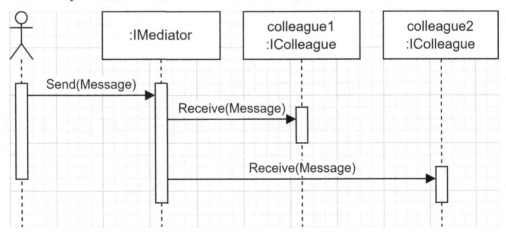

Figure 14.4: Sequence diagram of a mediator relaying messages to colleagues

That is also valid for colleagues; if they need to talk to each other, a colleague must also use the mediator. We could update the diagram as follows:

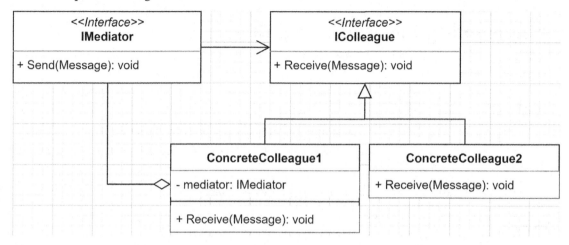

Figure 14.5: Class diagram representing the Mediator pattern including colleagues' collaboration

In that diagram, `ConcreteColleague1` is a colleague but also the consumer of the mediator. For example, that colleague could send a message to another colleague using the mediator, like this:

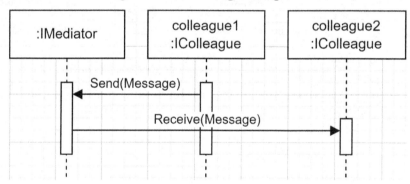

Figure 14.6: Sequence diagram representing colleague1 communicating with colleague2 through the mediator

From a mediator standpoint, its implementation will most likely contain a collection of colleagues to communicate with, like this:

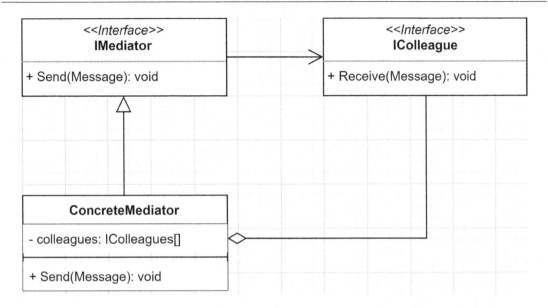

Figure 14.7: Class diagram representing a simple hypothetical concrete mediator implementation

All of those UML diagrams are useful, but enough of that; it is now time to look at some code.

Project – Mediator (IMediator)

The Mediator project consists of a simplified chat system using the Mediator pattern. Let's start with the interfaces:

```
namespace Mediator;

public interface IMediator
{
    void Send(Message message);
}
public interface IColleague
{
    string Name { get; }
    void ReceiveMessage(Message message);
}
public class Message
{
    public Message(IColleague from, string content)
    {
        Sender = from ?? throw new ArgumentNullException(nameof(from));
        Content = content ?? throw new ArgumentNullException(nameof(content));
```

```
    }

    public IColleague Sender { get; }
    public string Content { get; }
}
```

The system is composed of the following:

- IMediator, which sends messages.
- IColleague, which receives messages and has a Name property (to output something).
- The Message class, which represents a message sent by an IColleague implementation.

Now to the implementation of the IMediator interface. ConcreteMediator broadcasts the messages to all IColleague instances without discrimination:

```
public class ConcreteMediator : IMediator
{
    private readonly List<IColleague> _colleagues;
    public ConcreteMediator(params IColleague[] colleagues)
    {
        ArgumentNullException.ThrowIfNull(colleagues);
        _colleagues = new List<IColleague>(colleagues);
    }

    public void Send(Message message)
    {
        foreach (var colleague in _colleagues)
        {
            colleague.ReceiveMessage(message);
        }
    }
}
```

That mediator is simple; it forwards all the messages it receives to every colleague it knows. The last part of the pattern is ConcreteColleague, which delegates the messages to an IMessageWriter<TMessage> interface:

```
public class ConcreteColleague : IColleague
{
    private readonly IMessageWriter<Message> _messageWriter;
    public ConcreteColleague(string name, IMessageWriter<Message>
messageWriter)
    {
        Name = name ?? throw new ArgumentNullException(nameof(name));
```

```
        _messageWriter = messageWriter ?? throw new
 ArgumentNullException(nameof(messageWriter));
    }
    public string Name { get; }
    public void ReceiveMessage(Message message)
    {
        _messageWriter.Write(message);
    }
}
```

That class could hardly be simpler: it takes a name and an IMessageWriter<TMessage> implementation when created, then it stores a reference for future use.

The IMessageWriter<TMessage> interface serves as a presenter to control how the messages are displayed and has nothing to do with the Mediator pattern. Nevertheless, it is an excellent way to manage how a ConcreteColleague object handles messages. Here is the code:

```
namespace Mediator;
public interface IMessageWriter<Tmessage>
{
    void Write(Tmessage message);
}
```

Let's use that chat system now. The consumer of the system is the integration test defined in the MediatorTest class:

```
public class MediatorTest
{
    [Fact]
    public void Send_a_message_to_all_colleagues()
    {
        // Arrange
        var (millerWriter, miller) = CreateConcreteColleague("Miller");
        var (orazioWriter, orazio) = CreateConcreteColleague("Orazio");
        var (fletcherWriter, fletcher) = CreateConcreteColleague("Fletcher");
```

The test starts by defining three colleagues with their own TestMessageWriter implementation (names were randomly generated).

```
        var mediator = new ConcreteMediator(miller, orazio, fletcher);
        var expectedOutput = @"[Miller]: Hey everyone!
[Orazio]: What's up Miller?
[Fletcher]: Hey Miller!
";
```

In the second part of the preceding Arrange block, we create the subject under test (mediator) and register the three colleagues. At the end of that Arrange block, we also define the expected output of our test. It is important to note that we control the output from the TestMessageWriter implementation (defined at the end of the MediatorTest class).

```
// Act
mediator.Send(new Message(
from: miller,
content: "Hey everyone!"
));
mediator.Send(new Message(
from: orazio,
content: "What's up Miller?"
));
mediator.Send(new Message(
from: fletcher,
content: "Hey Miller!"
));
```

In the preceding Act block, we send three messages through mediator, in the expected order.

```
// Assert
Assert.Equal(expectedOutput, millerWriter.Output.ToString());
Assert.Equal(expectedOutput, orazioWriter.Output.ToString());
Assert.Equal(expectedOutput, fletcherWriter.Output.ToString());
}
```

In the Assert block, we ensure that all colleagues received the messages.

```
private (TestMessageWriter, ConcreteColleague)
CreateConcreteColleague(string name)
{
    var messageWriter = new TestMessageWriter();
    var concreateColleague = new ConcreteColleague(name, messageWriter);
    return (messageWriter, concreateColleague);
}
```

The CreateConcreteColleague method is a helper method that encapsulates the creation of the colleagues, enabling us to write the one-liner declaration used in the Arrange section of the test.

```
private class TestMessageWriter : IMessageWriter<Message>
{
    public StringBuilder Output { get; } = new StringBuilder();
    public void Write(Message message)
    {
```

```
                Output.AppendLine($"[{message.Sender.Name}]: {message.Content}");
        }
    }
}// Closing the MediatorTest class
```

Finally, the `TestMessageWriter` class writes the messages into `StringBuilder`, making it easy to assert the output. If we were to build a GUI for that, we could write an implementation of `IMessageWriter<Message>` that writes to that GUI; in the case of a web UI, it could be using **SignalR**, for example.

To summarize the sample: the consumer (the unit test) sent messages to the colleagues through the mediator. Those messages were written in the `StringBuilder` instance of each `TestMessageWriter`. Finally, we asserted that all colleagues received the expected messages. That illustrates that using the Mediator pattern allowed us to break the direct coupling between the colleagues; the messages reached them without them knowing about each others'.

In theory, colleagues should communicate through the mediator, so the Mediator pattern would not be complete without that. Let's implement a chatroom to tackle that concept.

Project – Mediator (IChatRoom)

In the last code sample, the classes were named after the Mediator pattern actors, as shown in the diagram of *Figure 14.7*. While this example is very similar, it uses domain-specific names instead and implements a few more methods to manage the system showing a more tangible implementation. Let's start with the abstractions:

```
namespace Mediator;
public interface IChatRoom
{
    void Join(IParticipant participant);
    void Send(ChatMessage message);
}
```

The `IChatRoom` interface is the mediator and it defines two methods instead of one:

- `Join`, which allows `IParticipant` to join `IChatRoom`.
- `Send`, which sends a message to the others.

  ```
  public interface IParticipant
  {
      string Name { get; }
      void Send(string message);
      void ReceiveMessage(ChatMessage message);
      void ChatRoomJoined(IChatRoom chatRoom);
  }
  ```

The IParticipant interface also has a few more methods:

- Send, to send messages.
- ReceiveMessage, to receive messages from the other IParticipant objects.
- ChatRoomJoined, to confirm that the IParticipant object has successfully joined a chatroom.

```csharp
public class ChatMessage
{
    public ChatMessage(IParticipant from, string content)
    {
        Sender = from ?? throw new ArgumentNullException(nameof(from));
        Content = content ?? throw new
ArgumentNullException(nameof(content));
    }
    public IParticipant Sender { get; }
    public string Content { get; }
}
```

ChatMessage is the same as the previous Message class, but it references IParticipant instead of IColleague.

Let's now look at the IParticipant implementation:

```csharp
public class User : IParticipant
{
    private IChatRoom? _chatRoom;
    private readonly IMessageWriter<ChatMessage> _messageWriter;
    public User(IMessageWriter<ChatMessage> messageWriter, string name)
    {
        _messageWriter = messageWriter ?? throw new
ArgumentNullException(nameof(messageWriter));
        Name = name ?? throw new ArgumentNullException(nameof(name));
    }
    public string Name { get; }
    public void ChatRoomJoined(IChatRoom chatRoom)
    {
        _chatRoom = chatRoom;
    }
    public void ReceiveMessage(ChatMessage message)
    {
        _messageWriter.Write(message);
    }
    public void Send(string message)
    {
        if (_chatRoom == null)
```

```
        {
            throw new ChatRoomNotJoinedException();
        }
        _chatRoom.Send(new ChatMessage(this, message));
    }
}
public class ChatRoomNotJoinedException : Exception
{
    public ChatRoomNotJoinedException()
        : base("You must join a chat room before sending a message.") { }
}
```

The User class represents our default IParticipant. A User instance can chat in only one IChatRoom; that is set when calling the ChatRoomJoined method. When it receives a message, it delegates it to its IMessageWriter<ChatMessage>. Finally, a User instance can send a message by delegating it to the mediator (IChatRoom). The Send method throws a ChatRoomNotJoinedException to enforce that the User has joined a chat room before sending messages (code-wise: the _chatRoom field is nullable).

We could create a Moderator, Administrator, SystemAlerts, or any other IParticipant implementation as we see fit, but not in this sample. I am leaving that to you to experiment with the Mediator pattern.

Now to the IChatRoom implementation:

```
public class ChatRoom : IChatRoom
{
    private readonly List<IParticipant> _participants = new
List<IParticipant>();
    public void Join(IParticipant participant)
    {
        _participants.Add(participant);
        participant.ChatRoomJoined(this);
        Send(new ChatMessage(participant, "Has joined the channel"));
    }
    public void Send(ChatMessage message)
    {
        _participants.ForEach(participant => participant.
ReceiveMessage(message));
    }
}
```

ChatRoom is even slimmer than User; it allows IParticipant to join in and sends ChatMessage to all registered participants. When joining a ChatRoom, it keeps a reference on that IParticipant, tells that IParticipant that it has successfully joined, then sends a ChatMessage to all participants announcing the newcomer.

That's it; we have a classic Mediator implementation. Before moving to the next section, let's take a look at the `Consumer` instance of `IChatRoom`, which is another integration test:

```
public class ChatRoomTest
{
    [Fact]
    public void ChatRoom_participants_should_send_and_receive_messages()
    {
        // Arrange
        var (kingChat, king) = CreateTestUser("King");
        var (kelleyChat, kelley) = CreateTestUser("Kelley");
        var (daveenChat, daveen) = CreateTestUser("Daveen");
        var (rutterChat, _) = CreateTestUser("Rutter");
        var chatroom = new ChatRoom();
```

We created four users with their respective `TestMessageWriter` instances in the `Arrange` section, as we did before (names were also randomly generated).

```
        // Act
        chatroom.Join(king);
        chatroom.Join(kelley);
        king.Send("Hey!");
        kelley.Send("What's up King?");
        chatroom.Join(daveen);
        king.Send("Everything is great, I joined the CrazyChatRoom!");
        daveen.Send("Hey King!");
        king.Send("Hey Daveen");
```

In the `Act` block, our test users join the `chatroom` instance and send messages into it.

```
        // Assert
        Assert.Empty(rutterChat.Output.ToString());
```

Since Rutter did not join the chatroom, we expect no message.

```
        Assert.Equal(@"[King]: Has joined the channel
[Kelley]: Has joined the channel
[King]: Hey!
[Kelley]: What's up King?
[Daveen]: Has joined the channel
[King]: Everything is great, I joined the CrazyChatRoom!
[Daveen]: Hey King!
[King]: Hey Daveen
", kingChat.Output.ToString());
```

Since King is the first to join the channel, he is expected to have received all messages.

```
        Assert.Equal(@"[Kelley]: Has joined the channel
[King]: Hey!
[Kelley]: What's up King?
[Daveen]: Has joined the channel
[King]: Everything is great, I joined the CrazyChatRoom!
[Daveen]: Hey King!
[King]: Hey Daveen
", kelleyChat.Output.ToString());
```

Kelley was the second user to join the chatroom, so the output contains almost all messages, except the line saying [King]: Has joined the channel.

```
        Assert.Equal(@"[Daveen]: Has joined the channel
[King]: Everything is great, I joined the CrazyChatRoom!
[Daveen]: Hey King!
[King]: Hey Daveen
", daveenChat.Output.ToString());
    }
```

Daveen joined after King and Kelley exchanged a few words, so the conversation is expected to start later.

```
    private (TestMessageWriter, User) CreateTestUser(string name)
    {
        var writer = new TestMessageWriter();
        var user = new User(writer, name);
        return (writer, user);
    }
```

The CreateTestUser method helps simplify the Arrange section of the test case, similar to before.

```
    private class TestMessageWriter : IMessageWriter<ChatMessage>
    {
        public StringBuilder Output { get; } = new StringBuilder();
        public void Write(ChatMessage message)
        {
            Output.AppendLine($"[{message.Sender.Name}]: {message.Content}");
        }
    }
} // Close the ChatRoomTest class

// As a reference, the IMessageWriter interface
// is the same as the previous project.
public interface IMessageWriter<TMessage>
```

```
{
    void Write(TMessage message);
}
```

The `TestMessageWriter` implementation is the same as the previous example, accumulating messages in a `StringBuilder` instance.

To summarize the test case, we had four users; three of them joined the same chatroom at a different time and chatted a little. The output is different for everyone since the time you join now matters. All participants are loosely coupled, thanks to the Mediator pattern, allowing us to extend the system without impacting the existing pieces. Leveraging the Mediator pattern can help us create more maintainable systems; many small pieces are easier to manage and to test than a large component handling all the logic itself.

Conclusion

As we explored in the two preceding projects, a **mediator** allows us to decouple the components of our system. **The mediator is the middleman between colleagues,** and it served us well in the small chatroom samples where each colleague can talk to the others without knowing how and without any need of even knowing them.

Now let's see how the Mediator pattern can help us follow the **SOLID** principles:

- S: The mediator extracts the communication responsibility from colleagues.
- O: With a mediator relaying the messages, we can create new colleagues and change the existing colleagues' behaviors without impacting the others. If we need a new colleague, we can register one with the mediator, and voilà! Moreover, if we need new mediation behavior, we can implement a new mediator and reuse the existing colleagues' implementations.
- L: N/A
- I: The system is divided into multiple small interfaces (`IMediator` and `IColleague`).
- D: All actors of the Mediator pattern solely depend on other interfaces.

Next, we explore CQRS, which allows us to separate commands and queries, leading to a more maintainable application. After all, all operations are queries or commands, no matter how we call them.

Implementing the CQRS pattern

CQRS stands for **Command Query Responsibility Segregation**. We can apply CQRS in two ways:

- Dividing requests into commands and queries.
- Applying the CQRS concept to a higher level, leading to a distributed system.

We stick with the first one here and tackle the second definition in *Chapter 16, Introduction to Microservices Architecture*.

Goal

The goal is to divide all requests into two categories: commands and queries.

- **A command mutates the state of an application.** For example, creating, updating, and deleting an entity are commands. In theory, commands do not return a value. In practice, they often do.
- **A query reads the state of the application but never changes it.** For example, reading an order, reading your order history, and retrieving your user profile are all queries.

Dividing operations into mutator requests (write/command) and accessor requests (read/query) creates a clear separation of concerns, leading us toward the SRP.

Design

There is no definite design for this, but for us, the flow of a command should look like the following:

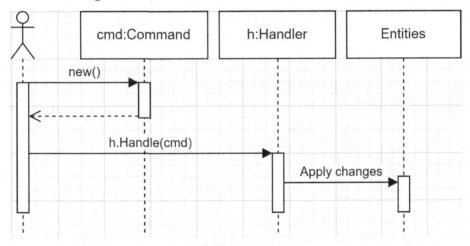

Figure 14.8: Sequence diagram representing the abstract flow of a command

The consumer creates a command object and sends it to a command handler, applying mutation to the application. In this case, I called it Entities, but it could have sent a SQL UPDATE command to a database or a web API call over HTTP; the implementation details do not matter.

The concept is the same for a query, but it returns a value instead. Very importantly, the query must not change the state of the application but query for data instead, like this:

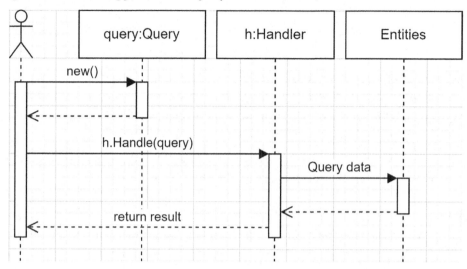

Figure 14.9: Sequence diagram representing the abstract flow of a query

Like the command, the consumer creates a query object and sends it to a handler, which then executes some logic to retrieve and return the requested data. You can replace `Entities` with anything that your handler needs to query the data.

Enough talk—let's look at the CQRS project.

Project – CQRS

Context: We need to build an improved version of our chat system. The old system worked so well that we now need to scale it up. The mediator was of help to us, so we kept that part, and we picked CQRS to help us with this new, improved design. A participant was limited to a single chatroom in the past, but now a participant should be able to chat in multiple rooms simultaneously.

The new system is composed of three commands and two queries:

- A participant must be able to join a chatroom.
- A participant must be able to leave a chatroom.
- A participant must be able to send a message into a chatroom.
- A participant must be able to obtain the list of participants that joined a chatroom.
- A participant must be able to retrieve the existing messages from a chatroom.

The first three are commands, and the last two are queries. The system is backed by a mediator that makes heavy use of C# generics as follows:

```
public interface IMediator
{
    TReturn Send<TQuery, TReturn>(TQuery query)
```

```
        where TQuery : IQuery<TReturn>;
    void Send<TCommand>(TCommand command)
        where TCommand : ICommand;

    void Register<TCommand>(ICommandHandler<TCommand> commandHandler)
        where TCommand : ICommand;
    void Register<TQuery, TReturn>(IQueryHandler<TQuery, TReturn>
commandHandler)
        where TQuery : IQuery<TReturn>;
}
public interface ICommand { }
public interface ICommandHandler<TCommand>
where TCommand : ICommand
{
    void Handle(TCommand command);
}
public interface IQuery<TReturn> { }
public interface IQueryHandler<TQuery, TReturn>
where TQuery : IQuery<TReturn>
{
    TReturn Handle(TQuery query);
}
```

If you are not familiar with generics, this might look daunting, but that code is way simpler than it looks. First, we have two empty interfaces: `ICommand` and `IQuery<TReturn>`. We could omit them, but they help identify the commands and the queries; they help describe our intent.

Then we have two interfaces that handle commands or queries. Let's start with the interface to implement for each type of command that we want to handle:

```
public interface ICommandHandler<TCommand>
where TCommand : ICommand
{
    void Handle(TCommand command);
}
```

That interface defines a `Handle` method that takes the command as a parameter. The generic parameter `TCommand` represents the type of command handled by the class implementing the interface. The query handler interface is the same, but it specifies a return value as well:

```
public interface IQueryHandler<TQuery, TReturn>
where TQuery : IQuery<TReturn>
{
    TReturn Handle(TQuery query);
}
```

The mediator abstraction allows registering command and query handlers using the generic interfaces that we just explored. It also supports sending commands and queries. Then we have the `ChatMessage` class, which is similar to the last two samples (with an added creation date):

```
public class ChatMessage
{
    public ChatMessage(IParticipant sender, string message)
    {
        Sender = sender ?? throw new ArgumentNullException(nameof(sender));
        Message = message ?? throw new ArgumentNullException(nameof(message));
        Date = DateTime.UtcNow;
    }

    public DateTime Date { get; }
    public IParticipant Sender { get; }
    public string Message { get; }
}
```

Next is the updated `IParticipant` interface:

```
public interface IParticipant
{
    string Name { get; }
    void Join(IChatRoom chatRoom);
    void Leave(IChatRoom chatRoom);
    void SendMessageTo(IChatRoom chatRoom, string message);
    void NewMessageReceivedFrom(IChatRoom chatRoom, ChatMessage message);
    IEnumerable<IParticipant> ListParticipantsOf(IChatRoom chatRoom);
    IEnumerable<ChatMessage> ListMessagesOf(IChatRoom chatRoom);
}
```

All methods of the `IParticipant` interface accept an `IChatRoom` parameter to support multiple chatrooms. Then, the updated `IChatRoom` interface has a name and a few basic operations to meet the requirement of a chatroom, like adding and removing participants:

```
public interface IChatRoom
{
    string Name { get; }
    void Add(IParticipant participant);
    void Remove(IParticipant participant);
    IEnumerable<IParticipant> ListParticipants();
    void Add(ChatMessage message);
    IEnumerable<ChatMessage> ListMessages();
}
```

Before going into commands and the chat itself, let's take a peek at the Mediator class:

```
public class Mediator : IMediator
{
    private readonly HandlerDictionary _handlers = new
    HandlerDictionary();
    public void Register<TCommand>(ICommandHandler<TCommand> commandHandler)
    where TCommand : ICommand
    {
        _handlers.AddHandler(commandHandler);
    }
    public void Register<TQuery, TReturn> (IQueryHandler<TQuery, TReturn>
commandHandler)
    where TQuery : IQuery<TReturn>
    {
        _handlers.AddHandler(commandHandler);
    }
    public TReturn Send<TQuery, TReturn>(TQuery query)
    where TQuery : IQuery<TReturn>
    {
        var handler = _handlers.Find<TQuery, TReturn>();
        return handler.Handle(query);
    }
    public void Send<TCommand>(TCommand command)
    where TCommand : ICommand
    {
        var handlers = _handlers.FindAll<TCommand>();
        foreach (var handler in handlers)
        {
            handler.Handle(command);
        }
    }
}
```

The Mediator class supports registering commands and queries as well as sending a query to a handler or sending a command to zero or more handlers.

Note

I omitted the implementation of HandlerDictionary because it does not add anything, and it is just an implementation detail. It is available on GitHub (https://adpg.link/ CWCe).

Now to the commands. I grouped the commands and the handlers together to keep it organized and readable, but you could use another way to organize yours. Moreover, since this is a small project, all the commands are in the same file, which would not be viable for something bigger. Remember we are playing LEGO® blocks, this chapter covers the CQRS pieces, but you can always use them with bigger pieces like Clean Architecture or other types of architecture. Let's start with the `JoinChatRoom` class:

```
public class JoinChatRoom
{
    public class Command : ICommand
    {
        public Command(IChatRoom chatRoom, IParticipant requester)
        {
            ChatRoom = chatRoom ?? throw new
ArgumentNullException(nameof(chatRoom));
            Requester = requester ?? throw new
ArgumentNullException(nameof(requester));
        }
        public IChatRoom ChatRoom { get; }
        public IParticipant Requester { get; }
    }
    public class Handler : ICommandHandler<Command>
    {
        public void Handle(Command command)
        {
            command.ChatRoom.Add(command.Requester);
        }
    }
}
```

The `JoinChatRoom.Command` class represents the command itself, a data structure that carries the command data. The `JoinChatRoom.Handler` class handles that type of command. When executed, it adds the specified `IParticipant` to the specified `IChatRoom`, from the `ChatRoom` and `Requester` properties (highlighted line). Next command:

```
public class LeaveChatRoom
{
    public class Command : ICommand
    {
        public Command(IChatRoom chatRoom, IParticipant requester)
        {
            ChatRoom = chatRoom ?? throw new
ArgumentNullException(nameof(chatRoom));
            Requester = requester ?? throw new
```

```
ArgumentNullException(nameof(requester));
        }
        public IChatRoom ChatRoom { get; }
        public IParticipant Requester { get; }
    }
    public class Handler : ICommandHandler<Command>
    {
        public void Handle(Command command)
        {
            command.ChatRoom.Remove(command.Requester);
        }
    }
}
```

That code represents the exact opposite of the JoinChatRoom command, the LeaveChatRoom handler removes an IParticipant from the specified IChatRoom (highlighted line). To the next command:

```
public class SendChatMessage
{
    public class Command : ICommand
    {
        public Command(IChatRoom chatRoom, ChatMessage message)
        {
            ChatRoom = chatRoom ?? throw new
ArgumentNullException(nameof(chatRoom));
            Message = message ?? throw new
ArgumentNullException(nameof(message));
        }
        public IChatRoom ChatRoom { get; }
        public ChatMessage Message { get; }
    }
    public class Handler : ICommandHandler<Command>
    {
        public void Handle(Command command)
        {
            command.ChatRoom.Add(command.Message);
            foreach (var participant in command.ChatRoom.ListParticipants())
            {
                participant.NewMessageReceivedFrom(
                    command.ChatRoom,
                    command.Message
                );
```

```
            }
        }
    }
}
```

The SendChatMessage command, on the other hand, handles two things (highlighted lines):

- It adds the specified Message to IChatRoom (which is now only a data structure that keeps track of users and past messages).
- It also sends the specified Message to all IParticipant instances that joined that IChatRoom.

We are starting to see many smaller pieces interacting with each other to create a more developed system. But we are not done; let's look at the two queries, then the chat implementation:

```
public class ListParticipants
{
    public class Query : IQuery<IEnumerable<IParticipant>>
    {
        public Query(IChatRoom chatRoom, IParticipant requester)
        {
            Requester = requester ?? throw new
ArgumentNullException(nameof(requester));
            ChatRoom = chatRoom ?? throw new
ArgumentNullException(nameof(chatRoom));
        }
        public IParticipant Requester { get; }
        public IChatRoom ChatRoom { get; }
    }
    public class Handler : IQueryHandler<Query, IEnumerable<IParticipant>>
    {
        public IEnumerable<IParticipant> Handle(Query query)
        {
            return query.ChatRoom.ListParticipants();
        }
    }
}
```

The ListParticipants query's handler uses the specified IChatRoom and returns its participants (highlighted line). Now, to the last query:

```
public class ListMessages
{
    public class Query : IQuery<IEnumerable<ChatMessage>>
    {
        public Query(IChatRoom chatRoom, IParticipant requester)
```

```
        {
            Requester = requester ?? throw new
ArgumentNullException(nameof(requester));
            ChatRoom = chatRoom ?? throw new
ArgumentNullException(nameof(chatRoom));
        }
        public IParticipant Requester { get; }
        public IChatRoom ChatRoom { get; }
    }
    public class Handler : IQueryHandler<Query, IEnumerable<ChatMessage>>
    {
        public IEnumerable<ChatMessage> Handle(Query query)
        {
            return query.ChatRoom.ListMessages();
        }
    }
}
```

The ListMessages query's handler uses the specified IChatRoom instance and returns its messages.

Note

All of the commands and queries reference IParticipant so we could enforce rules such as "IParticipant must join a channel before sending messages," for example. I decided to omit these details to keep the code simple, but feel free to add those features if you want to.

Next, let's take a look at the ChatRoom class, which is a simple data structure that holds the state of a chatroom:

```
public class ChatRoom : IChatRoom
{
    private readonly List<IParticipant> _participants = new
List<IParticipant>();
    private readonly List<ChatMessage> _chatMessages = new List<ChatMessage>();
    public ChatRoom(string name)
    {
        Name = name ?? throw new ArgumentNullException(nameof(name));
    }
    public string Name { get; }
    public void Add(IParticipant participant)
    {
        _participants.Add(participant);
    }
```

```
    public void Add(ChatMessage message)
    {
        _chatMessages.Add(message);
    }
    public IEnumerable<ChatMessage> ListMessages()
    {
        return _chatMessages.AsReadOnly();
    }
    public IEnumerable<IParticipant> ListParticipants()
    {
        return _participants.AsReadOnly();
    }
    public void Remove(IParticipant participant)
    {
        _participants.Remove(participant);
    }
}
```

If we take a second look at the ChatRoom class, it has a Name property, and it contains a list of IParticipant instances and a list of ChatMessage instances. Both ListMessages() and ListParticipants() return the list AsReadOnly() so a clever programmer cannot mutate the state of ChatRoom from the outside. That's it, the new ChatRoom class is a façade over its underlying dependencies.

Finally, the Participant class is probably the most exciting part of this system because it is the one that makes heavy use of our **Mediator** and **CQRS** implementations:

```
public class Participant : IParticipant
{
    private readonly IMediator _mediator;
    private readonly IMessageWriter _messageWriter;
    public Participant(IMediator mediator, string name, IMessageWriter
messageWriter)
    {
        _mediator = mediator ?? throw new
ArgumentNullException(nameof(mediator));
        Name = name ?? throw new ArgumentNullException(nameof(name));
        _messageWriter = messageWriter ?? throw new
ArgumentNullException(nameof(messageWriter));
    }
    public string Name { get; }
    public void Join(IChatRoom chatRoom)
    {
        _mediator.Send(new JoinChatRoom.Command(chatRoom, this));
```

```
    }
    public void Leave(IChatRoom chatRoom)
    {
        _mediator.Send(new LeaveChatRoom.Command(chatRoom, this));
    }
    public IEnumerable<ChatMessage> ListMessagesOf(IChatRoom chatRoom)
    {
        return _mediator.Send<ListMessages.Query, IEnumerable<ChatMessage>>(new
ListMessages.Query(chatRoom, this));
    }
    public IEnumerable<IParticipant> ListParticipantsOf(IChatRoom chatRoom)
    {
        return _mediator.Send<ListParticipants.Query,
IEnumerable<IParticipant>>(new ListParticipants.Query(chatRoom, this));
    }
    public void NewMessageReceivedFrom(IChatRoom chatRoom, ChatMessage message)
    {
        _messageWriter.Write(chatRoom, message);
    }
    public void SendMessageTo(IChatRoom chatRoom, string message)
    {
        _mediator.Send(new SendChatMessage.Command (chatRoom, new
ChatMessage(this, message)));
    }
}
```

Every method of the `Participant` class, apart from `NewMessageReceivedFrom`, sends a command or a query through `IMediator`, breaking the tight coupling between `Participant` and the system's operations (that is, the commands and queries). If we think about it, the `Participant` class is also a simple façade over its underlying dependencies, delegating most of the work to the mediator.

Now, let's look at how it works when everything is put together. I grouped several test cases that share the following setup code:

```
public class ChatRoomTest
{
    private readonly IMediator _mediator = new Mediator();
    private readonly TestMessageWriter _reagenMessageWriter = new();
    private readonly TestMessageWriter _garnerMessageWriter = new();
    private readonly TestMessageWriter _corneliaMessageWriter = new();

    private readonly IChatRoom _room1 = new ChatRoom("Room 1");
    private readonly IChatRoom _room2 = new ChatRoom("Room 2");
```

```
    private readonly IParticipant _reagen;
    private readonly IParticipant _garner;
    private readonly IParticipant _cornelia;

    public ChatRoomTest()
    {
        _mediator.Register(new JoinChatRoom.Handler());
        _mediator.Register(new LeaveChatRoom.Handler());
        _mediator.Register(new SendChatMessage.Handler());
        _mediator.Register(new ListParticipants.Handler());
        _mediator.Register(new ListMessages.Handler());


        _reagen = new Participant(_mediator, "Reagen", _reagenMessageWriter);
        _garner = new Participant(_mediator, "Garner", _garnerMessageWriter);
        _cornelia = new Participant(_mediator, "Cornelia", _
corneliaMessageWriter);
    }
    // Omited test cases and helpers
}
```

The test program setup is composed of the following:

- One `IMediator`, which enables all colleagues to interact with each other.
- Two `IChatRoom` instances.
- Three `IParticipant` instances and their `TestMessageWriter`.

In the constructor, all handlers are registered with the `Mediator` instance, so it knows how to handle commands and queries. The names of the participants are randomly generated. The `TestMessageWriter` implementation accumulates the data in a list of tuples (`List<(IChatRoom, ChatMessage)>`) to assess what is sent to what participant:

```
private class TestMessageWriter : IMessageWriter
{
    public List<(IChatRoom chatRoom, ChatMessage message)> Output { get; } =
new();

    public void Write(IChatRoom chatRoom, ChatMessage message)
    {
        Output.Add((chatRoom, message));
    }
}
```

Here is the first test case:

```
[Fact]
public void A_participant_should_be_able_to_list_the_participants_that_
joined_a_chatroom()
{
    _reagen.Join(_room1);
    _reagen.Join(_room2);
    _garner.Join(_room1);
    _cornelia.Join(_room2);
    var room1Participants = _reagen.ListParticipantsOf(_room1);
    Assert.Collection(room1Participants,
        p => Assert.Same(_reagen, p),
        p => Assert.Same(_garner, p)
    );
}
```

In that test case, Reagen and Garner join Room 1, and Reagen and Cornelia join Room 2. Then Reagen requests the list of participants from Room 1, which outputs Reagen and Garner. The code is easy to understand and use. Under the hood, it uses commands and queries through a mediator, breaking tight coupling between the colleagues. Here is a sequence diagram representing what is happening when a participant joins a chatroom:

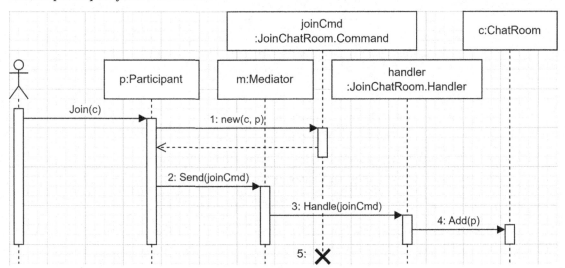

Figure 14.10: Sequence diagram representing the flow of a participant (p) joining a chatroom (c)

1. The participant (p) creates a JoinChatRoom command (joinCmd).
2. p sends joinCmd through the mediator (m).

3. m finds and dispatches joinCmd to its handler (handler).

4. handler executes the logic (adds p to the chatroom).

5. joinCmd ceases to exist afterward; commands are ephemeral.

That means Participant never interacts directly with ChatRoom or other participants.

Then a similar workflow happens when a participant requests the list of participants of a chatroom:

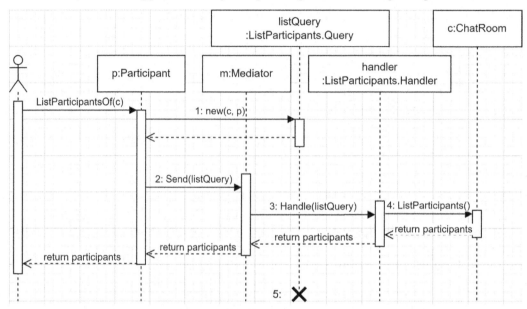

Figure 14.11: Sequence diagram representing the flow of a participant (p) requesting the list of participants of a chatroom (c)

1. Participant (p) creates a ListParticipants query (listQuery).

2. p sends listQuery through the mediator (m).

3. m finds and dispatches the query to its handler (handler).

4. handler executes the logic (lists the participants of the chatroom).

5. listQuery ceases to exist afterward; queries are also ephemeral.

Once again, Participant does not interact directly with ChatRoom.

Here is another test case where Participant sends a message to a chatroom, and another Participant receives it:

```
[Fact]
public void A_participant_should_receive_new_messages()
{
    _reagen.Join(_room1);
    _garner.Join(_room1);
    _garner.Join(_room2);
```

```
    _reagen.SendMessageTo(_room1, "Hello!");
    Assert.Collection(_garnerMessageWriter.Output,
    line =>
    {
        Assert.Equal(_room1, line.chatRoom);
        Assert.Equal(_reagen, line.message.Sender);
        Assert.Equal("Hello!", line.message.Message);
    }
);
}
```

In that test case, Reagen joins Room 1 while Garner joins Rooms 1 and 2. Then Reagen sends a message to Room 1, and we verify that Garner received it once. The SendMessageTo workflow is very similar to the other one that we saw, but with a more complex command handler:

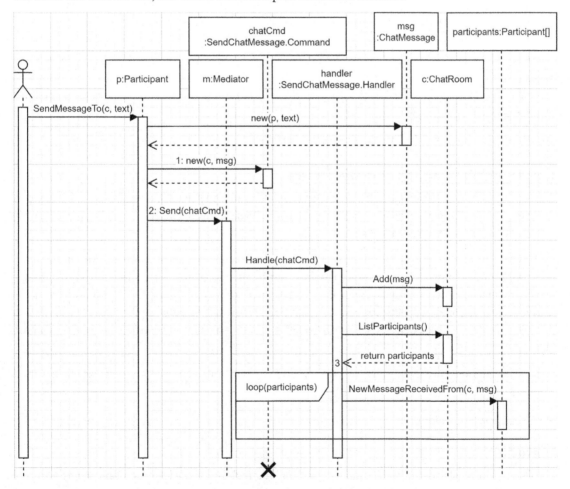

Figure 14.12: Sequence diagram representing the flow of a participant (p) sending a message (msg) to a chatroom (c)

From that diagram, we can observe that the logic was pushed to the `ChatMessage.Handler` class. All of the other actors work together with limited knowledge of each other (or even no knowledge of each other).

This demonstrates how CQRS works with a mediator:

1. A consumer (the participant in this case) creates a command (or a query).
2. The consumer sends that command through the mediator.
3. The mediator sends that command to one or more handlers, each executing their piece of logic for that command.

You can explore the other test cases to familiarize yourself with the program and the concepts.

> **Note**
>
> You can debug the tests in Visual Studio; use breakpoints combined with *Step Into (F11)* and *Step Over (F10)* to explore the sample.

I also created a `ChatModerator` instance that sends a message in a "moderator chatroom" when a message contains a word from the `badWords` collection. That test case executes multiple handlers for each `SendChatMessage.Command`. I'll leave you to explore these other test cases yourself, so we don't wander astray from our goal.

Before concluding CQRS, let's peek at marker interfaces.

Code smell – Marker Interfaces

We used the empty `ICommand` and `IQuery<TReturn>` interfaces in the code samples to make the code more explicit and self-descriptive. Empty interfaces are a sign that something may be wrong: a code smell. We call those **marker interfaces**.

In our case, they help identify commands and queries but are empty and add nothing. We could discard them without any impact on our system. On the other hand, we are not performing any kind of magic tricks or violating any principles, so it is OK to have them; they help define the intent. Moreover, we could leverage them to make the code more dynamic, like leveraging dependency injection to register handlers. Furthermore, I designed those interfaces this way as a bridge to the next project you are about to see.

Back to the marker interfaces, here are two types of marker interfaces that are code smells in C#:

- Metadata
- Dependency identifier

Metadata

Markers can be used to define metadata. A class "implements" the empty interface, and some consumer does something with it later. It could be an assembly scanning for specific types, a choice of strategy, or something else.

Instead of creating marker interfaces to add metadata, try to use custom attributes. The idea behind attributes is to add metadata to classes or members. On the other hand, interfaces exist to create a contract, and they should define at least one member; empty contracts are like a blank sheet.

In a real-world scenario, you may want to consider the cost of one versus the other. Markers are very cheap to implement but can violate the SOLID principles. Attributes could be as cheap to implement if the mechanism is already implemented or supported by the framework but could cost a lot more than a marker interface to implement if you need to program everything by hand. Before deciding, you must evaluate money, time, and the skills required as crucial factors.

Dependency identifier

If you need markers to inject some specific dependency in a particular class, you are most likely cheating the **inversion of control**. Instead, you should find a way to achieve the same goal using dependency injection, such as by contextually injecting your dependencies.

Let's start with the following interface:

```
public interface IStrategy
{
    string Execute();
}
```

In our program, we have two implementations and two markers, one for each implementation:

```
public interface IStrategyA : IStrategy { }
public interface IStrategyB : IStrategy { }
public class StrategyA : IStrategyA
{
    public string Execute() => "StrategyA";
}
public class StrategyB : IStrategyB
{
    public string Execute() => "StrategyB";
}
```

The code is barebones, but all the building blocks are there:

- StrategyA implements IStrategyA, which inherits from IStrategy.
- StrategyB implements IStrategyB, which inherits from IStrategy.
- Both IStrategyA and IStrategyB are empty marker interfaces.

Now, the consumer needs to use both strategies, so instead of controlling dependencies from the composition root, the consumer requests the markers:

```
public class Consumer
{
```

```
    public IStrategyA StrategyA { get; }
    public IStrategyB StrategyB { get; }
    public Consumer(IStrategyA strategyA, IStrategyB strategyB)
    {
        StrategyA = strategyA ?? throw new
ArgumentNullException(nameof(strategyA));
        StrategyB = strategyB ?? throw new
ArgumentNullException(nameof(strategyB));
    }
}
```

The Consumer class exposes the strategies through properties to assert its composition later. Let's test that out by building a dependency tree, simulating the composition root, and then asserting the value of the consumer properties:

```
[Fact]
public void ConsumerTest()
{
    // Arrange
    var serviceProvider = new ServiceCollection()
        .AddSingleton<IStrategyA, StrategyA>()
        .AddSingleton<IStrategyB, StrategyB>()
        .AddSingleton<Consumer>()
        .BuildServiceProvider();
    // Act
    var consumer = serviceProvider.GetRequiredService<Consumer>();
    // Assert
    Assert.IsType<StrategyA>(consumer.StrategyA);
    Assert.IsType<StrategyB>(consumer.StrategyB);
}
```

Both properties are of the expected type, but that is not the problem. The Consumer class controls what dependencies to use and when to use them by injecting markers A and B instead of two IStrategy instances. Due to that, we cannot control the dependency tree from the composition root. For example, we cannot change IStrategyA to IStrategyB and IStrategyB to IStrategyA, nor inject two IStrategyB instances or two IStrategyA instances, nor even create an IStrategyC instance to replace IStrategyA or IStrategyB.

How do we fix this? Let's start by deleting our markers and injecting two IStrategy instances instead (the changes are highlighted). After doing that, we end up with the following object structure:

```
public class StrategyA : IStrategy
{
    public string Execute() => "StrategyA";
```

```
    }
    public class StrategyB : IStrategy
    {
        public string Execute() => "StrategyB";
    }
    public class Consumer
    {
        public IStrategy StrategyA { get; }
        public IStrategy StrategyB { get; }
        public Consumer(IStrategy strategyA, IStrategy strategyB)
        {
            StrategyA = strategyA ?? throw new
    ArgumentNullException(nameof(strategyA));
            StrategyB = strategyB ?? throw new
    ArgumentNullException(nameof(strategyB));
        }
    }
```

The Consumer class no longer controls the narrative with the new implementation, and the composition responsibility falls back to the composition root. Unfortunately, there is no way to do contextual injections using the default dependency injection container, and I don't want to get into a third-party framework for this. But all is not lost yet; we can use a factory to help ASP.NET Core build the Consumer instance, like this:

```
// Arrange
var serviceProvider = new ServiceCollection()
    .AddSingleton<StrategyA>()
    .AddSingleton<StrategyB>()
    .AddSingleton(serviceProvider =>
    {
        var strategyA = serviceProvider.GetRequiredService<StrategyA>();
        var strategyB = serviceProvider.GetRequiredService<StrategyB>();
        return new Consumer(strategyA, strategyB);
    })
    .BuildServiceProvider();
// Act
var consumer = serviceProvider.GetRequiredService<Consumer>();
// Assert
Assert.IsType<StrategyA>(consumer.StrategyA);
Assert.IsType<StrategyB>(consumer.StrategyB);
```

From that point forward, we control the program's composition, and we can swap A with B or do anything else that we want to, as long as the implementation respects the IStrategy contract.

To conclude, using markers instead of doing contextual injection breaks the inversion of control principle, making the consumer control its dependencies. That's very close to using the new keyword to instantiate objects. Inverting the dependency control back is easy, even using the default container.

> **Note**
>
> If you need to inject dependencies contextually, I started an open source project in 2020 that does that. Multiple other third-party libraries add features or replace the default IoC container altogether if needed. See the *Further reading* section.

Conclusion

CQRS suggests dividing the operations of a program into **commands** and **queries**. A command mutates data, and a query returns data. We can apply the **Mediator** pattern to break the tight coupling between the pieces of the CQRS program, like sending the commands and queries.

Dividing the program helps separate the different pieces and focus on the commands and queries that travel from a consumer through the mediator to one or more handlers. The data contract of commands and queries becomes the program's backbone, trimming down the coupling between objects and tying them to those thin data structures instead, leaving the central piece (the mediator) to manage the links between them.

On the other hand, you may find the codebase more intimidating when using CQRS due to the multiple classes. However, keep in mind that each of those classes does less (having a single responsibility), making them easier to test than a more sizable class with many responsibilities. The way you organize the classes should also greatly help. We organize the pieces a certain way in the book, but you could organize them differently in a different context.

Now let's see how CQRS can help us follow the **SOLID** principles:

- **S:** Dividing an application into commands, queries, and handlers takes us toward encapsulating single responsibilities into different classes.
- **O:** CQRS helps extend the software without modifying the existing code, such as adding handlers and creating new commands.
- **L:** N/A
- **I:** CQRS makes it easier to create multiple small interfaces with a clear distinction between commands, queries, and their respective handlers.
- **D:** N/A

Now that we have explored CQRS and the Mediator pattern, it is time to get lazy and look at a tool that will save us some hassle.

Using MediatR as a mediator

In this section, we are exploring MediatR, an open source mediator implementation.

What is MediatR? Let's start with its maker's description from its GitHub repository, which brands it as this:

> *"Simple, unambitious mediator implementation in .NET"*

MediatR is a simple but very powerful tool doing in-process communication through messaging. It supports a request/response flow through commands, queries, notifications, and events, synchronously and asynchronously.

You can install the NuGet package using the .NET CLI: `dotnet add package MediatR`.

Now that I have quickly introduced the tool, we are going to explore the migration of our Clean Architecture sample but instead use MediatR to dispatch the `StocksController` requests to the core use cases.

Why migrate our Clean Architecture sample? The primary reason we are building the same project using different models is for ease of comparison. It is much easier to compare the changes of the same features than if we were building completely different projects.

What are the advantages of using MediatR in this case? It allows us to organize the code around use cases (vertically) instead of services (horizontally), leading to more cohesive features. We remove the service layer (the `StockService` class) and replace it with multiple use cases instead (the `AddStocks` and `RemoveStock` classes). MediatR also enables an MVC-like pipeline, which we can extend by programming pipeline behaviors. Those extensibility points allow us to manage cross-cutting concerns, such as requests validation, centrally without impacting the consumers and use cases. We explore request validation in *Chapter 15, Getting Started with Vertical Slice Architecture*.

Let's jump into the code now to see how it works.

Project – Clean Architecture with MediatR

Context: We want to break some more of the coupling in the Clean Architecture project that we built in *Chapter 12, Understanding Layering*, by leveraging the **Mediator** pattern and a **CQRS**-inspired approach.

The clean architecture solution was already solid, but MediatR will pave the way to more good things later. The only "major" change is the replacement of the `StockService` with two feature objects, `AddStocks` and `RemoveStocks`, that we explore soon.

First, we must install the `MediatR.Extensions.Microsoft.DependencyInjection` NuGet package in the web project. That package adds a helper method to scan one or more assemblies for MediatR handlers, preprocessors, and postprocessors. It adds those to the IoC container with a transient lifetime.

With that package in hand, in the `Program.cs` file, we can do this:

```
builder.Services.AddMediatR(typeof(NotEnoughStockException).Assembly);
```

Note that the `NotEnoughStockException` class is part of the core project. We can also specify more than one assembly here; as of version 9.0.0 of MediatR, there are six overloads to that method. Moreover, I picked the `NotEnoughStockException` class, but I could have chosen any class from the `Core` assembly.

MediatR exposes two types of messages, request/response and notifications. The first model executes a single handler, while the second allows multiple handlers to handle each message. The request/response model is perfect for both commands and queries, while notifications are more suited to an event-based model applying the Publish-Subscribe pattern. We cover the Publish-Subscribe pattern in *Chapter 16, Introduction to Microservices Architecture*.

Now that everything is "magically" registered, we can look at the use cases that replace the `StockService`. Let's have a look at the updated `AddStocks` code first:

```
namespace Core.UseCases;
public class AddStocks
{
    public class Command : IRequest<int>
    {
        public int ProductId { get; set; }
        public int Amount { get; set; }
    }

    public class Handler : IRequestHandler<Command, int>
    {
        private readonly IProductRepository _productRepository;
        public Handler(IProductRepository productRepository)
        {
            _productRepository = productRepository ?? throw new
ArgumentNullException(nameof(productRepository));
        }

        public async Task<int> Handle(Command request, CancellationToken
cancellationToken)
        {
            var product = await _productRepository.FindByIdAsync(request.
ProductId, cancellationToken);
            if (product == null)
            {
                throw new ProductNotFoundException(request.ProductId);
            }
            product.AddStock(request.Amount);
            await _productRepository.UpdateAsync(product, cancellationToken);
            return product.QuantityInStock;
        }
    }
```

```
        }
    }
```

Since we covered both use cases in the previous chapters and the changes are very similar, we will analyze both together, after the RemoveStocks use case:

```csharp
namespace Core.UseCases;
public class RemoveStocks
{
    public class Command : IRequest<int>
    {
        public int ProductId { get; set; }
        public int Amount { get; set; }
    }

    public class Handler : IRequestHandler<Command, int>
    {
        private readonly IProductRepository _productRepository;
        public Handler(IProductRepository productRepository)
        {
            _productRepository = productRepository ?? throw new
ArgumentNullException(nameof(productRepository));
        }

        public async Task<int> Handle(Command request, CancellationToken
cancellationToken)
        {
            var product = await _productRepository.FindByIdAsync(request.
ProductId, cancellationToken);
            if (product == null)
            {
                throw new ProductNotFoundException(request.ProductId);
            }
            product.RemoveStock(request.Amount);
            await _productRepository.UpdateAsync(product, cancellationToken);
            return product.QuantityInStock;
        }
    }
}
```

As you may have noticed in the code, I chose the same pattern to build the commands as I did with the CQRS sample, so we have a class per use case containing two nested classes: Command and Handler. I find this structure makes for very clean code when you have a 1-on-1 relationship between the command class and its handler.

By using the MediatR request/response model, the command (or query) becomes a request and must implement the `IRequest<TResponse>` interface. The handlers must implement the `IRequestHandler<TRequest, TResponse>` interface. Instead, we can also implement the `IRequest` and `IRequestHandler<TRequest>` interfaces for a command that returns nothing (void).

> **Note**
>
> There are more options that are part of MediatR, and the documentation is complete enough for you to dig deeper by yourself. Not that I want to, but I must limit the subjects that I talk about or risk writing an encyclopedia.

Let's analyze the anatomy of the `AddStocks` use case. Here is the old code as a reference:

```
namespace Core.Services;
public class StockService
{
    private readonly IProductRepository _repository;
    // Omitted constructor
    public async Task<int> AddStockAsync(int productId, int amount,
CancellationToken cancellationToken)
    {
        var product = await _repository.FindByIdAsync(productId,
cancellationToken);
        if (product == null)
        {
            throw new ProductNotFoundException(productId);
        }
        product.AddStock(amount);
        await _repository.UpdateAsync(product, cancellationToken);
        return product.QuantityInStock;
    }
    // Omitted RemoveStockAsync method
}
```

The first difference is that we moved the loose parameters (highlighted) into the `Command` class, which encapsulates the whole request:

```
public class Command : IRequest<int>
{
    public int ProductId { get; set; }
    public int Amount { get; set; }
}
```

Then the `Command` class specifies the handler's expected return value by implementing the `IRequest<TResponse>` interface, where `TResponse` is an `int`. That gives us a typed response when sending the request through MediatR. This is not "pure CQRS" because the command handler returns an integer representing the updated `QuantityInStock`. However, we could call that optimization since executing one command and one query would be overkill for this scenario (possibly leading to two database calls instead of one). Moreover, we are exploring MediatR using a CQRS-like approach, which is more than fine for in-process communication.

I'll skip the `RemoveStocks` use case to avoid repeating myself as it follows the same pattern. Instead, let's look at the consumption of those use cases. I omitted the exception handling to keep the code streamlined and because `try`/`catch` blocks would only add noise to the code in this case and hinder our study of the pattern:

```
app.MapPost("/products/{productId:int}/add-stocks", async (
    int productId,
    AddStocks.Command command,
    IMediator mediator,
    CancellationToken cancellationToken) =>
{
    command.ProductId = productId;
    var quantityInStock = await mediator.Send(command, cancellationToken);
    var stockLevel = new StockLevel(quantityInStock);
    return Results.Ok(stockLevel);
});
app.MapPost("/products/{productId:int}/remove-stocks", async (
    int productId,
    RemoveStocks.Command command,
    IMediator mediator,
    CancellationToken cancellationToken) =>
{
    command.ProductId = productId;
    var quantityInStock = await mediator.Send(command, cancellationToken);
    var stockLevel = new StockLevel(quantityInStock);
    return Results.Ok(stockLevel);
});
// Omitted code
public record class StockLevel(int QuantityInStock);
```

In both delegates, we inject an `IMediator` and a command object (highlighted). We also let ASP.NET Core inject a `CancellationToken`, which we pass to MediatR. The model binder loads the data from the HTTP request into the objects that we send using the `Send` method of the `IMediator` interface (highlighted). Then we map the result into the `StockLevel` DTO before returning its value and an HTTP status code of `200 OK`. The `StockLevel` record class is the same as before.

Note

The default model binder cannot load data from multiple sources. Because of that, we must inject `productId` and assign its value to the `command.ProductId` property manually. Even if both values could be taken from the body, the resource identifier of that endpoint would become less exhaustive (no `productId` in the URI).

With MVC, we could create a custom model binder.

With minimal APIs, we could create a static `BindAsync` method to manually do the model binding, which is not very extensible and would tightly couple the `Core` assembly with the `HttpContext`. I suppose we will need to wait for .NET 7+ to get improvements into that field.

Meanwhile, Damian Edwards, Principal Program Manager Architect for the .NET platform, has an experimental project underway that allows us to create binders like this:

```
public class AddStocksCommandBinder : IParameterBinder<AddStocks.
Command>
{
    public async ValueTask<AddStocks.Command?> BindAsync(HttpContext
context, ParameterInfo parameter)
    {
        if (!context.Request.HasJsonContentType())
        {
            throw new BadHttpRequestException(
                "The content-type must be JSON.",
                StatusCodes.Status415UnsupportedMediaType
            );
        }

        var command = await context.Request
            .ReadFromJsonAsync<AddStocks.Command>(context.
RequestAborted);
        if (command is null)
        {
            throw new BadHttpRequestException(
                "The request body must contain an AddStocks
Command."
            );
        }
        command.ProductId = int.Parse(context.
GetRouteValue("roductid")?.ToString() ?? "");
        return command;
    }
}
```

Then we need to register it with the container:

```
builder.Services
    .AddParameterBinder<AddStocksCommandBinder, AddStocks.Command>()
```

Such an approach allows breaking tight coupling between the class we need custom binding for and the code that contains the model binding logic. For example, we could have multiple components that reuse the same input model but leverage a different model binder to translate the data, like XML, JSON, or gRPC, to name a few. I've left the link in the *further reading* section at the end of the chapter.

All in all, it is almost the same code as before, but we use MediatR, the Mediator pattern, and a CQRS-inspired style instead.

Conclusion

With MediatR, we packed the power of a CQRS-inspired pipeline with the Mediator pattern into a Clean Architecture application. We were able to break the coupling between the request delegates and the use case handler (previously a service). A simple DTO such as a command object makes delegates (or controllers in the case of MVC) unaware of the handlers, leaving MediatR to be the middleman between the commands and their handlers. Due to that, the handlers could change along the way without having any impact on the controller.

Moreover, we could configure more interaction between the command and the handler with `IRequestPreProcessor`, `IRequestPostProcessor`, and `IRequestExceptionHandler`. These allow us to extend the MediatR request pipeline with crosscutting concerns like validation.

MediatR helps us follow the SOLID principles the same way as the Mediator and CQRS patterns combined. The only drawback (if it is one) is that the use cases now also control the API's input contracts. The command objects are now the input DTOs. If this is something that you must avoid in a project, you can input a DTO in the action method instead, create the command object, then send it to MediatR.

Summary

In this chapter, we looked at the Mediator pattern. That pattern allows us to cut the ties between collaborators, mediating the communication between them. Then we attacked the CQRS pattern, which advises the division of software behaviors into commands and queries. Those two patterns are tools that cut tight coupling between components.

Then we updated a Clean Architecture project to use MediatR, an open source generic Mediator implementation that is CQRS-oriented. There are many more possible uses than what we explored, but this is still a great start. This concludes another chapter where we explored techniques to break tight coupling and divide systems into smaller parts.

All of those building blocks are leading us to the next chapter, where we will be piecing all of those patterns and tools together to explore the Vertical Slice Architecture.

Questions

Let's take a look at a few practice questions:

1. Can we use a mediator inside a colleague to call another colleague?

2. In CQRS, can a command return a value?

3. How much does MediatR cost?

4. Imagine a design has a marker interface to add metadata to some classes. Do you think you should review that design?

Further reading

Here are a few links to build on what we have learned in the chapter:

*   MediatR: `https://adpg.link/ZQap`

*   To get rid of setting `ProductId` manually in the Clean Architecture with MediatR project, you can use the open source project `HybridModelBinding` or read the official documentation about custom model binding and implement your own:

    a. Custom Model Binding in ASP.NET Core: `https://adpg.link/65pb`

    b. `HybridModelBinding` (open source project on GitHub): `https://adpg.link/EyKK`

    c. Damian Edward's MinimalApis.Extensions project on GitHub: `https://adpg.link/M6zS`

*   `ForEvolve.DependencyInjection` is an open source project of mine that adds support for contextual dependency injection and more: `https://adpg.link/myW8`

15

Getting Started with Vertical Slice Architecture

In this chapter, we explore Vertical Slice Architecture, which moves elements from multiple layers to a centralized feature. It is almost the opposite of layering, but not totally. Vertical Slice Architecture also gives us a clean separation between requests, leading to an implicit **Command Query Responsibility Segregation (CQRS)** design. We piece all of that together using MediatR, which we explored in the previous chapter. Of course, you don't have to use those tools to apply the architectural style; you can replace any library with one of your choosing or even code part of the stack yourself.

The following topics are covered in this chapter:

- Vertical Slice Architecture
- A small project using Vertical Slice Architecture
- Continuing your journey: A few tips and tricks

Vertical Slice Architecture

As said at the beginning of the previous chapter, instead of separating an application horizontally, a vertical slice groups all horizontal concerns together to encapsulate a feature. Here is a diagram that illustrates that:

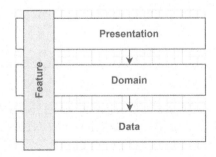

Figure 15.1: Diagram representing a vertical slice crossing all layers

Jimmy Bogard, who is a pioneer of this type of architecture and who promotes it frequently, says the following:

> *[The goal is to] minimize coupling between slices and maximize coupling within a slice.*

What does that mean? Let's split that sentence into two distinct points:

- "minimize coupling between slices" (improved maintainability, loose coupling)
- "maximize coupling within a slice" (cohesion)

We could see the former as one vertical slice should not depend on another. With that in mind, when you modify a vertical slice, you don't have to worry about the impact on the other slices because the coupling is minimal.

We could see the latter as: instead of spreading code around multiple layers, with potentially superfluous abstractions along the way, let's regroup that code. That helps keep the tight coupling inside a vertical slice to create a cohesive unit of code that serves a single purpose: handling the feature's logic.

Then we could wrap that to create software around the business problem that we are trying to solve instead of around the developer's concerns, which your client has no interest in (such as data access).

Now, what is a slice in more generic terms? I see slices as composites, or as a hierarchy if you prefer. For example, a shipping manager program has a multistep creation flow, a list, and a details page. Each step of the creation flow would be a slice responsible for handling its respective logic. When put together, they compose the create slice, which is responsible for creating a shipment (a bigger slice). The list and details pages are two other slices. Then, all of those slices become another bigger slice, leading to something like this:

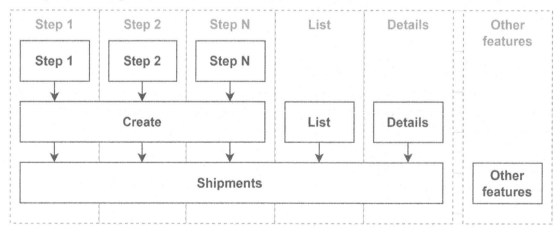

Figure 15.2: A diagram displaying a top-down coupling structure where smaller parts (top) depend on bigger parts (middle) of complex features (bottom) based on their cohesion with one another (vertically)

There is strong coupling inside **Step 1**, with limited coupling between the other steps; they share some creation code as part of the **Create** slice. **Create**, **List**, and **Details** also share some code, but in a limited way; they are all part of the **Shipments** slice and access or manipulate the same entity: one or more shipments. Finally, the **Shipments** slice shares no code (or very little) with **Other features**.

OK, this was my definition of a slice and how I see them; maybe other people have other points of view on that, which is fine. By following the pattern that I just described, I end up with limited coupling and maximum cohesion. The downside is that you need to continuously design the app, which requires stronger design skills than using a layered approach. We revisit this example in the *Continuing your journey* section near the end of the chapter.

Let's consider some further advantages and disadvantages in the next section.

What are the advantages and disadvantages?

On the upside, we have the following:

- We reduce coupling between features, making working on such a project more manageable. We only need to think about a single vertical slice, not *N* layers, improving **maintainability** by centralizing the code around a shared concern.
- We can choose how each vertical slice interacts with the external resources they require without thinking about the other slices. That adds **flexibility** since one slice can use T-SQL while another uses EF Core, for example.
- We can start small with a few lines of code (described as **Transaction Scripts** in *Patterns of Enterprise Application Architecture,* by Martin Fowler) without extravagant design or over-engineering. Then we can refactor our way to a better design when the need arises, and patterns emerge, leading to a **faster time to market**.
- Each vertical slice should contain precisely the right amount of code needed to be correct — not more, not less. That leads to a **more robust** codebase (less code means less extraneous code).
- It is easier for newcomers to find their way around an existing system since each feature is independent, grouped code, leading to a **faster onboarding time**.
- All that you already know from previous chapters still applies.

>
> **Tip**
>
> From my experience, features tend to start small and grow over time. While using software, the users often find out what they really need, updating the workflow they thought they initially required, which leads to changes in the software. I wish many projects I worked on were built using Vertical Slice Architecture instead of layering.

Now some downsides:

- It may take time to wrap your head around it if you're used to layering, leading to an adaptation period to learn a new way to think about your software.
- It is a "newer" type of architecture, and people don't like change.

> **Note**
>
> Another thing that I learned the hard way is to embrace change. I don't think that I've seen one project end as it was supposed to. Everyone figures out the missing pieces of the business processes while using the software. That leads to the following advice: release the software as fast as you can and have your customer use the software as soon as possible. That advice can be easier to achieve with Vertical Slice Architecture because you are building value for your customers instead of more or less useful abstractions and layers.
>
> At the beginning of my career, I was frustrated when specifications changed, and I thought that better planning would have fixed that. Sometimes better planning would have helped, but sometimes, the client just did not know how to express their business processes or needs and had to try the application to figure it out. My advice here is don't be frustrated when the specs change, even if that means rewriting a part of the software that took you days or more to code in the first place; that will happen all the time. Learn to accept that instead, and find ways to reduce the number of times it happens by helping your clients figure out their needs.

The following points are downsides that can become upsides:

- If you are used to working in silos, it may be harder to assign tasks by concerns (such as the data guys doing the data stuff). But in the end, it should be an advantage; everyone in your team (or teams) should work more closely together, leading to more learning and collaboration and possibly a new cross-functional team(s)—which is an excellent thing.
- Refactoring: strong refactoring skills will go a long way. Over time, most systems need some refactoring, which is even more true for Vertical Slice Architecture. That can be caused by changes in the requirements or due to technical debt. No matter the reason, if you don't, you may very well end up with a **Big Ball of Mud**. First, writing isolated code and then refactoring to patterns is a crucial part of Vertical Slice Architecture. That's one of the best ways to keep cohesion high inside a slice and coupling as low as possible between slices. This tip applies to all types of architecture.

> **Tip**
>
> A way to start refactoring that business logic would be to push the logic into the **domain model**, creating a **rich domain model**. You can also use other design patterns and techniques to fine-tune the code and make it more maintainable, such as creating services or layers. A layer does not have to cross all vertical slices; it can cross only a subset of them. Compared to other application-level patterns, such as layering, there are fewer Vertical Slice Architecture rules, leading to more choices on your end. *You can use all design patterns, principles, and best practices inside a vertical slice without exporting those choices application-wide.*

How do you organize a project into Vertical Slice Architecture? Unfortunately, there is no definitive answer to that, and it depends on the engineers working on the project. We explore one way in the next project, but you can organize your project as you see fit. Then we dig deeper into refactoring and organization. Before that, let's have a quick look at the **Big Ball of Mud** anti-pattern.

Anti-pattern — Big Ball of Mud

Big Ball of Mud describes a system that ended badly or was never properly designed. Sometimes a system starts great but evolves into a Big Ball of Mud due to pressure, volatile requirements, impossible deadlines, bad practices, or any other reasons. A Big Ball of Mud is often referred to as **spaghetti code**, which means pretty much the same thing.

This anti-pattern means a very hard-to-maintain codebase, code that is badly written, code that is difficult to read, lots of unwanted tight coupling, low cohesion, or worse: all that in the same codebase.

Applying the techniques covered in this book should help you avoid this anti-pattern. Aim at small, well-designed components that are testable. Enforce that using automated testing. Refactor and improve your codebase every time you can, iteratively (continuous improvement). Apply the SOLID principles. Define your application pattern before starting. Think of the best way to implement each component and feature; do research, make one or more proof of concept or experiments if unsure of the best approach to take. Make sure you understand the business requirements of the program you are building (this is probably the best advice of all). Those tips should help you avoid creating a Big Ball of Mud.

Next, let's jump into the Vertical Slice Architecture project.

Project — Vertical Slice Architecture

Context: We are getting tired of layering, and we got asked to rebuild our small demo shop using Vertical Slice Architecture.

Here is an updated diagram that shows how the project is conceptually organized:

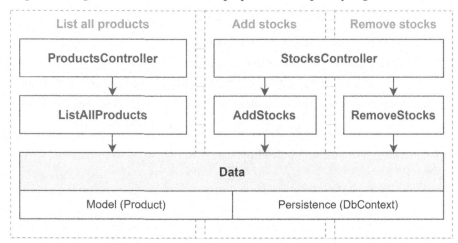

Figure 15.3: Diagram representing the organization of the project

Each vertical box is a use case (or slice), while each horizontal box is a cross-cutting concern or some shared components. This is a small project, so the data access code (DbContext) and the Product model are shared between the three use cases. That sharing has nothing to do with Vertical Slice Architecture, but it is hard to split it more in a small project such as this one. I'll go into more detail at the end of the section.

In this project, I decided to go with web API controllers instead of minimal APIs and an anemic product model instead of a rich one. We could have used minimal APIs as well, a rich model, or any combination. I chose this so you have a glimpse of using controllers, as this is something you might very well end up using.

Here are the actors:

- ProductsController is the web API entry point to manage products.
- StocksController is the web API entry point to manage inventory (add or remove stocks).
- AddStocks, RemoveStocks, and ListAllProducts are the same use cases we have copied in our project since *Chapter 12, Understanding Layering.*
- The persistence "layer" consists of an EF Core DbContext that persists the Product model.

We could add other crosscutting concerns on top of our vertical slices, such as authorization, error management, and logging, to name a few. In this case, we explore only validation.

Next, let's look at how the project is organized.

Project organization

Here is how we organized the project:

- The Data directory contains EF Core-related classes.
- The Features directory contains the features. Each subfolder contains its underlying use cases (vertical slices), including controllers, exceptions, and other support classes required to implement the feature.
- Each use case is self-contained and exposes the following classes:
    1. Command represents the MediatR request.
    2. Result is the return value of that request.
    3. MapperProfile instructs AutoMapper how to map the use case-related objects (if any).
    4. Validator contains the validation rules to validate the Command objects (if any).
    5. Handler contains the use case logic: how to handle the request.
- The Models directory contains the domain model.

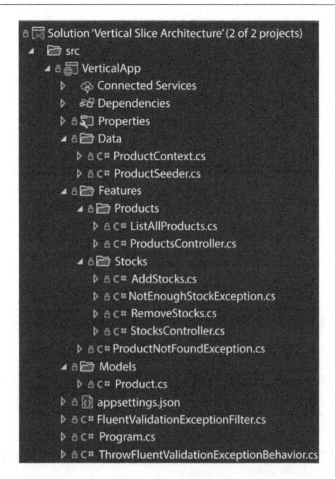

Figure 15.4: Solution Explorer view of the file organization

In this project, we support request validation using **FluentValidation**, a third-party NuGet package; see the *Further reading* section. You could also use System.ComponentModel.DataAnnotations or any other validation system that you want. What is great about FluentValidation is that it is easy to keep the validation within our vertical slice but outside of the class to be validated (compared to DataAnnotations, for example). Moreover, it is easy to test and extend.

Like other tools, FluentValidation can scan assemblies for validators with the following highlighted line (Program.cs):

```
var currentAssembly = typeof(Program).Assembly;
var builder = WebApplication.CreateBuilder(args);
builder.Services
    // Plumbing/Dependencies
```

```
    .AddAutoMapper(currentAssembly)
    .AddMediatR(currentAssembly)
    .AddSingleton(typeof(IPipelineBehavior<,>),
typeof(ThrowFluentValidationExceptionBehavior<,>))

    // Data
    .AddDbContext<ProductContext>(options => options
        .UseInMemoryDatabase("ProductContextMemoryDB")
        .ConfigureWarnings(builder => builder.Ignore(InMemoryEventId.
TransactionIgnoredWarning))
    )

    // Web/MVC
    .AddControllers(options => options.Filters
        .Add<FluentValidationExceptionFilter>())
        .AddFluentValidation(config => config
            .RegisterValidatorsFromAssembly(currentAssembly,
                lifetime: ServiceLifetime.Singleton)
;
var app = builder.Build();
app.MapControllers();
using (var seedScope = app.Services.CreateScope())
{
    var db = seedScope.ServiceProvider.GetRequiredService<ProductContext>();
    await ProductSeeder.SeedAsync(db);
}
app.Run();
```

The preceding code adds the bindings we already explored in previous chapters, FluentValidation, and other validation pieces required to connect the dots. We explore the validation pieces under the *Request validation* subsection of the project. Meanwhile, the highlighted line registers FluentValidation and scans the currentAssembly for validator classes. The validators themselves are part of each vertical slice. The lifetime named parameter tells FluentValidation to register those validators with a singleton lifetime so they can be injected into our custom MediatR behavior. FluentValidation binds validators as scoped services by default, and we can't inject a scoped service into a singleton service. Before digging too much into request validation, let's look at features.

Exploring a feature

In this subsection, we explore the RemoveStocks feature with the same logic as in previous samples but organized differently (which is pretty much the difference between one architectural style and another). Since we are using an anemic product model, the add and remove stocks logic has been moved from the Product to the Handler classes. Let's look at the code next. I describe each nested class along the way.

The sample starts with the `RemoveStocks` class that contains the nested classes. That helps organize the feature and saves us some headaches about naming collision. We could use namespaces instead, but tools like Visual Studio will always recommend adding a `using` statement and removing the inline namespace, which I find annoying. Here is the `RemoveStocks` class breakdown:

```
namespace VerticalApp.Features.Stocks;

public class RemoveStocks
{
    public class Command : IRequest<Result>
    {
        public int ProductId { get; set; }
        public int Amount { get; set; }
    }
}
```

The `Command` class is the **input of the use case**: the request. The request contains everything needed to execute the operation; remove stocks from the inventory. The `IRequest<TResult>` interface tells MediatR that the `Command` class is a request and should be routed to its handler. The `Result` class (which follows here) is the return value of that handler:

```
public class Result
{
    public int QuantityInStock { get; set; }
}
```

The `Result` class represents the **output of the use case**. That's what the handler will return:

```
public class MapperProfile : Profile
{
    public MapperProfile()
    {
        CreateMap<Product, Result>();
    }
}
```

The mapper profile is optional and allows encapsulating AutoMapper *maps* that are related to the use case. The preceding `MapperProfile` class registers the mapping from a `Product` instance to a `Result` instance:

```
public class Validator : AbstractValidator<Command>
{
    public Validator()
    {
        RuleFor(x => x.Amount).GreaterThan(0);
    }
}
```

The validator is also optional and allows validating the input (Command) before it hits the handler.

> **Note**
>
> To make validation work, we need to implement an IPipelineBehavior<TRequest, TResponse> interface and add it to the MediatR pipeline. We cover that after we are done exploring the RemoveStock feature.

Next is the Handler class, which implements the use case logic:

```csharp
    public class Handler : IRequestHandler<Command, Result>
    {
        private readonly ProductContext _db;
        private readonly IMapper _mapper;

        public Handler(ProductContext db, IMapper mapper)
        {
            _db = db ?? throw new ArgumentNullException(nameof(db));
            _mapper = mapper ?? throw new ArgumentNullException(nameof(mapper));
        }

        public async Task<Result> Handle(Command request, CancellationToken
cancellationToken)
        {
            var product = await _db.Products.FindAsync(new object[] { request.
ProductId }, cancellationToken);
            if (product == null)
            {
                throw new ProductNotFoundException(request.ProductId);
            }
            if (request.Amount > product.QuantityInStock)
            {
                throw new NotEnoughStockException(product.QuantityInStock,
request.Amount);
            }

            product.QuantityInStock -= request.Amount;
            await _db.SaveChangesAsync(cancellationToken);

            return _mapper.Map<Result>(product);
        }
    }
} // RemoveStocks class
```

The `Handler` class implements the `IRequestHandler<Command, Result>` interface, which links it to the `Command` and `Result` classes. It implements the same logic as the previous implementations, from *Chapter 12*, *Understanding Layering*, onward.

To summarize, the `RemoveStocks` class contains all the required sub-classes for that specific use case. As a reminder, now that we read the code, the pieces of each use case are the following:

- `Command` is the input DTO.
- `Result` is the output DTO.
- `MapperProfile` is the AutoMapper profile that maps feature-specific classes to non-feature-specific classes and vice versa.
- `Validator` validates the input before an instance hits the `Handler` class (the `Command` class).
- `Handler` encapsulates the use case logic.

Let's now look at the `StocksController` class, which translates the HTTP requests to the MediatR pipeline:

```
namespace VerticalApp.Features.Stocks;

[ApiController]
[Route("products/{productId}/")]
public class StocksController : ControllerBase
{
    private readonly IMediator _mediator;
    public StocksController(IMediator mediator)
    {
        _mediator = mediator ?? throw new
ArgumentNullException(nameof(mediator));
    }
    // Omitted action methods
}
```

We inject an `IMediator` implementation in the controller since we are using it in all of the actions that follow. Next, we look at the add stocks action method, part of `StocksController`:

```
[HttpPost("add-stocks")]
public async Task<ActionResult<AddStocks.Result>> AddAsync(
    int productId,
    [FromBody] AddStocks.Command command
)
{
    try
    {
        command.ProductId = productId;
```

```
            var result = await _mediator.Send(command);
            return Ok(result);
        }
        catch (ProductNotFoundException ex)
        {
            return NotFound(new
            {
                ex.Message,
                productId,
            });
        }
    }
}
```

In the preceding code, we read the content of an `AddStocks.Command` instance from the body, and then we set `ProductId` to finally send the `command` object into the MediatR pipeline, for the reasons discussed in the note near the end of *Chapter 14, Mediator and CQRS Design Patterns*. From there, MediatR routes the request to the handler we explored previously before returning the result of that operation with an HTTP `200` `OK` status code. Next, we look at the `RemoveStocks` action method, part of `StocksController`:

```
[HttpPost("remove-stocks")]
public async Task<ActionResult<RemoveStocks.Result>> RemoveAsync(
    int productId,
    [FromBody] RemoveStocks.Command command
)
{
    try
    {
        command.ProductId = productId;
        var result = await _mediator.Send(command);
        return Ok(result);
    }
    catch (NotEnoughStockException ex)
    {
        return Conflict(new
        {
            ex.Message,
            ex.AmountToRemove,
            ex.QuantityInStock
        });
    }
    catch (ProductNotFoundException ex)
```

```
    {
        return NotFound(new
        {
            ex.Message,
            productId,
        });
    }
}
```

The `remove-stocks` action has the same logic as the `add-stocks` one, with the added `catch` block like the previous implementations of this code.

> **Note**
>
> I did not map exceptions to typed DTOs for the only reason that it would be more optimal to handle those in an exception filter instead of in each action. The filter would allow centralizing exception handling and return a standardized error object. As an example, we implement a `FluentValidationExceptionFilter` that translates `ValidationException` to `BadRequestObjectResult` in this chapter.

One of the differences between the preceding code and previous implementations is that we moved the DTOs to the vertical slice itself. Each vertical slice defines the input, the logic, and the output of that feature, as follows:

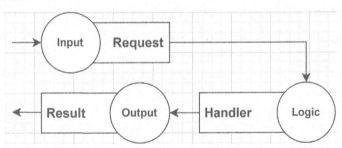

Figure 15.5: Diagram representing the three primary pieces of a vertical slice

When we add input validation, we have the following:

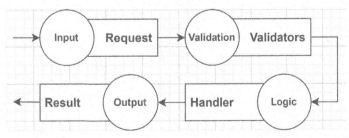

Figure 15.6: Diagram representing the three primary pieces of a vertical slice, with added validation

All in all, the code of the controller is thin, creating a tiny layer between HTTP and our domain, mapping the HTTP requests to the MediatR pipeline and the responses back to HTTP. That thin piece represents the presentation of the API and allows access to the domain logic, the feature. When controllers grow, it is often a sign that part of the feature logic is in the wrong place, most likely leading to code that is harder to test because the HTTP and other logic become intertwined.

In the code, we still have the extra line for the productId and that try/catch block, but we could get rid of these using custom model binders and exception filters; see the end of the chapter for some additional resources.

It is now straightforward to add new features to the project with that in place. Visually, we end up with the following vertical slices (bold), possible vertical expansions (normal), and shared classes (italics):

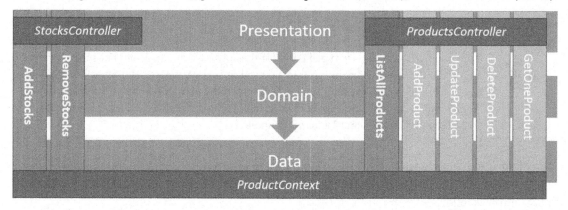

Figure 15.7: Diagram representing the project and possible extensions related to product management

The diagram shows the grouping of the two main areas, products and stocks. On the products side, when including the expansions, we have a CRUD-like feature bundle. In our tiny application, it is very hard to divide the data access part into more than one DbContext, so ProductContext is used by all slices to create a shared data access layer. In other cases, you should create multiple smaller DbContext instead of a big one that deserves the whole application (this has nothing to do with Vertical Slice Architecture but is just a best practice overall). Think about grouping features together, as long as they are cohesive and fit together, under the same domain area.

Next, we add the missing parts to use those IValidator implementations.

Request validation

We now have most of the code to run our little project. However, we still have no validation in our MediatR pipeline, only validators.

Fortunately, MediatR has an `IPipelineBehavior<in TRequest, TResponse>` interface we can use to extend the request pipeline. It works like an MVC filter. Speaking of which, we also need an MVC filter to control the HTTP response when a validation error occurs. That will allow us to encapsulate validation logic in two small classes. Those two classes will intercept and handle all validation exceptions thrown by any feature.

Let's start with a high-level view:

- The HTTP request passes through the ASP.NET Core MVC pipeline up to the controller.
- The controller sends a command that passes through the MediatR pipeline:

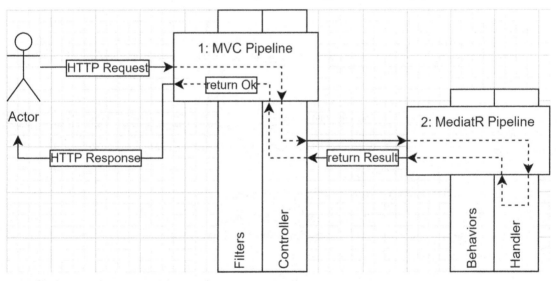

Figure 15.8: High-level flow of a successful HTTP request

What we want to do is the following:

1. Add an `IExceptionFilter` that catches `ValidationException` (from FluentValidation) in the MVC pipeline (in the **Filters** section of the diagram).

2. Add a MediatR `IPipelineBehavior` that validates requests and throws a `ValidationException` when the request validation fails (in the **Behaviors** section of the diagram).

After adding those two pieces, our request flow will become something like this:

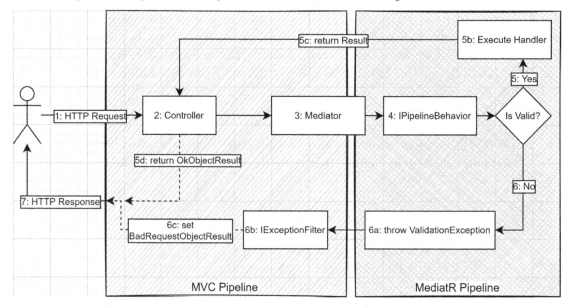

Figure 15.9: Request flow including request validation details

1. The user sends an HTTP request.
2. The controller sends a command through the mediator.
3. The mediator runs the request through its pipeline.
4. The `IPipelineBehavior` implementation validates the request.
5. If the request is valid, the following occurs:

    a. The request continues through the MediatR pipeline until it reaches the handler.
    b. The `Handler` is executed.
    c. The `Handler` returns a `Result` instance.
    d. The controller transfers that `Result` object into an `OkObjectResult` object.

6. If the validation of the request fails, the following occurs:

    a. The `IPipelineBehavior` implementation throws a `ValidationException`.
    b. The `IExceptionFilter` implementation catches and handles the exception.
    c. The filter sets the action result to a `BadRequestObjectResult`.

7. MVC transforms the resulting `IActionResult` into a `200 OK` (success) or a `400 BadRequest` (validation failure) response and serializes the resulting object into the response body.

Now that we understand the changes' theoretical aspects, let's start by coding the `IPipelineBehavior` implementation.

I named it `ThrowFluentValidationExceptionBehavior` because it throws a `ValidationException` (from FluentValidation) and is a MediatR behavior.

We start by implementing the `IPipelineBehavior<TRequest, TResponse>` interface. Our class forwards both generic parameters to the `IPipelineBehavior` interface to serve all types of requests, as long as the request implements `IRequest<TResponse>`. Then the magic happens by injecting a list of `IValidator<TRequest>` instances, which gives access to the validators of the current request to the pipeline behavior. This works for any type of `TRequest` object. I'll let you look at the code and then explain the `Handle` method:

```
namespace VerticalApp;

public class ThrowFluentValidationExceptionBehavior<TRequest, TResponse> :
IPipelineBehavior<TRequest, TResponse>
    where TRequest : IRequest<TResponse>
{
    private readonly IEnumerable<IValidator<TRequest>> _validators;
    public
ThrowFluentValidationExceptionBehavior(IEnumerable<IValidator<TRequest>>
validators)
    {
        _validators = validators ?? throw new
ArgumentNullException(nameof(validators));
    }

    public Task<TResponse> Handle(TRequest request, CancellationToken
cancellationToken, RequestHandlerDelegate<TResponse> next)
    {
        var failures = _validators
            .Select(v => v.Validate(request))
            .SelectMany(r => r.Errors);
        if (failures.Any())
        {
            throw new ValidationException(failures);
        }
        return next();
    }
}
```

Finally, in the `Handle` method, we run all validators (see the highlighted code) and project the errors into the `failures` variable. If there are any failures, it throws a `ValidationException` that contains all the failures. If the validation succeeds, it invokes the next element of the pipeline and returns its result. This concept is similar to the **Chain of Responsibility** pattern, which we explored in *Chapter 10, Behavioral Patterns*.

Next, we must register it in the composition root to make it work. Since we don't want to register it for every feature in our project, we are going to register it as an **unbound generic** like this (in the Program.cs file):

```
.AddSingleton(
    typeof(IPipelineBehavior<,>),
    typeof(ThrowFluentValidationExceptionBehavior<,>)
);
```

This code means: "add an instance of ThrowFluentValidationExceptionBehavior in the pipeline for all types of requests." That way, our behavior runs every time, no matter the type of request.

If we run the code, we get the following error, which is not elegant:

```
1   FluentValidation.ValidationException: Validation Failed:
2   -- Amount: 'Amount' must be greater than '0'.
3     at verticalApp.ThrowFluentValidationExceptionBehavior`2.
      Core\C14\Vertical Slice Architecture\src\VerticalApp\
4     at MediatR.Internal.RequestHandlerWrapperImp`2.<>c__
5     at MediatR.Pipeline.RequestExceptionProcessorBehavior`2.
6     at MediatR.Pipeline.RequestExceptionProcessorBehavior`2.
7     at MediatR.Pipeline.RequestExceptionActionProcessor
```

Figure 15.10: The result of ThrowFluentValidationExceptionBehavior without the MVC filter

To manage how our application outputs those exceptions, we can add an IExceptionFilter to the MVC pipeline. I decided to call it FluentValidationExceptionFilter because it is an exception filter that handles exceptions of type FluentValidation.ValidationException. That class looks like the following:

```
namespace VerticalApp;
public class FluentValidationExceptionFilter : IExceptionFilter
{
    public void OnException(ExceptionContext context)
    {
        if (context.Exception is ValidationException ex)
        {
            context.Result = new BadRequestObjectResult(new
            {
                ex.Message,
                ex.Errors,
            });
            context.ExceptionHandled = true;
        }
    }
}
```

The preceding code validates whether the value of the Exception property (the current exception) is a ValidationException. If it is, it sets the Result property's value to an instance of BadRequestObjectResult. It creates an anonymous object with two properties directly taken from the ValidationException object: Message and Errors. The Message property is the error message, while the Errors property references a collection of ValidationFailure objects.

Afterward, it sets the ExceptionHandled property to true, so MVC knows the exception was handled and stops caring about it like it never happened. Those few lines of code are the equivalent of returning a BadRequest(new {...}) instance from a controller action but applied globally for all controller actions.

One last step: we must register it with the MVC pipeline, so the code gets executed. In the Program.cs file, we can add the filter as part of the .AddControllers() method call, like the following (highlighted):

```
.AddControllers(options => options
    .Filters.Add<FluentValidationExceptionFilter>())
```

That adds a filter to the MVC pipeline, in this case, the FluentValidationExceptionFilter class we just created. From now on, whenever an unhandled exception occurs, the filter is executed.

Now, if we run a request that should not pass validation (such as *add 0 new stock*), we get the following result:

```
                                        400 Bad Request    178 ms    608 B    Save Response ▼

Pretty     Raw      Preview     Visualize     JSON ▼    ⥲                                    ☐ Q

 1   {
 2       "message": "Validation failed: \r\n -- Amount: 'Amount' must be greater than '0'.",
 3       "errors": [
 4           {
 5               "propertyName": "Amount",
 6               "errorMessage": "'Amount' must be greater than '0'.",
 7               "attemptedValue": 0,
 8               "customState": null,
 9               "severity": 0,
10               "errorCode": "GreaterThanValidator",
11               "formattedMessageArguments": [],
12               "formattedMessagePlaceholderValues": {
13                   "ComparisonValue": 0,
14                   "ComparisonProperty": "",
15                   "PropertyName": "Amount",
16                   "PropertyValue": 0
17               },
18               "resourceName": "GreaterThanValidator"
19           }
20       ]
21   }
```

Figure 15.11: The result of ThrowFluentValidationExceptionBehavior handled by FluentValidationExceptionFilter

That is more elegant and can be handled by clients more efficiently. You can also customize the exception you throw in your implementation of the `IPipelineBehavior` interface and the object you serialize in your implementation of `IExceptionFilter`. Since it is MVC, you can also leverage a custom implementation of the `IExceptionFilter` interface in non-MediatR-based projects. There are other types of filters too. Filters are really good at handling crosscutting concerns in MVC.

If you are not using MVC, you can achieve a similar result by creating middleware instead. Middlewares are run before MVC filters and could be applied to minimal APIs.

Next, we explore a bit of testing. I won't test the whole application, but I'll get into a few advantages of testing Vertical Slice Architecture versus other architecture types.

Testing

For this project, I wrote one integration test per use case outcome, which lowers the number of unit tests required while increasing the level of confidence in the system at the same time. Why? Because we are testing the features themselves instead of many abstracted parts independently. We could also add as many unit tests as we want. I'm not telling you to stop writing unit tests; on the contrary, I think this approach helps you to write fewer but better feature-oriented tests, diminishing the need for mock-heavy unit tests.

Let's look at the `StocksTest` class first:

```
namespace VerticalApp.Features.Stocks;
public class StocksTest
{
    private static async Task SeederDelegate(ProductContext db)
    {
        db.Products.RemoveRange(db.Products.ToArray());
        await db.Products.AddAsync(new Product(
            id: 4,
            name: "Ghost Pepper",
            quantityInStock: 10
        ));
        await db.Products.AddAsync(new Product(
            id: 5,
            name: "Carolina Reaper",
            quantityInStock: 10
        ));
        await db.SaveChangesAsync();
    }
    public class AddStocksTest : StocksTest
    {
        // omitted test methods
    }
```

```
        public class RemoveStocksTest : StocksTest
        {
            // omitted test methods
        }
        public class StocksControllerTest : StocksTest
        {
            // omitted test methods
        }
    }
```

The SeedAsync method removes all products and inserts two new ones in the in-memory test database so the test methods can run using a predictable set of data. The AddStocksTest and RemoveStocksTest classes contain the test methods for their respective use case. StocksControllerTest tests the MVC part. Let's explore the happy path of the AddStocksTest class:

```
[Fact]
public async Task Should_increment_QuantityInStock_by_the_specified_amount()
{
    // Arrange
    await using var application = new VerticalAppApplication();
    await application.SeedAsync(SeederDelegate);
    using var requestScope = application.Services.CreateScope();
    var mediator = requestScope.ServiceProvider.
GetRequiredService<IMediator>();

    // Act
    var result = await mediator.Send(new AddStocks.Command
    {
        ProductId = 4,
        Amount = 10
    });

    // Assert
    using var assertScope = application.Services.CreateScope();
    var db = assertScope.ServiceProvider.GetRequiredService<ProductContext>();
    var peppers = await db.Products.FindAsync(4);
    Assert.NotNull(peppers);
    Assert.Equal(20, peppers!.QuantityInStock);
}
```

In the *Arrange* section of the preceding test case, we create an instance of the application, create a scope to simulate an HTTP request, access the EF Core DbContext, and then get an IMediator instance to act on.

In the *Act* block, we send a valid `AddStocks.Command` through the MediatR pipeline.

We create a new scope in the *Assert* block then and get a `ProductContext` out of the container. With that `DbContext`, we find the product, make sure it's not null, and validate the quantity in stock is what we are expecting. Using a new `ProductContext` ensures we are not dealing with any cached items from the previous one, and the transaction has been saved as expected.

With that test case, we know that if a valid command is issued to the mediator, that handler gets executed and successfully does what it should: increment the stock property by the specified amount.

> **Note**
>
> The `VerticalAppApplication` class inherits from `WebApplicationFactory<TEntryP oint>`, creates a new `DbContextOptionsBuilder<ProductContext>` instance that has a configurable database name, implements a `SeedAsync` method that allows seeding the database, and allows altering the application services. I omitted the code for brevity reasons, but you can consult the complete source code in the GitHub repository (`https://adpg.link/QzwS`).

Then we can test the MVC part to make sure the controller is configured correctly. In the `StocksControllerTest` class, the `AddAsync` class contains the following test method:

```
public class AddAsync : StocksControllerTest
{
    [Fact]
    public async Task Should_send_a_valid_AddStocks_Command_to_the_mediator()
    {
        // Arrange
        var mediatorMock = new Mock<IMediator>();
        AddStocks.Command? addStocksCommand = default;
        mediatorMock
            .Setup(x => x.Send(It.IsAny<AddStocks.Command>(),
It.IsAny<CancellationToken>()))
            .Callback((IRequest<AddStocks.Result> request, CancellationToken
cancellationToken) => addStocksCommand = request as AddStocks.Command)
            ;
        await using var application = new VerticalAppApplication(
            afterConfigureServices: services => services
                .AddSingleton(mediatorMock.Object)
        );
        var client = application.CreateClient();
        var httpContent = JsonContent.Create(
            new { amount = 1 },
            options: new JsonSerializerOptions(JsonSerializerDefaults.Web)
        );
```

```
        // Act
        var response = await client.PostAsync("/products/5/add-stocks",
httpContent);

        // Assert
        Assert.NotNull(response);
        Assert.NotNull(addStocksCommand);
        response.EnsureSuccessStatusCode();
        mediatorMock.Verify(
            x => x.Send(It.IsAny<AddStocks.Command>(),
It.IsAny<CancellationToken>()),
            Times.Once()
        );
        Assert.Equal(5, addStocksCommand!.ProductId);
        Assert.Equal(1, addStocksCommand!.Amount);
    }
}
```

The highlighted code of the preceding test case *Arrange* section is new. That code mocks the `IMediator` and saves what is passed to the `Send` method in the `addStocksCommand` variable. We are using that value in the *Assert* section. When creating the `VerticalAppApplication` instance, we register that mock with the container to use it instead of the MediatR one. We then create an `HttpClient` that is connected to our in-process application.

Finally, we craft a valid HTTP request to add stocks that we post in the *Act* section.

The code of the *Assert* block makes sure the request was successful, verifies the mock method was hit once, and makes sure `AddStocks.Command` was configured correctly.

From the first test, we know the MediatR piece works. With this second test in place, we know the HTTP piece works. We are now almost certain that a valid add stocks request will hit the database with those two tests.

Note

I say "almost certain" because our first test runs using an in-memory database, which is different from a real database engine (for example, it has no relational integrity and the like). In case of more complex database operations that affect more than one table, or just to ensure the correctness of the feature, you can run the tests against a real database.

In the test project, I added more tests that cover exceptions, remove stocks, and list all products' features, and AutoMapper configuration correctness. Feel free to browse the code. I omitted them here as they become redundant. The objective here was to explore testing a feature almost end to end with very few tests (two for the happy path, to be precise in this case), and I think we covered that.

The vertical slice version of the project shows how we were able to remove abstractions while keeping the objects loosely coupled. We also organized the project into features (verticals) instead of layers (horizontals). We leveraged CQRS, Mediator, and MVC patterns. Conceptually, the layers are still there; for example, the controllers are part of the presentation layer, but they are not organized that way, making them part of the feature. The sole dependency that crosses all our features is the ProductContext class, making sense since our model is composed of a single class (Product). We could, for example, add a new feature that leverages minimal APIs instead of a controller, which would be okay because each slice is independent.

We can significantly reduce the number of mocks required by testing each vertical slice with integration tests. That could also lower the number of unit tests significantly, testing features instead of mocked units of code. Our focus should be on producing features, not on the details behind querying the infrastructure or the code itself (OK, that's important too).

Note

It is important to note that you can still write as many unit tests as you need; nothing from Vertical Slice Architecture stops you from doing that. That's one of the advantages: you can leverage all you know in the slice you are working on without the need to export it globally to other slices.

Next, we look at a few tricks and processes to get started with a bigger application. These are ways that I found work for me and will hopefully work for you too. Take what works for you and leave the rest; we are all different and work differently.

Continuing your journey

The previous project was tiny. It had a shared model that served as the data layer because it was composed of a single class. When building bigger applications, you have more than one class, so I'll try to give you a good starting point to tackle bigger apps. The idea is to create slices as small as possible, limit interactions with other slices as much as possible, and refactor that code into better code. We cannot remove coupling, so we need to organize it instead.

Depending on your workplace, chances are you only have one role to play, and others cover the rest. If that is not the case (for any reason), here is a workflow that we could call "start small and refactor" to help you out (this approach might work given either of the two previous cases):

1. Write the contracts that cover your feature (input and output).
2. Write one or more integration tests covering your feature, using those contracts; the Query or Command class (IRequest) as input and the Result class as output.
3. Implement your Handler, Validator, MapperProfile, and any other bit that needs to be coded. At this point, the code could be a giant Handler; it does not matter.
4. Once your integration tests pass, refactor that code by breaking down your giant Handler. Handle method as needed.
5. Make sure your tests still pass.

During *step 2*, you may also test the validation rules with unit tests. It is way easier and faster to test multiple combinations and scenarios from unit tests, and you don't need to access a database for that. The same also applies to any other parts of your system that are not tied to an external resource.

During *step 4*, you may find duplicated logic between features. If that's the case, it is time to encapsulate that logic elsewhere, in a shared place. That could be to create a method in the model, create a service class, or any other pattern and technique that you know might solve your logic duplication problem. Working from isolated features and extracting shared logic will help you design the application. You want to push that shared logic outside of a handler, not the other way around (well, once you have that shared logic, you can use it wherever needed). Here, I want to emphasize *shared logic*, which means a business rule. When a business rule changes, all consumers of that business rule must also change their behavior. Avoid sharing *similar code* but do share business rules.

What is very important when designing software is to focus on the functional needs, not the technical ones. Your clients and users don't care about the technical stuff; they want results, new features, bug fixes, and improvements. Simultaneously, beware of the technical debt and don't skip that refactoring step, or your project may end up in trouble. That advice also applies to all types of architecture.

Another piece of advice is to keep all the code that makes a vertical slice as close as possible. You don't have to keep all use case classes in a single file, but I feel that often helps. Partial classes are a way to split classes into multiple files.

You can also create a folder hierarchy where the deeper levels share the previous levels. For example, I recently implemented a workflow in an MVC application related to shipments. The creation process was in multiple steps. So I ended up with a hierarchy that looked like the following (the directories are in bold):

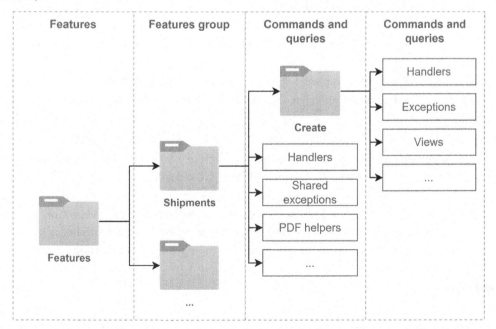

Figure 15.12: The organizational hierarchy of directories and elements

Initially, I coded all the handlers one by one, then I saw patterns emerge, so I took that shared logic and encapsulated it into shared classes. Then I reused some upper-level exceptions, so I moved those up from the `Features/Shipments/Create` folder (and namespace) to the `Features/Shipments` folder (and namespace). I also extracted a service class to manage shared logic between multiple use cases and more (I'll skip all the details as they are irrelevant). In the end, I have only the code that I need, no duplicated logic, and the collaborators (classes, interfaces) are close to each other. I registered only three interfaces with the IoC container for that workflow, and two of them are related to PDF generation. The coupling between features is minimal, while parts of the system work in synergy (cohesion). Moreover, there is very little to no coupling with other parts of the system. If we compare that result to another type of architecture such as layering, I would most likely have needed more abstractions such as repositories, services, and whatnot; the result with Vertical Slice Architecture was simpler.

The key point here is to code your handlers independently, organize them the best you can, keep an eye open for shared logic and emerging patterns, extract and encapsulate that logic, and try to limit interactions between use cases and slices.

Conclusion

Overall, we explored a modern way to design an application that aligns well with Agile, which helps generate value for your customers.

Before moving to the summary, let's see how Vertical Slice Architecture can help us follow the **SOLID** principles:

- **S:** Each vertical slice (feature) becomes a cohesive unit that changes as a whole, leading to the segregation of responsibilities per feature. Based on a CQRS-inspired approach, each feature splits the application's complexity into commands and queries, leading to multiple small pieces. Each piece handles a part of the process. For example, we can define an input, a validator, a mapper profile, a handler, a result, an HTTP bridge (controller), and as many more pieces as we need to craft the slice.
- **O:** We can enhance the system globally by extending the ASP.NET Core, MVC, or MediatR pipelines. The features themselves can be designed as one sees fit, having a limited direct impact on the OCP.
- **L:** N/A
- **I:** By organizing features by units of domain-centric use cases, we create many client-specific components instead of general-purpose elements, like layers.
- **D:** The slice pieces depend on interfaces and are tied together using dependency injection. Furthermore, by cutting the less useful abstractions out of the system, we simplify it, making it more maintainable and concise. By having so many pieces of a feature living close to each other, the system becomes easier to maintain with improved discoverability.

Summary

This chapter overviewed Vertical Slice Architecture, which flips layers by 90°. Vertical Slice Architecture is about writing minimal code to generate maximum value by getting superfluous abstractions and rules out of the equation by relying on the developers' skills and judgment instead.

Refactoring is a critical factor in a Vertical Slice Architecture project; success or failure will most likely depend on it. We can use all patterns with Vertical Slice Architecture. It has lots of advantages over layering with only a few disadvantages. Teams who work in silos (horizontal teams) may need to rethink switching to Vertical Slice Architecture and first create or aim at creating multi-functional teams instead (vertical teams).

We replaced the low-value abstraction with commands and queries (CQRS-inspired). Those are then routed to their respective `Handler` using the Mediator pattern (helped by MediatR). That allows encapsulating the business logic and decoupling it from its callers (the controllers in the sample). Those commands and queries ensure that each bit of domain logic is centralized in a single location.

Depending on where we want that concern handled, we can encapsulate crosscutting concerns using a classic MVC filter, an ASP.NET middleware, or a MediatR `IPipelineBehavior`. We can also implement a composite solution using many options, as we did with the validation.

Of course, if you start with a strong analysis of your problem, you will most likely have a head start, like with any project. Nothing stops you from building a strong domain model and then using it in your slices. The more requirements you have, the easier the initial project organization will be. To reiterate, engineering practices that you know still apply.

The next chapter explores another architectural style and talks about microservices.

Questions

Let's take a look at a few practice questions:

1. What design patterns can we use in a vertical slice?
2. Is it true that when using Vertical Slice Architecture, you must pick a single ORM and stick with it, such as a data layer?
3. What will likely happen if you don't refactor your code and pay the technical debt in the long run?
4. Can we handle crosscutting concerns using behaviors and MVC filters in other types of applications or are they enabled by Vertical Slice Architecture?
5. What does cohesion mean?
6. What does tight coupling mean?

Further reading

Here are a few links to build upon what we learned in the chapter:

- For UI implementations, you can look at how Jimmy Bogard upgraded ContosoUniversity:

    a. ContosoUniversity on ASP.NET Core with .NET Core: `https://adpg.link/UXnr`

    b. ContosoUniversity on ASP.NET Core with .NET Core and Razor Pages: `https://adpg.link/6Lbo`

- FluentValidation: `https://adpg.link/xXgp`

- ExceptionMapper is an open source project of mine, which is an ASP.NET Core middleware that reacts to exceptions. You can map certain exception types to HTTP status codes, automatically serialize them as JSON `ProblemDetails`, and so on: `https://adpg.link/i8jb`

- AutoMapper: `https://adpg.link/5AUZ`

- MediatR: `https://adpg.link/ZQap`

- To avoid setting `ProductId` manually in the Vertical Slice project, you can use the open source HybridModelBinding project or read the official documentation about custom model binding and implement your own:

    a. Custom Model Binding in ASP.NET Core: `https://adpg.link/65pb`

    b. HybridModelBinding: `https://adpg.link/EyKK`

Join our book's Discord space

Join the book's Discord workspace for *Ask me Anything* session with the authors:

`https://packt.link/ASPdotNET6DesignPatterns`

16

Introduction to Microservices Architecture

This chapter is the last chapter that talks about application design before we move on to a few user interface chapters. The chapter covers some essential microservices architecture concepts. It is designed to get you started with those principles and give you a good idea of the microservices architecture.

This chapter aims to give you an overview of the concepts surrounding microservices, which should help you make informed decisions about whether you should go for a microservices architecture or not.

Since microservices architecture is larger in scale than the previous application-scale pattern we visited and usually involves advanced components, there is no C# code in the chapter. Instead, I explain the concepts and list open source or commercial offerings that you can leverage to apply these patterns to your applications. Moreover, you should not aim to implement many of the pieces discussed in the chapter because it can be a lot of work to get them right, and they don't add business value, so you are better off just using an existing implementation instead and extending it if needed. There is more context about this throughout the chapter.

That said, monolithic architecture patterns, such as Vertical Slice and Clean Architecture, are still good to know, as you can apply those to individual microservices. Don't worry—all of the knowledge you have acquired since the beginning of this book is not forfeit and is still worthwhile.

The following topics are covered in this chapter:

- What are microservices?
- An introduction to event-driven architecture
- Getting started with message queues
- Implementing the Publish-Subscribe pattern
- Introducing Gateway patterns
- Revisiting the CQRS pattern
- The Microservices Adapter pattern

Let's get started!

What are microservices?

Besides being a buzzword, microservices represent an application that is divided into multiple smaller applications. Each application, or microservice, interacts with the others to create a scalable system. Usually, microservices are deployed to the cloud as containerized or serverless applications.

Before getting into too many details, here are a few principles to keep in mind when building microservices:

- Each microservice should be a cohesive unit of business.
- Each microservice should own its data.
- Each microservice should be independent of the others.

Furthermore, everything we have studied so far—that is, the other principles of designing software— applies to microservices but on another scale. For example, you don't want tight coupling between microservices (solved by microservices independence), but the coupling is inevitable (as with any code). There are numerous ways to solve this problem, such as the Publish-Subscribe pattern.

There are no hard rules about how to design microservices, how to divide them, how big they should be, and what to put where. That being said, I'll lay down a few foundations to help you get started and orient your journey into microservices.

Cohesive unit of business

A microservice should have a single business responsibility. Always design the system with the domain in mind, which should help you divide the application into multiple pieces. If you know **Domain-Driven Design (DDD)**, a microservice will most likely represent a **Bounded Context**, which in turn is what I call a *cohesive unit of business*. Basically, a cohesive unit of business (or bounded context) is a self-contained part of the domain that has limited interactions with other parts of the domain.

Even if a **microservice** has *micro* in its name, it is more important to group logical operations under it than to aim at a micro-size. Don't get me wrong here; if your unit is tiny, that's even better. However, suppose you split a unit of business into multiple smaller parts instead of keeping it together (breaking cohesion).

In that case, you are likely to introduce useless chattiness within your system (coupling between microservices). This could lead to performance degradation and to a system that is harder to debug, test, maintain, monitor, and deploy.

Moreover, it is easier to split a big microservice into smaller pieces than assemble multiple microservices back together.

Try to apply the SRP to your microservices: a microservice should have only one reason to change unless you have a good reason to do otherwise.

Ownership of data

Each microservice is the source of truth of its cohesive unit of business. A microservice should share its data through an API (a web API/HTTP, for example) or another mechanism (integration events, for example). It should own that data and not share it with other microservices directly at the database level.

For instance, two different microservices should never access the same relational database table. If a second microservice needs some of the same data, it can create its own cache, duplicate the data, or query the owner of that data but not access the database directly; **never**.

This data-ownership concept is probably the most critical part of the microservices architecture and leads to microservices independence. Failing at this will most likely lead to a tremendous number of problems. For example, if multiple microservices can read or write data in the same database table, each time something changes in that table, all of them must be updated to reflect the changes. If different teams manage the microservices, that means cross-team coordination. If that happens, each microservice is not independent anymore, which opens the floor to our next topic.

Microservice independence

At this point, we have microservices that are cohesive units of business and own their data. That defines **independence**.

This independence offers the systems the ability to scale while having minimal to no impact on the other microservices. Each microservice can also scale independently, without the need for the whole system to be scaled. Additionally, when the business requirements grow, each part of that domain can evolve independently.

Furthermore, you could update one microservice without impacting the others or even have a microservice go offline without the whole system stopping.

Of course, microservices have to interact with one another, but the way they do should define how well your system runs. A little like Vertical Slice architecture, you are not limited to using one set of architectural patterns; you can independently make specific decisions for each microservice. For example, you could choose a different way for how two microservices communicate with each other versus two others. You could even use different programming languages for each microservice.

Tip

I recommend sticking to one or a few programming languages for smaller businesses and organizations as you most likely have fewer developers, and each has more to do. Based on my experience, you want to ensure business continuity when people leave and make sure you can replace them and not sink the ship due to some obscure technologies used here and there (or too many technologies).

Now that we've defined the basics, let's jump into the different ways microservices can communicate using event-driven architecture. We first explore ways to mediate communication between microservices using message queues and the Publish-Subscribe pattern. We then learn ways to shield and hide the complexity of the microservices cluster using Gateway patterns. After that, we dig into more detail about the CQRS pattern and provide a conceptual serverless example.

An introduction to event-driven architecture

Event-driven architecture (**EDA**) is a paradigm that revolves around consuming streams of events, or data in motion, instead of consuming static states.

What I define by a static state is the data stored in a relational database table or other types of data stores, like a NoSQL documents store. That data is dormant in a central location and waiting for actors to consume and mutate it. It is stale between every mutation and the data (a record, for example) represents a finite state.

On the other hand, data in motion is the opposite: you consume the ordered events and determine the change in state that each event brings.

What is an event? People often interchange the words event, message, and command. Let's try to clarify this:

- A message is a piece of data that represents something.
- A message can be an object, a JSON string, bytes, or anything else your system can interpret.
- An event is a message that represents something that happened in the past.
- A command is a message sent to tell one or more recipients to do something.
- A command is sent (past tense), so we can also consider it an event.

A message usually has a payload (or body), headers (metadata), and a way to identify it (this can be through the body or headers).

We can use events to divide a complex system into smaller pieces or have multiple systems talk to each other without creating tight couplings. Those systems could be subsystems or external applications, such as microservices.

Like **Data Transfer Objects** (**DTO**) of web APIs, events become the data contracts that tie the multiple systems together (coupling). It is essential to think about that carefully when designing events. Of course, we cannot foresee the future, so we can only do so much to get it perfect the first time. There are ways to version events, but this is out of the scope of this chapter.

EDA is a fantastic way of breaking tight coupling between microservices but requires rewiring your brain to learn this newer paradigm. Tooling is less mature, and expertise is scarcer than more linear ways of thinking (like using point-to-point communication and relational databases), but this is slowly changing and well worth learning (in my opinion).

Before moving further, we can categorize events into the following overlapping buckets:

- Domain events

- • Integration events
- • Application events
- • Enterprise events

As we explore next, all types of events play a similar role with different intents and scopes.

Domain events

A domain event is a term based on DDD representing an event in the domain. This event could then trigger other pieces of logic to be executed subsequently. It allows a complex process to be divided into multiple smaller processes. Domain events work well with domain-centric designs, like Clean Architecture, as we can use them to split complex domain objects into multiple smaller pieces. Domain events are usually application events. We can use MediatR to publish domain events inside an application.

To summarize, **domain events integrate pieces of domain logic together while keeping the domain logic segregated**, leading to loosely coupled components that hold one domain responsibility each (single responsibility principle).

Integration events

Integration events are like domain events but are used to propagate messages to external systems, to integrate multiple systems together while keeping them independent. For example, a microservice could send the new user registered event message that other microservices react to, like saving the user id to enable additional capabilities or sending a greeting email to that new user.

We use a message broker or message queue to publish such events. We cover those next, after covering application and enterprise events.

To summarize, **integration events integrate multiple systems together while keeping them independent**.

Application events

An application event is an event that is internal to an application; it is just a matter of scope. If the event is internal to a single process, that event is also a domain event (most likely). If the event crosses microservices boundaries that your team owns (the same application), it is also an integration event. The event itself won't be different; it is the reason why it exists and its scope that describes it as an application event or not.

To summarize, **application events are internal to an application**.

Enterprise events

An enterprise event describes an event that crosses internal enterprise boundaries. These are tightly coupled with your organizational structure. For example, a microservice sends an event that other teams, part of other divisions or departments, consume.

The governance model around those events should be different from application events that only your team consumes.

Someone must think about who can consume that data, under what circumstances, the impact of changing the event schema (data contract), schema ownership, naming conventions, data-structure conventions, and more, or risk building an unstable data highway.

Note

I like to see EDA as a central **data highway** in the middle of applications, systems, integrations, and organizational boundaries, where the events (data) flow between systems in a loosely coupled manner.

It's like a highway where cars flow between cities (without traffic jams). The cities are not controlling what car goes where but are open to visitors.

To summarize, **enterprise events are integration events that cross organizational boundaries**.

Conclusion

We defined events, messages, and commands in this quick overview of event-driven architecture. An event is a snapshot of the past, a message is data, and a command is an event that suggests other systems to take action. Since all messages are from the past, calling them events is accurate. We then organized events into a few overlapping buckets to help identify the intents. We can send events for different objectives, but whether it is about designing independent components or reaching out to different parts of the business, an event remains a payload that respects a certain format (schema). That schema is the data contract (coupling) between the consumers of those events. That data contract is probably the most important piece of it all; break the contract, break the system.

Now, let's see how event-driven architecture can help us follow the **SOLID** principles at cloud-scale:

- S: Systems are independent of each other by raising and responding to events. The events themselves are the glue that ties those systems together. Each piece has a single responsibility.
- O: We can modify the system's behaviors by adding new consumers to a particular event without impacting the other applications. We can also raise new events to start building a new process without affecting existing applications.
- L: N/A
- I: Instead of building a single process, EDA allows us to create multiple smaller systems that integrate through data contracts (events) where those contracts become the messaging interfaces of the system.
- D: EDA enables systems to break tight coupling by depending on the events (interfaces/abstractions) instead of communicating directly with one another, inverting the dependency flow.

EDA does not only come with advantages; it also has a few drawbacks that we explore in subsequent sections of the chapter.

Next, we explore message queues followed by the Publish-Subscribe pattern, two ways of interacting with events.

Getting started with message queues

A **message queue** is nothing more than a queue that we leverage to send ordered messages. A queue works on a **First In, First Out (FIFO)** basis. If our application runs in a single process, we could use one or more Queue<T> instances to send messages between our components or a ConcurrentQueue<T> instance to send messages between threads. Moreover, queues can be managed by an independent program to send messages in a distributed fashion (between applications or microservices).

A distributed message queue can add more or fewer features to the mix, which is especially true for cloud programs that have to handle failures at more levels than a single server does. One of those features is the **dead letter queue**, which stores messages that failed some criteria in another queue. For example, if the target queue is full, a message could be sent to the **dead letter queue** instead. One could requeue such messages by putting the message back at the end of the queue (beware, this changes the initial order in which messages were sent).

Many messaging queue protocols exist; some are proprietary, while others are open source. Some messaging queues are cloud-based and used *as a service*, such as Azure Service Bus and Amazon Simple Queue Service. Others are open source and can be deployed to the cloud or on-premises, such as Apache ActiveMQ.

If you need to process messages in order and want each message to be delivered to a single recipient at a time, a **message queue** seems like the right choice. Otherwise, the **Publish-Subscribe** pattern could be a better fit for you.

Here is a basic example that illustrates what we just discussed:

Figure 16.1: A publisher that enqueues a message with a subscriber that dequeues it

For a more concrete example, in a distributed user registration process, when a user registers, we could want to do the following:

- Send a confirmation email.
- Process their picture and save one or more thumbnails.
- Send an onboarding message to their in-app mailbox.

To sequentially achieve this, one operation after the other, we could do the following:

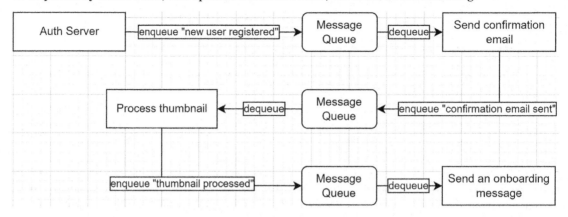

Figure 16.2: A process flow that sequentially executes three operations that happen after a user creates an account

In this case, if the process crashes during the *Process Thumbnail* operation, the user would not receive the *Onboarding Message*. Another drawback would be that to insert a new operation between the *Process Thumbnail* and *Send an onboarding message* steps, we'd have to modify the *Send an onboarding message* operation (tight coupling).

If the order does not matter, we could queue all the messages from the *Auth Server* instead, right after the user's creation, like this:

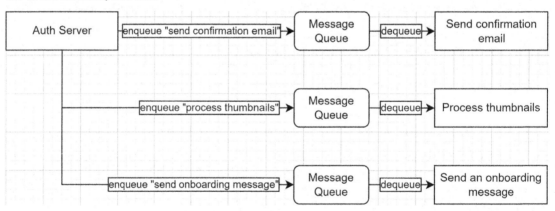

Figure 16.3: The Auth Server is queuing the operations sequentially while different processes execute them in parallel

This process is better, but the *Auth Server* is now controlling what should be happening once a new user has been created. The *Auth Server* was queuing an event in the previous workflow that told the system that a new user was registered. However, now, it has to be aware of the post-processing workflow to queue each operation sequentially. Doing this is not wrong in itself and is easier to follow when you dig into the code, but it creates tighter coupling between the services where the *Auth Server* is aware of the external processes.

According to the SRP, I don't see how an authentication/authorization server should be responsible for anything other than authentication, authorization, and managing that data.

If we continue from there and want to add a new operation between two existing steps, we would only have to modify the *Auth Server*, which is less error-prone than the preceding workflow.

If we want the best of both worlds, we could use the **Publish-Subscribe** pattern instead, which we cover next. We revisit this example there.

Conclusion

If you need messages to be delivered sequentially, a queue might well be the right tool to use. The example that we explored was "doomed to failure" from the beginning, but it allowed us to explore the thinking process behind designing the system. Sometimes, the first idea is not the best and can be improved by exploring new ways of doing things or learning new skills. Being open-minded to the ideas of others can also lead to better solutions.

Message queues are amazing at buffering messages for high-demand scenarios where an application may not be able to handle spikes of traffic. In that case, the messages are enqueued so the application can catch up at its own speed, reading them sequentially.

Implementing distributed message queues requires a lot of knowledge and effort and is not worth it for almost all scenarios. The big cloud providers like AWS and Azure offer fully managed message queue systems as a service. You can also look at **ActiveMQ**, **RabbitMQ**, or any **Advanced Message Queuing Protocol (AMQP)** broker.

One essential aspect of choosing the right queue system is whether you are ready and have the skills to manage your own distributed message queue. If you want to speed up development and have enough money on hand, you should use a fully managed offering for at least your production environment, especially if you are expecting a large volume of messages. On the other hand, using a local or on-premise instance for development or smaller scale usage may save you a considerable sum of money. Choosing an open source system with fully managed cloud offerings is a good way to achieve both: low local development cost with an always available high-performance cloud production offering that the service provider maintains for you.

Another aspect is to base your choice on needs. Have clear requirements and ensure the system you choose does what you need. Some offerings can also cover multiple use cases like queues and pub-sub (which we are exploring next), leading to learning or requiring fewer skills that enable more possibilities.

Before moving to the next pattern, let's see how message queues can help us follow the **SOLID** principles at the app scale:

- S: Helps centralize and divide responsibilities between applications or components without them directly knowing each other, breaking tight coupling.
- O: Allows us to change the message producer's or subscriber's behaviors without the other knowing about it.
- L: N/A

- I: Each message and handler can be as small as needed, while each microservice indirectly interacts with the others to solve the bigger problem.

- D: By not knowing the other dependencies (breaking tight coupling between microservices), each microservice depends only on the messages (abstractions) instead of concretions (the other microservices API).

One drawback is the delay between enqueuing a message and processing a message. We talk about delay and latency in more detail in subsequent sections.

Implementing the Publish-Subscribe pattern

The **Publish-Subscribe** pattern (Pub-Sub) is very similar to what we did using **MediatR** and what we explored in the *Getting started with message queues* section. However, instead of sending one message to one handler (or enqueuing a message), we publish (send) a message (event) to zero or more subscribers (handlers). Moreover, the publisher is unaware of the subscribers; it only sends messages out, hoping for the best (also known as **fire and forget**).

> **Note**
>
> Using a message queue does not mean you are limited to only one recipient.

We can use **Publish-Subscribe** in-process or in a distributed system through a **message broker**. The message broker is responsible for delivering the messages to the subscribers. That is the way to go for microservices and other distributed systems since they are not running in a single process.

This pattern has many advantages over other ways of communication. For example, we could recreate the state of a database by replaying the events that happened in the system, leading to the **event sourcing** pattern. More on that later.

The design depends on the technology that's used to deliver the messages and the configuration of that system. For example, you could use **MQTT** to deliver messages to **Internet of Things** (**IoT**) devices and configure them to retain the last message sent on each topic. That way, when a device connects to a topic, it receives the latest message. You could also configure a **Kafka** broker that keeps a long history of messages and asks for all of them when a new system connects to it. All of that depends on your needs and requirements.

> **MQTT and Apache Kafka**
>
> If you were wondering what MQTT is, here is a quote from their website `https://adpg.link/mqtt`:
>
> *"MQTT is an OASIS standard messaging protocol for the Internet of Things (IoT). It is designed as an extremely lightweight publish/subscribe messaging transport [...]"*
>
> Here is a quote from Apache Kafka's website `https://adpg.link/kafka`:
>
> *"Apache Kafka is an open-source distributed event streaming platform [...]"*

We cannot cover every single scenario of every single system that follows every single protocol. Therefore, I'll highlight some shared concepts behind the Pub-Sub design pattern so that you know how to get started. Then, you can dig into the specific technology that you want (or need) to use.

A topic is a way to organize events, a channel, a place to read or write specific events so consumers know where to find them. As you can probably imagine, sending all events to the same place is like creating a relational database with a single table: it would be suboptimal, hard to manage, use, and evolve.

To receive messages, subscribers must subscribe to topics (or the equivalent of a topic):

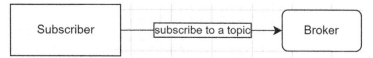

Figure 16.4: A subscriber subscribes to a pub-sub topic

The second part of the Pub-Sub pattern is to publish messages, like this:

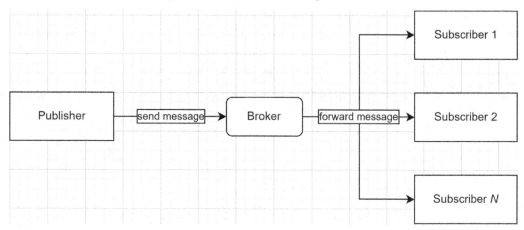

Figure 16.5: A publisher is sending a message to the message broker. The broker then forwards that message to N subscribers, where N can be zero or more

Many abstracted details here depend on the broker and the protocol. However, the following are the two primary concepts behind the Publish-Subscribe pattern:

- Publishers publish messages to topics.
- Subscribers subscribe to topics to receive messages when they are published.

Note

For example, one crucial implementation detail that is not illustrated here is security. Security is mandatory in most systems, and not every subsystem or device should have access to all topics.

Publishers and subscribers could be any part of any system. For example, many Microsoft Azure services are publishers (for example, Blob storage). You can then have other Azure services (for example, Azure Functions) subscribe to those events and react to them.

You can also use the **Publish-Subscribe** pattern inside your applications—there's no need to use cloud resources for that; this can even be done inside the same process.

The most significant advantage of the Publish-Subscribe pattern is breaking tight coupling between systems. One system publishes events while others consume them without the systems knowing each other.

That loose coupling leads to scalability, where each system can scale independently and where messages can be processed in parallel using the resources it requires. It is easier to add new processes to a workflow as well since the systems are unaware of the others. To add a new process that reacts to an event, you only have to create a new microservice, deploy it, then start to listen to one or more events and process them.

On the downside, the message broker can become the application's single point of failure and must be configured appropriately. It is also essential to consider the best message delivery policies for each message type. An example of a policy could be to ensure the delivery of crucial messages while delaying less time-sensitive messages and dropping unimportant messages during load surges.

If we revisit our previous example using Publish-Subscribe, we end up with the following simplified workflow:

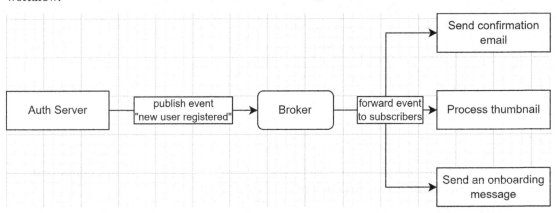

Figure 16.6: The Auth Server is publishing an event representing the creation of a new user. The broker then forwards that message to the three subscribers that then execute their tasks in parallel

Based on this workflow, we decoupled the Auth Server from the post-registration process. The Auth Server is not aware of the workflow, and the individual services are unaware of each other. Moreover, if we want to add a new task, we only have to create or update a microservice that subscribes to the right topic (in this case, the "new user registered" topic).

The current system does not support synchronization and does not handle process failures or retries, but it is a good start since we combine the pros of the message queue examples and leave the cons behind.

Now that we have explored the Publish-Subscribe pattern, we look at message brokers, then dig deeper into EDA and leverage the Publish-Subscribe pattern to create a persistent database of events that can be replayed: the Event Sourcing pattern.

Message brokers

A message broker is a program that allows us to send (**publish**) and receive (**subscribe**) messages. It plays the mediator role at scale, allowing multiple applications to talk to each other without knowing each other (**loose coupling**). The message broker is usually the central piece of any event-based distributed system that's implementing the publish-subscribe pattern.

An application (**publisher**) publishes messages to topics, while other applications (**subscribers**) receive messages from those topics. The notion of **topics** may differ from one protocol or system to another, but all systems I know have a topic-like concept to route messages to the right place. For example, you can publish to the `Devices` topic using Kafka, but to `devices/abc-123/do-something` using MQTT.

How you name your topics depends significantly on the system you are using and the scale of your installation. For example, MQTT is a lightweight event broker that recommends using a path-like naming convention. On the other hand, Apache Kafka is a full-featured event broker and event streaming platform that is not opinionated about topic names, leaving you in charge of that. Depending on the scale of your implementation, you can use the entity name as the topic name or may need prefixes to identify who in the enterprise can interact with what part of the system. Due to the small scale of the examples of the chapter, we stick with simple topic names, which also makes the examples easier to understand.

The message broker is responsible for forwarding the messages to the registered recipients. The lifetime of those messages can vary by broker or even per individual message or topic.

There are multiple message brokers out there using different protocols. Some brokers are cloud-based, such as Azure Event Grid. Other brokers are lightweight and more suited for IoT, such as Eclipse Mosquitto/MQTT. In contrast to MQTT, others are more robust and allow for high-velocity streaming of data, such as Apache Kafka.

What message broker to use should be based on the requirements of the software that you are building. Moreover, you are not limited to one broker. Nothing stops you from picking a message broker that handles the dialogs between your microservices and uses another to handle the dialogs with external IoT devices. If you are building a system in Azure, want to go serverless, or prefer paying for SaaS components that scale without investing maintenance time, you can leverage Azure services such as Event Grid, Service Bus, and Queue Storage. If you prefer open source software, you can choose Apache Kafka and even run a fully managed cloud instance as a service using Confluent Cloud if you don't want to manage your own cluster.

The event sourcing pattern

Now that we have explored the Publish-Subscribe pattern, learned what an event is, and talked about event brokers, it is time to explore **how to replay the state of an application**. To achieve this, we can follow the **event sourcing pattern**.

The idea behind event sourcing is to **store a chronological list of events** instead of a single entity, where that collection of events becomes the source of truth. That way, every single operation is saved in the right order, helping with concurrency. Moreover, we could replay all of these events to generate an object's current state in a new application, allowing us to deploy new microservices more easily.

Instead of just storing the data, if the system propagates it using an event broker, other systems can cache some of the data as one or more **materialized views**.

Materialized views

A materialized view is a model that's created and stored to serve a specific purpose. The data can come from one or more sources, leading to improved performance when querying that data. For example, the application returns the materialized view instead of querying multiple other systems to acquire the data. You can view the materialized view as a cached entity that a microservice stores in its own database.

One of the drawbacks of event sourcing is data consistency. There is an unavoidable delay between when a service adds an event to the store and when all the other services update their materialized views. This is named **eventual consistency**.

Eventual consistency

Eventual consistency means that the data will be consistent at some point in the future, but not outright. The delay can be from a few milliseconds to a lot longer, but the goal is usually to keep that delay as small as possible.

Another drawback is the complexity of creating such a system compared to a single application that queries a single database. Like the microservices architecture, event sourcing is not just rainbows and unicorns. It comes at a price: **operational complexity**.

Operational complexity

In a microservices architecture, each piece is smaller, but gluing them together has a cost. For example, the infrastructure to support microservices is more complex than a monolith (one app and one database). The same goes for event sourcing; all applications must subscribe to one or more events, cache data (materialized view), publish events, and more. This operational complexity represents the shift of complexity from the application code to the operational infrastructure. In other words, it requires more work to deploy and maintain multiple microservices and databases, as well as to fight the possible instability of network communication between those external systems than it does for a single application containing all of the code. Monoliths are simpler: they work or don't; they rarely partially work.

A crucial aspect of event sourcing is appending new events to the store and never changing existing events (append-only). In a nutshell, microservices communicating using the Pub-Sub pattern publish events, subscribe to topics, and generate materialized views to serve their clients.

Example

Let's explore an example of what could happen if we mix what we just studied together. **Context:** We need to build a program that manages IoT devices. We begin by creating two microservices:

- The `DeviceTwin` microservice, which handles an IoT device's twin's data (that is, a digital representation of the device).
- The `Networking` microservice, which manages the networking-related information of IoT devices (that is, how to reach a device).

As a visual reference, the final system could look as follows (we cover the `DeviceLocation` microservice later):

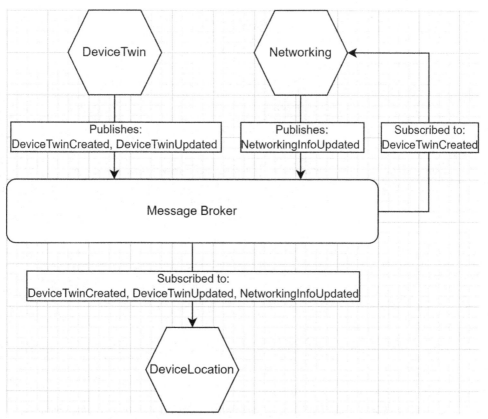

Figure 16.7: Three microservices communicating using the Publish-Subscribe pattern

Here are the user interactions and the published events:

1. A user creates a twin in the system named Device 1. The `DeviceTwin` microservice saves the
    data and publishes the `DeviceTwinCreated` event with the following payload:

```
{
    "id": "some id",
    "name": "Device 1",
    "other": "properties go here..."
}
```

In parallel, the `Networking` microservice needs to know when a device is created, so it subscribed
to the `DeviceTwinCreated` event. When a new device is created, the `Networking` microservice
creates default networking information for that device in its database; the default is unknown.
This way, the `Networking` microservice knows what devices exist or not:

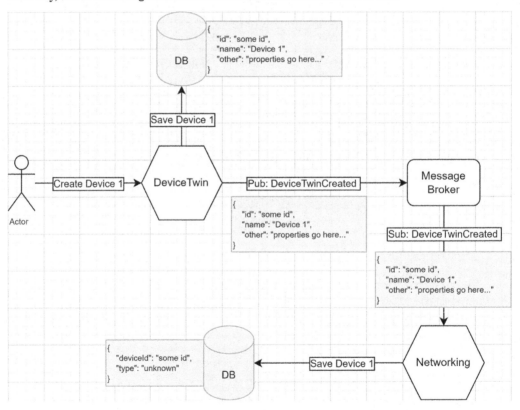

*Figure 16.8: A workflow representing the creation of a device twin and its default networking
information*

2. A user then updates the networking information of that device and sets it to MQTT. The Networking microservice saves the data and publishes the NetworkingInfoUpdated event with the following payload:

```json
{
    "deviceId": "some id",
    "type": "MQTT",
    "other": "networking properties..."
}
```

This is demonstrated by the following diagram:

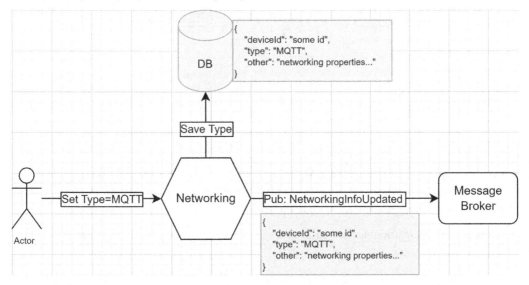

Figure 16.9: A workflow representing updating the networking type of a device

3. A user changes the device's display name to Kitchen Thermostat, which is more relevant. The DeviceTwin microservice saves the data and publishes the DeviceTwinUpdated event with the following payload. The payload uses **JSON patch** to publish only the differences instead of the whole object (see the *Further reading* section for more information):

```json
{
    "id": "some id",
    "patches": [
        { "op": "replace", "path": "/name", "value": "Kitchen Thermostat"
},
    ]
}
```

This is demonstrated by the following diagram:

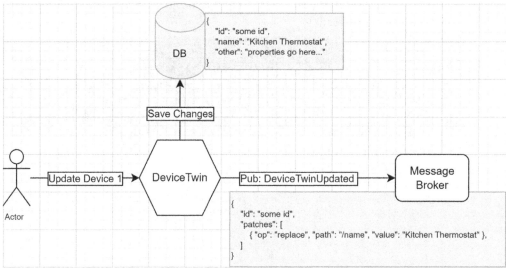

Figure 16.10: A workflow representing a user updating the name of the device to Kitchen Thermostat

From there, let's say another team designed and built a new microservice that organizes the devices at physical locations. This new `DeviceLocation` microservice allows users to visualize their devices' location on a map, such as a map of their house.

The `DeviceLocation` microservice subscribes to all three events to manage its materialized view, like this:

- When receiving a `DeviceTwinCreated` event, it saves its unique identifier and display name.
- When receiving a `NetworkingInfoUpdated` event, it saves the communication type.
- When receiving a `DeviceTwinUpdated` event, it updates the device's display name.

When the service is deployed for the first time, it replays all events from the beginning (**event sourcing**); here is what happens:

1. `DeviceLocation` receives the `DeviceTwinCreated` event and creates the following model for that object:

```
{
    "device": {
        "id": "some id",
        "name": "Device 1"
    },
    "networking": {},
    "location": {...}
}
```

This is demonstrated by the following diagram:

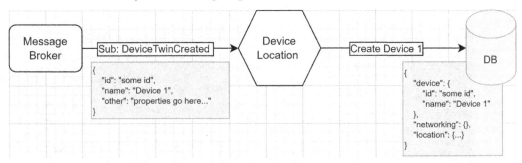

Figure 16.11: The DeviceLocation microservice replaying the DeviceTwinCreated event to create its materialized view of the device twin

2. The `DeviceLocation` microservice receives the `NetworkingInfoUpdated` event, which updates the networking type to `MQTT`, leading to the following:

```
{
    "device": {
        "id": "some id",
        "name": "Device 1"
    },
    "networking": {
        "type": "MQTT"
    },
    "location": {...}
}
```

This is demonstrated by the following diagram:

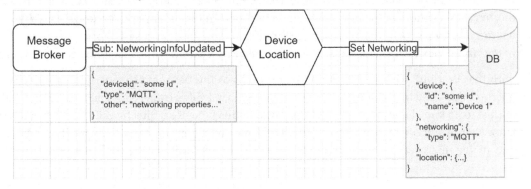

Figure 16.12: The DeviceLocation microservice replaying the NetworkingInfoUpdated event to update its materialized view of the device twin

3. The `DeviceLocation` microservice receives the `DeviceTwinUpdated` event, updating the device's name. The final model looks like this:

```
{
    "device": {
        "id": "some id",
        "name": "Kitchen Thermostat"
    },
    "networking": {
        "type": "MQTT"
    },
    "location": {...}
}
```

This is demonstrated by the following diagram:

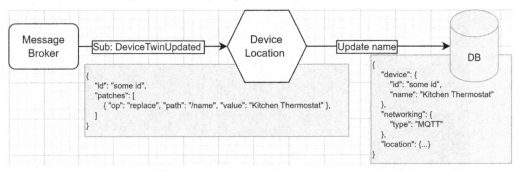

Figure 16.13: The DeviceLocation microservice replaying the DeviceTwinUpdated event to update its materialized view of the device twin

From there, the `DeviceLocation` microservice is initialized and ready. A user could set the kitchen thermostat's location on the map or continue to play with the other parts of the system. When a user queries the `DeviceLocation` microservice for information about `Kitchen Thermostat`, it displays the **materialized view**, which contains all the required information without sending external requests.

With that in mind, we could spawn new instances of the `DeviceLocation` microservice or other microservices, and they could generate their materialized views from past events—all of that with very limited to no knowledge of other microservices. In this type of architecture, a microservice can only know about events, not the other microservices. How a microservice handles events should be relevant only to that microservice, never to the others. The same applies to both publishers and subscribers.

This example illustrates the event sourcing pattern, integration events, the materialized view, the use of a message broker, and the Publish-Subscribe pattern.

In contrast, using direct communication (HTTP, gRPC, and so on) would look like this:

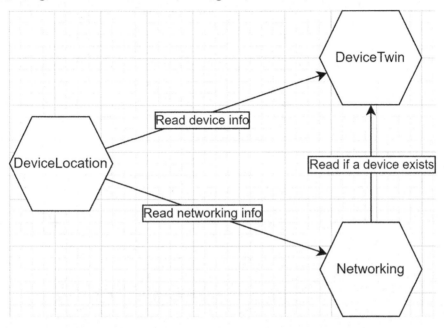

Figure 16.14: Three microservices communicating directly with one another

If we compare both approaches, by looking at the first diagram (*Figure 16.7*), we can see that the message broker plays the role of a **mediator** and breaks the direct coupling between the microservices. By looking at the preceding diagram (*Figure 16.14*), we can see the tight coupling between the microservices, where the DeviceLocation microservice would need to interact with the DeviceTwin and Networking microservices directly to build the equivalent of its materialized view. Furthermore, the DeviceLocation microservice translates one interaction into three since the Networking microservice also talks to the DeviceTwin microservice, leading to indirect tight coupling between microservices, which can negatively impact performance.

Suppose eventual consistency is not an option, or the Publish-Subscribe pattern cannot be applied or could be too hard to apply to your scenario. In this case, microservices can directly call each other. They can achieve this using HTTP, gRPC, or any other means that best suit that particular system's needs.

I won't be covering this topic in this book, but one thing to be careful of when calling microservices directly is the indirect call chain that could bubble up fast. You don't want your microservices to create a super deep call chain, or your system will most likely become very slow, very fast. Here is an abstract example of what could happen to illustrate what I mean. A diagram is often better than words:

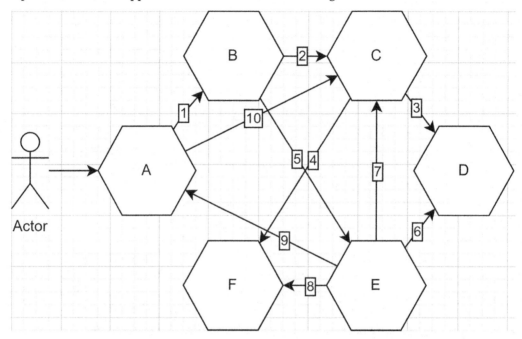

Figure 16.15: A user calling microservice A, which then triggers a chain reaction of subsequent calls, leading to disastrous performance

In terms of the preceding diagram, let's think about failures (for one). If microservice C goes offline, the whole request ends with an error. No matter the measures we put in place to mitigate the risks, if microservice C cannot recover, the system will remain down; goodbye to microservices' promise of independence. Another issue is latency: ten calls are made for a single operation; that takes time.

Such chatty systems have most likely emerged from an incorrect domain modeling phase, leading to multiple microservices working together to handle trivial tasks. Now think of *Figure 16.15* but with 500 microservices instead of 6. That could be catastrophic!

This type of interdependent microservices system is known as the **Death Star anti-pattern**. Personally, I see the Death Star anti-pattern as a *distributed big ball of mud*. One way to avoid such pitfalls is to ensure the bounded contexts are well segregated and that responsibilities are well distributed.

A good domain model should allow you to avoid building a Death Star and create the "most correct" system possible instead. No matter the type of architecture you choose, if you are not building the right thing, you may well end up with a big ball of mud or a Death Star. Of course, the Pub-Sub pattern can help us break the tight coupling between microservices to avoid such issues.

Conclusion

The Publish-Subscribe pattern uses events to break tight coupling between parts of an application. In a microservices architecture, we can use a message broker and integration events to allow microservices to talk to each other indirectly. The different pieces are now coupled with the data contract representing the event (its schema) instead of each other, leading to a potential gain in flexibility. One risk of this type of architecture is breaking events' consumers by publishing breaking changes in the event's format without letting consumers know or without having events versioning in place so consumers can self-manage themselves. Therefore, it is critical to think about event schema evolutions thoroughly. Most systems evolve, as will events, but since schemas are the glue between systems in a Publish-Subscribe model, it is essential to treat them as such. Some brokers, like Apache Kafka, offer a schema store and other mechanisms to help with these; some don't.

Then, we can leverage the event sourcing pattern to persist those events, allowing new microservices to populate their databases by replaying past events. The event store then becomes the source of truth of those systems. Event sourcing can also become very handy for tracing and auditing purposes since the whole history is persisted. We can also replay messages to recreate the system's state at any given point in time, making it very powerful for debugging purposes. The storage size requirement for the event store is something to consider before going down the event sourcing path. The event store could grow quite large because we keep all messages since the beginning of time and could grow fast based on the quantity of events sent. You could compact the history to reduce the data size but lose part of the history. Once again, you must decide based on the requirements and ask yourself the appropriate questions. For example, is it acceptable to lose part of the history? How long should we keep the data? Do we want to keep the original data in cheaper storage if we need it later? Do we even need replaying capabilities? Can we afford to keep all the data forever? Craft your list of questions based on the specific business problem you want to solve. This advice applies to all aspects of software engineering: clearly define the business problem first, then find how to fix it.

Such patterns can be compelling but can also take time to learn and implement. Like with message queues, cloud providers offer fully managed brokers as a service. Those can be faster to get started with than building and maintaining your own infrastructure. If building servers is your thing, you can use open source software to "economically" build your stack or just pay for managed instances of such software to save yourself the trouble. The same tips as with message queues apply here; for example, you can leverage a managed service for your production environment and a local version on the developer's machine.

Apache Kafka is one of the most popular event brokers that enables advanced functionalities like event streaming. Kafka has partially and fully managed cloud offerings like Confluent Cloud. Redis Pub/Sub is another open source project that has fully managed cloud offerings. Redis is also a key-value store trendy for distributed caching scenarios. Other offerings are (but are not limited to) Solace PubSub+, RabbitMQ, and ActiveMQ. Once again, I suggest comparing the offerings with your requirements to make the best choice for your scenarios.

Now, let's see how the Publish-Subscribe pattern can help us follow the **SOLID** principles at cloud-scale:

- **S:** Helps centralize and divide responsibilities between applications or components without them directly knowing each other, breaking tight coupling.
- **O:** Allows us to change how publishers and subscribers behave without directly impacting the other microservices (breaking tight coupling between them).
- **L:** N/A
- **I:** Each event can be as small as needed, leading to multiple smaller communication interfaces (data contracts).
- **D:** The microservices depend on events (abstractions) instead of concretions (the other microservices), breaking tight coupling between them and inverting the dependency flow.

As you may have noticed, pub-sub is very similar to message queues. The main difference is the way messages are read and dispatched:

- Queues: messages are pulled one at a time, consumed by one service, then disappear.
- Pub-Sub: messages are also read in order and are sent to all consumers instead of to only one, like with queues.

Observer design pattern

I intentionally kept the Observer pattern out of this book since we rarely need it in .NET. C# offers multicast events, which are well versed in replacing the Observer pattern (in most cases). If you don't know the Observer pattern, don't worry–chances are, you will never need it anyway. Nevertheless, if you already know the Observer pattern, here are the differences between it and the Pub-Sub pattern.

In the Observer pattern, the subject keeps a list of its observers, creating direct knowledge of their existence. Concrete observers also often know about the subject, which leads to even more knowledge of other entities, leading to more coupling.

In the Pub-Sub pattern, the publisher is not aware of the subscribers; it is only aware of the message broker. The subscribers are not aware of the publishers either, only of the message broker. The publishers and subscribers are linked only through the data contract of the messages they are either publishing or receiving.

We could view the Pub-Sub pattern as the distributed evolution of the Observer pattern or more precisely, like adding a mediator to the Observer pattern.

Next, we explore some patterns that directly call other microservices by visiting a new kind of **Façade:** the **Gateway**.

Introducing Gateway patterns

When building a microservices-oriented system, the number of services grows with the number of features; the bigger the system, the more microservices you have.

When you think about a user interface that has to interact with such a system, this can become tedious, complex, and inefficient (dev-wise and speed-wise). Gateways can help us achieve the following:

- Hide complexity by routing requests to the appropriate services.
- Hide complexity by aggregating responses, translating one external request into many internal ones.
- Hide complexity by exposing only the subset of features that a client needs.
- Translate an external request into another protocol that's used internally.

A gateway can also centralize different processes, such as logging and caching requests, authenticating and authorizing users and clients, enforcing request rate limits, and other similar policies.

You can see gateways as façades, but instead of being a class in a program, it is a program of its own, shielding other programs. There are multiple variants of the Gateway pattern, and we explore many of them here.

Regardless of the type of gateway you need, you can code it yourself or leverage existing tools to speed up the development process.

>
>
> **Tip**
>
> Beware that there is a strong chance that your homemade gateway version 1.0 has more flaws than a proven solution. This tip is not only applicable to gateways but to most complex systems. That being said, sometimes, there is no proven solution that does exactly what we want, and we have to code it ourselves, which is where the real fun begins!

An open source project that could help you out is Ocelot (`https://adpg.link/UwiY`). It is an application gateway written in .NET Core that supports many things that we expect from a gateway. You can route requests using configuration or write custom code to create advanced routing rules. Since it is open source, you can contribute to it, fork it, and explore the source code if you need to.

A gateway is a **reverse proxy** that fetches the information that's been requested by a client. That information can come from one or more resources, possibly located on one or more servers. Microsoft is working on a reverse proxy named YARP, which is also open source (`https://adpg.link/YARP`). Microsoft claims they are building it for their internal teams, so it will most likely evolve and be maintained over time (my guess).

Now, let's explore a few types of gateways.

Gateway Routing pattern

We can use this pattern to hide the complexity of our system by having the gateway route requests to the appropriate services.

For example, let's say that we have two microservices: one that holds our device data and another that manages device locations. We want to show the latest known location of a specific device (id=102) and display its name and model.

To achieve that, a user requests the web page, and then the web page calls two services (see the following diagram). The DeviceTwin microservice is accessible from service1.domain.com, and the Location microservice is accessible from service2.domain.com. From there, the web application has to keep track of what services use what domain name. The UI has to handle more complexity as we add more microservices. Moreover, if at some point we decide to change service1 to device-twins and service2 to location, we'd need to update the web application as well. If there is only a UI, it is still not so bad, but if you have multiple user interfaces, that means each of them has to handle that complexity.

Furthermore, if we want to hide the microservices inside a private network, it would be impossible unless all the user interfaces are also part of that private network (which exposes it):

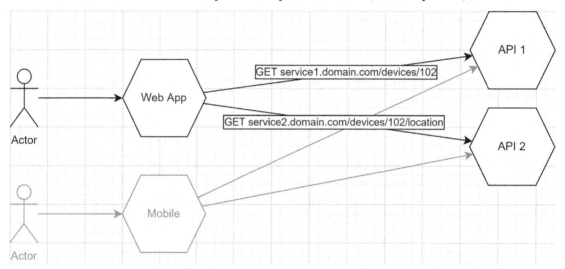

Figure 16.16: A web application and a mobile app that are calling two microservices directly

To fix some of these issues, we can implement a gateway that does the routing for us. That way, instead of knowing what services are accessible through what sub-domain, the UI only has to know the gateway:

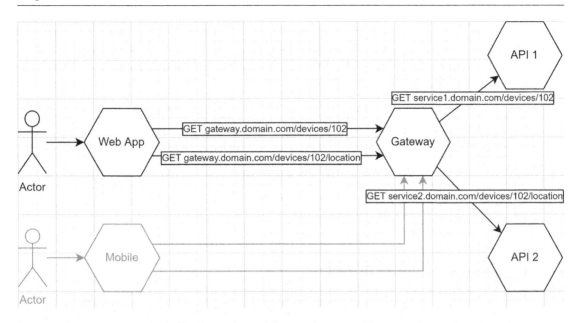

Figure 16.17: A web application and a mobile app that are calling two microservices through a gateway application

Of course, this brings some possible issues to the table as the gateway becomes a single point of failure. You could consider using a load balancer to ensure that you have strong enough availability and fast enough performance. Since all requests pass through the gateway, you may need to scale it up at some point.

You should also ensure the gateway supports failure by implementing different resiliency patterns, such as **Retry** and **Circuit Breaker**. The chances that an error will occur on the other side of the gateway increase with the number of microservices you deploy and the number of requests sent to those microservices.

You can also use a routing gateway to reroute the URI to create easier-to-use URI patterns. You can also reroute ports; add, update, or remove HTTP headers; and more. Let's explore the same example but using different URIs. Let's assume the following:

Microservice	URI
API 1 (get a device)	`internal.domain.com:8001/{id}`
API 2 (get a device location)	`internal.domain.com:8002/{id}`

UI developers would have a harder time remembering what port is leading to what microservice and what is doing what (and who could blame them?). Moreover, we could not transfer the requests as we did earlier (only routing the domain). We could use the gateway as a way to create memorable URI patterns for developers to consume, like these:

Gateway URI	Microservice URI
`gateway.domain.com/devices/{id}`	`internal.domain.com:8001/{id}`
`gateway.domain.com/devices/{id}/location`	`internal.domain.com:8002/{id}`

As you can see, we took the ports out of the equation to create usable, meaningful, and easy-to-remember URIs.

However, we are still making two requests to the gateway to display one piece of information (the location of a device and its name/model), which leads us to our next Gateway pattern.

Gateway Aggregation pattern

Another role that we can give to a gateway is to aggregate requests to hide complexity from its consumers. Aggregating multiple requests into one makes it easier for consumers of a microservices system to interact with it; clients need to know about one endpoint instead of multiple. Moreover, it moves the chattiness from the client to the gateway, which is closer to the microservices, lowering the many calls' latency, thus making the request-response cycle faster.

Continuing with our previous example, we have two UI applications that contain a feature to show a device's location on a map before identifying it using its name/model. To achieve this, they must call the device twin endpoint to obtain the device's name and model, as well as the location endpoint to get its last known location. So, two requests to display a small box, times two UIs, means four requests to maintain for a simple feature. If we extrapolate, we could end up managing a near-endless number of HTTP requests for a handful of features.

Here is a diagram showing our feature in its current state:

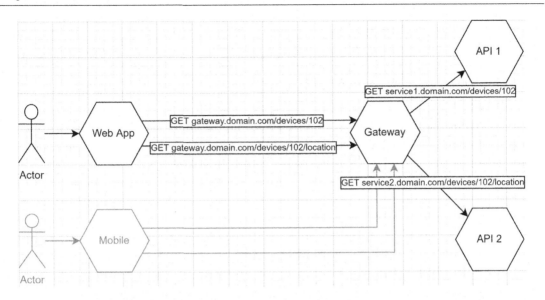

Figure 16.18: A web application and a mobile app that are calling two microservices through a gateway application

To remedy this problem, we can apply the Gateway Aggregation pattern to simplify our UIs and offload the responsibility of managing those details to the gateway.

By applying the Gateway Aggregation pattern, we end up with the following simplified flow:

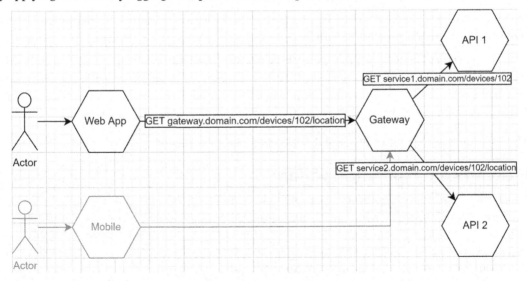

Figure 16.19: A gateway that aggregates the response of two requests to serve a single request from both a web application and a mobile app

In the previous flow, the Web App calls the Gateway that calls the two APIs, then crafts a response combining the two responses it got from the APIs. The Gateway then returns that response to the Web App. With that in place, the Web App is loosely coupled with the two APIs, with the Gateway playing the middleman. With only one HTTP request, the Web App has all the information it needs, aggregated by the Gateway.

Next, let's explore the steps that occurred. In the following diagram, we can see the Web App makes a single request (1), while the gateway makes two calls (2 and 4). In the diagram, the requests are sent in series, but we could have sent them in parallel to speed things up:

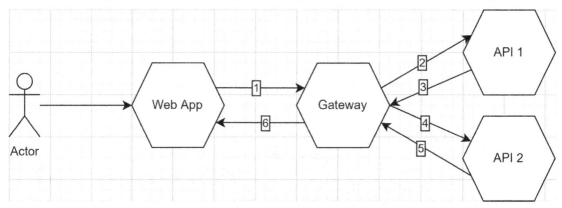

Figure 16.20: The order in which the requests take place

Like the routing gateway, an aggregation gateway can become the bottleneck of your application and a single point of failure, so beware of that.

Another important point to note is the latency between the gateway and the internal APIs. If the latency is too high, your clients are going to wait for every response. So, deploying the gateway close to the microservices it interacts with could become crucial for system performance. The gateway can also implement caching to improve performance so that subsequent requests are faster.

Next, we explore another type of gateway that creates specialized gateways instead of generic ones.

Backends for Frontends pattern

The Backends for Frontends pattern is yet another variation of the Gateway pattern. With Backends for Frontends, instead of building a general-purpose gateway, we build a gateway per user interface (or for an application that interacts with your system), lowering complexity. Moreover, it allows for fine-grained control of what endpoints are exposed. It removes the chances of app B breaking when changes are made to app A. Many optimizations can come out of this pattern, such as sending only the data that's required for each call instead of sending data that only a few applications are using, saving some bandwidth along the way.

Let's say that our Web App needs to display more data about a device. To achieve that, we would need to change the endpoint and send that extra information to the mobile app as well.

However, the mobile app doesn't need that information since it doesn't have room on its screen to display it. Here is an updated diagram that replaces the single gateway with two gateways, one per frontend.

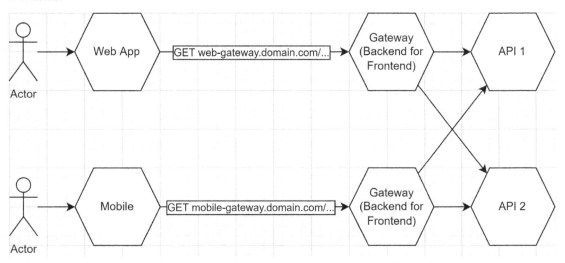

Figure 16.21: Two backends for frontends gateways; one for the Web App and one for the Mobile App

By doing this, we can now develop specific features for each frontend without impacting the other. Each gateway is now shielding its particular frontend from the rest of the system and the other frontend. This is the most important benefit this pattern brings to the table: independence between clients.

Once again, the Backends for Frontends pattern is a gateway. And like other variations of the Gateway pattern, it can become the bottleneck of its frontend and its single point of failure. The good news is that the outage of one backend for frontend gateway limits the impact to a single frontend, shielding the other frontends from that downtime.

Mixing and matching gateways

Now that we've explored three variations of the Gateway pattern, it is important to note that we can mix and match them, either at the codebase level or as multiple microservices.

For example, a gateway can be built for a single client (backend for frontend), perform simple routing, and aggregate results.

We can also mix them as different applications, for example, by putting multiple backend for frontend gateways in front of a more generic gateway to simplify the development and maintenance of those backends for frontends.

Beware that each hop has a cost. The more pieces you add between your clients and your microservices, the more time it will take for those clients to receive the response (latency). Of course, you can put mechanisms in place to lower that overhead, such as caching or non-HTTP protocols such as gRPC, but you still must consider it. That goes for everything, not just gateways.

Here is an example illustrating this:

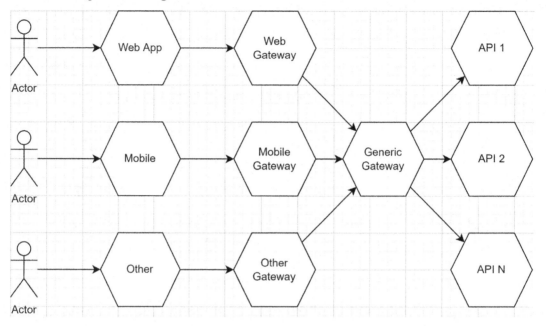

Figure 16.22: A mix of the Gateway patterns

As you've possibly guessed, the Generic Gateway is the single point of failure of all applications, while at the same time, each backend for frontend gateway is a point of failure for its specific client.

Service mesh

A service mesh is an alternative to help microservices communicate with one another. It is a layer, outside of the application, that proxies communications between services. Those proxies are injected on top of each service and are referred to as **sidecars**. The service mesh can also help with distributed tracing, instrumentation, and system resiliency. If your system needs service-to-service communication, a service mesh would be an excellent place to look.

Conclusion

A gateway is a façade or reverse proxy that shields or simplifies access to one or more other services. In this section, we explored the following:

- **Routing:** This forwards a request from point A to point B.
- **Aggregation:** This combines the result of multiple sub-requests into a single response.
- **Backends for Frontends:** This is used in a one-to-one relationship with a frontend.

We can use any microservices pattern, including gateways, and like any other pattern, we can mix and match them. Just consider the advantages, but also the drawbacks, that they bring to the table. If you can live with them, well, you've got your solution.

Gateways often end up being the single point of failure, so that is a point to consider. On the other hand, a gateway can have multiple instances running simultaneously behind a load-balancer (see *Appendix B* for more information about scaling). Moreover, we must also consider the delay that's added by calling a service that calls another service since that slows down the response time.

All in all, a gateway is a great tool to simplify consuming microservices. They also allow hiding the microservices topology behind them, possibly even isolated in a private network. They can also handle cross-cutting concerns such as security.

> **Note**
>
> It is imperative to use gateways as a requests passthrough and avoid coding business logic into them; gateways are just reverse proxies. Think single responsibility principle: a gateway is a façade in front of your microservices cluster. Of course, you can unload specific tasks into your gateways like authorization, resiliency (retry policies, for example), and similar cross-cutting concerns, but the business logic must remain in the backend microservices.

I strongly recommend against rolling out your own gateway and suggest leveraging existing offerings instead. This is why I chose not to add C# code in this section. There are many open source and cloud gateways that you can use in your application. Using existing components leaves you more time to implement the business rules that solve the issues your program is trying to tackle.

Of course, cloud-based offerings exist, like Azure Application Gateway and Amazon API Gateway. Both are extendable with cloud offerings like load-balancers and **web application firewalls** (**WAF**). For example, Azure Application Gateway also supports autoscaling, zone redundancy, and can serve as **Azure Kubernetes Service** (**AKS**) Ingress Controller (in a nutshell, it controls the traffic to your microservices cluster). For more information about Kubernetes and containers, see *Appendix B*.

If you want more control over your gateways or to deploy them with your application, you can leverage one of the options that are out there. For simplicity, I picked two to talk to you about: Ocelot and Envoy.

Ocelot is an an open source production-ready API Gateway programmed in .NET. Ocelot supports routing, request aggregation, load-balancing, authentication, authorization, rate limiting, and more. It also integrates well with Identity Server, an **OpenID Connect** (**OIDC**) and OAuth 2.0 implementation, written in .NET. The biggest advantage of Ocelot, in my eyes, is the fact that you create the .NET project yourself, install a NuGet package, configure your gateway, then deploy it like you would any other ASP.NET Core application. Since Ocelot is written in .NET, it is easier to extend it if needed or contribute to the project or its ecosystem by sharing your improvements.

Envoy is an *"open source edge and service proxy, designed for cloud-native applications,"* to quote their website. Envoy is a **Cloud Native Computing Foundation** (**CNCF**) graduated project, originally created by Lyft. Envoy was designed to run as a separate process from your application, allowing it to work with any programming language. Envoy can serve as a gateway and has an extendable design through TCP/UDP and HTTP filters, supports HTTP/2 and HTTP/3, gRPC, and more.

Which offering to choose? If you are looking for a fully managed service, look at the cloud provider's offering of your choice. Consider Ocelot if you are looking for a configurable HTTP gateway that supports the patterns covered in this chapter. If you have complex use cases that Ocelot does not support, you can look into Envoy, a proven offering with many advanced capabilities. Please keep in mind that these are just a few possibilities that can play the role of a gateway in a microservices architecture system and are not intended to be a complete list.

Now, let's see how gateways can help us follow the **SOLID** principles at cloud-scale:

- **S**: A gateway can handle routing, aggregation, and other similar logic that would otherwise be implemented in different components or applications.
- **O**: I see many ways to attack this one, but here are two takes on this:
    a.   Externally, a gateway could reroute its sub-requests to new URIs without its consumers knowing about it, as long as its contract does not change.
    b.   Internally, a gateway could load its rules from configurations, allowing it to change without updating its code (this one would be an implementation detail).
- **L**: We could see the previous point (b) as *not changing the correctness of the application*.
- **I**: Since a backend for frontend gateway serves a single frontend system, that means one contract (interface) per frontend system, leading to multiple smaller interfaces instead of one big general-purpose gateway.
- **D**: We could see a gateway as an abstraction, hiding the real microservices (implementations) and inverting the dependency flow.

Next, we revisit CQRS on a distributed scale.

Revisiting the CQRS pattern

Command Query Responsibility Segregation (CQRS), explored in *Chapter 14, Mediator and CQRS Design Patterns*, applies the **Command Query Separation** (CQS) principle. Compared to what we saw in *Chapter 14, Mediator and CQRS Design Patterns*, we can push CQRS further using microservices or serverless computing. Instead of simply creating a clear separation between commands and queries, we can divide them even more by using multiple microservices and data sources.

CQS is a principle stating that a method should either return data or mutate data, but not both. On the other hand, **CQRS** suggests using one model to read the data and one model to mutate the data.

Serverless computing is a cloud execution model where the cloud provider manages the servers and allocates the resources on-demand, based on usage. Serverless resources fall into the platform as a service (PaaS) offering.

Let's use IoT again as an example; we queried the last known location of a device in the previous examples, but what about the device updating that location? This can mean pushing many updates every minute. To solve this issue, we are going to use CQRS and focus on two operations:

- Updating the device location.
- Reading the last known location of a device.

Simply put, we have a Read Location microservice, a Write Location microservice, and two databases. Remember that each microservice should own its data. That way, a user can access the last known device location through the read microservice (query model), while a device can punctually send its current position to the write microservice (command model). By doing that, we split the load from reading and writing the data as both occur at different frequencies:

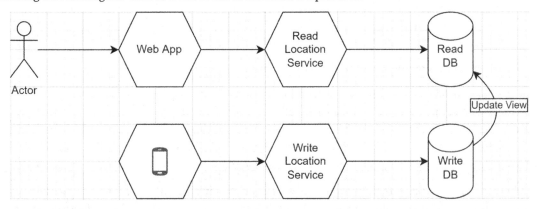

Figure 16.23: Microservices that apply CQRS to divide the reads and writes of a device's location

In the preceding schema that illustrates the concept, the reads are queries, and the writes are commands. How to update the Read DB once a new value is added to the Write DB depends on the technology at play. One essential thing in this type of architecture is that, per the CQRS pattern, a command should not return a value, enabling a "fire and forget" scenario. With that rule in place, consumers don't have to wait for the command to complete before doing something else.

Note

Fire and forget does not apply to every scenario; sometimes, we need synchronization. Implementing the Saga pattern is one way to solve coordination issues.

Conceptually, we can implement this example by leveraging serverless cloud infrastructures, such as Azure Functions and Table Storage. Let's revisit this example using those components:

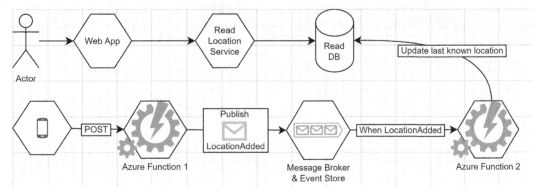

Figure 16.24: Using Azure services to manage a CQRS implementation

The previous diagram illustrates the following:

1. The device sends its location at a regular interval by posting it to Azure Function 1.
2. Azure Function 1 then publishes the `LocationAdded` event to the event broker, which is also an event store (the Write DB).
3. All subscribers to the `LocationAdded` event can now handle the event appropriately; in this case, Azure Function 2.
4. Azure Function 2 updates the last known location of the device in the Read DB.
5. Any subsequent queries should result in getting the new location.

The message broker is also the event store in the preceding diagram, but we could store events elsewhere, such as in an Azure Storage Table, in a time-series database, or in an Apache Kafka cluster. Azure-wise, the datastore could also be CosmosDB. Moreover, I abstracted this component for multiple reasons, including the fact that there are multiple "as-a-service" offerings to publish events in Azure, and there are multiple ways of using third-party components as well (both open source and proprietary).

Furthermore, the example demonstrates **eventual consistency** well. All the last known location reads between *steps 1* and *4* get the old value while the system processes the new location updates (commands). If the command processing slows down for some reason, a longer delay could occur before the next read database updates. The commands could also be processed in batches, leading to another kind of delay. No matter what happens with the command processing, the read database would be available all that time whether it has the latest data or not and whether the write system is overloaded or not. This is the beauty of this type of design, but it is more complex to implement and maintain.

Time-series databases

Time-series databases are optimized for temporally querying and storing data, where you always append new records without updating old ones. This kind of NoSQL database can be useful for temporal-intensive usage.

Once again, we used the Publish-Subscribe pattern to get another scenario going. Assuming that events are persisted forever, the previous example could also support event sourcing. Furthermore, new services could subscribe to the `LocationAdded` event without impacting the code that has already been deployed. For example, we could create a SignalR microservice that pushes the updates to its clients. It is not CQRS-related, but it flows well with everything that we've explored so far, so here is an updated conceptual diagram:

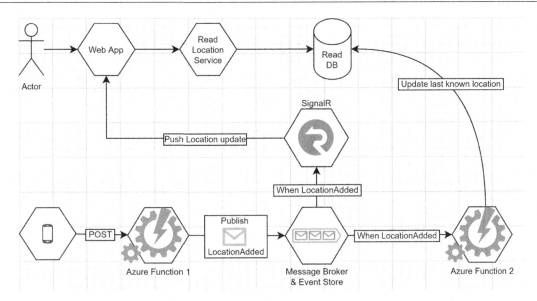

Figure 16.25: Adding a SignalR service as a new subscriber without impacting the other part of the system

The SignalR microservice could be custom code or an Azure SignalR Service (backed by another Azure Function); it doesn't matter. Here I wanted to illustrate that it is easier to drop new services into the mix when using a Pub-Sub model than with point-to-point communication.

As you can see, a microservices system adds more and more small pieces that indirectly interconnect with each other over one or more message brokers. Maintaining, diagnosing, and debugging such systems is harder than with a single application; that's the **operational complexity** we talked about earlier. However, containers can help deploy and maintain such systems; see *Appendix B* for more information about containers.

Starting in ASP.NET Core 3.0, the ASP.NET Core team invested much effort into **distributed tracing**. Distributed tracing is necessary to find failures and bottlenecks related to an event that flows from one program to another (such as microservices). If something bugs out, it is important to trace what the user did to isolate the error, reproduce it, and then fix it. The more independent pieces there are, the harder it can become to make that trace possible. This is outside the scope of this book, but it is something to consider before jumping into the microservices adventure.

Conclusion

CQRS helps divide queries and commands and helps encapsulate and isolate each block of logic independently. Mixing that concept with serverless computing or microservices architecture allows us to scale reads and writes independently. We can also use different databases, empowering us with the tools we need for the transfer rate required by each part of that system (for example, frequent writes and occasional reads or vice versa).

Major cloud providers like Azure and AWS provide serverless offerings to help support such scenarios. Each cloud provider's documentation should help you get started. Meanwhile, for Azure, we have Azure Functions, Event Grid, Event Hubs, Service Bus, Cosmos DB, and more. Azure also offers bindings between the different services that are triggered or react to events for you, removing a part of the complexity.

Now, let's see how CQRS can help us follow the **SOLID** principles at the cloud scale:

- **S:** Dividing an application into smaller reads and writes applications (or functions) leans toward encapsulating single responsibilities into different programs.
- **O:** CQRS, mixed with serverless computing or microservices, helps extend the software without the need for us to modify the existing code by adding, removing, or replacing applications.
- **L:** N/A
- **I:** CQRS set us up to create multiple small interfaces (or programs) with a clear distinction between commands and queries.
- **D:** N/A

Exploring the Microservice Adapter pattern

The Microservice Adapter pattern allows adding missing features, adapting one system to another, or migrating an existing application to an event-driven architecture model, to name a few possibilities. The Microservice Adapter pattern is similar to the Adapter pattern we cover in *Chapter 9, Structural Patterns* but applied to a microservices system that uses event-driven architecture instead of creating a class to adapt an object to another signature.

In the scenarios we cover in this section, the microservices system represented by the following diagram can be replaced by a standalone application as well; this pattern applies to all sorts of programs, not just microservices, which is why I abstracted away the details:

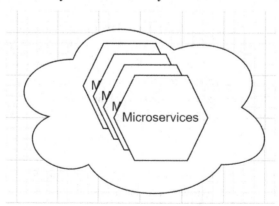

Figure 16.26: Microservice system representation used in the subsequent examples

Here are the examples we are covering next and possible usages of this pattern:

- Adapting an existing system to another.
- Decommissioning a legacy application.
- Adapting an event broker to another.

Let's start by connecting a standalone system to an event-driven one.

Adapting an existing system to another

In this scenario, we have an existing system of which we don't control the source code or don't want to change, and we have a microservices system built around an event-driven architecture model. We don't have to control the source code of the microservices system either as long as we have access to the event broker.

Here is a diagram that represents this scenario:

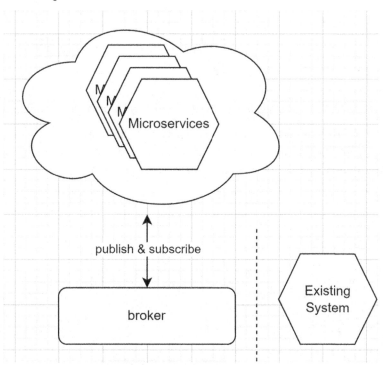

Figure 16.27: A microservices system that interacts with an event broker and an existing system that is disconnected from the microservices

As we can see from the preceding diagram, the existing system is disconnected from the microservices and the broker. To adapt the existing system to the microservices system, we must subscribe or publish certain events. In this case, let's see how to read data from the microservices (subscribe to the broker) then update that data into the existing system.

In a scenario where we control the existing system's code, we could open the source code, subscribe to one or more topics, and change the behaviors from there. In our case, we don't want to do that or can't, so we can't directly subscribe to topics, as demonstrated by the following diagram:

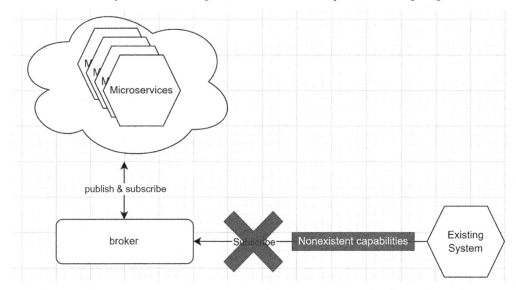

Figure 16.28: Missing capabilities to connect an existing system to an event-driven one

This is where the microservice adapter comes into play and allows us to fill the capability gap of our existing system. To add the missing link, we create a microservice that subscribes to the appropriate events, then apply the changes in the existing system, like this:

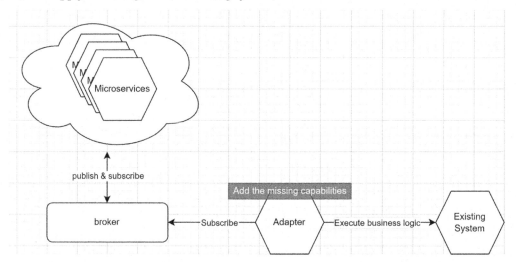

Figure 16.29: An adapter microservice adding missing capabilities to an existing system

As we can see in the preceding diagram, the Adapter microservice gets the events (subscribes to one or more topics) then uses that data from the microservices system to execute some business logic on the existing system.

In this design, the new `Adapter` microservice allowed us to add missing capabilities to a system we had no control over with little to no disruption to users' day-to-day activities.

The example assumes the existing system had some form of extensibility mechanism like an API. If the system does not, we would have to be more creative to interface with it.

For example, the microservices system could be an e-commerce website and the existing system a legacy inventory management system. The adapter could update the legacy system with new orders data.

The existing system could also be an old **customer relationship management (CRM)** system that you want to update when users of the microservices application execute some actions, like changing their phone number or address.

The possibilities are almost endless; you create a link between an event-driven system and an existing system you don't control or don't want to change. In this case, the microservice adapter allows us to follow the **Open-Closed principle** by extending the system without changing the existing pieces. The primary drawback is that we are deploying another microservice that has direct coupling with the existing system, which may be best for temporary solutions. On that same line of thought, next, we replace a legacy application with a new one with limited to no downtime.

Decommissioning a legacy application

In this scenario, we have a legacy application that we want to decommission and a microservices system we want to connect some existing capabilities to. To achieve this, we can create one or more adapters to migrate all features and dependencies to the new model.

Here is a representation of the current state of our system:

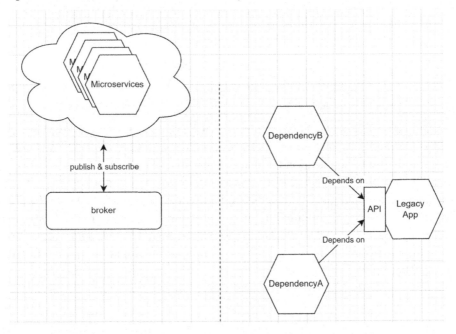

Figure 16.30: The original legacy application and its dependencies

The preceding diagram shows the two distinct systems, including the legacy application we want to decommission. Two other applications, dependency A and B, directly depend on the legacy application. The exact migration flow is strongly dependent on your use case. In the case you want to keep the dependencies, we want to migrate them first. To do that, we can create an event-driven `Adapter` microservice that breaks the tight coupling between the dependencies and the legacy application, like this:

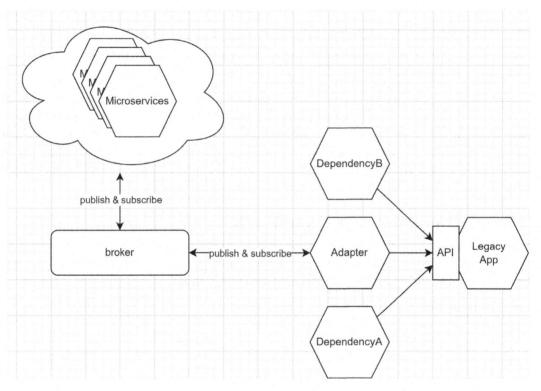

Figure 16.31: Adding a microservice adapter that implements the event-driven flow required to break tight coupling between the dependencies and the legacy application

The preceding diagram shows an `Adapter` microservice and the rest of a microservices system that communicates using an event broker. As we explored in the previous example, the adapter was placed there to connect the legacy application to the microservices. The focus of our scenario is to remove the legacy application and migrate its two dependencies. Here, we carved out the required capabilities using the adapter, allowing us to migrate the dependencies to an event-driven model and break tight-coupling with the legacy application. Such migration could be done in multiple steps, migrating each dependency one by one, and we could even create one adapter per dependency. For the sake of simplicity, I chose to draw only one adapter. If your dependencies are large or complex, you may want to revisit this choice.

Once we are done migrating the dependencies, our systems look like the following:

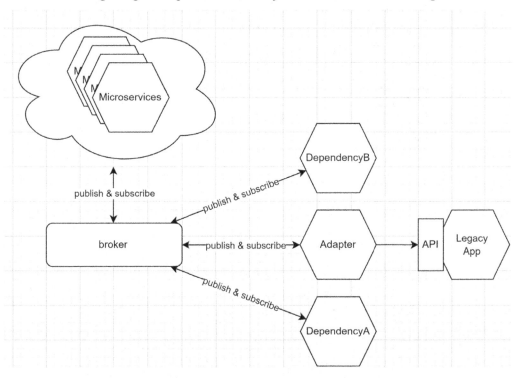

Figure 16.32: The dependencies are now using an event-driven architecture, and the adapter microservice is bridging the gap between the events and the legacy system

In the preceding diagram, the Adapter microservice executes the operations against the legacy application API that the two dependencies were doing before. The dependencies are now publishing events instead of using the API. For example, when an operation happens in DependencyB, it publishes an event to the broker. The Adapter microservice picks up that event and executes the original operation against the API. Doing this creates more complexity and is a temporary state.

With this new architecture in place, we can start migrating existing features away from the legacy application into the new application without impacting the dependencies; we broke tight coupling.

Note

From this point forward, we are applying the **Strangler Fig Application** pattern to migrate the legacy system piece by piece to the new architecture of our choosing. For the sake of simplicity, think of the Strangler Fig Application pattern as migrating features from one application to another, one by one. In this case, we replaced one application with another, but we could use the same patterns to split an application into multiple smaller applications as well (like microservices).

I left a few links in the further reading section in case migrating legacy systems is something you do or simply if you want to know more about that pattern.

The following diagram is a visual representation that adds the modern application we are building to replace the legacy application. That new modern application could also be a purchased product you are putting in place instead; the concepts we are exploring apply to both use cases, but the exact steps are directly related to the technology at play.

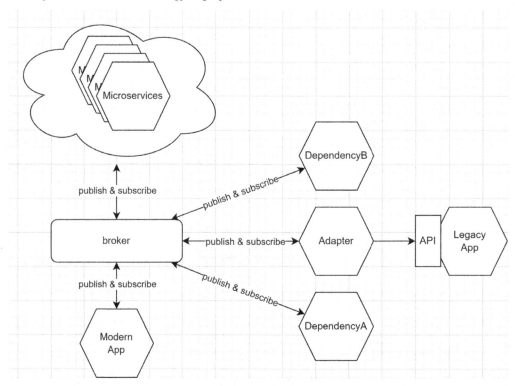

Figure 16.33: The modern application to replace the legacy application is starting to emerge by migrating capabilities to that new application

In the preceding diagram, we see the new modern application has appeared. Each time we deploy a new feature to the new application, we can remove it from the adapter, leading to a graceful transition between the two models. At the same time, we are keeping the legacy application in place to continue to provide the capabilities that are not yet migrated.

Once all features we want to keep are migrated, we can remove the adapter and decommission the legacy application, leading to the following system:

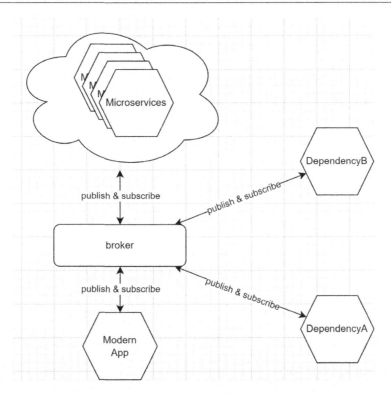

Figure 16.34: The new system topology after the retirement of the legacy application, showing the new modern application and its two loosely coupled dependencies

The preceding diagram shows the new system topology encompassing a new modern application and the two original dependencies that are now loosely coupled through event-driven architecture. Of course, the bigger the migration, the more complex it will be and the longer it will take, but the Adapter Microservice pattern is one way to help do a partial or complete migration from one system to another.

Like the preceding example, the main advantage is adding or removing capabilities without impacting the other systems, which allows us to migrate and break the tight coupling between the different dependencies. The downside is once again the added complexity of this temporary solution. Moreover, during the migration step, you will most likely need to deploy both the modern application and the adapter in the correct sequence to ensure both systems are not handling the same events twice, leading to duplicate changes. For example, updating the phone number to the same value twice should be all right because it leads to the same final data set. However, creating two records instead of one should be more important to mitigate as it may lead to integrity errors in the data set. For example, creating an online order twice instead of once could create some customer dissatisfaction or internal issues.

And voilà, we decommissioned a system using the Microservice Adapter pattern without breaking its dependencies. Next, we look at an **Internet of Things** (**IoT**) example.

Adapting an event broker to another

In this scenario, we are adapting an event broker to another. In the following diagram, we look at two use cases, one that translates events from broker B to broker A (left) and the other that translates events from broker A to broker B (right). Afterwards, we explore a more concrete example:

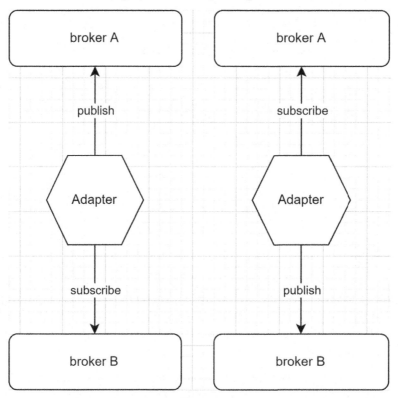

Figure 16.35: An adapter microservice that translates events from broker B to broker A (left) and from broker A to broker B (right)

We can see the two possible flows in the preceding diagram. The first flow, on the left, allows the adapter to read events from broker B and publish them to broker A. The second flow, on the right, enables the adapter to read events from broker A and publish them to broker B. Those flows allow us to translate or copy events from one broker to another by leveraging the Microservice Adapter pattern once more.

> **Note**
>
> In *Figure 16.35*, there is one adapter per flow. I did that to make the two flows as independent as possible, but the adapters could be a single microservice.

This can be very useful for an IoT system where your microservices leverage Apache Kafka internally for its full-featured suite of event-streaming capabilities but MQTT is used to communicate with the low-powered IoT devices that connect to the system. An adapter can solve this problem by translating the messages from one protocol to the other. Here is a diagram that represents the complete flows, including a device and the microservices:

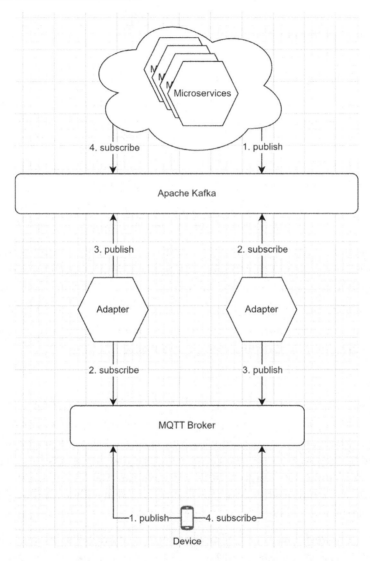

Figure 16.36: Complete protocol adapter flows, including a device and microservices

Before we explore what the events could be, let's explore both flows, step by step. The left flow allows getting events inside the system, from the devices, through the following sequence:

1. A device publishes an event to the MQTT broker.
2. The adapter reads that event.

3. The adapter publishes a similar or different event to the Kafka broker.

4. Zero or more microservices subscribed to the event act on it.

On the other hand, the right flow allows getting events out of the system to the devices through the following sequence:

1. A microservice publishes an event to the Kafka broker.

2. The adapter reads the event.

3. The adapter publishes a similar or different event to the MQTT broker.

4. Zero or more devices subscribed to the event act on it.

You don't have to implement both flows; the adapter could be bidirectional (supporting both flows), we could have two unidirectional adapters that support one of the flows or allow the communication to flow only one way (in or out but not both). The choice relates to your specific use cases.

Concrete examples of sending a message from a device to a microservice (left flow) could be to send its GPS position, send a status update (the light is now on), or a message indicating a sensor failure.

Concrete examples of sending a message to a device (right flow) could be to remotely control a speaker's volume, flip a light on, or send a confirmation that a message has been acknowledged.

In this case, the adapter is not a temporary solution but a permanent capability. We could leverage such adapters to create additional capabilities with minimal impact on the rest of the system. The primary downside is deploying one or more other microservices, but your system and processes are probably robust enough to handle that added complexity when leveraging such capabilities.

This third scenario that leverages the Microservice Adapter is our last. Hopefully, I sparked your imagination enough to leverage this simple yet powerful design pattern.

Conclusion

We explored the Microservice Adapter pattern that allows us to connect two elements of a system by adapting one to the other. We explored how to push information from an event broker into an existing system that does not support such capabilities. We also explored how we can leverage an adapter to break tight coupling, migrate features into a newer system, and decommission a legacy application seamlessly. We finally connected two event brokers through an adapter microservice, allowing a low-powered IoT device to communicate with a microservices system without draining their battery and without the complexity it would incur to use a more complex communication protocol.

This pattern is very powerful and can be implemented in many ways, but it all depends on your exact use cases, which is why I did not write code into the chapter. You can write an adapter using a serverless offering like an Azure function, no-code/low-code offerings like Power Automate, or C#. Of course, these are just a few examples. The key to designing the correct system is to nail down the problem statement because once you know what you are trying to fix, the solution becomes clearer.

Now, let's see how the Microservice Adapter pattern can help us follow the **SOLID** principles at cloud-scale:

- S: the microservice adapter can help you correct the responsibilities segregation by helping to migrate legacy systems to a better design. An adapter can play a single role in a system, like bridging the communication between IoT devices and internal microservices.

- O: You can leverage microservice adapters to dynamically add or remove features without impacting or with limited impact on the rest of the system. For example, in the IoT scenario, we could add support for a new protocol like AMQP without changing the rest of the system.

- L: N/A

- I: Adding smaller adapters can make changes easier and less risky than updating large legacy applications. As we saw in the legacy system decommissioning scenario, we could also leverage temporary adapters to split large applications into smaller pieces.

- D: A microservice adapter inverts the dependency flow between the system it adapts. For example, in the legacy system decommissioning scenario, the adapter reversed the flow from the two dependencies to the legacy system by leveraging an event broker.

Summary

The microservices architecture is something different from everything else that we've covered in this book and how we build monoliths. Instead of one big application, we split it into multiple smaller ones that we call microservices. Microservices must be independent of one another; otherwise, we will face the same problems associated with tightly coupled classes, but at the cloud scale.

We can leverage the Publish-Subscribe design pattern to decouple microservices while keeping them connected through events. Message brokers are programs that dispatch those messages. We can use event sourcing to recreate the application's state at any point in time, including when spawning new containers. We can use application gateways to shield clients from the microservices cluster's complexity and publicly expose only a subset of services.

We also took a look at how we can build upon the CQRS design pattern to decouple reads and writes of the same entities, allowing us to scale queries and commands independently. We also looked at using serverless resources to create that kind of system.

Finally, we explored the Microservice Adapter pattern that allowed us to adapt two systems together, decommission a legacy application, and connect two event brokers. This pattern is simple but powerful at inverting the dependency flow between two dependencies in a loosely coupled manner. The use of the pattern can be temporary like we saw in the legacy application decommissioning scenario, or permanent, as we saw in the IoT scenario.

On the other hand, microservices come at a cost and are not intended to replace all that exists. Building a monolith is still a good idea for many projects. Starting with a monolith and migrating it to microservices when scaling is another solution. This allows us to develop the application faster (monolith). It is also easier to add new features to a monolith than it can be to add them to a microservice application. Most of the time, mistakes cost less in a monolith than in a microservices application. You can also plan your future migration toward microservices, which leads to the best of both worlds while keeping operational complexity low. For example, you could leverage the Publish-Subscribe pattern through MediatR notifications in your monolith and migrate the events dispatching responsibility to a message broker later when migrating your system to microservices architecture (if the need ever arises).

I don't want you to discard the microservices architecture, but I just want to make sure that you weigh up the pros and cons of such a system before blindly jumping in. Your team's skill level and ability to learn new technologies may also impact the cost of jumping into the microservices boat.

DevOps (development [Dev] and IT operations [Ops]) or **DevSecOps** (adding security [Sec] to the DevOps mix), which we do not cover in the book, is essential when building microservices. It brings deployment automation, automated quality checks, auto-composition, and more. Your microservices cluster will be very hard to deploy and maintain without that.

Microservices are great when you need scaling, want to go serverless, or split responsibilities between multiple teams, but keep the operational costs in mind.

This chapter concludes the application-scale section of this book at a cloud-scale level. Next, we explore user interface options provided by ASP.NET Core, including Blazor and the Model-View-Update pattern.

Questions

Let's take a look at a few practice questions:

1. What is the most significant difference between a **message queue** and a **pub-sub** model?
2. What is **event sourcing**?
3. Can an **application gateway** be both a **routing gateway** and an **aggregation gateway**?
4. Is it true that real CQRS requires the use of a serverless cloud infrastructure?

Further reading

Here are a few links that will help you build on what you learned in this chapter:

- Event Sourcing pattern by Martin Fowler: `https://adpg.link/oY5H`
- Event Sourcing pattern by Microsoft: `https://adpg.link/ofG2`
- Publisher-Subscriber pattern by Microsoft: `https://adpg.link/amcZ`
- Event-driven architecture by Microsoft: `https://adpg.link/rnck`
- Microservices architecture and patterns on microservices.io: `https://adpg.link/41vP`
- Microservices architecture and patterns by Martin Fowler: `https://adpg.link/Mw97`
- Microservices architecture and patterns by Microsoft: `https://adpg.link/s2Uq`
- RFC 6902 (JSON Patch): `https://adpg.link/bGGn`
- JSON Patch in ASP.NET Core web API: `https://adpg.link/u6dw`

Strangler Fig Application pattern:

- Martin Fowler: `https://adpg.link/Zi9G`
- Microsoft: `https://adpg.link/erg2`

Section 5: Designing the Client Side

In this section, we explore the options given by ASP.NET Core to build user interfaces, the client-side aspect of our programs. We dig into the possibilities provided by ASP.NET Core Razor Pages and multiple ways to divide our UIs into smaller, easier-to-reuse components. Finally, we cover a type-oriented way to build complex UIs. Most content applies to both Razor Pages and MVC.

Afterward, we move on to Blazor, enabling us to build full-stack .NET programs. We quickly explore Blazor Server and dig into Blazor WebAssembly, a .NET SPA framework. We explore different ways to create Razor components, and we explore the Model-View-Update (MVU) pattern. We complete the section with a medley of Blazor features that I cannot cover in more detail in the book, but I give you an outline and many pointers to help you start your Blazor journey.

This section comprises the following chapters:

- *Chapter 17, ASP.NET Core User Interfaces*
- *Chapter 18, A Brief Look into Blazor*

17

ASP.NET Core User Interfaces

This chapter explores different ways to create user interfaces using ASP.NET Core and its extensive offerings. As macro-models, we have MVC, Razor Pages, and Blazor (*Chapter 18, A Brief Look into Blazor*). Then to micro-manage our UIs, we have partial views, view components, Tag Helpers, display templates, editor templates, and Razor components.

Furthermore, the .NET ecosystem includes other non-web technologies to build UIs, such as WinForms, WPF, UWP, and Xamarin. This chapter aims to give you a good understanding of the numerous ASP.NET Core options by exploring the tools you have at your disposal when programming web user interfaces to make your life easier.

Tip

Knowing many options is often better than being an expert in only one area because you can pick the right tool at the right time instead of systematically doing the same thing every time.

The following topics are covered in this chapter:

- Getting familiar with Razor Pages
- Organizing the user interface
- Display and Editor Templates

Getting familiar with Razor Pages

As its name implies, Razor Pages is a server-side way of rendering web content organized into pages. That applies very well to the web, as people visit pages, not controllers. Razor Pages shares many components with MVC under the hood.

If you want to know if using MVC or Razor Pages is best for your project, ask yourself if organizing your project into pages would be more suitable for your scenario. If yes, go with Razor Pages; otherwise, pick something else, such as MVC or a **single-page application** (SPA).

If the solution is still unclear, we can also use both Razor Pages and MVC in the same application, so there is no need to choose only one. You can, for example, create Razor Pages for some part of your system, use MVC for CRUD modules (Create-Read-Update-Delete), and even add some APIs consumed by your client-side code. This is one of the powerful features of the ASP.NET Core opt-in offering: you enable what you need.

To create a Razor Pages project, we can use the `webapp` project template using the CLI, like this:

```
dotnet new webapp
```

Using Razor Pages is very similar to MVC. In the `Program.cs` file, instead of `builder.Services.AddControllersWithViews()` or `builder.Services.AddControllers()`, we can call the `builder.Services.AddRazorPages()` extension method.

The same applies to the `Startup.Configure` method where we must map Razor Pages routes using the `endpoints.MapRazorPages();` method.

The use of the other middlewares is the same. Here is an example of `Program.cs`:

```
var builder = WebApplication.CreateBuilder(args);

// Add services to the container.
builder.Services.AddRazorPages();

var app = builder.Build();
// Configure the HTTP request pipeline.
if (!app.Environment.IsDevelopment())
{
    app.UseExceptionHandler("/Error");
    // The default HSTS value is 30 days. You may want to change this for
production scenarios, see https://aka.ms/aspnetcore-hsts.
    app.UseHsts();
}

app.UseHttpsRedirection();
app.UseStaticFiles();
app.UseRouting();
app.UseAuthorization();
app.MapRazorPages();
app.Run();
```

ASP.NET handles the routing and the model binding for us with the two highlighted lines, as with MVC.

Design

Each page can handle one or more GET or POST methods. The idea is that each page is self-sufficient (following the SRP). To get started, a page consists of two parts: a view and a model. The model must inherit from PageModel. The view must use the @model directive to link to its page model, and the @ page directive tells ASP.NET that it is a Razor page, not just an MVC view.

Here is a visual representation of that relationship:

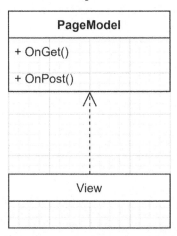

Figure 17.1: Diagram representing a Razor page

Here is an example that I scaffolded using Visual Studio. The @page and @model directives are highlighted in the following snippet, taken from the Pages\Employees\Create.cshtml file:

```
@page
@model PageController.Pages.Employees.CreateModel
@{
    ViewData["Title"] = "Create";
}
<h1>Create</h1>
<h4>Employee</h4>
<hr />
<div class="row">
    div class="col-md-4">
        <form method="post">
            <div asp-validation-summary="ModelOnly" class="text-danger"></div>
            <div class="form-group">
                <label asp-for="Employee.FirstName" class="control-label"></
label>
                <input asp-for="Employee.FirstName" class="form-control" />
```

```
                    <span asp-validation-for="Employee.FirstName" class="text-
danger"></span>
            </div>
            <div class="form-group">
                <label asp-for="Employee.LastName" class="control-label"></
label>
                <input asp-for="Employee.LastName" class="form-control" />
                <span asp-validation-for="Employee.LastName" class="text-
danger"></span>
            </div>
            <div class="form-group">
                <input type="submit" value="Create" class="btn btn-primary" />
            </div>
        </form>
    </div>
</div>
<div>
    <a asp-page="Index">Back to List</a>
</div>
@section Scripts {
    @{await Html.RenderPartialAsync ("_ValidationScriptsPartial");}
}
```

Next is PageModel, taken from the Pages\Employees\Create.cshtml.cs file, which we discuss here:

```
namespace PageController.Pages.Employees
{
    public class CreateModel : PageModel
    {
        private readonly EmployeeDbContext _context;
        public CreateModel(EmployeeDbContext context)
        {
            _context = context;
        }
        public IActionResult OnGet()
        {
            return Page();
        }
        [BindProperty]
        public Employee Employee { get; set; }
        public async Task<IActionResult> OnPostAsync()
        {
```

```
                    if (!ModelState.IsValid)
                    {
                        return Page();
                    }
                    _context.Employees.Add(Employee);
                    await _context.SaveChangesAsync();
                    return RedirectToPage("./Index");
                }
            }
        }
```

From that code, we can see both parts: the view and the model. In the PageModel code, the [BindProperty] attribute is what tells ASP.NET to bind the form post to the Employee property. That's the equivalent of an MVC action that looks like this:

```
[HttpPost]
public Task<IActionResult> MyAction([FromForm] Employee employee) {…}
```

Visually, a user requesting a page would look like this:

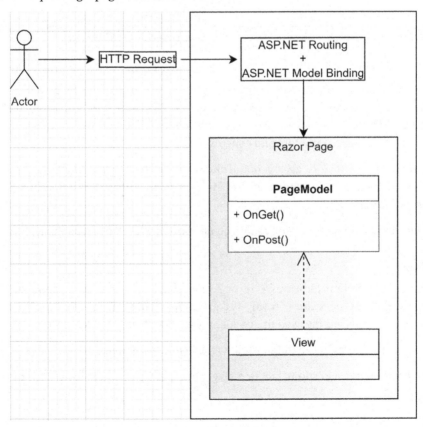

Figure 17.2: User requesting a page

By default, pages live under the Pages directory instead of the Views directory. The layout mechanism of MVC is also available with Razor Pages. The default layout is in the Pages/Shared/_Layout.cshtml file; the Pages/_ViewStart.cshtml and Pages/_ViewImports.cshtml files play the same role as their MVC equivalent, but for Razor Pages.

Routing

In MVC, we can control the routing by creating global route patterns or with attributes. In Razor Pages, we can also control those routes. By default, the routing system automatically creates routes based on the filesystem, making it faster to get started. We must include the @page directive at the top of the page to use automatic routing, and ASP.NET Core does the magic for us.

The routing system used by Razor Pages is simple yet powerful. The default pattern is the page's location without the Pages folder and the .cshtml extension with the Index.cshtml pages being optional (like the Index view of MVC). Instead of endless explanations, let's look at some examples:

Razor page file location	URL/Route
/Pages/Index.cshtml	/ or /index
/Pages/Contact.cshtml	/contact
/Pages/Employees/Index.cshtml	/employees or /employees/index
/Pages/Employees/Details.cshtml	/employees/details

In Razor Pages, the routing system chooses the page to be displayed based on the URL.

We can also replace those defaults with custom routes. The way to replace the default route of a page is by providing a route template after the @page directive, such as @page "/some-route". That page now handles the /some-route URL instead of the default one. The template supports the same MVC routes patterns, including parameters and constraints.

Covering every aspect of Razor Pages is out of the scope of the current book, but I encourage you to dig deeper into that way of building websites and web applications. It is enjoyable, powerful, and sometimes simpler than MVC.

However, Razor Pages might not be for you if you need other HTTP methods than GET and POST.

Conclusion

Razor Pages is an excellent alternative to organize your website or web application by pages instead of controllers. Many features from MVC are supported, such as validation (ModelState and ValidationSummary), the routing system, model binding, Tag Helpers, and more.

Now let's see how Razor Pages can help us follow the **SOLID** principles:

- S: Each PageModel is responsible for a single page, an essential point of Razor Pages.
- O: N/A
- L: N/A

- **I:** N/A
- **D:** N/A

The single-responsibility principle

One could see the "single responsibility" of a Razor page as multiple responsibilities. It handles both reads and writes, the page model, HTTP requests, and could play with the HTTP response.

Keep in mind that the goal of a Razor page is to manage a page, which is a single responsibility, which does not have to translate into a single operation. That said, if you think there is too much code in one of your Razor pages, there are ways to help diminish that burden by extracting and delegating part of those responsibilities to other components, leaving the **PageModel** with fewer responsibilities and less code. For example, you could leverage Vertical Slice Architecture, Clean Architecture, or any other architectural style that fits your needs.

Now that we know about Razor Pages and MVC, it is time to explore the options that ASP.NET Core offers to us to organize our UIs.

Want to know more?

Pattern-wise, we could see a Razor page as a simplified **Page Controller.** That pattern is covered in Martin Fowler's 2002 book **Patterns of Enterprise Application Architecture (PoEAA)** and is partially available online (see the *Further reading* section for more information). Why simplified? Because ASP.NET does most of the **Page Controller** work for us, leaving us only the **model** (domain logic) and the **view** to implement. Knowing about the Page Controller pattern is not necessary to work with Razor Pages.

Organizing the user interface

In this section, we will explore three options:

- **Partial views** to encapsulate reusable UI parts.
- **Tag Helpers,** which enable us to write HTML-like Razor code instead of a C#-like syntax.
- **View components,** which allow encapsulating logic with one or more views to create reusable components.

Keep in mind that we can use these options in both MVC and Razor Pages.

Partial views

A partial view is a part of a view created in a `cshtml` file, a Razor file. The content (markup) of the partial view is rendered at the location it was included by the `<partial>` Tag Helper or the `@Html.PartialAsync()` method. ASP.NET introduced the concept in MVC, hence the view. For Razor Pages, you could see partial views as partial pages.

We can place partial view files almost anywhere in our projects, but I'd suggest keeping them close to the views that use them (in the same folder, for example). You can also keep them in the Shared folder. As a rule of thumb, the filename of a partial view begins with _, like _CreateOrEditForm.cshtml.

Partial views are good at simplifying complex views and reusing part of the UI in multiple other views. Here is an example that helps simplify the _Layout.cshtml file:

```
<div class="container">
    @Html.PartialAsync("_CookieConsentPartial")
    <partial name="_CookieConsentPartial" />
    <main role="main" class="pb-3">
    @RenderBody()
  </main>
</div>
```

The two highlighted lines are doing the same thing, so only one is needed. They are the two code styles to load partial views; pick the one you prefer. This example inserts the content of the Pages/Shared/_CookieConsentPartial.cshtml file at that location in the page. Partial views are very similar to the good old **includes** from ASP and PHP, but they don't have direct access to the caller's scope (a very good thing).

By default, the current value of the Model property is sent to the partial view, but it is possible to send a different model, like this:

```
@{
    var myModel = "My Model";
}
@Html.PartialAsync("_SomePartialView", myModel)
<partial name="_SomePartialView" model="myModel" />
```

In this case, myModel is a string, but it could also be an object of any type.

Partial views are more robust than the **includes** were, with added flexibility. Let's now dig into some code.

Project – Shared form

One of the possibilities of partial views is to share presentation code. The create and edit forms are often very similar in a CRUD project, so we can leverage partial views to simplify such duplication maintenance. This is similar to the project implemented in *Chapter 4, The MVC Pattern Using Razor*, but using Razor Pages instead of MVC.

The initial Razor code for this project has been scaffolded by Visual Studio, based on the Employee class below:

```
namespace PageController.Data.Models
{
```

```
    public class Employee
    {
        public int Id { get; set; }
        [Required]
        [StringLength(50)]
        public string? FirstName { get; set; }
        [Required]
        [StringLength(50)]
        public string? LastName { get; set; }
    }
}
```

Next, we explore a way to centralize the form shared by both pages to enhance our module's maintainability. First, we must extract the shared portion of CreateModel and EditModel so the form can use it. The ICreateOrEditModel interface contains that shared contract, taken from the Pages/Employees/ICreateOrEditModel.cs file:

```
public interface ICreateOrEditModel
{
    Employee Employee { get; set; }
}
```

Then both CreateModel and EditModel must implement it:

```
// From Pages/Employees/Create.cshtml.cs
public class CreateModel : PageModel, ICreateOrEditModel
{
    ...
    [BindProperty]
    public Employee Employee { get; set; }
    ...
}
// From Pages/Employees/Edit.cshtml.cs
public class EditModel : PageModel, ICreateOrEditModel
{
    ...
    [BindProperty]
    public Employee Employee { get; set; }
    ...
}
```

Then we can isolate the shared portion of the forms and move that to the `_Form.cshtml` partial view (you can name it as you want):

Pages/Employees/_Form.cshtml

```
@model ICreateOrEditModel
<div class="form-group">
    <label asp-for="Employee.FirstName" class="control-label"></label>
    <input asp-for="Employee.FirstName" class="form-control" />
    <span asp-validation-for="Employee.FirstName" class="text-danger"></span>
</div>
<div class="form-group">
    <label asp-for="Employee.LastName" class="control-label"></label>
    <input asp-for="Employee.LastName" class="form-control" />
    <span asp-validation-for="Employee.LastName" class="text-danger"></span>
</div>
```

In the preceding code, we are using the `ICreateOrEditModel` interface as the `@model` to access the `Employee` property of both the create and edit page models. Then we can include that partial view in both of our create and edit pages:

Pages/Employees/Create.cshtml

```
@page
@model PageController.Pages.Employees.CreateModel
...
<div class="row">
    <div class="col-md-4">
        <form method="post">
            <div asp-validation-summary="ModelOnly" class="text-danger"></div>
            <partial name="_Form" />
            <div class="form-group">
                <input type="submit" value="Create" class="btn btn-primary" />
            </div>
        </form>
    </div>
</div>
```

Pages/Employees/Edit.cshtml

```
@page
@model PageController.Pages.Employees.EditModel
...
<div class="row">
    <div class="col-md-4">
```

```
            <form method="post">
                <input type="hidden" asp-for="Employee.Id" />
                <div asp-validation-summary="ModelOnly" class="text-danger"></div>
                <partial name="_Form" />
                <div class="form-group">
                    <input type="submit" value="Save" class="btn btn-primary" />
                </div>
            </form>
        </div>
    </div>
```

With that in place, we have one form to maintain and two pages that do different things. In this case, the form is trivial, but that could save us a lot of time for more substantial entities.

Beware that complex logic within a partial view can become more problematic than the time saved by having it. If you see the amount of conditional code grow in a partial view, I'd recommend investigating whether another technique/pattern would be better. Getting rid of the partial view or creating multiple partial views used in fewer places could also be solutions. Sometimes we think that sharing is a good idea, but it turns out it is not. When that happens, admit your failure, then fix the problem.

Conclusion

Partial views are a great way to reuse parts of a UI or divide a complex page into smaller, more manageable elements. Partial views are the most basic way of encapsulating chunks of UI. Use them when the display logic is limited; we explore other options in the following subsections for more advanced use cases.

Now let's see how partial views can help us follow the **SOLID** principles:

- S: Extracting manageable parts of the UI into partial views can lead to the encapsulation of component-like views with each managing a single display responsibility.
- O: N/A
- L: N/A
- I: N/A
- D: N/A

Next, we explore other ways to divide our complex views into smaller pieces by digging into the built-in tag helpers and how to create custom ones.

Tag Helpers

Tag Helpers are server-side helpers allowing developers to write more HTML-like code in Razor views, reducing the amount of C#-like code mixed into the view. We used Tag Helpers in the last example, maybe without knowing it.

Let's start by having a second look at the `Pages/Employees/_Form.cshtml` file:

```
@model ICreateOrEditModel
<div class="form-group">
    <label asp-for="Employee.FirstName" class="control-label"></label>
    <input asp-for="Employee.FirstName" class="form-control" />
    <span asp-validation-for="Employee.FirstName" class="text-danger"></span>
</div>
<div class="form-group">
    <label asp-for="Employee.LastName" class="control-label"></label>
    <input asp-for="Employee.LastName" class="form-control" />
    <span asp-validation-for="Employee.LastName" class="text-danger"></span>
</div>
```

In that partial view, we used built-in ASP.NET Tag Helpers to enhance the HTML `label`, `input`, and `span` tags. When rendered to HTML, the Tag Helpers' properties add additional HTML capabilities, like HTML attributes and validation support. The `asp-*` attributes are used to set the values of certain built-in Tag Helpers' properties.

For example, the **Label Tag Helper** generates the value of the HTML `for` attribute automatically, based on its `asp-for` attribute. Moreover, it generates the text of the label based on the property name or its `[Display(Name = "Custom name")]` attribute if the model property was decorated by one.

The Anchor Tag Helper (`<a>`) is incredibly convenient to set the `class` attribute without an anonymous object, and an escape character (if you've used HTML helpers before, you'll know what I mean).

To get the same output using HTML helpers, let's look at the partial view `Pages/Employees/_Form-HtmlHelpers.cshtml`:

```
@model ICreateOrEditModel
<div class="form-group">
    @Html.LabelFor(x => x.Employee.FirstName, new { @class = "control-label" })
    @Html.TextBoxFor(x => x.Employee.FirstName, new { @class = "form-control"
})
    @Html.ValidationMessageFor(x => x.Employee.FirstName, null, new { @class =
"text-danger" })
</div>
<div class="form-group">
    @Html.LabelFor(x => x.Employee.LastName, new { @class = "control-label" })
    @Html.TextBoxFor(x => x.Employee.LastName, new { @class = "form-control" })
    @Html.ValidationMessageFor(x => x.Employee.LastName, null, new { @class =
"text-danger" })
</div>
```

In both cases, the `FirstName` form-group is rendered as the following HTML:

```html
<div class="form-group">
    <label class="control-label" for="Employee_FirstName">FirstName</label>
    <input class="form-control valid" type="text" data-val="true" data-val-
length="The field FirstName must be a string with a maximum length of 50."
data-val-length-max="50" data-val-required="The FirstName field is required."
id="Employee_FirstName" maxlength="50" name="Employee.FirstName" value="Bob"
aria-describedby="Employee_FirstName-error" aria-invalid="false">
    <span class="text-danger field-validation-valid" data-valmsg-for="Employee.
FirstName" data-valmsg-replace="true"></span>
</div>
```

I find the use of Tag Helpers more elegant than the old HTML helpers (C#), but that's my personal preference. Nevertheless, we can choose and mix both options.

Built-in Tag Helpers

There are many built-in Tag Helpers in ASP.NET Core. Some can help load different elements depending on the environment (production or development); others help build the `href` attribute of the `<a>` tag; and more.

Let's have a quick overview of the options available. If you want to learn more afterward, the official documentation is getting better and better since Microsoft open-sourced it. I've added a few links in the *Further reading* section at the end of the chapter. Afterward, we will explore how to create custom Tag Helpers.

The Anchor Tag Helper

The Anchor Tag Helper enhances the `<a>` tag to generate the `href` attribute based on a controller action or a Razor page.

Here are a few examples for Razor Pages:

Tag	href value
`<a asp-page="/Index">...</a>`	`/`
`<a asp-page="/Employees/Index">...</a>`	`/Employees`
`<a asp-page="/Employees/Create">...</a>`	`/Employees/Create`
`<a asp-page="./Edit" asp-route-id="@item.Id">...</a>`	`/Employees/Edit/{item.Id}`

It is similar for MVC controllers:

Tag	href value
`<a asp-controller="Home" asp-action="Index">...</a>`	`/`
`<a asp-controller="Employees" asp-action="Index">...</a>`	`/Employees`
`<a asp-controller="Employees" asp-action="Create">...</a>`	`/Employees/Create`

`<a asp-controller="Employees" asp-action="Edit" asp-route-id="@item.Id">...</a>`	`/Employees/Edit/{item.Id}`

The Anchor Tag Helper is very useful in creating links that look like HTML in Razor. The `asp-route-id` attribute is a little different than the others. The `asp-route-*` attributes allow specifying the value for a parameter, such as id. So if the `GET` action looks like this:

```
[HttpGet]
public IActionResult Details(int something){ ... }
```

You would need a link that specifies the `something` parameter, which could be declared like this:

```
<a asp-controller="Employees" asp-action="Details" asp-route-
something="123">...</a>
```

There are many more options behind this Tag Helper that we are not covering here, but with what we did, you know that you can leverage ASP.NET to generate links based on pages and controllers.

The Link Tag Helper

The Link Tag Helper allows you to define a fallback CSS `href` in case the primary one does not load (that is, if the CDN is down). Here is an example:

```
<link rel="stylesheet" href="https://cdnjs.cloudflare.com/ajax/libs/twitter-
bootstrap/4.1.3/css/bootstrap.min.css"
    asp-fallback-href="~/lib/bootstrap/dist/css/bootstrap.min.css"
    asp-fallback-test-class="sr-only"
    asp-fallback-test-property="position"
    asp-fallback-test-value="absolute"
    crossorigin="anonymous"
    integrity="sha256-eSi1q2PG6J7g7ib17yAaWMcrr5GrtohYChqibrV7PBE=" />
```

ASP.NET renders the required HTML and JavaScript to test if the CSS was loaded, based on the specified `asp-fallback-test-*` attributes. If it was not, it swaps it for the one specified in the `asp-fallback-href` attribute.

The Script Tag Helper

The Script Tag Helper allows you to define a fallback JavaScript file in case the primary one does not load (that is, if the CDN is down). Here is an example:

```
<script src="https://cdnjs.cloudflare.com/ajax/libs/twitter-bootstrap/4.1.3/js/
bootstrap.bundle.min.js"
    asp-fallback-src="~/lib/bootstrap/dist/js/bootstrap.bundle.min.js"
    asp-fallback-test="window.jQuery && window.jQuery.fn && window.jQuery.
fn.modal"
    crossorigin="anonymous"
    integrity="sha256-E/V4cWE4qvAeO5MOhjtGtqDzPndRO1LBk8lJ/PR7CA4=">
</script>
```

ASP.NET renders the required HTML and JavaScript to test if the script was loaded based on the specified `asp-fallback-test` attribute. If the script does not load, the browser swaps the source for the one specified in the `asp-fallback-href` attribute. This is the equivalent of the `<link>` tag but for `<script>` tags.

The Environment Tag Helper

The Environment Tag Helper allows rendering certain parts of the UI only for specific environments. For example, you could render some debugging information only when in `Development`.

The Environment Tag Helper is also a good complement to the `<link>` and `<script>` Tag Helpers, allowing us to load local non-minified scripts when developing and CDN-hosted minified files in production.

We can define what environment to target by including or excluding environments using the `include` and `exclude` attributes, respectively. The value of those attributes can be a single environment name or a comma-separated list. Here are some examples:

```
<environment include="Development">
    <div>Development Content.</div>
</environment>
```

The preceding snippet displays the `<div>` only when the environment is `Development`.

```
<environment exclude="Development">
    <div>Content not to display in Development.</div>
</environment>
```

The preceding snippet displays the `<div>` for all environments but `Development`.

```
<environment include="Staging,Production">
    <div>Staging and Production content.</div>
</environment>
```

The preceding snippet displays the `<div>` only for the `Staging` and `Production` environments.

```
<environment exclude="Staging,Production">
    <div>Content not to display in Staging nor Production.</div>
</environment>
```

The preceding snippet displays the `<div>` for all environments but `Staging` and `Production`.

The Caching Tag Helpers

ASP.NET Core also provides the following caching-related Tag Helpers:

- The Cache Tag Helper
- The Distributed Cache Tag Helper
- The Image Tag Helper

The **Cache Tag Helper** allows caching part of a view for 20 minutes, by default, and leverages the ASP.NET Core cache provider mechanism. A basic example could be caching a random number like this:

```
<cache>@(new Random().Next())</cache>
```

Multiple attributes can also be set to control how the cache is invalidated and what it targets. We could want to cache the greeting to a user, for example, but if we write the following, all users would see the greeting of the first user to trigger the cache:

```
<cache>Hello @this.User.Identity.Name!</cache>
```

To fix that issue, we can set the `vary-by-user` attribute to `true`:

```
<cache vary-by-user="true">
    Hello @this.User.Identity.Name!
</cache>
```

Multiple other `vary-by-*` attributes can be used in other cases, such as `vary-by-header`, `vary-by-query`, `vary-by-route`, and `vary-by-cookie`.

To control how the cache is invalidated, we can set the `expires-on` attribute to a `DateTime` object or the `expires-after` or `expires-sliding` attributes to a `TimeSpan` object.

If that is not enough, ASP.NET Core also provides a **Distributed Cache Tag Helper** that leverages the `IDistributedCache` implementation that you register. You must configure the distributed cache provider in the `Startup` class, or the Tag Helper will use the in-memory provider. You must also specify a unique key for each element by setting the `name` attribute. The other attributes are the same as the Cache Tag Helper.

The last cache-related Tag Helper is the **Image Tag Helper**. That Tag Helper allows invalidating images when they change. To do that, ASP.NET appends a version to its enhanced `<img>` tags that get invalidated when the file changes.

> **Note**
>
> One caching mechanism of web clients (like a browser) is to cache resources (like images), so they don't download them from the server with every request, leading to a faster web browsing experience. The Image Tag Helper generates a string based on the image itself and appends it as a query string. When the image changes, ASP.NET Core sends a new string representing the latest version of the image to the client, forcing the client to redownload it. The client uses the cached image as long as the image does not change and the cache is not expired. This technique is a good way to force invalidating cached resources.

Since the **Image Tag Helper** enhances the `<img>` tag, there is no new tag here. To use this functionality, you must set an `asp-append-version` attribute to `true` on an `<img>` tag that has an `src` attribute like this:

```
<img src="~/images/some-picture.jpg" asp-append-version="true">
```

Here is an example of the generated HTML, where the string `TKD5TTR1kXQlmE53RcZCqbCQ34tLDrRwe` `cFcA3mkrAQ` is the version number generated by the Image Tag Helper:

```
<img src="/images/NetCoreLogo.
png?v=TKD5TTR1kXQlmE53RcZCqbCQ34tLDrRwecFcA3mkrAQ">
```

While using one or more of those three Tag Helpers, it is easier than ever to cache part of your views, but caching is a subject of its own that I prefer not to dig too deeply into here.

The Form Tag Helpers

ASP.NET Core provides multiple Tag Helpers when the time comes to create forms. Since forms are the way to gather user inputs, they are quite essential. Here, we cover the **Form Tag Helper** first, which extends the `<form>` HTML tag.

Its first advantage is the automatic rendering of an `input[name="__RequestVerificationToken"]` element to prevent **cross-site request forgery** (CSRF or XSRF). **Razor Pages does the verification automatically**, but **MVC does not**. To enable XSRF/CSRF protection when using MVC, we need to decorate the action or the controller with the `[ValidateAntiForgeryToken]` attribute.

The second advantage is to help with routing. The Form Tag Helper exposes the same attributes as the Anchor Tag Helper when routing time comes, like the `asp-controller`, `asp-action`, `asp-page`, and `asp-route-*` attributes.

To submit the form, you can proceed like any normal HTML `<form>` tag: with a `button[type="submit"]` or an `input[type="submit"]`. We can also set different actions on different buttons by using the same routing attributes.

Next, let's explore the **Input Tag Helper** that we saw earlier. The key attribute of the Input Tag Helper is `asp-for`. When setting it to a property of the view's model, ASP.NET automatically generates the name of the `<input>` tag, its value, the validation information, the id, and the type of that input. For example, a `bool` is rendered as `input[type=checkbox]` while a `string` is rendered as `input[type=text]`. We can decorate our view models with data annotations to control the type of input to be generated, like `[EmailAddress]`, `[Url]`, or `[DataType(DataType.*)]`.

Tip

When you have a property on your model representing a collection, you should use a `for` loop (not a `foreach`) to generate your form. Otherwise, in many cases, ASP.NET Core will not render the elements correctly, and you will receive a `null` value for those fields on the server after posting the form. Here is an example that works:

```
@for (var i = 0; i < Model.Destinations.Count; i++)
{
    <input type="text" asp-for="@destinations[i].Name"
class="control-label"></label>
    <input type="text" asp-for="@destinations[i].Name"
class="form-control" />
}
```

Another advantage of Tag Helpers that enhance HTML tags is that all standard HTML attributes are usable. So when you want to create an input[type=hidden] for the Id property of the model being edited, you can set the type attribute directly and override the defaults, like this:

```
<input type="hidden" asp-for="Employee.Id" />
```

We then have the **Textarea Tag Helper**, which generates a <textarea> tag like this:

```
<textarea asp-for="Employee.Description"></textarea>
```

Then comes the **Label Tag Helper**, which helps render <label> tags, like this:

```
<label asp-for="Employee.Description"></label>
```

Finally, the **Select Tag Helper** helps render <select> tags using the values specified in its asp-items attribute. The items must be an IEnumerable<SelectListItem> collection. The asp-for attribute serves the same purpose as the other Tag Helpers. Here is an example of a manually generated list of items bound to the SomeProperty property of the Model:

```
@{
    var items = new[]
    {
        new SelectListItem("Make a selection", ""),
        new SelectListItem("Choice 1", "1"),
        new SelectListItem("Choice 2", "2"),
        new SelectListItem("Choice 3", "3"),
    };
}
<select asp-items="items" asp-for="SomeProperty"></select>
```

Tip: ENUM

You can use the Html.GetEnumSelectList<TEnum>() method to generate the list from an enum, where TEnum is the type of your enum. The generated <option> tags will have a numerical value equal to the value of the enum element and its text set to the textual representation of the enum element, like <option value="2">SecondOption</option>.

To customize the text of each option, you can decorate your enum members with attributes, like the [Display(Name = "Second option")] attribute, which would render <option value="2">Second option</option> instead, improving readability. Here's an example:

```
public enum MyEnum {
    [Display(Name = "Second option")]
    SecondOption = 2
}
```

To conclude this subsection, we have two more form-related Tag Helpers to cover, the **Validation Message Tag Helper** and the **Validation Summary Tag Helper**. They exist to help validate form inputs on the client side.

The Validation Summary Tag Helper is used to display the list of error messages of the `ModelState` property (`ModelStateDictionary`). That property is accessible in most MVC and Razor Pages-related base classes, such as `PageModel`, `PageBase`, `ControllerBase`, and `ActionContext` (accessible from `RazorPageBase.ViewContext` in an MVC view). The following code creates a validation summary:

```
<div asp-validation-summary="ModelOnly" class="text-danger"></div>
```

The value of the `asp-validation-summary` attribute can be `None`, `ModelOnly`, or `All`:

- `None` means that no summary will be displayed.
- `ModelOnly` means that only errors not related to the model's properties will be displayed in the validation summary (the name is counter-intuitive if you ask me).
- `All` means that all errors, including property errors, will be displayed in the validation summary.

If you are using the Validation Message Tag Helper for your properties, I'd recommend setting that value to `ModelOnly`, which will allow sending custom validation messages from your page or action without duplicating the messages of the model's properties on the page.

The Validation Message Tag Helpers allow us to display the error message of a single property. Usually, these are displayed close to the element they represent, but they don't have to be. Here is an example:

```
<span asp-validation-for="Employee.FirstName" class="text-danger"></span>
```

The `asp-validation-for` attribute acts as the `asp-for` attribute but tells the element that it is for validation purposes instead of creating a form input. If the property (in this case, `Employee.FirstName`) is not valid, the error message is displayed; otherwise, it is not.

`class="text-danger"` is a Bootstrap class that sets the text to a red color.

If we take a look again at the previous section's example, we will see that the following Razor code (first block) is rendered to the following HTML code (second block), with the Razor code highlights being translated to the HTML code highlights:

```
<div class="form-group">
    <label asp-for="Employee.FirstName" class="control-label"></label>
    <input asp-for="Employee.FirstName" class="form-control" />
    <span asp-validation-for="Employee.FirstName" class="text-danger"></span>
</div>
<div class="form-group">
    <label class="control-label" for="Employee_FirstName">FirstName</label>
    <input class="form-control" type="text" data-val="true" data-val-
length="The field FirstName must be a string with a maximum length of 50."
data-val-length-max="50" data-val-required="The FirstName field is required."
id="Employee_FirstName" maxlength="50" name="Employee.FirstName" value="">
```

```
      <span class="text-danger field-validation-valid" data-valmsg-for="Employee.
    FirstName" data-valmsg-replace="true"></span>
    </div>
```

The validation attributes (data-val-length, data-val-length-max, data-val-required, and maxlength) and the type attribute come from the Employee.FirstName property, which is defined as follows:

```
[Required]
[StringLength(50)]
public string FirstName { get; set; }
```

To conclude, the Form Tag Helpers provided by ASP.NET Core are very handy at crafting readable forms, fast, and packed with functionalities.

The Partial Tag Helper

We already used the Partial Tag Helper in the previous subsection about partial views, but here are a few more use cases. The most trivial one involves setting only the name attribute as we did before:

```
<partial name="_Form" />
```

We can also specify a path instead of a name, like this:

```
<partial name="Employees/_PieceOfUI" />
```

That would load the _PieceOfUI.cshtml partial view from one of the following three files: /Pages/Employees/_PieceOfUI.cshtml, /Pages/Shared/Employees/_PieceOfUI.cshtml, or /Views/Shared/Employees/_PieceOfUI.cshtml.

We can also pass a custom model to a partial view using the model attribute. Let's start with the model defined in the Pages/Employees/PieceOfUIViewModel.cs file:

```
public record PieceOfUIViewModel(bool GenerateRandomNumber);
```

The PieceOfUIViewModel record class is a view model that we pass to the PieceOfUI partial view as follows. Records are a new C# 9 feature (see *Appendix A* for more info). For now, think of PieceOfUIViewModel as a class with a read-only property named GenerateRandomNumber.

Here is the partial view that renders that model, taken from the Pages/Employees/_PieceOfUI.cshtml file:

```
@model PieceOfUIViewModel
Piece of UI
@if (Model.GenerateRandomNumber) {
    <text>| </text>
    @(new Random().Next())
}
```

We render the preceding partial view in the next block, taken from the `Pages/Shared/_Layout.cshtml` file:

```
@using PageController.Pages.Employees
…
<partial name="Employees/_PieceOfUI" model="new PieceOfUIViewModel(true)" />
…
```

In that example, we pass an instance of `PieceOfUIViewModel` to the partial view, which in turn renders a random number or not (`true` or `false`), depending on the value of the `GenerateRandomNumber` property.

The `for` attribute of the Partial Tag Helper allows similar behavior but through the model of the current view itself. If we go back to our shared form but create a new partial view **without the need to implement any interface**, we could end up with the following code instead, taken from the `_FormFor.cshtml` file:

```
@using PageController.Data.Models
@model Employee
<div class="form-group">
    <label asp-for="FirstName" class="control-label"></label>
    <input asp-for="FirstName" class="form-control" />
    <span asp-validation-for="FirstName" class="text-danger"></span>
</div>
<div class="form-group">
    <label asp-for="LastName" class="control-label"></label>
    <input asp-for="LastName" class="form-control" />
    <span asp-validation-for="LastName" class="text-danger"></span>
</div>
```

In the preceding code, the highlighted lines represent the generation of the HTML markup based on that partial view model. That enables us to leverage the Partial Tag Helper for the attribute's capabilities. Here is the code that both the `Create` and `Edit` views should use to load the partial view and leverage this feature:

```
…
<partial name="_FormFor" for="Employee" />
…
```

Even if the partial view (`_FormFor.cshtml`) is unaware of the `Employee` property on the original `Model`, it still renders the same form because the `for` attribute preserved that context for us. Next is the generated first name field, with the validation data omitted to improve readability where we can see from the highlighted lines that Razor knew about the `Employee` property of the model even if the partial view did not:

```
<input class="form-control" type="text" id="Employee_FirstName" maxlength="50"
name="Employee.FirstName" value="">
```

One last attribute is `view-data`, allowing us to pass a `ViewDataDictionary` instance to the partial view. I recommend sticking with fully typed objects instead of playing with dictionaries and magic strings, but if you need it one day for some obscure cases, well, you know that the attribute exists.

The Component Tag Helper

The **Component Tag Helper** is used to render **Razor components** into an MVC or Razor Pages application. We explore Razor components in *Chapter 18, A Brief Look into Blazor,* and briefly explore this Tag Helper as well.

Creating a custom Tag Helper

Now that we've sprinted through the built-in Tag Helpers, we can also create our own quite easily. We have two options; we can extend an existing tag or create a new tag.

In this example, we are creating the `<pluralize>` tag. The objective behind it is to replace code like this:

```
<p class="card-text">
    @Model.Count
    @(Model.Count > 1 ? "Employees" : "Employee")
</p>
```

With code like this:

```
<p class="card-text">
    <pluralize count="Model.Count" singular="{0} Employee" plural="{0}
Employees" />
</p>
```

There is less context-switching with that code than with the first block as the whole block looks like HTML now.

> **Side effect**
>
> It would also be easier to localize a UI built using the `<pluralize>` Tag Helper than a UI filled with tertiary operators. As a quick change, we could inject `IStringLocalizer<T>` into our `PluralizeTagHelper` class to localize the content of the `Singular` or `Plural` property before formatting it using `string.Format()`.
>
> Don't get me wrong here: I'm not telling you to stop writing C# into your views; I'm just pointing out another possible advantage of this versus using plain C#.

For that component, we need to create a `PluralizeTagHelper` class that we save into the `TagHelpers` directory. A Tag Helper must implement the `ITagHelper` interface but can also inherit from the `TagHelper` class. We are opting for the `TagHelper` class, which exposes a synchronous `Process` method that we can use.

Note

The TagHelper class does nothing more than add the Process method to override and a default empty implementation of the ITagHelper interface.

The PluralizeTagHelper class that we are programming looks like this:

```
namespace PageController.TagHelpers
{
[HtmlTargetElement("pluralize", TagStructure = TagStructure.WithoutEndTag)]
```

This attribute tells Razor that we're extending the <pluralize> tag and that we can omit the end tag and write it like <pluralize /> instead of <pluralize></pluralize>.

```
public class PluralizeTagHelper : TagHelper
{
    public int Count { get; set; }
    public string? Singular { get; set; }
    public string? Plural { get; set; }
```

The name of the properties directly translate to attributes in **kebab-case** format. So Singular translates to singular, while a property named ComplexAttributeName would translate to complex-attribute-name.

```
    public override void Process(TagHelperContext context, TagHelperOutput
output)
    {
        var text = Count > 1 ? Plural : Singular;
        if (text is not null)
        {
            text = string.Format(text, Count);
        }
```

The preceding code is the logic that chooses whether we display the singular or the plural version of the text.

```
        output.TagName = null;
```

Setting the TagName property to null ensures that Razor does not render the content inside a <pluralize> tag; we only want to generate text.

```
        output.Content.SetContent(text);
    }
  }
}
```

Finally, we set the value of what we want to output with the `SetContent` method of the `TagHelperContent` class. The `TagHelperContent` class exposes multiple other methods to append and set the content of the Tag Helper.

Like any other Tag Helper, we need to register it. We will register all Tag Helpers of the project, in a few pages, in *Project – Reusable employee count*.

When loading a page that displays the Pluralize Tag Helper, we end up with the following outputs:

```
# When count = 0
0 Employee
# When count = 1
1 Employee
# When count = 2
2 Employees
```

That's it for this one. Of course, we could create more complex Tag Helpers, but I'll leave that to you and your projects.

Tip

You can also download existing Tag Helpers from `NuGet.org` and publish your Tag Helpers on `NuGet.org` (or the third-party service of your choice) as NuGet packages.

Next, we explore how to modify the `<head>` of the page by adding an RSS feed `<link>` tag without changing the HTML markup itself.

Creating an RSS feed TagHelperComponent

Context: We want to dynamically add a `<link>` tag into the `<head>` of every page without changing the `_Layout.cshtml` file. The expected output looks like the following:

```
<link href="/feed.xml" type="application/atom+xml" rel="alternate"
title="Chapter 17 Code Samples App">
```

We can do that by implementing the `ITagHelperComponent` interface or by inheriting from the `TagHelperComponent` class. We do the latter because the `TagHelperComponent` class already defines the members and adds a synchronous `Process` method. Inheriting that class allows us to simply override the method or property that we need. Like we are about to see, we only need the `Process` method.

Let's first look at the `RssFeedTagHelperComponent` class and its options:

```
namespace PageController.TagHelpers
{
    public class RssFeedTagHelperComponentOptions
    {
        public string Href { get; set; } = "/feed.xml";
        public string Type { get; set; } = "application/atom+xml";
```

```
        public string Rel { get; set; } = "alternate";
        public string Title { get; set; } = "";
    }
```

The `RssFeedTagHelperComponentOptions` class contains some properties with default values about what to write into the `<link>` tag, for convenience.

Next, `RssFeedTagHelperComponent` looks like this:

```
    public class RssFeedTagHelperComponent : TagHelperComponent
    {
        private readonly RssFeedTagHelperComponentOptions _options;
        public RssFeedTagHelperComponent(RssFeedTagHelperComponentOptions
options)
        {
            _options = options ?? throw new
ArgumentNullException(nameof(options));
        }
        public override void Process(TagHelperContext context, TagHelperOutput
output)
```

The `Process` method is where the magic happens. That can also be in the `ITagHelperComponent.ProcessAsync` method if you have asynchronous code to run.

```
        {
            if (context.TagName == "head")
```

Two sections can be extended by a Tag Helper component: the `<head>` and the `<body>`. We want to append content to the `<head>`, so we are looking for that.

```
            {
                output.PostContent.AppendHtml(
                $@"<link href=""{_options.Href}"" type=""{_options.Type}""
rel=""{_options.Rel}"" title=""{_options.Title}"">"
                );
            }
        }
    }
}
```

Finally, we append the `<link>` tag itself to the `<head>`, using our `options` object.

That code does nothing on its own; for it to run, we need to tell ASP.NET about it. To do that, we have multiple options, but as a big fan of **Dependency Injection**, that's the way that I chose here.

In the `Program.cs` file, we must register the `RssFeedTagHelperComponentOptions` and the `RssFeedTagHelperComponent` classes. Let's start with the options, which is a design choice and has nothing to do with the `ITagHelperComponent` itself:

```
builder.Services
    .Configure<RssFeedTagHelperComponentOptions>(
        builder.Configuration.GetSection("RssFeed")
    )
    .AddSingleton(sp => sp.GetRequiredService<
        IOptionsMonitor<RssFeedTagHelperComponentOptions>
    >().CurrentValue)
;
```

Here, I decided to leverage the **Options** pattern, which allows overriding our default values from any configuration source like the `appsettings.json` file. Then I needed a raw `RssFeedTagHelperCompo`nentOptions instance, so I registered it as is (see *Chapter 8*, *Options and Logging Patterns*, for more information about this workaround).

Now that our options are registered, we can register `RssFeedTagHelperComponent` as an `ITagHelperComponent`. Since the component is stateless, we can register it as a singleton, like this:

```
services.AddSingleton<ITagHelperComponent, RssFeedTagHelperComponent>();
```

That's it. When loading any page, the `<link>` tag is added to the `<head>` with the options that we defined! That's ASP.NET Core extensibility magic!

When we think about it, the options are endless; we could have components self-registering their CSS files or even minifying the `<head>` or the `<body>` or both. Here is an example of a minifier:

```
namespace PageController.TagHelpers;
public class MinifierTagHelperComponent : TagHelperComponent
{
    public override int Order => int.MaxValue;

    public async override Task ProcessAsync(TagHelperContext context,
TagHelperOutput output)
    {
        var childContent = await output.GetChildContentAsync();
        var content = childContent.GetContent();
        var result = Minify(content);
        output.Content.SetHtmlContent(result);
```

```
    }

    private static string Minify(string input) { ... }
}
```

That is probably not the optimal way of doing minification (I did not benchmark it), but I built it because it crossed my mind and as a quick second example to trigger your imagination. All of the code is available in Git (`https://adpg.link/EcSc`).

More Info

The `ITagHelper` interface inherits from `ITagHelperComponent`, so you can technically create a Tag Helper that adds resources to the `<head>` or `<body>` of the page by combining both methods into one class.

Conclusion

Tag Helpers are a great way to create new HTML-like tags or expand existing ones to lower the friction from switching context between C# and HTML in Razor code. ASP.NET Core is packed with existing Tag Helpers, and you may have used some without even knowing it.

Now let's see how creating Tag Helpers can help us follow the **SOLID** principles:

- **S:** Tag Helpers can help us encapsulate tag-related logic into reusable pieces of code.
- **O:** N/A
- **L:** N/A
- **I:** N/A
- **D:** N/A

Next, we explore view components, which opens new ways to divide our user interface into smaller, more manageable pieces.

View components

Now to a new concept: **view components**. A view component is a mix between a partial view and a controller action in the sense that you render it using one or more Razor views and you program its logic in a class, returning the partial-like view using a similar concept that controller actions do.

View components are composed of two parts:

- A class that inherits from `ViewComponent` or is decorated with a `[ViewComponent]` attribute. This class contains the logic.
- One or more `cshtml` views. These are the views that know how to render the component.

There are multiple ways to organize the files that compose a view component. Since I prefer it when the files related to a feature are close together, I like to see all of the classes live in the same directory as the view itself (let's call that vertical slice-inspired), like this:

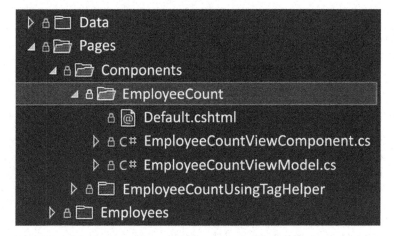

Figure 17.3: A way to organize view components keeping all files together

Project — Reusable employee count

Context: We want to create a view component in the same Razor Pages project. That component should display the number of employees in the database and should always be visible.

The widget is a Bootstrap card that looks like this:

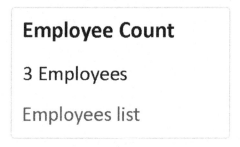

Figure 17.4: The result, rendered in a browser, of the employee count view component

I decided to make my life easier by inheriting from ViewComponent to leverage the helper methods, such as View(), making it trivial to implement the feature. One advantage of view components is the ability to code C# logic in a class instead of a Razor file.

I decided to leverage **record classes** (see *Appendix A*) to implement the EmployeeCountViewModel class that we use as the view component's view model. The view model exposes a Count property (taken from the Pages/Components/EmployeeCount/EmployeeCountViewModel.cs file):

```
public record EmployeeCountViewModel(int Count);
```

The `EmployeeCountViewModel` class is virtually the same as a class with a `public int Count { get; }` property. Next, we look at the view taken from the `Pages/Components/EmployeeCount/Default.cshtml` file:

```
@model PageController.Pages.Components.EmployeeCount.EmployeeCountViewModel
<div class="card">
    <div class="card-body">
        <h5 class="card-title">Employee Count</h5>
        <p class="card-text">
            @Model.Count
            @(Model.Count > 1 ? "Employees" : "Employee")
        </p>
        <a asp-page="Employees/Index" class="card-link">Employees list</a>
    </div>
</div>
```

As we saw in the *View Model design pattern* section of *Chapter 4, The MVC Pattern Using Razor*, we inject a model specifically crafted for this view, which is the default view of our view component, then we render the component using it. Now, to the view component, taken from the `Pages/Components/EmployeeCount/EmployeeCountViewComponent.cs` file:

```
public class EmployeeCountViewComponent : ViewComponent
{
    private readonly EmployeeDbContext _context;
    public EmployeeCountViewComponent(EmployeeDbContext context)
    {
        _context = context ?? throw new ArgumentNullException(nameof(context));
    }
```

Here, we inject `EmployeeDbContext` so we can count the employees in the `InvokeAsync` method down below:

```
    public async Task<IViewComponentResult> InvokeAsync()
    {
        var count = await _context.Employees.CountAsync();
        return View(new EmployeeCountViewModel(count));
    }
}
```

A view component's logic must be placed inside an `InvokeAsync` method that returns a `Task<IViewComponentResult>` value or an `Invoke` method that returns an `IViewComponentResult` value. In our case, we access a database, so we better go async to ensure we don't block a thread while waiting for the database. Then, similar to a controller action, we use the `View<TModel>(TModel model)` method of the `ViewComponent` base class to return a `ViewViewComponentResult` value that contains an `EmployeeCountViewModel` instance.

To render a view component, we can use the `Component.InvokeAsync()` extension method, like this:

```
@await Component.InvokeAsync("EmployeeCount")
```

The name of the view component must exclude the `ViewComponent` suffix.

For a more refactor-friendly method, we can also pass the type instead of its name:

```
@await Component.InvokeAsync(typeof(PageController.Pages.Components.
EmployeeCount.EmployeeCountViewComponent))
```

We can also use Tag Helpers to invoke our view components. To do so, we can register all view components as Tag Helpers by adding the following line to the `_ViewImports.cshtml` file:

```
@addTagHelper *, PageController
```

`PageController` is the name of the assembly to scan for view components (the name of the project).

Then we can use the `<vc:[view-component-name]></vc:[view-component-name]>` Tag Helper instead, like this:

```
<vc:employee-count></vc:employee-count>
```

We can achieve many things with view components, including passing arguments to the `InvokeAsync` method. Moreover, with view components and the power of dependency injection, we can create powerful UI pieces that are reusable and encapsulate complex logic, leading to a more maintainable application. We can also register components independently, without the need to register them all at once.

Conclusion

View components are a mix between a partial view and a controller action, with the possibility of having a Tag Helper-like syntax. They support dependency injection for extensibility and optional parameters when using both the Tag Helper syntax and the `Component.InvokeAsync()` methods. The default places where we can save the views are limited but could be extended if we want to.

In a nutshell, if you want a controller-like piece of UI that has logic or that needs to access external resources, a view component could be the right choice for you. On the other hand, if you want to create composable pieces of UI, Razor components might be a better fit (we cover those in the *Getting familiar with Razor components* section of *Chapter 18, A Brief Look into Blazor*).

Now let's see how creating view components can help us follow the **SOLID** principles:

- S: A view component helps us extract pieces of UI logic into independent components.
- O: N/A
- L: N/A
- I: N/A
- D: N/A

Next, we explore two other ways to divide complex user interfaces into smaller pieces, but those pieces are built for types this time.

Display and editor templates

This section uses **display and editor templates** to divide our UIs into model-oriented partial views. These have been available since MVC on the .NET Framework and are not new to ASP.NET Core. Unfortunately, they are often forgotten or overlooked at the expense of brand-new things that come out.

Display templates are Razor views that override the default rendering template of a given type. Editor templates are the same but override the editor's view of a given type.

Each type can have a display template and an editor template. They are also stored hierarchically so that each type can have globally shared templates and specific ones per area, controller, section, or page. In a complex application, this could be very handy to override an individual template for a particular section of the app.

A **display template** must be created in a DisplayTemplates directory, and an **editor template** must be created in an EditorTemplates directory. These directories can be placed at different levels. Moreover, the directory structure depends on whether you're using MVC or Razor Pages.

ASP.NET loads them in order of priority, from the more specific to the more general. That allows us to create a shared template between all pages or all controllers, then override it for a particular controller or page.

For MVC, the order in which they are loaded is as follows:

1. Views/[some controller]/DisplayTemplates
2. Views/Shared/DisplayTemplates

For Razor pages, the order in which they are loaded is as follows:

1. Pages/[some directory]/DisplayTemplates
2. Pages/Shared/DisplayTemplates

> **Note**
>
> The same logic applies to areas; MVC searches for display and editor templates like any other view.

Both display and editor templates are .cshtml files with an @model directive that points to the type they are for. For example, Views/Shared/DisplayTemplates/SomeModel.cshtml should have an @model SomeModel directive at the top. The same goes for Views/Shared/EditorTemplates/SomeModel.cshtml.

Let's start with display templates.

Display templates

Let's use a CRUD UI to manage the employees that we scaffolded again for this section. See the TransformTemplateView project.

Context: We want to encapsulate the way employees are displayed in both the `Details` and `Delete` pages. Instead of creating a partial view, we have decided to use a display template.

We don't want that template to be used elsewhere, so we create it specifically in the `Pages/Employees` directory. Let's start with the display template, taken from the `Pages/Employees/DisplayTemplates/Employee.cshtml` file:

```
@model Data.Models.Employee
<dl class="row">
    <dt class="col-sm-2">
        @Html.DisplayNameFor(model => model.FirstName)
    </dt>
    <dd class="col-sm-10">
        @Html.DisplayFor(model => model.FirstName)
    </dd>
    <dt class="col-sm-2">
        @Html.DisplayNameFor(model => model.LastName)
    </dt>
    <dd class="col-sm-10">
        @Html.DisplayFor(model => model.LastName)
    </dd>
</dl>
```

That file is a copy of the scaffolded files that we had. To render a display template, we must call one of the `@Html.DisplayFor()` extension methods. In the details and delete views, we can replace the old code with `@Html.DisplayFor(x => x.Employee)`. From there, the rendering engine of ASP.NET Core will find the template and render it (as easy as that).

Next, we look at the two pages that consume that display template. First we explore the `Pages/Employees/Details.cshtml` file:

```
@page
@model TransformTemplateView.Pages.Employees.DetailsModel
@{
    ViewData["Title"] = "Details";
}
<h1>Details</h1>
<div>
    <h4>Employee</h4>
    <hr />
    @Html.DisplayFor(x => x.Employee)
</div>
<div>
    <a asp-page="./Edit" asp-route-id="@Model.Employee.Id">Edit</a> |
```

```
        <a asp-page="./Index">Back to List</a>
    </div>
```

Next, we explore the Pages/Employees/Delete.cshtml file:

```
@page
@model TransformTemplateView.Pages.Employees.DeleteModel
@{
    ViewData["Title"] = "Delete";
}
<h1>Delete</h1>
<h3>Are you sure you want to delete this?</h3>
<div>
    <h4>Employee</h4>
    <hr />
    @Html.DisplayFor(x => x.Employee)
    <form method="post">
        <input type="hidden" asp-for="Employee.Id" />
        <input type="submit" value="Delete" class="btn btn-danger" /> |
        <a asp-page="./Index">Back to List</a>
    </form>
</div>
```

Just like that, we centralized the display of an employee to one cshtml file, located and loaded automatically by its type, not by a string like partial views. But that's not it—display templates are more powerful than that, as we are about to see after our overview of editor templates.

Editor templates

Editor templates work the same way as **display templates**, so let's rebuild the same thing that we did with a partial view, but with an editor template.

Reminder: We want to encapsulate the Employee form and reuse it in both Create and Edit views.

Once again, we don't want that template to be used elsewhere, so we create it at the same level, under Pages/Employees. Let's take a look at the code in the Pages/Employees/EditorTemplates/Employee. cshtml file:

```
@model Data.Models.Employee
<div class="form-group">
    <label asp-for="FirstName" class="control-label"></label>
    <input asp-for="FirstName" class="form-control" />
    <span asp-validation-for="FirstName" class="text-danger"></span>
</div>
<div class="form-group">
    <label asp-for="LastName" class="control-label"></label>
```

```
            <input asp-for="LastName" class="form-control" />
            <span asp-validation-for="LastName" class="text-danger"></span>
    </div>
```

That's the same view as the partial view that we created in a previous sample. It is important to remember that the display and editor templates are designed around a type, the Employee class.

To tell ASP.NET Core to create an editor for a model, we can use one of the @Html.EditorFor() extension method overloads. In both the Create and Edit views, we are replacing the form with a call to @Html. EditorFor(m => m.Employee). Let's start with the Pages/Employees/Create.cshtml file:

```
@model TransformTemplateView.Pages.Employees.CreateModel
@{
    ViewData["Title"] = "Create";
}
<h1>Create</h1>
<h4>Employee</h4>
<hr />
<div class="row">
    <div class="col-md-4">
        <form method="post">
            <div asp-validation-summary="ModelOnly" class="text-danger"></div>
            @Html.EditorFor(m => m.Employee)
            <div class="form-group">
                <input type="submit" value="Create" class="btn btn-primary" />
            </div>
        </form>
    </div>
</div>
```

Next, let's look at the Pages/Employees/Edit.cshtml file:

```
@page
@model TransformTemplateView.Pages.Employees.EditModel
@{
    ViewData["Title"] = "Edit";
}
<h1>Edit</h1>
<h4>Employee</h4>
<hr />
<div class="row">
    <div class="col-md-4">
        <form method="post">
            <div asp-validation-summary="ModelOnly" class="text-danger"></div>
```

```
                <input type="hidden" asp-for="Employee.Id" />
                @Html.EditorFor(m => m.Employee)
                <div class="form-group">
                    <input type="submit" value="Save" class="btn btn-primary" />
                </div>
            </form>
        </div>
</div>
```

And like the display templates, that's the only thing that we need to do. When running the project, both the create and edit pages use the same form, explicitly crafted for the Employee class.

We are about to explore the power of display templates in the next example. Keep in mind that you can achieve the same with editor templates.

Project – Composite BookStore revisited

Context: We want to revisit how we display the composite bookstore's UI that we built earlier, in *Chapter 3, Architectural Principles*, and *Chapter 9, Structural Patterns*. The goal is to get the display logic out of the classes, decoupling them from their HTML output.

What could be better than display templates to encapsulate those small blocks of UI?

Let's first inspect the steps to take:

1. Update the model classes.
2. Create the views and transfer the rendering logic there (the HTML).

Let's start by updating the model classes, taken from the Models/*.cs files:

```
namespace TransformTemplateView.Models;
public interface IComponent
{
    void Add(IComponent bookComponent);
    void Remove(IComponent bookComponent);
    int Count();
}
```

First, we removed the Display method and the Type property from IComponent. Both are used to display the IComponent instance.

```
public class Book : IComponent
{
    public Book(string title)
    {
        Title = title ?? throw new ArgumentNullException(nameof(title));
```

```
        }

        public string Title { get; set; }

        public int Count() => 1;

        public void Add(IComponent bookComponent)
            => throw new NotSupportedException();
        public void Remove(IComponent bookComponent)
            => throw new NotSupportedException();
    }
```

Then we did the same for the Book class (both members were part of the IComponent interface).

```
public abstract class BookComposite : IComponent
{
    protected readonly List<IComponent> children;
    public BookComposite(string name)
    {
        Name = name ?? throw new ArgumentNullException(nameof(name));
        children = new List<IComponent>();
    }

    public string Name { get; }
    public virtual ReadOnlyCollection<IComponent> Components => new
ReadOnlyCollection<IComponent>(children);

    public virtual string Type => GetType().Name;
    public virtual void Add(IComponent bookComponent) => children.
Add(bookComponent);
    public virtual int Count() => children.Sum(child => child.Count());
    public virtual void Remove(IComponent bookComponent) => children.
Remove(bookComponent);
    public virtual void AddRange(IComponent[] components) => children.
AddRange(components);
}
```

Then, we stripped all the display code from BookComposite, added a property named Components that exposes its children to the display template, and the AddRange method to make it easier to add multiple IComponent instances.

The Corporation, Section, and Store classes that follow are only organizational types since we are keeping the bookstore logic to a minimum to explore patterns and features, not the business model of a fake store:

```
public class Corporation : BookComposite
{
    public Corporation(string name) : base(name) { }
}
public class Section : BookComposite
{
    public Section(string name) : base(name) { }
}
public class Store : BookComposite
{
    public Store(string name) : base(name) { }
}
```

The Set class is a little different. It is an organizational type, but it requires some books (see the books parameter of its constructor here):

```
public class Set : BookComposite
{
    public Set(string name, params IComponent[] books)
        : base(name)
    {
        AddRange(books);
    }
}
```

That code represents our first step and is conceptually very similar to what we had in the original code, without the display logic.

Now, to create the new, updated display code, we create the following three Razor files:

1. The Razor Page itself, displayed when a client requests it, in the Pages/BookStore/Index. cshtml file.
2. The View Template to render the books, in the Pages/BookStore/DisplayTemplates/Book. cshtml file.
3. The View Template to render all of the other BookComposite objects, in the Pages/BookStore/ DisplayTemplates/BookComposite.cshtml file.

Let's look at how the files are organized, then at the code:

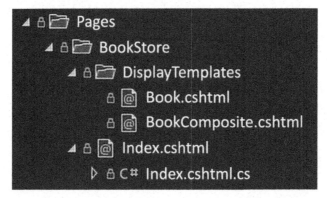

Figure 17.5: Solution Explorer's view of the revised BookStore display templates and Index page

Let's start with the page model in `Pages/BookStore/Index.cshtml.cs`:

```
using Microsoft.AspNetCore.Mvc.RazorPages;
using System;
using System.Collections.ObjectModel;
using TransformTemplateView.Models;
using TransformTemplateView.Services;
namespace TransformTemplateView.Pages.BookStore
{
    public class IndexModel : PageModel
    {
        private readonly ICorporationFactory _corporationFactory;
        public IndexModel(ICorporationFactory corporationFactory)
        {
            _corporationFactory = corporationFactory ?? throw new
ArgumentNullException(nameof(corporationFactory));
        }
```

First, we use **constructor injection** to gain access to `ICorporationFactory`.

```
        public ReadOnlyCollection<IComponent> Components { get; private set; }
= new(Array.Empty<IComponent>());
```

Then we expose a collection of `IComponent` instances that the view needs to render the page.

```
        public void OnGet()
        {
            var corporation = _corporationFactory.Create();
            Components = new ReadOnlyCollection<IComponent>(new IComponent[] {
corporation });
        }
```

```
        }
    }
}
```

Finally, when someone sends a GET request to that page, it builds the ReadOnlyCollection<IComponent> instance by calling the _corporationFactory.Create() method.

Next, the page's view, from Pages/BookStore/Index.cshtml:

```
@page
@model TransformTemplateView.Pages.BookStore.IndexModel
@{
    ViewData["Title"] = "My BookStore";
}
<section class="card">
    <h1 class="card-header">@ViewData["Title"]</h1>
    <ul class="list-group list-group-flush">
        @Html.DisplayFor(x => x.Components)
    </ul>
</section>
```

That markup creates a Bootstrap 4 .card to hold our bookstore data. The key to that view is the DisplayFor() call (highlighted).

Note

If you are creating a new project, it should include Bootstrap 5 instead, which may change the HTML markup slightly, so you may see a few differences when browsing the applications. Bootstrap is not the focus of the book, only a way to make the page a bit better looking, so I'll leave you to apply the required updates or use plain HTML/CSS if you prefer.

Since the Components property of our PageModel is a ReadOnlyCollection<T> that implements IEnumerable<T>, which inherits from IEnumerable, ASP.NET Core loops and renders all elements of the Components collection. In our case, that's only one Corporation object, but it could be more.

For each of those elements, ASP.NET Core tries to find the right **display template** for that type. Since we don't have a Corporation template, it goes up the inheritance chain to find the BookComposite template and renders the element. Let's look at those templates now, starting with BookComposite from Pages/BookStore/DisplayTemplates/BookComposite.cshtml:

```
@model BookComposite
<li class="list-group-item">
    <section class="card">
        <h5 class="card-header">
            @Model.Name
            <span class="badge badge-secondary float-right">@Model.Count()</
```

```
span>
        </h5>
        <ul class="list-group list-group-flush">
            @Html.DisplayFor(x => x.Components)
        </ul>
        <div class="card-footer text-muted">
            <small class="text-muted text-right">@Model.Type</small>
        </div>
    </section>
</li>
```

The `@model BookComposite` directive instructs the framework about the type it knows how to render.

The template renders a Bootstrap 4 `.card` inside a `.list-group-item`. Since the page renders the `Components` inside `<ul class="list-group list-group-flush">`, those `<li>` elements will make a nice-looking UI.

The template does the same as the page and calls `@Html.DisplayFor(x => x.Components)`, which allows rendering any type that implements the `IComponent` interface.

Highlights

That's the power of the display templates right there; with them, we can craft a complex model-based recursive UI with little effort.

In more detail, what happens is the following:

1. `ReadOnlyCollection<T>` implements `IEnumerable<T>`, so ASP.NET Core loops and renders all its content. In our case, that's a collection containing two `Store` instances.
2. For each element, ASP.NET tries to find the right display template for that type. Since we don't have a `Store` template, it goes up the inheritance chain to find the `BookComposite` template and renders the elements.
3. Then, for each `Store`, it renders its children; in our case, instances of `Section` and `Set`, using the `BookComposite` template (we don't have `Set` or `Section` templates).
4. From those `Section` and `Set` objects, the `Book` objects are rendered using the `Book` template (which we are about to look at), while other, non-book objects are rendered using the `BookComposite` template.

Let's start with the Razor code to render `Book` instances, in `Pages/BookStore/DisplayTemplates/Book.cshtml`:

```
@model Book
<li class="list-group-item">
    @Model.Title
    <small class="text-muted">(Book)</small>
```

```
    </li>
```

The Book template is a leaf of the tree and displays the details of a Book, nothing more (instructed by the @model Book directive).

If we compare that code with the initial model that we had, it is very similar. The BookComposite template is also very similar to what we were building in the BookComposite.Display() method.

The most significant difference is the level of difficulty that was required to write the presentation code. It is feasible to render a small element using a StringBuilder, but generating a complex web page would be tedious. **Display templates** allowed us to write that same code very easily with IntelliSense and tooling support.

Important Note

Display templates and editor templates are excellent ways to create a type-oriented UI design (model-oriented).

If we take a subset of our BookStore, what happens in the background is the following:

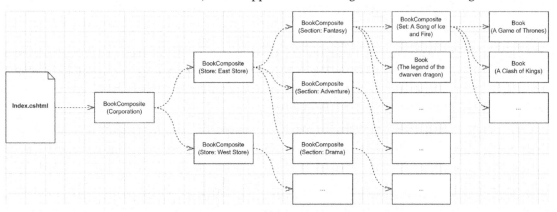

Figure 17.6: A subset of the rendering flow done by ASP.NET, based on our display templates

This completes our example. With those few lines of code, we were able to render a complex UI that supports a non-linear composite data structure. We could extend that UI by rendering each class differently, such as including a logo for Corporation objects or cover images for BookSet objects.

Conclusion

In this chapter, we discovered many ways to render components and parts of a page, but display and editor templates are convenient ones that are often overlooked. We can render complex polymorphic UIs with little effort.

Now let's see how this approach can help us follow the **SOLID** principles:

- **S**: By extracting the rendering of objects from the models, we divided both responsibilities into two different pieces.

- **O:** By managing independent, type-related pieces of the UI, we can change how a type is rendered without impacting it directly or its consumers.
- **L:** N/A
- **I:** N/A
- **D:** N/A

>
>
> **Note**
>
> We could see the display and editor templates as **Transformers** from the **Transform View** pattern and see **Razor** as an implementation of the **Template View** pattern. Martin Fowler introduced those patterns in his book, *PoEAA*, in 2002. See the *Further reading* section for more information.

Summary

This chapter explored **Razor Pages**, which allowed us to organize our web applications by page instead of controller. Razor Pages leverages the same tools as **MVC**, and both technologies can be combined and used together, allowing you to build parts of your application using Razor Pages and other parts using MVC.

Then we tackled **partial views**, allowing reusing parts of a UI and breaking down complex UI into smaller pieces. When we have complex logic, we can move from partial views to **view components**, a controller action-like view. We also tackled **Tag Helpers** to create reusable UI parts, extend existing HTML elements, or just consume the built-in ones.

Finally, we explored another way to divide UIs into smaller pieces, oriented around the model classes themselves. **Display and editor templates** give us the power to dynamically build a model-based UI for both display and modification purposes.

With all of that, we've almost dipped into everything that ASP.NET Core has to offer in terms of web UIs, but we are not done yet; we still have Blazor to explore in the next chapter to complete our full-stack journey into modern .NET.

Questions

Let's take a look at a few practice questions:

1. What are **Razor Pages** good for?
2. When using **Razor Pages**, do we have access to model binding, model validation, and routing of MVC?
3. Can we use a **partial view** to query a database?
4. Can we extend existing tags with **Tag Helpers**?
5. Can we use **view components** to query a database?
6. How many display templates can a class have?
7. To what do we link (or associate) a display or an editor template?

Further reading

Here are a few links to build upon what we learned in the chapter:

- Partial views in ASP.NET Core: `https://adpg.link/p1oW`
- View components in ASP.NET Core: `https://adpg.link/DNsE`
- Tag Helpers in ASP.NET Core: `https://adpg.link/JaZQ`
- Page Controller (Martin Fowler, PoEAA): `https://adpg.link/LLQg`
- Template View (Martin Fowler, PoEAA): `https://adpg.link/TFM9`
- Transform View (Martin Fowler, PoEAA): `https://adpg.link/4Gom`

Join our book's Discord space

Join the book's Discord workspace for *Ask me Anything* session with the authors:

`https://packt.link/ASPdotNET6DesignPatterns`

18

A Brief Look into Blazor

In this chapter, we look at Blazor. Blazor is the new kid on the block, enabling full stack .NET. Blazor is a great piece of technology. It is still relatively new, but it improved remarkably between its experimental stage, first official release, and current state. In only a few years, it went from being an idea for the distant future to reality. Daniel Roth, a Principal Program Manager at Microsoft on the ASP.NET team, was most likely the most fervent believer who preached Blazor over that period. For a time, Blazor was the only thing I heard about (or maybe that was the internet spying on me).

Fun fact

Back in the day, we could use server-side JavaScript with classic ASP, making classic ASP the first full stack technology (that I know of).

Blazor is two things:

- A client-side **single-page application (SPA)** framework compiling .NET to **WebAssembly (Wasm)**. WebAssembly is a low-level language that runs in the browser at near-native speed. C# compiles to WebAssembly, and then the resulting Wasm code is sent to the browser. This is known as the **Blazor WebAssembly** hosting model.
- A client-server link over SignalR that acts as a modern `UpdatePanel` with superpowers. SignalR enables real-time web features, like server code calling client code over WebSocket. This is known as the **Blazor Server** hosting model.

A bit of history

If you don't know what an `UpdatePanel` is, you haven't missed much. It was an ASP.NET Web Forms control released with .NET Framework 3.5 that helped run AJAX calls "automagically."

Blazor also comes bundled with **Razor components** (why not Blazor components? I don't know). It has some experimental projects revolving around it, a growing ecosystem of libraries accessible through NuGet, and a `BlazorWebView` control in .NET **Multi-platform App UI (MAUI)**.

Now that I have laid that out, the following topics are covered in this chapter:

- Overview of Blazor Server
- Overview of Blazor WebAssembly
- Getting familiar with Razor components
- The Model-View-Update pattern
- A medley of Blazor features

Overview of Blazor Server

Blazor Server is an ASP.NET Core web application that initially sends a page to the browser. Then, the browser updates part of the UI over a SignalR connection. The application becomes an automated AJAX client-server app on steroids. It is a mix of classic web apps and a SPA model, where the client loads the UI pieces to update from the server. So, less processing for the client and more processing for the server. There can also be a short delay (latency) since you must wait for a server response (*steps 2 to 4*); for example:

1. You click a button in the browser.
2. The action is dispatched to the server through SignalR.
3. The server processes the action.
4. The server returns the HTML diff to the browser.
5. The browser updates the UI using that diff.

To make that diff (*step 4*), the server keeps a graph of the application state. It constructs that graph using components, which translates into **Document Object Model (DOM)** nodes.

Blazor Server makes stateful applications that must keep track of the current state of all visitors. It may be hard to scale up or would cost a lot of money in cloud hosting. I don't want you to discard the option just yet; the model may fit your application's needs. Moreover, paying more for hosting can save development costs, depending on many factors.

On the other hand, a Blazor Server application is smaller than a Blazor WebAssembly one because the server only sends the requested page to the browser instead of the whole source code compiled to Wasm binary code. Blazor Server can be used with clients that do not support Wasm since the code is executed on the server, like a classic ASP.NET Core application. Razor components can be used in both Blazor Server and Blazor WebAssembly; we explore them after the Blazor WebAssembly overview.

Blazor Server can also be used to prerender a Blazor WebAssembly app and speed up the initial load time.

Disclaimer

I have not deployed nor participated in building any Blazor Server applications yet. Nonetheless, it looks like an improved remake of Web Forms. That might just be me, but a "magic" SignalR connection, latency, and everything processed in a stateful server sound like going back to the past. I might be wrong. I recommend you do your experiments and research and judge for yourself. I may even change my mind in the future; the technology is still young.

To create a Blazor Server project, you can run the `dotnet new blazorserver` command. That's it for Blazor Server.

Next, we look into Blazor WebAssembly, which is way more promising (once again, my opinion).

Overview of Blazor WebAssembly

Before getting into **Blazor WebAssembly**, let's look at **WebAssembly** itself. WebAssembly allows browsers to run code that is not JavaScript (such as C# and C++). Wasm is an open standard, so it is not a Microsoft-only thing. Wasm runs in a sandboxed environment close to native speed (that's the goal) on the client machine, enforcing browser security policies. Wasm binaries can interact with JavaScript.

As you may have "foreseen" from that last paragraph, Blazor WebAssembly is all about running .NET in the browser! And the coolest part is that it follows standards. It's not like running VBScript in Internet Explorer (oh, I don't miss that time). I think Microsoft's new vision to embrace open standards, open source, and the rest of the world is very beneficial for us developers.

But how does that work? Like Blazor Server and other SPAs out there, we compose the application using **components**. A component is a piece of UI that can be as small as a button or as big as a page. Then, when a client requests our application, the following happens:

1. The server sends a more or less empty shell (HTML).
2. The browser downloads external resources (Wasm binaries, JS, CSS, and images).
3. The browser displays the application.

It is the same experience as any other web page so far. The difference is that when a user carries out an action, such as clicking a button, the action is executed by the client. Of course, the client can call a remote resource, as you would using JavaScript in React, Angular, or Vue. However, the important part here is that you don't have to. You can control your user interface on the client using C# and .NET.

A significant advantage of Blazor Wasm is hosting: the compiled Blazor Wasm artifacts are only **static resources**, so you can host your web application in the cloud almost for free (provisioning Azure Blob storage and a **Content Delivery Network** (**CDN**), for example).

That leads to another advantage: scaling. Since each client runs the frontend, you don't need to scale that part—only the delivery of static assets.

On the other hand, you can also use a server-side ASP.NET application to prerender your Blazor Wasm app if you prefer. That leads to a faster initial load time for the clients at an increased hosting cost.

Nevertheless, there is one significant disadvantage: it runs on .NET. But why would I have a problem with that? That's blasphemy, right? Well, the browser must download the Wasm version of the .NET runtime, which is massive. Fortunately, the people at Microsoft worked on a way to trim unused parts, so browsers only download the required bits. Blazor also supports lazy-loading Wasm assemblies, so a client doesn't need to download everything at once. That said, all in all, the minimum download size is still around 2 MB. With high-speed internet, 2 MB is small and fast to download, but it can take a bit longer for people living in a remote area. So, think about your audience before making a choice.

We can also leverage **ahead-of-time** (AOT) compilation to optimize performance-intensive applications while making the binaries bigger. So far, every version has improved the performance, size, and capabilities, which makes me hopeful to see Blazor shine in the future (at least for .NET developers).

To create a Blazor Wasm project, you can run the `dotnet new blazorwasm` command.

Next, we explore Razor components and look at what Blazor has to offer.

Getting familiar with Razor components

Everything is a **Razor component** in Blazor Wasm, including the application itself, which is defined as a **root component**. In the `Program.cs` file, that root component is registered as follows:

```
builder.RootComponents.Add<App>("#app");
```

The App type is from the `App.razor` component (we cover how components work later), and the string `"#app"` is a CSS selector. The `wwwroot/index.html` file contains a `<div id="app">Loading...</div>` element that is replaced by the Blazor App component once the application is initialized. #app is the CSS selector identifying an element that has an `id="app"` attribute. The `wwwroot/index.html` static file is the default page served to clients; it is your Blazor app starting point. It contains the basic HTML structure of the page, including scripts and CSS. And that's how a Blazor application is loaded.

The `App.razor` file defines a `Router` component that routes the requests to the right page. When the page exists, the `Router` component renders the `Found` child component. It displays the `NotFound` child component when the page does not exist. Here is the default content of the `App.razor` file:

```
<Router AppAssembly="@ typeof(Program).Assembly">
    <Found Context="routeData">
        <RouteView RouteData="@routeData" DefaultLayout="@typeof(MainLayout)"
/>
        <FocusOnNavigate RouteData="@routeData" Selector="h1" />
    </Found>
    <NotFound>
        <PageTitle>Not found</PageTitle>
        <LayoutView Layout="@typeof(MainLayout)">
            <p>Sorry, there's nothing at this address.</p>
```

```
            </LayoutView>
        </NotFound>
    </Router>
```

Pages are **Razor components**, with a @page "/some-uri" directive at the top, similar to Razor Pages. You can use most, if not all, of the same things as you can with Razor Pages to compose those routes.

A **Razor component** is a C# class that implements the IComponent interface. You can also inherit from ComponentBase, which implements the following interfaces for you: IComponent, IHandleEvent, and IHandleAfterRender. All of these live in the Microsoft.AspNetCore.Components namespace.

Next, we take a look at how to create Razor components.

Creating Razor components

You can create your components anywhere in your project, unlike Razor Pages and view components. I like to create my pages under the Pages directory, so it is easier to find pages. Then you can create the non-page components wherever you see fit.

There are three ways to create a component:

- Using only C#
- Using only Razor
- Using a mix of C# (code-behind) and Razor

You don't have to pick only one way for the whole application; you can choose one per component. All three approaches end up compiled into a single C# class. Let's take a look at those three ways of organizing components.

C#-only components

C#-only components are as simple as creating a class. In the following example, our component inherits from ComponentBase, but we could implement only the interfaces we need.

Here is the first component (CSharpOnlyComponent.cs):

```
namespace WASM
{
    public class CSharpOnlyComponent : ComponentBase
    {
    [Parameter]
    public string? Text { get; set; }
```

The Parameter attribute allows setting the value of the Text property when consuming the component. Officially, it becomes a **component parameter**. We see this in action once we are done with this class.

The BuildRenderTree method, next, is responsible for rendering our component:

```
    protected override void BuildRenderTree(RenderTreeBuilder builder)
    {
```

```
        builder.OpenElement(0, "h1");
        builder.AddAttribute(1, "class", "hello-world");
        builder.AddContent(2, Text);
        builder.CloseElement();
    }
  }
}
```

By overriding this method, we control the render tree. Those changes are eventually translated into DOM changes. Here, we are creating an H1 element with a hello-world class. In it is a text node that contains the value of the Text property.

Sequence numbers

The sequence numbers (0, 1, and 2 in the BuildRenderTree method) are used internally to generate the diff tree that .NET uses to update the DOM. It is recommended to write those manually to avoid performance degradation in more complex code such as conditional logic blocks. See the *ASP.NET Core Blazor advanced scenarios* link in the *Further reading* section for more info.

Now, in the Pages/Index.razor page, we can use that component like this:

```
@page "/"
<CSharpOnlyComponent Text="Hello World from C#" />
```

The name of the class becomes the name of its tag. That's automatic; we have nothing to do to make it happen. We can set the value of the properties identified with the Parameter attribute as HTML attributes. In this case, we set the value of the Text property to Hello World from C#. We could mark more than one property with that attribute and use them as we would any normal HTML attribute.

When rendering the page, our component is rendered to the following HTML:

```
<h1 class="hello-world">Hello World from C#</h1>
```

With those few lines of code, we created our first Razor component. Next, we will create a similar component using the Razor-only syntax.

Razor-only components

Razor-only components are created in .razor files. They are compiled into a C# class. The default namespace of that class depends on the directory structure where it is created. For example, a component created in the ./Dir/Dir2/MyComponent.razor file generates the MyComponent class in the [Root Namespace].Dir.Dir2 namespace. Let's look at some code (RazorOnlyComponent.razor):

```
<h2 class="hello-world">@Text</h2>
@code{
    [Parameter]
```

```
        public string? Text { get; set; }
    }
```

If you like Razor, you probably prefer this one already. That listing is straightforward and allows us to code the same component as the previous section but more concisely and with less code. In the @code{} block, we can add properties, fields, methods, and pretty much anything we would in a regular class, including other classes. We can also override ComponentBase methods there if we need to. We can use this component the same way we did in the previous example; the same goes for parameters.

Next is the page consuming the RazorOnlyComponent (Pages/Index.razor):

```
@page "/"
<CSharpOnlyComponent Text="Hello World from C#" />
<RazorOnlyComponent Text="Hello World from Razor" />
```

The rendering is also very similar, but we went for an H2 instead of an H1:

```
<h2 class="hello-world">Hello World from Razor</h2>
```

And with those few lines of code, we created our second component. Next, we create a hybrid of the two styles.

Razor and C# hybrid components

This third model can separate the C# code (known as code-behind) from the Razor code. This hybrid counterpart leverages **partial classes** to achieve the same as the other models and generates a C# class.

For this, we need two files:

- [component name].razor
- [component name].razor.cs

Let's remake our previous component for the third time but render an H3 this time. Let's begin with the Razor code (CodeBehindComponent.razor):

```
<h3 class="hello-world">@Text</h3>
```

This code could barely be leaner; we have an H3 tag with the Text property as its content. The .razor file in this model replaces the BuildRenderTree method. The compiler translates the Razor code into C#, generating the BuildRenderTree method's content for us.

The Text parameter is defined in the following code-behind file (CodeBehindComponent.razor.cs):

```
public partial class CodeBehindComponent
{
    [Parameter]
    public string? Text { get; set; }
}
```

It's the same code as the previous two samples—we just divided it into two files. The key is the partial class. It allows compiling a single class from multiple files. In this case, there is our partial class and the autogenerated one from the CodeBehindComponent.razor file. We can use the CodeBehindComponent in the same way as the other two.

Next is the page that consumes the CodeBehindComponent (Pages/Index.razor):

```
@page "/"
<CSharpOnlyComponent Text="Hello World from C#" />
<RazorOnlyComponent Text="Hello World from Razor" />
<CodeBehindComponent Text="Hello World from Code-Behind" />
```

That renders the same way as the others, but as an H3 with different content:

```
<h3 class="hello-world">Hello World from Code-Behind</h3>
```

Using code-behind can be very useful for two things:

- Keeping your .razor file clean of C# code
- Getting better tooling support

The tooling for .razor files tends to explode on us from time to time, includes weird bugs, or provides half-support. It seems that handling HTML, C#, and Razor in a single file is not as easy as it sounds. On a more positive note, it is getting better, so I can only see more stable tooling in the future. I could see myself writing all the code of a component in a single .razor file if the tooling was on par with the C# tooling (in many scenarios). That would lead to fewer files and closer proximity of all parts of the component (leading to better maintainability).

Next, we take a look at skinning our components with CSS, but with a twist...

CSS isolation

Like other SPAs, Blazor allows us to create CSS styles scoped to a component. That means that we don't have to worry about naming conflicts.

Unfortunately, this does not seem to work with C#-only components, so we will skin only two of the three components. Each of them has the same CSS class (hello-world). We are about to change the text color by defining simple .hello-world CSS selectors for both.

To achieve that, we must create a .razor.css file named after our component. The following code represents the content of the RazorOnlyComponent.razor.css file (RazorOnlyComponent):

```
.hello-world {
    color: red;
}
```

The following code represents the content of the CodeBehindComponent.razor.css file (CodeBehindComponent):

```
.hello-world {
```

```
    color: aqua;
}
```

As you can see from those two files, they define the same `.hello-world` selector with a different color.

In the `wwwroot/index.html` file, the `dotnet new blazorwasm` template added the following line:

```
<link href="[name of the project].styles.css" rel="stylesheet" />
```

That line links the bundled component-specific styles into the page. Yes, you did read **bundled**. The Blazor CSS isolation feature also bundles all those styles into a single `.css` file, so the browser only loads one file.

If we load the page, we see this (without the layout):

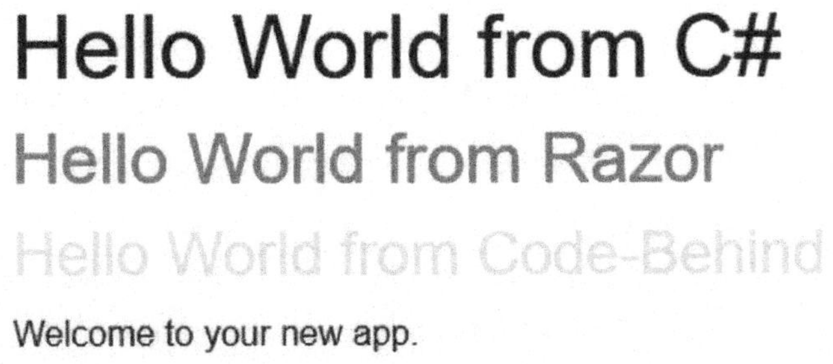

Hello World from C#

Hello World from Razor

Hello World from Code-Behind

Welcome to your new app.

Figure 18.1: Output after loading the page

So it worked! But how? Blazor autogenerated random attributes on each HTML element and used those in the generated CSS. Let's first look at the HTML output:

```
<h1 class="hello-world">Hello World from C#</h1>
<h2 class="hello-world" b-cjkj1dpci4>Hello World from Razor</h2>
<h3 class="hello-world" b-0gygcymdih>Hello World from Code-Behind</h3>
```

Those two highlighted attributes are the "magic" links. Now, with the following CSS code, you should understand their usage and why they have been generated:

```
/* /CodeBehindComponent.razor.rz.scp.css */
.hello-world[b-0gygcymdih] {
    color: aqua;
}
/* /RazorOnlyComponent.razor.rz.scp.css */
.hello-world[b-cjkj1dpci4] {
    color: red;
}
```

If you are not too familiar with CSS, [...] is an **attribute selector**. It allows you to do all kinds of things, including selecting an element with the specified attribute (as in this case). That's what we need here.

The first selector means that all elements with the `hello-world` class and an attribute named `b-0gygcymdih` should have their color updated to aqua. The second selector is the same, but for elements with an attribute named `b-cjkj1dpci4` instead.

With that pattern in place, we can define component-scoped styles with a high level of confidence that they won't conflict with other components' styles.

Next, let's explore the life cycle of those components.

Component life cycle

The components, including the root components, must be rendered as DOM elements for the browser to display them. The same goes for any changes that subsequently occur. Two distinct phases compose the components' life cycle:

- Initial rendering, when a component is rendered for the first time.
- Re-rendering, when a component needs to be rendered because it changed.

During the first rendering, if we get rid of the duplicated sync/async methods, the life cycle of a Razor component looks like this:

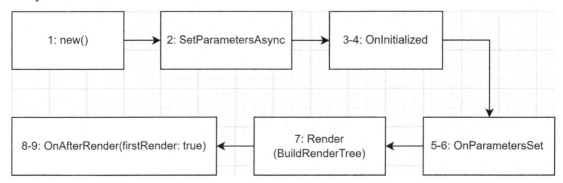

Figure 18.2: Life cycle of a Razor component

1. An instance of the component is created.
2. The `SetParametersAsync` method is called.
3. The `OnInitialized` method is called.
4. The `OnInitializedAsync` method is called.

5. The OnParametersSet method is called.

6. The OnParametersSetAsync method is called.

7. The BuildRenderTree method is called (the component is rendered).

8. The OnAfterRender(firstRender: true) method is called.

9. The OnAfterRenderAsync(firstRender: true) method is called.

During re-rendering, if we get rid of the duplicated sync/async methods, the life cycle of a Razor component is leaner and looks like this:

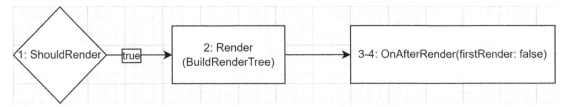

Figure 18.3: Re-rendered version of a Razor component life cycle

1. The ShouldRender method is called. If it returns false, the process stops here. If it is true, the cycle continues.

2. The BuildRenderTree method is called (the component is re-rendered).

3. The OnAfterRender(firstRender: false) method is called.

4. The OnAfterRenderAsync(firstRender: false) method is called.

Note

Don't worry if you have worked with Web Forms before and dread the Blazor life cycle's complexity. It is leaner and doesn't contain any postback. They are two different technologies. Microsoft is trying to push Blazor as the next logical step to migrate from Web Forms (which makes sense based on the current state of .NET), but the only significant similarity that I see is that the component model of Blazor is close to the control model of Web Forms. So if you moved away from Web Forms, don't be afraid to look into Blazor; they are not the same — Blazor is all that Web Forms is not, with one similarity: they are both component-oriented.

I created a component named `LifeCycleObserver` in the WASM project (see `https://adpg.link/ntqD`). That component outputs its life cycle information to the console, leading to the following trick: `Console.WriteLine` writes in the browser console, like this:

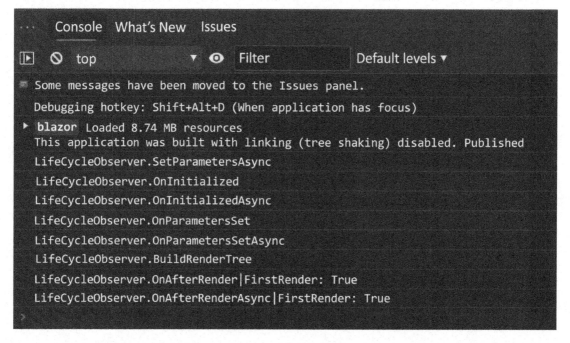

Figure 18.4: The browser debug console displaying the life cycle of the LifeCycleObserver component

Here is an example (highlighted) from the `LifeCycleObserver` class:

```
public class LifeCycleObserver : ComponentBase
{
    public override Task SetParametersAsync(ParameterView parameters)
    {
        Console.WriteLine("LifeCycleObserver.SetParametersAsync");
        return base.SetParametersAsync(parameters);
    }
    // Omitted members
}
```

Next, we look at event handling and how to interact with our components.

Event handling

So far, we've displayed the same component built using three different techniques. Now it is time to interact with a component and see how it works. There are multiple events in HTML that can be handled using JavaScript. In Blazor, we can handle most of them using C# instead.

I slightly modified the `FetchData.razor` page component that comes with the generated project to show you two different event handler patterns:

- Without passing an argument
- With an argument

Both ways call `async` methods, but the same can be done with synchronous methods as well. Let's now explore that code. I'll skip some irrelevant markup, such as H1 and P tags, to focus only on the real code, which starts with this:

```
@page "/fetchdata"
@inject HttpClient Http
```

At the top of the file, I left the injection of the `HttpClient` and the `@page` directive. These allow us to reach the page when navigating to the `/fetchdata` URL and query resources over HTTP. The `HttpClient` is configured in the `Program.cs` file (the composition root). Then, I added a few buttons to interact with. Here is the first:

```
<button class="btn btn-primary mb-4" @onclick="RefreshAsync">Refresh</button>
```

All buttons of this code example have an `@onclick` attribute. That attribute is used to react to click events, like the HTML `onclick` attribute and the JavaScript `"click"` `EventListener`. That button delegates the click event to the `RefreshAsync` method:

```
private Task RefreshAsync() => LoadWeatherAsync();
private async Task LoadWeatherAsync()
{
    forecasts = await Http
        .GetFromJsonAsync<WeatherForecast[]>(_uriList.Next());
}
```

The refresh method then calls the `LoadWeatherAsync()` method, which in turn queries a resource returning an array of `WeatherForecast`. The forecasts are three static JSON files located in the `wwwroot/sample-data` directory. `_uriList` is an instance of the `Cycle` class that cycles through a series of strings. Its code is simple but helps simplify the rest of the page in an OOP manner:

```
private class Cycle
{
    private int _currentIndex = -1;
    private string[] _uris;
    public Cycle(params string[] uris) => _uris = uris;
    public string Next() => _uris[++_currentIndex % _uris.Length];
}
```

When the forecasts change (when we click on the **Refresh** button), the component is reloaded automatically, leading to an updated weather forecast table.

We can also access the event argument like we would in JavaScript. In the case of a click, we have access to the `MouseEventArgs` instance associated with the event. Here is a quick sample displaying possible usage:

```
<button class="btn btn-primary mb-4" @onclick="DisplayXY">Display (X, Y)</
button>
@code {
    public void DisplayXY(MouseEventArgs e)
    {
        Console.WriteLine($"DOM(x, y): ({e.ClientX}, {e.ClientY}) | Button(x,
y): ({e.OffsetX}, {e.OffsetY}) | Screen(x, y): ({e.ScreenX}, {e.ScreenY})");
    }
}
```

In that code, the `@onclick` attribute is used the same way as before, but the `DisplayXY` method expects `MouseEventArgs` as a parameter. The `MouseEventArgs` argument is provided automatically by Blazor. Then, the method will output the mouse position in the browser's DevTools console (*F12* on Chromium-based browsers), which looks like this:

```
DOM(x, y): (921, 175) | Button(x, y): (119, 4) | Screen(x, y): (-999, 246)
DOM(x, y): (809, 197) | Button(x, y): (7, 26) | Screen(x, y): (-1111, 268)
```

To generate those coordinates, I clicked the top-right corner of the button, then the bottom-left corner. As we can deduce from the negative screen *x* position, my browser was on my left monitor.

Another possibility is to use lambda expressions as inline event handlers. Those lambda expressions can also call a method. Here is an example:

```
<button class="btn btn-primary mb-4" @onclick="@(e => Console.
WriteLine($"DOM(x, y): ({e.ClientX}, {e.ClientY})"))">Lamdba (X, Y)</button>
```

That button outputs only the client (*x, y*) coordinate to improve readability.

That's it for our overview of event handling. Next, we look into another way to manage the component's state other than each component doing its own thing.

The Model-View-Update pattern

Unless you've never heard of React, you've most likely heard of Redux. Redux is a library that follows the **Model-View-Update** (**MVU**) pattern. MVU comes from The Elm Architecture. If you don't know Elm, here is a quote from their documentation:

> *Elm is a functional language that compiles to JavaScript.*

Next, let's see what the goal behind MVU is.

Goal

The goal of MVU is to simplify the **state management** of applications. If you've built a stateful UI in the past, you probably know it can become hard to manage an application's state. MVU takes the two-way binding complexity out of the equation and replaces it with a linear one-way flow. It also removes mutations from the picture by replacing them with immutable states, where state updates are moved to pure functions.

Design

The MVU pattern is a **unidirectional data flow** that routes an **action** to an **update function**. An update function must be **pure**. A pure function is **deterministic** and has **no side effects**. A model is a **state**, which must be **immutable**. A state must have an **initial state**. A **view** is the code that knows how to display a state.

Depending on the technology, there are many synonyms. Let's get into more details. It may sound confusing at first, but don't worry, it's not that bad.

An **action** is called a **command** or a **request** in MediatR. It is called an **action** in Redux, and a **message** in Elm. I will use **action**. An **action** is the equivalent of the commands that we used in our CQRS examples in *Chapter 14, Mediator and CQRS Design Patterns*. There is no notion of a query in MVU because a view always renders the current state.

Terminology	MediatR	Redux	Elm
Action	Command Request	Action	Message

An **update function** is called a **handler** in MediatR. It is called a **reducer** in Redux and an **update** in Elm. I will use **reducer**. The **reducer** is a pure function that always returns the same output for any given input (it's deterministic). The pure function must have no impact on external actors (having no side effects). So, no mutation of external variables, no mutation of the input value: no side effects. One significant advantage of a pure function is testing. It is easy to assert the value of its output based on a given input since it is deterministic.

Terminology	MediatR	Redux	Elm
Reducer	Handler	Reducer	Update

A **view** is a **component** in React and Blazor and is a **view function** in Elm. I will mostly use **view** because **component** can be ambiguous and easily confused with Razor components, view components, or the plain notion of a UI component.

Terminology	MediatR	Redux	Elm
View	Component	Component	View function

A model or **state** cannot be altered and must be immutable. Every time a state changes, an altered copy of the state is created. The current state then becomes that copy. Elm calls the **state** a **model**; it is a **state** in Redux. We are using the term **state** as I find it defines the intent better.

Terminology	Redux	Elm
State	State	Model

Here is a diagram that represents this **unidirectional data flow**:

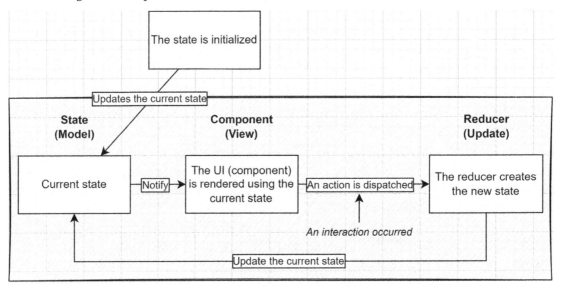

Figure 18.5: Unidirectional data flow chart

1. When the application starts, the state is initialized. That initial state becomes the current state.
2. The current state change triggers the UI to render.
3. When an interaction occurs, such as the user clicking a button, then an **action** is dispatched to a **reducer**.
4. The reducer *creates an instance* of the updated state.
5. That new state *replaces* the current state.
6. Go back to *step 3* of the current list.

It may be hard to wrap your head around this at first. Like all new things, we must take the time to create new paths in our brains to get something fully. Don't worry; we are about to see that in action.

All in all, it is straightforward; the flow goes only one way. Whenever the state changes, the component is re-rendered. Since states are immutable, we cannot alter them directly, so we must pass by reducers.

Project — Counter

For this project, we will use an open source library that I created in 2020 while experimenting with C# 9 record classes. Since a record is immutable, it is a perfect candidate to represent an MVU state.

Moreover, it allows our example to be streamlined in a limited amount of space.

Note

There are multiple similar libraries, but they were all created before C# 9, so there's no direct record support.

Context: We are building a counter page to increment and decrement a value.

I know it does not sound very exciting, but since many MVU libraries showcase one, as well as Blazor itself, I believe this is a good way to compare Blazor with others.

First, we need to install the library by loading the `StateR.Blazor` NuGet package. In this case, we are using a prerelease version.

Redux DevTools

I also installed the `StateR.Blazor.Experiments` NuGet package in the project. That project has a few experimental features, including a Redux DevTools connector. Redux DevTools is a browser extension that allows the tracking of states and actions. It also allows time travel between states.

Next, let's code the `Counter` feature (`Features/Counter.cs`):

```
using StateR;
using StateR.Reducers;
namespace WASM.Features
{
    public class Counter
    {
        public record State(int Count) : StateBase;
```

The `State` record is our **state**. It exposes one `init-only` property. It inherits from `StateBase`, which is an empty record class. `StateBase` serves as a generic constraint to make sure the state class is a record class so we can leverage the `with` expression. States in StateR must be records; it is mandatory.

```
        public class InitialState : IInitialState<State>
        {
            public State Value => new(0);
        }
```

The `InitialState` class, by implementing the `IInitialState<State>` interface, represents the **initial state** of the `State` record.

```
        public record Increment : IAction;
        public record Decrement : IAction;
```

Here, we declare two **actions**. They are records, but they could have been classes instead. Being a record is not a requirement but a shortcut to writing less code. In StateR, an action must implement the IAction interface.

```
        public class Reducers : IReducer<Increment, State>, IReducer<Decrement,
    State>
```

The Reducers class implements the **pure functions** that handle the **actions**. In StateR, a reducer must implement the IReducer<TAction, TState> interface. TAction must be an IAction, and TState must be a StateBase. The interface defines only a Reduce method that inputs a TAction and TState and that outputs the updated TState.

```
        {
            public State Reduce(Increment action, State state)
                => state with { Count = state.Count + 1 };
```

The Increment **reducer** returns a copy of State with its Count incremented by 1.

```
            public State Reduce(Decrement action, State state)
                => state with { Count = state.Count - 1 };
        }
      }
    }
```

Finally, the Decrement **reducer** returns a copy of State with its Count decremented by 1.

Using a with expression like that makes very clean code, especially if the State record has more than one property. Moreover, the record classes help enforce the immutability of the states, which is in line with the MVU pattern.

That is all that we need to cover the model (state) and the update (actions/reducers). Now to the view (component) portion. The view is the following Razor component (Features/CounterView.razor):

```
@page "/mvu-counter"
@inherits StatorComponent
@inject IState<Counter.State> State
<h1>MVU Counter</h1>
<p>Current count: @State.Current.Count</p>
<button class="btn btn-primary" @onclick="() => DispatchAsync(new Counter.
Increment())">+</button>
<button class="btn btn-primary" @onclick="() => DispatchAsync(new Counter.
Decrement())">-</button>
```

There are only a few lines, but quite a lot of things to discuss here. First, the Razor component is accessible at the /mvu-counter URL.

Then, it inherits from StatorComponent. This is not required, but it is convenient. The StatorComponent class implements a few things for us, including managing the component's re-rendering when an IState<TState> property changes.

That leads to the next line, the injection of an IState<Counter.State> interface implementation accessible through the State property. That interface wraps the TState instance and gives access to the current state through its Current property. The @inject directive enables **property injection** in Razor components.

Next, we display the page. @State.Current.Count represents the current count. Following that are two buttons. Both have an @onclick attribute that calls a lambda expression that represents the action to be executed when a user clicks the button. The DispatchAsync method comes from StatorComponent. As its name implies, it **dispatches actions** through the StateR pipeline. It is similar to the MediatR Send and Publish methods.

Each button dispatches a different action; one is Counter.Increment and the other is Counter.Decrement. StateR knows the reducers and sends the action to the appropriate reducers.

That code creates a centralized state and uses the MVU pattern to manage it. If we need Counter.State elsewhere, we only need to inject it, as we did here, and the same state would be shared between multiple components or classes. In this example, we injected the state in a Razor component, but we could also use the same pattern in any code.

One more thing: we need to initialize StateR. To do that, in the Program.cs file, we need to register it like this:

```
using StateR;
using StateR.Blazor.ReduxDevTools; // Optional
// ...
builder.Services
    .AddStateR(typeof(Program).Assembly)
    .AddReduxDevTools() // Optional
    .Apply()
;
```

The builder.Services property is an IServiceCollection. The AddStateR method creates an IStatorBuilder and registers StateR's static dependencies.

Then, the optional AddReduxDevTools method call links StateR to the *Redux DevTools* browser plugin that I mentioned previously. That helps to debug applications from the browser. Other optional mechanisms can be added here. A developer could also code their own extensions to add missing or project-specific features. StateR is DI-based.

Finally, the Apply method initializes StateR by scanning the specified assemblies for every type that it can handle. In this case, we are scanning only the Wasm application assembly (highlighted). The initialization is a two-stage process, completed by the Apply method call.

With that in place, we can run the application and play with our counter. I hope that you liked this little piece of Redux/MVU with StateR. If you did, feel free to use it. If you find missing features, bugs, or performance issues, or want to share your ideas, feel free to open an issue on GitHub (https://adpg.link/Z7Ej).

Conclusion

The MVU pattern uses a **model** to represent the current **state** of the application. The **view** renders that **model**. To **update** the **model**, an **action** is dispatched to a **pure function** (a **reducer**) that returns the new **state**. That change triggers the **view** to re-render.

The **unidirectional flow** of MVU reduces state management's complexity. Having all state changes flowing in the same direction makes it easier to monitor, trace, and debug data flow errors.

Now let's see how the MVU pattern can help us follow the **SOLID** principles:

- S: Each part of the pattern (states, views, and reducers) has its own responsibility.
- O: We can add new elements without impacting existing ones. For example, adding a new action does not impact existing reducers.
- L: N/A
- I: By segregating responsibilities, each part of the pattern implicitly has a smaller surface (interface).
- D: This depends on how you implement it. Based on what we did using StateR, we depended only on interfaces and DTOs (state and actions).

Next, we take a quick peek at other Blazor information to give you an idea of what is available if you want to get started.

A medley of Blazor features

Your Blazor journey has just begun, and there are so many more features to Blazor than what we covered. Here are a few more possibilities to give you a glimpse of the options.

You can integrate Razor components with MVC and Razor Pages using the `Component` Tag Helper. When doing so, you can also prerender your applications (the `App` component) by setting the `render-mode` attribute to `Static`, leading to a faster initial render time. Prerendering can also be used to improve **search engine optimization** (SEO) and the initial load time of the page. The "drawback" is the need for an ASP.NET Core server to execute the prerendering logic.

Another lovely thing about full-stack C# is sharing code between the client and the server. Say we have a web API and a Blazor Wasm application; we could create a third project, a class library, and share the DTOs (API contracts) between the two.

In our component, we can also allow arbitrary HTML between the opening and closing tags by adding a `RenderFragment` parameter named `ChildContent` to that component. We can also catch arbitrary parameters and *splat* them on an HTML element of the component. *Attribute splatting* in Blazor means accepting multiple parameters in a single `Dictionary<string, object>` property and splitting them into multiple HTML properties during rendering. In the following code, we capture any non-specified attributes (`CaptureUnmatchedValues = true`) and render them as HTML attributes. Here is an example combining those two features (`Card.razor`):

```
<div class="@($"card {Class}")" @attributes="Attributes">
    <div class="card-body">
```

```
            @ChildContent
        </div>
    </div>
    @code{
        [Parameter]
        public RenderFragment? ChildContent { get; set; }
        [Parameter(CaptureUnmatchedValues = true)]
        public Dictionary<string, object> Attributes { get; set; } = new()
        [Parameter]
        public string? Class { get; set; }
    }
```

The Card component renders a Bootstrap card and allows consumers to set any attributes they want on it. The content between the <Card> and </Card> tags can be anything. That content is rendered inside the div.card-body. The highlighted lines represent that child content.

The Class parameter is a workaround to allow consumers to add CSS classes while enforcing the card class's presence. The Attributes parameter becomes a catch-all by setting the CaptureUnmatchedValues property of the Parameter attribute to true.

Next is an example that consumes the Card component (Pages/Index.razor):

```
<Card style="width: 25%;" class="mt-4">
    <h5 class="card-title">Card title</h5>
    <h6 class="card-subtitle mb-2 text-muted">Card subtitle</h6>
    <p class="card-text">Some quick example text to build on the card title and
make up the bulk of the card's content.</p>
    <a href="#" class="card-link">Card link</a>
    <a href="#" class="card-link">Another link</a>
</Card>
```

We can see that the Card component (the highlighted lines) is filled with arbitrary HTML (from the official Bootstrap documentation). There are two attributes specified as well, a style and a class.

Here is the rendered result:

```
<div class="card mt-4" style="width: 25%;">
    <div class="card-body">
        <h5 class="card-title">Card title</h5>
        <h6 class="card-subtitle mb-2 text-muted">Card subtitle</h6>
        <p class="card-text">Some quick example text to build on the card title
and make up the bulk of the card's content.</p>
        <a href="#" class="card-link">Card link</a>
        <a href="#" class="card-link">Another link</a>
    </div>
</div>
```

The highlighted lines represent the Card component. Everything else is the ChildContent. We can also notice how the attribute splatting added the style attribute. The Class attribute appended the mt-4 class to card. Here is what it looks like in a browser:

Card title

Card subtitle

Some quick example text to build on the card title and make up the bulk of the card's content

Card link   Another link

Figure 18.6: The Card component rendered in a browser

The Virtualize component allows the number of rendered items to be reduced to just those visible on the screen. You can also control the number of offscreen elements that are rendered to reduce the frequency at which elements are rendered while scrolling. I've left a link to the *ASP.NET Core Blazor component virtualization* documentation page in the *Further reading* section, at the end of the chapter.

As we saw in the counter project, Blazor has full support for dependency injection. For me, that's a requirement. That's also why I learned Angular 2 when it came out and not React or Vue. Blazor's DI support is way better than all of the JavaScript IoC containers that I have seen so far, so this is a major benefit.

There are many other built-in features in Blazor, including an EditForm component, validation support, and a ValidationSummary component, as you'd expect in any MVC or Razor Pages application, but client-side.

Quick tip

Should you ever need to force the rendering of a component, you can call the StateHasChanged method from ComponentBase.

As mentioned earlier in this chapter, .NET code can interact with JavaScript and vice versa. To execute JavaScript code from C#, inject and use the IJSRuntime interface. To execute C# code from JavaScript, use the DotNet.invokeMethod or DotNet.invokeMethodAsync functions. The C# method must be public static and decorated with the JSInvokable attribute. There are multiple other ways in which C# and JavaScript can interact, including non-static methods. By supporting this, developers can build wrappers around JavaScript libraries or use JavaScript libraries as is. It also means that we can implement features that Blazor does not support in JavaScript or even write browser-optimized code in JavaScript if Blazor is slower in one area or another. This also allows tapping into browsers' APIs, like the Fetch API, Storage API, and Canvas API.

You can even write 2D and 3D games using a JavaScript wrapper around a canvas (such as *BlazorCanvas*) or a full-fledged game engine such as *WaveEngine*.

The last bit of additional information that I can think of is an experimental project named *Blazor Mobile Bindings*. That project is a Microsoft experiment that allows Blazor to run in a phone app. It allows native performance by wrapping Xamarin.Forms controls with Razor components. It also supports loading Blazor Wasm in a `WebView` control, allowing for better reusability between mobile and web apps, but at a performance cost.

I've left a long list of links in the *Further reading* section to complement this chapter's information.

Summary

Blazor is a great new piece of technology that could bring C# and .NET to a whole new level. In its present state, it is good enough to develop apps with. There are two main models; Server and WebAssembly.

Blazor Server links the client with the server over a SignalR connection, allowing the server to push updates to the client whenever needed (such as when a user carries out an action). Blazor WebAssembly is a .NET SPA framework that compiles C# to WebAssembly using AOT compilation or sends the **Intermediate Language** (**IL**) code to the browser where a .NET interpreter implemented in WebAssembly interprets that code. That allows .NET code to run in the browser. We can interact with JavaScript using `IJSRuntime` and vice versa.

Blazor is component-based, meaning that every piece of UI in Blazor is a component, including pages. We explored three ways to create components: C#-only, Razor-only, and a hybrid that combines C# and Razor in two different files. A component can also have its own isolated CSS without the need to worry about conflicts.

We explored the life cycle of a Razor component, which is very simple yet powerful. We also took a look at handling events and how to react to them.

We then dug into the MVU pattern, which is very well suited for stateful user interfaces like Blazor. We used an open source library and leveraged C# 9.0 record classes to implement a basic example.

Finally, we took a look at the other possibilities that Blazor has to offer.

I will close this chapter with a personal opinion. I would like to see a Blazor-like model become the unified way to build user interfaces in .NET. I appreciate writing Razor way more than writing XAML, to name only one other way of writing UI code.

Questions

Let's take a look at a few practice questions:

1. Is it true that Blazor Wasm is compiled to JavaScript?
2. Out of the three methods explored to create a Razor component, which one is the best?
3. What are the three parts of the MVU pattern?
4. In the MVU pattern, is it true that it is recommended to use two-way binding?
5. Can Blazor interact with JavaScript?

Further reading

Here are a few links to build upon what we have learned in the chapter:

- WebAssembly:

    a. WebAssembly.org: `https://adpg.link/kod8`

    b. Mozilla Developer Network (MDN): `https://adpg.link/PDh5`

- Stator (StateR) is a simple, dependency injection-oriented, Redux-inspired, or MVU experiment using C# 9.0+: `https://adpg.link/Z7Ej`

- ASP.NET Core Blazor hosting models: `https://adpg.link/N8Do`

- Component Tag Helper in ASP.NET Core: `https://adpg.link/mjqL`

- Create and use ASP.NET Core Razor components: `https://adpg.link/iDVh`

- ASP.NET Core Blazor WebAssembly performance best practices: `https://adpg.link/HrLJ`

- ASP.NET Core Blazor advanced scenarios: `https://adpg.link/nBRc`

- ASP.NET Core Blazor component virtualization: `https://adpg.link/6DTq`

- *Prerendering a Client-side Blazor Application* (by Chris Sainty): `https://adpg.link/Lwhj`

- Blazor Mobile Bindings:

    a. Documentation: `https://adpg.link/yj6T`

    b. Source code (GitHub): `https://adpg.link/shFz`

- Call JavaScript functions from .NET methods in ASP.NET Core Blazor: `https://adpg.link/Wk9z`

- Call .NET methods from JavaScript functions in ASP.NET Core Blazor: `https://adpg.link/93CZ`

- MudBlazor is an amazing UI kit containing many customizable components and inspired by material design: `https://adpg.link/Csfi`

The last time I did 2D/3D development was back when XNA was a thing. I also used Ogre3D in C++ for a school project. That said, I hinted about 2D and 3D games in the chapter, so here are a few resources that I found for those of you who are interested:

- Here are the resources that I found about using HTML5 Canvas in C#:

    a. David Guida (GitHub): `https://adpg.link/3ksk`

    b. Stefan Lörwald (GitHub): `https://adpg.link/zJep`

    c. Blazor Extensions (GitHub): `https://adpg.link/XRAe`

- For games, Evergine supports 2D, 3D, VR, and AR. It is totally free, multiplatform, and has paid enterprise options: `https://adpg.link/fQZj`.

An end is simply a new beginning

This may be the end of the book, but it is also the beginning of your journey into software architecture and design. No matter who you are, I hope you found this to be a refreshing view of design patterns and how to design SOLID web apps.

Depending on your goal and current situation, you may want to explore one or more application-scale design patterns in more depth, start your next personal project, start a business, apply for a new job, or all of those at the same time. No matter your goal, keep in mind that designing software is technical but also an art. There is rarely one right way of implementing a feature, but multiple acceptable ways of doing so. Experience is your best friend, so keep programming, learn from your mistakes, and move forward. Remember that we are all born knowing next to nothing, so not knowing something is expected; we need to learn. Please ask your teammates questions, learn from them, and share your knowledge with others.

Now that this book is complete, I'll get back to writing blog posts, so you can always learn new things there (`https://adpg.link/blog`). Feel free to hit me up on social media, such as Twitter `@CarlHugoM` (`https://adpg.link/twit`). I hope you found the book educational and approachable and that you learned many things. I wish you success in your career.

Appendices

Appendix A

This appendix describes different C# features that we use or are related to topics we use in the book. I cannot cover all C# features in an appendix, but I did my best to pick the most relevant ones.

We are covering the following:

- **Older C# features** covering C# 1 to 8
- **What's new in .NET 5 and C# 9?** covering features from C# 9
- **What's new in .NET 6 and C# 10?** covering features from C# 10

Older C# features

This section covers a list of C# features that are useful, less known, or I want to make sure you are aware of since we are leveraging or mentioning them in the book.

The null-coalescing operator (C# 2.0)

The null-coalescing (??) operator is a binary operator written using the following syntax: result = left ?? right. It expresses to use the right value when the left value is null. Otherwise, the left value is used.

Here is a console application using the null-coalescing operator:

```
Console.WriteLine(ValueOrDefault(default, "Default value"));
Console.WriteLine(ValueOrDefault("Some value", "Default value"));

static string ValueOrDefault(string? value, string defaultValue)
{
    return value ?? defaultValue;
}
```

The ValueOrDefault method returns defaultValue when value is null; otherwise, it returns value. Executing that program outputs the following:

```
Default value
Some value
```

The null-coalescing (??) operator is very convenient as it saves us from writing code like the following equivalent method:

```
static string ValueOrDefaultPlain(string? value, string defaultValue)
{
    if (value == null)
```

```
    {
        return defaultValue;
    }
    return value;
}
```

Interesting Fact

C# 2.0 is also the version they added generics, which were a very welcome addition. Try to imagine C# without generics.

Expression-bodied member (C# 6-7)

Expression-bodied members allow us to write an expression (a line of code) after the arrow operator (=>) instead of the body of that member (delimited by { }). We can write methods, properties, constructors, finalizers, and indexers this way.

Here is a small program that leverages this capability:

```
Console.WriteLine(new Restaurant("The Cool Place"));
Console.WriteLine(new Restaurant("The Even Cooler Place"));

public class Restaurant
{
    public readonly string _name;
    public Restaurant(string name)
        => _name = name;

    public string Name => _name; // read-only property

    public override string ToString()
        => $"Restaurant: {Name}";
}
```

Executing the program yields:

```
Restaurant: The Cool Place
Restaurant: The Even Cooler Place
```

The equivalent with bodies would be the following code:

```
public class RestaurantWithBody
{
    public readonly string _name;
    public RestaurantWithBody(string name)
```

```
    {
        _name = name;
    }

    public string Name
    {
        get
        {
            return _name;
        }
    }

    public override string ToString()
    {
        return $"Restaurant: {Name}";
    }
}
```

As we can see from the preceding example, expression-bodied members allow us to make the code denser with less noise (less {}).

> **Note**
>
> I find that expression-bodied members reduce readability when the right-hand expression is complex. I rarely use expression-bodied constructors and finalizers as I find they make the code harder to read. However, read-only properties and methods can benefit from this construct as long as the right-hand expression is simple.

Throw expressions (C# 7.0)

This feature allows us to use the throw statement as an expression, giving us the possibility to throw exceptions on the right side of the null-coalescing operator (??).

The good old-fashioned way of writing a guard clause, before throw expressions, was as follows:

```
public HomeController(IHomeService homeService)
{
    if (homeService == null)
    {
        throw new ArgumentNullException(nameof(homeService));
    }
    _homeService = homeService;
}
```

In the preceding code, we first check for null, and if homeService is null, we throw an

ArgumentNullException; otherwise, we assign the value to the field _homeService.

Now, with throw expressions, we can write the preceding code as a one-liner instead:

```
public HomeController(IHomeService homeService)
{
    _homeService = homeService ?? throw new
ArgumentNullException(nameof(homeService));
}
```

Before C# 7.0, we could not throw an exception from the right side (it was a statement), but now we can (it is an expression).

> **Note**
>
> From C# 10 onward, we can now write guards using the static ThrowIfNull method of the ArgumentNullException class, like this:
>
> ```
> public HomeController(IHomeService homeService)
> {
>     ArgumentNullException.ThrowIfNull(homeService);
>     _homeService = homeService;
> }
> ```
>
> This makes the intent a little more explicit but does not assign the value to the field, which is less than ideal for a constructor guard. If the objective is only to validate for nulls, like in a method, this new method can be handy.

Tuples (C# 7.0+)

A tuple is a type that allows returning multiple values from a method or stores multiple values in a variable without declaring a type and without using the dynamic type. Since C# 7.0, tuple support has greatly improved.

> **Note**
>
> Using dynamic objects is OK in some cases, but beware that it could reduce performance and increase the number of runtime exceptions thrown due to the lack of strong types. Moreover, dynamic objects bring limited tooling support, making it harder to discover what an object can do; it is more error-prone than a strong type, there is no type checking, no auto-completion, and no compiler validation. Compile-time errors can be fixed right away, without the need to wait for them to arise during runtime, or worse, be reported by a user.

The C# language adds syntactic sugar regarding tuples that makes the code clearer and easier to read. Microsoft calls that **lightweight syntax**.

If you've used the Tuple classes before, you know that Tuple members are accessed through Item1,

Item2, and ItemN properties. The ValueTuple struct also exposes similar fields. This newer syntax is built on top of the ValueTuple struct and allows us to eliminate those generic names from our codebase and replace them with meaningful user-defined ones. From now on, when referring to tuples, I refer to C# tuples, or more precisely an instance of ValueTuple. If you've never heard of tuples, we explore them right away.

Let's jump right into a few samples, coded as xUnit tests. The first shows how we can create an unnamed tuple and access its fields using Item1, Item2, and ItemN, which we talked about earlier:

```csharp
[Fact]
public void Unnamed()
{
    var unnamed = ("some", "value", 322);
    Assert.Equal("some", unnamed.Item1);
    Assert.Equal("value", unnamed.Item2);
    Assert.Equal(322, unnamed.Item3);
}
```

Then, we can create a named tuple—very useful if you don't like those 1, 2, 3 fields:

```csharp
[Fact]
public void Named()
{
    var named = (name: "Foo", age: 23);
    Assert.Equal("Foo", named.name);
    Assert.Equal(23, named.age);
}
```

Since the compiler does most of the naming, and even if IntelliSense is not showing it to you, we can still access those 1, 2, 3 fields:

```csharp
[Fact]
public void Named_equals_Unnamed()
{
    var named = (name: "Foo", age: 23);
    Assert.Equal(named.name, named.Item1);
    Assert.Equal(named.age, named.Item2);
}
```

Note

If you loaded the whole Git repository, a Visual Studio analyzer should tell you not to do this by underlining those members with red error-like squiggly lines because of the configuration I've made in the .editorconfig file, which instructs Visual Studio how to react to coding styles. In a default context, you should see a suggestion instead.

Moreover, we can create a named tuple using variables where names follow "magically":

```
[Fact]
public void ProjectionInitializers()
{
    var name = "Foo";
    var age = 23;
    var projected = (name, age);
    Assert.Equal("Foo", projected.name);
    Assert.Equal(23, projected.age);
}
```

Since the values are stored in those 1, 2, 3 fields, and the programmer-friendly names are compiler-generated, equality is based on field order, not field name. Partly due to that, comparing whether two tuples are equal is pretty straightforward:

```
[Fact]
public void TuplesEquality()
{
    var named1 = (name: "Foo", age: 23);
    var named2 = (name: "Foo", age: 23);
    var namedDifferently = (Whatever: "Foo", bar: 23);
    var unnamed1 = ("Foo", 23);
    var unnamed2 = ("Foo", 23);

    Assert.Equal(named1, unnamed1);
    Assert.Equal(named1, named2);
    Assert.Equal(unnamed1, unnamed2);
    Assert.Equal(named1, namedDifferently);
}
```

If you don't like to access the tuple's members using the dot (.) notation, we can also deconstruct them into variables:

```
[Fact]
public void Deconstruction()
{
    var tuple = (name: "Foo", age: 23);
    var (name, age) = tuple;
    Assert.Equal("Foo", name);
    Assert.Equal(23, age);
}
```

Methods can also return tuples and can be used the same way that we saw in previous examples:

```
[Fact]
public void MethodReturnValue()
{
    var tuple1 = CreateTuple1();
    var tuple2 = CreateTuple2();
    Assert.Equal(tuple1, tuple2);

    static (string name, int age) CreateTuple1()
    {
        return (name: "Foo", age: 23);
    }

    static (string name, int age) CreateTuple2()
        => (name: "Foo", age: 23);
}
```

Note

The methods are local functions, but the same applies to normal methods as well.

To conclude on tuples, I suggest avoiding them on public APIs that are exported (a shared library, for example). However, I find they come in handy internally to code helpers without creating a class that holds only data and is used once or a few times.

I think that tuples are a great addition to .NET, but I prefer fully defined types on public APIs for many reasons. The first reason is encapsulation; tuple members are fields, which breaks encapsulation. Then, accurately naming classes that are part of an API (contract/interface) is essential.

Tip

When you can't find an exhaustive name for a type, the chances are that some business requirements are blurry, what is under development is not exactly what is needed, or the domain language is not clear. When that happens, try to word a clear statement about what you are trying to accomplish and if you still can't find a name, try to rethink that API.

For example, "I want to calculate the sales tax rate of the specified product" could yield a `CalculateSalesTaxRate(...)` method in a `Product` class or a `CalculateSalesTaxRate(Product product, ...)` in another class.

An excellent alternative to tuples for public APIs is record classes, keeping additional code minimal.

Default literal expressions (C# 7.1)

Default literal expressions were introduced in C# 7.1 and allow us to reduce the amount of code required to use **default value expressions**.

Previously, we needed to write this:

```
string input = default(string);
```

Or this:

```
var input = default(string);
```

Now, we can write this:

```
string input = default;
```

It can be very useful for optional parameters, like this:

```
public void SomeMethod(string input1, string input2 = default)
{
    // ...
}
```

In the method defined in the preceding code block, we can pass one or two arguments to the method. When we omit the input2 parameter, it is instantiated to default(string), which is null.

We can use default literal expressions instead, which allow us to do the following:

* Initialize a variable to its default value.
* Set the default value of an optional method parameter.
* Provide a default argument value to a method call.
* Return a default value in a return statement or an expression-bodied member (the arrow =>
  operator introduced in C# 6 and 7).

Here is an example covering those use cases:

```
public class DefaultLiteralExpression<T>
{
    public void Execute()
    {
        // Initialize a variable to its default value
        T? myVariable = default;

        var defaultResult1 = SomeMethod();

        // Provide a default argument value to a method call
        var defaultResult2 = SomeOtherMethod(myVariable, default);
    }
```

```
    // Set the default value of an optional method parameter
    public object? SomeMethod(T? input = default)
    {
        // Return a default value in a return statement
        return default;
    }

    // Return a default value in an expression-bodied member
    public object? SomeOtherMethod(T? input, int i) => default;
}
```

We used the generic T type parameter in the examples, but that could be any type. The default literal expressions become handy with complex generic types such as Func<T>, Func<T1, T2>, or tuples.

Here is a good example of how simple it is to return a tuple and return the default values of its three components using a default literal expression:

```
public (object, string, bool) MethodThatReturnATuple()
{
    return default;
}
```

It is important to note that the default value of reference types (classes) is null, but the default of value types (struct) is an instance of that struct with all its fields initialized to their respective default value. C# 10 introduces the ability to define a default parameterless constructor to value types, which initializes that struct's default instance when using the default keyword, overriding the preceding assertion about default fields. Moreover, many built-in types have custom default values; for example, the default for numeric types and enum is 0 while a bool is false.

Switch expressions (C# 8)

This feature was introduced in C# 8 and is named **switch expressions**. Previously, we had to write this (code taken from the Strategy pattern code sample from *Chapter 6, Understanding the Strategy, Abstract Factory, and Singleton Design Patterns*):

```
string output = default;
switch (input)
{
    case "1":
        output = PrintCollection();
        break;
    case "2":
        output = SortData();
        break;
```

```csharp
    case "3":
        output = SetSortAsc();
        break;
    case "4":
        output = SetSortDesc();
        break;
    case "0":
        output = "Exiting";
        break;
    default:
        output = "Invalid input!";
        break;
}
```

Now, we can write this:

```csharp
var output = input switch
{
    "1" => PrintCollection(),
    "2" => SortData(),
    "3" => SetSortAsc(),
    "4" => SetSortDesc(),
    "0" => "Exiting",
    _   => "Invalid input!"
};
```

That makes the code shorter and simpler. Once you get used to it, I find this new way even easier to read. You can think about a switch expression as a `switch` that returns a value.

Note

Switch expressions also support **pattern matching** introduced in C# 7. C# received more pattern matching features in subsequent versions. We are not covering pattern matching here.

Discards (C# 7)

Discards were introduced in C# 7. In the following example (code taken from the GitHub repo associated with the Strategy pattern code sample from *Chapter 6, Understanding the Strategy, Abstract Factory, and Singleton Design Patterns*), the discard became the `default` case of the `switch` (see the highlighted line):

```csharp
var output = input switch
{
    "1" => PrintCollection(),
```

```
        "2" => SortData(),
        "3" => SetSortAsc(),
        "4" => SetSortDesc(),
        "0" => "Exiting",
        _   => "Invalid input!"
};
```

Discards (_) are also useable in other scenarios. It is a special variable that cannot be used, a placeholder, like a variable that does not exist. Using discards doesn't allocate memory for that variable, which helps optimize your application.

It is useful when deconstructing a tuple and to use only some of its members. In the following code, we keep the reference on the name field but discard age during the deconstruction:

```
var tuple = (name: "Foo", age: 23);
var (name, _) = tuple;
Console.WriteLine(name);
```

It is also very convenient when calling a method with an out parameter that you don't want to use, for example:

```
if (bool.TryParse("true", out _))
{
    Console.WriteLine("true was parsable!");
}
```

In that last code block, we only want to do something if the input is a Boolean, but we do not use the Boolean value itself, which is a great scenario for a discard variable.

Async main (C# 7.1)

From C# 7.1 onward, a console application can have an async Main method, which is very convenient as more and more code is becoming asynchronous. This new feature allows the use of await directly in the Main() method, without any quirks.

Previously, the signature of the Main method had to fit one of the following:

```
public static void Main() { }
public static int Main() { }
public static void Main(string[] args) { }
public static int Main(string[] args) { }
```

Since C# 7.1, we can also use their async counterpart:

```
public static async Task Main() { }
public static async Task<int> Main() { }
public static async Task Main(string[] args) { }
public static async Task<int> Main(string[] args) { }
```

Now, we can create a console application that looks like this:

```csharp
class Program
{
    static async Task Main(string[] args)
    {
        Console.WriteLine("Entering Main");
        var myService = new MyService();
        await myService.ExecuteAsync();
        Console.WriteLine("Exiting Main");
    }
}
public class MyService
{
    public Task ExecuteAsync()
    {
        Console.WriteLine("Inside MyService.ExecuteAsync()");
        return Task.CompletedTask;
    }
}
```

When executing the program, the result is as follows:

```
Entering Main
Inside MyService.ExecuteAsync()
Exiting Main
```

Nothing fancy, but it allows us to take advantage of the await/async language feature directly from the Main method.

> **Note**
>
> From .NET Core 1.0 to .NET 5, all types of applications start with a Main method (usually Program.Main), including ASP.NET Core web applications. This addition is very useful and well needed. The minimal hosting model for ASP.NET Core introduced in .NET 6 is built on top of top-level statements, introduced in .NET 5, and they make this construct implicit since the compiler generates the Program class and the Main method for us. It is still there, good to know, but chances are you won't need to write that code manually.

User-defined conversion operators (C# 1)

User-defined conversion operators are user-defined functions crafted to convert one type to another implicitly or explicitly. Many built-in types offer such conversions, such as converting an int to a long without any cast or method call:

```csharp
int var1 = 5;
```

```
long var2 = var1; // This is possible due to a class conversion operator
```

Next is an example of custom conversion. We convert a string to an instance of the SomeGenericClass<string> class without a cast:

```
using Xunit;
namespace ConversionOperator;

public class SomeGenericClass<T>
{
    public T? Value { get; set; }

    public static implicit operator SomeGenericClass<T>(T value)
    {
        return new SomeGenericClass<T>
        {
            Value = value
        };
    }
}
```

The SomeGenericClass<T> class defines a generic property named Value that can be set to any type. The highlighted code block is the conversion operator method, allowing conversion from the type T to SomeGenericClass<T> without a cast. Let's look at the result next:

```
[Fact]
public void Value_should_be_set_implicitly()
{
    var value = "Test";
    SomeGenericClass<string> result = value;
    Assert.Equal("Test", result.Value);
}
```

That first test method uses the conversion operator we just examined to convert a string to an instance of the SomeGenericClass<string> class. We can also leverage that to cast a value (a float in this case) to a SomeGenericClass<float> class, like this:

```
[Fact]
public void Value_should_be_castable()
{
    var value = 0.5F;
    var result = (SomeGenericClass<float>)value;
    Assert.Equal(0.5F, result.Value);
    Assert.IsType<SomeGenericClass<float>>(result);
}
```

Conversion operators also work with methods, as the next test method will show you:

```
[Fact]
public void Value_should_be_set_implicitly_using_local_function()
{
    var result1 = GetValue("Test");
    Assert.IsType<SomeGenericClass<string>>(result1);
    Assert.Equal("Test", result1.Value);

    var result2 = GetValue(123);
    Assert.Equal(123, result2.Value);
    Assert.IsType<SomeGenericClass<int>>(result2);

    static SomeGenericClass<T> GetValue<T>(T value)
    {
        return value;
    }
}
```

The preceding code implicitly converts a string into a SomeGenericClass<string> object and an int into a SomeGenericClass<int> object. The highlighted line returns the value of type T as an instance of the SomeGenericClass<T> class directly; the conversion is implicit.

This is not the most important topic of the book, but if you were curious, this is how .NET does this kind of implicit conversion (like returning an instance of T instead of an ActionResult<T> in MVC controllers). Now you know that you can implement custom conversion operators in your classes too when you want that kind of behavior.

Local functions (C# 7) and a static local function (C# 8)

In the previous example, we used a static local function, new to C# 8, to demonstrate the class conversion operator.

Local functions are definable inside methods, constructors, property accessors, event accessors, anonymous methods, lambda expressions, finalizers, and other local functions. Those functions are private to their containing members. They are very useful for making the code more explicit and self-explanatory without polluting the class itself, keeping them in the consuming member's scope. Local functions can access the declaring member's variables and parameters, like this:

```
[Fact]
public void With_no_parameter_accessing_outer_scope()
{
    var x = 1;
    var y = 2;
    var z = Add();
```

```
    Assert.Equal(3, z);

    x = 2;
    y = 3;
    var n = Add();
    Assert.Equal(5, n);

    int Add()
    {
        return x + y;
    }
}
```

That is not the most robust function because the inner scope (inline function) depends on the outer scope (method variables x and y). Nonetheless, the code shows how a local function can access its parent scope's members, which is necessary in some cases.

The following code block shows a mix of inline function scope (the y parameter) and outer scope (the x variable):

```
[Fact]
public void With_one_parameter_accessing_outer_scope()
{
    var x = 1;
    var z = Add(2);
    Assert.Equal(3, z);

    x = 2;
    var n = Add(3);
    Assert.Equal(5, n);

    int Add(int y)
    {
        return x + y;
    }
}
```

That block shows how to pass an argument and how the local function can still use its outer scope's variables to alter its result. Now, if we want an independent function, decoupled from its outer scope, we could code the following instead:

```
[Fact]
public void With_two_parameters_not_accessing_outer_scope()
{
```

```
    var a = Add(1, 2);
    Assert.Equal(3, a);

    var b = Add(2, 3);
    Assert.Equal(5, b);

    int Add(int x, int y)
    {
        return x + y;
    }
}
```

This code is less error-prone than the other alternatives; the logic is contained in a smaller scope (the function scope), leading to an independent inline function. But it still allows someone to alter it later and to use the outer scope since there is nothing to tell the intent of limiting access to the outer scope, like this (some unwanted outer scope access):

```
[Fact]
public void With_two_parameters_accessing_outer_scope()
{
    var z = 5;
    var a = Add(1, 2);
    Assert.Equal(8, a);

    var b = Add(2, 3);
    Assert.Equal(10, b);

    int Add(int x, int y)
    {
        return x + y + z;
    }
}
```

To clarify that intent, we can leverage static local functions. They remove the option to access the enclosing scope variables and clearly state that intent with the static keyword. The following is the static equivalent of a previous function:

```
[Fact]
public void With_two_parameters()
{
    var a = Add(1, 2);
    Assert.Equal(3, a);
```

```
        var b = Add(2, 3);
        Assert.Equal(5, b);

        static int Add(int x, int y)
        {
            return x + y;
        }
    }
}
```

Then, with that clear definition, the updated version could become the following instead, keeping the local function independent:

```
[Fact]
public void With_three_parameters()
{
    var c = 5;
    var a = Add(1, 2, c);
    Assert.Equal(8, a);

    var b = Add(2, 3, c);
    Assert.Equal(10, b);

    static int Add(int x, int y, int z)
    {
        return x + y + z;
    }
}
```

Nothing can stop someone from removing the static modifier, maybe a good code review, but at least no one can say that the intent was not clear enough since the following would not compile:

```
[Fact]
public void With_two_parameters_accessing_outer_scope()
{
    var z = 5;
    var a = Add(1, 2);
    Assert.Equal(8, a);

    var b = Add(2, 3);
    Assert.Equal(10, b);

    static int Add(int x, int y)
    {
```

```
        return x + y + z;
    }
}
```

Using the enclosing scope can be useful sometimes, but I prefer to avoid that whenever possible, for the same reason that I do my best to avoid global stuff: the code can become messier, faster.

To recap, we can create a local function by declaring it inside another supported member without specifying any access modifier (`public`, `private`, and so on). That function can access its declaring scope, expose parameters, and do almost everything a method can do, including being `async` and `unsafe`. Then comes C# 8, which adds the option to define a local function as `static`, blocking the access to its outer scope and clearly stating the intent of an independent, standalone, private local function.

What's new in .NET 5 and C# 9?

In this section, we explore the following C# 9 features:

- Top-level statements
- Target-typed new expressions
- Init-only properties
- Record classes

We use top-level statements to simplify code samples, leading to one code file with less boilerplate code. Moreover, top-level statements are the building blocks of the .NET 6 minimal hosting model and minimal APIs. We dig into the new expressions, which allow creating new instances with less typing. The init-only properties are the backbone of the record classes used in multiple chapters and are foundational to the MVU example presented in *Chapter 18, A Brief Look into Blazor*.

Top-level statements

Starting from C# 9, it is possible to write statements before declaring namespaces and other members. Those statements are compiled to an emitted `Program.Main` method.

With top-level statements, a minimal .NET "Hello World" program now looks like this:

```
using System;
Console.WriteLine("Hello world!");
```

Unfortunately, we also need a project to run, so we have to create a `.csproj` file with the following content:

```
<Project Sdk="Microsoft.NET.Sdk">
    <PropertyGroup>
        <TargetFramework>net5.0</TargetFramework>
        <OutputType>Exe</OutputType>
    </PropertyGroup>
</Project>
```

From there, we can use the .NET CLI to dotnet run the application.

> **Note**
>
> I left the TargetFramework as net5.0 because this is related to .NET 5. We revisit top-level statements in the *What's new in .NET 6 and C# 10?* section.

We can also declare other members, like classes, and use them as in any other application. Classes must be declared after the top-level code. Be aware that the top-level statement code is not part of any namespace, and it is recommended to create classes in a namespace, so you should limit the number of declarations done in the Program.cs file to what is internal to its inner workings.

Top-level statements are a great feature for getting started with C# and writing code samples by cutting out boilerplate code.

Target-typed new expressions

Target-typed new expressions are a new way of initializing types. C# 3 introduced the var keyword back in the day, which became very handy to work with generic types, LINQ return values, and more (I remember embracing that new construct with joy).

This new C# feature does the opposite of the var keyword by letting us call the constructor of a known type, like this:

```
List<string> list1 = new();
List<string> list2 = new(10);
List<string> list3 = new(capacity: 10);
var obj = new MyClass(new());
AnotherClass anotherObj = new() { Name = "My Name" };

public class MyClass {
    public MyClass(AnotherClass property)
        => Property = property;
    public AnotherClass Property { get; }
}
public class AnotherClass {
    public string? Name { get; init; }
}
```

The first highlight shows the ability to create new objects when the type is known using the new() keyword and omitting the type name. The second list is created the same way, but we passed the argument 10 to its constructor. The third list uses the same approach but explicitly specifies the parameter name, as we could with any standard constructor. Using a named parameter makes the code easier to understand.

The instance of MyClass assigned to the obj variable is created explicitly, but new() is used to create an instance of AnotherClass, which is inferred because the parameter type is known.

The final example demos the use of class initializers. As you may have noticed, the `AnotherClass` class has an init-only property, which is our next subject.

I can see the target-typed new expressions simplify many codebases. I started using them, and they are a great addition to C# 9.0. Please be careful not to make your code harder to read by abusing target-typed new expressions; only use them when the type is clear, like `MyType variable = new()`.

Init-only properties

Init-only properties are read-only properties that can be initialized using class initializers. Previously, read-only properties could only be initialized in the constructor or with property initializers (such as `public int SomeProp { get; } = 2;`).

For example, let's take a class that holds the state of a counter. A read-only property would look like `Count`:

```
public class Counter
{
    public int Count { get; }
}
```

Without a constructor, it is impossible to initialize the `Count` property, so we can't initialize an instance like this:

```
var counter = new Counter { Count = 2 };
```

That's the use case that init-only properties enable. We can rewrite the `Counter` class to make use of that by using the `init` keyword, like this:

```
public class Counter
{
    public int Count { get; init; }
}
```

With that in place we can now use it like this:

```
var counter = new Counter { Count = 2 };
Console.WriteLine($"Hello, Counter: {counter.Count}!");
```

Init-only properties enable developers to create immutable properties that are settable using a class initializer. They are also a building block of **record classes**.

Record classes

A record class uses init-only properties and allows making reference types (classes) **immutable**. The only way to change a `record` is to create a new one. Let's convert the `Counter` class into a record:

```
public record Counter
{
    public int Count { get; init; }
```

```
    }
```

Yes, it is as simple as replacing the `class` keyword with the `record` keyword. Since .NET 6, we can keep the `class` keyword as well to differentiate (and make consistent) the new **record struct**, like this:

```
public record class Counter
{
    public int Count { get; init; }
}
```

But that's not all:

- We can simplify record creation.
- We can also use the `with` keyword to simplify "mutating" a record (creating a mutated copy without changing the source).
- Records support **deconstruction**, like the **tuple** types.
- .NET auto-implements the `Equals` and `GetHashCode` methods. Those two methods compare the value of the properties instead of the reference to the object. That means that two different instances with equal values would be equal.
- .NET auto-overrides the `ToString` method that outputs a better format, including property values.

All in all, that means we end up with an immutable reference type (`class`) that behaves like a value type (`struct`) without the copy allocation cost.

Simplifying the record creation

If we don't want to use a **class initializer** when creating instances, we can simplify the code of our records to the following:

```
public record class Counter(int Count);
```

> **Note**
>
> That syntax reminds me of **TypeScript**, where you can define fields in the constructor, and they get implemented automatically without the need to write any plumbing code.

Then, we can create a new instance like with any other class:

```
var counter = new Counter(2);
Console.WriteLine($"Count: {counter.Count}");
```

Running that code would output `Count: 2` in the console. We can also add methods to the record class:

```
public record class Counter(int Count)
{
    public bool CanCount() => true;
}
```

You can do everything with a record that you would do with a class and more. The record class is a class like any other.

The with keyword

The with keyword allows us to create a copy of a record and change only the value of certain properties without altering the others. Let's take a look at the following code:

```
var initialDate = DateTime.UtcNow.AddMinutes(-1);
var initialForecast = new Forecast(initialDate, 20, "Sunny");
var currentForecast = initialForecast with { Date = DateTime.UtcNow };

Console.WriteLine(initialForecast);
Console.WriteLine(currentForecast);

public record class Forecast(DateTime Date, int TemperatureC, string Summary)
{
    public int TemperatureF => 32 + (int)(TemperatureC /
    0.5556);
}
```

When we execute that code, we end up with a result similar to this:

```
Forecast { Date = 9/22/2020 12:04:20 AM, TemperatureC = 20, Summary = Sunny,
TemperatureF = 67 }
Forecast { Date = 9/22/2020 12:05:20 AM, TemperatureC = 20, Summary = Sunny,
TemperatureF = 67 }
```

The power of the with keyword allows us to create a copy of the initialForecast record and only change the Date property's value.

> **Note**
>
> The formatted output is provided by the overloaded ToString method that comes by default with record classes. We have nothing to do to make this happen.

The with keyword is a very compelling addition to the language.

Deconstruction

We can **deconstruct** record classes like a tuple:

```
var current = new Forecast(DateTime.UtcNow, 20, "Sunny");
var (date, temperatureC, summary) = current;

Console.WriteLine($"date: {date}");
Console.WriteLine($"temperatureC: {temperatureC}");
Console.WriteLine($"summary: {summary}");
```

```
public record class Forecast(DateTime Date, int TemperatureC, string Summary)
{
    public int TemperatureF => 32 + (int)(TemperatureC / 0.5556);
}
```

By default, all **positional members** (defined in the constructor) are deconstructable. In that example, we cannot access the TemperatureF property by using deconstruction because it is not a positional member.

We can create a custom **deconstructor** by implementing one or more Deconstruct methods that expose out parameters of the properties that we want to be deconstructable, like this:

```
using System;
var current = new Forecast(DateTime.UtcNow, 20, "Sunny");
var (date, temperatureC, summary, temperatureF) = current;

Console.WriteLine($"date: {date}");
Console.WriteLine($"temperatureC: {temperatureC}");
Console.WriteLine($"summary: {summary}");
Console.WriteLine($"temperatureF: {temperatureF}");

public record Forecast(DateTime Date, int TemperatureC, string Summary)
{
    public int TemperatureF => 32 + (int)(TemperatureC / 0.5556);
    public void Deconstruct(out DateTime date, out int temperatureC, out string
summary, out int temperatureF)
        => (date, temperatureC, summary, temperatureF) = (Date, TemperatureC,
Summary, TemperatureF);
}
```

With that updated sample, we can also access the TemperatureF property's value when deconstructing the record.

Lastly, by adding Deconstruct methods, we can control the way our record classes get deconstructed.

Equality comparison

As mentioned previously, the default comparison between two records is made by their values and not their memory addresses, so two different instances with the same values are equal. The following code proves this:

```
var employee1 = new Employee("Johnny", "Mnemonic");
var employee2 = new Employee("Clark", "Kent");
var employee3 = new Employee("Johnny", "Mnemonic");
Console.WriteLine($"Does '{employee1}' equals '{employee2}'? {employee1 ==
```

```
employee2}");
Console.WriteLine($"Does '{employee1}' equals '{employee3}'? {employee1 ==
employee3}");
Console.WriteLine($"Does '{employee2}' equals '{employee3}'? {employee2 ==
employee3}");


public record Employee(string FirstName, string LastName);
```

When running that code, the output is as follows:

```
Does 'Employee { FirstName = Johnny, LastName = Mnemonic }' equals 'Employee {
FirstName = Clark, LastName = Kent }'? False
Does 'Employee { FirstName = Johnny, LastName = Mnemonic }' equals 'Employee {
FirstName = Johnny, LastName = Mnemonic }'? True
Does 'Employee { FirstName = Clark, LastName = Kent }' equals 'Employee {
FirstName = Johnny, LastName = Mnemonic }'? False
```

In that example, even if `employee1` and `employee3` are two different objects, the result is `true` when we compare them using `employee1 == employee3`, proving that values were compared, not instances.

Once again, we leveraged the `ToString()` method of record classes, which is returning a developer-friendly representation of its data. The `ToString()` method of an object is called implicitly when using string interpolation, like in the preceding code block, hence the complete output.

On the other hand, if you want to know if they are the same instance, you can use the `object.ReferenceEquals()` method like this:

```
Console.WriteLine($"Is 'employee1' the same as 'employee3'? {object.
ReferenceEquals(employee1, employee3)}");
```

This will output the following:

```
Is 'employee1' the same as 'employee3'? False
```

Conclusion

Record classes are a great new addition that creates immutable types in a few keystrokes. Furthermore, they support deconstruction and implement equality comparison that compares the value of properties, not whether the instances are the same, simplifying our lives in many cases.

Init-only properties can also benefit regular classes if one prefers class initializers to constructors.

What's new in .NET 6 and C# 10?

.NET 6 and C# 10 have brought many new features. We cannot visit them all but we explore a selection of those features that are leveraged in the book or that I thought were worth mentioning.

In this section, we explore the following C# 10 features:

- File-scoped namespaces
- Global using directives
- Implicit using directives
- Constant interpolated strings
- Record struct
- Minimal hosting model
- Minimal APIs
- Nullable reference types (added in C# 8 and enabled by default in .NET 6 templates)

File-scoped namespaces

Declaring a file-scoped namespace reduces the horizontal indentation of our code files by removing the need to declare a block ({}).

We previously wrote:

```
namespace Vehicles
{
    public interface IVehicleFactory
    {
        // Omitted members
    }
}
```

We now can write:

```
namespace Vehicles;
public interface IVehicleFactory
{
    // Omitted members
}
```

Saving four spaces at the beginning of each line may sound insignificant, but I feel it helps reduce the cognitive load by removing some indentation, and it gives us more screen space for meaningful code.

Global using directives

Before .NET 6, there was always a long list of using directives at the top of each file. Global using directives allow us to define some using directives globally, so those namespaces are automatically imported into every file of the project.

You can add global using directives in any project file, but I recommend centralizing them, so they are not spread around the whole project. There are two places I feel they would fit:

- In the Program.cs file because that's the entry point of the program.
- In a specific file, named meaningfully, like GlobalUsings.cs.

Here is an example that is comprised of three files:

```
// GlobalUsings.cs
global using GlobalUsingDirectives.SomeCoolNamespace;

// SomeClass.cs
namespace GlobalUsingDirectives.SomeCoolNamespace;
public class SomeClass {  }

// Program.cs
Console.WriteLine(typeof(SomeClass).FullName);
```

When executing the program, we obtain the following output:

```
GlobalUsingDirectives.SomeCoolNamespace.SomeClass
```

Since there is no using directive in the Program.cs file, that proves the global using declared in the GlobalUsings.cs was used, and the whole thing worked as expected.

Implicit using directives

To continue in the way of global using directives, the .NET team gave us a treat: implicit using directives. It is an opt-in feature that is enabled by default in .NET 6 templates by the following property (placed in a PropertyGroup) of your .csproj file:

```
<ImplicitUsings>enable</ImplicitUsings>
```

The imported namespaces are stored in an auto-generated [project name].GlobalUsings.g.cs file saved under the obj/Debug/[version] folder. The content varies depending on the project type. As of the time of writing, for console applications, the file contains the following code:

```
// <auto-generated/>
global using global::System;
global using global::System.Collections.Generic;
global using global::System.IO;
global using global::System.Linq;
global using global::System.Net.Http;
global using global::System.Threading;
global using global::System.Threading.Tasks;
```

With this enabled, we don't have to bother with those redundant using directives. We can now write a Hello World program as a one-liner (OK, plus an eight-line csproj file). We can also register our own global using directives in our own files to complement this.

If you don't like this, you can opt out by deleting the ImplicitUsings property from your project file or by setting its value to disable.

Constant interpolated strings

We do not use this feature in the book, but I felt it was worth mentioning. It happened a few times in my career that I needed this feature.

Note

As a workaround, I used static properties instead, but constants are replaced at build time and are equivalent to hardcoding their value with a lower maintenance overhead (1 constant instead of hardcoded values in multiple places). Using constants is more performant than accessing a property.

Before .NET 6, we could not initialize a constant through interpolation. Now we can as long as all the interpolated values are also string constants. Here is an example:

```
const string DotNetVersion = "6";
const string BookTitle = $"An Atypical ASP.NET Core {DotNetVersion} Design
Patterns Guide";

Console.WriteLine(BookTitle);
```

That code outputs the following:

```
An Atypical ASP.NET Core 6 Design Patterns Guide
```

That code has the same performance as the following:

```
Console.WriteLine("An Atypical ASP.NET Core 6 Design Patterns Guide");
```

That's it, a little more that we can do using C#.

Record struct

This is another feature we do not use in the book but is worth mentioning. These are very similar to record classes but for structure types. As you can see from the following program, the syntax is very similar:

```
var client1 = new MutableClient("John", "Doe");
client1.Firstname = "Jane";
Console.WriteLine(client1);

var client2 = new ImmutableClient("John", "Doe");
```

```
Console.WriteLine(client2);

public record struct MutableClient(string Firstname, string Lastname);
public readonly record struct ImmutableClient(string Firstname, string
Lastname);
```

What is strange compared to record classes is that the positional properties of a record struct are mutable. To make positional properties immutable we must use the readonly record struct keywords instead of record struct.

Executing the code outputs the following result:

```
MutableClient { Firstname = Jane, Lastname = Doe }
ImmutableClient { Firstname = John, Lastname = Doe }
```

You should apply the same decision process to record struct versus record class that you'd do to struct versus class. As a rule of thumb, when you are not sure if you should create a struct or a class create a class (the same for record).

Note

Remember that structure types are passed by copy instead of by reference, so a copy occurs every time the struct "moves."

Minimal hosting model

With the appearance of top-level statements in .NET 5, ASP.NET Core 6 brings a minimal hosting model, which removes the need to create a Program and a Startup class. You can still use the old model, but you don't need to anymore; you have two options. ASP.NET Core 6 templates leverage this new hosting model by default now.

Concretely, the minimal hosting model is an auto-generated Program class that leverages top-level statements to remove as much plumbing as possible. Here is an example (Program.cs):

```
var builder = WebApplication.CreateBuilder(args);
// Configure builder.Services here
var app = builder.Build();
// Configure app here
app.Run();
```

Those three lines of code replace two classes, three methods, the constructor injection of the configuration, and so on. I personally find this more elegant. If your application is larger than a small code sample or you want to test pieces of the registration, nothing stops you from creating extension methods to Add[Feature name] and Use[Feature name] instead of hardcoding everything in the Program.cs file.

As a side note, the auto-generated Program class has an internal visibility modifier, requiring some workaround to test. We explore workarounds in *Chapter 2, Automated Testing*.

Minimal APIs

With that new hosting model, a few APIs moved to the top of the line, like registering HTTP endpoints. We leverage minimal APIs throughout the book, but the idea is to get rid of as much plumbing as possible and write only what is needed. When building web APIs, we want to create endpoints. Those endpoints don't always fit well in controllers, and sometimes, even if they do, that seems overkill to do so.

Minimal APIs have a smaller overhead than MVC (fewer features) but offer model binding and dependency injection in a route-to-delegate model. Here is an example (Program.cs) from the GitHub repo associated with *Chapter 8, Options and Logging Patterns*:

```
using CommonScenarios;

var builder = WebApplication.CreateBuilder(args);
builder.Services.Configure<MyOptions>("Options1", builder.Configuration.
GetSection("options1"));
builder.Services.Configure<MyOptions>("Options2", builder.Configuration.
GetSection("options2"));
builder.Services.Configure<MyDoubleNameOptions>(builder.Configuration.
GetSection("myDoubleNameOptions"));
builder.Services.AddTransient<MyNameServiceUsingDoubleNameOptions>();
builder.Services.AddTransient<MyNameServiceUsingNamedOptionsFactory>();
builder.Services.AddTransient<MyNameServiceUsingNamedOptionsMonitor>();
builder.Services.AddTransient<MyNameServiceUsingNamedOptionsSnapshot>();

var app = builder.Build();
app.MapGet("/", (HttpContext context) => new[] {
    new { expecting =  "Options 1", uri = $"https://{context.Request.Host}/
options/true" },
    new { expecting =  "Options 2", uri = $"https://{context.Request.Host}/
options/false" },
    new { expecting =  "Options 1", uri = $"https://{context.Request.Host}/
factory/true" },
    new { expecting =  "Options 2", uri = $"https://{context.Request.Host}/
factory/false" },
    new { expecting =  "Options 1", uri = $"https://{context.Request.Host}/
monitor/true" },
    new { expecting =  "Options 2", uri = $"https://{context.Request.Host}/
monitor/false" },
    new { expecting =  "Options 1", uri = $"https://{context.Request.Host}/
snapshot/true" },
```

```
        new { expecting = "Options 2", uri = $"https://{context.Request.Host}/
    snapshot/false" },
    });
    app.MapGet("/options/{someCondition}", (bool someCondition,
    MyNameServiceUsingDoubleNameOptions service)
        => new { name = service.GetName(someCondition) });
    app.MapGet("/factory/{someCondition}", (bool someCondition,
    MyNameServiceUsingNamedOptionsFactory service)
        => new { name = service.GetName(someCondition) });
    app.MapGet("/monitor/{someCondition}", (bool someCondition,
    MyNameServiceUsingNamedOptionsMonitor service)
        => new { name = service.GetName(someCondition) });
    app.MapGet("/snapshot/{someCondition}", (bool someCondition,
    MyNameServiceUsingNamedOptionsSnapshot service)
        => new { name = service.GetName(someCondition) });
    app.Run();
```

Hopefully, it is easy enough to read in the book; essentially, the preceding code leverages the minimal hosting model, registers dependencies with the IoC container, creates the app, then registers five GET endpoints.

The first endpoint creates a JSON menu so you can navigate the project more easily when executing the code. In this endpoint's delegate, the IoC container injects an HttpContext that is associated with the current request. We can use the context parameter to handle HTTP requests manually. In this case, the code uses the context.Request.Host, but we could use the context.Response.WriteAsync method if we wanted to write to the response stream manually. Here, we return an array of anonymous objects to keep it simple. With minimal APIs, returning an object makes ASP.NET Core serialize it and return it to the client with a 200 OK status code.

The four other endpoints do the same thing but with a different service parameter type. Compared to the first endpoint, these have two parameters:

- A bool that comes from the route pattern.
- A service that comes from the IoC container.

Those endpoints leverage the same feature as the first endpoint and return an object that gets serialized automatically and returns it to the client with a 200 OK status code.

Now, if we want to control the output a little more than hoping the framework will do what we want, we can return an implementation of the IResult interface (part of the Microsoft.AspNetCore.Http namespace). Fortunately for us, we do not need to create those implementations and can leverage the static methods of the Results class (same namespace), like this (from the Wishlist example of *Chapter 7, Deep Dive into Dependency Injection*):

```
app.MapPost("/", async (IWishList wishList, CreateItem? newItem) =>
{
```

```
    if (newItem?.Name == null)
    {
        return Results.BadRequest();
    }
    var item = await wishList.AddOrRefreshAsync(newItem.Name);
    return Results.Created("/", item);
}).Produces(201, typeof(WishListItem));
```

If you want to define OpenAPI specs, you can also leverage extension methods that are part of the same namespace to describe the endpoints, as we did with the `Produces` method; explicitly defining this endpoint returns a status code of 201 with a body containing a serialized `WishListItem` instance.

This new model is a great addition to ASP.NET Core and can be very useful to remove plumbing while remaining optional. If MVC is better for your project, you can call the `AddControllers()` method and go back to what is best for your project. You can even mix both in the same project.

Nullable reference types

.NET 6 enables nullable reference type checking by default in templates. If you are migrating an existing project, you can enable this feature by adding the following property to your `csproj` file:

```
<Nullable>enable</Nullable>
```

That tells Visual Studio and the .NET compiler to run static code analyzers to detect possible null references. For example, the following code yields a few warnings (highlighted):

```
var obj = Create(true);
Console.WriteLine($"Hello, {obj.Name}!");

static MyClass? Create(bool shouldYieldANullResult)
{
    return shouldYieldANullResult
        ? default
        : new()
    ;
}

public class MyClass
{
    public string Name { get; set; }
}
```

The first warning is:

```
CS8602 Dereference of a possibly null reference.
```

Which informs us the return value of the `Create` method can be `null` (`MyClass?`). We could fix this by testing if `obj` `is` `null` or with the null-conditional operator (`?.`), like this:

```
Console.WriteLine($"Hello, {obj?.Name}!");
```

The second warning is:

```
CS8618 Non-nullable property 'Name' must contain a non-null value when exiting
constructor. Consider declaring the property as nullable.
```

This message informs us that the `Name` property of the `MyClass` class can be `null` but was defined as not nullable (`string`). We can fix this one by marking the property as a nullable string instead, like this:

```
public class MyClass
{
    public string? Name { get; set; }
}
```

There are also many attributes available in the `System.Diagnostics.CodeAnalysis` namespace to deal with null references like `NotNull`, `NotNullWhen`, `MemberNotNull`, and `MemberNotNullWhen`.

Here is a good resource from Microsoft to help you get started with this, titled *Learn techniques to resolve nullable warnings* (`https://adpg.link/Ljo8`).

The .NET team started to update the framework for a few versions before .NET 6, and the default is still just enabled in the template, so if you have a large codebase, you may want to address this iteratively.

Moreover, this feature relies on static analyzers, and the generated IL code is the same as before, so if external consumers call your code or if you call external consumers, runtime errors can still occur. In those cases, it is very important not to put blind confidence in this feature. It is a very good step forward and should help .NET developers write better code, but that's it.

For example, writing a guard clause to make sure injected values are not null is still useful if the IoC container is not used (or maybe used by someone other than you) or another third-party container is set up in the project. If you rely solely on the .NET IoC container and the analyzers (null-state analysis), no external consumer exists, and you believe that's safe enough for your project, you can avoid writing guard clauses. If you are writing libraries that consumers could use and have disabled null checks, I suggest writing some. Moreover, guards are pretty cheap to write, so they should not negatively impact the cost of the product you are working on. On the contrary, catching precise errors early can save you time and money.

Appendix B

This appendix covers a few additional notions that relate to microservices architecture and the technology that supports that type of architecture. As a reminder, the biggest downside of microservices architecture is the complexity of the infrastructure required to host such applications (known as operational complexity).

We are covering the following:

- An overview of containers
- Docker and Docker Compose
- Orchestration with Project Tye and Kubernetes
- Scaling

An overview of containers

Containers are an evolution of virtualization. With containers, we virtualize applications instead of machines. To share resources, we can leverage virtual or physical machines. A container contains everything that is required for the containerized app to run, including an OS.

Containers can help us set up environments, ensure the correctness of applications when moving them between environments (local, staging, and production), and more. By packaging everything into a single container image, our application becomes more portable than ever before; no more "it was working on my machine." Another perk of containers is the possibility to configure the networking and relationships between containers. Moreover, containers are lightweight, allowing us to create a new one in a matter of seconds, leading to on-demand provisioning of resources that can scale up with traffic spikes, then scale back down when the demand decreases.

Containers can be very abstract and seem very complicated at first glance. However, nowadays, the tools have matured and improved, making it easier than ever to understand and debug containers, but it can still be a steep learning curve. The upside is that once you grasp it, it is hard to go back to non-containerized applications.

In this section, we explore the following topics related to containers:

- **Docker**, which is a container engine.
- **Docker Compose**, which allows us to compose complex Docker applications.
- **Orchestration**, which is the concept of managing complex containerized applications.
- **Scaling**, which is a key point of using containers and microservices, where each microservice can scale independently.

Let's get started with Docker.

Docker

Docker is by far the most popular container engine out there. Getting started is now easy, but mastering it is another story. You can use Docker on Linux or Windows. You can even use Docker on Linux on Windows by leveraging **Windows Subsystem for Linux** (**WSL**) or WSL 2. The Getting Started page (see *Further reading*) describes how to install Docker and what Docker Hub is.

The following are a few key concepts behind Docker:

- **Docker Desktop** is the runtime environment that allows you to run containers locally (you must install it first). It also comes bundled with the docker and docker-compose CLIs.
- **Docker Hub** is a web-based repository to publish, share, and download **Docker images**.
- A **Docker image** is the plan to build a **Docker container**. It's similar to a **Virtual Machine** (**VM**) image but to spawn containers instead of VMs.
- A **Docker container** is a running **Docker image**; basically, the running application. You can run multiple instances (containers) of an image.
- A Dockerfile is a text file that describes the building process of a **Docker image**.
- A .dockerignore file works similarly to a .gitignore file and allows you to exclude certain files from being copied to the image by the ADD and COPY instructions (continue reading for more info on them).
- **Docker Compose** is a utility that allows you to build a complex topology that could include multiple Docker images, public and private networks, volumes, and more. Docker Compose uses YAML files as configuration (the default is docker-compose.yml) and is run using the docker-compose CLI or the docker compose command.

> **Note**
>
> The docker compose command, Compose V2, comes with Docker Desktop 3.4.0+, and should work similarly to docker-compose. Just replace the dash (-) with a space if you need to.

Regarding these concepts, both Visual Studio and Visual Studio Code have very useful tools that help with Docker. Moreover, the newer Docker Desktop user interface is very convenient and includes a dashboard, settings, and more.

Here is the basic idea around getting started:

1. Install Docker and other prerequisites (you only need to do this once).
2. Create a Dockerfile per application.
3. Create a docker-compose.yml file to manage multiple applications as a whole (optional).
4. Deploy your images to an image repository (locally, Docker Hub, or any cloud provider).
5. Run your images as containers (using Docker, container as a service, Kubernetes, or something else).

To create a Dockerfile, from Visual Studio, do the following:

1. Right-click the project that you want to dockerize.
2. In the contextual menu, select **Add > Docker Support**.
3. Choose Linux or Windows.

> **Note**
>
> I tend to run all my .NET code on Linux nowadays to gain performance, save hosting costs, and skip wrestling against IIS (or any other Windows features you feel fit this category).

The generated Dockerfile of a web project named WebApp (Linux) looks as follows:

```
FROM mcr.microsoft.com/dotnet/aspnet:6.0 AS base
WORKDIR /app
EXPOSE 80
EXPOSE 443


FROM mcr.microsoft.com/dotnet/sdk:6.0 AS build
WORKDIR /src
COPY ["WebApp.csproj", "."]
RUN dotnet restore "./WebApp.csproj"
COPY . .
WORKDIR "/src/."
RUN dotnet build "WebApp.csproj" -c Release -o /app/build


FROM build AS publish
RUN dotnet publish "WebApp.csproj" -c Release -o /app/publish


FROM base AS final
WORKDIR /app
COPY --from=publish /app/publish .
ENTRYPOINT ["dotnet", "WebApp.dll"]
```

Microsoft's engineers, working on Docker tools, leveraged a Docker feature named **multistage build** to generate optimized layers (highlighted lines), making sure the final image is as small as possible while still having access to the .NET SDK during the build process. You can spot the base, build, publish, and final stages using the highlighted lines.

> **Visual Studio tip**
>
> When using Visual Studio tools to run and debug Docker containers, Visual Studio only uses the first stage, so if you have logic that must run during startup or any other dependencies such as fonts that need to be installed in the micro-Linux distro, you have to put that logic into the **base** layer.

An essential part of the Dockerfile is the `FROM [base image] AS [alias]` instruction. `FROM` loads an existing Docker image as its base image. It's similar to inheriting from a class; we inherit from the whole base image. Then, we can add more content to that image, creating a new image of our own. Furthermore, each `FROM` defines a new stage of a multi-stage build.

.NET SDK versus runtime images

In the preceding Dockerfile, the first stage contains the .NET runtime (`mcr.microsoft.com/dotnet/aspnet:6.0`), while the second contains the SDK (`mcr.microsoft.com/dotnet/sdk:6.0`). This opens up the possibility of building the application inside Docker using the SDK and publishing the app inside an image (stage) that only contains the runtime. The runtime is much lighter than the full SDK. The smaller the resulting image, the faster it will be to download and start a new container from it.

The `WORKDIR` instruction specifies the execution context's directory from which other instructions are executed, such as `RUN`, `COPY`, `EXPOSE`, and `ENTRYPOINT`:

- `RUN` executes the specified command inside the container's OS. It could be a simple `dotnet build` command, a more complex one, or a series of commands that download and install the .NET SDK, for example.
- `COPY` does what you think it does; it copies files from your machine to the image.
- `EXPOSE` tells Docker what ports the application is listening to. These ports must also be opened using the `-p` (one port) or `-P` (all exposed ports) flags. Don't forget that your application must listen to the ports that you expose; otherwise, nothing will happen when you query your container. We can also open and map ports inside the `docker-compose.yml` file.
- `ENTRYPOINT` represents the executable that runs when you start a container. In this case, it is `dotnet WebApp.dll`, which runs the web application by using the .NET CLI.

More information

For more information about the way Microsoft builds Dockerfiles, take a look at `https://adpg.link/L2PD`.

For more information about the Dockerfiles syntax, take a look at `https://adpg.link/j1Kv`.

Docker comes with a CLI, which could take a whole book to describe, but here are a few useful commands. I think these snippets will help you get started with Docker.

`docker build` allows you to create an image. The `--rm` flag removes intermediate containers, the `-f` flag points to the Dockerfile, and the `-t` flag allows you to specify a tag (which is useful for identifying and running the image). Here is an example (the `.` at the end is important and represents the current directory):

```
docker build --rm -f "WebApp/Dockerfile" -t webapp:latest .
```

docker run allows you to start a container based on an image. If you don't want the shell to be attached, you can run a container in the background (detached mode) using the -d flag. The --rm flag removes the container when it exits, which is very useful when developing. Here is an example:

```
docker run --rm -d -p 443:8443/tcp -p 80:8080/tcp webapp:latest
```

Specifying tcp is optional and is the default value when mapping ports. It can also be replaced by another value, such as udp. The --name flag can be handy for accessing the container later, by name; for example:

```
docker run --rm -d -p 8080:80 --name MyWebApp webapp:latest
```

docker image ls lists all Docker images, while docker ps lists all running images (containers). docker stop stops a running container, while docker rm removes a stopped container. For example, we could start, stop, and then remove a container using the following commands:

```
docker run -d -p 8080:80 --name MyWebApp webapp:latest
docker stop MyWebApp
docker rm MyWebApp
```

For an unnamed container, we'd need to use its ID (run docker ps to find the ID of a running container). We can stop and remove a container by ID like so:

```
docker stop 0d5bffe4071f
docker rm 0d5bffe4071f
```

You can label your containers with both the docker CLI and docker-compose. You can then use those labels for many useful things, such as filtering. We can use the -l option when executing docker build to label a container. We can also use the --filter "label=[label to filter here]" option when executing a docker ps command to filter running containers that share a label; for example:

```
docker run -d -p 8080:80 --name MyWebApp -l webapp webapp:latest
docker ps --filter "label=webapp"
```

Here, we have two more options of the docker ps command. The first is the -a flag, which can come in handy for listing stopped containers (such as when they crash or did not start properly). The second is the -q flag, which only outputs IDs (which can be useful for chaining commands). For example, if you want to stop all containers that are labeled webapp, you could run the following command (in both Bash and PowerShell):

```
docker stop $(docker ps --filter "label=webapp" -a -q)
```

That's enough Docker CLI commands for now; let's peek at docker-compose.

Docker Compose

Docker Compose allows you to create a complex system and link multiple applications together by creating one or more YAML files. Both Visual Studio and Visual Studio Code offer tools that can help you create and edit docker-compose files, which can be very useful when you're just starting out.

Visual Studio creates two complementary files: the default `docker-compose.yml` file and one for local overrides called `docker-compose.override.yml`. You can use any number of files that you want when using the `docker-compose` CLI so that you can define overrides for *staging*, *production*, and whatnot. Here is a slightly modified version of that `docker-compose.yml` file:

```
version: '3.4'
services:
    webapp:
        image: ${DOCKER_REGISTRY-}webapp
        build:
            context: .
            dockerfile: WebApp/Dockerfile
        container_name: MyWebApp
        ports:
            - '8080:80'
        labels:
            - webapp
```

This file does the same as the previous command that we executed to run the container; it maps the ports, adds the `webapp` label, names the container `MyWebApp`, and uses `WebApp/Dockerfile`.

To build the images, we can use the `docker-compose build` command. The `--no-cache` flag is convenient in making sure that we are rebuilding the images; caches can sometimes be a pain. The `--force-rm` flag acts like the `docker build --rm` flag and removes intermediate containers. The following command builds the images using the `docker-compose.yml` file combined with the `docker-compose.override.yml` file (if one exists):

```
docker-compose build --no-cache --force-rm
```

To specify certain files and the order in which they are applied, we can use the `-f` option, like this:

```
docker-compose -f docker-compose.yml build --no-cache --force-rm
```

It is important to note that `-f` options must be located **before** `build`, not after, like the other options. It is also possible to specify multiple files, like this:

```
docker-compose -f docker-compose.yml -f another-docker-compose-file.yml build
--no-cache --force-rm
```

To run (start) the system, we can use `docker-compose up`. Like the `build` command, we can specify one or more files, using the `-f` option before the up command. You can also use the `-d` flag to run containers in detached mode and the `--build` flag to build the images before you start them. Here is an example:

```
docker-compose -f docker-compose.yml up --build -d
```

Finally, to take down the system, we can use the docker-compose down command, which also supports the -f option, like this:

```
docker-compose -f docker-compose.yml down
```

Now that we've explored all of those commands, let's add a SQL Server instance to the docker-compose.yml file and make our WebApp depend on it. Achieving this is as easy as adding a service to the docker-compose.yml file and, optionally, specifying that our WebApp depends_on it:

```
version: '3.4'
services:
    webapp:
        image: webapp:latest
        build:
            context: .
            dockerfile: WebApp/Dockerfile
        container_name: MyWebApp
        ports:
            - '8080:80'
        labels:
            - webapp
        depends_on:
            - sql-server
    sql-server:
        image: 'mcr.microsoft.com/mssql/server'
        ports:
            - '1433:1433'
        environment:
            SA_PASSWORD: Some_Super_Strong_Password_123
            ACCEPT_EULA: 'Y'
        labels:
            - db
```

The WebApp could use the following connection string:

```
Server=sql-server;Database=[database name here];User=sa;Password=Some_Super_
Strong_Password_123;
```

The server name in the connection string (highlighted) matches the service name (highlighted) from the docker-compose.yml file. This is because Docker Compose automatically creates a DNS entry based on the service name. These DNS entries are accessible from the other containers.

Now that we've created a connection string, we don't want the password in the docker-compose.yml file so that we don't accidentally commit that value into Git. We could do this in many ways, such as passing environment variables to the docker/docker-compose commands, but we are going to create a .env file instead.

> **Tip**
>
> When using Git, add your `.env` file to your `.gitignore` file so that you don't commit it to your repository. Moreover, don't forget to document the values that should go there, without the secret values, so your colleagues (or yourself at a later time) can create and update their personal `.env` file. For example, you could create a `.env.template` file that contains the keys but not the sensitive values, and check that file into Git.

At the same level of the `docker-compose.yml` file, if we add a `.env` file, we can reuse the environment variables that we define in there, like this:

`.env`:
```
# Don't commit this file in Git
SQL_SERVER_SA_PASSWORD=Some_Super_Strong_Password_123
SQL_SERVER_CONNECTION_STRING=Server=sql-server;Database=webapp;User=sa;Password
=Some_Super_Strong_Password_123;
```

`docker-compose.yml`:
```
version: '3.4'
services:
    webapp:
        image: webapp:latest
        build:
            context: .
            dockerfile: WebApp/Dockerfile
        container_name: MyWebApp
        ports:
            - '8080:80'
        environment:
            - ConnectionString=${SQL_SERVER_CONNECTION_STRING}
        labels:
            - webapp
        depends_on:
            - sql-server
    sql-server:
        image: 'mcr.microsoft.com/mssql/server'
        ports:
            - '1433:1433'
        environment:
            SA_PASSWORD: ${SQL_SERVER_SA_PASSWORD}
            ACCEPT_EULA: 'Y'
        labels:
            - db
```

With these two files, when we run `docker-compose` up, two containers start up: a SQL server and an ASP.NET Core web application that connects to that SQL server. Moreover, we opened and mapped port 1433 to itself, allowing us to connect to that container using SQL Management Studio or the tool of your choosing.

Tip

Port 1433 is the default SQL Server port. Don't leave port 1433 open in production, except to the containers. The fewer attack vectors that you leave open, the harder it will be for intruders to breach your system. This tip works for everything that should be hidden inside your container cluster, not just SQL Server.

From a .NET perspective (inside the web application), we have access to the connection string like we have access to any other setting (_configuration is of the IConfiguration injected into the Startup class or accessed in the Program.cs file):

```
var connectionString = _configuration
    .GetValue<string>("ConnectionString");
```

Note

The ConnectionString can come from any settings supported by ASP.NET Core. In this case, it is an environment variable defined in the preceding docker-compose.yml file.

And we could load an Entity Framework Core context from there as well, like this:

```
services.AddDbContext<MyDbContext>(options => options.
UseSqlServer(connectionString))
```

Now that we've explored Docker in more detail, let's look at tools to manage a production environment.

Orchestration

Once we have a containerized microservices application, we need to deploy it. The challenges pass from the number of features in a single application (monolith) to the number of applications to deploy, maintain, and orchestrate.

Each cloud provider has its own offering, which can be serverless, such as **Azure Container Instances (ACI)** and **Azure Kubernetes Service (AKS)**. You can also maintain your own VMs in the cloud or on-premises.

There are many tools to help with orchestrating and deploying containers, and we can't cover them all here. That is also why I've kept this section as lean as possible; I don't want to overwhelm you with information about tools that may become irrelevant or that you may never use. Instead, I think it is important to lay out some foundations to help you get started. Let's start with Project Tye, before we explore Kubernetes jargon.

Project Tye

Project Tye (`https://adpg.link/tye`) is an open source experiment started by Microsoft employees David Fowler, Glenn von Breadmeister, Justin Kotalik, and Ryan Nowak. The .NET Foundation now sponsors the project. Here is their README description:

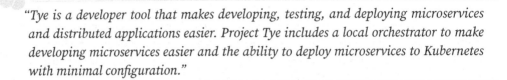

> *"Tye is a developer tool that makes developing, testing, and deploying microservices and distributed applications easier. Project Tye includes a local orchestrator to make developing microservices easier and the ability to deploy microservices to Kubernetes with minimal configuration."*

If you did not watch Build 2020, many praised the tool, so I figured that I would include a short introduction in this book.

In a nutshell, Tye is another YAML-based tool that allows you to compose multiple programs for a distributed application (that was my initial thought). Now, I see Tye as a tool for simplifying distributed .NET application development, the initial cost of setup, and deployment. It is important to remember that it is an experiment, as pointed out by the following quote from the project:

> *"[They] are using [Tye] to try radical ideas to improve microservices developer productivity and see what works. [...] consider every part of the tye experience to be volatile."*

Tye offers many features, including the following:

- A dashboard that shows your application and services
- The ability to load Docker images
- A proxy server that allows you to easily configure an **ingress**, which does the job of a **routing gateway**
- **Distributed tracing**
- **Service discovery**
- The ability to connect to **log aggregation systems**, such as **Elastic Stack** and **Seq**
- The ability to deploy to Kubernetes
- The ability to deploy to cloud providers, such as AKS

I only played slightly with Tye, but it sounds very promising. For example, I started an existing solution by only executing the `dotnet tye` command without any additional configuration (tye is a global tool installed via NuGet). That solution contains about 15 `docker-compose` files, 15 Dockerfiles, and most of the containers started.

Enough with the Tye experiments; let's look at Kubernetes next.

Kubernetes

Kubernetes is the most popular container orchestrator out there. It allows you to deploy, manage, and scale containers. Kubernetes can help you manage multiple VMs, add load balancing, monitor your containers, auto-scale based on demands, and more.

K8s

Kubernetes is also called **K8s**, short for "K", 8 other letters, and then "s". K8s is pronounced **K-eights**.

A tool that can help you get started with K8s, when using Docker Compose, is **Kompose** (https://adpg.link/NKqu). It is an open source project that converts docker-compose YAML files into K8s YAML files. This process can also be automated in a **continuous integration** (CI) pipeline by running the following command:

```
kompose convert -f docker-compose.yaml
```

This section exposes you to foundational concepts related to Kubernetes, so you gain a good base to help you learn more about K8s. When deploying a microservices application, containers are foundational. So are orchestrators, which is why we are covering K8s here.

A **cluster** is a group of nodes. A **node** is a machine (physical or virtual) that contains pods. Containers run inside **pods**. Pods are volatile; to quote the official documentation:

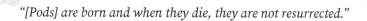

> *"[Pods] are born and when they die, they are not resurrected."*

Services come to the rescue by identifying a set of pods that serve a resource – say, the *DeviceLocation microservice*. Services are the conceptual identifiers of the applications running inside Kubernetes, so external clients don't have to know about the pods getting spawned and destroyed all the time.

Ingress exposes services outside the cluster. **Volumes** are directories where you store files. They outlive containers but die with their associated pod. **Persistent Volumes** (**PVs**) are dedicated resources used to store files in the cluster. PVs can be provisioned on a **Network File System** (**NFS**), iSCSI, or cloud storage system. Beware that the lifetimes of the files saved inside a container are tied to the life of that container.

Tip

A container can be destroyed at any time, so don't store important files inside a container; otherwise, you will lose them. Each container has its own filesystem, so files are not shared between them, even if two containers come from the same image. Use volumes or PVs instead, depending on your needs.

I understand this sub-section contains many concepts and, at the same time, not that much information. However, I think this high-level overview of Kubernetes is sufficient to save you hours of reading and deciphering information from diverse sources. You can always come back to this chapter later and use it as a reference.

Scaling

Everyone is talking about scaling; all the cloud providers are selling auto-scaling and near-unlimited scaling capabilities, but what does that mean, microservices-wise?

Let's go back to our IoT example from *Chapter 16, Introduction to Microservices Architecture*. Let's say that there are so many devices sending real-time information about their location that the server needs more power to run the *Location microservice*. What we can do here is put more power into the server (CPU and RAM), which is called **vertical scaling**. Then, at some point, when a single server is not enough, we can add more servers, which is called **horizontal scaling**. However, more servers means multiple instances of the application running on all of those servers. Using containers and an orchestrator such as Kubernetes makes it possible to create containers when the demand gets high enough, then remove them when it goes back to normal. Moreover, we can run a minimum number of instances so that if one crashes, there is always one or more others running to serve the requests while the one that crashed gets restarted (more precisely, it gets removed while a new one starts).

When multiple instances of the same application are running simultaneously, the requests need to be routed to the right node (server). For that to be possible, all nodes hosting that app must have a common entry point. None of the consumers can be in charge of reaching the instance they want, or it would create chaos (and be unmanageable). To overcome that, we can use a load balancer to balance the load between the different applications running on different servers (or nodes).

A load balancer is a sort of routing gateway; it takes a request and routes it to the right server while managing the load between servers. We will not go into the implementation details of all of this, but here is a contextual diagram that represents this:

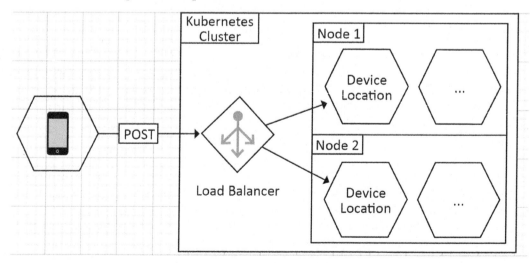

Figure 1: A device that sends its location to a Kubernetes cluster. Then, a load balancer dispatches the request to the right instance of the DeviceLocation microservice

That is a little simplified, but it shows the idea behind load balancing:

1. A request enters the cluster and reaches the load balancer.
2. The load balancer dispatches the request to the appropriate instance of the *DeviceLocation microservice*.

Some load balancers can also serve the same server to the same client after subsequent calls, allowing stateful applications to be more dependable.

Summary

Containers are very helpful for creating portable applications. Docker Compose and orchestrators such as K8s come in handy to compose and deploy complex applications. All of this leads to scaling individual parts of the system more easily than ever before.

Containers also come in handy to automate end-to-end testing since you can spawn the whole cluster, run tests against it, then tear it down.

Further reading

Here are a few links that will help you build on what you learned in this appendix:

*   *Docker Getting Started*: `https://adpg.link/1zfM`
*   *Learn Kubernetes Basics*: `https://adpg.link/oS2G`

Assessment Answers

The answers to the practice questions for each chapter are as follows:

Chapter 1

1. No. However, sending a body with a GET request is not forbidden by the HTTP specifications, but such a request semantic is not defined either. It is preferable to avoid sending GET requests with a body.
2. Long methods are indicators that a method handles too many responsibilities and should be split into multiple methods or have some of the responsibilities extracted to other classes.
3. No. Target .NET Standard 2.0 when you want to support most runtime versions, like .NET Framework and .NET 6+. Target .NET Standard 2.1 to share code between Mono and Xamarin. Otherwise, target .NET 6+ directly.
4. A code smell represents a potential design flaw that could benefit from being rewritten.

Chapter 2

1. Yes, it is true.
2. To test a unit of code, such as the logical code path of a method.
3. As small as possible. A unit test aims at testing the smallest possible unit of functionality in isolation.
4. Integration tests are usually used for that kind of task.
5. No, there are multiple ways of writing code, TDD being only one of them.

Chapter 3

1. Five: S.O.L.I.D. (SRP, OCP, LSP, ISP, and DIP).
2. No, the idea is the opposite: create smaller components that interact with each other in a loosely coupled manner.
3. No, you want to encapsulate similar logic, not similar-looking blocks of code.
4. Yes, it is easier to reuse smaller pieces than adapt enormous ones.
5. It is the SRP, but the separation of concerns principle states that too.

Chapter 4

1. The **controller** manipulates the **model** and chooses what **view** to render.
2. The @model directive.
3. A **view model** should have a one-to-one relationship with a **view**.
4. Yes.
5. Yes.

Chapter 5

1. 201 CREATED.
2. The [FromBody] attribute.
3. The GET method.
4. Yes, those are precisely the objectives of a DTO: loosely coupling the *ins* and *outs* from the **model**.
5. Yes.

Chapter 6

1. It helps manage behaviors at runtime, such as changing an algorithm in the middle of a running program.
2. The creational patterns are responsible for creating objects.
3. v1 and v2 are two different instances. The code next to the arrow operator is executed every time you call the property's getter.
4. Yes, it is true. That's the primary goal of the pattern, as we demonstrated in the MiddleEndVehicleFactory code sample.
5. The Singleton pattern violates the SOLID principles and encourages the use of global (static) variables when it can be avoided.

Chapter 7

1. Transient, Scoped, Singleton.
2. The composition root holds the code that describes how to compose the program's object graph—the types bindings.
3. Yes, it is true. Volatile dependencies should be injected instead of instantiated.
4. The Strategy pattern.
5. The Service Locator pattern is all three. It is a design pattern used by DI libraries, internally, but becomes a code smell in application code. If misused, it is an anti-pattern that has the same drawbacks as using the new keyword directly.

Chapter 8

1. Singleton.
2. Scoped.
3. Transient.
4. Yes, you can configure as many providers as you want. One could be for the console, and another could be used to append entries to a file.
5. No, you should not log trace-level entries in production. You should only log debug-level entries when debugging an issue.

Chapter 9

1. Yes, we can decorate decorators by depending only on interfaces because they are just another implementation of the interface, nothing more.
2. The Composite pattern adds simplicity when it comes to managing complexity.
3. Yes, we could use an adapter for this.
4. We usually use façades to simplify the use of one or more subsystems, creating a wall in front of them.
5. The Adapter and Façade design patterns are almost the same but are applied to different scenarios. The Adapter pattern adapts an API to another API, while the Façade pattern exposes a unified or simplified API, hiding one or more complex subsystems.

Chapter 10

1. False; you can create as many abstract (required) or virtual (optional) extension points as you need, as long as the class stays cohesive and does not break architectural principles. For example, ensure the class has a single responsibility.
2. Yes, there is no reason not to.
3. No, there is no greater limit than with any other code.
4. Yes, you can have one handler per message or multiple handlers per message. It is up to you and your requirements.
5. It helps divide responsibilities between classes by encapsulating the shared logic into one or more base classes.

Chapter 11

1. Yes. Actually, the HttpResponseMessage instance returned by the HttpMessageInvoker.Send method is an operation result. HttpClient inherits from HttpMessageInvoker and exposes other methods that also return an instance of HttpResponseMessage.
2. We implemented two **static factory methods**.
3. Yes, returning an object is faster than throwing an exception leading to a marginal performance gain which is a situational optimization technique. In most cases, you should not solely use the Operation Result pattern for that speed gain.

Chapter 12

1. No, you can have as many layers as you need, and you can name and organize them as you want.
2. No, both have their place, their pros, and their cons.
3. Yes. A DbContext is an implementation of the Unit of Work pattern. DbSet<T> is an implementation of the Repository pattern.
4. No, you can query any system, any way you want. For example, you could use ADO.NET to query a relational database, manually create the objects using a DataReader, track changes using a DataSet, or do anything else that fits your needs. Nonetheless, ORMs can be very convenient.

624   *Assessment Answers*

5. Yes. A layer can never access outward layers, only inward ones.

Chapter 13

1. Yes, it can, but not necessarily. Moving dependencies around does not fix design flaws; it just moves those flaws elsewhere.

2. Yes, mappers should help us follow the SRP.

3. No, it may not be suitable for every scenario. For example, when the mapping logic becomes complex, think about not using AutoMapper.

4. Yes, use profiles to organize your mapping rules cohesively.

5. Four or more. Once again, this is just a guideline; injecting four services into a class could be acceptable.

Chapter 14

1. Yes, you can. That's the goal of the Mediator pattern: to mediate communication between colleagues.

2. In the original sense of CQRS: no, a command can't return a value. The idea is that a query reads data while commands mutate data. In a looser sense of CQRS, yes, a command could return a value. For example, nothing stops a create command from returning the created entity partially or totally. You can always trade a bit of modularity for a bit of performance.

3. MediatR is a free, open source project licensed under Apache License 2.0.

4. Yes, you should; using Marker Interfaces to add metadata is generally wrong. Nevertheless, you should analyze each use case individually, considering the pros and cons before jumping to a conclusion.

Chapter 15

1. Any pattern and technique that you know that can help you implement your solution. That's the beauty of it: you are not limited; only by yourself.

2. No, you can pick the best tool for the job inside each vertical slice; you don't even need layers.

3. The application will most likely become a Big Ball of Mud and be very hard to maintain, which is not good for your stress level, the product quality, time to market of changes, and so on.

4. We can create MVC filters in any ASP.NET Core MVC application. We can augment the MediatR pipeline using behavior in any application that uses MediatR. We can also implement ASP.NET Core middlewares in non-MVC applications or to execute code before getting into the MVC pipeline.

5. Cohesion means elements that should work together as a united whole.

6. Tight coupling describes elements that cannot change independently; that directly depend on one another.

Chapter 16

1. The message queue gets a message and has a single subscriber dequeue it. If nothing dequeues a message, it stays in the queue indefinitely (FIFO model). The Pub-Sub model gets a message and sends it to zero or more subscribers.

2. Event sourcing is the process of chronologically accumulating events that happened in a system instead of persisting the current state of an entity. It allows you to recreate the state of the application by replaying those events.

3. Yes, you can mix Gateway patterns (or sub-patterns).

4. No, you can deploy micro-applications (microservices) on-premises if you want to. Moreover, in *Chapter 14, Mediator and CQRS Design Patterns*, we saw that we can use CQRS even inside a single application.

Chapter 17

1. Razor Pages is best at creating web page-oriented applications.

2. Yes, we have access to mostly the same things as with MVC.

3. Technically, yes, you could, but you should use partial views only to render part of the UI and presentation logic, not domain logic and database queries.

4. Yes, you can. You can also create new tags.

5. Yes, you can. View components are like component-based, single-action controllers rendering one or more views.

6. A class can have as many display templates as there are levels in the views/pages hierarchy.

7. Display and editor templates are directly related to a type.

Chapter 18

1. No, it is compiled to WebAssembly (AOT compilation) or leverages the .NET Wasm runtime (JIT compilation) and runs the .NET binaries in the browser.

2. None. All three are acceptable options—it depends on what you are building and with whom.

3. Model (State), View (Component), Update (Reducer).

4. No. The MVU pattern is all about a unidirectional flow of data to simplify state management.

5. Yes. Blazor can interact with JavaScript and vice versa.

Join our book's Discord space

Join the book's Discord workspace for *Ask me Anything* session with the authors:

https://packt.link/ASPdotNET6DesignPatterns

Acronyms Lexicon

Here is the list of all the acronyms used throughout the book:

- ACI: Azure Container Instances
- AKS: Azure Kubernetes Service
- AOP: Aspect-Oriented Programming
- API: Application Programming Interface
- ATDD: Acceptance Test-Driven Development
- BDD: Behavior-Driven Development
- BLL: Business Logic Layer
- CDN: Content Delivery Network
- CI: Continuous Integration
- CLI: Command-Line Interface
- CQS: Command Query Separation
- CQRS: Command Query Responsibility Segregation
- CRUD: Create, Read, Update Delete
- CSRF (or XSRF): Cross-site Request Forgery
- DAL: Data Access Layer
- DDD: Domain-Driven Design
- DI: Dependency Injection
- DIP: Dependency Inversion Principle
- DOM: Document Object Model
- DRY: Don't Repeat Yourself
- DTO: Data Transfer Object
- EF Core: Entity Framework Core
- FIFO: First in, First Out
- GoF: Gang of Four
- Grpc: gRPC Remote Procedure Calls
- GUI: Graphical User Interface
- IOC: Inversion of Control
- IoT: Internet of Things
- ISP: Interface Segregation Principle
- K8s: Kubernetes
- LSP: Liskov Substitution Principle
- MQTT: MQ Telemetry Transport

- MVC: Model View Controller
- MVU: Model -View-Update
- MVVM: Model-View-ViewModel
- NFS: Network File System
- OCP: Open/Closed principle
- OOP: Object-Oriented Programming
- ORM: Object-Relational-Mapper
- PoEAA: Patterns of Enterprise Application Architecture
- PV: Persistent Volume
- E2E: End-to-End
- REST: Representational State Transfer
- RPC: Remote Procedure Call
- SEO: Search Engine Optimization
- SME: Small-to-Medium-sized-Enterprise
- SOLID: SRP, OCP, LSP, ISP, DIP
- SPA: Single-Page Application
- SQL: Structured Query Language
- SRP: Single Responsibility Principle
- TDD: Test-Driven Development
- TLD: Top-Level Domain
- UML: Unified Modeling Language
- URI: Uniform Resource Identifier
- URL: Uniform Resource Locator
- VM: Virtual machine
- Wasm: WebAssembly
- Yagni: You aren't gonna need it

packt.com

Subscribe to our online digital library for full access to over 7,000 books and videos, as well as industry leading tools to help you plan your personal development and advance your career. For more information, please visit our website.

Why subscribe?

- Spend less time learning and more time coding with practical eBooks and Videos from over 4,000 industry professionals
- Improve your learning with Skill Plans built especially for you
- Get a free eBook or video every month
- Fully searchable for easy access to vital information
- Copy and paste, print, and bookmark content

At www.packt.com, you can also read a collection of free technical articles, sign up for a range of free newsletters, and receive exclusive discounts and offers on Packt books and eBooks.

Other Books You May Enjoy

If you enjoyed this book, you may be interested in these other books by Packt:

C# 10 and .NET 6 – Modern Cross-Platform Development, Sixth Edition

Mark J Price

ISBN: 9781801077361

- Build rich web experiences using Blazor, Razor Pages, the Model-View-Controller (MVC) pattern, and other features of ASP.NET Core
- Build your own types with object-oriented programming
- Write, test, and debug functions
- Query and manipulate data using LINQ

- Integrate and update databases in your apps using Entity Framework Core, Microsoft SQL Server, and SQLite
- Build and consume powerful services using the latest technologies, including gRPC and GraphQL
- Build cross-platform apps using .NET MAUI and XAML

Software Architecture with C# 10 and .NET 6, Third Edition

Gabriel Baptista

Francesco Abbruzzese

ISBN: 9781803235257

- Use proven techniques to overcome real-world architectural challenges
- Apply architectural approaches such as layered architecture
- Leverage tools such as containers to manage microservices effectively
- Get up to speed with Azure features for delivering global solutions
- Program and maintain Azure Functions using C# 10
- Understand when it is best to use test-driven development (TDD)
- Implement microservices with ASP.NET Core in modern architectures
- Enrich your application with Artificial Intelligence
- Get the best of DevOps principles to enable CI/CD environments

Packt is searching for authors like you

If you're interested in becoming an author for Packt, please visit authors.packtpub.com and apply today. We have worked with thousands of developers and tech professionals, just like you, to help them share their insight with the global tech community. You can make a general application, apply for a specific hot topic that we are recruiting an author for, or submit your own idea.

Share your thoughts

Now you've finished *An Atypical ASP.NET Core 6 Design Patterns Guide, Second Edition*, we'd love to hear your thoughts! Scan the QR code below to go straight to the Amazon review page for this book and share your feedback or leave a review on the site that you purchased it from.

https://packt.link/r/1803249846

Your review is important to us and the tech community and will help us make sure we're delivering excellent quality content.

Index

Symbols

.NET 9
.NET 5, versus .NET Standard 10
.NET applications, testing 21
.NET base class library (BCL) 284
.NET program structure 35
.NET runtime 9
.NET SDK, versus runtime 9

A

Abstract Factory design pattern 141
design 141-143
goal 141
project 143-147
SOLID principles 147, 148

abstraction 41

abstract layers 339-341

acceptance test-driven development (ATDD) 19

ActiveMQ 459

Adapter design pattern
Adapter interface 262
design 262, 263
goal 261
Greeter project 263, 264
implementing 261

Advanced Message Queuing Protocol (AMQP) 459

ahead-of-time (AOT) compilation 550

Ambient Context pattern 148, 152-154

Anchor Tag Helper 514-516

anemic domain model 331, 332

anti-patterns 3

Apache Kafka broker 460
reference link 460

API contracts
defining 128-131

application event 455

applications 10

architectural principles
Don't repeat yourself (DRY) 88
keep it simple, stupid (KISS) 89
separation of concerns 87
SOLID principles 41

Arrange, Act, Assert (AAA) 31

arrow operator 151

aspect-oriented programming (AOP) 87

ASP.NET Core
integration tests, implementing 35

ASP.NET Core MVC anatomy 95, 96
controller 97, 98
default routing 100
directory structure 96, 97
model 98
SOLID principles 101
view 99

ASP.NET Core web APIs anatomy 113
attribute routing 117-119
controller 114
directory structure 114
entry point 113
returning values 115-117

assemblies 328
versus layers 328, 329

assertions 23, 24

Made in the USA
Coppell, TX
10 July 2022